The Wars of the
Middle Eastern Succession

1914 – 2016

Second Edition

———

By

Curtis F. Jones

First Edition 2017
Second Edition 2018

ISBN 13: 978-1725899209
ISBN-10: 1725899205

To Enlightened Government,
in the spirit of those three who contributed
to this enterprise

Objectives

This book was written with three intentions:

- To integrate a century of Middle East military history in one volume.
- To calendar the consequential events of the century.
- To articulate an objective appraisal of American policy in that time and place.

Thesis

Comprehensive review of 5000 years of the history of the peoples that have inhabited southwest Asia and the adjoining corner of Africa indicates that these areas comprise a discrete segment of the planet that is irrevocably conjoined by valleys, plateaus, routes, and rivers, while separated from neighboring lands by deserts, seas, and mountain ranges.

The geographic coherence of the region thus delineated has imparted to its inhabitants an overlay of cultural and political commonality. It has a geopolitical identity that has received conventional recognition as the Middle East.

Any foreign policy formulated in disregard of this identity is doomed to fail. In the opinion of the author, since World War II American policymakers have fallen deep into this geopolitical trap, costing the United States a gratuitous toll of frustration, expenditure, and lives.

Transliteration

Most foreign words and names are spelled as they appear in the *Encyclopaedia Britannica,* Fifteenth Edition, 1995. Aside from established spellings of place and author names, Arabic words and names are spelled in accordance with the system established by the United States Board of Geographic Names, wherein the guide is printed text, not pronunciation (which is subject to dialectal variation). Some Iraqi names contain a borrowed (from Turkish?) ch – as in much – which is customarily represented in Arabic text as a triple-dotted jim; the borrowed p may be represented by two dots under a ba'.

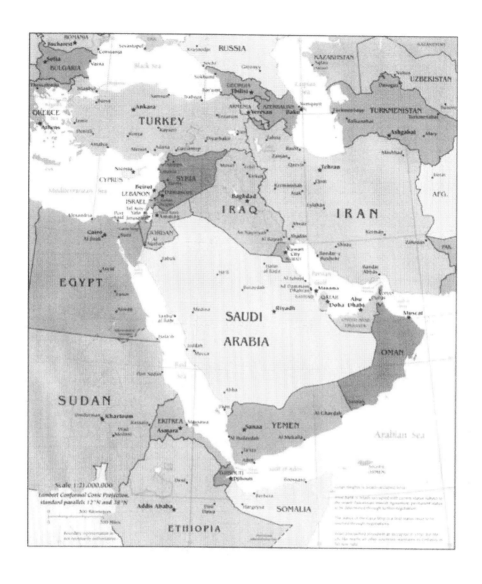

[For a full-color map, see *The World Factbook* at
https://www.cia.gov/library/publications/the-world-factbook/docs/refmaps.html]

Contents

Preface: From War to Politics

Homo Sapiens: A Martial Scenario

War has always been with us. It is cited in national anthems: "rockets' red glare" in America, "rules the waves" in Britain, "stand on guard" in Canada, "l'étendard sanglant" in France, "über alles" in Germany. After two world wars, and endemic violence worldwide, war has been exposed, to all but the hawks, as a curse.

Is it necessary?

In *Scientific American* of August 2015, Curtis Marean of Arizona State University assembled evidence in support of his evolutionary chronology for humanity:

-   200,000 years ago: Emergence in Africa of homo sapiens, anatomically modern, capable of complex cognition.
-   70,000 years ago: Still confined to Africa, humans developed projectile weaponry – sticks to spears to atlatls (spear-hurlers) to bow and arrow.
-   55,000 years ago: Humans expanded their geographic range and evolved the skill of communal cooperation, which enabled them to kill big game, defend communal living space, and exterminate rival homonins.

- <u>Today</u>: Humans are hardwired to fight rival tribes, ethnicities, and nationalities, but they have the intelligence to appreciate scientific ways other than war to match living space to population. The antidote to war is enlightened culture.

War is insidious. It has resisted every effort to curb it. The criterion of military success is statistical, not ethical. War is won by the side that manages to inflict the most damage and death on its adversary. As technology has evolved, casualties have risen and tactics have proliferated: hand-to-hand, firearms, chemical (starting with "Greek fire"), biological (starting with throwing bodies of deceased into the path of the enemy), aircraft, cyberwar, and now remote combat with missiles and drones.

The American drone has presented the US with the convenience of conducting attacks with metronomic regularity, with negligible risk to the attackers – but subsequent risks of generating implacable hatreds.

Geopolitics: From War to Politics

This text is based on the following postulates:

1) Human society has evolved into a number of variant cultures. Their similarities are established by universal elements of the evolutionary process. Their differences derive from their varying geographic and social circumstances. These differences tend to cluster in distinct global neighborhoods. Some ten or fifteen geopolitical regions comprise the habitable lands of Planet Earth.

2) From the dawn of history, every region has oscillated between the hypothetical poles of unity and disunity. Unity promotes stability; disunity promotes instability. For examples of relative stability in recent times, see North America, Europe – even the Middle East back when the power structure had been reduced to two rivals: the Ottoman and Safavid Empires.

3) In each region, the evolution of the political system is determined by the vicissitudes of the power equation. Of the six basic arenas of power – geographic, demographic, cultural, economic, military,

2

and political – the military has the most immediate consequences. The other five can alter the more lasting characteristics of a regional society, but they generally take more time. To keep up with political evolution in real time, watch the wars.

The Battle for Control of the Middle East

History seems to have divided the Middle Eastern region into six sub-regions, or sectors: In northeast Africa and Asian Sinai – Egypt; in southwest Asia – The Southern Caucasus, Iran, Arabia, The Fertile Crescent, and Anatolia (which includes the corner of Europe assimilated into the Middle Eastern Region, as a unique consequence of the adventitious European site of the ancient oriental city of Constantinople).

The closest the region ever came to unification of all six sectors under one central authority was in the 600's, when the impassioned warriors of the Islamic Caliphate exploded out of Arabia and, taking advantage of the mutual exhaustion of the Byzantines, based in Anatolia, and the Sassanians, based in Persia, briefly overran all six regions <u>except</u> Anatolia; in Constantinople and its Asian outskirts, the Byzantines held out against Islam.

Since then, the region has fluctuated between eras of political consolidation under two or three rival empires, and eras of splintering. The most recent indigenous consolidation was achieved between 1500 and 1800 by the rival Ottomans and Safavids. As both empires collapsed, they were replaced by the extra-regional imperialisms of Britain, France, and Russia.

During World War II, these same three states unceremoniously appropriated the Middle East – minus neutral Turkey – as one of their seven major military bases against the Nazis: The UK, the Soviet Union, the Middle East, North Africa, the Atlantic Ocean, the Mediterranean Sea, and the Arabian Sea.

The region's last seventy years have been an era of splintering: In the natural course of events, a more viable power structure should already be emerging, but the age-old process has been prolonged a century or two by the venal intervention of Western imperialism – European before and during the two world wars, American since the second one. From 1914 through 2016, twelve regional wars have dictated the political process in the Middle East. The six wars that are still underway leave the region in political limbo.

In the unfinished contest for control of the region, Britain and France are out of the running. Britain was discredited by its mismanagement of the Palestine Mandate, and subsequently forced by postwar economic crisis to cut back its investment in empire. France needed time to overcome the effects of the Vichy occupation. As they have fitfully disengaged, the Middle East has been afflicted by a frenzied contest for control that has been dominated by five indigenous contenders – Turks, Iranians and their Shiite associates, Kurds, Sunni Arabs, and Israelis – and two foreign interlopers, the United States and Russia.

Since 2011, Middle East violence has flooded Europe with refugees, and converted parts of the Fertile Crescent into no man's lands. The most dreadful case is that of the Syrian regime, which by elevating the Alawite cause above that of any other community, in disregard of its responsibility for the welfare of 23,000,000 Syrians, has allowed or caused millions of citizens to suffer displacement, hundreds of thousands to want for adequate food, and at least 400,000 to lose their lives. According to the 2017 *World Almanac*, there were only 17,000,000 Syrians left in country.

Section I: Eighteen Wars

1914-58 – The British Subjugation of Iraq

Rise of the British Empire – In the ancient battle for preeminence in Europe, England had a permanent advantage in its insularity. Perhaps its dynastic rivalries were just as violent as those of its continental rivals, but England was sheltered from direct foreign intervention by the English Channel. Twenty miles of ocean acted as a filter that allowed free exchange of knowledge but kept invaders out, notably the troops on board the ships of the Spanish Armada in 1588, and the Nazis in World War II. It afforded the United Kingdom (England, plus Wales in 1536, Scotland in 1707, and Ireland in 1801) the opportunity to develop a language, a culture, and a political system that in essence were adopted in America and which have been widely embraced in many countries.

The genesis of British imperialism has been variously identified. For John Hobson, the impetus came from British financiers looking for new opportunities for investment; for Joseph Schumpeter, the prime movers were the principals of an oversize British war machine: *Empires*, Michael W. Doyle. Another theory: British imperialism was invited in to the Middle East by venal rulers: For example, in 1882, Egyptian Khedive Tawfiq asked the UK to send troops back in to suppress a rebellion by anti-imperialist Ahmad 'Urabi: *EB*: 11:583.

In the 1650's, Oliver Cromwell built the state-of-the-art fleet that unseated the Dutch Navy as the best in the world, and became the keystone of empire. It made possible the conquest of India in the 1600's, the destruction of the French fleet off the coast of Egypt by Admiral

Horatio Nelson in 1798, the suppression of Egypt's Muhammad 'Ali in 1839, the 1875 takeover of the Suez Canal after Disraeli bought the shares held by the bankrupt Khedive of Egypt, the 1882 invitation from the Khedive to British troops to keep order in Egypt, and the conversion of five Gulf shaykhdoms to British protectorates in the late 1800's.

World War I clinched British preeminence in the Middle East. To preempt the Axis, the Allies reinforced their garrisons there. The long-failing Ottoman Empire subsided into oblivion, leaving the Allies in charge. We learn from two world wars that the winners of a war habitually occupy the territories of the losers. So it was in the Middle East – except that the British and French meant to stay. For Britain, permanent domination of new possessions meant doubling down on its military posture. Before World War I, naval power had sufficed. After the war, Britain had to plunge into action on the ground, and supplement it from the air. The first case was Iraq:

Timeline: 1914-58 – On 10/28/14, the Ottoman Empire made a rash decision to side with the Central Powers (Germany and Austria-Hungary) in World War I, and bombarded Russian ports on the Black Sea. The Triple Alliance (France, Russia, and Great Britain) declared war on the Ottomans: *EB*: 28:963.

1914 – To protect Persian oil wells from the risk of Ottoman attack, on 11/22/14 an Anglo-Indian force occupied Basrah, Iraq: *Times Atlas of World History*, HarperCollins, London.

1914 – In December, to consolidate its longtime control over Egypt, Britain declared the country a protectorate: *EB*.

1915 – The storied passage between the Aegean and Black Seas, from west to east, consists of the Dardanelles Strait, the Sea of Marmara, and the Bosporus Strait. The passage has not been given its own name. In the early 1900's, as a general war was beginning to threaten Europe, British pre-planning including a naval operation against the city of Gallipoli, to take the sinuous peninsula that is the north shore of the Dardanelles (38 miles long, down to a width of less than a mile), followed by a land operation to take Istanbul, 127 miles east of Gallipoli. In February and March of 1915, the naval operation against Gallipoli was tried, and failed. Three obsolete battleships were damaged, and three sunk. In the summer of 1915, General Mustafa Kemal scored his first military victory by repelling British attempts to land ground troops. By the end of 1915, the Gallipoli debacle was history. Its chief protagonist, First Lord of the Admiralty Winston Churchill, resigned from the government and went to France to command an infantry battalion: *EB*: 3:884.

1915 – The UK had decided that it would take advantage of an Allied victory in WW I to carve up the Ottoman Empire. Its main target was to be Iraq, as a likely source of oil: *A Peace to End All Peace*, David Fromkin.

1915 – In October, British forces marched on Baghdad, but were repelled by Ottoman troops and forced to surrender at Kut in April 1916: *Atlas of World History.*

1915 – British forces in Egypt blocked an Ottoman effort to cross the Suez Canal.

1916 – On May 9, Britain and France made a secret land-grab deal: After winning the war, they would divide the Ottomans' northern Arab territories – Lebanon, Syria, and northern Iraq to France; Palestine and the rest of Iraq to Britain. The deal was later publicized as the Sykes-Picot Agreement, but Sykes (British) and Picot (French) were acting under closely-held instructions from British Secretary of State for War Horatio Kitchener – idolized by the British public, but known to his peers in government as an eccentric incompetent: Fromkin. The conspiracy contradicted three British commitments: McMahon's written assurances of 1915 to the Sherif of Mecca; the false pretenses of the Balfour Declaration of 1917; and the duplicitous effusions of the Allies' mandate system.

1916 – British forces from Egypt expelled German-led Ottoman troops from Sinai and Gaza.

1916 – A British force under General Edmund Allenby entered Palestine.

1917 – Over stiff resistance from Turkish troops, but with the help of Iraqis who had been officers in the Ottoman service, Allenby's forces took Baghdad on 3/10/17: *Atlas of World History.*

1918 – To maximize its control of Mesopotamian oil, Britain prevailed on France to swap northern Iraq in return for partnership with Britain in the exploitation of Mawsil (Mosul)-area oil. This revision was formalized by the Treaty of Sèvres of 8/10/20.

1918-19 – Three pro-independence secret societies had been formed in Iraq.

1918 – In September an Arab force occupied Damascus and hailed Prince Faysal bin Husayn as King of Syria: *EB*: 4:706.

1918 – By the Armistice of Mudros (10/30/18), the Ottoman Empire dissolved its armed forces and left the war. Allied troops occupied Constantinople on 11/13/18.

1919 – In May, Shaykh Mahmud Barzanji (sic) arrested British officials in his district and sparked an uprising in the Kurdish-populated area of northeastern Iraq.

1920 – In March, Faysal bin Husayn was proclaimed King of Syria.

1920 – In March, speaking in the House of Commons, Prime Minister Winston Churchill mused that the most efficient way to keep order in Iraq might be "aerial policing" – bombing trouble spots from aircraft.

1920 – In April, a conference at San Remo, France, awarded Britain and France "mandates" over the territories assigned in the Sykes-Picot fraud. They were designated "Class A", meaning the countries under mandate were early candidates for independence.

1920 – In May, mass demonstrations against the mandate erupted in Iraq. All ethnic communities participated. There was no visible support for British rule. New British legislation, including revision of land ownership laws, and a tax on the worldwide practice of devout Shiites to arrange for burial in Najaf, was widely condemned. Shiite Ayatallah Muhammad Taqy al Shirazi declared by *fatwa* (legal opinion) that the service of Muslims in a British administration was unlawful; non-Muslims could never rule Muslims. Shirazi called for *jihad* (holy war).

1920 – In June, Shirazi issued another fatwa: If Britain continued to deny the rights of the Iraqis, they should resort to force. Zawalim tribesmen stormed a prison and released a colleague. The uprising had escalated into a revolt that had started along the middle Euphrates and spread to the lower Euphrates and Baghdad.

1920 – In July, the French occupied Damascus. Prince Faysal was caught in the dispute between Syrian nationalism and French imperialism. Imperialism prevailed, and Faysal was forced into exile: *EB*: 4:707.

1920 – The Iraqi revolt had engulfed the whole country, though it was inhibited by the British garrisons in Mawsil, Baghdad, and Basrah: *EB*: 21:988. A simultaneous revolt was ongoing in Iraqi Kurdistan. Churchill had sent in troop reinforcements from garrisons in Iran and India, including two squadrons of the RAF, whose bombers, after shipment by sea and reassembly in the Middle East, had played a huge role in suppressing the revolt. A particularly successful model was the British De Havilland 9A, a light biplane with an American Liberty engine. The number of British and Indian troops deployed to Iraq in 1920 had exceeded 100,000: *BBC News Magazine*, 10/7/2014, Marek Pruszewicz.

1920 – On 8/10/20, the Allies vented their pique over the Gallipoli disaster by forcing the successors of the Ottoman regime to sign the Treaty of Sèvres, which provided for an autonomous Kurdish entity and a Greek presence in western Anatolia, gave the Allies control of Turkish finances, and virtually internationalized the Straits.

1920 – In October, Sir Percy Cox arrived as British High Commissioner to the state of Iraq. Most of the officials of the Iraqi branches of the Ottoman civil service were being replaced with Britons: *EB*: 3:699.

1920 – As the rebels ran out of supplies and the British built up the forces of the occupation, the revolt lost momentum. It expired by the end of October, although incidents of unrest sputtered off and on for the next two decades. The Mesopotamian wings of the RAF dealt severely with each episode, wiping out troublesome villages in the process: *The Outlaw State*, Elaine Sciolino.

1920 – The loss of life from the Iraqi-British fighting was estimated at 6-10,000 Iraqis, 500 British and Indian ground troops, and nine from the RAF. British funding to put down the revolt was believed to exceed

British funding for the Arab Revolt of 1917-18 against the Ottomans, which brought renown to T. E. Lawrence.

1921 – In Cairo in March, Churchill (now Colonial Secretary) convened British officials to review British policy for Iraq. The consensus was to invite the recently unemployed king, Faysal bin Husayn, older son of the Sherif of Mecca, scion of the Hashemite clan to which the Prophet had belonged, to take the throne in Iraq. Although he would face strong disapproval from Iraqi devotees of Arab Nationalism, he accepted, provided that the mandate could be nullified, in keeping with Iraq's right to be a sovereign state. London agreed to conclusion of a treaty of British-Iraqi alliance, which seemed to meet Faysal's requirement. Such a treaty was ratified on 6/11/24, long after the crowning of King Faysal of Iraq on 8/23/21.

1921 – The Cairo Conference also agreed on the formation of an Iraqi Army. Its officers would be required to have had previous service as (Sunni) officers in the Ottoman Army. Lower ranks would be chosen from Iraq's Shiite community.

1921 – The British established an Iraqi government on the Indian model, with a legal code based on the Anglo-Indian precedent, and staffed to a large extent by Indian nationals.

1922 – The unpopular Anglo-Iraqi Treaty of 10/10/22 incorporated the terms of the mandate. The Arabic equivalent for "mandate" is *intidab*, a derivative of the root NDB, whose many meanings include appoint and assign.

1922 – On 11/1/22, the Ottoman Empire was abolished by Kemal's new parliament: *EB*: 28:964.

1922 – High Commissioner Cox, who was called on to arbitrate a complex boundary dispute in northeast Arabia, incorporated his decision on 12/2/22 in the Treaty of 'Uqayr (in Iraq), by which new borders between the Sultanate of Najd and its northern neighbors, Kuwait and Iraq, were established. The sultanate was later incorporated into the Kingdom of Saudi Arabia.

1922 – In December, Cox allowed inveterate rebel Mahmud Barzani to come back to Kurdistan, in the hope that the Barzani tribe might be induced to cooperate with the new regime in Baghdad. Instead, Mahmud pronounced himself King of Kurdistan on 12/25/23. The British sent troops to Kurdistan, the RAF dropped bombs, some of them delayed-action, against targets in the Sulaymaniyyah district, including Mahmud's house. Mahmud went back into exile.

1923 – In March and April, British troops expelled Turkish troops from Iraq to Persia.

1923 – Ancient tribal rivalries welled up along the Saudi-Iraqi border. Ibn Sa'ud and the British High Commissioner in Iraq were engaged in talks aimed at preventing anti-Saudi border tribes from sending raiding parties into Iraq. RAF planes bombed "Ikhwan" raiders in late 1923 and early 1924: *The Making of Saudi Arabia, 1916-1936*, published in cooperation with the Moshe Dayan Center and the Shiloah Institute for Middle Eastern and African Studies, Oxford University Press, 1993, Joseph Kostiner.

1923 – In April, units of the RAF flew 280 Sikh troops from India to Kirkuk. It was Britain's first airborne troop deployment.

1923 – On 7/24/23, the Treaty of Lausanne replaced the Treaty of Sèvres: *EB*: 28:969.

1923 – On 10/29/23, Kemal's new assembly proclaimed the Republic of Turkey: *EB*: 28:964.

1924 – On 3/3/24, Turkey abolished the Ottoman Caliphate.

1930 – An updated treaty of alliance between Great Britain and Iraq gave the British access to two main air bases, and allowed British troops to stay on until 1942.

1932 – The end of the mandate made Iraq an independent state in theory, and a member of the League of Nations, but it was still incapable of maintaining domestic order or self-defense without the help of the RAF: *The British Mandate in Iraq, 1920-32*, Toby Dodge.

1933 – Continued political disorder caused King Faysal to write, shortly before his death, "There is not yet in Iraq an Iraqi people." He was succeeded by his incompetent son, Ghazi.

1939 – King Ghazi, on one of his DUI jaunts, crashed and died. His successor was his infant son, whom Regent 'Abd al Ilah represented. The Regent received valuable cooperation from Nuri al Sa'id, pro-British and pro-Hashimite, who served as Prime Minister on fourteen separate occasions between 1930 and 1958: *EB*.

1939 – Nuri's desire to declare war on Germany was blocked by the influence of Arab Nationalists in the Iraqi Army.

1941 – In April, Prime Minister Rashid 'Ali al Kaylani (Gaylani) fronted for a military coup that took over the government and began secret negotiations with the Axis powers. Nuri and the Regent fled into exile. British reinforcements arrived and went into action. In 30 days of conflict in mid-1941, the British forces ousted the military government, hanged four of its leaders, and reinstated the monarchists, who declared war on the Axis in January 1942. British forces also took control of Syria.

1941-58 – Seventeen years of bitter dissension followed between the traditionalists in the government and the Arab Nationalists in the army. The tipping point came on July 14, 1958, when a cabal headed by Brigadier 'Abd al Karim Qasim ended the monarchy, declared Iraq a republic and a component of the Arab Nation, and executed the young king and the crown prince – leaving the various factions of the military to continue the wrangling on their own: *EB*: 8:832, 21:989.

Nuri, in disguise, tried to escape on foot, but he was recognized, killed, and dragged through the streets of Baghdad.

1917-48 – The British Subjugation of Palestine

(The following summary is based on
A History of Modern Palestine, 2nd edition, 2006, Ilan Pappe.)

1650-1923 – The rise of the British Navy as the world's preeminent maritime force enabled the expansion of a global empire that came to dominate, inter alia, the politics of the Middle East, by virtue of supremacy over the eastern and southern coasts of Arabia, the Suez Canal, Cyprus, Egypt, Iraq, and the Levant. These conquests enhanced Britain's license from the League of Nations to govern the Palestine Mandate in any way it saw fit.

1917 – On 12/9/17, Gen. Edmund Allenby, Commander-in-Chief of a British Expeditionary Force from Egypt, occupied Jerusalem and established a preliminary framework for administering occupied Palestine (population 800,000, including 60,000 Jews). The military government was hampered by the British commitment in the Balfour Declaration – issued by Foreign Secretary Arthur Balfour on 11/2/17, on instructions from pro-Zionist Prime Minister David Lloyd George – to establish a Jewish homeland in that Arab country.

1920 – The military governor of Palestine was replaced by pro-Zionist High Commissioner Sir Herbert Samuel, governing through a civil administration.

1920's – Jews were allowed to pray at the Western Wall in Jerusalem.

14

1922 – On 7/24/22, the Council of the League of Nations confirmed (in draft) the terms of a British mandate committed to the Balfour Declaration.

1922-39 – The pro-Zionist policy of the mandatory authority put the Arab side at an increasing disadvantage.

1929 – Zionist politics were being run in Jerusalem by the Jewish Agency, whose first president was Chaim Weizmann. The quintessential strongman of the Agency was David Ben-Gurion. The Palestinians, who generally thought of themselves as Syrians, looked to their local notables, but the Husaynis, Nashashibis, and Khalidis were too mired in local feuds to be of much help.

1929 – On August 15, Jewish demonstrators raised the Zionist flag at the Western Wall and claimed ownership of the site: *LRB*, 10/6/16.

1929 – Arab-Jewish violence broke out, causing 300 deaths on each side. Many Palestinians had become frustrated with Britain's pro-Zionist policy. In reaction, the Zionist leadership organized its own defense force, the Haganah.

1929 – Britain separated the economic system of the Mandate between a Jewish and an Arab section. Jews paid twice as much in total taxes as Palestinians did. By economic separation, the Mandatory authorities enhanced the ability of Ben-Gurion to entrench the Zionist leadership in its inflexible position – to the lasting disadvantage of the Arab majority. After 1929, external Jewish investment in Palestine enabled the Jewish community to prosper. The Zionist Trade Union, the Histadrut, was an additional power base for Ben-Gurion's almost total control of the Jewish political system – in stark contrast to the absence of any centralized Arab leadership.

1929-36 – While the Zionist leadership concentrated on the acquisition of land and the eviction of the tenant laborers, London subjected the Empire to a beggar-the-colonies policy, which in the Mandate further contributed to the pauperization of rural Palestine.

1936 – In May, Mufti Amin al Husayni, through his Arab Higher Committee (the unofficial government of the Palestinians until 1948), declared a general strike. British police fired on demonstrators, and the strike escalated into the Arab Revolt. London dimly saw the violence as inspired by German and Italian provocation. In Palestine, British forces rounded up Palestinian nationalists. Pro-Zionist intelligence officer Orde Wingate organized night patrols to defend Jewish communities against Arab raiders.

1936-7 – The mandatory authorities expelled from Palestine Hajj Amin al Husayni and the other leaders of the 1936 rebellion: *The Arab-Israeli Wars*, Chaim Herzog.

1939 – As the befuddled policymakers in London began to open their eyes to impending war in Europe, they made a feeble, belated effort to appease Arab resentment of misrule in Palestine by issuance of a White Paper purporting to check Zionist expansion. This initiative failed in its futile objective, but it unleashed Zionist death squads. Law and order were crumbling as Arabs attacked Jews and Jews attacked British.

1939 – The Arab Revolt ended in March. Total deaths were 3,000 Palestinians, 2,000 Jews, and 600 British: *Fallen Pillars*, Donald Neff.

1939 – On 9/3/39, Britain and France declared war on Germany.

1946 – On 7/22/46, Irgun operatives, disguised as Arabs, bombed the King David Hotel, which housed the headquarters of the British Armed Forces in Palestine and Transjordan.

1946-47 – A bad winter in Britain, and US pressure for repayment of Britain's war debt, created an economic crisis that led to British abdication of some of its imperial responsibilities in India and Palestine.

1947 – After the failure of various hopeless stabs at a belated diplomatic resolution of the Arab-Israeli conflict, London abjectly submitted to the UN the mess it had made of Palestine. Taking opportunistic advantage of British confusion and UN inexperience, Washington bulldozed through the neophyte General Assembly on 11/29/47 Resolution 181, which called for the partition of Palestine into an Arab state and a Jewish state. It was all the authority Israel needed to qualify for UN membership and, by 1967, to conquer all the territory of the Palestine Mandate. While the Zionists made maximum use of their noteworthy advantages, the Arabs never mustered leadership able to prevent mass sales of Palestinian land to Zionists, to grasp the import of UN decisions, or to read the Zionist handwriting figuratively emblazoned on every wall.

1947 – The Occupation authorities hanged three Irgunists. In retaliation, Begin hanged two British soldiers. London never hit on a way out of the Palestinian dilemma. On the contrary, the Mandate compounded that dilemma by favoring Jewish immigration. In 1920, 640,000 Arabs faced 76,000 Jews: "Interim Report on the Civil Administration of Palestine". In 1948, 1,300,000 Arabs were confronted by 600,000 Jews: UNSCOP Report.

1948 – War for Israeli Independence

Israel arose from Zionist resolve, Arab incapacity, British opportunism, Soviet arms supply, and American domestic politics. All these syndromes were in frenzied operation before and during the war of 1948.

The following encapsulation of Israel's war of independence leans on two antithetical accounts: *The Arab-Israeli Wars*, published in 1982 by Chaim Herzog, just before he became President of Israel; *The Ethnic Cleansing of Palestine*, published in 2006 by Israeli scholar Ilan Pappe. Whoever reads them both may get the impression they report on two different wars.

1906 – David Green (Gruen) arrived in Palestine and became David Ben-Gurion, the father of the Israeli state.

1920 – As leader of the Histadrut, Ben-Gurion turned the labor movement into a dominant political force: *NYR*, 1/14/16, Avishai Margalit.

1937 – Britain's Peel Commission recommended partition between Arab and Jewish Palestine – the first official endorsement of a persistent but never viable concept.

1940 – The Haganah set up a permanent armed force of volunteers under a salaried General Staff. The elected leadership of the Yishuv (Jewish community) determined its policy. Two paramilitary groups also materialized, the IZL (Irgun) and LEHI (Stern Gang). The Haganah cooperated with the British forces in World War II. The IZL collaborated until Allied victory became certain; LEHI never collaborated: *The Israeli Army*, Edward Luttwak and Dan Horowitz.

1941 – The Haganah (illegal in British eyes) set up a "national" command, which formed a full-time mobile force, the Palmach. Two Palmach companies provided guides for the British troops during the Allied invasion of Syria/Lebanon. Among them were Yigal Allon and Moshe Dayan (who lost an eye there): *The Israeli Army*.

1944 – The Jewish Brigade Group, set up by the UK to help in World War II, saw little active service, but its officers and NCO's received timely training for the 1948 war. The UK did not accept the Zionist offer of a Jewish division, but 27,000 members of the Yishuv volunteered as individuals in the British forces.

1944 – In January, the IZL began acts of sabotage and assassination against British police and army in Palestine. Ben-Gurion assigned the Haganah to security protection for a time against IZL attack on the British.

1945 – The Palmach, youthful and energetic, was becoming the nucleus of the Israeli armed forces.

1945 – In October, the Haganah, the IZL, and LEHI formed the United Resistance Movement, which sabotaged British targets: *MEP*, Summer 2015.

1945 – The British Labor Party, pro-Zionist while it was in opposition, became anti-Zionist in office. It limited Jewish immigration to Palestine to 1500 a month, and set up a blockade to restrict influx of arms. The Haganah moved into cooperation with the IZL and LEHI: *The Israeli Army*.

1946 – The IZL, which had doubled in size, was destroying infrastructure needed by the British authorities to govern Palestine. LEHI was destroying anything British, and killed a British minister: *How Israel Was Won*, Baylis Thomas.

1946 – On 7/22/46, the IZL collaborated in the bombing that destroyed a wing of the King David Hotel, killing 95, including British personnel assigned to offices in the building. Blaming the IZL for not giving their victims adequate warning, the Haganah suspended its cooperation: Herzog. The Haganah continued to violate the British arms blockade.

1946 – When the Yishuv refused to help round up the King David Hotel bombers, the British instituted a virtual police state, and also resorted to illegal tactics versus the subversives: Thomas.

1946 – Late in the year, the Jewish Agency opened with King 'Abdallah negotiations that led to agreement in principle on a top-secret deal: Jordan to get 20 percent of Palestine (later known as The West Bank), in return for Jordanian neutrality between Palestinians and Jews: Pappe; *The Fateful Triangle*, Noam Chomsky. The Zionists saw 'Abdallah as an Arab leader who would accept a Jewish state. 'Abdallah saw an opportunity to realize his dream of a Greater Syria under Jordanian leadership: *The Iron Wall*, Avi Shlaim.

1946 – Palestinian Arab violence was largely directed against Arabs guilty of selling land to Jews. Jewish violence was mitigated for many observers by the age-old persecution of Jews in Europe: Thomas.

1946 – Ben-Gurion had the foresight to realize that the time had come for the Yishuv to start building an army: Margalit.

1947 – In February, with 80,000 troops tied down in Palestine, losing lives to steady IZL and LEHI attack, the UK asked the UN to take over: Thomas. The UNGA set up a special committee (UNSCOP) to decide the future of Palestine. It recommended partition, except for direct UN control of Jerusalem. For sentimental reasons, UNSCOP proposed freakish borders that would assign 56 percent of Palestine to 499,000 Jews (and 438,000 Palestinians), and 42 percent to 818,000 Palestinians (and 10,000 Jews); Jerusalem would have 200,000 residents, equally divided: Pappe.

1947 – The Arab League boycotted UNSCOP, whereas the Zionists established a congenial relationship – until the partition plan had been adopted by the UNGA. Thereafter, the only one of its provisions accepted by the Zionists was the recognition of the legality of a Jewish state: Pappe.

1947 – The Arab League Council resolved in mid-October that it would mount military action against any solution other than an independent Arab state.

1947 – Fawzi Qawuqji, training an anti-Zionist volunteer force in Syria (the Arab Liberation Army – ALA), received arms aid from Egypt, which reserved its support for anti-Hashemites – none for Jordan or its Palestinian following: *The Middle East in World Affairs*, George Lenczowski. Iraq withheld arms from Palestinians suspected of loyalty to Hajj Amin al Husayni: Lenczowski.

1947 – On November 2, Ben-Gurion told his associates that, to prevent the Palestinians in Zionist territory from becoming a fifth column, the Zionist forces would have to expel them.

1947 – On 11/17/47, with British concurrence, 'Abdallah and Golda Meir secretly agreed on the mutual non-belligerency of Israel and Jordan, and that any part of Palestine not annexed by Israel would be annexed by Jordan: *Fallen Pillars*, Donald Neff; *NYR*, 11/4/99, *Collusion Across the Jordan*, Avi Shlaim; the UK approved of their agreement: *JPS*, Benny Morris. (With this agreement in mind, Jordan's General Glubb viewed the 1948 conflict as a "phony war".)

1947 – **The Partition Resolution** – On 11/29/47, UNGA Resolution 181 authorized implementation of the UNSCOP recommendations, including partition. The Arab-Jewish conflict escalated to civil war between Jewish forces (Haganah – 43,000, most of them poorly trained; Palmach – 3000, well trained; IZL; LEHI) and a dedicated but incoherent band of some 3000 Palestinian volunteers and 2500 incoming ALA volunteers: Herzog; Pappe.

1947 – From 11/30/47 on, the Haganah, the IZL, and LEHI colluded in a campaign of terror against the Palestinian people: Pappe. Attacks on selected villages implemented Ben-Gurion's Plan Dalet – the systematic expulsion of Palestinians from their country by fear or force, and the country-wide extermination of activists whose names had been assembled by meticulous intelligence work over the years: Pappe. Early examples were the demolition of homes and the killing of 15 villagers in Khisas on 12/18/47, the massacre of residents of Balad al Shaykh on 12/31/47, and a demolition/expulsion in a Haifa neighborhood on 12/31/47: Pappe.

1947 – In December, the Arab League agreed on the supply of arms to the Palestinians, whose supplies were short, particularly because each of the feuding pro and anti Hashemite factions had been trying to block the acquisition of arms by the other faction. The League approved the appointment of Syrian Fawzi al Qawuqji as commander of the volunteer ALA. He was not recognized by the Palestinian leadership, which named the Mufti's nephew, 'Abd al Qadir al Husayni, commander of the Army of the Holy War. Qawuqji was a protégé of Syria and Iraq, which opposed the Husaynis: Pappe. In combat, he actually colluded with the Haganah against the forces of his Palestinian rivals: Thomas. He also dealt in secret with the Jewish Agency. Ben-Gurion knew from the outset that the Zionists would win the war.

1948 – The Zionists began incorporating Druze and Circassians into the Border Police, which were later used primarily to oppress Palestinians in the Occupied Territories (OT): Pappe.

1948 – In January, the Palmach erased a Haifa neighborhood, the IZL and LEHI increased air attacks, and the British gave up security duty: Pappe.

1948 – On 2/1/48, the twin authorities of the Yishuv (Jewish Agency and Va'ad Leumi) called for general mobilization. The Zionist army was larger and better trained than the opposing Arab forces: Thomas. Haganah took over the Field Guard (the *Hish*): *The Israeli Army*. According to Shlaim, IDF strength, 35,000 at the start of the war, had increased by December 1948 to 96,000.

1948 – **The War of the Roads** – On 2/15/48, the Zionists undertook to wipe out Arab villages whose sites obstructed their battle plans. Villagers were expelled or killed: Pappe.

1948 – Through all the early violence between Jews and Arabs, the British forces took no action except for their own defense against the Zionists' underground war, and support for Haganah's defense against the ALA: Pappe.

1948 – On 3/2/48, British Foreign Secretary Ernest Bevin endorsed the secret proposal for the Transjordanian takeover of east Jerusalem and a land link thereto.

1948 – In early March, Qawuqji brought his first ALA unit across the Allenby Bridge. In April, he directed artillery fire against Jewish positions. In the ensuing eight months, his forces were repeatedly routed, and they gave up the ghost in October, having done no service to anyone but the Zionists, who considered ALA operations a convenient pretext for the Zionist excesses imposed by the secret Plan Dalet: Pappe.

1948 – Plan Dalet, Ben-Gurion's program for ethnic cleansing of Palestine, was officially adopted on 3/10/48: Pappe.

1948 – In April, the Zionists went on the offensive: Herzog.

1948 – In early April, Haganah fought a bitter six-day battle for control of the access road to Jerusalem. The battle ended in Israel's favor after the death of Palestinian commander 'Abd al Qadir al Husayni, which demoralized the Arab forces. The participation of a Druze unit was the Druzes' last fight on the Arab side. Later on, they became loyal fighters for the Israelis: Herzog.

1948 – By April 7, all villages on the Haifa-Tel Aviv, Haifa-Janin, and Jerusalem-Jaffa roads had been wiped out.

1948 – **The Massacre of Dayr Yasin** – IZL and LEHI had been committing various anecdotal atrocities, including torture, but their most notorious crime was the massacre of Dayr Yasin on 4/9/48. On a hill west of Jerusalem, some 250 villagers were killed, bodies were thrown down wells, women were raped, and some Palestinians were trucked through Jerusalem in a victory parade and then killed: Thomas. Menachem Begin and Yitzhak Shamir, then leaders of the IZL and LEHI, would later become prime ministers of Israel: *Atlantic*, Milan Kubik, former Middle East correspondent for *Newsweek*.

1948 – The villages of Abu Ghawah and Nabi Samawil exemplified the strange vicissitudes of war. They were on Haganah's list for demolition, but they were saved by the intervention of LEHI, with which Arab mukhtars had built a working relationship: Pappe.

1948 – On April 18, the first Palestinian city to fall to the Zionist onslaught was Tiberias, on the western shore of Lake Tiberias.

1948 – **Massacre in Haifa** – On April 21, the British garrison in Haifa was preparing to evacuate. As the IDF's Carmeli Brigade entered the city, British commander Major General Hugh Stockwell informed remaining Arab and Jewish notables of the situation; he passed on word from the Jewish attackers that Haifa's Arabs had to surrender their arms,

23

but should stay; the Mufti and Qawuqji had advised the Arabs to leave until the Jews had been "driven out"; Stockwell advised the Arabs to leave: Herzog.

Pappe's version is more comprehensive, and grimmer: The Zionists had been committing acts of terror against the Arabs of Haifa since December 1947. On 4/22/48, with British soldiers as onlookers, the Carmelis acted to take Haifa without the Haifans. As Jewish loudspeakers goaded Arab residents to leave before it was too late, the Carmelis invaded under orders to "kill any Arab you encounter". Panic-stricken Arabs bolted to the harbor to find boats, while Carmelis looted.

British inaction was later recognized as a shameful chapter in their history. In a subsequent letter to Palestinian leaders, Stockwell apologized for his British superiors' lack of sympathy. The letter infuriated Foreign Secretary Bevin, but Field Marshal Montgomery defended Stockwell. As for the Palestinians, many died under Jewish artillery fire, and many drowned in the harbor: Pappe.

1948 – The Palestinian Mandate expired on 5/5/48.

1948 – Acre on the coast and Baysan in the east fell to the Jews 5/6/48. During the siege of Acre, a typhoid epidemic broke out. The Red Cross team in the city suspected that outsiders (Haganah?) had poisoned the water supply with typhoid bacilli. On May 27 Egypt caught – and later executed – two Jews in Gaza on that same charge: Pappe.

1948 – **The Battle for Jerusalem** – The greatest handicap of the Jewish side at the start of the war was the country-wide dispersal of its 650,000 people. However, their largest community – 100,000 residents in Jerusalem – gave them a head start toward securing the country's capital.

In February, the Haganah had captured Jerusalem's Shaykh Jarrah district (west of Mount Scopus, north of the Old City), which was to become the nucleus of postwar west Jerusalem. By late March, Palestinian control of the 50-mile Tel Aviv-Jerusalem highway had subjected Jerusalem to rationing of food and water: Thomas. The Jews' priority military objective had to be securing the highway in order to break the siege. The timely (and illegal) arrival of the first Czech rifles and machine guns on 4/1/48 enabled the Jews to open the highway and

24

on 4/8/48 to kill 'Abd al Qadir al Husayni: Pappe, Herzog. In late April, the Palmach took additional segments of the city and its approaches from Palestinian and ALA forces.

The British forces in the Jerusalem area stood aside, except for blocking a Jewish effort to cleanse Shaykh Jarrah: Pappe. In another neighborhood, they disarmed the Palestinian resisters, promising to defend them against any Jewish attack, but they later reneged on this promise: Pappe.

On May 2, in a top-secret meeting, an Israeli official informed two senior officers (British) of Jordan's Arab Legion that the Jewish forces were strong enough to take all of Palestine, but this was a political issue: If 'Abdallah would stay neutral between Jews and Palestinians, the Jewish forces would stay clear of east Jerusalem (the "Old City") and a block of land between it and Transjordan. This plan suited 'Abdallah, whose devious strategy was to project his image as defender of Palestine while striking a deal for a foothold in the holy city and a land link thereto.

In the later heat of battle, Ben-Gurion changed his mind and ordered his forces to contest the Old City – in violation of the understanding with 'Abdallah: *JPS*, Benny Morris. From May 8 to 14, there was bitter fighting between the Jewish and Palestinian/ALA forces for control of Latrun, which is 20 miles west of Jerusalem but a crucial point on the access road to Jerusalem from Tel Aviv. On May 16 Israel secured west Jerusalem – up to the walls of the Old City.

On May 18, in accordance with the secret understanding with the Jews, 'Abdallah ordered Major General Sir John Glubb, commander of the Arab Legion, to occupy the Old City and the land link to Transjordan. The secret understanding between the Jewish Agency and King 'Abdallah had made no mention of a sector of special concern to the Jews – the Old City's Jewish Quarter. In May, in desperate fighting, the Legion took the Quarter from the Israelis. The engagement was the Legion's signal achievement of the war, and the Israelis' worst defeat: Herzog. The Legion expelled IZL militiamen from northern west Jerusalem, interrupted Jewish cleansing operations in the city, and carried out shelling that made life in west Jerusalem almost intolerable (Herzog), but in equally intense combat, the Israelis salvaged it.

25

The war was to end with the new city (west Jerusalem), under Israeli control, and the old city (east Jerusalem), Kfar Etzion, and the Latrun salient under Transjordanian control. (That situation, in Jewish eyes, was rectified in 1967.)

According to Pappe, the Jews' capture of Ramallah was vitiated by their massacre of 400 citizens, and the deaths of many more dispatched on a long march to exile without food or water.

1948 – Israeli Declaration of Independence; Arab Invasion – On 5/14/48, the Jewish Agency proclaimed the founding of the State of Israel. It was immediately recognized by the US and the USSR. Begin announced the end of Irgun's underground activities.

The proclamation precipitated the reluctant decisions of Egypt, Syria, Lebanon, and Iraq to invade Palestine – ostensibly to rescue its people in the service of the nebulous mystique of Pan-Arabism, more probably to compete for available pieces of Palestine. According to conventional estimates, the invaders included 10,000 Egyptians, 8000 Syrians, 2000 Lebanese, and 10,000 Iraqis. Shlaim offers a lower estimate of 25,000 total.

According to General Glubb, the main motivation for the Arab invasions was the pressure of public opinion on the four governments: *MEP*, Summer 2015, Albert B. Wolf. None of their contributions would be decisive: Thomas. All Arab invaders were handicapped by the arms embargo imposed on the Palestine conflict by their traditional supplier, the UK, and especially by the shaky status of the neophyte governments that sent them.

The Egyptian force consisted of a few thousand regulars and 2,000 untrained but fervent Muslim-Brotherhood volunteers, who saw Palestine as a central battlefield in the war against European imperialism: Pappe. The Egyptian regulars were resolute on defense, but unimaginatively commanded. Toward the end of the war, only British and American warnings kept the Israelis from invading Sinai: Lenczowski.

The invaders had two strategic objectives: to subdue the Israelis, and – Iraq excepted – to prevent Transjordan from inheriting Palestinian territory. They soon outran their supply lines. Their coordination was hopeless – especially given the Arab League's tone-deaf choice of King 'Abdallah as commander-in-chief.

1948 – The expulsion of Jaffa's 50,000 Arab residents on 5/13/48 had completed the depopulation of most of the Arab cities and towns in Palestine: Pappe. After Israel's UDI (Unilateral Declaration of Independence) on May 15, its forces continued to press on all fronts regardless of UN truces or Arab invasions. In May, they took Safad, Jaffa, the northern Negev, the coastal plain, and the valleys of Galilee. By the end of May, the cleansing process was complete in a coastal rectangle ten miles wide and sixty miles long between Haifa and Tel Aviv (the only all-Jewish city in prewar Palestine). The cleansing campaign featured a Jewish "killing spree" of young Arab men in the village of Tantura. A hooded informer matched names of prewar activists with faces: Pappe.

1948 – The Arab Legion took the Jewish Quarter in east Jerusalem on May 20: *The Israeli Army*. On May 24, the arrival of more arms from the Soviet Bloc coincided with the Israeli capture of several Arab districts in west Jerusalem. The advent of Israeli statehood had theoretically converted the British mandatory authorities to neutral observation, but their disorderly departure added to the chaos; they seemed to think that by leaving a political vacuum behind, they could prevent 'Abdallah's seizure of the West Bank: *The Israeli Army*. However, there was no vacuum. Palestine had already split into <u>two</u> entities – one Jewish, one Arab.

1948 – **The UN: Abortive Mission** – Before May 15, the UK had excluded UN representation from Palestine. Thereafter, the UN lacked the resources to honor its commitment under UNGA 181 to keep law and order. Its one accomplishment was its prevention of Israeli occupation of Syria's Golan: Pappe.

UN Mediator Count Folke Bernadotte arrived in Palestine on May 20. His appointment had been endorsed by the Jews: As President of the Swedish Red Cross, he had saved Jewish lives in Europe during World War II. The Jews didn't realize that his approach to the Palestine problem would be equally humanitarian: Pappe.

1948 – **Political Assassination: Episode One** – On May 22, returning from consultation with the new mediator, American Consul General Tom Wasson was shot down. He was wearing a "bullet-proof" vest (which had been a subject of merriment in the State Department when he took leave), but the Israeli (?) sniper was skilled enough to put a fatal bullet through the armhole.

1948 – On 5/26/48, as the fighting intensified, Israel founded the Israeli Defense Force (IDF).

1948 – Bernadotte's first truce (June 11 to July 8) was the turning point of the war: Pappe. While affording both sides a badly needed respite, it gave Israel more time to get on with ethnic cleansing, and to deploy a welcome shipment of up-to-date fighter planes (Messerschmitts). Later in the war, Israeli pilots – few in numbers but experienced from World War II – would "outshine" their Arab and British adversaries. (See different version by Donald Neff below.)

1948 – On June 20, the IZL's SS Altalena, carrying arms and recruits, arrived offshore near Netanya. Ben-Gurion offered a plan for division of the arms between the IDF and the IZL. Begin rejected it. In an exchange of small-arms fire (deaths: IDF – 2; Irgun – 6), the IDF took over and ordered the ship to sail to Tel Aviv. On the coast of Tel Aviv, fire was exchanged among IDF soldiers on shore and in corvettes, and IZL fighters on shore and on the Altalena (deaths: IDF – 1; IZL – 10). The ship caught fire, was beached (?), and later sunk. On June 28, the IZL's military wing ceased to exist: Herzog; Pappe. Shortly thereafter, Ben-Gurion had the members of the IZL and LEHI integrated into the IDF: *MEP*, Summer 2015.

Israel also took advantage of the first truce to level villages previously depopulated. At the start of the war, the Yishuv had owned 5.8 percent of Palestine. By July, the Israeli forces had occupied 78 percent.

When the war resumed on 7/9/1948, the IDF – now numbering 60,000 – took the initiative with even more ferocity than before. The first targets were Lod and Ramallah, just southeast of Tel Aviv. They were still in the hands of local Arab forces, Transjordanian tribesmen, and small detachments of the Arab Legion. In the seizure of Lod, 426 Palestinian villagers died: Pappe; *My Promised Land*, Ari Shavit, cited by

Jonathan Freedland, *NYR*. Ramallah fell July 14, Nazareth July 16. Western journalists reported on "riddled corpses", and Palestinians forced into exile on foot without food or water. There was simultaneous hard fighting between the IDF and the Legion for east Jerusalem: Pappe; Herzog.

Israel's outstanding field commander in the war was Yigal Allon, ably backed by Yitzhak Rabin; Moshe Dayan's small unit had mounted a crucial defense against the Syrians: Herzog. The Syrians went home: Pappe. The ALA was eliminated.

1948 – **Political Assassination: Episode Two** – Bernadotte's second truce was proclaimed 7/18/48. The IDF ignored it.

Bernadotte had infuriated the Israelis by his recommendations to the UN: repatriate the refugees and re-divide Palestine (western Galilee to Israel; Ramallah and the Negev to the Arabs; put Jerusalem and Lod under UN control; Arab Palestine to be administered by Transjordan): Herzog. On September 17 in Jerusalem, Bernadotte was assassinated by three assailants, who escaped. Herzog writes they "were generally assumed to be Jewish." Pappe writes what most observers believe – that they were operatives of Shamir's LEHI. According to Fred Jerome, writing in *The Link* of July 2015: The assassination was ordered by Israel Eldad, Nathan Yellin-Mor, and Yitzhak Shamir of LEHI (split off from Menachem Begin's Irgun in 1940, headed by Begin since 1942); it was perpetrated by Yitzhak Ben Moshe, Gingi Zinger, Meshulam Makover, and Yehoshua Cohen of LEHI; in 1991 Eldad and Makover gave the details of the killing to a jolly TV audience on the Israeli program "This Is Your Life"; Jerome also reported that Resolution 194, based on Bernadotte's plan, was adopted by "the UN" 12/11/48, but never implemented. Bernadotte's final report, released on September 20 by the UNGA, included his recommendations. They were rejected by both parties. Bernadotte was replaced by a committee, the UN's Palestine Conciliation Commission (PCC).

1948 – Ben-Gurion ordered the IZL to disband, and detained LEHI's leaders. The Israelis were in danger of UNGA adoption of the resolutions of the martyred mediator, but they were saved by Egypt, which blocked Israeli access to routes across the Negev, thereby justifying Israeli counteraction, and consigning the Bernadotte report to oblivion.

1948 – In September, the Egyptians (including Jamal 'Abd al Nasir) and a Saudi unit were the last Arab invaders still fighting. The Israeli-Arab war had essentially become an Israeli-Egyptian war, and the Egyptians were on the defensive: *JPS*, Winter 1998, Benny Morris. The Saudis were too few and too late to affect the outcome (*Imperialism and Nationalism in the Fertile Crescent*, Richard Allen), although they put up a good fight. According to Herzog, when they ran out of ammunition, they fought with their teeth – as their female ancestors reportedly did in ancient tribal warfare.

1948 – In October, the IDF launched several offensives of unprecedented effectiveness. In the south, it took Beersheba from the Egyptians and the Saudis. In the north, the villages of Galilee – reinforced by Iraqis who had disregarded orders calling them home – put up an impassioned defense. Some villages defended themselves so staunchly that they survived the war, as the nucleus of the Arab minority in Israel. Most of the Galileeans disappeared. The Israelis massacred 450 villagers in Dawaymah (Pappe), crossed the border, and went north to one of their ultimate goals, the Litani River. They were unopposed by the Lebanese army, but the UK and the US ordered them back to the prewar border: Herzog.

1948 – In November Israel completed the occupation of the Negev and the village of Umm Rashrash (now Eilat). In December, Egypt's defenses collapsed: Herzog. Israeli forces entered Sinai. They were challenged by aircraft from Britain's major air base in the Suez Canal Zone. Four British Spitfires were shot down by the Israeli Air Force, another by Israeli ground fire: Herzog. Neff offers a different version: On 1/7/49, the day of the ceasefire, Israeli warplanes shot down five unsuspecting British aircraft. The Israelis moved the wreckage into Israel to support their claim that the British had been the violators.

1949 – On January 1, the US Ambassador to Israel delivered an ultimatum from the UK: withdraw from Sinai, or face British intervention under the Anglo-Egyptian Treaty of 1936. Israel complied, but on January 7 extracted a ceasefire from defeated Egypt. The war was over.

1949 – The Arab capitulations were formalized in four armistice agreements:

Egypt – 2/24/49
Lebanon – 3/23/49
Jordan – 4/3/49
Syria – 7/20/49
Iraq, Saudi Arabia – No agreements

These covenants established the original borders of the new State of Israel: Herzog.

Israel – The lives of 4500 soldiers and 1200 civilians were lost in the war – almost 1 percent of the population of the Yishuv (650,000): *The Israeli Army*; *How Israel Was Won*, Baylis Thomas. The prize was most of Palestine. The Arab invasions paid off for Israel by enhancing its permanent claim to the territory it had conquered: Awarded 55 percent of Palestine under the subtext of UNGA Resolution 181, Israel came out of the war with 79 percent: Shlaim. Israel also claimed full sovereignty over the Israeli-Syrian demilitarized zones: *Times*, 7/19/77, Norman Dacey. Territory already controlled by the Yishuv at the start of hostilities had gone largely unchallenged: Thomas.

Herzog stresses that of all the leaders on both sides, Ben-Gurion's charisma and insight put him head and shoulders above the rest. Herzog does not warn that Ben-Gurion put the forces of Zionism on a path of ruthlessness that may come back to haunt them, or that the mystique of Zionism itself may be found wanting.

Palestinians – The prewar Arab population of Palestine numbered between 1.1 million (*The Arab-Israeli Wars*, Chaim Herzog) and 1.4 million (*The Ethnic Cleansing of Palestine*, Ilan Pappe). Back then, they were the putative heirs of the "mandate". At the end of the war, they were disinherited and catastrophically dispersed, with only 92,000 still in Israeli Palestine, versus 716,000 Jews: Shlaim.

The forces of Palestine and their Arab allies had fought bravely, but they were doomed to lose by the Israeli forces' greater numbers, and their own inferior coordination. That handicap was most detrimental in

31

darkness, so the Israelis learned to launch most of their attacks at night: Herzog. Equally detrimental to the Palestinian cause was inter-Arab bickering: Herzog.

Most of the Palestinians fled their homes – over 300,000 by choice, to escape Jewish rule, another 400,000 in panic, after massacres in Dayr Yasin, Haifa, and elsewhere – for a total of 725,000: Thomas. 531 villages had been destroyed, and 11 urban areas depopulated: Pappe.

Transjordan – 'Abdallah wisely chose not to enlist his diminutive Arab Legion (5000 troops: Thomas) in the Arab invasion, but Ben-Gurion's breach of promise with 'Abdallah forced the Legion to demonstrate its professionalism. The acquisition of 2263 square miles of Palestine converted Transjordan to Jordan. Jordan's generous grant of citizenship to all Palestinian applicants created a troublesome rift between West-Bankers and East-Bankers, but in 2016 the throne of Jordan seemed to be on its way to successful assimilation of its subjects. From combat with Israeli forces in 1948, Jordan moved rapidly to the status of protectorate of Israel – as first demonstrated in the civil war of 1970.

Arab Invaders – Palestine's Arab neighbors, appalled by the Jewish swallowing of an Arab country before their eyes, were chafing to abort that process or, failing that, pick up some of the territorial leftovers. However, they were handicapped by the British arms embargo, and hogtied by domestic squabbles. Contrary to other estimates, Thomas doubts that their expeditionary forces totaled as many as 10,000 soldiers.

Egypt came out of the war in control of 140 square miles, which were to acquire disproportionate political importance, and the inelegant name of the Gaza Strip. (In this text, "Gaza Strip" is simplified to "Gaza".) An Egypt-Israel Mixed Armistice Commission (EIMAC) was formed, with headquarters in the Egyptian village of Al 'Awjah: Thomas. For some years after the war, the Arab League maintained a boycott of trade with Israel, and a denial of Arab-controlled waterways to Israeli shipping.

In *Thirteen Days in September*, Lawrence Wright described how "… the [Arab] soldiers returned [from Palestine] to take revenge on their governments. Military coups … turned the region into a vast barracks state.": *NYR*, 12/4/14. Peace with Israel was the furthest prospect from their thoughts. The most traumatic consequences: 1949 – a military coup in Syria; 1951 – the assassination of Jordan's King 'Abdallah by agents of Hajj Amin; 1952 – a military coup in Egypt; 1958 – a military coup in Iraq. From 1949 to the present day, there has been a large community of second-class Palestinian citizens in Israel, a seething community of Palestinians in occupied Palestine, a lost community under Israeli lockdown in Gaza, an indigestible community of stateless Sunni Palestinians in pathologically sectarian Lebanon, and overall in the region millions of Palestinian refugees on the UNRWA dole.

1956 – Suez War

———

Ever since 1929, the Arab-Israeli conflict has been a political volcano, always active, periodically erupting in all-out war. The second eruption came in 1956.

1949 – France and Israel began sharing the results of their nuclear research.

1951 – On 5/18/51 the UNSC adopted Resolution 93 that condemned an Israeli action of 2/2/51 that had been described by the Egyptian-Israeli Mixed Armistice Commission as an attack by forces of the Israeli regular army against forces of the Egyptian regular army in Gaza.

1952 – "Paunchy, balding, and bloated" (Richard Cavendish, *History Today*, 7/7/02), "uneducated, lazy, untruthful" (Sir Miles Lampson) British puppet King Faruq was ousted by a group of Egyptian officers, headed by Col. Jamal ʿAbd al Nasir.

1954 – The outbreak of the Algerian war of independence further alienated France from the Arab world.

1954 – Israeli agents in Egypt damaged American Embassy offices with incendiary devices that Washington was supposed to blame on Nasir, Egypt's new leader. Instead, his intelligence service unearthed the plot and hanged the plotters.

1954 – In December, British efforts to enroll Jordan in the pro-Western "Baghdad Pact" precipitated the dismissal of General Glubb and his British officers, and King Husayn's switch to alliance with Nasir.

1954 – Shimon Peres, Director of Israel's Defense Ministry, was in Paris in November to lobby the French Government.

1955 – Nasir's cautious foreign policy had promoted a tranquility along the border that was frustrating Israel – which needed border tension that could be exploited for conquest of the rest of Israel's alleged birthright: The West Bank, the Gaza Strip, and Sinai. In "retaliation" for the 1954 hangings, Israel raided Gaza in February 1955, killing 39 members of the Egyptian garrison.

1955 – Under domestic political pressure, Nasir responded to the Gaza raid by sponsoring pinprick raids on Israeli targets by Palestinian guerrillas (fedayeen – *fida'iyyin*) based in Gaza.

1955 – Egypt and Syria established a joint military command. Jordan joined in 1956.

1955 – France escalated its shipments of arms to Israel.

1955 – Alarmed by arms supply to Israel from France and Canada, Nasir applied to the USSR. In September, the Soviets readily agreed to sell Egypt a huge quantity of weapons, including MiG jet fighters, Ilyushin bombers, and main battle tanks.

1955 – As soon as Israel got word of the Soviet-Egyptian transaction, it determined to go to war to eliminate Nasir before Egypt could deploy the new weapons.

1956 – In March, British Prime Minister Anthony Eden decided that Nasir had to be removed, whereas Eisenhower was still looking for ways to do business with Nasir – short of selling arms to an adversary of Israel.

1956 – In April, Peres was back in Paris to inform the French that Israel was going to war against "genocidal maniac Nasir".

1956 – Probably in retaliation for US concurrence in Canadian shipment of jets to Israel, and to line up an alternative source of arms, Nasir on 5/16/56 recognized Washington's bête noire, Communist China. This was the last straw for Eisenhower and Dulles. Nasir had failed to obtain a Soviet counteroffer to Washington's agreement in late 1955 to lend Egypt financing for a giant new dam on the Nile. His belated acceptance of the American offer was badly timed: The American cotton farmers were opposed to Egyptian competition – which would be increased by the extra irrigation from the High Dam;

Congress resented the Egyptian resistance to Israeli expansion; if the US was going to the rescue of any Positive Neutralist, let it be Tito: *The Prize*, Daniel Yergin. Washington's July 19 withdrawal of its High-Dam offer was insulting in its tone, and in its suggestion that Egypt's economy was not up to the size of the project.

1956 – On July 26, Nasir riposted by nationalizing the Suez Canal. Nasir's three adversaries were already furious. Now came the nationalization – an intolerable act of insolence to France, patron of *La Compagnie du Canal de Suez*, to Britain, guardian of the canal and the Canal Zone, and to the US, the would-be warden of the Middle East. In their paranoia, Britain and France saw the nationalization as a mortal threat to Western oil supplies: *Strategic Geography and the Changing Middle East*, Geoffrey Kemp/Robert Harkavy.

The Western powers had swallowed their own propaganda that Egypt lacked the expertise to run the canal on its own. Before announcing the withdrawal of High Dam aid, the secretariat of the State Department had solicited the views of at least two bureaus about Nasir's political situation. The Bureau of Intelligence and Research (INR) was not given all the relevant facts: The writer (who, despite recent service in Port Said, had failed to foresee the nationalization) was charged with producing a rush assessment of the political significance of the High Dam project to the Nasir regime. His conclusion – that the regime would not stand or fall on the completion of the project – was probably accurate in isolation, but it had no relevance to the actual circumstances, some of which were unknown to INR.

1956 – Secretary Dulles spent the summer on another of America's futile efforts to diplomatize a Middle Eastern stalemate out of existence. His problem was exacerbated by Nasir's determination to deny Israeli ships access to the Canal – and to the Strait of Tiran. This seven-mile-wide waterway between the tip of Sinai and Saudi Arabia, Israel's only maritime access to the Red Sea, was hostage to artillery batteries on the Egyptian coast. In the dog-eat-dog Middle East, the dignified provisions of the Egypt-Israel Armistice Agreement, and of UNSC Resolution 93 of 1951, were irrelevant.

1956 – Meanwhile, even wilder melodrama was brewing behind the scenes. Prime Minister Anthony Eden, failing in health and judgment, was irrevocably locked in to the mystique of British Empire. He was drawing false analogies with Sarajevo and Munich: Yergin. His obsession was to annul the British evacuation of the Canal Zone prescribed in the Anglo-Egyptian Treaty of 1954. France was infuriated by Nasir's support for Algeria's fierce resistance to the demented French idea that Algeria was part of France. Israel was committed to aborting Egypt's de facto control of the Gaza Strip, opening the Canal and the Strait, and bringing the mythical (?) Kingdom of David back to life.

On 6/17/56, Moshe Dayan and Shimon Peres met in secret with French officials to propose joint military operations against the Arabs. France was unconvinced: *Warriors at Suez*, Donald Neff.

1956 – Ben-Gurion's replacement of conciliator Moshe Sharett as Prime Minister enabled him to arrange and implement the Suez War conspiracy: Shlaim.

1956 – In July, Eden ordered his chiefs of staff to plan for war with Egypt. On July 29, the French cabinet decided to go to war in alliance with Israel. On August 7 Peres assured the French that Israel was ready to attack Egypt in concert with France: Neff. On September 1, the Israeli Military Attaché in Paris transmitted word of French sentiment in favor of Israeli participation in an Anglo-French invasion of the Canal Zone: Herzog. In a September 26 talk with Eden, French Prime Minister Guy Mollet withheld report of the secret talks between France and Israel: Neff; Israel was concerned that Britain might oppose any Israeli attempt to take the West Bank. On October 7, out of concern that Iraq might send troops to help Jordan against Israeli invasion of the West Bank, France let Eden in on its joint war plans with Israel. Good news: Eden was delighted: Neff. With fedayeen raids into Israel from Gaza at an all-time high (Herzog), final war plans were drawn up at Sèvres on October 21 by Prime Minister Mollet, Foreign Minister Selwyn Lloyd, and Ben-Gurion, Peres, and Dayan: Herzog; *Washington Post Weekly*, review of *Battling for Peace*, published in 1995 by Shimon Peres. According to Peres's postwar analysis, Israel's primary motive for participation was the

French promise to reward Israel by clandestine construction of a nuclear reactor at Dimona: *NYR*, 5/9/96, Avishai Margalit.

1956 – In the elaborate invasion scenario, Israel was comfortably typecast as the villain, although it did try to put an innocent face on its intrusion into the Gaza Strip and Sinai on October 29 as defense against "action by Egyptian forces" (there was none) and "to eliminate fedayeen bases". Israel had additional objectives it didn't broadcast: To reinstate Western control of the Canal, pulverize Egyptian forces, and oust Nasir: Neff; Lenczowski. Israel hoped the magnitude of these offenses would be muted by the Canal crisis, and the concomitant US electoral campaign and Hungarian revolution.

Having feinted toward Jordan, Israel began its invasion of Egypt by a paradrop that was supposed to be misread by the Egyptians as just one more reprisal raid. The ruse worked – delaying an adequate Egyptian response by one valuable day – in part because Field Marshal 'Amir, a political appointee, was an alcoholic incompetent. It gave Israel more time to strafe positions in Sinai, cut telephone lines by treetop flights, and launch a ground attack. More important, it gave Israel more leeway to disengage if Britain and France should get cold feet: Herzog.

The invasion secured the Strategic Mitla Pass (35 miles east of the south end of the Canal), took Al 'Arish November 2, the Gaza Strip November 3, Sharm al Shaykh November 5. Israel had Sinai, and meant to keep it: *The Iron Wall*, Avi Shlaim.

England and France vetoed a pacific UNSC resolution October 30, and then – in accordance with their elaborate prewar scenario – issued an ultimatum to the warring parties to withdraw their forces ten miles from the Canal, Israeli to the east, Egyptian to the west. Israel "accepted". Egypt obviously refused to disavow sovereignty over Sinai. From bases in Cyprus, the British and French began air attacks on Canal Zone targets October 31. France had already flown 72 jets to Israel to help maintain air cover of Israel and its invading forces. On November 6, British ground troops from Cyprus landed at Port Said, west of the Canal, French troops at Port Fu'ad, east of the Canal. Also on October 31, the Egyptian frigate Ibrahim al Awwal shelled port and refinery facilities in Haifa for four hours, before it surrendered and became a unit of the Israeli fleet.

Against the invasion, Nasir adopted the martyrdom strategy – outfitting his troops in mufti and deploying them in civilian neighborhoods, so that if the invaders chose to return fire, which they did, the populace took heavy casualties.

The conspiratorial invasion of the Canal Zone was a military cakewalk but a political disaster.

On the military side, the British and French air forces went into action on October 31, destroying 95 percent of the Egyptian Air Force on the ground. Nasir had made the mistake of crediting the British and French with enough sense not to act on their professions of belligerence: Thomas. In late October, Nasir suspended civil liberties and seized Jewish businesses. (Later on, 25,000 Jews left Egypt for Israel.) On November 1, Egypt seized British and French properties in Egypt, notably their oil companies, and accepted the UNGA demand for a ceasefire, leaving the three conspirators in a "ridiculous position": Neff. On November 2, Egypt sank a blockship in the Canal.

On November 6, the UNGA called for a ceasefire, and the replacement of British and French forces in Egypt by UNEF (Expeditionary Force). Britain and France ignored the UNGA resolution, vetoed a similar UNSC proposal, and put in ground troops November 5 and 6, while Israel consolidated its hold on Sinai up to the secret ten-mile-wide buffer strip stipulated by its allies.

The plans of Britain and France began to fall apart even before the landings. Israel caused early embarrassment on November 4: Having met its own objectives by taking Sinai and the Gaza Strip, it blew its allies' cover by accepting a ceasefire – leaving them with no warring forces to "separate": Thomas. The UK accepted the ceasefire November 6. France had to follow suit.

For once, the imperturbable Eisenhower was perturbed. The blatant conspiracy was an insult to his intelligence. The clandestine violation of NATO solidarity and the UN Charter was an affront. Taking charge from Dulles, Eisenhower asked over the trans-Atlantic telephone if Eden had lost his mind. He also withheld alternative sources of oil from the invaders, threatened to pull the rug out from under the pound sterling by blocking British access to IMF loans, and ordered Israel to evacuate Sinai and Gaza or lose American arms and financial aid, both public and (tax-exempt) private: *NYR*, 7/16/98; *The Passionate Attachment*, George Ball; Shlaim; Thomas.

In the circumstances, Eisenhower's fiat was law. He had a powerful case, which he took to the people, in the first ultimatum an American President had dared to impose on the State of Israel. (For the next US ultimatum to Israel, see the 10/28/73 Yom Kippur War entry.) Dulles later made the impossible claim that no secret concessions had been made to Israel. Israel has always gotten secret concessions. In this case, the US extracted from Nasir a promise to rein in the fedayeen, and an American tanker brought a special shipment of crude oil to Eilat: *Counterpunch*, 3/16/07.

Eden had come to the end of the line. His invasion had split the House of Commons – even the High Command. Opposition leader Hugh Gaitskell condemned the "disastrous folly". The European troops were gone by December 22: Lenczowski. On November 8 Ben-Gurion announced the cabinet's decision to withdraw the troops from Sinai – subject to satisfactory arrangements for installation of a UN force.

Nasir's People's War suffered the predictable disproportionate casualty rates: deaths – British, 16; French, 10; Israeli, 231; Egyptian, 3000 soldiers, 1000 civilians or more.

Israel held out stubbornly for continuation of its occupation of Sinai and Gaza, but capitulated to Eisenhower's pressure after a few months, while effectively demilitarizing Sinai by demolishing Egyptian military installations. Israel came out of the war with "mountains of Egyptian military equipment" (Yergin), and the French commitment to make it a nuclear power. The only adverse development for Israel was Egypt's reoccupation of Gaza in 1957.

The UN played its usual anemic role: UNEF, barred from Israeli territory, moved in on 11/15/56 on the Egyptian side of the border as a tripwire, but not as a defensive force – as demonstrated in 1967.

1967 – Six-Day War

―――――

After the Suez War, Israel remained fixed on the objectives unfulfilled in 1956: The ouster of Nasir, the destruction of the Egyptian armed forces, and the expansion of Israel's territory. Ben-Gurion had a "grand design" to extend Israeli rule to the Suez Canal in Egypt, the Jordan River in Palestine, and the Litani River in Lebanon: Shlaim.

In early 1965, the writer had occasion to review Israel's strategic concerns with America's country teams in Embassies Cairo, Baghdad, and Damascus. The consensus of all three was that Israel would take the first political opportunity to occupy The West Bank, the Gaza Strip, and Syria's Golan. Opportunity knocked in 1967, by which time violent clashes on Israel's borders with Syria, Jordan, and Egypt had raised tension to the explosion point for the third time since 1948.

On May 13, 1967, a Soviet delegation in Cairo joined the alarmist camp by imparting to the Egyptian government a false report that Israel was massing troops along the Syrian border: *The Arab-Israeli Wars*, Chaim Herzog. Herzog concluded that the Soviets were trying to spook Nasir into massing troops on the Israeli border – an action that would ease the military pressure on Syria, the USSR's foothold in the Middle East. In fact, by May 20 there were 100,000 Egyptian troops along the Israeli border.

Another hint of Soviet provocation was the report that Soviet pilots in Foxbat fighter jets overflew Dimona just before the Six-Day War broke out: *MEJ*, June 1967, Richard B. Parker; *Foxbats Over Dimona*, Isabella Ginor/Gideon Remez.

On May 17, Nasir demanded that the UN withdraw UNEF. On May 19, UN Secretary-General U Thant ordered compliance, allegedly without consulting the UNSC or the UNGA. This order was widely criticized as dereliction of the UN's responsibility to keep the peace, but in 1968 Indian Major General Indar Rikhye, then Military Adviser to the Secretary-General, told a group from the Naval War College, including the writer, that U Thant had no choice: The Egyptian Army had started dropping artillery shells near UNEF posts. The UNEF force, numbering 6000 in February 1957, had fallen to 3400 by May 1967. Most of them were evacuated before the Six-Day War began, but some were still in place, to be caught up in the fighting. Fifteen were killed.

On May 22, Nasir cast the die by declaring reclosure of the Tiran Strait to Israeli ships and strategic cargoes. Israel declared the reclosure an act of aggression, and began full-scale mobilization: *Body of Secrets*, James Bamford. On May 26, as troops from Kuwait, Algeria, and other Arab states were arriving in Egypt, Nasir told the Arab Trade Union Congress that "it was their intention to destroy Israel": Herzog. On May 29, Nasir publicly identified the central issue as "the rights of the Palestinian people".

On May 30, to appease public opinion and avert the risk of a military coup, King Husayn switched sides again. Previously branded "lackey of imperialism" by Nasir, he suddenly flew to Cairo, signed an Egypt-Jordan defense agreement, and concurred in the designation of an Egyptian officer as commander of Arab troops in Jordan. Husayn took this step, not out of naïve enthusiasm, but canny cynicism. The Palestinian component of his subjects, including many military officers and civil service officials, approaching two-thirds of Jordan's population, were dedicated to Nasir and his premature faith in Arab nationalism and Arab military prowess. Correctly anticipating a war that Israel would win, Husayn saw no option other than following his deluded subjects into a doomed enterprise. By accepting Egypt's overall command, he saddled it with responsibility for the inevitable defeat: *Diplomatic History*.

Israeli Prime Minister Levi Eshkol, like Husayn, was under pressure from his subjects and his armed forces. On June 1, he formed a national unity cabinet by bringing in war hero Moshe Dayan as Minister of Defense, and opposition leader Menachem Begin: *Warriors for Jerusalem*, Donald Neff.

Nasir was now in the mystifying position of having dismissed UNEF, reoccupied Sinai, and challenged Israel – while 50,000 Egyptian soldiers were engaged on the rebel side of a civil war in Yemen. Nasir knew Israel had proclaimed the Tiran closure a casus belli. According to his confidant Muhammad Haykal (*A Political Biography of Gamal Abdel Nasser*), Nasir did not want war, and thought that the mass Arab mobilization on the frontier would deter Israel into backing down. According to Neff, Nasir expected war, but had been instilled with false confidence by his incompetent generals. Patrick Seale concluded that Nasir felt compelled to mass troops on the Egyptian front, against the risk of Syrian provocation of Israel. In *The New York Review* of 10/5/95, Avishai Margalit speculated that one of Nasir's reasons for confronting Israel was to create a pretext for extracting his troops from the quagmire in Yemen. Egyptian General 'Abd al Muhsin Murtaji later wrote that for Nasir the June war was a desperate effort to wipe out his failures – the Egyptian-Syrian union and the Yemen war.

Perhaps Nasir had illusions that Washington would come to his rescue as it had in 1956-7. (If so, he had to lure Israel into attacking first. Under the Tripartite Declaration of 1950, America, Britain, and France had made a quixotic commitment to counter any aggression from either side (or both?) across the Arab-Israeli armistice lines of 1949: Shlaim. Britain and France disavowed that ill-conceived decision late in the Suez War.) Like some of us in the State Department, Nasir may have been slow in realizing that Johnson had secretly scrapped Kennedy's more evenhanded policy of trying to "do business with Nasir".

Unfortunately for Nasir, his former colleagues in the Egyptian armed forces were creatures of habit: An alert every morning at dawn; at 07:45, coffee break for pilots, breakfast for senior officers: Neff. For Israel, that coffee break and breakfast meant Open Sesame. On June 5, 1967, 183 Israeli jets took off on schedules timed to bring them over targets in

43

Egypt during its pilots' quiet time, on routes over water (Mediterranean and Red Sea), at altitudes low enough to evade Egyptian air defenses – even if they had been functioning. They had been shut down to ensure the safety of Commander-in-Chief 'Abd al Hakim 'Amir as he flew to a meeting with his subordinates in Sinai.

In eighty minutes, the air attack destroyed 189 Egyptian planes on the ground, smashed 16 radar stations, and cratered six airfields. A second wave of 164 planes destroyed another 120 jet fighters and bombers. According to Alfred Lilienthal, these operations were facilitated by Israeli access to American high-altitude photography. The two air attacks coincided with a ground invasion of the Gaza Strip and Sinai.

Before noon, Jordanian planes strafed an Israeli airfield. The gratified Israelis' response was to wipe out the Jordanian air force, and invade east Jerusalem. Shortly thereafter, Israel replied to Syrian air attacks by destroying most of Syria's warplanes, and to an Iraqi air attack by destroying 10 Iraqi planes at Habbaniyyah Air Base, on the Euphrates between Al Fallujah and Al Ramadi.

On 6/6/67, major Arab oil producers reached a decision to impose oil embargoes on states aiding the Israeli war effort. The war ended too soon for the decision to have serious effect. The war was terminated by the Khartoum Resolution of 9/1/67.

On Friday, June 9, according to the Israeli version, Dayan made a split-second change in battle plans by sending ground troops into Syria's Golan. Donald Neff and Patrick Seale accept this version.

Recap: The Six Days that Shook the Middle East

Day One (Monday, June 5) – Israel shattered the air forces of Egypt, Syria, and Jordan, preempted air action by Iraq, and launched ground attacks on Egypt's Sinai, Jordan's east Jerusalem and West Bank, and the Gaza Strip.

Day Two (Tuesday, June 6) – Israel overran the Gaza Strip (hereafter called "Gaza" in this text) and took Nabulus in the West Bank.

<u>Day Three</u> (Wednesday, June 7) – Israel took East Jerusalem and The West Bank.

<u>Day Four</u> (Thursday, June 8) – Israel took Sinai, and began air and artillery attacks on Syrian positions.

<u>Day Five</u> (Friday, June 9) – Israel overran most of Syria's Golan.

<u>Day Six</u> (Saturday, June 10) – Israel reached the Canal and reopened the Strait of Tiran. Ceasefires went into effect on all fronts.

The Secret of Israeli Success – The Six-Day War endowed Israel with defense-in-depth on all fronts. The Arab side suffered the most crushing defeat in the history of the modern Middle East. In his single-minded reliance on unrelenting force, Ben-Gurion had initiated the conversion of Jewish townsmen and kibbutzniks into a latter-day Sparta, united by a common tradition, and fighting for home and family. Further, Israel had organized a highly effective hierarchy of officers and noncoms, guided in every enterprise by meticulous planning. Herzog's detailed account of the fighting suggests that Israeli artillery surpassed Arab artillery in range and accuracy. And once again, Israel dominated the air, losing 26 planes in the first two days of the war, against 416 Arab planes: Herzog. Most of Israel's combat aircraft were French: Mirages, Mystères, and Super-Mystères: *Living by the Sword*, Stephen Green. The IDF also made heavy use of napalm: Thomas.

In stark contrast was the miscellaneous makeup of the Arab opposition, featuring foot soldiers who could slug it out man-to-man, but were under the command of leaders whose imagination, defective in the realm of military planning, was overactive in the issuance of self-destructive propaganda. Bizarre claims of Egypt's successful repulse of Israel's surprise air attack lured King Husayn into mounting his own attack, which was to cost Jordan – and the Palestinians – the West Bank.

Reportedly, the fevered claims even misled Nasir. For a time, the Egyptian propaganda machine tried to explain away the military fiasco by alleging US planes had participated in the June 5 raids on Egypt.

Casualties – Israel: 983 dead. Arabs: 4296 dead.

Global Repercussions of the War – President Johnson was alerted about the Israeli attack at 4:30 a.m. June 5. Just over three hours later he

45

received a direct call from Soviet Premier Aleksey Kosygin: Neff. It was the first time the Hot Line had been used since its installation in August 1963: Neff. The two leaders agreed on efforts to stop the fighting.

On June 10, the USSR, frustrated at Israel's continued operations on the Egyptian and Syrian fronts, broke relations with Israel. Israel's acceptance of a ceasefire was finally extracted on June 10 by Washington, alarmed by the risk of Soviet intervention.

A few days after the ceasefire, Soviet President Podgorny visited Egypt, Syria, and Iraq. Soon after, all three states received Soviet arms to replace those lost in the war. Egypt admitted Soviet military advisors in force. The USSR acquired access to four Egyptian ports on the Mediterranean, plus virtual control of seven Egyptian air bases: Neff.

Contrary to France's collaboration with Israel in 1956, President de Gaulle declared France neutral during the Six-Day War: *Times*, February 1977, Arthur Sulzberger.

More Palestinian Refugees – By UN estimate, 178,000 Palestinians fled from the West Bank – most of them to Jordan: Thomas. Those Palestinians staunch enough to hold out during the war struck a critical blow for the Palestinian side. Their community has at least deferred the Israeli interest in annexation of the West Bank. Some who left, but tried to sneak back home, were shot on sight.

Arabs who stayed on in the West Bank and Gaza received Israeli ID cards, but not citizenship. Arabs who stayed in Jerusalem were awarded the higher status of "resident aliens". For Israel, any prewar resident of the OT who was out of the country during the war became a foreigner.

Economics – The occupation has been a moneymaker for Israel: new subjects to pay taxes, and a captive market for Israeli products: *NYR*, 12/19/02, Amos Elon. The channeling of trade from the Territories to Israel, instead of to Arab neighbors, was also lucrative for the Israeli economy: *MEP*, October 1998. Exportation from the Territories to Israel has necessarily been subject to rigorous security restrictions.

Israeli Expansionism – Herzog takes the standard Israeli line that the de facto annexation of Jerusalem, the West Bank, and Gaza were afterthoughts. In the writer's opinion, all were clearly premeditated. This conclusion does not rest solely on tradition ("next year in Jerusalem"), or on aggressive Zionist practice in 1948. There is a compelling body of direct evidence:

- The report that, before the war, the IDF's Attorney General, Meir Shamgar, was drafting plans for governing the coveted Palestinian territories: *MEP*, citing an article from *Davar* of 3/8/94.

- Herzog undermines his own parroting of the party line by his eloquent assessment of the importance of these very territories to Israel's overall security.

- Israel's expeditious elimination of Palestinian villages along the western approaches to Jerusalem, taken with the brisk incorporation of an expanded east Jerusalem into a unified metropolis, suggested that this course of action had been meticulously worked out in advance. Knesset Law 5727 provided that Israeli law, jurisdiction, and administration should prevail in any designated part of Eretz Yisrael. East Jerusalem was so designated. In the midst of the 1967 war, Israeli sound trucks were intimidating residents into flight from strategic districts of the West Bank, like villages along the Tel Aviv-Jerusalem highway, and the city of Qalqilyah, where the onetime Jordan border squeezed Israel into a ten-mile-wide isthmus between Jordan and the sea: Thomas.

- Israel repudiated the four 1949 armistice agreements on the last day of the Six-Day War.

- Israel expanded the area of Jerusalem from 2.3 square miles to 27, and "annexed" it as their undivided capital.

- By June 11, all but 6400 of the 130,000 residents of Golan (most of them Sunnis) had fled or been expelled to unoccupied Syria: *MER*, July 1996. The residents of four Druze villages and one Alawite village stayed in place: *The Link*, April 2000. In those villages, the school curricula were immediately switched from Syrian to Israeli. (The Golan Druze who stayed on have remained loyal to Syria; most have declined Israeli citizenship.)

47

The obvious Israeli objective was annexation: *The Link*. The first Jewish settlement was planted within two weeks of the Israeli occupation: *The Link*. Israel designated its earliest settlements in Golan as "temporary" military outposts, to evade citation of the Fourth Geneva Convention, but their purpose was to preempt the final status of the territory: *The Accidental Empire*, Gershom Gorenberg.

Aftermath of the War – On 12/14/81, Israel's Golan Heights Law provided for the imposition of Israeli law, jurisdiction, and administration over Golan. The law did not use the term annexation. The timing may have been meant to protest a contemporary rapprochement between the US and Saudi Arabia, and/or to take advantage of Soviet and American preoccupation with a crisis in Poland, and/or to impede Arab-Israeli peace talks. The motivation is obvious: The strategic value of Golan matches that of occupied Palestine. It encompasses some of the Jordan River's headwaters, and it affords a commanding optical and radar view of Damascus, 30 miles distant, and control of the escarpment from which Syrian artillery used to sweep the upper Jordan River and the eastern shores of the Sea of Galilee during the contest for control of the demilitarized zones laid out after the 1948 war.

On 11/22/67, UNSC Resolution 242 called for withdrawal of all Israeli armed forces from "territories occupied in the recent conflict". This language was vague enough to allow Israel to procrastinate.

In the heady days after the Six-Day War, many Israelis were determined to bypass the international consensus that annexation of the territories overrun in the war would violate UNSC Resolution 242, UNGA Resolution 194, The Hague Regulations of 1907, and the Fourth Geneva Convention. Since none of the great powers was inclined to press these issues, and the UN has no army, Israel's only requirement was to avoid provoking its patron, the US. During the administration of Lyndon Johnson, this was not a difficult assignment. He didn't challenge Israel's contention that the Geneva Convention was irrelevant because the prewar sovereignty of post-Ottoman Palestine had never been

48

established. For Israel, the mention of "belligerent occupation" in The Hague Regulations was enough: *MEP*, Ian Lustick. The joining of the 71 square kilometers of expanded east Jerusalem "did not constitute annexation": *JPS*, Autumn 2000, Ian Lustick.

The Golan Heights Law has received no international recognition. It was declared null and void by unanimous adoption of UNSC Resolution 497 on 12/17/81. Israel has treated the territory, without penalty, as an integral part of the state.

In 2016, the population of Golan was 42,000 – 22,000 Syrian Druze and 20,000 Jewish settlers: *Times*, 4/18/16.

Jordan's Losses – Jordan lost the West Bank, including the Old City of Jerusalem. The price was high. On the economic side, the West Bank had been contributing up to 40 percent of Jordan's GDP: Albert B. Wolf. On the political side, Jordan had lost the prestigious role of defender of the *Haram al Sharif* (Noble Sanctuary), and the influx of West Bankers had disrupted Jordan's tight little tribal demography.

The Three Noes - In Khartoum on 9/1/67 Arab League envoys encapsulated their hypothetical belligerence with the mantra "no peace with Israel, no recognition of Israel, and no negotiation with [Israel]…"

Moment of Truth – According to a witness, one of the most affecting events in modern Arab history occurred on June 9, when Nasir apologized to the Egyptian people, resigned his office, and named Zakariyya Muhy al Din to replace him. (He refused.) Nasir's words evoked an outpouring of support for the anguished leader. The flooding of the streets by Cairo's millions was so obviously heartfelt that the resignation was retracted on June 10.

1969-70 – War of Attrition

———

In the sequence of Arab-Israeli conflicts, Nasir's War of Attrition was an oddity – not dominated by a contest for territory. It started that way in March 1969 with an Egyptian effort to dislodge Israeli troops from the east bank of the Suez Canal (*Asad*, Seale), but Israel didn't respond in kind. It was perfectly happy with the Canal as a western frontier, so for the next three years it fought an escalating campaign to subdue the Egyptian resistance – ideally by precipitating the overthrow of Jamal 'Abd al Nasir, the apostle of Arab Nationalism.

Phase One – At the outset, Egypt was reassured by Soviet resupply of arms lost in the Six-Day War, and by Soviet pressure for a continuing effort by the Arabs to reverse their territorial losses: Herzog. On July 1, 1967, there was a heavy artillery exchange across the Canal: Green. On October 21, 1967, Egypt introduced missiles into the Arab-Israeli conflict, sinking the Israeli destroyer Eilat. Forty-seven Israeli sailors died.

Phase Two – Israel was quick to retaliate. Its air, artillery, and naval attacks in and around the Canal Zone drove out thousands of civilian refugees: Green. On October 24 the industrial complex in Suez City was ravaged and 80 percent of Egypt's refining capacity was eliminated: Green.

Phase Three – Nine months of quiet, as Israel went back to the business of consolidating its new territories, and Egypt to repairing the damage.

Phase Four – Resupply of Soviet artillery enabled Egypt to punish the Israeli positions on the east bank of the Canal. Fifteen Israelis died on October 26, 1968. The morale of the Egyptian army surged.

Phase Five – The Israeli response was to upgrade its east-bank fortifications (the Bar Lev line), and initiate a new strategy of deep penetration – air and commando attacks on targets all over Egypt. The damage to the Egyptian infrastructure compelled the army to suspend shelling along the Canal in favor of setting up a nation-wide militia, and to upgrade Egypt's air defense system with Soviet SAM-2's.

Israeli air action had been boosted by receipt of Phantom F-4's from the US. In 1970, Israel trumped successes of Egyptian commandos along the Canal by the exploits of its air force, including helicopter raids and air attacks. On 9/9/69 an Israeli armored force wearing Egyptian uniforms, in violation of The Hague regulations, killed 100 Egyptians along the Red Sea coast. On 1/22/70 Israeli commandos killed 80 Egyptians on Shadwan Island, at the southern end of the Gulf of Suez. The targets of Israeli air raids between January and May 1970 included a scrap metal plant (70 dead), a Cairo suburb (32 dead), Mansurah (3 dead), Mansurah missile sites (12 dead), a school in Bahr al Baqr (46 dead). On 5/16/70 Israeli aircraft sank an Egyptian destroyer and a missile boat.

Phase Six: Climax – On 1/22/70 a desperate Nasir made a secret visit to Moscow to demand Soviet help, reportedly on pain of his switching his appeal from the USSR to the US. In return for continued access to four ports on the Mediterranean, and a huge new airbase near Alexandria, the USSR agreed to take over Egypt's air defense. By the end of 1970, there were 200 Soviet pilots, 15,000 Soviet soldiers, and 5,000 Soviet technicians in Egypt. By May 1970, Soviet pilots were flying operational missions over the Canal Zone: Green.

On June 30, the combination of Western aircraft and Israeli pilots reaffirmed Israeli domination of Middle Eastern skies by shooting down four MiG's piloted by Soviet airmen. However, by advancing SAM's to the Canal, the Soviets had begun to bring down Israeli jets. In June, Soviet missiles shot down two F-4's, and Soviet anti-aircraft guns downed a Skyhawk: Green. The War of Attrition was stalemated. The strategic situation did not demand an all-out military effort from Israel.

51

On the crucial day of July 23, 1970, Soviet and American negotiators managed to dispel the specter of Soviet-American confrontation. Nasir and Israel accepted the powers' ceasefire proposal. Egypt lost another three jets in a dogfight 7/30/70, but the War of Attrition had ended – in stalemate, with one momentous exception: On the west bank of the Canal, it left the missiles that would check Israeli air power at the outset of the Yom Kippur War.

When heavy civilian casualties ensue from IDF action, Israeli spokesmen usually have two stock answers: "It was an accident," or "It didn't happen." In "unguarded moments", leading Israeli officials have sometimes acknowledged that Israel has employed terrorism as an instrument of policy. In 1978 IDF Chief of Staff Mordechai Gur said, "I've been in the army 30 years. Do you think I don't know what we've been doing all those years?" As an example, Gur cited Israeli bombardment of Jordanian sites during the Israeli-Egyptian War of Attrition: "The whole Jordan Valley was evacuated...": *MEP*, Fall 2015, "Terrorism and the Israeli-Palestinian Conflict", Jerome Slater.

1970-71 – Jordan-PLO War

────────

1949-50 – Transjordan acquired the Palestinian West Bank (2263 square miles, just over one-fifth of the area of the Mandate) from Israel as a consequence of the Israeli War of Independence. Transjordan was renamed Jordan.

1952 – At the orders of the Prime Minister of Israel, Major Ariel Sharon was returned to active service at age 24 as founder and commander of Unit 101, whose role was to mount reprisals against Palestinian fedayeen incursions into Israel.

1959 – In the Palestinian diaspora, Al Fatah, a Palestinian nationalist organization, was taking shape. The leading cofounder was Yasir 'Arafat ('Abd al Ra'uf al Qudwah). 'Arafat was born in Gaza (?) of Palestinian parents, trained in Cairo as a civil engineer, joined the Egyptian branch of the Muslim Brotherhood, served in the Egyptian army during the Suez War, and was employed as an engineer in Kuwait.

1964 – Egyptian President Nasir convened the first Summit of the Arab League, which announced the formation of a Palestine Liberation Organization (PLO) to represent the world's Palestinians, estimated to number 4.5 million. The League also created the Palestine Liberation Army (PLA), which subsequently evolved under the direction of its host government, usually Syria. Egypt promoted the founding of the Palestine National Council (PNC), which set up a PLO Executive Council.

1964 – The PLO Executive Council promulgated the Palestinian Covenant, which proclaimed a Palestinian state in all of Palestine.

1965 – In January, Fatah sent its first raid into Israel.

1966   Ariel Sharon led a major raid against Sammu' in Jordan. Arab casualties were heavy. Jordan accused Syria of colluding in the operations of the Fedayeen. Syria called for the overthrow of King Husayn.

1967 – The Arab debacle in the Six-Day War convinced the PLO that, if their country were ever liberated, it would be by their own devices. The only Arabs to benefit from the war were the 'Arafat faction, which later replaced the puppet leadership set up by Egypt.

1967 – Palestinian George Habash (Greek Orthodox) founded the secularist Popular Front for the Liberation of Palestine (PFLP).

1967 – Israel captured the West Bank from Jordan.

1968 – On 3/21/68, in destroying a PLO base in Karamah, Jordan, the IDF took an unusually high percentage of total casualties. Killed: 200 PLO, 40 Jordanians, 28 IDF. 'Arafat's prestige skyrocketed. Friction was mounting between the monarchy and the PLO, which was acting like a state within a state.

1968 – On 7/23/68, the PFLP hijacked an El Al airliner and ordered it flown to Algiers. The non-Israeli passengers were sent to France. The twelve Israeli passengers and the crew of ten were held as hostages for five weeks, then released in exchange for 16 Arabs reportedly held by Israel.

1968 – 'Arafat, leader of Al Fatah, became Chairman of the Palestine Liberation Organization (PLO), the new umbrella organization of the Palestinian resistance to Israeli occupation.

1968 – Israel's Labor government began to allow Jewish squatters to settle on lands in the Palestinian territories occupied during and after the Six-Day War.

1969 – Under its new chairman, Yasir 'Arafat, the PNC called for the establishment of a democratic secular state of Arabs and (some) Jews in Palestine. Dissenters (Arab Nationalists and Islamists) formed the Rejection Front.

1970 – In February, after consultation with Jamal 'Abd al Nasir and President Nixon, Husayn published an edict restricting activities of the Palestinian Liberation Organization (PLO) in Jordan. On February 11 fighting broke out between Jordanian security forces and Palestinian groups in the streets of Amman, resulting in some 300 deaths.

1970 – By September, the PLO had established a "government" in Irbid (45 miles north of Amman): *MEP*, Summer 2015, Albert Wolf.

1970 – On 9/1/70, there were several attempts to assassinate Husayn.

1970 – On 9/7/70, to precipitate a Palestinian showdown with Husayn, PFLP (Popular Front for the Liberation of Palestine) operatives hijacked a Swissair and a TWA airliner to Jordan, and a Pan Am airliner to Cairo. On 9/9/70, a BOAC airliner was hijacked to Jordan. The planes that landed in Jordan were blown up in front of TV cameras.

1970 – On 9/15/70, Husayn declared martial law. His forces ravaged Palestinian bases, and managed to restore order, while remaining watchful of an Iraqi armored division in Jordan, and Syrian troop movements along the border. Syrian Minister of Defense Hafiz al Asad, having just bested previous dictator Salah Jadid in a power struggle, was master of Syria in all but name: *Asad*, Seale. Asad controlled all Syria's armed forces, including the Palestinian Liberation Army (PLA). Salah Jadid's Palestine force, *Al Sa'iqah* (The Thunderbolt), had been neutralized. As soon as fighting broke out in Jordan, Asad sent arms to the PLO forces in Jordan.

1970 – On 9/18/70, Asad sent into Jordan soldiers of the Syrian branch of the PLA, and Syrian soldiers under PLA cover. Asad told Patrick Seale later their sole motive was to protect the Palestinians from massacre. He withheld the air force to "prevent escalation": Seale.

1970 – On 9/21/70, the Syrians broke through Jordanian lines. Husayn asked the US, the UK, and possibly Israel to intervene.

1970 – On 9/22/70, Husayn deployed an armored brigade that knocked out large numbers of Syrian tanks. The rest of the Syrian force went back home. Activation of the Jordanian air force was the deciding factor in the military action: Seale.

1970 – More decisive, however, was the diplomatic action behind the scenes. On 9/20/70, Husayn had notified Washington that if the US could not protect Jordan from Syria, he would accept Israeli intervention. On 9/21/70, Henry Kissinger and Yitzhak Rabin, the

Israeli ambassador in Washington, had agreed that, if necessary, the IDF Air Force would attack the Syrians on 9/22. Asad knew better than to put Syrian planes into battle against the Israeli Air Force. It seems that the only persuasion Asad needed to withdraw Syria's ground forces from Jordan was the report that the Israeli Air Force had gone on alert.

1970 – 9/28/70: Death of Nasir, the Arab champion against Israel.

1971 – On 6/5/71, the PLO called for the deposition of Husayn, but its forces were routed by Jordan's Arab Legion, and forced to move from Jordan to Lebanon.

1973 – Yom Kippur War

After the debacle of 1967, Egyptian Commander-in-Chief 'Abd al Hakim 'Amir reportedly committed suicide – to avoid trial on a charge of plotting the death of President Nasir. Nasir, a broken man, had a fatal heart attack 9/28/70. He was succeeded on 10/15/70 by his Vice President, Anwar al Sadat.

The central plank of Sadat's political platform was recovery of Sinai. By devious manipulation of Israel's strategic concerns, meticulous military planning, a bewildering sequence of military "exercises", changing in midstream from the Soviet camp to the American, and selling out his Syrian allies and the Palestinians, he would succeed: *Warriors Against Israel*, Donald Neff.

Meanwhile, the USSR was resupplying arms to Egypt in a volume greater than to Vietnam, and raising the number of its military advisors in Egypt to several thousand. The Soviets' special access to Cairo West Airport and key Mediterranean ports was enabling the USSR to expand its Mediterranean fleet: Neff.

On 5/27/71, USSR President Nikolai Podgorny and Sadat signed a treaty of Soviet-Egyptian friendship by which the Soviets issued their first security guarantee to a non-Communist country: Neff. Egypt was confirmed as a member of the Soviet camp in the Soviet-American Cold War.

From 1971 on, Sadat issued a series of bellicose statements, which the Israelis, complacent in the glow of their historic victory of 1967, tended to write off as typical Arab bluster:

3/28/71 – Israel's arrogance had taken Egypt to the end of the diplomatic road.

6/22/71 – 1973 would be Egypt's year of decision.

1/13/72 – Sadat had rescinded his order to attack in December 1972 because the USSR had diverted arms shipments from Egypt to the higher priority of India in its war with Pakistan.

3/31/72 – War with Israel was inevitable.

4/25/72 – The occupied territories would be liberated within a year.

This rhetorical barrage did nothing to alter the stalemate in the Arab-Israeli conflict. Stalemate was fine with Israel, anathema to Sadat. In microcosm, the Israeli-Egyptian conflict corresponded with the American-Soviet conflict, and it was so recognized by the policymakers in Washington. On the American side, that correspondence was enhanced by the mysterious bond between anti-Semitic Richard Nixon and pro-Zionist Henry Kissinger. That mystery is the central topic in Walter Isaacson's 800-page biography, *Kissinger*. All we onlookers can know for sure is that Nixon was a challenge for the psychoanalysts, Kissinger starred in the art of ingratiation, and the adventitious concurrence of the Watergate crisis and the Yom Kippur War gave a foreign-born pragmatist unconstitutional authority in a time of national crisis – domestic and foreign.

In 1968, still outside the government, old-pol Kissinger had impressed old-pol Nixon, presidential candidate, by slipping him inside tips on the Vietnam peace talks being conducted in Paris by the Johnson administration: Isaacson. In 1969 new President Nixon brought Kissinger into his administration as National Security Adviser, and his old friend William P. Rogers as Secretary of State. Rogers' greater objectivity soon clashed with Kissinger's personal biases. In the bureaucratic jungle, Rogers was no match for Kissinger. Rogers told Nixon, accurately, that the 1971 Soviet-Egyptian treaty favored American interest in reopening the Suez Canal. Kissinger's assessment was the opposite, because the treaty jeopardized the stalemate favored by Israel: Neff.

In July 1971, at Kissinger's recommendation, Nixon obstructed State Department initiatives for progress toward an Arab-Israeli settlement. Rogers countered on 10/4/71 with an address at the UN urging Israel to negotiate an interim agreement for Israeli withdrawal from its occupation of the east bank of the Canal. Israel refused: Neff.

In November 1971, under a US-Israel memorandum of understanding, which reflected opportunistic pressure from 78 Senators, Washington granted Israel, not just weapons, but state-of-the-art technology to make its own weapons. On October 11, Sadat was in Moscow to complain that the Soviet supply of arms to Egypt was not matching American supply to Israel. On October 12, the State Department dropped the whole mediation effort. In a White House meeting with Prime Minister Meir on 12/2/71, Nixon accepted the Israeli (!) request that Kissinger establish a secret back channel that would bypass the State Department: Neff. Prime Minister Golda Meir (Goldie Mabovitch) was a persuasive interlocutor. Born in Kiev, she emigrated with her family to the US in 1906 at age 8, then emigrated to Palestine in 1921 with her husband Morris Myerson.

Rogers hung on until his replacement in September 1973 by Kissinger, subsequently wearing both diplomatic hats.

On 1/1/72, David Elazar became Israeli Chief of Staff. He introduced a hard line that included two lethal reprisal raids into Lebanon, and the upgrading of the Bar Lev Line, whose central purpose was to protect a system of electronic sensors meant to rule out any surprise Egyptian invasion of Sinai – such as the upcoming Yom Kippur War.

For Anwar Sadat, 1972 was a year of frustration: Fizzle of State Department mediation; failure of the USSR to match US arms aid to Israel; USSR tilt toward Cold War détente – notably by opening the gates for emigration of Russian Jews to Israel. On 7/18/72, Sadat demonstrated his facility at thinking outside the box: He announced the expulsion (?) of the 15,000 Soviet military advisors, on the grounds that the USSR had lagged in arms supply to Egypt. (The literature is vague on this point. According to *Russiapedia*, the announcement was made in consonance with a Soviet-Egyptian plot to conceal from Israel the reality that the departing Russians were troops, whereas the military advisors were staying in Egypt. Possible relevance to this mystery lies in the fact that in December 1972 Sadat renewed the five-year agreement on Soviet access to Egyptian ports; Saudi Arabia was to help finance Soviet arms shipments: Neff.)

In February 1972, the Soviets had advised Egypt that, in preparation for the next war, it should build a crushing air defense system of anti-aircraft guns and SAM-2's, SAM-3's (mobile), and SAM-6's (agile), and a deep-penetration arsenal of Scud ground-to-ground missiles: *The Arab-Israeli Wars*, Chaim Herzog. Egyptian-Syrian planning for a joint surprise attack began in January 1973. Delivery of Soviet Scuds to Egypt began in April. Sadat and Syrian President Hafiz al Asad met secretly in Cairo in April (*Asad*, Patrick Seale) and in Damascus in June.

In 1972, American drivers began to find themselves stuck in lines of vehicles waiting to buy gas, as world demand began to exceed supply.

On 2/23/73, Hafiz Isma'il, Sadat's National Security Adviser, was in Washington to deliver to Nixon a note warning that "explosion" was near. On Nixon's orders, Kissinger and Isma'il had secret talks in New York City, with no results. Kissinger didn't even tell Rogers about the secret meetings: Neff.

Also in February, King Husayn met with Nixon, and told him Sadat had expelled the Soviet advisors because Moscow opposed war (?), and Nixon had promised Meir more arms: Neff.

On 3/26/73, Sadat told Parliament he was taking over as Prime Minister, in addition to his presidency, to prepare for war with Israel.

In the summer of 1973, while Egypt was trying to project a public image of a country lost in confusion, back-up aircraft were arriving from Iraq and Libya, plus continued Soviet supply of aircraft, SAM's, and antitank missiles (Herzog; *Living by the Sword*, Stephen Green), and its troops were rehearsing canal-crossing on a mock-up canal in the desert of upper Egypt. The Canal is an excellent anti-tank ditch – 673 feet wide, with concrete sides, and waters roiled by tides: Herzog.

On 8/23/73, in anticipation of war, Saudi King Faysal and Sadat met in Riyadh and agreed that, if war came, the Arab producers would use the oil weapon against nations taking the Israeli side.

Meanwhile Washington was oblivious, except that back in the spring of 1973 Roger Merrick, Egyptian analyst in the State Department's intelligence bureau, had initiated a warning of early Egyptian attack. After massaging by superiors, the warning had presumably reached the desk of Kissinger, still at the NSC. By the fall of 1973, many of us – missing the significance of the resumption of diplomatic relations between Jordan and Egypt in September – had been inclined, by a CIA report of an imminent Saudi oil embargo on the US, to regard Merrick's warning as premature.

We were wrong. So was Israel: Herzog. On Israel's northern front, Syria was taking delivery of Soviet SAM's: Herzog. On September 13 Israel staged in Syria a test overflight that led to a dogfight in which Syria lost 12 jets, Israel one: Neff. Asad withheld Syria's new SAM-6's as a surprise for the upcoming war.

October arrived with Israel more frustrated than ever by its perennial dilemma: If attack was imminent, full mobilization was indicated. But if no attack materialized, mobilization would drain the economy, and look trigger-happy in the upcoming general election. The high command tried to split the difference – a halfway measure that turned out to be a costly mistake: *The Iron Wall*, Shlaim.

In early October, the Soviet Union began shipping more arms to Egypt.

On October 3, the Soviets committed a major breach of Egyptian and Syrian security by evacuating nonessential personnel from both countries. Israel issued its first all-out alert since 1967, but did not declare full mobilization. Egypt even got away with a negligent order of October 5 cancelling commercial flights.

At 4:30 a.m. October 6, Israel picked up a report accurate in substance (attack was imminent), inaccurate in detail ("zero hour: 6

p.m.”), and too vague to act on: Dayan feared that Israeli preemption, whatever the circumstances, would damage its credit in Washington: Neff.

Saturday, 10/6, Attack – At 1:55 p.m. (with the sun behind the Egyptians), Egypt and Syria launched attacks coordinated in time and impetus, but not in objective: Asad had only 460 square miles of Golan to recover; Sadat was inhibited by the reliance of his forces on the SAM umbrella, which reached only ten miles east of the Canal: Herzog; Neff. Sadat had to hope that military success in that limited range would have decisive impact on the terms of the ultimate settlement. Sadat was dishonest with Asad – letting him believe that the Egyptian forces intended to fight their way across all of Sinai: Seale.

Before the Israeli Air Force could get overhead, Egyptian and Syrian jets were active in the reduction of Israeli defenses. Then came artillery barrages. Then the ground attack.

10/6, Syrian Attack – 1400 Syrian tanks invaded occupied Golan. Israel's 188 Brigade was almost completely destroyed, but held out long enough for Israel to bring up reserves, which checked the Syrian advance just short of the border of Israel proper: Herzog.

10/6, Egyptian Attack – The barriers were the Canal, plus the acclaimed Bar Lev Line – a berm of sand 70 feet high, rising sharply from the eastern bank, studded along the top by a chain of formidable forts, backed by concentrations of tanks. It was an oriental Maginot Line, minus the end-around option. The Egyptians had learned from experimentation that a huge sand pile is a quasi-living organism with the ability to instantly refill holes dug into it. Their recourse was high-pressure water hoses – with the exception of a site that had to be bulldozed: Neff.

The Egyptians benefitted from the Syrians' near-breakthrough into Israel proper, diverting the Israelis' attention from the Egyptian front. The execution of the Egyptian crossing was as competent as its planning: Neff; Green. The first landing was at 2:30 p.m. By boat, pontoon, and amphibious vehicle, 8000 foot soldiers crossed the Canal and scaled the berm. Before Israeli tanks could get into firing position, they were being taken out by shoulder-fired, wire-guided missiles.

By nightfall there were 32,000 Egyptians on the berm, and half the Bar Lev forts had been captured. Overnight, pontoon bridges were put in place, the berm was being perforated with passages, and tanks were pouring into Sinai. The Bar Lev Line had been exposed as a liability – too vulnerable to serve its defensive purpose, too substantial to abandon: Herzog. The Egyptians had expected as many as 10,000 dead during the crossing. Actual deaths were 208: Herzog.

Saturday, October 6, Jordanian Front – No action for several days to come. Having been burned in 1967, Husayn had adopted a strategy of wait-and-see.

Saturday/Sunday, October 6-7, Washington "Front" – Israel kept Washington up to the minute on the extent of its military shock. The American Joint Chiefs needed no prodding. Not taking the time to go through channels, they preempted their civilian superiors by ordering transfer of unprecedented quantities of AWACS, air-to-air missiles, cluster bombs, and other emergency weapons direct from Seventh Army stocks in Europe to Israel: Green. A larger shipment was proceeding through more conventional channels; Kissinger produced the two billion dollars to finance this enterprise.

Sunday, October 7, Syrian Front – The Syrians were advancing with so much determination that they sacrificed some units unnecessarily: Neff. At a cost of 30 planes, Israeli forces stopped the Syrians just short of Israel's Lake Tiberias. By the end of the day, tank reserves had arrived to turn the tide of battle: Neff.

Sunday, October 7, Egyptian Front – By the second day in Sinai, Israeli tank units had lost two-thirds or more of their machines: Herzog. Egypt had moved 850 tanks and 5000 artillery pieces as far as 5 miles inland, plus 40,000 men and 11,000 vehicles. (Israel had needed all available reserves to stop the Syrian advance.) The IAF had lost 70 planes. Many Israeli units were in full retreat.

Monday, October 8, Syrian Front – Israeli outposts survived a second armored attack because the Syrians were short of anti tank weapons: Herzog. Concentrating on the Syrian front, the Israelis defeated a superior force: Herzog. At dusk a Syrian force with the advantage of night vision devices was demoralized by the death of its General, 'Umar Abrash: Neff.

Monday, October 8, Egyptian Front – Israel's first counterattack failed. Tanks were lost because of inadequate infantry support: Herzog. After two days of crushing losses, the Israelis finally checked the Egyptian advance into Sinai: Neff. From 10/8 on, Sharon's disregard for orders from his superiors disrupted the Israeli resistance. He and General Adan shared a deep hatred of each other, but Sharon enjoyed political influence back home. Two attempts to replace him were overruled: Herzog. Under the pressure, Defense Minister Dayan was freaking out: Green.

Tuesday, October 9, Syrian Front – The Syrians, overextended, finally broke: Herzog. Syria's air defenses had been knocked out: Neff. The turning point had arrived: Green.

The US resumed arms supply to Israel.

1973 – At an unspecified point in the Yom Kippur War, Israel sensed that its back was against the wall, and it put eight nuclear-armed F-4's on alert: *The Nation*, 3/12/2015, William Greider, cited by *WRMEA*.

Tuesday, October 9, Egyptian Front – End of the Egyptian advance: Herzog. Israel had needed three days to accomplish full mobilization. The massive American airlift had convinced Sadat that Egypt's military drive had run its course. Both sides were exhausted: Neff. An Egyptian spokesman cited Egypt's objectives: 1) recovery of Sinai; 2) Israeli recognition of Palestinian rights: Neff.

Wednesday, October 10, Syrian Front – Having regained total control of the air, and returned to the lines of 10/6/73, the Israelis used 10/10 to recuperate from four terrible days. The 1400 Syrian tanks that attacked 10/6 had been eliminated: Herzog.

Wednesday, October 10, Egyptian Front – Israel was able to transfer more planes from the Syrian front to increase the pressure on the Egyptian forces: Green. Flights of the American emergency arms airlift were landing in Al 'Arish.

Wednesday, October 10, Global Diplomacy – For the US and the USSR, the Yom Kippur War was a major event in the Cold War. Each power supported its client – though not so recklessly as to invite Soviet-

American confrontation. Neither would tolerate any humiliation of its client state. Kissinger would have regarded a defeat of Israel by Soviet arms as a geopolitical disaster: Neff. He would have regarded Egyptian recovery of Sinai as a Soviet victory in the proxy war; Defense Secretary James Schlesinger: not so much, since Sinai was Egyptian territory: *NYR* 8/13/09, Brian Urquhart. Israel calibrated the depth of its entry into Syria proper so as not to risk direct Soviet intervention: Herzog. The USSR was pressing for a ceasefire in place on the Syrian front (leaving Golan in Syrian hands), and for further Egyptian advance into Sinai. That didn't happen; American arms and financial aid had enabled Israel to occupy still more Egyptian territory: Thomas.

Thursday, October 11, Syrian Front – Israel was about to acquire more Syrian territory as well. Israeli forces entered Syria proper against stiff resistance from Syrian and Moroccan forces: Herzog. Their first conquest was Al Qunaytirah.

Friday, October 12, Syrian Front – A few days earlier, as the Syrian offensive had stalled, Asad had called for a ceasefire, but Sadat had declined. By 10/12, a desperate Asad was appealing to the Soviets. In Syria, Iraqi, Saudi, and Jordanian forces had belatedly entered the fighting, but their zeal was neutralized by defective tactics and lack of coordination: Herzog.

Saturday, October 13 – In Washington, under heavy political pressure from Israel, Nixon dismissed his concerns about an Arab oil embargo and ordered a massive C-5A airlift of arms to Israel: Neff. Israel was receiving two American airlifts – the emergency shipments from Germany initiated by the Pentagon, and the later shipments ordered by the White House: Green.

Sunday, October 14, Egyptian Front – Sadat issued a rash order for abandonment of his forces' hedgehog crouch in favor of an advance deeper into Sinai. He would cite it later as compliance with Asad's appeal, although his real concern was that Syria would just stop fighting, allowing Israel to mass all its resources against Egypt. The result of the advance was catastrophic. The engagement of 2000 tanks – one of the largest tank battles ever – under total Israeli control of the air was an Israeli turkey shoot.

With hundreds of Egyptian tanks destroyed, and many more scattered in Sinai, Sharon got his showboat wish – leadership of the Israeli crossing of the Canal: Herzog.

Tuesday, October 16, Egyptian Front – The initial Israeli crossing, just north of Great Bitter Lake, was accomplished between Egypt's second (northern) and third (southern) armies, after midnight. Israeli intelligence had spotted Egypt's crucial failure to maintain adequate communication across the hinge between the two armies: Neff; *The Economist*, Edgar O'Ballance, 2/2/80. By 8:00 a.m., Israel had a three-mile-wide bridgehead, but no assured supply route. There was still heavy fighting on the eastern bank north of the lake, but the more significant action was the destruction by Sharon's forces of Egyptian air defenses west of the Canal: Herzog. Later in the week, when Kissinger asked INR about the risk that an Egyptian pincer movement could cut off the Israeli salient, we were able to show him aerial photographs from DOD and/or CIA of Israeli formations lined up in orderly fashion east of the Canal, waiting patiently to cross, versus Egyptian armored vehicles, west of the Canal, largely dispersed or destroyed. Israel's basic problem on the Canal front had been the High Command's need to keep Sharon from getting too far ahead of the rear echelon: Neff.

Soviet Premier Kosygin rushed to Cairo to urge an Israeli-Egyptian ceasefire in place: Seale.

Tuesday, October 16, OPEC – The Arab oil states imposed a punitive rise in the posted price of a barrel of crude from $3.01 to $5.12: Neff.

Wednesday, October 17 – The Arab members of OPEC (Organization of Petroleum Exporting Countries), plus Egypt and Syria, proclaimed an embargo on the sale of oil to Canada, Japan, the Netherlands, the UK, and the US.

Thursday, October 18, Egyptian Front – Israel set up a bridgehead on the western bank of the canal: Herzog; Neff.

Friday, October 19 – Israel was stalling on Soviet pressure for a ceasefire, in its efforts to recapture the Mt. Hermon observation post in Golan, and nail down its bridgehead west of the Canal: Neff.

Friday, October 19, OPEC – Nixon asked Congress for 2.2 billion dollars in emergency aid to Israel. In retaliation, Qadhafi announced that Libya was raising the price of its premium oil to 8.25 dollars a barrel, and suspending the shipment of oil to the US: Neff.

Saturday, October 20, Global Diplomacy – Kissinger was in Moscow at the Soviets' invitation. Now that Israel was the clear winner on both fronts, Kissinger turned his attention to his secondary objective – preservation of the Soviet-American détente. In a belated show of objectivity, he joined Brezhnev in confronting Israel with three proposals: 1) ceasefire in place; 2) an immediate start toward the implementation of UNSC Resolution 242; 3) direct Arab-Israeli negotiations for a just and durable peace – a formula to be embodied in UNSC Resolution 338. Kissinger also pressured Israel into allowing Egypt to supply its Third Army, which had been trapped in Sinai – to the great annoyance of the USSR.

Saturday, October 20, OPEC – Other major producers joined the oil embargo against the US. The price of oil was to rise to around 12 dollars a barrel until 1986. States in Western Europe, much more dependent than the US on Middle East oil, adopted more pro-Arab policies and were not embargoed. The UK and France denied the US Air Force the use of their airfields.

Monday, October 22, Global Diplomacy – The adoption of UNSC Resolution 338, which called for a ceasefire, was a major advance for Israel. It ignored the Arab bid for prior implementation of the vague territorial language of UNSC 242, concluded after the Six-Day War. Israel recaptured the Mt. Hermon observation post, just before accepting the first ceasefire along with Egypt. An Israeli attempt to take Isma'iliyyah failed: Neff. Syria accepted the first ceasefire, but still rejected Resolutions 242 and 338. Israel had won sufficient military advantage to drive all the way to Cairo, but any such deployment was blocked by the risk of Soviet intervention: Herzog.

Tuesday, October 23, Egyptian Front – Claiming Egypt had broken the ceasefire, Israeli forces continued their effort to encircle the Third Army. Heavy fighting resumed on the Canal. Brezhnev denounced

Israeli "treachery" to Kissinger: Neff. The US continued its resupply of arms to Israel.

Wednesday, October 24, Egyptian Front – Ignoring a second call for a ceasefire, Israel sought to score one last military coup by capturing the city of Suez, at the south end of the Canal. The attempt was a costly failure: Neff. Sadat shocked Washington with the news that he had asked Moscow to send troops. Late that day, Dobrynin phoned to inform Kissinger that the Kremlin was thinking of asking the UNSC to endorse a joint US-Soviet force for the Middle East. For a few hours, Kissinger was confronted with three thunderbolts: In the throes of impeachment panic, Nixon was in break-down mode, leaving Kissinger for practical purposes the acting President of the United States (see Isaacson); Kissinger had to deal with Brezhnev's threat to take unilateral action to save the Third Army – and Egypt's honor; Kissinger was drawn into the role of Nixon's psychologist. The distraught Nixon had pleaded with Kissinger to tell Congress of Nixon's "indispensable" role in resolving the Middle East crisis: Neff.

At 11:41 p.m. Washington time, Kissinger and top US officials – minus Nixon – raised the Defense Condition from DefCon IV (heightened alert) to DefCon III (possibility of war). Neff reports the change as reflecting a full-scale crisis. Ambassador Dobrynin later wrote that Brezhnev was play-acting – that Moscow well understood that the declaration of DefCon III was a Kissinger ploy to deflect public attention away from Watergate, which really was a crisis, inflicted on the nation by a sorry excuse for a President. In retrospect, Dobrynin's analysis seems sounder. Kissinger later admitted that the US had proclaimed DefCon III without consultation with NATO: *The Alliance*, Richard J. Barnet.

Wednesday, October 24, Syrian Front – Syria accepted Resolution 338 on Sadat's assurance that the USSR had guaranteed total Israeli withdrawal.

Thursday, October 25 – A UNSC Resolution demanded an immediate ceasefire, and provided for creation of a peacekeeping force of nonpermanent members of the UNSC. The tension evaporated. The DefCon alert was cancelled.

Sunday, October 28 – Israeli interruption of the Cairo-Suez road had cut the supply lines of the Third Army, still in Sinai. With characteristic determination, or obstinacy, Israel pursued its relentless blockade of the Third Army until Washington took action that it should have taken some days earlier: It issued that rarest of political phenomena – an American ultimatum to Israel: If the blockade was not lifted, the US Armed Forces would fly in relief supplies: *Times*, 12/20/74, Moshe Dayan. In the first direct Arab-Israeli talks of the war, Egyptian and Israeli representatives met at Kilo 101 on the Cairo-Suez road. Israel agreed to admit an Egyptian relief convoy to the Third Army: *Kissinger*, Walter Isaacson. The war was over.

After the war, Kissinger laboriously negotiated Israeli-Egyptian and Israeli-Syrian agreements on partial disengagement from Syrian territory and total disengagement from Egypt and Gaza, and deployment of UN Disengagement and Observer Forces (UNDOF). A military disengagement agreement was signed by Israel and Egypt on 1/18/74, by Israel and Syria on 5/31/74.

On 1/18/74, Kissinger extracted from Israel agreement to withdraw its troops from Egypt to Sinai. By 3/5/74, they were back east of the Suez Canal.

By March 1974, all Arab oil embargoes but that of Libya had been lifted.

Recap

Military – By shaking the complacency of the modern state of Israel, so solidly reinforced by history's greatest superpower, Egypt and Syria achieved the Arab World's greatest military effort in centuries. Meticulous planning, skilled tactics, conservative strategy (at first), and unprecedented surprise enabled Sadat's Egypt to seize the military advantage for the first seven days of the war. The canal-crossing and crushing of the Bar Lev Line was a major achievement. However, the Egyptians never broke into Israeli territory.

Sadat lost the advantage by sending his troops too far into Sinai. On October 14, by letting his forces get sucked into a war of movement,

Sadat subjected them to counterattack by an enemy force favored by superior command and control, better equipment and training, and – out in the wilds of Sinai – complete control of the air: Green. They were further handicapped by the defensive bias of Soviet military doctrine.

On the northern front, Syrian courage and numerical advantage were neutralized by Israel's longer tradition of military professionalism, and the inspiration of Israelis fighting for their hallowed country's survival. At the outset, the Israelis had been undercut by overconfidence and a shortage of infantrymen to complement the tank forces. The initiative shifted from the Syrians to the Israelis on October 9.

In nineteen days of combat, Egypt lost almost 300 aircraft, and 5000 lives. Syria lost over 200 aircraft, and 3100 lives. Israel lost 102 aircraft (5 to Egyptian pilots, the rest to SAM's 2, 3, and 6: *Aviation Week*, 1/16/12, Alon Ben David), and 2838 lives. Of all Arab-Israeli wars to date, the Yom Kippur War was the hardest: Neff; Herzog.

On the naval side, the Israeli navy, much improved since the Six-Day War, sank a number of Egyptian and Syrian missile boats, and established control of the southeastern Mediterranean and the Gulf of Suez: Herzog. Egypt blockaded the Red Sea between Port Sudan and Aden.

The greater mechanization of Israeli forces in the Yom Kippur War, as compared with the Six-Day War, led Israel to do most of its fighting in daylight: Herzog.

Political – Sadat lost the military effort, but won Kissinger's admiration by achieving his political objectives: breaking the Arab-Israeli statemate and recovering Sinai: *The Link*, December 1992, Norman Finkelstein. He did so by a seismic shift in Egypt's political alignment: 1) entry into America's imperialist structure; 2) conclusion of a separate peace with Israel – the option that Nasir rejected in 1967, and that 'Abd al Fattah Sisi was to reinforce in 2014 by joining the anti-Hamas coalition.

In adopting this radical new posture, Sadat had to abandon three long-time allies – the USSR, which had enabled his political triumphs; Syria, Egypt's recent comrade-in-arms; and the Palestinians, in whose nominal cause Egypt had fought five bloody wars over the previous 19 years. He also had to turn his back on the nine Arab states that had rallied to the pan-Arab cause during the Yom Kippur War.

Unanswered Questions – According to unconfirmed reports, Ashraf Marwan, son-in-law of President Nasir, was a double agent for Egypt versus Israel, or Israel versus Egypt. Before the outbreak of the Yom Kippur War, he was believed to have delivered official Egyptian documents to a London drop of Israeli intelligence, followed by two warnings of imminent Egyptian attack – the second on October 6, 1973, but inaccurate as to the hour of attack. On 12/17/10 *Ha'aretz* reported that Marwan had been a reliable source for Israel, but not privy to Sadat's secrets. On 6/2/07, he died in London, having gone off a fourth-floor balcony. Egypt gave him a state funeral: *Times*, 7/13/07; "Sixty Minutes", 5/10/09; *Ha'aretz*, 12/17/10.

According to a later report, Ashraf Marwan was an Israeli agent, but the improbability of Nasir's son-in-law's being a traitor prevented the Israelis from taking his assertions seriously: *The Angel*, Uri Bar-Joseph.

Another question relates to a postwar story, given credence by some chroniclers, that before the Yom Kippur attack Egypt had to seal pipes through which Israel planned to frustrate any Egyptian attempt to cross the Canal by flooding it with petroleum, to be ignited. According to *The Encyclopedia of the Arab-Israeli Conflict*, edited by Spencer C. Tucker, the scheme never materialized because the delivery pipes had been crushed by the over-burden of sand. Herzog reported that such pipes were never installed.

1978-2000 – Israel-Lebanon War

The IDF had established military supremacy over the Arabs in the Six-Day War, but the transfer of the PLO militia from Jordan to south Lebanon in the early 1970's was a prelude to explosion. Lebanon was sliding into civil war (1975-90).

1978 – The PLO's domination of south Lebanon was interrupted on 3/14/78 by Israeli occupation of a strip along the Lebanon-Israel border. A thousand Palestinians died resisting that operation: *NYTBR*, 9/14/14. The action put a temporary stop to PLO forays into Israel, such as a maritime incursion that had killed 38 Israelis near Tel Aviv: *Times*, 4/2/98.

1978 – In June a small UN force moved into the area, under UNSC Resolution 425. The Israeli forces withdrew, but began to supply arms, money, and troop support to anti-PLO Christian forces in the "Security Zone": *EB*, 22:900.

1981 – On 4/28/81, the IDF was invited into the Lebanese civil war by the Phalange (*Kata'ib*), a Maronite Christian faction. At Phalangist request, the Israeli Air Force intervened in the fighting in <u>central</u> Lebanon, shooting down two of the Syrian helicopters that had been punishing the Christian town of Zahlah: *The Arab-Israeli Wars*, Chaim Herzog.

1981 – In July the PLO directed heavy fire against many communities in northern Galilee: Herzog. The Israeli response was a major air campaign against targets in Lebanon. The professed objective was to subdue bases of the PLO. In Stephen Green's view (*Living By the Sword*), the real aim was to destabilize Lebanon. As exchanges between PLO artillery and Israeli aircraft intensified, Reagan sent out Philip Habib as a special representative. In July, Habib negotiated among the PLO, Syria, and Israel an understanding that called for a ceasefire, brought Syria back into the realm of international diplomacy after four years in the wilderness, and gave political status to the PLO – even though Habib was prohibited from direct contact with 'Arafat by a blanket commitment Kissinger had made to Israel in the aftermath of the Yom Kippur War.

1981 – The Habib accord troubled Ariel Sharon, named Minister of Defense in June 1981. A quiet border obstructed his plans for combat that would discredit the PLO and eliminate West Bankers' resistance to Israeli settlement: *How Israel Was Won*, Baylis Thomas. Sharon actually laid out to Habib his intention to invade Lebanon, expel PLO and Syrian forces there, hand the Presidency of Lebanon to Bashir Jumayyil (Gemayel), leader of the militia of the Phalange, and if possible annihilate the PLO and the Syrian armed forces: *Times*, 5/26/85, per the Israeli *Davar*, 5/24/85. To complete the radical surgery, Sharon favored replacement of the Jordanian monarchy with a Palestinian government: *Beyond Alliance*, Camille Mansour.

1981 – On 7/17/81, Israel bombed PLO headquarters in West Beirut, killing over 300 civilians.

1982 – In January, Sharon had a secret meeting in Beirut on joint strategy with Phalangist leader Bashir Jumayyil, who also made a secret visit to Prime Minister Begin on 2/16/82: Shlaim.

1982 – US arms shipments to Israel rose sharply in the first quarter: *Green Light in Lebanon*, Ze'ev Schiff.

1982 – An Israeli air strike of 5/9/82 on fedayeen targets in the area of Damur (coastal town between Beirut and Sidon) precipitated fedayeen rocket and artillery fire into Israel; the shells landed in empty fields: *Asad*, Patrick Seale. Also in May, Washington sent two carrier groups into Lebanese waters to provide air cover for Israel and its operations in Lebanon: Schiff.

1982 – In May, Secretary of State Haig told the media the Lebanese civil war required a radical solution.

1982 – The wounding of the Israeli ambassador in London on 6/3/82 by agents of the maverick Abu Nidal faction of Palestinians provided the flimsy pretext for Sharon's invasion of Lebanon: Seale. Washington voted for UNSC Resolution 509 calling for Israeli withdrawal, but Haig reportedly favored Israeli intervention to knock out the Soviets' Palestinian and Syrian "proxies".

1982 – On 6/4/82 Israel bombed PLO targets, counting on the PLO to retaliate. It complied, firing artillery that wounded 16 people in Israel. On June 5, the IDF began subjecting refugee camps in Lebanon to saturation bombing: Seale.

1982 – **Invasion** – On 6/6/82, 76,000 Israeli troops with 1250 tanks assaulted a defense line of 40,000 Lebanese, Syrians, and fedayeen. In the air, Syrian pilots put up a courageous resistance despite the inferiority in aircraft, pilot training, and military intelligence. (Israel was familiar with Syria's SAM-6 batteries, courtesy of Egypt, via the Pentagon.) Results of two days of air combat: Syrian planes lost – 64; Israeli planes lost – none: Seale. Ignoring a decision of the Israeli cabinet that put a 40-kilometer limit on Israeli penetration of Lebanon, Sharon aimed for Beirut. He met strong resistance, especially from Syrian ground troops (*WRMEA*, August 1992; Israel Shahak; Seale), but reached the outskirts of Beirut in three days. After a Soviet warning of "global consequences", Reagan ordered Israel not to block Syrian access along the Damascus-Beirut road, but Haig voided Habib's ceasefire accord of June 11 by persuading Reagan not to demand Israeli withdrawal.

On 6/8/82, the US vetoed draft UNSC Resolution 509 calling for Israeli withdrawal.

1982 – On 6/9/82, in one of history's biggest air battles (Shlaim), 100 Israeli jets destroyed SAM's that Syria had just moved into the Lebanese Biqa' along the Beirut-Damascus highway. The IAF shot down 23 Syrian MiG's without losing a single aircraft: Shlaim. *The New York Review* of 11/24/83 carried comments on the battle by former Deputy Secretary of State George Ball: "Israel gratuitously humiliated the Soviet

Union by misusing our advanced weapons to annihilate Syria's second-class Soviet equipment ..."

1982 – Habib was getting mixed signals from Washington. The President was sympathetic to Israel's concerns. Secretary of State Haig, Israel's foremost champion in the administration, reportedly gave the invasion a green light. National Security Adviser William Clark told Habib on 6/10/82 to assure Syrian ruler Hafiz al Asad that Reagan favored Israeli withdrawal, but Haig chimed in with instructions to give Israel more time. Syria lost 150 tanks that day. Israel also had heavy ground losses. Habib negotiated another brief ceasefire on June 11. IDF forces, advantaged by their mastery of the air, advanced against stiff Palestinian and Syrian resistance. On June 13, they reached Beirut, where they linked up with Phalangist forces. Beirut was surrounded by the IDF and the Phalangist militia. Asad was in Moscow arranging for Soviet arms resupply. Begin had informed Reagan 6/10/82 that Israel could not comply with the US request to withdraw from Lebanon until Lebanon had a new government that would no longer let the PLO use that country as its base of operations.

1982 – On 6/14/82 the IDF took the 'Ayn Hilwah refugee camp. Inside Beirut the Lebanese and PLO continued to resist: Shlaim; Mansour; Seale.

1982 – The siege of Beirut went on for 70 days (6/13 to 8/12), while Israeli aircraft and gunboats pounded west Beirut, Sidon, Damur, and Tyre. East Beirut was under Christian control. Anarchic west Beirut was under Muslim control: EB: 14:845. Lebanese and Palestinian deaths approached 20,000: Herzog; Seale; Thomas. West Beirut (Palestinian neighborhoods included) was largely destroyed: *EB*, 14:845. The Phalangist forces still ringed Beirut, but they resisted Israeli pressure to join the siege. They concentrated on reducing the PLO presence down the coast. Thomas Friedman's coverage of the devastation of west Beirut (for the *Times*) was to win him his first Pulitzer Prize.

1982 – **Haig Out** – On 6/25/82, as a second ceasefire was proclaimed in Lebanon, Reagan came into focus and dumped Haig from the cabinet. Haig had strayed on many policy issues, but his tolerance of Israeli overreaching was the last straw. Reagan bought the expulsion of the PLO forces from Lebanon, but not the plan to convert Lebanon to a puppet state. The new Secretary of State was George Shultz.

1982 – During the siege of Beirut, the Israeli-Syrian conflict continued in eastern Lebanon. On 7/24/82 Israel lost a Phantom F-4 to a Syrian SAM-6. Syria lost its batteries of SAM-8's – new to Lebanon – to Israeli jets.

1982 – Another Israeli F-4 was shot down by a Syrian SAM-6 on 7/25/82.

1982 – On 8/1/82 Reagan told the press the bloodshed in Beirut had to stop.

1982 – On 8/4/82 the IDF captured south Beirut and the Lebanese international airport at Khalidah (Herzog), and raided the Palestinian Quarter.

1982 – During the first half of August, Israel's shelling of West Beirut intensified to carpet-bombing: Thomas; *Going All the Way*, Jonathan Randall. (The editors of the *Times* characteristically deleted the term "indiscriminate" from one of Thomas Friedman's submissions.) One objective of these barrages was to kill Yasir 'Arafat.

1982 – On August 12, Habib, back in Lebanon, prevailed on the White House to order a stop to saturation bombing of the Palestinian sector of Beirut; Michael Deaver had reportedly threatened to resign if Reagan didn't intervene.

1982 – **Reagan Intervenes: Washington's Third Ultimatum to Israel?** – Reagan's patience had run out. His phone conversation with Begin led to Israeli proclamation of a ceasefire. The Palestinians' killing of 19 Israelis and wounding of 64 was the "victory" the PLO needed for its acceptance of its evacuation from Lebanon, which began 8/21/82. Reagan all but forced Begin to lift the bloody siege of Beirut. Soon after, Begin left public life: *FT*, 3/7/15.

1982 – **Entry of US Marines** – In mid-August, Habib negotiated a multinational agreement: a ceasefire, the evacuation of Syrian and PLO troops from Beirut, and the introduction of a French/Italian/US Multinational Force (MNF) to keep the peace in Lebanon. As part of the MNF, 850 US Marines arrived in Beirut on 8/25/82. Reagan reportedly agreed to send the Marines to Lebanon in return for Israeli agreement to withdraw its forces from Beirut: *Post*, Edwin Yoder.

1982 – Israel turned Beirut's water system back on 8/8/82, electricity 8/22.

1982 – **PLO Away to its own Diaspora** – On 8/23/82, Parliament elected Bashir Jumayyil President of Lebanon. Washington supported the choice. By 9/1/82 the Syrians, the PLA, and the PLO had left Beirut. Some 10,000 Palestinian combatants were to evacuate Lebanon, bound for eight Arab countries. (No country would take them all.) 'Arafat's headquarters moved to Tunisia.

1982 – **Marines Depart** – By 9/10/82 the 850 Marines were gone. Habib had guaranteed that Israeli forces would stay out of Beirut, and Palestinian noncombatants would not be harmed.

1982 – **Bashir Assassinated** – On 9/14/82, in a grim reminder that the Israeli invasion was carried out in the midst of Lebanon's sectarian civil war, President Bashir Jumayyil was assassinated by Habib Shartuni, a member of the SSNP (Syrian Social Nationalist Party), and a presumed agent of the Baathist regime in Damascus: *MEJ*, Winter 2013. In panic, the IDF occupied the Muslim section of Beirut: Randall; Shlaim; *From Beirut to Jerusalem*, Thomas Friedman.

1982 – On 9/15/82 a special Israeli unit assassinated 63 Palestinian intellectuals, residents of Beirut.

1982 – **Massacre in the Camps** – Sharon had lied to Habib. After the Lebanese government refused the IDF's request to search the Sabra neighborhood and Shatila Palestinian refugee camp for hidden members of the PLO, the commander of IDF forces in Beirut, Brigadier General Amos Yaron, arranged for the Phalangist militia to wipe out (nonexistent) "terrorist nests" in the camps. On 9/16/82 1500 militiamen – most of them from the Phalange, some reportedly from the South Lebanon Army (SLA, an Israeli mercenary force commanded by renegade Lebanese Major Sa'd Haddad) – entered the Sabra neighborhood and the Shatila refugee camp and began shooting residents on sight. The order to shoot reportedly came from Phalangist official Elie Hubaykah. The dead numbered over 1000, including Palestinians, Lebanese, Syrians, and Egyptians. IDF collusion was blatant: illumination of the kill zones by flares during the night of 9/16-17; allowing the mayhem to continue into 9/18; maintenance of a perimeter that bottled up the victims: Friedman; Randall; Shlaim; *JPS*, Autumn 2002; *Begin*, Eric Silver; *NYTBR*, 2/16/14. The atrocity was a wholesale violation of Philip Habib's commitment to 'Arafat – endorsed by Washington – to assure the safety of Palestinian civilians after the PLO forces had left Lebanon. The objective of the Phalangists was extermination of the Palestinians, in retaliation for previous massacres committed by the PLO. The motives of Sharon were to ingratiate Israel with the Maronites (Seale), exterminate the PLO, and possibly precipitate Palestinian flight back to Jordan: *WRMEA*, March 1999, Richard Curtiss. Herzog's version: The IDF commanders on the scene demanded evacuation of the Phalangist militia on 9/17, "when they first learned that noncombatants were being killed".

1982 – On 9/20/82, Reagan expressed horror at the massacre, called for IDF withdrawal from Beirut, and announced agreement with France and Italy on formation of a second MNF to help the Lebanese government restore order in west Beirut. Sharon and Chief of Staff Rafael Eitan denied responsibility for the massacre, and accused "the Americans" of shared responsibility because of Habib's role: *Living by the Sword*, Stephen Green. Eitan accused the Americans of plotting to steal the West Bank from Israel: *Times*, 2/10/83, Anthony Lewis.

1982 – On 9/24/82, the UNSC condemned the massacre and called on Israel to withdraw from Lebanon at once.

1982 – **Israeli Mass Protest** – Whereas no Arab country allowed public protests of Sabra-Shatila (for fear of riots), on 12/21/82 400,000 Israelis went into the streets to demand a public inquiry: Seale. Before the war ended, appalling destruction had been visited on Beirut and Sidon, 17,500 Arabs had lost their lives, and the PLO forces had left Lebanon for Syria, Iraq, Yemen, and Tunisia. (Egypt, Saudi Arabia, and the Gulf shaykdoms had denied them entry.)

1982 – **Marines Return** – On 9/29/82, Sharon withdrew his forces from Beirut, and 1200 US Marines, members of a second MNF, returned in penitence. Reagan on TV: They would stay until Syrian and Israeli forces had left Lebanon. USG spokesman: They would stay until the

Lebanese Government had reestablished its authority: Seale. They were to learn from escalating fire from the pro-Syrian faction in the Shuf (a mountainous district southeast of Beirut) that they had walked into a civil war.

1982 – 67 Israelis died on 11/11/82 in the bombing of the IDF headquarters in Tyre.

1982 – After Israeli missiles destroyed Syria's SAM-6 system, the Soviets supplied SAM-5's (manned by Russians), less vulnerable to missile attack: *Times*.

1983 – On 2/3/83, an international commission charged Israel with aggression against Lebanon. It charged Israel and the Phalange with culpability in the Sabra-Shatila massacre.

1983 – In support of an effort to bring south Lebanon under de facto Israeli administration, Israel backed the emergence of the South Lebanon Army (SLA) under command of Sa'd Haddad, who claimed control of south Lebanon from the Israeli border to the Awali River. The SLA consisted of 1500 militiamen, mostly Christian. Its main garrison was to be in Sidon. *CSM*; *Times*.

1983 – In February, General Secretary Andropov authorized installation in Syria of state-of-the-art SAM-5's, protected by Soviet troops: Herzog.

1983 – **Kahan Commission** – On 2/8/83, under domestic and international pressure, Israel set up the Kahan Commission to investigate the Sabra-Shatila massacre. Chairman Yitzhak Kahan was President of the Israeli Supreme Court: Herzog. His commission blamed the Phalange for direct responsibility, Sharon and the IDF for indirect responsibility. Sharon was slapped on the wrist by demotion from Minister of Defense to Minister without portfolio: Shlaim. The report also faulted Prime Minister Begin and Foreign Minister Shamir: Herzog. Chief of Staff Rafael Eitan was found guilty of failure to order the Phalangist militiamen out of the area: *WRMEA*, citing *Ma'ariv*. *Times*, 4/6/84.

On 2/21/83, *Time* reported that one day before the Sabra/Shatila massacre, Sharon had discussed with Bashir's family taking revenge on Palestinian civilians in those two neighborhoods, and that an unpublished appendix of the Kahan Commission's report had contained evidence of that conversation.

In the Tel Aviv District Court, Sharon sued *Time* for libel. On 1/22/86, Sharon and *Time* announced an out-of-court settlement: *Time* told the court the reference to a Sharon/Jumayyil conversation was erroneous, and agreed to pay for part of Sharon's legal fees. Sharon dropped the suit: *Times*, 1/23/86, Thomas Friedman.

Richard Falk condemned the Kahan Report as having whitewashed the full participation of the Israeli state: *MER*, June 1983.

1983 – **Embassy Bombing** – On 4/18/83, a car bomb attributed to Hizballah demolished the center of the US Embassy building in Beirut, killing 63, including 17 Americans, wounding 100. One of the dead was Robert Ames, the CIA's able trouble-shooter in the Middle East. An anonymous phone call to *Agence France Presse* said the bombing was part of the campaign of the Iranian revolution against imperialism: *Pity the Nation*, Robert Fisk. NSA found evidence of Iranian and Syrian complicity: *Times*.

1983 – Five thousand Soviets were helping Syria build an integrated air defense system: *Times*.

1983 – Israel had four major military bases in south Lebanon, and a logistics base at Marj'uyun: *Times*.

1983 – **Shultz: Abortive Treaty** – Secretary of State George Shultz forced Amin Jumayyil, weak successor of his brother Bashir as President of Lebanon, to sign on 5/17/83 a pie-in-the-sky "treaty" that arranged for reciprocal withdrawal of Israeli and Syrian troops from Lebanon, and purported to award Israel hegemony in Lebanon, in blatant disregard of the fact that Syria was the dominant power there. Hafiz al Asad's rejection of the arrangement soured Shultz on all Arabs: Seale; Friedman.

1983 – By this time the balance of power in Lebanon was undergoing a radical shift as a consequence of Iranian skill in inventing Hizballah, its new anti-Western force, and of Israeli clumsiness in alienating Lebanon's previously quiescent Shiite community, which had welcomed Israeli elimination of the overbearing PLO. Israel managed to cancel out that advantage by imposing a tax on Lebanese villagers (*Pity the Nation*, Robert

Fisk), inflicting gratuitous devastation on Lebanese villages, and operating with the characteristic disdain of occupying armies.

1983 – On 5/20/83, the US lifted its embargo on the provision of F-16's to Israel.

1983 – The IDF had been taking continuous casualties in central Lebanon from the resistance operations of Syria and its Lebanese allies. In August, Israel sought escape by moving its defense perimenter south of the Awali River, which flows from the Lebanon Range to the Mediterranean just north of Sidon. By vacating central Lebanon, the Israelis left it wide-open for its people to get back to their own war: Friedman.

1983 – **US Forces Enter the War** – In late August, US Marine positions near the Beirut Airport began taking mortar and rocket fire. On 8/29/83, two Marines were killed and 14 wounded. In Washington, a sharp debate was building between advocates of US engagement (Secretary Shultz) and opponents (Defense Secretary Casper Weinberger).

1983 – On 9/1/83, the IDF withdrew from the Shuf (the district [*Qadha*] about 25 miles south of Beirut), while agreeing to supply arms to its people. Since most of them are Druze, Israel's 50,000 Druze citizens take an interest in their welfare: *Economist*.

1983 – On 9/8/83, in defense of the Marines, US destroyers shelled resistance positions in the hills east of Beirut.

1983 – On 9/9/83, Lebanese government units (pro-West) based at Suq al-Gharb, a strategically located suburb of 'Alayh, ten miles east of Beirut, reported that they were in danger of being overrun by pro-Syrian Druze. White House aide Robert McFarlane, then on a visit to Lebanon, relayed to Washington a Lebanese government request for help. On 9/11/83, Reagan authorized the Marines to attack the forces of the resistance if Marine Commander Col. Timothy Geraghty thought the Lebanese apprehension was justified. McFarlane asked Geraghty to request the US ships to return fire. Geraghty reportedly demurred on the ground that return fire would violate the Marines' neutrality and his mission directives.

1983 – On 9/12/83, two thousand more Marines arrived off the Lebanese coast, bringing the total of US ground forces in Lebanese waters to 12,000. If attacked, the Marines had been authorized by Reagan to act in defense of themselves and Lebanese forces, and to call for supporting fire from US ships.

1983 – From 9/16/83 to 9/25/83, US warships shelled Druze positions on a strategic ridge controlled by anti-West forces. According to one source, that shelling was in retaliation for resistance fire on the US Embassy and the Lebanese Ministry of Defense.

1983 – On 9/19/83, Sixth Fleet units fired on Arab forces in the hills east of Beirut (*Times*), and the Marines fired on local assailants.

1983 – On 9/25/83, the USS New Jersey, the only battleship still in service, arrived on the scene and shelled positions in the mountains for nine hours: *Times*. According to James Kilpatrick's column, this barrage brought enemy fire to a stop. The New Jersey fired 301 rounds of 2250 pounds each. These "flying Volkswagens" wreaked destruction with every impact and killed hundreds of civilians (*Harper's*), but the New Jersey's rounds were wildly inaccurate, and did their greatest damage to random targets: *Counterpunch*, 4/19/13, Franklin Lamb. The cause of the inaccuracy was also random: The powder for the cannons was a mistaken remix of variant burning rates: *Chicago Tribune*, Tim McNulty.

1983 – On 9/29/83, under the War Powers Act of 1973, Congress drafted a resolution that would allow the Marines to stay in Lebanon up to eighteen months.

1983 – Excerpts from Reagan's simplistic and largely irrelevant radio address of 10/8/83: "Can the United States stand by and see the Middle East incorporated into the Soviet Bloc?" "... didn't we assume a moral obligation to the continued existence of Israel?" "Syria ... has some 5000 Soviet advisers ... and new Soviet equipment ..." "The presence of our Marines as part of the multi-national force demonstrates that Lebanon does not stand alone."

1983 – On 10/16/83, an armed Israeli convoy precipitated a final break with Lebanon's Shias by trying to barge through a religious procession in Nabatiyyah on 'Ashurah, their holiest day. In the consequent dustup, several Nabatiyyans were wounded and two killed.

On 10/17 a Shiite fatwa identified the Israelis as enemies, and sparked a feud that has haunted Israel ever since: Friedman.

1983 – **Marine Barracks Bombing** – At dawn on 10/23/83, a smiling driver drove a truck-bomb into the Marine compound in Beirut, killing 241 Marines. Minutes later another truck-bomb killed 58 French paratroopers at their compound. These operations were widely viewed as Shiite (Hizballah and/or Iranian) retaliation for the French and American entry into the Lebanese War on the Israeli/Maronite side. US intelligence found that Iran gave direct support to the barracks bombing: *Washington Post Weekly*. US officials suspected that Iran had supplied the ten tons of TNT that powered the explosion: *Times*. Thomas Friedman put a share of the blame on the naïveté, if not venality, of Reagan, Shultz, McFarlane, Weinberger, Casey, and Haig (?) for giving Israel a blank check to invade Lebanon with American weapons, and compounding the offense by ordering US forces to support the invasion: *From Beirut to Jerusalem*.

1983 – In the aftermath, Reagan resorted to the usual bluster about America's immunity to terrorist blackmail, but on 2/7/84, after Lebanon was out of the headlines, Marines were ordered out.

1983 – The bizarre "invasion" of Grenada began 10/25/83. Ron Steel speculated that it was Reagan's way of diverting attention from the 10/23/83 bombing of the Marine barracks: *The Boston Globe*, 7/28/91.

1983 – On 11/4/83, a truck-bomb killed 39 Israelis and Arabs at the IDF headquarters in Tyre. Suspected in this operation was *Hizballah* (Party of God), a Shiite militia lately assembled and trained in the Lebanese Biqa' by the new Islamic Revolutionary Guard Corps (IRGC). The Israeli Air Force retaliated against Hizballah targets, killing 60 militants of Hizballah's Islamic Jihad, which had claimed responsibility for the Marine barracks bombing and the Tyre attack. The suicide bomb remains as one of Hizballah's contributions to history: *Sacred Rage*, Robin Wright; *Atlantic*, David Brooks.

1983 – During an Israeli air attack on Sa'iqah (pro-Syrian Palestinian faction) and General Command bases in the Shuf, a Syrian SAM-7 shot down an Israeli plane. The Lebanese Army returned the pilot to the IDF.

1983 – On 11/16/83, IDF jets attacked Hizballah bases in the Biqa', in retaliation for the 11/4/83 truck bombing in Tyre.

1983 – Israel exchanged 4000 PLO militiamen who had been held in south Lebanon and elsewhere for 6 IDF soldiers held by the PLO: *Economist*.

1983 – On 12/4/83, in retaliation for Syrian anti-aircraft attacks on US recon planes, US jets attacked Syrian targets. A US A-6 and an A-7 were shot down.

1983 – 12/13/83: Renewed Syrian fire on US recon planes; the Sixth Fleet shelled Syrian anti-aircraft batteries for the second time in two weeks.

1983 – On 12/14/83, in retaliation for Syrian SAM attacks on US recon aircraft, the New Jersey fired eleven 16-inch projectiles at Druze positions in Lebanon.

1983 – On 12/23/83, Italian President Pertini called for the withdrawal of Italian troops from Lebanon, on the grounds that the US was using its troops there for the defense of Israel, not for peace.

1983 – The Long Commission, set up by Defense Secretary Weinberger to investigate the Marine barracks bombing of 10/23/83, reported on 12/28/83 that among the causes of the catastrophe were major failures of intelligence, policy, and command – notably perversion of the Marines' mission from peace-keeping to unrelated policy objectives.

1983 – Tapline, running from Dhahran to Beirut, had ceased to function north of Jordan.

1984 – An Israeli raid of 1/4/84 on Hizballah bases in the northern Biqa' wounded 400, killed 40. Many of the victims were civilians.

1984 – In January the US tightened restrictions on exports to Iran on the grounds that its support for bombings, abductions, and hijackings in Lebanon had made it a sponsor of international terrorism: Seale.

1984 – **US Forces Back Again in the War** – On 2/8/84, in retaliation for renewed Muslim and Druze shelling of Beirut, the battleship New Jersey (16" guns) and the destroyer Caron (5" guns) destroyed a number of Druze and Syrian gun batteries in the mountains east of Beirut, and a Syrian command post in the Biqaʿ. One of the dead in the Biqaʿ was the commander of Syrian forces in Lebanon.

1984 – The withdrawal of the Marines was completed on 2/26/84. During their stay in Lebanon, 265 soldiers had been killed.

1984 – Lebanese Shiites, Sunnis, and Druze joined Syrians and remaining Palestinians in harrying Israeli forces back toward the border. In February Muslim and Druze militiamen overran the Muslim sector of Beirut.

1984 – **End of Shultz's Treaty** – On March 5, Amin Jumayyil, who had signed the Lebanese-Israeli accord of 5/17/83, went to see Hafiz al Asad in Damascus, Jumayyil's Canossa, and scrapped the accord. The action marked the end of the brief Israeli-American era in Lebanon. In the contest for primacy, Syria had won: Seale; Shlaim. Reagan had been "outmaneuvered by a master player" (Asad): *CSM*, Joseph Harsch. By June, Israeli forces had been pushed back to the "Security Zone", controlled by the SLA with IDF support. Having had to abandon the effort to run Lebanese affairs, Israel had fallen back on trust in its Christian proxies in south Lebanon: Shlaim.

1984-85 – Washington continued to support Israel at the UN, vetoing a 1984 draft calling on Israel to respect international law in Lebanon, and one of 1985 condemning Israeli killings of civilians in south Lebanon.

1985 – On 1/14/85 the Israeli cabinet approved a plan for IDF withdrawal in three stages from Lebanon proper, but leaving the "Security Zone" under control of the SLA. The first stage – withdrawal to south of the Litani River – was completed in mid-February.

1985 – Hours after a suicide bomber killed 12 IDF soldiers, the IDF conducted a reprisal raid on Zrariyyah, killing 24 of its Lebanese defenders – soldiers and militiamen – under Israel's "iron fist" strategy.

1985 – On 6/6/85 Israel completed the withdrawal of its combat forces from Lebanon, except for the "Security Zone" (440 square miles), which remained under Israeli/SLA control.

US Intervention: Recap

US Marines have had three deployments in Lebanon. None of them was productive. In 1958, Eisenhower sent a force to save President Camille Sham'un (Maronite Christian) from Muslim insurgency. The Commander of the Lebanese Army – also a Maronite, but neutral in the dispute – resolved matters and took Sham'un's place as President of Lebanon. In 1982, Reagan sent Marines to Lebanon to help keep the peace as the PLO left the country. The Marines arrived 8/25/82 and departed by September 10 without serious incident. The traumatic Syrian (?) assassination of Maronite President Bashir Jumayyil, plus the collusion of the Phalangists and the IDF in the Sabra-Shatila massacre, required Reagan to send Marines back to Lebanon two weeks later to help supervise the evacuation of Israeli and Syrian forces from the country. He allowed the Marines and the warships offshore to enter the fighting on the Israeli/Phalangist side on 9/16/83 (?). The reprisal bombing of the Marines' barracks demonstrated that, short of military occupation, there was no way the US could restore peace in Lebanon. The Marine contingent was withdrawn in February 1984, and the US warships soon after.

Israeli Occupation of Lebanon: Recap

The Syrian Claim to Lebanon – Syria and Lebanon are a geographic, cultural, and economic unit. In detail, Lebanon is distinguished by its close-knit Maronite (Catholic) community, which emerged in the northern mountains of the Lebanon Range around 400 A.D., and won independence from the Byzantine Empire in 684: *EB*, 7:867. In the 1800's, the Ottoman rulers of Syria incited the Druze against the Maronites. In 1860, a Druze massacre of Maronites moved France, which had long since assumed the role of protector of the Maronites, to persuade the Ottoman Emperor to award them their own autonomous province (Mount Lebanon). Under the French mandate of 1923, Syria and Lebanon were administered separately; in 1946, Lebanon became an independent state (*EB*, 7:227), although its ethnic division among Maronites, Greek Orthodox Christians, Sunni Muslims, and Shia Muslims was bound to lead to civil war: *EB*, 22:898.

Since the separation imposed by France in 1920, Lebanon had gone its own way. The Lebanese civil war of 1975-90 was fought between two coalitions – one pro-West, one anti-West. Neither one had advocated rule by Syria, but the civil war was Syria's opportunity to close the artificial gap. With cold-blooded pragmatism, the Alawite regime in Damascus outlasted the Israeli-American invasion of 1982-2000 and deployed Syrian army and intelligence forces to preserve an approximate balance of power between the pro-West (largely Christian and Sunni) and anti-West (largely Shiite and Druze) factions, and ultimately to win authentication from the Arabs and the West of Syria's role as peacekeeper in a Lebanon which had demonstrated no ability to keep the peace on its own. Tempering his dictatorial instincts with broad consultation among the embittered parties, and trading on Washington's eagerness to enlist Syria in the 1991 coalition to expel Iraq from Kuwait, Hafiz al Asad achieved a signal political victory in Lebanon. Foreshadowed by the Ta'if Accord of October 1989, the dual Syrian-Lebanese regime was sealed by the military defeat inflicted on the Lebanese separatists in 1990 by a Syrian-Lebanese force commanded by Lebanese Colonel Amil Lahhud.

To assure Syrian control, Asad stationed a large garrison in Lebanon, worked through like-minded Lebanese (notably Lahhud, who became President of Lebanon in 1998), and concluded a series of bilateral agreements. A 1991 Treaty of Coordination was followed up by an agreement recognizing Syria's right to a voice in the internal affairs of the Lebanese "region" (*qutr*). However, the two systems had evolved so differently that Asad excluded any hint of annexation from the discussions.

As Asad's health declined, the Damascus regime adhered to standard dynastic practice (not unknown even in Western democracies). Assad's older son, groomed for succession, had died in a traffic accident, so the mantle fell on second son Bashar, who was meekly studying ophthalmology in London, and had shown no interest in politics. Called back from England, Bashar was given a crash course in dictatorship, notably including the formidable assignment of running Lebanon. As President of the Syrian Computer Society, Bashar opened Syria to cell phones and the Internet. After the death of Hafiz in 2000, the Syrian Baath power structure (nominally operating through the National Progressive Front) moved rapidly to qualify Bashar for the Presidency by appointing him Secretary General of the Baath National Command and Commander-in-Chief of the Armed Forces, and by lowering the Presidential age minimum in the Syrian Constitution. On June 27, 2000, the Syrian Parliament unanimously elected Bashar al Asad President of Syria. 'Abd al Halim Khaddam (Sunni) stayed on as Vice President. An orderly transition had been accomplished. In 2001, Bashar symbolized the objective of Alawite-Sunni assimilation (under Alawite control) by marrying Asma Akhras, a Londoner of Sunni Syrian origin who had been employed by J.P. Morgan.

By 2004, problems had arisen in the other half of Bashar's hermaphroditic realm. As Lebanese never tire of recounting, their society had been cosmopolitan since the Phoenicians first colonized Mediterranean shores and sailed out into the Atlantic. (Hiram of Tyre established a colony in Utica, modern Tunisia, perhaps as early as 1000 BCE: *EB*: 22:895.) In modern Lebanon, the term "Phoenician" had become politically incorrect, having been appropriated as a code word for "Christian".

As memories of the savage civil war faded, Lebanese grew impatient of Syrian domination. When the pro-West faction swept the Lebanese Parliamentary elections of 2000, activists began to agitate for reduction of the Syrian presence. Syria's staunch ally, Hizballah, counter-demonstrated, and the agitation subsided.

However, as Israel's most formidable neighbor (after Egypt's neutralization), Syria has had to contend with automatic hostility from the US. As a refuge of Palestinian resistance leaders, it has long been on Washington's list of "terrorist" states. In 2003, Bush 43 signed the Syrian Accountability and Lebanese Sovereignty Restoration Act, which would impose minor economic sanctions against Syria until it terminated its support for Hizballah and the Palestinian resistance, closed the border with Iraq, and withdrew its troops from Lebanon. In 2004, Washington managed to extract from the UN Security Council Resolution 1559, which mentioned neither sanctions nor Syria, but called for the dismantling of all militias in Lebanon and the withdrawal of all foreign forces. (Russia and China abstained.)

By these two initiatives, Washington posed a threat to vital Syrian interests. Lebanon employed hundreds of thousands of Syrian workers, its free-enterprise economy was Syria's main source of hard currency, and Beirut was Damascus' natural entrepot (as Latakia is for Aleppo – now that Alexandretta is lost to Turkey). More crucially, Lebanon's southern border, staunchly defended by Hizballah, not by the separatists, was a major sector in Syria's natural line of defense against any Israeli encroachment.

Bashar met the separatist challenge head-on in September 2004 by persuading the Lebanese Parliament to revise the Constitution and extend the tenure of President Lahhud for another three years. From that time on, Syria's trajectory was all downhill: withdrawal of troops from Lebanon; streaming into Syria of a million Iraqi refugees from the consequences of the American invasion of Iraq; *Middle East Policy*'s citation of speculation that Syria's primary motivation in pulling out of Lebanon was apprehension that it was next on Washington's hit list; and then Syria's final tocsin – collapse into its own civil war.

Israeli Policy Errors – In Israel's 67 years, its survival has hung on two essentials: 1) From the outset, reliance on superpower support; 2) Ultimately, acceptance by the Middle East power structure.

Israel's most intimate association with an Arab state was its intrusion into Lebanon (1978-2000). That reckless venture was a severe setback to the goal of regional acceptance. It exacerbated Sunni enmity, antagonized the initially neutral Shia (*The Shia Revival*, Vali Nasr), and lost their only friends in Lebanon, the Maronites, who were soured by the arrogance of the Israeli leadership, notably when it condescended to an infuriated President Bashir Jumayyil.

During the Israeli invasion of Lebanon, international sympathy for the refugees from the Holocaust was attenuated by Israeli carpet-bombing (Shlaim), violations of international law, ferocity (15,000 Lebanese and Palestinians killed: *NYR*), looting (*Going All the Way*,

Jonathan Randall), illegal use of cluster bombs against civilian targets (*Times*), and of white phosphorus (Fisk), and blatant collusion with the Phalange in the Sabra-Shatila massacre: *JPS*, Autumn 2002.

Israel's atrocities were whitewashed in part on 2/7/83 by the Kahan Report, although its mission was confined to examination of the Sabra-Shatila atrocity. It assigned indirect responsibility to Begin and his ranking officials: Neff; *WRMEA*, January 1998.

US Policy Errors – Responsibility for Israel's strategic myopia in Lebanon was shared by its guarantor, the US. Reagan's inattention to the multitudinous hazards lurking in Haig's green light embroiled America in Israel's self-sabotage, the rise of Hizballah, the Lebanese epidemic of abduction (most of whose victims were reportedly held in Ras al 'Ayn in the northern Biqa' – Shiite country), aircraft hijacking, US supply to Israel of cluster bombs, the opportunity for Iranian intrusion into the Arab World, exacerbation of the Cold War, and Washington's incomprehensible contravention of the prohibition against deploying US and Israeli forces in the same conflict – all this culminating in Shultz's lapse of 5/17/83, the US-Lebanon "treaty" that had already been preempted by the Syrian victory over Israel in their contest for influence in Lebanon.

1980-88 – Iraq-Iran War

———

By 1800, a long period of indigenous empire in the Middle East was drawing to a close; in Iran, the Safavid Empire had vanished; in the eastern Arab World, the Ottoman Empire was collapsing. For the rapacious European imperialists, the resultant power vacuum was an irresistible invitation.

Over the next one hundred years, Britain and France fought their way from enmity to alliance. One of the more myopic enterprises of that alliance was the 1916 Sykes-Picot Agreement: Three of its products were the ungovernable states of Syria, Lebanon, and Iraq. All three were centers of political innovation. They introduced Baathism – a secularist form of Arab Nationalism, too advanced for the sect-ridden Arab World, but still professed by the dictatorships of Syria and Iraq at the time the Iran-Iraq War was being fought.

The Baathist partnership between Syria and Iraq never got off the ground. Syria was a Sunni country, ruled by Alawite Shiites. Its enemy was Israel. Iraq, home of a restless Shiite majority, had been ruled since Ottoman times by Sunnis. Its enemy was Iran. Syrian assistance for Iraq against Iran was negligible. The rancor between Iraq and Iran was a war waiting to happen.

Ethnic Challenges in Iraq – In 1958-9, Shiite leader Muhammad Baqir al Sadr presided over the founding of *Al Da'wah al Islamiyyah* (the Islamic Call). Its original mission was to promote social justice and an Islamic state: *The Oxford Dictionary of Islam*, John Esposito. As the Ba'th won control of Iraq, Al Da'wah was drawn into bitter conflict with the regime, which from 1968 on became increasingly synonymous with the person of Saddam Husayn, who designated membership in Al Da'wah a capital crime: *Current History*, Juan Cole.

From 1974 on, Saddam resorted to execution of activist Shiite leaders. The 2/11/80 bombing of the hallowed Mustansiriyyah University, and the attempt on the life of Deputy Prime Minister Tariq 'Aziz, were charged to Al Da'wah. On April 9, 1980, Grand Ayatallah Muhammad Baqir al Sadr was forced to watch the torture and death of his sister, Bint al Huda, before his own torture and execution – allegedly by the hammering of spikes into his head.

The mountains of northeastern Iraq were the stronghold of the Iraqi Kurds, who had been agitating for autonomy for decades. Their insurrection was a surrogate Iranian war versus Iraq: *The Reckoning*, Sandra Mackey.

The Iraqi-Iranian Feud – In the early 1500's Iran emerged as an integrated country with a majority language (Persian), a Shiite dynasty, and fairly precise geographic frontiers: in the east, the Kopet-Dag Range, the Kavir Desert, and the Lut Desert; in the west, the Zagros Mountains. From prehistoric times, the shifting peoples of Persia have looked infrequently to the east – mostly when the conquests of their imperial regimes extended to the Indus River (Achaemenids, Alexandrines, the Caliphate), but more often to the alluring river valleys and pioneering civilizations to the west.

Iran has been properly classified as part of the Middle East. It has been an active participant in the power struggles of that region, including a contentious relationship with the rulers of Iraq. Persian language and Shiite fervor have given Iranian culture its own persona, distinct from the other dominant cultures in the region: of the Arabs to the west, and of the Turks to the northwest.

In 1969, the Shah of Iran abrogated a 1937 agreement that had equated Iraq's eastern frontier with the east bank of the Shatt al 'Arab (confluence of the Tigris and Euphrates rivers), in favor of the Iranian claim that the frontier should follow the *Thalweg* (the deepest course of the riverbed).

In 1975 Saddam Husayn and the Shah suddenly mended their fences in the Algiers Accord, by which Iraq renounced its claim to Khuzistan (the Iranian area populated by Persian-speakers of Arab extraction), and conceded the Shah's position on the frontier. In return, the Shah closed the border between Iran and Iraqi Kurdistan – terminating the flow of logistic support provided to the rebellious Barzani Kurds by Iran, Israel, and America. Baghdad was then able to cripple the Kurdish rebellion. Mustafa Barzani fled Iraq and died in exile: Mackey. Ever since, the Iraqi Kurds have reviled Carter and Kissinger for betraying earlier promises of continuing support: *NY*, 9/29/14, Dexter Filkins.

The Rise of Khomeini: From Ayatollah to Imam – In 1979, as often happens in history, one individual radically altered the course of human events: Around 1900 a member of Iran's landlord class had ordered the death of a mullah who was survived by an infant son. The child grew up to become Grand Ayatollah Ruhollah Khomeini, outspoken critic of the Shah's campaign to revise Iranian society along Western secularist lines. Exiled from Iran in 1964, Khomeini later settled in Iraq, where he continued his denunciations of the Shah. In 1978, Saddam fortified détente with the Shah by expelling Khomeini from Iraq.

On 2/1/79, at the invitation of the Shiite clergy – who were the base of the Iranian power structure – Khomeini astounded the Shah, Saddam, and Washington by returning to a euphoric welcome in Tehran as the leader of Iran's second revolution: *EB*. (The first was the constitutional revolution of 1905-11.)

By the fall of 1979, Khomeini was well on his way to establishing an Iranian theocracy under the rule of a jurisprudent cleric (*velayat-e faqih*) – a concept advanced by the late Ali Shariati: Vali Nasr. He had purged the monarchists still in office. Prime Minister Mehdi Bazargan resigned 11/6/79. Khomeini was projecting a vehemently anti-American stance. He gave a warm welcome to PLO head Yasir 'Arafat, conveyed the Israeli Embassy building to the PLO, and in return for the support he had enjoyed from the PLO promised to work for the elimination of Israel.

93

The Shah in the US – Under browbeating from Henry Kissinger and other friends of the former Shah, Carter took the risk of admitting him into the US for urgent medical treatment. Khomeini cried conspiracy, and encouraged Iranians to take action. Student groups, uniformly critical of the US for its long record of interference in Iranian affairs, agitated for action against the US Embassy. Khomeini liked the idea. On 11/4/79, as the Iranian guard on the Embassy disappeared, students stormed the building, strewed the streets with sensitive American documents, and took over 50 Americans hostage: *All Fall Down*, Gary Sick. Khomeini endorsed the takeover, which was so popular that the hostages could not be released for a year.

A desperate US raid to rescue the hostages by helicopter was vanquished by desert dust.

The student wardens of the immobile Embassy conditioned release of the hostages on the departure of the Shah from the US. He left a few weeks later. Carter's final humiliation was their release on 1/20/81 – twenty minutes after Reagan's inauguration.

On April 1, 1980, Khomeini followed up his landslide endorsement in a national referendum by proclaiming Iran an Islamic Republic: *EB*. Khomeini assumed the awesome title of Imam, evoking the twelve Imams who served as Caliphs before the evolution of the Shiite faith.

Khomeini Provokes Saddam – From late 1979 on, Khomeini mounted a series of challenges to the secular regime in Iraq: A prediction that Iraq would be the next Shiite theocracy; a suggestion that the Saddam regime should be replaced by Al Da'wah: *NYTBR*, 1/29/95, Ephraim Karsh; public denunciations of Saddam's "Satanic regime"; clandestine support for rebellious Iraqi Shiites and Kurds. There were skirmishes along the Iraq-Iran border. Iraqi Shiite leader Muhammad Baqir al Hakim was allowed to issue from Tehran a call for armed uprising against Saddam.

If Khomeini had Iranian-Iraqi unification in mind, he was overreaching. Iraqi Shiites were basically closer to Sunni Arabs than to Iranian Shiites; language is the key. Iraqi Shiites were not disposed to slavish imitation of Persian practice. All they wanted was help in ousting their Sunni rulers – which was to come twenty years later with the fatuous invasion ordered by George Bush 43.

Saddam's Response – The overreaching came from Saddam. Whether Khomeini knew it or not, he was playing with fire. Power corrupts. No one has more power than a dictator. Saddam's precipitation of a war against a country with a three-to-one population advantage would have seemed hare-brained – except for special circumstances:

- Iraq had a large army, armed and trained by the Soviets, and military superiority in the air.
- Many of Iran's cadre of military officers had been jailed as suspected monarchists.
- Most of the Arab world stood with Iraq.
- Saddam presumably recognized that, if war was inevitable, the sooner it came, the better Iraq's chances.

Arab States – In case of war with Iran, massive financial aid would be forthcoming from Arabia's oil states, which had historical grounds for suspicion of Persian intentions: Persian dynasties ruled Yemen from 575 to 628, Bahrain from 1602 to 1783, and Oman from 1737 to 1749: *EB*. According to rumor, Iran was still saving two seats in its parliament for Bahrain, a state with a Shiite majority. The Saudis suspected Khomeini of complicity in the bloody occupation of Mecca's Great Mosque in November 1979. In case of war with Iran, Iraq would have the use of Saudi airfields: Sciolino. Assistance would also come from Iraq's traditional partner, Jordan. With the closure of Iraqi ports on the Gulf, Iraq's wartime traffic would come and go via 'Aqaba, Jordan's port on the Gulf of 'Aqaba (access to the Red Sea). King Husayn would mobilize Jordanian transport vehicles in the service of Iraq. The economies of Iraq and Jordan would be integrated: *Iraq*, Dilip Hiro.

Invasion

1980 – On 9/17/80, Saddam tore up a copy of the Algiers Agreement on television. On 9/22, he sent Iraqi planes to attack Iranian positions; the results were unimpressive. On 9/23, he launched a full-scale invasion of Iran at four points along the 730-mile border, with the immediate goal of precipitating a major uprising in Khuzistan against the regime in Tehran; it didn't happen.

The Iranian military, police, IRGC, Basij, and air force staged counterattacks, individually impressive, but indecisive because of lack of coordination.

Since ground action was impeded on the central and northern fronts by the Zagros Mountains, and on the south-central front by the riverine marshes, most of the fighting took place in the far south along the Shatt, where Iran had greater strategic depth, and was able to obstruct the Iraqis' advance by flooding areas in their path: *Strategic Geography and the Changing Middle East*, Kemp/Harkavi. The initial Iraqi advance was also hindered by low morale among the foot soldiers, and the inadequacy of officers chosen more for loyalty to the regime than for military expertise. Nevertheless, in the first few weeks of the war, the Iraqi forces did serious damage to the Abadan oil refinery, then one of the largest in the world: *EB*; *The Prize*, Daniel Yergin. (The city of Abadan was founded in the 700's at the point where the Shatt then flowed into the Gulf. Today, the alluvial deposit of thirteen centuries has left Abadan 33 miles from the Gulf, but still on the Shatt: *EB*.)

The Iraqis also captured Khorramshahr, a major port at the confluence of the Karun River and the Shatt, just north of Abadan, but the operation took long enough for Iran to deploy defenses in force. Having suffered heavy casualties, the Iraqi offensive ground to a halt in November: *The Reckoning*, Sandra Mackey.

1980 – On September 30, two Iranian Phantoms did light damage to Iraq's nuclear reactor at Osirak. French engineers repaired the damage.

"October Surprise" – Jimmy Carter had to pay the price for the misjudgement of Republican predecessor Eisenhower, who in 1953 authorized the CIA to collude with British colleagues in the ouster of elected Prime Minister Mohammad Mossadeq and the reinstatement of unpopular Reza Shah Pahlavi.

On 2/1/79, on invitation from the Shiite clergy, Ruhollah Khomeini returned to a tumultuous welcome in Tehran, and designation as Supreme Leader of the Islamic Republic of Iran. He embarked on a foreign policy that was critical of US policy and dismissive of Israel. Nine months later, a mob of students stormed the US Embassy, took its diplomatic staff hostage, and ignited a new wave of anti-Americanism. Gratified by the enthusiastic reaction of the Iranian public, Khomeini got on board the students' initiative. By holding on to the hostages he deepened Carter's humiliation. A desperate American effort to rescue the hostages by helicopter got only as far as the Iranian desert, where it fell apart. Carter's reputation for leadership fell along with it: *EB*: 2:907.

On January 20, 1981, twenty minutes after Reagan's inauguration, Iran released the American Embassy hostages. Former Iranian President Abolhassan Bani-Sadr alleged flatly that the Reagan campaign staff had concluded with Iranian clerics a secret deal not to release them during Carter's tenure. The Iranian collusion was thought to reflect Khomeini's resentment of the solicitude Carter had shown for the health of the Shah. According to Richard Curtiss in *Middle East Policy*, the timing was a signal to the Reagan team that Iran expected the new Republican administration to supply it arms (separately from the Iran-Contra deal).

1981 – The war went on. In March, Iran stalled the Iraqi offensive. For the next five months, the front was relatively quiet, as both sides prepared for a longer war than they had expected.

1981 – Syria reopened the Kirkuk-Tripoli pipeline, which had been closed in 1976 by civil-war violence. The reopening was ascribed to Syrian interest in winning Iraqi support against Israeli annexation of the Golan. (No such luck; Israel proclaimed de facto annexation on 12/14/81.) The Kirkuk-Baniyas pipeline was opened in 1980.

1981 – In April, the Iraqi Air Force came out of hiding. Eight Phantoms and four Tomcats destroyed 30-40 Iranian jet fighters.

1981 – In May, phase one of the Tanker War began with an Iraqi proclamation that all ships going in or out of Iranian ports would be subject to attack (by jets).

1981 – In Iran the Mujahedeen–e Khalq, founded by Iranian leftists in 1965, staged bombings that killed hundreds of Iranian officials, including President Mohammed-Ali Rajai. One attack wounded Khomeini. Government retaliation killed thousands of leftists. The MEK finally gave up. Leader Massoud Rajavi fled to Paris, many of his followers to Iraq: *Frontline*, 10/23/07; *NY*, 3/6/06.

1981 – On 6/7/81, Israeli F-15's and F-16's put the Osirak reactor out of operation.

1981 – The Iranian war effort had recruited thousands of teen-age "martyrs". Armed with plastic "keys to heaven", they were sent into the front lines to flood the enemy lines by "human-wave" attacks. They were sometimes used to clear minefields by the elementary technique of running across them: Robin Wright.

1981 – By November, the Iranian forces had broken the siege of Abadan and taken the offensive: Ramazani; Sciolino; *Oil, Turmoil, and Islam in the Middle East*, Sheikh Ali. Iraq had been reduced to declaring that the battle lines – still in Iranian territory – were the new frontier. However, by switching from offense to defense, the Iraqi forces were getting better results. In the huge tank battle around Dezful (just east of the Iraq-Iran border, north of Abadan) an Iranian division reportedly advanced too far and was almost entirely wiped out.

1982 – On 1/3/82 the Kirkuk-Tripoli pipeline was cut northeast of Tripoli by bombing, probably by pro-Iranian Shia.

1982 – Jordan announced 1/28/82 that Jordanian enlistments for service in the Iraqi armed forces would be accepted. Egypt was allowing retired officers to serve in the Iraqi army.

1982 – **US Support for the Iraqi War Effort** – In March, Reagan removed Iraq from the list of "terrorist" countries: *Living by the Sword*, Stephen Green. From that point on, he supported the Iraqi war effort by authorizing the sales of military equipment, the sharing of intelligence on Iranian deployment, and CCC (Commodity Credit Corporation) loans: Mackey; *Times*, 1/26/92, Seymour Hersh.

1982 – **Syrian Support for the Iranian War Effort** – March 1982, conclusion of a ten-year economic agreement with Iran; 4/8/82, closure of the Syrian border with Iraq; 4/10/82, closure of the Kirkuk-Baniyas pipeline (in return for 100 million dollars' worth of Iranian crude): *Times*, 3/26/92; 4/1/82, Syrian call for Saddam's overthrow; subsequent Syrian supply of Soviet-made arms to Iran.

1982 – **Saudi-Egyptian Support for the Iraqi War Effort** – In April 1982, Egypt agreed to supply 1.5 million dollars' worth of arms, to be financed by Saudi Arabia. On 5/10/82, Iraq terminated its boycott of

Egypt (reprisal for the 1979 peace treaty with Israel). Iraq landed an airliner in Cairo.

1982 – **Lineup of Arab States** – Pro-Iran: Syria, South Yemen, Libya, Algeria. Pro-Iraq: Bahrain, Egypt, Jordan, Kuwait, Qatar, Saudi Arabia, Sudan. Neutral: Oman and the UAE (torn between Abu Dhabi's preference for Iraq, and Dubai's preference for Iran).

1982 – On May 25 Iran recaptured Khorramshahr (Ramazani) and advanced to the outskirts of Basrah but never captured it. Iran had developed an effective three-wave strategy of attack: first, the infantry of the Basij (rural youth); second, the devout Revolutionary Guards; third, army regulars. All were short of armor, and were finally stopped by the Iraqi defenses, which by this time had probably introduced chemical weapons: *MEP*, Fall 2012; *NYR*, 3/26/92, Stephen C. Pelletiere/Douglas V. Johnson, II; Kemp/Harkavy; Mackey. Saddam executed 10-12 ranking officers whose units failed to get results.

1982 – In June Reagan issued a National Security Decision Directive (NSDD) stating that the national interest required an Iraqi victory.

1982 – The Soviet leaders, angered by the Iranian restrictions on the Tudeh Party, stepped up arms supply to Iraq.

1982 – Israel invaded Lebanon June 6. Elaine Sciolino speculated that the attack on Israeli Ambassador Argov in London (which was Sharon's pretext for invading Lebanon) had been contrived by Iraq to precipitate hostilities between Israel and Syria: *Times*, 4/28/86. The suspected culprits in the attack on Argov were the Abu Nidal group, long financed by Iraq.

1982 – On June 20, Saddam announced that Iraqi forces were being withdrawn from Iranian territory, and he proposed a ceasefire. Khomeini rejected a ceasefire. Since the war would drag on for another six years, Khomeini's holdout for the ouster of Saddam was a major strategic error: Sciolino. The Israeli invasion of Lebanon, taken with Saddam's prediction of troop withdrawal from Iran, moderated Khomeini's determination to invade Iraq. By this time, Iran had re conquered most of its occupied territory.

1982 – From mid-1982, Saudi Arabia contributed a million dollars a month to the Iraqi war effort. The Arab monarchies had been stirred by Khomeini's declaration that "monarchies are illegitimate".

1982 – On 7/13/82, Iran captured Iraq's Faw Peninsula.

1982 – On 10/27/82, Iraqi Scuds fell on Dezful: wounded – 107; killed – 21.

1982 – **Iranian Offensive Stalled** – With help from East German advisors, Iraqi "hunter-killer" helicopter operations finally checked the Iranian offensive against Basrah.

1982 – December: With the USSR holding back on arms supply to Iraq, France had become a major supplier, but late in 1982 the USSR supplied Iraq with tanks and helicopter gunships.

1982 – In Iran, Al Da'wah and other anti-Baathist Iraqi factions founded SCIRI (The Supreme Council of the Islamic Revolution in Iraq): Hiro; *Times*, 11/5/04. In 1984, Muhammad Baqir al Hakim became its leader. Its paramilitary branch, the Badr Corps, was commanded by Muhammad Baqir's brother, 'Abd al 'Aziz al Hakim: Juan Cole Blog, 8/12/04. The IRGC supported the operations of the Badr Corps: *MEP*, Summer 2003.

1982 – To counter Shiite rebellion, Saddam downplayed Baathist secularism, and added the legend *Allahu Akbar* (God is Great) to the Iraqi flag: Mackey. Baghdad's creative propaganda traced the lineage of the Iraqis (Semitic) back to the Assyrians and Babylonians, who were also Semites, and to the Sumerians, who were not: Mackey.

1983 – April: By use of chemical weapons, Iraq again repelled an Iranian offensive: Hiro. Iraq continued to use chemical weapons at key intervals throughout the war: *Scientific American*, December 1996; *MER*, Summer 2000. Eric Margolis discovered that the UK had sent scientists to Iraq in the 1980's to develop biological weapons for use against Iran: *WRMEA*, January 2015, *EricMargolis.com*.

1983 – May: Iran outlawed the pro-Soviet Tudeh Party, and sent 20 Soviet diplomats home.

1983 – On 6/2/83, Assistant Secretary of State Nicholas Veliotes told a subcommittee of the House Foreign Affairs Committee the US was neutral in the Iraq-Iran war.

1983 – July: Iraq's two rival Kurdish factions were at odds again: The PUK (Talabani) wanted to negotiate with Jordan; the KDP (Barzani) joined the Shiite Badr Corps and Iranian forces in an offensive that used mustard gas. Iraq abducted several thousand KDP soldiers who were never seen again: Mackey; *The Nation*, Andrew Cockburn.

1983 – On 9/23/83, an onboard bomb downed an airliner of Gulf Air (Bahrain), killing 112: *Times*, 9/12/01.

1983 – October: Iran rejected UNSC Resolution 540, which called for a ceasefire between Iraq and Iran.

1983 – November: The NSC concluded that an Iranian defeat of Iraq would be a major blow to US interests: *Times*, 6/18/01.

1983 – December: The Arab freeze against Egypt for its peace with Israel was giving way to the general desire for Egyptian adherence to the common front against Iran.

US Escalates Support for Iraq

1983 – The US joined an Arab arms embargo on Iran.

1983 – 12/19/83, Donald Rumsfeld was in Baghdad with an offer from Reagan to Saddam to resume diplomatic relations. Washington was looking for opportunities to undermine the anti-US, anti-Israel regime in Tehran. On 8/18/02, a *Times* article cited reports from anonymous US military officers that in 1983 Washington was supplying massive supplies of arms to Iraq, including helicopters equipped to spray poison gas, thus feeding Iraq's chemical-weapons habit. In 1984, Iraq was buying pathogens from American firms: Mackey. On 6/17/04, *Counterpunch* assembled press allegations that Washington was colluding in Iraq's development of chemical, biological, and nuclear weapons.

1984 – In January the US Government designated the Iranian regime as a sponsor of terrorism, and imposed additional export controls on Iran: Seale.

1984 – January: 350,000 Shia had fled from Iraq to Iran: Ramazani. Iraq's prosperity of 1980 had evaporated, despite generous subsidies from Kuwait and Saudi Arabia. Basrah was still under Iraqi control, but it had been bombed and burned: Mackey.

1984 – February: Start of phase one of Iraq's "War of the Cities" against Iran, by strategic bombers.

1984 – February: Iranian zeal was confronted by Iraqi heavy and amphibious equipment and mustard gas, in "The Battle of the Marshes": *US-Arab Relations*, Frederick Axelgard; Sciolino.

1984 – On 2/27/84, Iraq shot down 49 of 50 Iranian helicopters in the Battle of the Marshes.

1984 – On 3/5/84, the Department of State condemned Iraqi use of chemical weapons. Iraq denied the charge. By global consensus, Iraq was culpable, but no sanctions were imposed on it by the UNSC: *Times*, 3/14/06.

1984 – On 3/24/84, Rumsfeld was back in Iraq on instructions to tell Saddam that, despite the State Department's accusation of 3/5/84, preventing an Iranian victory was an American priority; in 2003 Rumsfeld said he recalled no such instructions: *Times*, 12/23/03. Alexander Cockburn reported in *The Nation* that, despite State Department condemnation of Iraqi use of chemical weapons, Rumsfeld said nothing in Baghdad about use of mustard gas (western origin) versus Iranian and pro-Iran Kurds and Shiites. The US had allowed Iraq to buy chemical materiel from western companies: Juan Cole Blog, 12/30/06.

1984 – **The Tanker War** – Iraqi attacks on Iranian tankers and oil-processing facilities on Khark Island were followed by an Iranian attack on a Kuwaiti tanker conveying Iraqi oil, 5/13/84, and on a Saudi tanker 5/16/84. Oil prices and marine insurance rates for Gulf shipping rose sharply. UNSC Resolution 552 condemned Iranian attacks on neutral shipping in the Persian Gulf: Axelgard. Iran had blockaded the southern Gulf against Iraq.

1984 – In May, over the opposition of the Israeli lobby, the Reagan administration stated it would send Saudi Arabia 400 Stingers (heat-seeking shoulder-fired anti-aircraft missiles) for protection of oil installations and tankers.

1984 – All jet fighters in the Saudi and Iranian air forces were US-made. The Saudis flew F-15's guided by AWACS (Airborne Warning And Control System), the Iranians F-4's guided by F-14's. Iranian and Saudi flight crews were US-trained. The Saudi crews were supported by

American refuellers and AWACS technicians. On 6/5/84, two Saudi-piloted F-15's shot down two Iranian F-4's.

1984 – In November, shortly after his reelection, Reagan met with Tariq 'Aziz in Washington and reestablished full diplomatic relations with Iraq, after a hiatus of 17 years: Axelgard; Sciolino.

1984 – Iraq had spent most of its foreign reserves on the war and was now living hand to mouth on Saudi and Kuwaiti subsidies. The Iraqi dinar had fallen from $3.30 to $.90: Mackey.

1985 – MEK forces in Iran began joint operations with Iraqi forces.

1985 – Combat between Iraq and Iran had bogged down into trench warfare: Mackey. "A war of attrition": Hiro.

1985 – To undermine the Iranian economy, Saudi Arabia raised its oil output, flooding the oil market. The price fell below ten dollars a barrel: *LRB*, 2/4/16, Joost Hilterman, from *The Iran-Iraq War*, Pierre Razoux.

1986 – Saddam closed the universities, drafted all able-bodied males, and complied with his generals' demand for control of military operations. The Iraqi Army was growing to be twice the size of the Iranian Army.

1986 – In February, after Iran had abandoned the human-wave attacks, and trained troops for amphibious operations, it took advantage of bad flying weather to cross the Shatt and occupy the Faw Peninsula, Iraq's only coastline: Sciolino.

1986 – In March Iraq and Iran exchanged Scud attacks ("War of the Cities", phase two). On the ground, Iran seemed to be winning.

1986 – **Resumption of the Tanker War** – In May Iran resumed air attacks on Saudi and Kuwaiti tankers: Mackey. Iraq reacted by another attempt to shut down by air attack Iran's giant oil terminal on Khark Island. Saudi increase in oil production lowered its price, and Iranian revenue along with it. There was a widely-held theory that the Saudis meant the price of oil to fall and force Iran to sue for peace – as may well have happened: *FT*, 11/10/14.

1986 – Reagan named sixteen maritime "choke points" that the USSR had contingency plans to block. They included the Suez Canal, the Bab al Mandab, and the Strait of Hormuz.

1986 – France expelled MEK leader Rajavi, who recruited 7000 Iranian exiles into the National Liberation Army, encamped in Iraq: *NY*, 3/6/06.

1986 – On 11/1/86, Kuwait appealed for help against Iranian strikes on tankers serving Kuwait.

1986 – On 11/3/86, the Lebanese magazine *Al Shira'* (reportedly on the basis of an Iranian leak) reported that Reagan aide Robert McFarlane had gone to Tehran to discuss the fate of American hostages held in Lebanon by Hizballah. The *Times* reported the story on 11/4/86, precipitating the Reagan regime's biggest scandal: *The National Security Archive*, 11/4/2014, Malcolm Byrne.

1986 – In December, Iran launched its last major offensive of the war: Sciolino.

1987 – January: In the Battle of Basrah, Iraq finally stopped the Iranian advance. The morale of Iranian troops and the Iranian public was declining.

1987 – **American Intervention in the Tanker War** – Kuwait's appeal of November 1986 to both the US and the USSR for tanker protection did what Iraq had failed to do – bring US forces into the war: Sciolino. Washington was now under political pressure on two counts: 1) Cold War rivalry, as Soviet ships came to Kuwait's defense; 2) After the *Al Shira'* leak of 11/3/86, the need to reassure the Arab side that the US was not backing away from its support for Iraq and its allies against Iran.

1987 – January: A Soviet frigate escorted four Soviet merchant ships carrying arms for offloading at Kuwait.

1987 – Iraq had escalated its role in the Tanker War by introducing Super-Étendard jets. Iran likewise, by the introduction of Chinese Silkworm missiles.

1987 – The USSR began chartering tankers carrying Kuwaiti oil. The US responded on 3/7/87 by agreeing to let tankers for Kuwait fly the American flag – hence coming under the protection of the US Navy: *With Friends Like These*, Bruce Jentleson; *The Prize*, Daniel Yergin.

1987 – Washington accepted the Iraqi explanation that a 5/17/87 attack by an Iraqi Mirage on the frigate USS Stark, killing 37 sailors, was a case of misidentification. Iraq paid compensation. Some Americans suspected an Iraqi scheme to draw the US into the war: Sciolino.

1987 – On 5/18/87, Washington undertook to protect 11 reflagged Kuwaiti tankers against Iranian attack. US aims: to reassure the Arabs that the US-Iranian arms deal did not mean the US was defecting from the Iraqi cause; to block Soviet infiltration; and to support Chevron, which had an interest in Kuwaiti oil, and was a major contributor to Reagan political campaigns: Sciolino; *The Nation*, 6/13/87; *MEJ*, Ray Takeyh, Summer 2010.

1987 – As the Tanker War escalated, Lloyds of London counted 546 commercial ships damaged, 430 civilian sailors killed.

1987 – In July, a USN ship operating under Operation Prime Chance scuttled an Iranian minelayer.

1987 – On 9/24/87, USN Seals boarded an Iranian minelayer, detained the crew, and scuttled the ship: *Times*, 1/20/08. On 9/24/87, Seals captured an Iranian minelayer.

1987 – From 7/24/87 to 9/28/88, under Operation Earnest Will, ships of the Third, Sixth, and Seventh Fleets protected Kuwaiti tankers. US carrier and battleship task forces in the Arabian Sea and the Persian Gulf helped maintain the flow of Gulf oil.

1987 – On 10/8/87, USN ships sank four Iranian patrol boats.

1987 – On 10/15/87, an Iranian missile hit a reflagged tanker. On 10/18/87, USN ships shelled two Iranian oil platforms and sank three Iranian patrol boats. Patrol boats were the mainstay of Iranian naval operations in the Gulf: *US Navy in Desert Shield*, Edward Marolda. A US merchant ship and a US-flagged tanker were damaged by mines during these actions.

1987 – Hafiz al Asad's attendance at a February Arab Summit was widely construed as a signal to Iran that Syria opposed an Iranian invasion of Iraq.

1987 – In April, Iraqi Sukhoi bombers gassed the Iraqi Kurdish village of Shaykh Wisan, killing 238: Mackey.

1987 – In July, the KDP and PUK tried ending their feud once more, this time under the title of the Iraqi-Kurdistan Front, which undertook the overthrow of the Iraqi Ba'th. With Kurdish support, Iran made another try to open a northern front.

1987 – On 7/31/87, pilgrims in Mecca staged an anti-Saudi demonstration that sparked a clash in which security forces killed some 400 pilgrims, including 275 Iranians: *MEP*, June 1998; *MEJ*, Summer 2006.

1987 – **Anfal Campaign** – In the summer of 1987, in retaliation for Kurdish collusion with Iran, Saddam ordered his cousin, 'Ali Hasan al Majid, to assume the direction of Al Anfal, a campaign to suppress the Kurdish insurrection once and for all. Al Majid's reliance on poison gas had won him the nickname "Chemical 'Ali". In July, his force rounded up Kurdish males of ages 12-50 and trucked them off, never to be seen again: Mackey. Between 80,000 and 100,000 Kurds were executed: *LRB*, 2/4/16, Joost Hilterman.

1987 – Iraq was running out of Iraqis. To prosecute the war it was recruiting men from Egypt and other Arab states. Iran was short of planes. Iraq was receiving more planes from the USSR, and invaluable intelligence from the US. On 10/8/87, the US ships destroyed 2 oil rigs and 4 Iranian speedboats.

1987 – Late in the year, US (air?) forces were supporting Iraqi attacks on Iran's infrastructure.

1988 – In Iran, growing war-weariness had great military significance in a country that relied on volunteers, not conscription. In Iraq, still on defense on the ground, but on the offensive in the air war, new tanks and planes were flowing in from the USSR. Iraq had a 5-1 advantage in tanks, 10-1 in aircraft. Its armed forces were up to a strength of 500,000 men.

1988 – Iraqi Kurds were suffering terrible losses from the Anfal campaign. Their hatred for their Arab rulers matched Arab hatred for Kurds who fought on the Iranian side. Baghdad's troops were demolishing Kurdish communities and farms, killing farm animals, sending residents to concentration camps: Mackey. Although Iran also used poison gas, the American media fixed on Iraq as by far the worst offender. Chemical weapons figured largely in the May 1988 recapture of the Faw Peninsula by a new Iraqi force, the Republican Guard (Sciolino; Mackey), and in the Anfal Campaign.

In retaliation for Kurdish participation in an Iranian thrust into Iraqi Kurdistan, Iraq was accused of an operation in March that saturated the Iraqi village of Halabjah, 150 miles northeast of Baghdad, with mustard gas, cyanide, sarin, tabun, VX, and napalm. Halabjah had been captured by Iranian and Kurdish forces: Mackey, Sciolino, Friedman, the *Times*, major American periodicals, the Senate Foreign Relations Committee, and Human Rights Watch. The Iraqis followed up anti-Kurd air attacks with a scorched-earth offensive that destroyed 2000-3000 Kurdish villages.

1988 – The Iraqi threat to drop gas-armed Scuds on Tehran sparked a flight from the city: *LRB*, Hilterman.

1988 – On 2/29/88, Iraq began a four-month pounding of Iranian cities (third phase) by Soviet-made Scud surface-to-surface missiles: Hiro. Iranian morale plummeted. In Tehran, 2000 residents were killed, and three million took flight: Mackey.

1988 – On 4/14/88, during operation Praying Mantis, a USN frigate was destroyed by an Iranian mine. In retaliation, at the cost of a helicopter and its two pilots, USN ships damaged two Iranian frigates, destroyed two Iranian oil platforms, sank 6 Iranian ships, and damaged a seventh; *Times*. CIA assets bombed factories in Iran.

1988 – In *Middle East Policy* of June 1988, R. K. Ramazani wrote that American ships had destroyed most of the Iranian Navy. This assertion should be evaluated in the light of the Kemp/Harkavy assessment that at that time no Middle Eastern country had a blue-water navy, and of the possibility that some USN operations in the Gulf were withheld from the media.

1988 – The Soviet decision to withdraw from Afghanistan in 1988 produced a Soviet-US deal whereby Gorbachev would press Khomeini to end the Iraq-Iran War, and Reagan would persuade Pakistan and Saudi Arabia to facilitate Soviet withdrawal from Afghanistan: *LRB*, Hilterman.

107

1988 – On 5/25/88, Iraq launched a major counter-offensive against Iranian troops in the increasingly desiccated marshes, leading to the recapture of the Faw Peninsula.

1988 – On 7/3/88 the USS Vincennes allegedly mistook Iranian Air Lines Flight 655 for an attacking fighter plane, and shot it down, killing all 290 on board.

1988 – On July 20, Ayatollah Khomeini, distressed by growing chaos in the cities of Iran, suspecting that the American destruction of the airliner was intentional, and backed by Rafsanjani and other moderates, accepted the UNSC's resolution 598 of 7/20/87, which called for a ceasefire along prewar borders: Sciolino; Mackey; Vali Nasr; *MEP*, October 1999; Fall 2012, Ahmed Hashim.

1988 – On 8/20/88 Iraq accepted the ceasefire, which took effect on that date. Five days later Iraqi forces carried out chemical attacks on 49 Kurdish villages, killing tens of thousands, triggering mass flight of Iraqi Kurds to Turkey: *NYR*, 5/13/04, Peter Galbraith; *MER*, Summer 2009, Hilterman. Total estimated dead from the Al Anfal campaign: *MER*, Spring 2002 – 100,000; *NY*, 4/7/03 – 50-100,000; Los *Angeles Times*, 12/6/03 – over 100,000; *Times*, 12/17/04 – 150,000; *NYTBR* review of *A Modern History of the Kurds*, David McDowall – 200,000. The Iraqi culprits in the campaign were assisted by Kurdish collaborators: *Los Angeles Times*.

1988 – Saddam saw the war as his Qadisiyyah (the Islamic defeat of Persia in 636): Hilterman.

Stalemate – The postwar reaffirmation of the prewar frontier between Iraq and Iran seemed to validate the consensus that – even though the military balance had begun to shift in Iraq's favor – the eight-year war had ended in stalemate: Yergin; *MEP*, June 1994, Cordesman. Iran's domination of the Gulf (*Zones of Conflict*, John Keegan/Andrew Wheatcroft) had been superseded by the intervention of the US Navy. Air superiority had been maintained by Iraq's jet fighters and Scuds. On the ground, Iraq had finally gained the advantage by virtue of its greater firepower in conventional and chemical weapons, its more effective control of its armed forces (Kemp/Harkavy), and the professionalism of the Republican Guard: Sciolino. A quick Iranian victory had been

108

averted by Iraq's natural defenses – Zagros foothills and southern marshlands. A slow Iranian victory had been blocked by American intervention. By 1988, the Iranian economy was deteriorating.

Khomeini's hypnotic leadership had been crippled by the peculiar circumstances of his elevation. Whereas Saddam had risen to power by the exercise of raw armed force, culminating in twelve years of dictatorship, Khomeini was a cleric with no military experience and only twenty months to learn the business of governing before the war had intruded. Over all, he did well to preserve all Iranian territory, still circumscribed by the favorable frontier Iran had extracted from the Algiers Accord.

The Iraq-Iran War: Recap

In his review of *The Iran-Iraq War*, by Pierre Razoux, Graeme Wood wrote: "Few modern wars have so thoroughly broken, traumatized, and destroyed both sides": *NYTBR*, 1/3/16.

Casualties – Estimates of Arab Iraqi deaths range from 100,000 to 200,000; of Iranian dead, from 250,000 to half a million.

Phases – Elaine Sciolino saw three phases in the eight-year war: Phase one, 1980 to mid-1982, Iraq on the offensive; phase two, 1982-6, Iran on the offensive; phase three, 1987-8, Iraq regained the offensive, bringing in foreign workers to man the economy, and building the armed forces up to 500,000 men.

Costs – Over one trillion dollars, divided approximately 50-50 between Iraq and Iran.

Saddam's Miscalculations – According to Ramazani, Saddam overlooked some basic considerations:

He did not appreciate that Iran had the whip hand over Iraqi oil exports. In dictating the Treaty of 'Uqayr (1922), British High Commissioner Cox had awarded Najd (the Saudis) new land at Kuwait's expense, but Kuwait had acquired new land at Iraq's expense. Iraqi access to the Gulf had been squeezed to a maritime outlet, the Khawr 'Abdallah, only twenty miles wide. The Iranian "navy" of the 1980's, largely exempt from the political disruption of 1979, was far superior to that of Iraq. Iran's ability to bottle up Britain's "contrived political entity" (Iraq: Sandra Mackey's phrase) released Iran from any military requirement to shut down the Strait of Hormuz – an enterprise easy enough, by artillery fire from the Iranian coast, but problematic for Iran's own exportation: Ramazani. The closure of Khawr 'Abdallah, plus Syria's later shutdown of the pipeline from Kirkuk to Baniyas on the Syrian coast, were to reduce Iraqi oil exports from three million barrels a day to one million or less: Mackey.

Saddam overestimated Soviet interest in supplying arms to Iraq, versus its interest in cultivating the new regime in Tehran.

Calculating from the modest baseline of the patriotism of the average Iraqi soldier, Saddam underestimated the nationalistic and pious fervor of the Iranian Shiite masses: Ramazani.

Saddam knew that Iran's new theocracy had imprisoned or exiled thousands of army officers suspected of loyalty to the monarchy. He didn't know that Bani-Sadr would sell Khomeini on a mass amnesty (*Bush in Babylon*, Tariq Ali), or that the all-new Islamic Revolutionary Guard Corps (IRGC) and the Basij would bear the military and ideological brunt of the war: Ramazani.

The Iran-Contra Transaction

During Reagan's second term, special interests of Israel, Iran, and the Reagan administration combined to produce The Iran-Contra Affair. It was a side issue in the Iraq-Iran War, but a central one in Israeli strategy and American politics. The Iranian interest was to reduce the imbalance between the extensive arsenal of Iraq and the depleted arsenal of Iran. The Israeli objective was to exploit its connections in Iran (derived from its dwindling Jewish community), and its special relationship with the US, to prolong the war – thus extending the travails of the two warring countries, both bitter enemies of Israel. The interests of the Reagan administration lay in supplying arms to Iran in return for Iranian pressure on its client, Hizballah, to release the American hostages Hizballah was holding, and periodically killing, in Lebanon. Washington needed secrecy, because any such deal would clash with US support for

110

the Iraqi side, and it would violate the Western ban on supply of arms to Iran, which had been designated a state sponsor of terrorism in January 1984. Washington saw a second advantage if profit from the sale could be diverted as a subsidy for the Contras – Nicaraguan authoritarians favored by Reaganites but disqualified by Congress. (Saudi Arabia reportedly gave the CIA 32 million dollars for the Contras: *Times*, 1/24/16.)

A prominent victim of Hizballah's wave of American abductions in the 1980's was Beirut CIA Station Chief William F. Buckley. He was seized on 3/16/84 by Islamic Jihad, which is thought to be a wing of Hizballah. Washington had reason to suspect that until Buckley's death fifteen months later, he was tortured for information on his operations. After his abduction, all his secret contacts vanished or were killed. On 12/27/91, his ravaged body was found lying on a Beirut highway: https://www.cia.gov/news-information; *Post*, 11/25/86; *Times*, 12/27/91; *Journey into Madness*, Gordon Thomas; "The Spy Who Never Came in from the Cold", Gordon Thomas.

In 1985, National Security Adviser Robert McFarlane told Reagan that a moderate Iranian faction had sent via Israel an offer to effect the release of Hizballah's hostages, then numbering seven, in return for Western arms. With Reagan's approval, Israel supplied to Iran between 8/20/85 and 10/28/86 substantial shipments of TOW anti-tank missiles and Hawk anti-aircraft missiles and parts. The Americans agreed to reimburse Israel for the arms (or replace them?).

On 9/15/85, the Islamic Jihad Organization released Reverend Benjamin Weir. On 12/4/85, as John Poindexter was appointed as replacement for McFarlane, NSC aide Oliver North proposed two changes in procedure: The US would provide the arms direct, and mark up the price to earn funds that could go to the Contras.

In July 1986 Hizballah released Father Lawrence Jenco, but in the fall three more Americans were abducted in Lebanon. Later on, David Jacobsen was released.

On 11/13/86, Reagan stated on television that arms had been sent to Iran, but not for hostages. (The professed policy of the US was never to negotiate for hostage release, as Nixon gratuitously told the nation on

3/2/73 after the abduction in Khartoum of American diplomats Cleo Noel and George C. Moore – who were killed by the abductors, the PLO, the same day.)

On 2/26/87, a special Review Board (The Tower Commission) sent Reagan a report that placed the primary blame for the Contra Affair on his subordinates, but faulted Reagan for inadequate supervision. In 1989 North and others went on trial, in the face of vivid testimony from, inter alia, North's secretary and Attorney General Edwin Meese, about subsidizing Contras and shredding government documents. Poindexter left the government. North was fired and sentenced, but all parties were ultimately pardoned. Bob Woodward's *Veil: The Secret Wars of the CIA 1981-1987* recounted the agency's role.

On 3/4/87 and later, Reagan told the country of his regret over these events, and took full responsibility for the whole affair, including actions he had been unaware of. He admitted he had authorized illegal sales of arms for the release of hostages.

In 1980, Saddam caught Washington in one of its pro-Iraq moods. Iran's lockup of staffers of Embassy Tehran had piqued America's knee-jerk sensitivity to indignities inflicted by uppity states, and it had ignited the short fuse of the neocon bloc by the opportunity to punish one of Israel's most dreaded enemies, if not both. The Carter administration cast wisdom and legality to the winds in a shameless campaign to promote Iraqi invasion: Hiro; *NYTM*, 7/11/04. The Reagan administration had already carried out a morally debased effort to foster mutual Iraqi-Iranian destruction by promoting war between them: *NY*, 4/6/15, Steve Coll. Now it would supply Iraq with trucks, helicopters, cluster bombs, intelligence, and half a billion dollars a year in credits toward US exports. An ancillary benefit to the US would be profits for the US arms industry: *The Link*, December 2002 and January 2005; *The Washington Monthly*, January 1995; *NYTM*, 7/11/04; *MER*, Spring 2005; *Times*, 3/14/06; *The Atlantic*, March 2005. According to unconfirmed reports, the Reagan administration also sold Iraq precursors for chemical and biological weapons: *NYTM*, 7/11/04; *Le Monde Diplomatique*, November 2004; *Resurrecting Empire*, Rashid Khalidi.

The Reagan Administration would cite various meretricious pretexts for siding with Iraq: resistance to Shiite Jihad; access to Iraqi oil; cooption of Iraq into Arab-Israeli peace-planning: *Times*, 3/14/06; *Washington Post Weekly*, 11/5/07. The hostage stalemate sealed Carter's defeat in the Presidential election of 1980: *NYR*, 9/25/14, Elizabeth Drew. Critics of the Reagan administration believed that the "October Surprise" had been a secret deal by the Republicans to sell arms to Iran if it would delay the release of the hostages and Reagan were reelected. Republican skullduggery in the matter was strongly suggested by the Iranian release of the hostages in 1981, fifteen minutes after Reagan was sworn in.

1985-? – Israel-Palestine War

———

1947 – From 1947 to 1964, the Palestinian resistance to the initial consolidation of Greater Israel was impassioned, but disorganized and ineffective.

1948 – Most of the Palestinians who managed to stay in Israel after independence became citizens of Israel, and elected Palestinian members of the Knesset. Many Knesset Palestinians had been "collaborators" before 1948: *LRB*, 10/4/16, Yonatan Mendel.

1948 – In keeping with Israel's adherence to the imperialist standby, divide-and-rule, Israel accorded Palestinian residents of Jerusalem special status. Later, Israel reinforced the separation by building a seven-meter wall between Jerusalem and the West Bank: *LRB*, 10/6/16, Mendel.

1964 – The first Summit meeting of the Arab League, held in Alexandria under Egyptian sponsorship, founded The Palestine Liberation Army (PLA) as the "military wing" of the PLO.

1965 – Fatah, an independent organization, carried out its first operation in Israel – a bomb meant to shut down the National Water Carrier. It failed to explode.

1965 – Under Chairman Yasir 'Arafat, the Palestinian National Council (PNC) called for a democratic secular state in Palestine of Arabs and selected Jews.

1967 – On 11/22/67, UNSC Resolution 242 called for "withdrawal of Israeli armed forces from territories occupied in the recent conflict" (the Six-Day War). By not specifying borders, 242 left the diplomatic track open for interminable debate while the IDF created "facts on the ground" in the territories occupied in the war.

1968 – On 11/22/68, a car bomb in Jerusalem killed 12 and wounded 52.

1968 – On 12/28/68, in reprisal for an attack of 12/26/68 by the Lebanon-based PFLP, IDF commandos and aircraft (?) raided the Beirut International Airport a few miles south of Beirut. They destroyed fourteen aircraft on the tarmac, including eight belonging to Middle East Airlines, of which 30 percent was owned by French investors and 70 percent by a combine of Lebanese, Kuwaiti, Qatari, and American investors.

1970 – In September 'Arafat was appointed Commander-in-Chief of the Palestinian Resistance Movement. The Egyptian-sponsored and independent resistance organizations merged.

1970 – Jordan expelled 'Arafat and his forces to Lebanon.

1972 – On 9/5-6/72, at the Summer Olympics in Munich, members of Black September (a creation of the PLO) killed two members of the Israeli Olympic team, seized nine others, and conditioned their release on Israeli release of 234 Palestinian prisoners and West German release of the two founders of the Red Army faction. During a clumsy rescue attempt by West German police, nine Israelis, one West German police officer, and five Palestinian attackers were killed. The surviving three Palestinians were released by West Germany after the hijacking of Lufthansa 615.

According to *The Local* of 6/17/02, a German neo-Nazi had helped the Palestinian attackers.

1973 – Nixon gave National Security Adviser Henry Kissinger the additional appointment of Secretary of State, making him the first strong supporter of Israel to hold high American office outside the White House: Neff.

Since 1973, IDF action was confined to low-level but highly lethal operations against Arab militias: the various factions of the Palestinian resistance based in Tunisia, the West Bank, and Gaza, and the Lebanese Hizballah, based along the Israel-Lebanon frontier.

1974 – The UNGA accorded the PLO observer status.

1975 – In September, during Kissinger's shuttle diplomacy to resolve Middle East borders after the Yom Kippur War, he included in the Sinai II accord a secret American pledge not to recognize the PLO, nor to negotiate with it: Neff.

1975 – On 11/12/75, Assistant Secretary of State Harold Saunders told the House Foreign Affairs Subcommittee on the Middle East that the Palestinians' interests must be taken into account in Arab-Israeli peace negotiations. The Zionist uproar led Kissinger to disown the Saunders statement, but it remained in the record as the first official American identification of Palestinians as a people, not mere impersonal refugees: Neff.

1976 – The Arab League granted the PLO full voting membership. Washington accepted a visit by midlevel PLO representatives.

1977 – On 7/28/77, Carter became the only President to declare that Israeli settlements in Occupied Palestine were illegal: Neff.

1978 – At Camp David, President Carter nagged Sadat and Begin into an agreement. It sold the Palestinians down the river, but set up the Israeli-Egyptian peace treaty of 3/26/79. The legal basis of that treaty, and the later treaty between Israel and Jordan, was UNSC Resolution 242 of 1967. Of all the Arab states, Egypt had made the greatest military effort against Israel, and suffered five military defeats, but the onlooker states still ostracized Egypt for several years for signing the treaty.

1981 – On 2/2/81, after less than a month in office, President Reagan characterized the controversial Israeli settlements as maybe provocative, but not illegal: Neff.

1982 – After Alexander Haig went overboard in his tolerance of Israeli aggression in Lebanon, Reagan named George Shultz to replace him as Secretary of State. Shultz's effort to follow an evenhanded policy enraged Israel and precipitated a firestorm of criticism in the US media. Shultz switched his stance to pro-Israeli, blocked a Yasir 'Arafat visit to the US, and finished his tour in a shower of plaudits for the "architect of the special relationship with Israel": Neff.

1982 – The Israeli invasion of Lebanon failed in its central objective to demolish the PLO, but it engineered the exile of 'Arafat and staff to Tunisia.

1985 – On 10/2/85, in retaliation for the PLO's killing of three Israeli intelligence officers in Cyprus, Israeli F-16's killed 51 Palestinians and 15 Tunisians in the PLO compound in Tunisia.

1987 – **Intifadah I** – A traffic accident in Gaza's Jabaliyah Refugee Camp on 12/9/87 killed four Palestinians, triggering Palestinian civil disobedience and throwing of stones and Molotov cocktails. The IDF responded with live rounds and beatings ("breaking Palestinian bones").

1987 – The outbreak of Intifadah I moved the Muslim Brotherhood to create *Hamas* (Zeal), the Islamist wing of the Palestinian Resistance Movement. Hamas is an acronym for *Harakat al Muqawamah al Islamiyyah* (Islamist Resistance Movement). When Fatah called for an Israeli-Palestinian peace conference, Hamas led the Palestinians who rejected negotiation: *Middle East Quarterly*, Spring 2003, Jonathan Schanzer (Washington Institute of Near East Policy).

1988 – On 4/16/88, an Israeli team of Mossad and IDF commandos, under the direction of Ehud Barak, came ashore in Tunisia, used stolen ID's to infiltrate PLO headquarters, and killed PLO chief 'Arafat's deputy, Khalil al Wazir. The US State Department condemned the killing. (In 2013, Israel admitted its responsibility for the operation.)

1988 – The PLO specified UNGA Resolution 181 as the legal basis for a Palestinian state in Palestine, endorsed UNSC resolutions 242 and 338, accepted the frontier of 1967 as permanent, and proclaimed Palestinian independence in the West Bank and Gaza.

1988 – The US recognized the PLO as representative of the Palestinian people. Over one hundred other states recognized a Palestinian state.

1989 – In Gaza, Hamas carried out its first attack, killing two IDF soldiers, Avi Saspartas and Ilan Sa'adon.

117

1989 – Hamas founder Shaykh Ahmad Yasin pleaded guilty of the deaths of four Palestinians suspected of collaboration with Israel. Shaykh Ahmad was sentenced by an Israeli court to life in prison.

1989 – Still operating underground, Hamas published a covenant calling for Jihad (Holy War) to liberate Palestine (all of the former Mandate).

1989 – Israel declared Hamas an illegal organization.

1990 – PLO support for the Iraqi invasion of Kuwait caused the Gulf states to expel hundreds of thousands of Palestinians, and many states to terminate aid programs for the PLO.

1990 – Hamas declined 'Arafat's invitation to join the PLC.

1990 – On 10/8/90, at the joint site of the Temple Mount (sacred to Judaism) and the Dome of the Rock (sacred to Islam), Jewish plans to lay a cornerstone led to Palestinian protests and rioting, and Israeli security measures that caused 20 Palestinian deaths, and many injuries. There were four Israeli deaths.

1991 – Hamas founded an elite militia, named for 'Izz al Din al Qassam, a Syrian cleric killed in a British manhunt in Palestine on 11/20/35, after he had attacked British soldiers.

1992 – Kissinger noted that, as the years passed with no Israeli compliance with international recommendations and Arab demands, those demands were relaxed. In the light of this trend, Israel chose procrastination as its best strategy: Neff.

1992 – On 6/7/92, PLO security officer for Europe 'Atif Busaysu was killed in Paris by two gunmen, suspected to be agents of Mossad.

1993 – **End of Intifadah I** – By accepting the Oslo Accord on 9/9/93, 'Arafat won Israeli recognition of the PLO as representative of the Palestinian people. By writing Prime Minister Rabin that the PLO recognized Israel, 'Arafat suspended the PLO's status as an armed contender. Despite a firestorm of criticism from rivals and allies, the 'Arafat faction projected a mistaken or feigned conviction that Israeli-Palestinian talks had shifted in favor of Palestinian statehood. Israel promoted this canard. Statements from Washington lent it verisimilitude: *MEP*, Summer 2015, Sara Roy.

1993 – On 9/13/93, on the Shite House lawn, with President Clinton presiding, Prime Minister Rabin and 'Arafat signed the Oslo Declaration of Principles. Israel approved the creation of the Palestine (National) Authority (PA): Neff.

1993 – Death toll from six years of Intifadah I: IDF – 60; other Israelis – 100; Palestinians – 1200; Palestinian "collaborators executed by the Palestinian Resistance" – 822.

1993 – In reaction to Hamas's continued suicide bombings, Israel dumped 413 Hamas adherents in an unpopulated area of Lebanon. (They got back years later.)

1994 – Clinton's Assistant Secretary of State for the Near East replaced the terms "occupied territories" and "disputed territories" with "a complicating factor": Neff.

1994 – 'Arafat's flimsy recognition of Israel in the Oslo Accord was all the cover King Husayn of Jordan needed to sign Israel's second peace treaty with an Arab state.

1995 – On 10/26/95, Fathi Shiqaqi, co-founder of the Islamic Jihad in Gaza, was killed in Malta by two gunmen from Mossad.

1996 – On 1/5/96, an Israeli double agent accomplished the assassination of Yahya 'Ayyash, "the Engineer", Hamas's explosives expert, by planting a cell phone rigged to explode when set off by a radio signal.

1996 – Yasir 'Arafat was elected President of the PA.

1997 – Israel failed in a furtive attempt to assassinate Hamas principal Khalid Mish'al on a street in Amman.

1999 – After a debate with Clinton over the Oslo Accord, Benjamin Netanyahu lost an election to Ehud Barak, who replaced him as prime minister: FT, 3/7/15.

1999 – At Sharm al Shaykh, 'Arafat and Ehud Barak signed a timetable for peace.

2000 – Clinton's meeting at Camp David with 'Arafat and Barak made no progress.

2000 – By this time, the Oslo Accord had been exposed as an Israeli scam. The Israeli occupation of Palestinian territories was no longer a simple matter of international concern. The situation was deteriorating from legalistic manipulation to war: Sara Roy.

2000 – **Intifadah II** – A contentious visit on 9/28/00 by Ariel Sharon to the Temple Mount, in the company of several hundred soldiers, swung the Palestinian mood toward the Islamists, set off Intifadah II, and helped Sharon become Prime Minister in February 2001. The PA Security Force, maintained by Israel and the US to keep order in the Occupied Territories, was deep down a Fatah protection society. At the outbreak of Intifadah II, it briefly turned its guns on IDF personnel. The Oslo Accord became a dead letter.

2001 – Shaykh Ahmad Yasin condemned the Al Qaʻidah attack of 9/11/01 on sites in the US.

2001 – On March 7, by ordering an incursion into Gaza, Prime Minister Sharon set a new trend of entering the Palestinians' assigned territory by force: *Arab-Israeli Military Forces in an Era of Asymmetric Wars*, Anthony Cordesman.

2001 – In April, for the first time in the Israel-Palestine conflict, the IDF used bulldozers to create "free-fire" zones: Cordesman.

2001 – In August and October the IDF seized military sites in the West Bank and Gaza: Cordesman.

2001 – On 10/17/01, operatives of the PFLP (The Popular Front for the Liberation of Palestine) assassinated Israeli Tourism Minister Rehavam Ze'evi, in alleged reprisal for Israeli killing of a PFLP leader in August. The four killers went into hiding in the Ramallah compound that housed Yasir ʻArafat's PA headquarters. Under the 1993 Oslo Agreement, the PA had assumed the awkward role of a resistance organization that was in an armed truce with Israel, condemned the Ze'evi assassination, and on 4/25/02 committed the four fugitives to the PA prison in Jericho on a charge of murder. It did call on Israel to cease the "targeted killing" of Palestinian militants.

In the never-never land of Israeli-Palestinian relations, the parties arranged for the US and the UK to provide forces to watch over the four prisoners, presumably to prevent their escape, or their elimination by an Israeli raid. The guardians arrived in May 2002. In January 2006, after the victory of Hamas in the Palestinian elections, Hamas leader Ismaʻil

Haniyah announced his intention to free them. On 3/14/06, the US/UK guard left Jericho. Israeli forces immediately attacked the prison with bulldozers, forcing the surrender of the four prisoners. They were sentenced by an Israeli court to the equivalent of life sentences. On 12/25/08, Ahmad Sa'dat was sentenced to 30 years on a charge of having ordered Ze'evi's death.

2001 – On 12/3/01, the IDF destroyed 'Arafat's three helicopters, confining him to his headquarters in Ramallah.

2002 – The first suicide bombings by Fatah were carried out by its new military wing, Al Aqsa Martyrs' Brigade. They were reprisals for Israel's targeted killings.

2002 – 'Arafat was under US pressure to close down the PLO's bitter rival, Hamas: *Post*, 1/2/02.

2002 – On 1/18/02, a day after another Arab attack took Israeli lives, IDF tanks confined 'Arafat to his Ramallah office.

2002 – On 3/29/02, the IDF confined 'Arafat to the basement of his office.

2002 – From February 27 to March 18, IDF troops entered several camps and cities in the West Bank, and Jabaliyah Camp in Gaza, and arrested thousands of Palestinians: Cordesman. Israeli forces killed dozens of civilians, destroyed hundreds of homes, attacked schools, ambulances, and hospitals, and methodically destroyed all the institutions of the PA. The Israeli objective was to terminate the governing capacity of 'Arafat and the PA, and intimidate Palestinian civilians from supporting attacks on Israel by Hamas and the Islamic Jihad: *MEP*, Fall 2015, Jerome Slater.

2002 – On 4/4/02, Secretary of State Powell made a three-hour visit to 'Arafat in his compound.

2002 – On 5/1/02, the PA handed six Palestinian prisoners over to Anglo-American custody, so that 'Arafat could be released from his basement.

2002 – On 6/18/02, a suicide bomber from Hamas killed 19 Israelis and wounded 74 on a bus in Jerusalem.

2002 – On 7/1/02, the Rome Statute that created and governs the International Criminal Court entered into force. The Court is an independent organization based in The Hague. The Palestinian Resistance Movement had been interested in winning its support against Israel: https://www.icc-cpi.int/.

2002 – On 7/22/02, an IDF plane fired a missile that killed the top name on Israel's most wanted list, Salah Shihadah, commander of Hamas' military wing, 'Izz al Din al Qassam. The missile also flattened an apartment building, killing 14 other Palestinians.

2002 – On 11/21/02, a Hamas suicide bomber killed 11, and wounded over fifty on a bus in Jerusalem.

2003 – On 3/5/03 a Hamas suicide bomber killed 17 Israelis on a bus in Haifa.

2003 – On 3/16/03, in Rafah, Gaza, an IDF bulldozer crushed Rachel Corrie, American member of the International Solidarity Movement, which was trying to prevent Israeli demolition of Palestinian residences. Her colleagues charged murder. There is no report that Washington conducted the standard inquiry into the death of an American citizen overseas – to determine: 1) why the demonstrators were not removed from the scene (as Jewish settlers were before the withdrawal from Gaza); 2) who was responsible for the death.

2003 – On 8/19/03 a Hamas suicide bomber killed 23 Israelis and wounded over 130 on or near a bus in Jerusalem.

2004 – The US was setting up a program, under the command of Lt. General Keith Dayton, US Security Coordinator, to train a PA security force to police Palestinian residents on the West Bank. Egyptian, Jordanian, and Turkish forces were to man a presidential guard under the jurisdiction of Fatah. The UK's MI6 was to help the PA draw up a plan to combat the Palestinian Islamist militias – Hamas and Islamic Jihad.

2004 – In retaliation for three Israeli deaths caused by homemade rockets from Gaza, Israel sent a major foray into Gaza's Jabaliyah Refugee Camp.

2004 – On 3/22/04, a Hellfire missile from an Apache helicopter killed Shaykh Ahmad Yasin as he was being wheeled out of morning prayer. Israel had long wanted him dead. The timing may have been chosen to show the proposed evacuation of Gaza was not a sign of weakness, or to squelch Shaykh Ahmad's unwelcome gesture of conciliation when he suggested an interim two-state arrangement. Shaykh Ahmad's replacement was Khalid Mish'al.

2004 – On 4/17/04 an IDF rocket killed Hamas leader 'Abd al 'Aziz al Rantisi and two others in Gaza City.

2004 – Hamas official 'Izz al Din al Shaykh Khalil was assassinated in Damascus on 9/26/04.

2004 – On 8/31/04, 16 Israelis died in the suicide bombing of a bus in Beersheba. Hamas claimed responsibility.

2004 – On 9/30/04, in retaliation for the killing of two Israelis in Sderot by a Qassam rocket, the IDF launched an offensive against the northern sector of Gaza.

2004 – The end of the Israeli offensive against northern Gaza: 10/16/04. Over 100 Gazans had died under Israeli fire. Population of Gaza: Palestinians – 1.3 million; Jews – 7500: *Times*.

2004 – The death of Yasir 'Arafat (under medical care in the Paris area) on 11/11/04.

2005 – On 1/9/05, Mahmud 'Abbas was elected to succeed 'Arafat as President of the PA.

2005 – On 1/13/05, a Gazan raiding team went into Israel via the Karni Crossing and killed six Israelis.

2005 – On 2/25/05, a suicide bomber killed five Israelis and wounded 50. The bombing was claimed by Islamic Jihad (based in Gaza).

2005 – **End of Intifadah II** – Israel and the Gazan militias concluded a truce in March. The PA was preoccupied with finding a replacement for 'Arafat.

Israeli Withdrawal from Gaza

2005 – On 9/12/05, Prime Minister Sharon bulled through by armed force the withdrawal of all Jews, and some Bedouin, from Gaza. This action was a terrible blow for Israel's Religious Zionists: *Times*, 2/7/16, Steven Erlanger. The total number of Jews from 21 settlements in Gaza and four in adjoining parts of the West Bank, plus the garrison, was only about 9000 – low enough to suggest that Israel had been reserving the withdrawal option. Some settlers put up extreme resistance. Sharon told them don't attack the IDF – attack me! The Israeli motivation – never publicized – was probably demographic. It seems that Sharon had concluded that the Jewish majority in Greater Israel had to be maintained. Counting Gaza, the Arab population of Greater Israel was closing in on the Jewish population in total number – close to six million each: *Post*, 8/18/05.

Once past the withdrawal deadline of midnight August 18, Israel had to decide the enclave's future. Annexation of an impoverished enclave of 139 square miles had been ruled out. According to Christopher Hitchens's anecdote, when an Israeli negotiator offered to cede The Gaza Strip, his Palestine opposite number said, "Fine. What do we get in return?"

Two theoretical options remained: Egypt, or independence.

In its postwar withdrawal into its badly bruised shell, Egypt didn't want the problem even Israel couldn't handle.

Independence? Gaza had become a de facto autonomous state. In the words of the 2014 *World Almanac*, "The Palestinian Authority [Hamas] is responsible for civil government."

So aside from random intervention from Israel, Gaza was independent. Within the IDF's barbaric confines, the Hamas regime dictated domestic policy. It even had a foreign policy, insofar as it could bypass Israeli anti-ballistic and Egyptian anti-tunnel defenses.

Rashid Khalidi pointed out in the *Times* that Israel's imprisonment of an entire people is doubly felonious under the Fourth Geneva Convention, as collective punishment, and as dereliction of the obligations of an occupying power – even if the occupation is by remote control. In *Counterpunch*, Kathleen and Bill Christison quoted Sara Roy that Israel seemed bent on denying the Gazans a solid economic base.

The evacuation of all Jews from Gaza was not conclusive. The IDF would find reason to charge back in on repeated occasions, but with no occupier on site, and no effective ally, the Gazan enclave was totally responsible for its own security. In its captive status, nonviolence was not an option. For Gaza, defense was resistance, and that responsibility had fallen primarily on the government, which had been Hamas.

2005 – **Israel-Palestine War Resumed** – After the exit of the Jewish colonists, Hamas and the smaller militias regularly rocketed adjoining areas of Israel. Israel regularly returned fire.

2006 – After winning the PNC Parliamentary election, Hamas rejected the demand of the Middle East Quartet (the UN, the US, the EU, and Russia) to give up violence and recognize Israel. The Quartet and Israel imposed sanctions on Gaza. A post-election government of national unity broke down in military conflict between Fatah and Hamas.

2006 – In April, Isma'il Haniyah became Prime Minister of the Gaza government formed by Hamas.

2006 – On 6/9/06, after eight Palestinian civilians were killed on the Gaza beach by Israeli fire, the Hamas military wing called off the Gaza-Israel truce of March 2005.

2006 – On 6/24/06, the IDF abducted two Palestinians from Gaza.

2006 – On 6/25/06, under political pressure from unpaid civil servants, Hamas raided an IDF post across the border, killed two IDF soldiers, wounded four, and abducted IDF soldier Gilad Shalit. The immediate objective was to retaliate for the two abductions of June 24. The longer-term objective was to swap Shalit for some of the thousands of Palestinians in Israeli prisons. The action served Hamas's interest in attracting worldwide attention. Iran and Qatar pledged compensatory aid.

2006 – **First Israeli Invasion of Gaza** – In immediate response, the IDF conducted ground attacks in northern Gaza, and air strikes that damaged bridges and destroyed several government offices and Gaza's only power station. Israel put 64 Hamas members of the PA cabinet and Legislative Council in jail. Gazan casualties were heavy. Gaza's borders with Israel were closed in an effort to starve the enclave into submission: *Times*, 7/1/06.

2006 – On 7/5/06, a Hamas Qassam rocket of new design reached the Israeli city of Ashqelon, 12 miles north of Gaza.

2006 – Washington vetoed a UNSC resolution that would have called on Israel to withdraw its troops from Gaza. On 7/26/06, these troops instituted a search for the militants who had been rocketing Israel.

2006 – On 9/26/06, a UN study declared the humanitarian situation in Gaza intolerable, as a result of Western cancellation of aid, and Israeli closure of the border.

2006 – October 11-14 was a period of intensified rocket fire between Israel and Hamas. Gazan casualties were heavy.

2006 – The IDF felt obligated to conduct periodic "mow-the-lawn" operations against Hizballah in Lebanon and Hamas in Gaza: *WRMEA*, September 2015. From 2000 through 2006, Israeli forces had killed 339 Gazans, most of them from helicopters: *LRB*. Nevertheless, the Israeli offensives had failed; Hamas was more firmly entrenched than ever (*NY*, January 2008, Lawrence Wright), but the price was high. Borders remained closed, supplies of electricity and fuel had been cut back, bank transactions halted, imports reduced, exports shut down, water and sewerage services impaired, schools and hospitals crippled, employment negligible, building materials embargoed, and Gazans condemned to living with destitution and a moldering infrastructure. An Israeli buffer zone blocked access to 30 percent of arable land. The sea front was fouled with sewage. With Gazan export crops rotting in the fields, UNRWA was feeding 825,000 refugees, and the World Food Program was feeding 250,000 non-refugees.

2006 – **End of the First Invasion** – On 11/25/06, Israel and Hamas concluded a ceasefire.

2006 – On 12/14/06, the Israeli Supreme Court ruled that <u>targeted killing</u> is a legitimate form of self-defense against "terrorism". As defined by an official American panel, targeted killings do not fall under the category of assassination. Under a precise retaliation program, Israel had carried out hundreds of such operations by poison, clandestine drive-by shooting, sniper, explosive, or helicopter. The program had included the protracted but comprehensive elimination of planners of and participants in the PLO attack on Israeli athletes at the Munich Olympics in 1972.

2007 – Mahmud 'Abbas named Salam Fayyad PA Prime Minister. On 6/14/07, the PLO and the international community recognized Fayyad's appointment. Hamas ignored it.

2007 – In March, Isma'il Haniyah formed a PA government in Gaza.

2007 – In the summer, while PA and Hamas forces were fighting for control of Gaza, the Gazan-Israeli front was also active, including a joint cross-border raid by militants of Islamic Jihad and Fatah's Al Aqsa Martyrs' Brigade: www.news.com.au, 6/11/07.

2007 – In September, Israel and Egypt sealed Gaza's borders. Israel couldn't abide an autonomous Palestine next door. It saw its only option as lockdown – seal the enclave, residents and all, under a three-dimensional carapace. By denying Hamas access to electric power, fuel, and staples, Israel hoped to bring Hamas' rocket barrages to a stop. To boost the PA against Hamas, Israel had released 100 million dollars from tax receipts to Fatah.

2007 – In the West Bank, there were 140 Jewish settlements, with a population of 270,000: Robinson. Over one-third of their land had been confiscated from Palestinian owners: *B'Tselem* (The Israeli Information Center for Human Rights in the Occupied Territories).

2008 – In January, Hamas blew temporary holes in Egypt's security fences, and Gazans had eleven days of riotous access to shops across the Egyptian border.

2008 – Egypt had halted NGO shipments of food and medicine to the Gazans: *Counterpunch*, 2/1/08.

2008 – On 2/27/08, three Gazan militias fired rocket barrages at Ashqelon.

2008 – On 2/28/08, Israel retaliated with ground action and a rocket barrage that killed 112 Palestinians.

2008 – On 6/19/08, Hamas and Israel agreed on a six-month ceasefire, under which Israel eased border-crossing controls, and Hamas suspended rocket fire into Israel. In the assessment of Uri Avnery, the ceasefire amounted to de facto Israeli recognition of Hamas, and evidence that the level of conflict between them was a draw – even though the Gazans were confined to a dog run with an invisible fence, intermittently perforated by the tunnels they kept digging.

2008 – On 11/4/08, as reported by Roger Cohen in *The New York Review of Books* and Henry Siegman in *The London Review of Books*, Israel broke the truce by a lethal raid against one of the tunnels. Hamas resumed rocket attacks on southern Israel, now supplementing its homemade Qassams with longer-range Katyushas. Israel resumed the embargo on the supply of all but a trickle of essential food and medicine, and it intercepted welfare payments from Fatah's PA to its personnel in Gaza. Egypt had begun to block selected tunnels to Gaza. Nighttime Gaza was darkening as Israel cut the fuel supply: *Times*, 11/15/08. In retaliation for Israel's resumption of the embargo and its 11/4/08 strike at the attack tunnel, Hamas rockets hit an Israeli hospital. In the West Bank, Israeli security guards were being replaced with US-trained Palestinians from the PA: *Times*, 11/15/08.

2008 – **Second Israeli Invasion** – In an effort to stop rocket fire into Israel and arms smuggling into Gaza, and to rescue Gilad Shalit, the IDF initiated Operation Cast Lead on 12/22/08: *The Link*, January 2016, Atef Abu Saif. On 12/27/08, an air campaign destroyed almost every public building in Gaza – even the American International School and the science lab at Islamic University. The invaders also attacked roads, bridges, power plants, factories, fuel depots, sewage plants, water tanks, orchards, greenhouses, fishing boats, and hospitals. Estimated Palestinian deaths were 1400 – Israeli civilian deaths were three: *MEP*, Slater. On its own border, Egypt set up machine gun posts to deter Gazan flight from the combat zone: *AP*, 1/3/09; *The Link*, 1/3/09. On 1/3/09, Israel mounted a ground invasion of Gaza.

2009 - On 1/4/09, the Bush 43 administration cold-bloodedly blocked a UNSC call for a ceasefire. On the West Bank, America's Fatah protégés in the PA were repelling pro-Hamas demonstrators with tear gas. In a radio address, Bush 43 identified PA President Mahmud 'Abbas as the legitimate leader of the Palestinian people.

2009 – On 1/13-15/09, Israeli forces attacked a rural area in southern Gaza with rockets armed with white phosphorus (a breach of international conventions: *Times*, 1/22/09). The Red Crescent's Al Quds Hospital was also damaged. The IDF had taken maximum advantage of its crushing technological superiority: *Times*, 1/17/09.

2009 – On 1/15/09, missiles ignited a UN compound with white phosphorus shells, destroying a warehouse full of food and medicine. UNRWA Director for Gaza John Ging (Irish national) denied the Israeli allegation that Hamas had fired from the site: *Times*, 1/17/09. [The UN

Relief and Works Agency was founded on 12/8/49 by UNGA Resolution 302 (IV) as a subsidiary organ of the UN. It began field operations on 5/1/1950. Its mission was to aid, protect, and advocate for Palestinian refugees in Jordan, Lebanon, Syria, the West Bank, and the Gaza Strip. Palestinian refugees elsewhere were a responsibility of the UN Office of the High Commissioner for Refugees (UNHCR).]

2009 – In Cast Lead, the IDF introduced a new projectile, DIME (Dense Inert Metal Explosive), that sprays bits of super-hard tungsten alloy: *WRMEA: Foreign Policy in Focus*, April 2009.

2009 – **End of the Second Invasion** – On January 18, under international pressure, without having achieved any of its objectives, Israel issued a unilateral ceasefire. Israel had lost 13 dead. Gaza had lost 1409: *The Link*, January 2016. On February 10 UN Secretary General Ban Ki-Moon demanded that Israel end its restraints on the passage of relief supplies. On the Egyptian border, the Palestinian business of tunnel repair was already under way. Once again the Israeli-American diarchy had demonstrated its capacity for destruction, but its incapacity for conciliation. The mayhem of those 22 days set off a chorus that blamed Israel for inflicting disproportionate damage and death: *NYR*, 2/12/09 ("wanton killing"); Ban Ki-Moon (condemnation of Hamas rocketing and Israeli devastation of Gaza: *Times*, 1/18/09); Amnesty International ("war crimes on both sides": 7/2/09). *McClatchy* estimated that replacement of the Gazan structures and residences (4000) destroyed would cost 1.5 billion dollars. The *Times* of 1/19/09 speculated that the Hamas militia had escaped heavy casualties by avoiding close combat. During Cast Lead, Hamas fired new rockets with greater range, reaching Beersheba and Ashdod.

2009 – Arab anger at the disproportionate casualties of Cast Lead was so intense that Arab governments felt compelled to put on a show of reviewing counter-options: *Times*, 3/27/09.

2009 – On 10/16/09, The UN Human Rights Council endorsed the Goldstone Report of September 2009, which found the blockade of Gaza, as collective punishment, unlawful. It charged Hamas with rocketing Israeli civilians, and Israel with executing civilians and attempting to cripple Gaza's economy and sow desperation among its people. Russia and China concurred. The UNGA endorsed the report in November. Under Israeli pressure, Goldstone had reneged on the assertion that "citizens were intentionally targeted", but the three other members of the drafting team held firm: *NY*, 11/9/09, 9/1/14.

2010 – On 1/19/10, Mossad agents killed Hamas operative Mahmud Mabhuh in a Dubai hotel. Mabhuh had reportedly been involved in the killing of two IDF soldiers in 1989.

2010 – In January three Gazan militiamen died in two Israeli air strikes against attack tunnels.

2010 – The professed objective of the Israeli blockade of Gaza was to cut arms supply, but implementation had been so ruthless that it suggested Israeli intent to tear down the Gazan entity piece by piece until the Hamas leadership was forced out – regardless of the consequences for its million and a half wretched residents.

While authorities in Washington and European capitals seemed inured to this medieval performance, Muslim exasperation mounted. The tipping point was when well-placed Turkish elements backed, with money and personnel, a stronger flotilla than altruistic Western volunteers had previously launched against the maritime component of the blockade. History was made, it seems, by the coincidence of two otherwise unrelated events – the Israeli blockade of Gaza, and the seismic redirection of Turkish foreign policy from cultivating new ties with the West to renewing old ties with the Arab East. On May 31, 2010, the rightist administration in Jerusalem characteristically overreacted against the latest foray, "Gaza Freedom Flotilla", by staging a boarding operation by commandos who, in the process of detaining the six Turkish ships and their several hundred passengers (most of them unarmed), managed to kill nine Turks on the lead ship.

The resultant outburst achieved official modification of the Israeli position, and it focused unprecedented condemnation on the blockade. The UN High Commissioner for Human Rights, Navi Pillay, asserted an "almost unanimous international view that the Gaza blockade is illegal." Russia charged Israel with "violation of the norms of international law." In response to public outrage, the Arab League, lowest common denominator of Arab audacity, boldly sent Secretary General Amr

Moussa to Gaza to visit Hamas Prime Minister Haniyah (at his home, not his office) with a call for an end to the Israeli siege. Turkish Prime Minister Erdogan charged Israel with state terrorism, and sent Foreign Minister Davutoglu to New York to demand action from the Security Council.

UNSC Resolution 1860, 1/8/09, even as watered down by the Obama administration, had called for an end to the blockade of Gaza. International opinion seemed to be coalescing behind the thesis that the blockade, legal or not, was politically unsustainable.

In the center of the firestorm was the Mubarak regime, whose antipathy to Arab Islamism and reliance on American money had made it a de facto collaborator in the blockade – reportedly even to the extent of planning to block Gaza's tunnel system by installing a US-designed steel barrier sixty feet deep along Egypt's nine-mile border with Gaza. Shaken by the impact of the Freedom Flotilla episode, Cairo deferred the underground barrier project, and cracked the border blockade to allow easier passage by selected Gazans.

2010 – Dubai police released a videocast which they said contained surveillance of the Israeli agents who killed Hamas commander Mahmud Mabhuh: *Times*, 8/13/15.

2010 – On 8/31/10, Hamas operatives killed four Israeli civilians near Kiryat Arba in the West Bank.

2011 – Aid levels to the PA: From the US – 450 million dollars a year; from Arab states (in principle) – 2010, 280 million dollars; 2011 – 110 million dollars; from Japan – 2010, 100 million dollars: *FA*, September 2011; *Times*, 9/12/11. After the PA acquired nonmember observer status in the UNGA, Congress again suspended US aid payments: *Times*, 1/11/13.

2011 – On 3/23/11, Hamas bombed a Jerusalem bus station, killing 1, wounding 39.

2011 – Egypt reopened the Rafah crossing.

2011 – On 4/7/11, Hamas bombed an Israeli school bus, killing one.

2011 – In March, Israel shut down the Karni crossing: *Times*, 8/5/15.

2011 – On 8/18/11, Palestinian and Egyptian militants killed eight in southern Israel. Five Egyptians died.

131

2011 – In November, Palestine became a member of UNESCO.

2011 – The UN's Palmer Report on Israel's assessment of its blockade of Gaza: The Israeli naval blockade of Gaza was legal and appropriate; the principals of the Gaza Freedom Flotilla acted recklessly; the Israeli boarding party used excessive force: *Times*, 9/2/11.

2011 – According to the UN Human Rights Council, and the Red Cross, the blockade of Gaza was illegal.

2011 – On 10/11/11 and 10/18/11, under the authorization of Prime Minister Netanyahu and Ahmad Ja'abari, head of Hamas's 'Izz al Din Qassam Force, Israel released 1027 Palestinian prisoners in exchange for the return of Gilad Shalit, abducted 6/25/06.

2011 – From early November, Israel had been withholding payment of the PA's share of tax and customs fees, on which the PA was largely dependent. Israeli motives: to protest amicable PA overtures to Hamas, and the PA effort to win UN membership. The monthly transfer of fees, mandated by the Oslo Accord, had been averaging 100 million dollars.

2012 – In February, Hamas broke relations with Syria, in support of the Sunni rebellion there. Hamas had emerged as the armed wing of the MB in Gaza: *MEP*, Spring 2016.

2012 – From 3/9 to 3/15/12, exchanges between Gazan rockets, Grad missiles, and mortar shells, and Israeli air strikes, wounded 23 Israelis and killed over 20 Palestinians.

2012 – In early August, a ceasefire announced by Netanyahu was preempted by the capture by Hamas of an Israeli officer. Israel then unleashed a four-day indiscriminate tank and artillery bombardment of a nearby Palestinian residential neighborhood: *MEP*, Slater.

2012 – On 9/21/12, Egyptian Islamist militants initiated a cross-border clash with IDF soldiers.

2012 – PA Prime Minister Salam Fayyad made some nominal reductions in government charges and a rise in the minimum wage to mitigate a firestorm of West Bank protest at chronic unemployment, wage decline, and rise in the cost of living: *MER*, September 2012.

2012 – **Third Israeli Invasion** – On 11/14/12, Israel launched against Gaza Operation Pillar of Defense that lasted only 8 days but hit 1500 targets, and killed 130 Palestinians, including Ahmad al Ja'abari, commander of Hamas's military wing, 'Izz al Din al Qassam. Six Israelis died under fire from 1400 rockets. Mursi's surprise ceasefire of 11/22/12 stipulated Israeli reopening of its Gazan crossings. Israel ignored that stipulation, but the rockets subsided: *FT*, 11/23/12; *NYR*, 9/25/14. Hamas put up a better fight in 2012 than in 2008-9, and gained an end to targeted assassinations: *LRB*, 11/21/12, Nathan Thrall.

2012 – **End of the Third Israeli Invasion** – On 11/21/12, Israel and Hamas agreed to a ceasefire promoted by Egyptian Prime Minister Mursi: *MEP*, Slater. It included a reciprocal end to assassinations, invasions, and economic warfare. Hamas complied. Israel continued its economic blockade.

2012 – By a crushing majority (138-9-41), UNGA Resolution 67/19 of 11/29/12 confirmed Palestine as a non-member observer state in the UN.

2013 – In April, Khalid al Mish'al was reelected head of Hamas' political bureau: *MEP*, Fall 2013.

2013 – In June, Rami Hamdallah took over as the Prime Minister of the PA: *Times*, 5/21/14.

2013 – During the year, eight minor incidents between Israelis and Palestinians caused 9 Palestinian deaths and 6 Israeli deaths. Hamas observed the ceasefire of 11/22/12. Israel repeatedly violated it: *MEP*: Fall 2015, Slater.

2013 – In mystifying disregard of Prime Minister Netanyahu's adamant rejection of Palestinian partition, Secretary of State Kerry was doggedly searching for a diplomatic point of entry. Meanwhile, US Gen. John Allen was groping for a breakthrough in talks with Israeli officials, and American, Jordanian, and EU military officers were working with Israel to build the cadre of security police from the PA. Their role was to round up Hamas sympathizers and other elements of the opposition in order to marshal the West Bankers behind the hypothetical peace process. Kerry's push for partition had eliminated all shreds of a peace process: *MER*.

2014 – Hamas executed two men on a charge of collaboration with Israel: *Times*, 5/8/14.

2014 – Hamas had lost two of its principal backers – Egypt and Syria. Its border with Israel had been largely closed since 2005, with Egypt since 2013: *Times*. Unemployment in Gaza was running around 50 percent: *Times*, 7/23/14, Anne Barnard.

2014 – On 6/12/14, three Israeli teenagers were abducted and killed in the West Bank. Israel accused Hamas operatives of committing the atrocity and instituted a harsh roundup of suspects. Door-to-door visits to West Bank homes of suspected Hamas sympathizers led to the arrest of hundreds and a number of Arab deaths. Hamas retaliated with new waves of rocket fire, but Israeli acquisition from the US of an advanced anti-missile defense, Iron Dome, afforded Israel unprecedented protection. Israel was banning routine travel between the West Bank and Gaza: *Times*, 6/13/14.

2014 – On 6/30/14, just after the bodies of the three teenagers were found near Hebron, Israeli jets and helicopters unleashed a blizzard of air attacks on Gaza. Mursi's ceasefire of 11/22/12 was over. Hamas resumed rocketing Israel. Hamas continued to deny responsibility for the teenagers' deaths – rightly so, it seems, given the evidence that the culprits were a local crime family not under Hamas discipline.

2014 – On 7/1/14, sixteen-year-old Muhammad Abu Khudayr was picked up off a street in Arab Jerusalem, beaten, and burned alive. On 7/7/14, three Jewish Israelis confessed to the crime.

2014 – **Fourth Israeli Invasion** – There had been no recent flurries of cross-border rocket fire, but at this point Israeli strategy was being determined more by rage than reason. Of all the rounds yet fought between Israel and Hamas, that of July 2014 was the bloodiest: *FT*, 4/24/15.

2014 – On 7/7/14, Israel launched Operation Protective Edge with concentrated air strikes whose claimed objective was to end rocket fire from Gaza. The major strategic targets of Israel firepower were the attack tunnels. The emotional targets were the residences of Hamas officials, and 83 UN schools: *NYR*, 9/25/14; *WRMEA*, May 2015. Hamas stepped up cross-border rocket fire in an effort to compel Israel to end its offensive, lift the blockade of Gaza, and release its Palestinian prisoners. Early in the exchange of direct fire, 44 Palestinian civilians huddled in seven UN schools were killed: *Times*, 7/12/14, 4/28/15.

2014 – On 7/17/14, Israel backed up its air attack with a massive ground assault, backed by 3 million bullets and 20,000 tons of explosives. The IDF made no distinction between civilians and militants: *51-Day War*, Max Blumenthal.

2014 – On 7/21/14, the IDF fired 7000 shells into an area less than a mile wide. Comment of an American military observer: The only possible motive was to kill the most people in the shortest time: *MER*, 7/21/14. UNRWA, which was operating 250 installations in Gaza, accused Israel of violating international law by shelling schools designated as public bomb shelters: *Times*, 7/31/14. A number of international and Israeli human rights organizations concluded that the Protective Edge attacks were war crimes. The Israeli military had been sullied by these operations. The UN Secretary General had spoken of moral outrage. The *Times* noted that shelling by 155mm artillery was inexcusable in a densely populated area. Even a spokesperson from the US Department of State, which tries harder than most to act as the apologist for Israel, stated that "Israel must do more to meet its own standards": *Times*, 8/4/14.

2014 – **End of the Fourth Invasion** – The fifty-one-day war (7/7-8/26/14) came to an end with the ceasefire of August 26.

2014 – The postwar curtain rose on a devastated Gaza: Twenty schools demolished. 16,000 housing units uninhabitable. Total deaths: Gazans – 2131 including 1400 militants. Israelis – 72, including six civilians: *Times*, 9/11/14: *FA*, Summer, July 2016, Aluf Benn. Gaza had lost its only power plant, its sewage system, its water system, and four of its 13 hospitals. Israel had managed to destroy 32 attack tunnels: *Times*, 8/6/14. A senior Israeli in military intelligence said Operation Protective Edge had resembled Operation Cast Lead of 2008-9, with the one exception that the newly built attack tunnels had afforded the Gazan rocket teams better protection from Israeli fire: *Times*, 9/3/14; *Nation*, 7/20/15; *The Link*, January 2016.

2014 – In July Khalid Mish'al told interviewer Charlie Rose the Gazans wanted autonomy (no blockade) and peace. Even Obama seemed to be looking in the direction of the lifting of the blockade of Gaza. The Israeli blockade had nearly smothered agricultural exports and building-material imports: *WRMEA*, May 2015.

2014 – Ghanim Nusaybah, scion of Jerusalem's oldest Arab family, holder of the key of the Holy Sepulcher (burial site of Jesus, exact site unknown), said that the Second Caliph, 'Umar Ibn al Khattab, had promised Sophronius, Patriarch of Jerusalem, that he would protect Christian inhabitants and end the Roman ban on Jewish entry to the city. Now the covenant was threatened by pressures that were causing Christians to flee: *FT*, 12/2/14.

2015 – Israel, the largest exporter of military drones, was maintaining a constant cover of recon drones over the 1.8 million Gazans, one of the most enlightened communities in the Arab World. In its schools and universities, mixed-gender classes were the norm: *The Link*, January 2016.

2015 – Amnesty International: Indiscriminate firing of mortars and rockets by Gazan militants in 2014 constituted war crimes: *Times*, 3/26/15; Israel was culpable of indifference and flagrant disregard for the lives of Gazan civilians: *Times*, 6/12/15.

2015 – A UN study condemned both Israel and Hamas for war crimes – especially Hamas' killing of 21 suspects of collaborating with Israel: *Times*, 6/23/15. Israel cited self-defense as grounds for exoneration of criminal charges. Obama and the US Senate espoused that argument. The ICJ (International Court of Justice) reportedly took the position that international law rejects a claim of self-defense from an occupying power. The National Lawyers' Guild wrote Obama on 2/10/15 that there had been no cross-border rocket fire from Gaza directly prior to Operation Protective Edge.

2015 – Qatar and Kuwait were the only donors to have resumed financial aid to Hamas for reconstruction of homes. Estimated cost of reconstruction of 7,000 Gazan homes razed and 89,000 damaged: 4-6 billion dollars, over 20 years.

2015 – ICC judges ordered its chief prosecutor to review her decision not to investigate the Israel raid on the Mavi Marmara flotilla of 5/31/10. *Times*, 7/17/15.

2015 – All but two or three Palestinian refugee camps in Syria had been destroyed in the ongoing civil war. The population of the Yarmuk camp in the suburbs of Damascus had fallen from 800,000 (160,000 Palestinians) to 18,000. The IS had taken it over: *WRMEA*, September 2015.

2015 – PA President Mahmud 'Abbas stated that the Palestinians were no longer bound by mutual agreement to Israel: *Times*, 10/1/15.

2015 – The joint site of the Jews' Temple Mount and the Muslims' Noble Sanctuary (*Al Haram al Sharif*) had an area of 37 acres, but no one knew where the two temples were situated. The site was administered by a Jordanian *waqf*. Non-Muslim prayer was banned: *Times*, Rick Gladstone, 10/9/15, 10/22/15.

2015 – Israel was suddenly faced with a wave of sporadic attacks on Jewish citizens in Jerusalem and the West Bank by Palestinian individuals protesting the occupation and rumors that the Jews were thinking of violating the prohibition against Jewish prayer on the Temple Mount: *FT*, 10/14/15.

2015 – The new Palestinian violence was the almost inevitable consequence of discrimination by Jewish authorities, and of the inattention of the PA: *Times*, 10/18/15.

2015 – Israeli security forces were meeting the spate of individual Palestinian violence with live fire and demolition of offenders' houses. There had been numerous dead and wounded, most of them Palestinian. Amnesty International and Human Rights Watch condemned all killings and the security forces' live fire: *Nation*, 11/9/15; *Times*, 11/13/15.

2015 – At the end of the year, the Islamic State was beginning to sign recruits in Gaza: *NYR*, 1/14/16.

2016 – In early May, an IDF force looking for secret tunnels attacked a Hamas unit in southern Gaza: *FT*, 5/7/16.

2016 – Israel was building an underground wall to block tunnel construction along the 40-mile border with Gaza.

1990-91 – The Kuwait Wars

——

The Lost Province – As long as Iraq exists, it will harbor the conviction that Kuwait is Iraqi territory. Oil makes Kuwait a widely-coveted piece of real estate, but the Iraqi argument is stronger than that:

As noted by Geoffrey Kemp and Robert Harkavy, Iraq has always based its claim to Kuwait on the grounds that in Ottoman times Kuwait was part of the governorate of Basrah. From their occupation of Mesopotamia in 1534 until the collapse of their empire in World War I, the Ottomans professed to rule the northeastern shore of the Arabian Peninsula. (The Kuwaiti counterargument rests on the European view that Kuwait was an autonomous shaykhdom from around 1756, and that its autonomy was reinforced in 1899 when Britain concluded with the Shaykh of Kuwait an agreement that placed Kuwait under British protection, in effect nullifying the Ottoman view that the Shaykh was the governor of an Ottoman district.) (According to Elaine Sciolino, the Ottomans never established complete sovereignty over Kuwait.)

In 1869-72, the new Ottoman Governor in Baghdad, Midhat Pasha, was not only responsible for the administration of the area stretching from Mawsil in the north to Al Hasa in the Arabian Peninsula, he actually made an inspection tour to Kuwait and Al Hasa. In the last decades of Ottoman rule, this area was re-divided into the three separate vilayets of Mawsil, Baghdad, and Basrah.

The elaborate frontier separating Saudi Arabia, Kuwait, and Iraq was the cavalier concoction of Sir Percy Cox, who imposed it in 1922 with minimal consultation with Ibn Sa'ud and none at all with the Kuwaitis or the Iraqis.

Cox's restriction of Iraq's frontier on the Gulf to a paltry 12 miles, solely for Britain's political convenience, was an intolerable derogation of an Iraq's vital economic and strategic interests. As a matter of simple geometry, Kuwait sits between Iraq and the Gulf.

In 1937 Iraqi King Ghazi massed troops in anticipation of annexation of Kuwait, but Britain squelched the initiative. In 1961, a bid by Iraqi dictator 'Abd al Karim Qasim collapsed when British, Egyptian, and Syrian troops arrived in Kuwait.

In 1988, after Saddam had failed to extend Iraq's seacoast on the Iranian side, he turned his attention to the Kuwaiti side. Because of its dependence on oil exports, landlocked Iraq was obsessed with enlarging its access to the Gulf: *MEP*, October 2000. Iraq was also driven by crushing postwar indebtedness at a time when Kuwait and Saudi Arabia had refused to talk debt cancellation, Kuwaiti overproduction had helped drive the price of crude down to eleven dollars a barrel (*Iraq*, Dilip Hiro). Saddam suspected Kuwait of slant drilling into rich Iraqi fields, and he coveted Kuwait's superior oil production system: Mackey.

Kuwait's political system has always been so dysfunctional that it might have profited from annexation by the modern Iraq that Saddam had built by 1980 – but that was the year Saddam's foreign policy went off the rails. By 1990, Iraq's economy and infrastructure had been so ravaged by the war with Iran (*MER*, Fall 2014) that it no longer qualified for the annexation business. The military superiority it had attained over Iran in 1988 was already impaired by the obsolescence of its equipment: *MEP*, June 1999, Cordesman.

Saddam's own frame of mind was another negative factor. Twenty years of absolute power is bound to corrupt a ruler's judgment – particularly someone simultaneously embittered by assassination attempts and military reverses, and misled by Washington's knee-jerk favoritism for any adversary of Iranian theocracy. To top it all off, eight years of sterile war had left Saddam with a million-man army, and no enemies in sight except the rebellious Kurds.

1983 – **The "Kuwaiti Seventeen"** – On 12/12/83, the American Embassy and five other sites in Kuwait were bombed. Six victims died. Iraq's Al Da'wah and Hizballah affiliate Islamic Jihad claimed responsibility. Both claims had circumstantial corroboration. Kuwait convicted and imprisoned seventeen Iraqis and Lebanese for complicity: *The Iran-Iraq War: Impact and Implications,* edited by Ephraim Karsh. They were allegedly motivated by an Iranian conspiracy to avenge Kuwait's support for Iraq versus Iran. For years Hizballah tried to exploit its regional operations to pressure Kuwait to release the seventeen. This effort was Hizballah's motive for the subsequent rash of abductions of Americans in Lebanon: *The Iran-Iraq War.* In the course of the Iraqi invasion, 1300 political prisoners escaped, presumably including the "Kuwaiti Seventeen".

1990 – Iraqi Invasion

On August 2, 120,000 Iraqi troops reached Kuwait City in one hour, and overran the country in 5 hours: Sciolino. The Kuwaiti Amir fled to Saudi Arabia with his family. His half-brother Fahd al Ahmad al Sabah, who stayed to fight, was crushed by an Iraqi tank. Dasman Palace was burned. On 8/8/90, Iraq proclaimed the annexation of its nineteenth province. In rejection of pragmatism and the Baathist doctrine of Arab brotherhood, the occupiers looted and destroyed with the same brutality that forces of the Iraqi regime and insurrectionists had used against each other. Kuwaiti vigilantes also resorted to torture and execution of Iraqis: Sciolino. The Kuwaiti army of 16,000 – most of them foreigners – was brushed aside, but no Kuwaitis collaborated with the invaders, and there was an appreciable level of civil resistance.

UNSC Resolution 662 unanimously declared the annexation invalid. UNSC Resolution 678 authorized military counteraction. UNSC Resolution 687 of 11/29/90 authorized use of "all necessary means" to expel Iraqi forces if still there as of 1/15/91. The Arab League condemned the invasion in a close vote. Iraq, Libya, and the PLO opposed the condemnation. Jordan, Yemen, Algeria, Sudan, and Mauritania abstained: Sciolino.

The American Switch: Yesterday's Friend, Today's Enemy – In the days of British supremacy, the American presence in Iraq was largely confined to two Jesuit schools, Baghdad College and Al Hikmah University. In 1959, the CIA adopted Saddam Husayn as a man of promise. Juan Cole's website cited Richard Sale's *UPI* report that the Agency subsidized Saddam in Baghdad, and in Cairo after his escape to Egypt.

In 1963, Iraqi dictator 'Abd al Karim Qasim showed up in Washington's sights because of his ties with the Communists. Those ties were probably less ideological than opportunistic – he needed their support for his land reform program, which was opposed by the Shiite merchant class – but, as reported by Hanna Batatu, and discussed in an article by retired FSO Jim Akins in *The Washington Report on Middle East Affairs* of January 2005, Washington authorized the CIA to subsidize the Baathist coup against Qasim, and to supply the new Baathist regime with the names of Communists (mostly Kurds) for elimination. Irony: In 1963, Washington paid Saddam to kill Kurds; in 2006 Washington hanged Saddam for killing Kurds.

In 1979, the Carter administration reportedly encouraged Iraq to attack America's new enemy, Iran. *The Washington Post* reported that Washington also had delusions of coopting Iraq into an Arab-Israeli peace settlement. In 1984, Donald Rumsfeld went to Baghdad to stress American support for the Iraqi war effort. Alexander Cockburn reported in *The Nation* that Rumsfeld said nothing about Saddam's use of mustard gas (imported from Western companies) against the Iranians and their Iraqi Kurdish and Shiite allies – despite the State Department's condemnation of the action. In 1988 the White House was still ascribing the notorious Halabjah gas attack to Iran, according to an analysis by Jon Anderson in *The New Yorker*.

During the Iraq-Iran War, a pattern of aggressive Iranian tactics against Saudi and Kuwaiti tankers, Iraqi counterattacks against Iranian tankers, and trench warfare on the Faw Peninsula had evolved by 1986 into a war of attrition that drew in American forces – to the point of putting American flags on Arab tankers, seconding Air Force officers to Iraqi units, and destroying most of Iran's navy and offshore oilfields.

141

By 1988, Juan Cole reports, America was blinding Iranian radar, providing Iraq with valuable intelligence on Iranian deployments, and according Iraq billions of dollars in credits. According to *Middle East Report*, in 1989 Bush 41 issued a secret national security directive authorizing the export of arms to Iraq.

On July 25, 1990, US Ambassador April Glaspie was called into an unexpected meeting with Saddam. She was an accomplished diplomat and a fluent Arabist, but on this tragic occasion two alien political systems were talking past each other. The public record does not suggest that the ambassador or her superiors in Washington appreciated that, once again, Saddam was going for broke.

When he complained that overproduction by the Gulf oil states was damaging Iraq's economy (already known to have been crippled by the war with Iran), the Americans seem to have inferred a possible intent to make a minor unilateral adjustment in Iraq's frontier with Kuwait. Preoccupied with their campaign to curb Islamist Iran, they apparently assumed that Saddam would continue to appreciate Washington's red lines. Saddam, after eight years of uncritical American support for Iraq against Iran, seems to have misread the importance of tiny Kuwait in Washington's vision of the Middle East. According to one report, Saddam went so far as to tell Glaspie the United States could not risk the loss of 10,000 soldiers' lives in the Middle East.

Glaspie's instructions did not authorize her to tell Saddam the US would repel an Iraqi invasion by force. The day before her meeting with Saddam, a State Department spokesman had told the press the US had made no defense commitments to Kuwait: *With Friends Like These*, Bruce Jentleson.

Iraq took Kuwait in a few hours, and America – after a few days of indecision – initiated a highly successful campaign to form an international coalition to go to Kuwait's rescue. The risks of deeper involvement in the Middle Eastern morass were outweighed by counter-considerations: 1) Bush 41 feared that an Iraq-Kuwait state would join Saudi Arabia as a powerful swing producer of oil. 2) Queen Noor of Jordan wrote in *Leap of Faith* that Bush told King Husayn he would not let a little dictator control a quarter of the world's oil. 3) Washington liked Middle Eastern frontiers the way they were, and particularly hated to see them altered by aggression.

By September of 1990, Washington had become so committed to armed intervention that, according to *The Christian Science Monitor*, it was issuing false allegations of Iraq's having massed troops on the Saudi border. Scott Silliman theorized that Washington saw to it that UNSC condemnations of the Iraqi invasion made no mention of Article 51 of the UN Charter in order to maximize American control of the countermeasures.

<u>1990 – US to the Rescue</u> – After a few days of commendable quandary ("Don't go all wobbly, George" was Margaret Thatcher's advice), Bush 41 assumed primary American responsibility for saving Kuwait, and building a coalition to this end. The skilled and energetic architect was Secretary of State James Baker. Saudi Arabia, ideally situated, and alarmed by the threat that Arab Nationalist Baathism posed to traditional Arab monarchy, invited US troops to stage their attack from Saudi territory, under the misimpression that the American forces would go home as soon as Kuwait had been freed.

Bush froze Iraqi and Kuwaiti assets in the US, banned most imports from Iraq, and authorized the CIA to work for the overthrow of Saddam: *The Commanders*, Robert Woodward. To justify Western intervention, which passed Congress by a close vote, the Bush administration looked for a cause that would ring the bell of public opinion. After "oil" and "aggression" didn't hack it, they settled on "elimination of Iraq's nuclear threat".

US Air Action

1991 – Intensive American bombing of Iraqi targets began January 17. Over the next six weeks, the US destroyed more Iraqi infrastructure than Iran had destroyed in eight years (Charles Tripp) – and in later years the US would spend billions to repair its own damage. The American barrage originated from Prince Sultan Air Base in Saudi Arabia, four seaports on the Gulf, three seaports on the Red Sea, and warships in the Gulf, the Red Sea, and the Mediterranean. Many hundreds of Iraqi civilians were "collateral" victims: Sciolino.

143

The Iraqi Air Force was not deployed. Saddam sent many of his fighter planes to safety in Iran – abruptly promoted from enemy to ally. Saddam's only hope was to lure Saudi Arabia's ground forces into battle – an objective reportedly shared by the Islamic State in 2015. The Royal Family, congenitally suspicious of its forces' loyalty, had never sent them abroad in force. On 1/29/91, after shelling of Saudi positions and oil storage tanks had failed to provoke reaction, Iraqi ground forces invaded Al Khafji, a town just south of the Kuwaiti-Saudi border. This salient was repelled by Saudi National Guardsmen and Qatari tank units, with support from coalition aircraft and US artillery. Iraq's only noteworthy action in the air was the firing by night, from mobile launchers in the Iraqi desert, of 88 Scud missiles – 47 against Saudi Arabia, 1 each against Bahrain and Qatar, the rest against Israel. One Scud hit a barracks in Dhahran, killing 28 American soldiers, wounding 100.

1991 – On 2/13/91, an American bunker-buster hit the Amiriyyah bomb shelter in Baghdad, killing 408 Iraqi civilians. Most of them burned to death. When called to account, the Pentagon mistakenly claimed the target had been an Iraqi command-and-control center: *Times*, 2/17/16.

1991 – American hyper-initiative in Iraq first raised its ugly head on 2/15/91, when Voice of America Radio carried a Bush 41 speech that genteelly called on the Iraqi people to "force Saddam to step aside". On 2/24/91 the CIA's Voice of Free Iraq radio urged Iraqis to rise up against Saddam.

Liberation

1991 – On February 24, the US launched a ground war from Saudi Arabia. Marines conceded to Saudis the honor of being first to enter the Kuwaiti capital: Sciolino. Four days later, Washington proclaimed victory. Saddam ordered evacuation of Kuwait 2/28/91 – the same day he began to put down the Shiite and Kurdish insurrections at home. With British, French, and Saudi help, 500,000 US troops had monopolized the liberation effort. Total coalition strength was 700,000.

1991 – On 2/28/91, a retreating Shiite (?) tank unit shot out one of the giant roadside pictures of Saddam: Mackey. It was the first shot in a mass Shiite rebellion to convert Iraq to a real republic. It was sparked by members of the Islamic Call (Al Da'wah) and the Supreme Council for the Islamic Revolution in Iraq (SCIRI, later ISCI – Islamic Supreme Council in Iraq) who had been lying low in Iraq and Iran. Their way of rising up was to kill every Baathist official in sight.

1991 – A chastened Bush, while maintaining he had never sought the overthrow of Saddam, tried to salvage the situation Washington had created. In March, he established a No-Fly Zone that banned Iraqi helicopters above the 36th parallel (Al Mawsil and north). UNSC Resolutions 687 (4/3/91) and 688 were cited as authority. Dilip Hiro contended that citation of 688 was groundless because it did not refer to Chapter VII of the UN Charter.

1991 – On 4/3/91, the series of UNSC pronouncements on the Gulf crisis culminated in UNSC Resolution 687, which conditioned the ceasefire on Iraq's elimination of any program to develop nuclear weapons, its dismantling of long-range missiles, its acceptance of UN demarcation of the Iraq-Kuwait border, its payment of compensation for war damage, and its return of looted Kuwaiti property and Kuwaiti POW's. Resolution 687 contained no enforcement mechanism, but the US was happy to oblige. In those days, aside from five-state veto power, "UNSC" tended to be synonymous with "US". In some cases, US initiative went far beyond that of the UNSC – as in American implementation of 687's vague allusion to "further steps as may be required". Examples: The institution of the "No-Fly Zones", the gratuitous American air attacks of 1998, and the unconscionable invasion of 2003.

1991 – In northern Iraq, the two Kurdish factions, KDP and PUK, buried their longtime feud in their own uprising.

1991 – Having lost control of 14 of Iraq's 18 provinces, Saddam reacted to the two simultaneous rebellions with brutality equal to theirs. On his side, Saddam had the Sunni minority, confirmed in their historic rule over Iraq – with one Persian interruption in the 1600's – ever since the Ottoman conquest of the country in 1534. Against the impassioned Shiite majority, Saddam had a subservient military (as Bashar al Asad and 'Abd al Fattah al Sisi have in Damascus and Egypt today). In Iraq of 1991, half the elite Republican Guard (mostly Sunni) had not been

145

touched by the American onslaught. The terms of the UNSC ceasefire banned Iraqi use of fixed-wing aircraft, but helicopters sufficed to control insurrection. The Iraq-based forces of the Iranian insurgent MEK supported Saddam's campaign of repression. Baathist rule was restored countrywide by early April. One hundred thousand insurgents, more or less, had been eliminated by gunfire, chemical ordnance, torture, execution, or being burned alive. Two million Kurds had fled to Turkey and Iran: *NY*, 9/19/14, Dexter Filkins.

1991 – Under UNSC 687, Iraq was fined billions in war reparations: Sciolino. Legality aside, a major unintended consequence of the American deployment into the northern sector, after its evacuation by Iraqi forces in October 1991 (Filkins), was the emergence of an autonomous Kurdish entity that by 2014 seemed bent on a unilateral declaration of independence when circumstance permitted. According to Dexter Filkins, the Iraqi Kurds outmaneuvered the American proconsuls in Baghdad by averting disbandment of their militia, the Peshmerga.

1991 – In the south, the ongoing persecution of Shiites moved Bush on 8/22/91 to institute a second No-Fly Zone barring the regime from sending helicopters south of the 32nd parallel (south of Al Najaf). The southern zone was policed by planes based on Bahrain, and as of April 2003 from the new CENTCOM command center at Al 'Udayd Air Base in Qatar. British and French aircraft helped in the defense of both zones until France ended its patrols of the southern zone in 1998 in protest of Clinton's air strikes on Iraq. Bush withheld full support from the Shia, out of suspicion of Iranian intentions. He had no thought of occupying Baghdad. The coalition had no mandate to do so. The Arab members of the coalition opposed any action that could lead to a Shiite takeover of Iraq.

1996 – The Southern No-Fly Zone was extended north, from the 32nd parallel to the 33rd (north of Karbala'). Citing Resolution 688, America bombarded Iraqi air defenses with cruise missiles in reprisal for Iraq's sending troops into the Northern Zone in support of the anti-Turk Kurdish faction, the PKK. The Senate endorsed the action with one opposing vote.

146

Immediate Consequences of the Kuwait Wars

Kuwait – In 1991, soundly defeated by the American forces and selected allies, bankrupt Iraq abrogated its claim of annexation of Kuwait, promised to pay compensation for damage done there, suffered a small but painful alteration of its southern frontier, and accepted stiff UNSC terms for a ceasefire – including scrapping all weapons of mass destruction. In 1994, in an effort to escape UN sanctions, Iraq formally recognized the independence of Kuwait.

Casualties – Iraq: Military deaths – 20,000 (?). Civilian deaths from bombing – 3500. Civilian deaths from collapse of the water, sewer, and public health systems – 100,000 (?). Kuwait: deaths – over 3000. US: deaths – 266 from all causes. (Iraq did not use chemical weapons. Reasons unknown.) Possible ill effects to American soldiers from exposure to depleted uranium in US munitions are reportedly still under study.

Costs – Total expense of the coalition – 61 billion dollars, of which 36 billion was paid by Saudi Arabia, 16 billion by other Arab states, 9 billion by the US.

Ecological Damage – On their way out of Kuwait, the Iraqi forces ignited or mined 600 of Kuwait's 950 oil wells, and dumped 400 million gallons of crude oil into the Gulf. The fires were extinguished by November 1991. As most dictators do, Saddam subordinated his country's welfare to his own caprice: To eliminate Shiite insurgents hiding out in the Qurnah Marshes, he had them drained. By November 1993, 7500 square miles of the Marsh Arabs' ancestral home had been converted to desert. Restoration is still underway.

1994-? – Palestinian Power Struggle

1979 – Ayatollah Khomeini, new ruler of Iran, acclaimed the Palestinian cause, but his ardor was cooled by PLO support for the Iraqi side in the Iraq-Iran War, and by the PLO's acceptance of the devious Oslo Accord of 1993. Iran and Syria then adopted the cause of Hamas, which welcomed their support, even through Syria's massacre of MB supporters in 1982. The link was severed when Hamas sided with the Sunnis in the Syrian civil war that broke out in 2011: *MEP*, Spring 2016, Ora Szekely.

1991-2 – Rivalry between Fatah and Hamas escalated into armed clashes, mainly in Nabulus: Jonathan Schanzer.

1993-94 – Isolated in Tunisia after the expulsion of the PLO from Lebanon, 'Arafat was alarmed by the emergence of rival PRM factions back in Palestine. After 25 years, 'Arafat got back there himself by buying into Israel's tricky Oslo process. Hamas had condemned it as sacrilege.

1993 – 'Imad 'Aqal, 23, founder of Hamas's 'Izz al Din Qassam Brigades, died in a shootout at an IDF checkpoint in Gaza: *AP*, 11/25/93.

1994 – 'Arafat set out to rebuild his power base in Occupied Palestine (the West Bank and Gaza). Foreign contributions and repatriation of private funds had sparked a building boom.

1994 – In November, clashes in Gaza between the PA (Fatah) and Islamists (Hamas) left 16 dead, 200 wounded: Schanzer.

1996 – In March, PA security forces backed by Israel and the CIA took control of Gaza and jailed hundreds of members of Hamas.

1996 – Fatah won the 9/20/96 elections for President ('Arafat) and legislature of the PA. Hamas boycotted them.

1999 – Hamas launched attacks on Israelis in Jerusalem and the West Bank during the summer.

2000-2001 – During the first year of Intifadah II, Fatah and Hamas joined forces against Israel: Schanzer.

2001 – Status of Palestinian residents: Jordan – most Palestinian immigrants were Jordanian citizens; Syria – most had travel permission, but none had a passport; Lebanon – all were stateless, unwelcomed by the government, and largely excluded from the professions; Occupied Palestine – some had Jordanian papers, some had PA papers: *MEP*, September 2001, Peter Gubser.

2001 – October marked the resumption of armed conflict between Fatah and Hamas. Five dead.

2003 – On 6/29/03, Hamas, Islamic Jihad, and Fatah agreed on a three-month ceasefire.

2006 – On 1/25/06, Hamas swept the election of the second Palestinian Legislative Council (PLC) of the Palestinian Authority (PA). Hamas owed its surprise victory to its effective social security system, to Fatah misrule, to a split in Fatah between an old guard that favored Mahmud 'Abbas and a young guard that favored Marwan Barghuti (long in Israeli prison), and to Fatah's quisling ties with the Israeli-American diarchy: *JPS*, Graham Usher; *Current History*, December 2007, Glenn Robinson. Perhaps word got out of the 2 million dollars the CIA reportedly donated to Fatah's campaign fund.

2006 – A post-election government of "national unity" broke down in military conflict.

2006 – The electoral contretemps soured Washington on democracy as a remedy for Arab "terrorism". The friends of Israel froze financial aid to the PA, and urged banks to avoid dealing with Hamas. The US sent more arms to Fatah.

2006 – In April Hamas formed a new Gazan government under Prime Minister Isma'il Haniyah.

149

2006 – September and October featured fierce clashes between Fatah and Hamas. Fatah/PA was advocating the two-state solution. Israel and Hamas opposed it with equal resolve. The presumed Palestine state would unite two noncontiguous remnants of Palestine: the West Bank (2263 square miles) and Gaza (139 square miles).

2007 – On 2/8/07, under the chairmanship of Saudi King 'Abdallah, the PA, Hamas, and representatives of interested Arab states approved the Mecca Agreement, which called for PA and Hamas to participate in a national unity government, with a cabinet of 15 ministers – nine from Hamas, six from Fatah. The proposal evaporated in June, but it was kept alive long enough to torpedo an American effort to disband Hamas: *FA*, David Ottaway; *Times*, 12/11/07.

2007 – In clashes from January 2006 to May 2007 between Fatah and Hamas, some 600 Palestinian militants died: *Times*, 5/21/14.

2007 – **Hamas Takes Over in Gaza** – On 6/10/07, the clashes resumed. On 6/17/07 a Hamas unit threw a Fatah officer off an 18-story building. Days later, a Fatah unit retaliated in kind. By the end of the month, Gaza was under Hamas control. Total Hamas and Fatah casualties in June: Dead – 118; wounded – 550.

2007 – Hamas's ransacking of Fatah's office in Gaza had led to discovery of documentary confirmation of Fatah collaboration with the CIA, including the targeting of Palestinian Islamists for assassination: *The Wall Street Journal*. The effort by Fatah's Muhammad Dahlan to deploy his CIA-armed and CIA-trained forces for the takeover of Gaza had been overwhelmed by the forces of Hamas. 'Abbas later exiled Dahlan for his defeat in Gaza: *FA*, July 2015, Grant Rumley/Amir Tibon; *Times*, 3/14/14.

On the West Bank, by truckling to their Israeli and American patrons, the principals of Fatah (Mahmud 'Abbas and Salam Fayyad) managed to preserve the pretense of autonomy. If the US and Saudi Arabia had not been arming Fatah, and Israel had not been piling up pro-Hamas West Bankers in prison, Hamas might have established underground control of the West Bank as well as Gaza. Either way, after sixty years of blatant favoritism in Washington for the Israeli cause, the proposition that Washington was ready to protect Palestine from relentless Israeli expansionism was hard to sell, and unity between the realistic leadership of Hamas and the housebroken leadership of the Palestinian Authority was out of the question – until the pressures of Israeli-American persecution of the Gazans had driven Hamas to the breaking point, when its only recourse lay in appeal to its disdained rival.

2007 – Since the definitive split between Hamas and Fatah, the Palestinian Legislature had been defunct: *Times*, 3/18/16.

2008-2012 – There was no radical change in the relative situation of the two rival organizations during these seven years. The ideological fragmentation of the Palestinian resistance "movement" was manifest at funerals in the simultaneous display of the yellow flag of Fatah, the green flag of Hamas, the black flag of Islamic Jihad, and the red flag of the PFLP – but no Palestinian flag.

All these factions split much more sharply over the fundamental issue of strategy. Mahmud 'Abbas's Fatah took the easier route of a loyal opposition faction. In return for colluding with the strong Israeli interest in maintaining essential law and order in the West Bank, they received adequate subsidies from Israel and its allies, while clinging to the hope that the glacial process of Israeli democratization would show results before the appeasers were disgraced as traitors.

The antithesis to Sunni Fatah was Shiite Hizballah, whose mountain retreat and Iran's dedicated patronage had twice enabled it to stand up to the IDF. Neither Hizballah's advantages of geography nor Fatah's advantages of cutting ideological corners accrued to stolid Hamas, which had taken on the grim responsibility for defending Gaza, Israel's 140-square-mile shooting gallery. Hamas's defenses were international empathy and doctrinal determination. Israel's advantage was that it held the whip hand.

Hamas's only achievement was, in the words of Husayn Ibish on 7/8/14, to project the image of indomitability, leaving Fatah to set renown aside and accept the oppressor's coin by helping round up his victims.

2008 – Early in the year, the 'Abbas administration was little more than a shell kept in place by the IDF; one of 'Abbas's officials went so far as to hint that an Israeli raid into Gaza might help. *The New York*

Times reported that the 'Abbas faction of the Palestinian Authority was paying salaries to its employees in Gaza, but that territory was under the stricter and more decisive control of Hamas – despite occasional clashes with pro-Fatah hold-outs. By summer, Hamas was arresting and abusing Fatah activists in Gaza, and Fatah was reciprocating on the West Bank. In Jerusalem an American military mission was trying to solidify 'Abbas's regime by training a presidential guard: *Post*, Jackson Diehl.

2008 – The PA was still paying the salaries of its 80,000 employees in Gaza, but the stricter Hamas was in control. Gaza was receiving some 70 truckloads a day of staples via Israel, and an appreciable amount of goods were being smuggled in by tunnel from Egypt. Hamas was taxing all imports: *Times*, 6/15/08.

2009 – More disciplined than Fatah, Hamas continued to maintain law and order, and license traffic to Egypt through hundreds of tunnels; Gaza's Bank of Palestine was electronically linked with the Nablus, Cairo, and Dubai stock markets: *Times*, 10/22/09; *LRB*, 10/22/09, Nicholas Pelham; *NYR*, 11/5/09, Max Rodenbeck. Washington continued to parrot the Israeli position that dialogue with Hamas was rejected until Hamas renounced violence and recognized Israel. In other words, Washington endorsed Israeli violence in violation of international law, but denounced violence on the part of the victims.

2009 – By November Hamas was maintaining law and order in Gaza, and controlling the tunnels (1000) by a system of licensing. Rocket fire into Israel from Gaza was subsiding. The regime's major handicap was the Gazans' grinding poverty: *NYR*, 11/5/09.

2009 – The failure of Hamas to appeal to the ICC for a ruling against Israeli offenses had moved some Gazans to form a rival Salafi group. In 2009, a clash between them caused 29 deaths: *NYR*, 1/14/16.

2010 – Hamas alleged that former Fatah officials Ahmad Hasanayn and Anwar Shekhaiber had participated in the 1/19/10 killing of Mahmud Mabhuh by Mossad.

2010 – Mahmud 'Abbas, whose Presidency had been scheduled to expire in February 2009, was still in office. His position was precarious: The members of the PLO Central Committee who had appointed him were his appointees. He was still committed to the moribund two-state solution.

2012 – Muhammad Bali', Supreme Leader of the Muslim Brotherhood, had ruled out peace with Israel, but Egypt's new President, Muhammad Mursi, had arranged the abrupt 11/22 ceasefire between Israel and Hamas. Hamas rode higher in international circles when a member of the Muslim Brothers was President of Egypt: *FT*, 11/23/12. Nevertheless, Hamas was on its last legs. There was a severe shortage of fuel. Over 90 percent of Gaza's aquifer was contaminated.

2012 – Most members of the Hamas politbureau operated in secret – an elementary precaution against assassination. For some years, the head of the politbureau had found refuge under the auspices of the Asad regime in Damascus. By 2012, Sunni Hamas's sympathy for the Syrian anti-Alawite insurgency ruled Damascus out as a refuge. Musa Abu Marzuq moved to Egypt. His successor, Khalid Mish'al, settled in Doha, Qatar. On 12/7/12, Mish'al made his first ever visit to Gaza, spoke at the homes of Hamas martyrs Ahmad al Ja'abiri and Shaykh Ahmad al Yasin, and met with Gazan Prime Minister Isma'il Haniyah: *Times*, 1/22/12, 1/28/12, 12/6/12, 12/7/12.

2013 – In April, Khalid al Mish'al was reelected head of Hamas's political bureau: *MEP*, Fall 2013.

2013 – In June, Rami Hamdallah took over as the Prime Minister of the PA: *Times*, 5/21/14.

2013 – Egypt destroyed most of Gaza's tunnels into Egypt, and in August stopped passage between Egypt and Gaza.

2014 – Whereas subsidy from the US and Israel was enabling the PA to pay its employees in the West Bank and Gaza, Hamas had lost its two major contributors, Saudi Arabia and Qatar, and its tunnel revenues had been cut off: *WRMEA*, March 2014.

2014 – Penniless Hamas had to succumb to the irony of inviting an all-PA government to assume nominal rule of Gaza per an accord of 4/23/14. 'Abbas was even allowed to assign several thousand PA security police to patrolling in Gaza. The provision in the 4/23/14 accord for the PA to pay Hamas's civil service was not implemented. In the West Bank, Arabs looked on sourly as PA police helped Israel round up Hamas sympathizers: *LRB*, 8/21/14, Nathan Thrall.

2014 – In reaction to the encroachment of Israeli settlements into territory claimed by the PRM, and Israeli refusal to release Palestinian prisoners, the PA was angling for UN support for Palestinian autonomy. The PA was proposing union with Hamas in Gaza: *FT*, 5/28/14.

2014 – The European Union was giving substantial financial aid to the PA: *Times*, 5/30/14.

2014 – The PA stopped paying the salaries of PA employees in Gaza. The 48,000 employees of Hamas had not been paid in months. PA Prime Minister Fayyad had become nominal head of a Gazan "cabinet" he had not chosen, but he had no power in Gaza. The Gazan cabinet's expenses were supposed to be met by world powers, including the US: *Times*, 6/24/14.

2014 – Gaza's border with Israel had been kept nearly shut since 2008, its border with Egypt since 2013. Unemployment in Gaza was about 50 percent: *Times*, 7/23/14, Anne Barnard.

2014 – Hamas's only visible recourse was to throw itself on the mercy of the PA, but Israel defeated that strategy by blocking any PA payment of the salaries of Hamas's civil servants: *NYR*, 9/25/14.

2015 – Since January, Israel had been withholding transfer of 127 million dollars per month in taxes collected on behalf of the Palestinian Authority. Motive: Retaliation for the PA's exercise of its right to communicate with the International Criminal Court (ICC).

2015 – On 4/1/15, Palestine became a member of the International Computer Network.

2015 – Gazans were beginning to look for some way to leave, on the grounds that they had no future in Gaza. Without access to a proper lifestyle or even to an education, a whole generation was being passed over: *MEP*, Summer 2015, report of a symposium held 4/21/15: Sara Roy. (Of course evacuation of every Arab resident of Gaza would be Israel's ideal solution.)

2015 – 'Abbas dissolved the Palestinian Government of National Consensus: *WRMEA*, August 2015, Mohammed Omer.

2015 – Hamas defeated Fatah in student elections at Bir Zayt University. (Hamas allowed no student elections in Gaza: *Times*, 5/2/15.)

2015 – In reaction to pro-IS (Islamic State) disturbances in Gaza, Hamas began to issue condemnations of Salafi doctrine: *Times*, 6/3/15.

2015 – Hamas forces cracked down on Islamic State supporters in Gaza on 6/30/15: *NYR*, 1/14/16.

2015 – In support of the volunteer activists in the West Bank, Hamas leader Isma'il Haniyah proclaimed a new Intifadah: *FT*, 10/10/15.

2016 – Municipal elections scheduled by the Palestinians in the West Bank and Gaza were cancelled – probably because the PA suspected Hamas would win big: *LRB*, 10/6/16, Mendel.

2001-? – US-Taliban War

The American response to Al Qa'idah's attacks of 9/11/01 was a disastrous overreaction – three unnecessary wars: invasion of Afghanistan; invasion of Iraq; "war against terrorism" – a multi-arena campaign against jihadist organizations. The war against Afghanistan had no justification, since the Taliban faction that happened to be in power on 9/11/01 had no known connection with Al Qa'idah's attacks, and no known advance knowledge of their planning.

The history of isolated Afghanistan's interaction with the Middle East should have been one of the shorter chapters. However, in the late 1900's it became the temporary refuge of Al Qa'idah, an Arab organization that was blazing new trails in the evolution of international subversion – particularly against the United States. This accidental constellation of circumstances was all it took for Washington to blunder into the longest conventional overseas war in its history. The following chronology (up to 2001) comes from *Encyclopaedia Britannica*, *The World Almanac* for 2016, *The 9/11 Commission Report* (undated), and *Foreign Policy*, May/June 2015, Yochi Dreazan and Stan Naylor.

1978 – On 4/27/78, a pro-Soviet coup produced the Democratic Republic of Afghanistan. In the subsequent violence, US Ambassador Adolph Dubs was killed on 2/14/79.

1979 – From 12/24/79, at Afghan request, Soviet troops occupied Afghanistan. Ten years of civil war ensued between a regime in Kabul that had Soviet support, and anti-Soviet mujahideen, including Arab

156

volunteers. The Arab mujahideen received financing from the Saudi Arabian government and private Saudi sources, and from the CIA via Pakistan's ISI (Inter-Services Intelligence). Afghan casualties over the ten-year period were reported to exceed one million.

1979 – President Carter added Afghanistan to the list of countries (Somalia, Ethiopia, Angola) where the United States was engaged in proxy wars against the Soviet Union. Washington authorized 500 million dollars for nonlethal aid to the mujahideen fighting the puppet regime in Kabul. Carter saw the Soviet intervention in Afghanistan as a bid for hegemony over the Persian Gulf.

1980's – During the Soviet-Afghan War, Pakistani President Mohammed Zia ul-Haq received financing from Saudi Arabia and the US. Zia instructed the ISI to train Afghan resistance fighters in west Pakistan.

1986 – Mohammed Najibullah, pro-Soviet, came to power in Kabul on 5/4/86, and was elected president in November 1987.

1988 – In April, the Soviet Union gave up its losing effort in Afghanistan and signed peace accords with Afghanistan and Pakistan.

1989 – By 2/15/89, the Soviet Union had completed the withdrawal of its troops, leaving the new Al Qa'idah with a battle-hardened paramilitary force, but no convenient enemy.

1990 – An anti-Communist regime was bidding to take over in Kabul, but the country was dissolving into civil war.

1991 – Islamist schools for Afghan refugees in Pakistan were giving rise in the Peshawar area to an obscurantist Salafi political movement known as the Taliban (students). Based on the community of forty million Pashtuns living on both sides of the Afghan-Pakistani border, the original Taliban gradually split into two separate organizations, each retaining the name, but adopting separate hierarchies and strategies. (Hereafter, the two are distinguished as "Afghan Taliban" and "Pakistani Taliban".) The Afghan Taliban took root in its own enclave in Afghanistan.

1992 – In April the rebels stormed Kabul, and Najibullah was ousted. Iran, Saudi Arabia, and Pakistan chose sides among the various factions fighting a multifarious civil war.

1994 – The Afghan Taliban, led by village mullah Muhammed Omar, conquered 12 Afghan Provinces, briefly including Kabul. From 1994 to 1999, there was heavy intermittent fighting across the northern Pak-Afghan border between the "Communist" but pro-Western Northern Alliance led by Ahmad Shah Massoud, and forces of Pakistan and the Pakistani Taliban.

1994-6 – The US backed the Afghan Taliban on the captious grounds that they were anti-Shia.

1996 – Under the grim leadership of Mullah Omar, the Afghan Taliban resorted to scorched-earth tactics and massacre against the forces of the government in Kabul and its NATO allies. Mullah Omar knew how to fight: His record was burnished by a story that, wounded in the face, he stayed in the battle, undismayed by the eye dangling from its connective tissue.

Kabul Falls to the Taliban

1996 – In September, the Afghan Taliban took Kabul. On 9/27/96, the Afghan Taliban founded The Islamic Emirate of Afghanistan with Mullah Omar as the Emir: *Times*. It was recognized by Pakistan, Saudi Arabia, and the UAE. The Afghan Taliban and its emirate had ISI support before and after the US invasion of 2001.

1998 – The Afghan Taliban won a key battle against forces of the Northern Alliance.

1998 – The US asked the Afghan regime to extradite bin Ladin. Mullah Omar stalled.

1998 – The Afghan Taliban's primacy in Kabul brought to world attention their zealotry – strict fundamentalist doctrine, discrimination against women, and reliance on massacre.

1999 – In retaliation for the failure of the Afghan Taliban in Kabul to extradite bin Ladin, Washington had the UNSC impose sanctions on the Kabul regime on 11/14/99.

2000 – On 12/19/00, the UNSC again acted on behalf of the US with Resolution 1333, which endorsed the freezing of the Afghan Taliban's overseas assets, and embargoed the provision of arms to them.

Arms continued to reach them from Pakistan, over which the US had already used up its leverage by outlawing political and economic assistance on the grounds that Pakistan's current leader, Pervez Musharraf, had come to power by military coup, and Pakistan had gone nuclear in violation of the anti-proliferation treaty. (No such penalty for Israel.)

2001 – The Taliban were not known to be privy to the 9/11 conspiracy. In general, they were understandably opposed to Al Qa'idah attacks on the US for fear of US retaliation. However, they were too dependent on Al Qa'idah, financially and politically, to exert harsh discipline. Case in point: suggestions that Al Qa'idah was implicated in the 9/9/01 assassination of Northern Alliance leader Ahmad Shah Massoud, a committed enemy of the Afghan Taliban.

2001 – On 9/20/01, in a speech to Congress, Bush 43 proclaimed a five-point ultimatum to the Afghan Taliban, demanding inter alia the closure of terrorist training camps and the delivery of all Al Qa'idah leaders to US authorities. Mullah Omar asked for proof of the US charges. Secretary of State Powell asked Saudi Arabia and the UAE to break relations with the Afghan Taliban regime in Kabul. America's blood was up. Bush's public approval rating had risen to 90 percent. Congress voted Bush broad powers to confront terrorism.

2001 – On 10/7/01, Hamid Karzai entered Afghanistan from Pakistan. The CIA had spirited Karzai from Afghanistan to Pakistan during the Soviet-Afghan War, then back to Afghanistan as the best hope of a leader who would stand up to the Taliban: *NYTBR*, 2/5/15.

Invasion

2001 – The allied invasion of Afghanistan began on 10/7/01 with US and British air attacks on Taliban and Al Qa'idah targets. The Afghan civil war resumed.

2001 – Writing in *Middle East Policy* of Winter, 2014-15, Dennis Jett asserted that the regime established in Kabul by the Taliban in September 1996 had practiced terrorism, as defined by the US State Department, but Washington had chosen not to proclaim the Kabul regime as a terrorist state because of embarrassment over its evolution from a militant movement that had enjoyed US support.

2001 – On 11/13/01, with US air support, the CIA-funded Northern Alliance headed a coalition that ousted the Afghan Taliban regime from Kabul. The defeated forces took refuge in Pakistan, as did most of Al Qa'idah's forces. Some of its leaders were thought to be hiding out in the Tora Bora caves, close to the Pakistan border, but the allied forces found the caves empty. Bin Ladin had taken refuge in Pakistan with his staff, except for Muhammad 'Atif, who was killed in Kabul 11/15/01.

2001 – The Afghan Islamists were welcomed by the Pakistani Islamists: *Times*, 12/17/14.

2001 – On 12/5/01, four anti-Taliban factions concluded an agreement naming Hamid Karzai, a Pashtun tribal leader of the Sunni faith, as chairman of an Interim Administration of Afghanistan. (Pronunciation of Hamid: ham plus id.) Also on 12/5/01, Karzai and others were wounded by friendly fire from US Air Force planes, and were sent to the US for therapy.

2001 – On 12/7/01, the Afghan Taliban lost their last major foothold in Afghanistan with the fall of Kandahar to the Northern Alliance.

2001 – UNSC Resolution 1386 of 12/20/01 authorized the establishment of an International Security Assistance Force (ISAF) to assist an Afghan Interim Authority (AIA) in the maintenance of security in Kabul "and its surrounding areas", under initial British command. The ISAF was to be manned by soldiers from 46 countries – half of them from the US.

2001 – On 12/22/01, Karzai was sworn in as leader of the AIA. (See previous entry.)

2002-4 – Reports were coming in of beheadings in Pakistan by Islamist militias: *FP*, November 2014.

NATO Intervenes in Kabul

2003 – On 8/11/03, NATO assumed control of the ISAF in Kabul. Half the NATO troops were to be under direct US command.

2004 – On 12/7/04 Hamid Karzai was installed as the elected President of Afghanistan – a tribal state mislabeled a democracy. Afghan girls went back to school.

2006 – In June, NATO assumed responsibility for the security of Afghanistan.

2006 – The tribal area known as Waziristan, along the Afghan border of Pakistan, was the base of the Pakistani Taliban, and a haven for Al Qa'idah refugees from Afghanistan. In February 2006, partisans in north Waziristan proclaimed an Islamic state. On 9/5/06, the Pakistani government acknowledged the tribal organization, but not the state. The leader of the organization was Maulavi Jalaluddin Haqqani, former anti-Soviet fighter supported by the US. In 2001, he had been commander of the Afghan Taliban against the Karzai regime, and secret ally of ISI.

2006 – The US and the Afghan Taliban were conducting wars of assassination against each other's Afghan allies.

2007 – In February, a number of Islamist militant groups in Waziristan united under the leadership of Baitullah Mehsud as the Tehrik-i-Pakistan – bitterly hostile to the Government of Pakistan – later on known as the Pakistani Taliban. In reaction, Pakistan set out in June to take military action against the "Talibanization" of Waziristan. The Afghan Taliban were at war with Kabul, but they ruled out hostilities with Pakistan.

2007 – After 9/11, Pakistani leader Musharraf had made the difficult decision to give US forces access to Afghanistan via Pakistan. He seemed to have adopted a policy of desperation – paradoxically sheltering the leaderships of the Afghan Taliban and Al Qa'idah in Pakistan as allies against India, but tolerating American efforts to destroy both. The Americans were inhibited from moving against Pakistan by their reliance on the Pakistani corridor to Afghanistan.

2007 – On 12/27/07, former Pakistani Prime Minister Benazir Bhutto, daughter of former Prime Minister Zulficar Ali Bhutto, was assassinated – reportedly by two of President Musharraf's police, and members of Baitullah Mehsud's Pakistani Taliban: *Times*, 12/17/14.

2009 – Pakistan went to war against the Pakistani Taliban in Waziristan. The *Times* reported that the CIA was taking out Al Qa'idah leaders in Pakistan with Predator drones, but that the vacancies were being filled by volunteers across the Muslim World, while the Taliban (both wings?) continued to derive guidance and inspiration from Al Qa'idah. *Middle East Policy* identified Al Qa'idah's new spokesman on the Internet as an American convert to Islam, Adam Gadahn.

2009 – On 8/5/09, Baitullah Mehsud was killed by a US drone. He was succeeded by his deputy, Hakimullah Mehsud.

2009 – Karzai was reelected President in October, despite his unpopularity stemming from corruption in his regime, including skimming of poppy profits, and from the ongoing civil war. Periodic arrivals of new US troops had brought the total in Afghanistan to 140,000. The increase was contrary to Obama's disengagement philosophy, but was probably a concession to the hawks in Congress.

2009 – New Pakistan President Asif Zardari admitted that Pakistan had mounted terrorist attacks against India, including ISI's direction of the Lashkar-e Taiba atrocity that killed 166 in Mumbai in 2008.

2010: In February, NATO troops on site launched an offensive against the Afghan insurgency. Pakistani support for the Afghan Taliban was being attenuated by political pressure from Washington.

2010 – The elections for a new Afghan Parliament in November were blighted by fraud, and by the hostility of the Afghan Taliban.

2011 – NATO forces continued their offensive against the Afghan Taliban and the Haqqani network in Waziristan.

2011 – In November Afghan tribal elders approved a ten-year Afghan-US accord.

2012 – In April, the Afghan Taliban staged an offensive against Kabul.

2012 – August was disrupted by a rash of attacks on NATO personnel by maverick Afghan police and soldiers.

2012 – On 10/9/12 an assassination attempt by the Pakistani Taliban failed against illustrious Pakistani teenager Malala Yousefzai, subsequently resident in Britain and the US.

2013 – In June, the Afghan army took over from NATO the responsibility for the defense of Afghanistan.

2013 – A *loya jirga* endorsed the continued deployment of some US troops after 1/1/15, the agreed date for withdrawal of US troops from Afghanistan.

2013 – In November, an American air strike killed Pakistani Taliban leader Hakimullah Mehsud: *Times*, 12/17/14. He was replaced by Maulana Fazlullah.

2014 – In January an Afghan Taliban suicide attack killed 13 foreigners in Kabul.

2014 – A siege of the Karachi airport on June 14 drew a major Pakistani ground attack against the Pakistani Taliban.

2014 – The June run-off election for President of Afghanistan between Ashraf Ghani and Abdullah Abdullah was massively fraudulent, according to European observers.

2014 – The Northern Alliance and the Karzai faction were sharing control of the Afghan government, which had granted the US permission to maintain 10,000 troops, subject only to US law, in Afghanistan after the UN mandate expired on 12/31/14: Internet, Eric Margolis. Whereas the Taliban regime had firmly reduced opium production, under the Karzai/US regime it was flourishing.

2014 – In September an agreement to share power in Afghanistan was reached between Ashraf Ghani (President) and Abdullah Abdullah (Chief Executive).

2014 – In October the US and the UK "ended combat operations" in Afghanistan.

2014 – In December, security forces were taking heavy losses in Helmand Province from an Afghan Taliban offensive: *Times*, 12/23/14.

2014 – Mullah Muhammed Omar, supposedly under cover in Karachi, had not been seen by the rest of the Afghan Taliban leadership in years. His deputy was Mullah Akhtar Muhammed Mansur: *Times*, 11/22/14, 12/29/14.

2014 – The Afghan Taliban were carrying out a barrage of attacks, bombings, and assassinations. The recent dead included 2 NATO personnel and 20 Afghans affiliated with the Kabul regime. The 10,000 American soldiers who were to stay on would defend against the operations of the Afghan Taliban, who since 2001 with Al Qa'idah help had killed 2200 US soldiers, 1300 NATO soldiers, and 4600 Afghans: *Post*.

2014 – America's longest conventional overseas conflict had cost a trillion dollars, and would cost several hundred billion more: *FT*, 12/15/14.

2014 – On 12/16/14, the Pakistani Taliban horrified most Pakistanis by staging an armed attack on a school in Peshawar that killed over 140 students and faculty: *Times*.

2014 – According to Pakistani officials, by 12/19/14 retaliatory raids by the armed forces had killed over 60 Pakistani Taliban militants. Their chief cleric, Maulana Abdul Aziz, and Hafiz Muhammed Saeed, head of Lashkar-e Taiba, were in disgrace for their perpetration of the Peshawar school massacre. Saeed, who had an American price of ten million dollars on his head, was a resident of Lahore, Pakistan: *Times*, 12/20/14.

2014 – On 12/20/14, an American drone killed a number of Pakistani Taliban militants: *Times*, 12/21/14.

2014 – For the first time since the US-Afghan War began, a majority of American poll respondents assessed it as a mistake. NATO forces were down to 13,000 in Afghanistan, and the Afghan Taliban were on the rise.

2015 – Formation of a new Afghan cabinet was blocked by dissension among Afghanistan's four ethnic groups and two political camps: *Times*, 1/21/15.

2015 – The US had spent 65 billion dollars on building the Afghan police and army, but had nothing to show for it but the resurgence of the Taliban forces: *Times*, 1/29/15. The corruption promoted by the seven Karzai brothers was winning new supporters for the Taliban: *Times*, 2/22/15, Sarah Chayes.

2015 – The new Afghan government readily signed an agreement allowing the US to maintain 10,000 troops in Afghanistan for an unspecified period, under American control. US planes were the only force keeping the Afghan Taliban at bay – and protecting the 500,000 acres of poppies that had financed the country since the Taliban were expelled from Kabul: Margolis online.

2015 – The death of Mullah Muhammed Omar in 2013 (?) was belatedly announced. Mullah Akhtar Mansur, who had been the only one with access to Mullah Muhammed's hideout, claimed to be his successor as leader of the Afghan Taliban. In the summer of 2015, Sirajuddin Haqqani was appointed the Deputy Leader of the Afghan Taliban, who had been declared terrorists by the State Department in 2012: *Times*, 5/8/16.

2015 – On 8/7/15, the Afghan Taliban staged a major raid on Kabul, including waves of suicide attacks.

2015 – On 8/22/15, a suicide attack on a NATO convoy killed ten soldiers, including three Americans: *AP*, 8/23/15.

2015 – There was a report of a power struggle for leadership of the Afghan Taliban between Mullah Akhtar and Mullah Mansur Dadullah: *Times*, 9/7/15.

2015 – General John Campbell, commander of US forces in Afghanistan, was working so closely with President Ashraf Ghani that he had been dubbed the Afghan Minister of Defense. The war against the Afghan Taliban was not going well: *Times*, 9/11/15.

2015 – In a distressing indicator for the Kabul regime, the Afghan Taliban captured the strategic city of Kunduz and held it for several days: *Times*, 9/28/15.

2015 – The US command in Afghanistan released the report of a misdirected US air attack that on 10/3/15 caused a number of deaths in an Afghan hospital: *Times*, 11/26/15.

2015 – Mullah Akhtar Muhammed Mansur had emerged as the dynamic leader of the Afghan Taliban. He was closely linked to Pakistan's ISI: *Times*, 10/5/15.

2015 – Obama announced a deferment in the departure schedule of US forces in Afghanistan. Some 10,000 would remain through 2016, and 5500 thereafter: *Times*, 10/15-16/15.

2015 – The Pakistani ISI was providing clandestine support to the Afghan Taliban, who were continuing to advance. The IS had established a foothold in Afghanistan: *FT*, Edward Luce.

2015 – The IS was recruiting in Afghanistan, offering a monthly wage that was attracting some of the Afghan Taliban's militants. US trainers in Afghanistan were being drawn into combat situations: *Times*, 10/14/15.

2015 – Kabul was a dying city. It was no longer safe for a foreigner to try to drive between the airport and the US Embassy: *Times*, 11/4/15.

2015 – The Afghan War was dragging on. For reasons unknown, Obama had backed away from earlier remarks about US disengagement. He had reportedly issued a secret order for expansion of the American force in Afghanistan.

2015 – The US invasion of Afghanistan was an ill-considered act of revenge (for the 9/11 attacks): *LRB*, Tariq Ali.

2015 – Pakistan was coddling the Afghan Taliban, and had helped Mullah Akhtar Muhammed Mansur maintain the fiction that Mullah Omar was alive – long after he had actually died. The objective was to facilitate Mansur's succession: *Dawn*, Cyril Almeida; *The Week*, 12/11/15.

2016 – The US stepped up its air campaign against Islamic State affiliates in Afghanistan by a factor of 3-1: *Times*, 3/19/16.

2016 – On May 21, a strike by a US drone killed Mullah Akhtar on the Iran-Pakistan border: *Time*, 6/6/16.

2016 – After the death of Mullah Akhtar, Mawlawi Haibatullah Akundzada was named his replacement. His Supreme Council was based in Quetta, Pakistan: *Times*, 7/12/16.

2016 – So far, the cost to the US of the US-Taliban War was over 800 billion dollars. It was a failed policy: *Times*, 9/19/16.

(Note: In South Asia, Islamic clerics are distinguished by honorifics – including *mullah*, *mawlawi*, *mawlani*, and *akhund*.)

166

2001-? – US-Jihadist War

―――――

Al Qa'idah's attacks of 9/11/01 demanded a response of equal import.

The US could have abandoned its habit of blatant interference in Middle East affairs, but the combative mood in Washington ruled out capitulation.

The US could have mounted a massive ground invasion of countries where jihadists were based, like Iraq and Syria, but most analysts would have pointed out that all-out war against a diminutive, clandestine cabal would be overkill. After Vietnam, the electorate would probably have exploded at the prospect of another imperialist war.

Washington's decision was compromise: a hole-and-corner exercise aimed at uprooting jihadist leaderships with no alarmist headlines and minimal risk of US casualties – kill them off from a safe distance by minimizing ground action and relying on ships, planes, and drones.

Timeline: 1980-2016 – Since 1980, the US had garrisoned the Middle East, and fought wars from bases in Pakistan, Afghanistan, Diego Garcia, the Seychelles, Djibouti, Egypt, and Bahrain. The Fifth Fleet included a carrier strike group.

2001 – On 9/11/01, civilian airliners hijacked by Al Qa'idah operatives destroyed the Twin Towers in New York City, did massive damage to the Pentagon in Arlington County, Virginia, and killed 2977 Americans. A furor of demented militarism perverted the American response. Although most of the operatives were Saudis, and none of them was involved in any official capacity, Washington hyper-escalated the episode into simultaneous wars against Afghanistan and Iraq – whose governments had no known connection with the attack. Congressional adoption of the Patriot Act of 10/26/01 strained the civil-rights provisions of the Constitution. The Defense Department and the CIA were hustled into a "war" of arbitrary assassinations and an open-ended drone campaign against a heterogeneous aggregation of Islamist jihadists (holy warriors) who felt vindicated by their election as the prime enemies of the superpower.

2001 – On 9/18/01, Congress adopted the Authorization for Use of Military Force (AUMF), empowering the President to employ necessary force against the planners of the 9/11/01 attacks, including assassination: *NYR*, 3/6/14, Mark Danner.

2001 – On 10/7/01, US and British jets attacked targets of Al Qaʻidah and the Afghan Taliban.

2001 – On 10/26/01, Bush signed the Patriot Act, a catchall document that had been adopted almost unanimously by both houses of Congress, and was meant to close loopholes that had obstructed intelligence agencies, and to promote their mutual cooperation. For Jean Edward Smith, author of *Bush*, the act may have been "the most ill-conceived piece of domestic legislation since the Alien and Sedition Acts of 1790": *Times*, 7/4/16, Peter Baker.

2002 – The Authorization for Use of Military Force Against Iraq was a joint resolution passed by Congress on 10/16/02. This resolution was the only legal basis for the US war on Al Qaʻidah and the IS: *NYR*, 3/24/16, Jessica Mathews.

2002 – On 11/3/02, a CIA Predator drone (UAV – Unmanned Aerial Vehicle) fired a Hellcat Missile that took out a vehicle carrying six AQAP operatives, including Salim al Harithi, suspect in the 10/23/00 bombing of the USS Cole in Aden Harbor. This may have been the first confirmed killing in America's drone war.

2003 – The Americans invaded Iraq. The subsequent occupation spawned The Islamic State: *Times*, 2/22/15, Maureen Dowd.

2004 – In June, America's first drone strike in Pakistan caused several deaths: *Times*, 4/23/15; *NYTM*, 7/26/15.

2008 – In Pakistan's Waziristan, a US drone killed Abu Bakr Naji, a leading philosopher of the Islamic State, author of *The Management of Savagery*, based on writings of Taqy al-Din Ibn Taymiyyah (1263-1328): *NYR*, 7/9/15, Malise Ruthven.

2010 – US drone strikes against insurgent targets in the Middle East and Afghanistan had peaked at about 15 per month: *Times*, 4/23/15.

2011 – On 5/2/11, in a clandestine raid into Pakistan, US Seals discovered Usamah bin Ladin, founder of Al Qa'idah, in his secret (?) retreat in Abbottabad, killed him, and committed his remains to the ocean. Bin Ladin was found in a residence one mile away from a prestigious Pakistani military academy. Obama had said he was determined to kill him: *NY*, 8/8/11, Nicholas Schmidle.

2011 – As of 8/31/11, Obama declared an end to the US combat role in Iraq.

2011 – On 9/30/11, Anwar al 'Awlaqi, a birthright American, who had served as an effective propagandist for the AQAP, was killed by a US drone on the specific order of President Barack Obama, who reportedly tried to hide the circumstances behind "national security". 'Awlaqi was not a militant, but Washington had classified him as a terrorist because of his scathing polemics in favor of attacks on Western targets. Due process was not invoked. The *Times* and the American Civil Liberties Union (ACLU) brought suit. The administration's claim to secrecy was upheld by a district court, but reversed by a three-judge panel of the federal appeals court. A contrary finding by the Department of Justice was rejected. The Fifth Amendment appears to be conclusive in such cases. The ACLU accused the Obama administration of trying to manipulate American public opinion: *FT*, 12/11/14; *Times*, 4/22/14, 1/11/15.

2011 – After the US forces withdrew from Iraq, the AQI (progenitor of the IS) did not follow them back to the US: *Atlantic*, March 2016, Beinart.

2012 – In January, the Nusrah announced its founding. In December, the US denounced it as terrorist: *The Syrian Jihad*, Charles Lister.

2013 – The recovery of Al Qusayr (20 miles south of Homs) by Damascus forces, with the help of thousands of Iranian, Iraqi, and Hizballah forces, was a major victory for the Damascus regime. For one observer, it was the "defining battle" of Syria's civil war.

2013 – American drone strikes against targets in Yemen were being launched from Djibouti and a CIA base in the Saudi desert: *Times*, 12/21/13.

2013 – Obama announced that the US was no longer in a war against terror.

Between 2008 and 2013, the US launched over 400 drone strikes at Taliban and Al Qa'idah targets in Pakistan. By conservative estimate, American military action was killing at least as many civilians as militants. The US government estimate was lower: *NY*, 11/24/14, Steve Coll.

2014 – Five men were on trial at Guantanamo for complicity in the 9/11/01 attacks, including Khalid Shaykh Muhammad, who had been waterboarded at least 183 times: *NYR*, 3/6/14, Mark Danner.

2014 – From January to March, the IS lost control of three Syrian governorates: Lister.

2014 – In March, Senator Dianne Feinstein released an exposé of the CIA's years of clandestine abduction, detention, interrogation, and torture. She accused the CIA of spying on the computers her intelligence committee had used in compiling the exposé. After the midterm election, she was replaced by Republican senator Richard Burr, who did not pursue her investigation. CIA Director John Brennan admitted the truth of some of Feinstein's charges. Director of National Intelligence James Clapper had lied to the committee, but kept his job: *FT*, 12/11/14.

2014 – An American bipartisan panel concluded that the Drone War had shown no evidence of success in its mission to eliminate anti-American factions in the Middle East: *Times*, 6/26/14.

2014 – The US Combined Air and Space Operation Center at the Al 'Udayd Air Base in Qatar was overseeing combat aircraft operations in

Afghanistan, and tracking US air traffic in the Middle East: *The Week*, 7/25/14.

2014 – In the summer, the IS overran Mawsil. By August, US aircraft had gone into action in Iraq, by September in Syria; anti-Americanism was rising among Sunnis: Lister.

2014 – On 8/7/14, to rescue Yazidis from IS attack in Iraq, US aircraft struck IS targets.

2014 – On 8/8/14, American F-18's and Predator drones began attacking IS positions in Iraq along the KAR border: *Times*, 8/9/14; *AP*, 10/8/14.

2014 – After US bombers softened up IS defenders of the Mawsil Dam on the Tigris, Kurdish and Iraq troops recaptured it: *Times*, 8/19/14. Those troops expelled IS units from Mt. Sinjar and the approaches to Arbil.

2014 – In August, the IS was pushing the Peshmerga back when the US forgot its sensitivity to Baghdad's wishes and unleashed the Air Force: *MEP*, Spring 2015, Michael M. Gunter.

2014 – In a speech from the White House, Obama laid out upcoming military plans: Step up air strikes on the IS, station more US military observers in Iraq, assemble an anti-IS coalition, and increase provision of arms and training to moderate Syrian rebels: *Times*, 9/10/14. The American political mood was more militant after two IS beheadings. Neocons were pressing for all-out war.

2014 – Since the IS was the most prominent Sunni militia, Obama's war against it was seen as pro-Shia. The Shia already had the benefit of four organized military forces on their side: the armed forces of Iran, Iraq, and Syria, plus the Hizballah militia. Sunnis were opposed to Washington's position and hostile to its Arab affiliates: *FT*, 9/11/14.

2014 – In September, Obama announced a campaign to degrade and ultimately destroy the Islamic State. The US air war began: *FT*, 9/14/15; *Times*, 12/20/15.

2014 – Secretary of State Kerry: "Islamic State first" (before Asad); "that's our policy": *McClatchy*, 9/18/14.

2014 – On 9/17/14, a bipartisan majority in the House authorized training and arming of (moderate) Syrian rebels: *Times*, 9/18/14.

2014 – Arms were being flown from the US to Lebanon for use by Hizballah against the IS: *Times*, 9/26/14.

2014 – On 9/21/14, the US and Arab allies began air attacks on IS and Nusrah forces in Syria: *Times*, 9/23/14. IS policy was brutal. So was that of US ally Saudi Arabia, for which beheading was a standard punishment for nonlethal crimes like drug-peddling – but the IS had gone so far as to torture and execute a female lawyer for criticizing IS destruction of offending mosques and schools: *Times*, 9/28/14, Maureen Dowd.

2014 – The US government was sentencing American volunteers for service with the "terrorist" IS to a fine of up to 250,000 dollars and/or to imprisonment up to fifteen years.

2014 – The failure of the US Air Force to attack Asad-regime targets was angering Syrian rebels and anti-Asad Arab states. US attacks on Nusrah's forces angered all Syrian Islamist rebels: *Times*, 9/26/14. These policies had won greater support for the IS and Islamist unity from Sunni Arabs, who perceived the US war against the IS as a US war against Islam: *FT*, 10/3/14.

2014 – Secularist rebels were increasingly outraged at the failure of US air forces to act against the Syrian Air Force, which was still barrel-bombing residential areas controlled by rebels: *Times*, 10/9/14.

2014 – Since the IS had acquired the Man-Portable Air Defense (Manpad) technology, the US had withheld its Apache helicopters from combat, but continued to fly AC-130 gunships: *Times*, 10/9/14, 10/27/14.

2014 – The US was staging its air campaign against the IS in Iraq and Syria from carriers in the Persian Gulf and bases in the Gulf states: *FT*, 10/14/14.

2014 – In October, the anti-IS coalition began air strikes against IS targets: *FT*, 12/16/14.

2014 – Media comment: Drones operated by the US and its allies had struck 370 targets in Iraq and Syria. It was a supercilious way to wage war, sowing death at minimum risk to the attackers – aside from the growing hostility of the communities under attack. For Obama, war was "part of the solution". How accurately had Washington identified the alleged problem?

2014 – The US was directing air strikes at Nusrah units in Syria and IS units in Iraq: *Times*, 11/7/14, 11/10/14.

2014 – Obama authorized the deployment to Iraq of another 1500 soldiers to train Iraqis. They would have no combat role. Nusrah attacked two CIA-sponsored rebel militias in Syria: the Syrian Revolutionaries' Front and the Iraqi People's Militia (*Al Hashd al Sha'bi*): *Times*, 11/7/14, 11/8/14.

2014 – In late 2014, the IS had stepped up its attacks on targets in the West, after the US had begun to bomb IS targets in defense of their victims, the Yazidis. France had joined the campaign. In November, the IS staged an attack in Paris: *Atlantic*, March 2016, Beinart.

2014 – Obama allotted 500 million dollars to promote the "moderate opposition" in Syria: *MEP*, Fall 2014.

2014 – US air strikes destroyed some of Nusrah's installations, but the consequent wave of sympathy for Nusrah may have tipped Idlib Province from the control of secularist militiamen to that of Nusrah: *McClatchy*, 11/14/14, quoting the leader of the secularist militiamen.

2014 – Nusrah had prevailed over the secularist rebels for control of Idlib Province. Both rebel factions were dedicated to the overthrow of Asad, the genocidist. Neither had any sympathy for Obama's opportunistic effort to switch the enemy from Asad to the IS, champion of the Sunnis: *The Week*, 11/14/14.

2014 – Syrians in Al Raqqah disliked IS austerity and regimentation, but they welcomed the return to law and order, and they resented American destruction of their infrastructure: *Times*, 11/14/14.

2014 – US aid for moderate Syrian rebels was going to four provinces: Aleppo, Idlib, Raqqah, and Dayr al Zawr: *NY*, 12/8/14, Robin Wright.

2014 – Since 2012, Obama had resisted advice from several of his top advisers to arm and train secularist rebels in Syria. He felt they lacked combat experience. Since the secularists had failed to establish a permanent base in Syria, they had sited their headquarters and that of the "Syrian Interim Government" in Gaziantep, a Turkish city of 1.5 million 70 miles across the border from Aleppo: *NY*, 12/8/14, Wright.

2014 – In Syria, US aerial bombing was focused on IS installations on the outskirts of Raqqah. Asad's planes were bombing the city itself: *Times*, 12/14/14.

2014 – US air strikes against IS supply lines were helping the Iraqi forces, but three-fourths of the missions had to be aborted because the IS was learning to disperse its convoys in small inconspicuous units: *Times*, 12/16/14.

2014 – Iraq was receiving up-to-date jet fighters from the US and Russia.

2014 – The USAF was now training more drone operators than jet pilots: *The Week*, 12/19/14.

2015 – Obama stated that there was no US-Russia coalition against the IS, that Turkey was an ally of the US in the war against terrorism, that the Syrian rebels being supported by the US were dependable and moderate, and that Asad must go: Seymour Hersh, 1/7/15.

2015 – Because the Damascus regime had punctiliously avoided provoking Israel, whereas the jihadists had advertised their designs on it, Washington had suspended its military opposition to the Damascus regime and concentrated on action against the IS: *Times*, 1/20/15.

2015 – At a symposium arranged by the Middle East Policy Council on wars in the Middle East, former officials in the CIA, the NSA, and the Defense Department made a presentation: Middle East political tensions, frozen by the international political situation (an apparent euphemism for European imperialism) for the past century, were exploding with terrible destructive power. Iraq, Syria, and Lebanon were gone, and they were not coming back. The regional power struggle had entered a new phase – confrontation between Shiites and Sunnis. This development contrasted with the secularization of European conflicts after the peace of Westphalia that ended the Thirty Years' War of 1618-48.

2015 – US air strikes in the Raqqah sector had targeted IS installations, making the IS job of taking over management of a city even more difficult: *NYR*, 2/5/15, Birke.

174

2015 – Since Obama went to war against the IS, the secularist rebellion in Syria had withered, and arms supply to the Kurds had been neglected, whereas the IS had doubled its Syrian domain: *Raleigh News and Observer*, 2/6/15, Charles Krauthammer.

2015 – Obama seemed more alarmed by the intermittent brutality of the IS than the calculated genocide of Asad. Syria was Obama's worst foreign policy failure: *Times*, 2/15/15, Nicholas Kristof.

2015 – Since 2002, the US had launched over 100 drone strikes in Yemen, killing close to 900 militants and dozens of civilians, and stoking strong anti-American feelings. Many Yemenis believed that the Salih-Hadi faction was submitting to US operatives as "terrorists" the names of political enemies. US forces were training Yemeni soldiers and conducting missions with them: *The Week*, 3/6/15.

2015 – The US drone war in Iraq and Syria had failed to check IS expansion: *WRMEA*, Juan Cole blog; *Counterpunch*, 3/11/15, Cockburn.

2015 – The tactics of the IS had enabled it to escape serious losses from the US drone campaign: *FA*, March 2015, Audrey Cronin.

2015 – In Iraq, US forces were in tacit alliance with Iranian forces; at the same time, the US was supporting the anti-Iranian forces in Yemen. The Obama administration had instituted a paradigm shift in policy, from Pax Americana (leadership of pro-US coalition) to "offshore balancing" (policing the region from offshore, intervening only when the balance of power had been dramatically upset). In Iraq, the aim was to transfer a rogue state into a model for the region. Washington was leaving direct intervention to Iran. The transfer plan wasn't working. Instead of getting the Americans out, it was pulling them back in: *Times*, 3/29/15, Ross Douthat.

2015 – Drones operated by the CIA and the DOD's Special Forces were hitting Iraq, Syria, Somalia, Pakistan, and Yemen. In May 2013, Obama stated that every US drone strike was preceded by spadework that insured the near-certainty that no civilians would be injured or killed. On 4/13/15, The Open Society of Justice Initiative (OSJI) released a finding that between 2012 and 2014, nine strikes in Yemen had killed 26 civilians. A National Security Council spokesman said that in those rare instances of civilian casualties, payments were sometimes made to the injured and to the families of those killed. The OSJI also questioned the adherence of the drone operators to the stated policy that, whenever feasible, terrorists would be captured rather than killed. Israel and Britain had also staged drone strikes: *Times*, 4/14/15, Scott Shane. The American media were generally euphemizing assassination by drone as "targeted killing": *Times*, 2/22/15.

2015 – Since the American electorate would not tolerate another Vietnam War, the US had no good military options against the IS, which held the Sunni (majority) franchise against a number of adversaries who were also hostile to each other. There was no effective indigenous force to stand up the IS: *FA*, March 2015, Cronin.

2015 – Washington considered Al Qa'idah (Nusrah) a terrorist organization. The IS was a pseudo-state run by a conventional army. Its predecessor, the AQI, had been almost wiped out in Iraq in 2006, but it had renewed itself under the leadership of Abu Bakr, and gone on to exploit the disorder in Iraq and the civil war in Syria. It had recruited 15,000 foreign fighters: *FA*, March 2015, Cronin.

2015 – Since the US began using drones in Yemen in 2009, a Predator or a Reaper had killed US citizen Anwar al 'Awlaqi in 2011, AQAP leader Sa'id al Shihri in 2013, and AQAP leader Ibrahim al Rubaysh in 2015: *Times*, 4/15/15, 4/16/15.

2015 – On 4/23/15, Washington revealed that an American drone strike in Pakistan in January 2015 had killed two Western hostages of Al Qa'idah who were not known to be at the site of the strike.

2015 – The frequency of strikes by American drones at jihadist targets fluctuated. In 2015 it had risen again to an average of five per month: *Times*, 4/23/15.

2015 – A US carrier group from the Persian Gulf was sent into the Arabian Sea to deter an Iranian convoy from landing arms in Yemen for the Huthis, and to reassure the Saudis that US support was solid: *Times*, 4/23/15.

2015 – The neatness of drone warfare appealed to Obama, who had escalated Bush 43's drone war in Pakistan and initiated a drone war in Somalia and Yemen: *Times*, 4/24/15, Scott Shane.

2015 – While the US was claiming that its drones were aimed only at "terrorist" targets, it was mounting aircraft and drone strikes at Afghan Taliban forces as they advanced toward Kabul: *Times*, 4/30/15.

2015 – The CIA's campaign of assassination by drone had been embedded in America's Middle East strategy by strong support from CIA officers who had built the campaign (and torture programs at black sites overseas) and had risen to senior ranks in the Agency. Liberal groups that followed the drone campaign estimated it had killed about 4000 people, including 500 civilians: *Times*, 4/26/15. White House officials recommended shifting most drone operations to DOD's Special Operations Command, but the CIA convinced the congressional intelligence committees that CIA strikes were more precise. The CIA was still conducting all strikes in Pakistan and most strikes in Yemen. Senator Richard Burr and Representative Mike Rogers were strong advocates of CIA's programs.

2015 – Obama's drone war was supposed to make jihadists face up to the American determination to exercise its right to exterminate anti-Americans, inconvenient neutrals, and the occasional Western hostage. The calculation had failed: *The Week*, 5/8/15.

2015 – Obama's air strikes had failed to prevent the IS capture of Ramadi, in Iraq's 'Anbar Province: *Times*, 5/17/15.

2015 – No US official had been held accountable for the hundreds of civilians killed by chance in America's drone offensive. No one could prove that it was reducing the incidence of anti-Americanism: *The Nation*, 5/18/15.

2015 – IS militants had seized territory in Syria's Hamah Province and in the Yarmuk District. Nusrah militants had expanded their area of control along the Jordan border with Syria: *Times*, May 2015. Of the three crossings between Syria and Iraq, the Kurds held the northern one. The IS held the other two: *FT*, 5/23/15.

2015 – Commentary from the *Times*: Observations of IS operations suggest its deployment plan looked years ahead, as illustrated by the sudden capture of Ramadi from Iraqi forces on 5/15/15, and of Palmyra from Asad's forces on 5/21/15 – after allowing several months for the defending forces to be hollowed out: *Times*, 5/22/15. At Palmyra, IS forces had executed scores of Alawite soldiers and others, and then set out to restore law and order: *Times*, 5/29/15.

2015 – In response to IS bombings, Shia in the Eastern Province of Saudi Arabia were forming civil defense groups: *FT*, 6/1/15.

2015 – Taking the long view as always, the IS seemed to have suspended its operations against Asad's forces (which held the western half of Aleppo), in order to concentrate on taking the eastern half from the secularist rebels: *Times*, 6/3/15.

2015 – According to Iraqi Prime Minister 'Abadi, 43 percent of the IS's 20,000 fighters in Iraq were foreigners: *NYR*, 6/4/15.

2015 – Although the IS's Iraqi leadership was a handicap in its Syrian operations, the IS had managed to project in Syria and Iraq the image of the guardian of the Sunnis and the sworn enemy of the Shia. Washington was absorbed in a futile effort to convince Sunnis to switch their hatred from the Alawites to the kindred IS: *Times*, 6/4/15.

2015 – The US effort to recycle the errant Arab World back to the Sykes-Picot pattern was running into major roadblocks:

-   Urban Sprawl: The IS militiamen might number only 20,000 – almost half of them foreign – but they hid out in cities, where they were hard to hit without wiping out civilians. Washington was abstaining from the carpet-bombing favored by the Asad Regime and some Saudis.

-   Ethnicity: There was no meeting of US and Sunni minds. Washington feared the implications of an expanding Islamic State. Sunnis disliked its draconianism, but feared the Shiite forces more. Grand Ayatallah 'Ali Sistani had issued a call to eliminate the jihadists. The pro-Iranian Badr Organization was among those who had answered it.

-   Epidemic of Partition: Iraq had been the quintessential police state. It had never recovered from Bremer's gutting of the armed forces. Prime Minister 'Abadi had seemed to reestablish control of a Shiite Baghdad, but ethnic partition was in the air: *NYR*, 6/4/15.

2015 – The Obama administration announced the opening of a new base in 'Anbar Province, manned by 450 soldiers, bringing the total of US troops in Iraq to 3550: *Times*, 6/12/15.

2015 – In Libya, a US airstrike took out a "terrorist" who had masterminded the seizure of a gas plant in Algeria: *Times*, 6/15/15.

2015 – The rise of the IS had sparked the demand for drones, but operators in the US were getting scarce. The psychological pressure of melding stateside life with going to war was reducing their number: The worse pressure of all was the fear of inflicting civilian casualties. Defense contractors were paying extra to drone operators: *Times*, 6/17/15.

2015 – In "Why We Lost", Lt. General Daniel Bolger had taken the position that the US had already lost the "War on Terrorism" because of arrogance, taking on too many enemies, and practicing imperialism – which always loses in the end because the people it targets are in the country to stay. Nevertheless, no senior officer had ever argued for withdrawal: *AP*, 6/17/15.

2015 – The US Air Force staged eighteen night airstrikes against IS targets in the Raqqah area, destroying 16 bridges and killing ten people: *AP*, 7/5/15.

2015 – Malise Ruthven condemned US strategy against the jihadists as crude and simplistic. The US wiped out IS operatives without any understanding of their roles.

2015 – US planes and drones were striking IS affiliates who had emerged lately in eastern Afghanistan: *Times*, 7/16/15.

2015 – From mid-2012 to mid-2015, cooperation between the secularist rebels and the jihadist Nusrah was growing. The US failure to boost the secularists had allowed the jihadists to take leadership of the Syrian rebellion: Lister.

2015 – Nusrah militiamen routed a group of secularist Syrians whom the US Special Forces from DOD were trying to organize to fight the IS. US planes staged a retaliatory raid against Nusrah on 7/31/15. The DOD efforts were severely undermined by lack of financing, by the emphasis on fighting the IS but not the Alawites, and by the abductions of US trainees: *Times*, 8/1/15, 9/7/15.

179

2015 – The US effort to create a non-Islamist coalition against the IS had already been stalled by Nusrah's abduction of the Syrian rebels, most of them Turkmens, whom Americans had been training to be members of a pro-US militia. The US seemed to have stumbled over the resolve of most Sunni militants to get rid of Bashar al Asad: *Times*, 8/11/15; *FT*, 8/14/15.

2015 – In a year of US air strikes against the IS, the US had saved Arbil from IS bombing, helped rescue Yazidis, and facilitated the YPG's acquisition of Syrian territory between Turkey and Raqqah, but the IS had gained more territory in Iraq and Syria. Shiite militias in Iraq were looking less to Prime Minister 'Abadi than to his predecessor, Maliki, who also had an office in the Green Zone. In the no-man's-land between the KAR and Iraq, the Peshmerga were fighting the IS and Baghdad. In northern Syria, the YPG, having overrun Kurdish-populated areas, had gone as far as it could go. Its war with Syrian rebels was over: *FT*, 8/26/15.

2015 – In July, Obama cited the death of Anwar al 'Awlaqi (9/20/11) as an occasion for patriotic rejoicing. 'Awlaqi had proclaimed that every Muslim's religious duty was to kill Americans. He had condemned the 9/11/01 attacks, but also condemned the American record in the Middle East. When federal security personnel looking for suspects had swept Muslim institutions in northern Virginia in March 2002, 'Awlaqi had alleged that the US was at war with Muslims, not terrorists. With 'Awlaqi in mind, an American Muslim had stated that those fighting a martyrdom culture should not make more martyrs: *NYTM*, 8/30/15.

2015 – So far, the IS had come out of Washington's air campaign stronger than ever: *FT*, 9/9/15.

2015 – The US was donating to Jordan troops (1000), trainers, arms, and a subsidy of one million dollars a year: *FT*, 9/10/15.

2015 – In Iraq, the Western advance against the rebels was slow. In Syria, the Coalition had been stalemated. Over the past year, the Coalition had recaptured Tikrit, but lost Ramadi: *FT*, 9/19/15.

2015 – Robert Ford, US Ambassador to Syria since 2010, lately non-resident, resigned out of disagreement with the policy of the Obama administration: *Times*, 9/20/15.

2015 – Columnist Nicholas Kristof recommended that the US set up a No-Fly Zone in southern Syria as a means of exerting leverage on Russian and Syrian operations – as by pressuring Syria to terminate its barrel-bombing: *Times*, 9/20/15.

2015 – Early in the year, Pentagon releases stressed reports of damage done by air strikes to oil refineries, apparently seeking to imply that IS revenues had been reduced – whereas the IS had largely escaped losses by shifting to clandestine makeshift refineries and selling their product on the black market: *Times*, 9/24/15.

2015 – One of Iran's ranking generals in Syria, Hossein Hamedani, was killed in combat against IS forces in the Aleppo theater: *FT*, 10/8/15.

2015 – The failure of the CIA to train an effective militia of "moderate" Syrians in western Syria had forced Washington to abandon the effort – suggesting that Washington had been reduced to the strategy of reaction. The Russian intervention was motivating the US to try to do better: *FT*, 10/10/15.

2015 – By concentrating its aerial fire against Nusrah forces, and by leaving FSA forces to their own feeble devices, Washington had enabled IS forces to advance in the Aleppo area: *Times*, 10/10/15.

2015 – The advent of the Russian forces was motivating the US to step up the supply of weapons, primarily TOW anti-tank missiles, that helped the rebels resist Russian attacks. Result: an all-out proxy war: *Times*, 10/13/15.

2015 – The Khorasan Group, 24 veteran jihadists with Nusrah, was being gradually attritted by CIA drones: *Times*, 10/19/15.

2015 – In September, President Hollande had authorized the French air force to join America's air campaign against the IS in Iraq and Syria. British flights were still confined to Iraq: *Times*, 10/21/15.

2015 – For up to a year, US aircraft from Qatar's Al 'Udayd Air Base had been escalating action against oil fields, oil refining, and oil delivery facilities that had been helping finance IS operations. Washington meant to put these targets out of service.

2015 – A year of American air strikes had not materially weakened the IS forces in Syria: *FT*, 10/24/15.

2015 – Armed with American-made missiles from the GCC states, Syrian rebels in northwest Syria had largely withstood the combined offensive of Alawite, Hizballah, and Russian forces. American air strikes in the area had fallen off sharply, allegedly because of weather, actually because of aggressive Russian aircraft deployment: *FT*, 10/31/15; *Times*.

2015 – Obama's Syrian policy was weak and indecisive. The deployment of 50 soldiers from the Special Forces was a case of mission creep: *FT*, 11/2/15.

2015 – US government statistics on civilian deaths from drones were fallacious: *Times*, 11/4/15; *Washington Post*: https://consortiumnews.com.

2015 – The 7000 air strikes delivered against the jihadis by the US and allies in October had failed to repel them. In May, the IS had taken Ramadi and Palmyra. There had been fewer air attacks against Nusrah and Free Men of Syria (*Ahrar al Sham*), which were the dominant rebel forces in northwest Syria: *LRB*, 11/5/15, Cockburn.

2015 – The US had no ground forces as allies except the Kurds, and they operated only in Kurdish-populated areas: *LRB*, 11/5/15, Cockburn.

2015 – The anti-IS offensive in the Sinjar sector by the Peshmerga, some PKK forces, and some Yazidis was supported by US jet fighters and bombers, with two dozen US Special-Force spotters on the ground: *Times*, 11/13/15.

2015 – Some Iraqis felt that the US had mounted a weak air defense against the IS capture of northwestern Iraq, but a strong air defense of the subsequent Kurdish campaign to recover the territory. Close US-Kurdish ties annoyed Iraq, Iran, and Russia, and alarmed Turkey: *Times*, 11/14/15.

2015 – The US reported that an American air strike had killed Wisam al Zubaydi, IS commander in Libya, on 11/13/15: *McClatchy*, 11/15/15.

2015 – As US concern about collateral casualties of air action dwindled, US planes destroyed 116 oil trucks: *Times*, 11/16/15.

2015 – Having been upended by the IS attack on *Charlie Hebdo* in Paris, after Obama had declared that the IS was contained, he wanted to step up the war against it. The US electorate had come around to favor that strategy. There were still 3500 US troops in Iraq: *FT*, 11/16/15.

2015 – The attack in Paris by the IS may have been a warning to the US to ease up its war against the IS. Or it may have been an attempt to lure the US into overreaction – as Al Qa'idah had done in 2001: *FT*, 11/16/15, David Gardner.

2015 – Washington was urging the Russians to switch the targets of their air strikes from FSA forces to IS forces: *Times*, 11/18/15.

2015 – The UNSC voted 15-0 to call on all parties to join the battle against the IS: *Times*, 11/20/15.

2015 – Recent US efforts to steer local Arab politics had been a series of embarrassing failures. The best defense against Islamic extremism was to promote better governments in the afflicted areas, and closer union among adjoining states. The militancy of the administration of Bush 43 had given the jihadists a new lease on life: *FA*, November 2015, Steven Walt.

2015 – The Obama administration, ruling out US ground action in Syria, failed to enlist effective Arab forces in a ground operation of their own: *Times*, 12/8/15.

2015 – The US had sensibly avoided the carpet bombing by which Bashar al Asad had disgraced his office. However, by confining its air attacks in Syria to surgical strikes, the US had allowed communities under IS rule to continue to function, and the IS to continue to pay its militiamen: *FT*, 12/15/15.

2015 – The US had assigned 150 aircraft to the air war against the IS: *The Week*, citing *The Guardian*, 12/18/15.

2015 – The IS had lost 40 percent of the Iraqi territory it had seized in June 2014: *Times*, 12/20/15.

2015 – Washington was handicapped in its campaign to assassinate IS leaders because of their adherence to a regimen of constant change in their location, and avoidance of fixed residence: *Times*, 12/20/15.

2015 – On 12/27/15, the US-supported Syrian Democratic Forces (Kurds) captured Tishrin Dam on the Euphrates in Syria.

2015 – Since July, the US had contributed 630 air strikes to the Iraqi siege of Ramadi: *FT*, 12/29/15.

2015 – In Baghdad, a US military spokesman stated that US-trained Sunni tribesmen were active in the siege of Ramadi, and that recent US air strikes had killed ten IS leaders: *Times*, 12/30/15.

2015 – The US War on Terror had been widely perceived among Muslims as a war on Islam. It was one cause for the flood of recruits to the IS: *MER*, Winter 2015, Chris Toensing.

2015 – In Bosnia, Kosovo, Afghanistan, Libya, Iraq, and Syria, the US had resorted to brute force instead of sound diplomacy. Force has the power of destruction, but no power of construction. US reliance on sanctions (against Iran, Iraq, and Libya) had also failed: *MEP*, Winter 2015, Chas Freeman.

2016 – US air strikes against jihadists in Iraq and Syria were being coordinated in Arbil, in the Kurdish Autonomous Region (KAR). A prime target was the infrastructure of oil facilities controlled by the IS. US strikes had taken out hundreds of tanker trucks, plus makeshift refineries and separation plants: *NY*, 1/18/16.

2016 – In Afghanistan, the US was directing commando raids and air strikes against units of the several thousand IS militiamen there: *Times*, 2/1/16.

2016 – Current US policy for Syria was to let Russia crush rebel groups of its choice, but gang up with Russia against the IS. Rationale: Millions of Syrian exiles would never come back. The Middle East would never know peace. The West's only vital interest in Syria was to defeat the IS: *FT*, 2/16/16, Michael Ignatieff.

2016 – In a region riven by several simultaneous wars, critics were saying the US concentration on only one of the challenges, the rise of the Islamic State, was a mistake: *Times*, 2/19/16.

2016 – While focusing on the narrow interests of the US, Obama was forgetting the global interest in ending the flow of refugees to Europe. Obama refused to match Russia's ground engagement in Syria. Obama should terminate the campaign against the Islamic State: *FT*, 2/19/16, Philip Stephens.

2016 – The US was conducting air strikes of opportunity against IS targets in Libya: *FT*, 2/20/16.

2016 – US air strikes had just demolished an IS training camp, killing 36. The number of IS militiamen in Syria was down to 25,000; in Libya, up to 6500. IS suicide attacks against Alawites in Homs and Damascus had killed over 100: *Times*, 2/22/16.

2016 – In *Blood Year*, David Kilcullen, a US army officer, contends that the US invasion of Iraq produced the jihadist movement that ignited war in Iraq and Syria: *FT*, 2/22/16.

2016 – A US Special Forces team of 200 that had lately arrived in Iraq had captured some IS operatives, who were being interrogated in Arbil in the Kurdish Autonomous Region (KAR): *Times*, 3/2/16.

2016 – Obama had opted for the Drone War to avoid being mired in conventional war. However, picking off a few hundred suspects was no way to end the jihadist threat. For every one we killed, several emerged. The Drone War should end: *LRB*, 3/3/16, review of *Objective Troy*, Scott Shane.

2016 – After the 9/11 attack, the US had started targeting killers with Hellfire missiles fired from drone aircraft. Obama continued the strategy. Amnesty International condemned it on two counts: 1) It made killing too easy; 2) Outside a war zone, it constituted extrajudicial execution. Moreover, it was bad strategy. Washington favored military regimes, like the one in Egypt, and feared that the jihadists could jeopardize the flow of oil and harm Israel: *LRB*, 3/3/16, Owen Bennett-Jones.

2016 – Obama had ordered the killing of talented propagandist Anwar al 'Awlaqi because he had begun to help AQAP killers: *LRB*, 3/3/16.

2016 – Obama had expanded the drone war started by Bush 43, enabling US forces to kill 5000 so far: *Times*, 3/8/16.

2016 – The IS had fired two rockets against a US base in northern Iraq, killing one, wounding several: *Washington Post*, 3/19/16.

2016 – To reinforce the siege forces being deployed south of Mawsil, 200 Marines had joined the operations of the US Air Force: *Times*, 3/25/16.

2016 – The ceasefire brokered by the US and Russia, excluding the IS and Nusrah, was holding fairly well: *AP*, 3/27/16.

2016 – The CIA had been training Syrian rebels to "keep pressure on" the Damascus Regime. The DOD had been training a force of Kurds and a few Arabs to repel the IS advance. Now Kurds and Arabs were fighting each other: *Tribune Newspapers*, 3/28/16.

2016 – The cost to the US of fighting the Islamic State since 2014 was 6.5 billion dollars: *FT*, 4/13/16.

2016 – Air strikes in Iraq and Syria since 2011 had killed 25,000. The IS had lost thousands of square miles of the territory it had conquered, but it was still on the rise in Afghanistan and North Africa: *Times*, 4/18/16.

2016 – The US was to provide 415 million dollars to the KRG, which was strapped by the fall in the price of oil: *FT*, 4/19/16.

2016 – US troops in Iraq were up to 4100, mostly Special Forces. Many assigned to the advise-and-assist mission would be embedded with Iraqi forces. The US forces had Baghdad's permission to use Apache helicopters against the IS.

2016 – The US Cyber Command, established in 2010, had previously focused on Russia, China, North Korea, and Iran. It had now been deployed against "the most dangerous organization in the world" – the IS. The Cyber Command would disrupt IS communications, drop "cyber-bombs", and sabotage electronic transfers of funds. The IS was already communicating through cyberspace.

2016 – Lisa Monaco, Obama's top adviser on counterterrorism, had said, "We are not going to kill our way out of this conflict": *Times*, 4/25/16.

2016 – Killing "Caliph" Abu Bakr was a top goal of Obama's security apparatus. However, Obama had said, "The Middle East is no longer terribly important to American interests": *Atlantic*, April 2016, Jeffrey Goldberg.

2016 – US forces had killed 26,000 IS fighters and recovered lands inhabited by 3,000,000 people. Lands still under IS control were inhabited by 6,000,000 people. Adding to the 5000 soldiers in Iraq, and the Marines on board three amphibious warships in the Gulf, the US was to send 250 more Special Forces troops to Syria: *The Week*, 5/6/16.

2016 – State Department officers sent through the US Dissent Channel a memorandum to the Obama administration criticizing Obama's emphasis on fighting the IS instead of the Asad regime in Damascus: *Times*, 6/17/16.

2016 – Having perpetrated the monstrous blunder of disbanding the Iraqi Army in 2003, Washington had spent 25 billion dollars in a failed attempt to rebuild it: *FT*, 6/24/16.

2016 – In the War on Terrorism, the DOD had been responsible for operations in Afghanistan, Iraq, and Syria, while the CIA had primary responsibility in Pakistan, Somalia, and Yemen. On June 14, Obama said these operations were making significant progress. Scott Shane of *The New York Times* wrote that the case for the drone campaign appeared increasingly threadbare: *Times*, 7/4/16, Shane.

2016 – Obama said that he would leave 8400 troops in Afghanistan until the end of his term: *Times*, 7/7/16.

2016 – The IS was spreading faster than the US, in Iraq and Syria, was defeating it. US military action in those two states should be stepped up: *Wall Street Journal* editorial, *The Week*, 7/15/16.

2016 – Since late May, by the estimate of the Syrian Observatory of Human Rights, over 100 civilians in the Manbij area had been killed by US and/or French air strikes: *Times*, 7/22/16; Saudi Arabia News Agency.

2016 – The US met the request of the government in Libya to conduct air attacks against IS targets in Surt: *AP*, 8/1/16. The legal authorization for these attacks was the US Authorization for Use of Military Force adopted 9/18/01. The Libyan faction supported by the US had set up the Government of National Accord: *Times*, 8/3/16.

2016 – The CIA was delaying arms supply to Nusrah, strongest rebel militia in Syria, since Washington had branded it terrorist: *AP*, 8/7/16. Washington was also concerned by the risk that weapons supplied to moderates could leak to the IS: *Times*, 9/22/16.

2016 – Obama had overseen US military operations in three countries of the Middle East – Iraq, Syria, and Yemen. He had put a stop to the CIA's torture program, but forces under his command were killing unproven "enemies" of the US. Under the laws of war, secret killing was illegal. In practice, "terrorists" have been fair game. The Drone War was probably creating more anti-Americans than it killed: *NYR*, 8/18/16, David Cole (also citing General Stanley McChrystal).

2016 – Drones threaten to erase the boundary between war and peace: *NYR*, 8/18/16, Hugh Gusterson, *Drone, Remote Control Warfare*.

2016 – After suspect Abu Zubaydah was cordially interrogated by the FBI, to whom he imparted useful intelligence, the CIA took him over, waterboarded him, and falsely claimed that he held high office in Al Qa'idah: *Times* editorial, 8/25/16.

2016 – The US military was playing a key role in the battle for Mawsil: air strikes, rockets, helicopters, drones, and heavy artillery from a base at Hammam al 'Ali, 15 miles south of Mawsil. IS drones were spooking Iraqi troops: *Times*, 2/27/17.

2016 – During the year, the US military conducted 38 drone strikes in the shadow war in Yemen. The AQAP militants had been pushed back into rural areas: *Times*, 3/4/17.

2003-11 – US-Iraq War

The American occupation of Iraq was a case of blatant imperialism – a quantum leap from the indirect imperialism the United States had previously pursued via its protectorates over seven Arab monarchies (Bahrain, Jordan, Kuwait, Oman, Qatar, Saudi Arabia, UAE), and its diarchy with Israel. Bush 43 took the American presence in the Middle East to a whole new level by invading a major Arab state, replacing its leadership with an American military regime, and embarking on a breathtakingly radical program to convert Iraq from a Sunni dictatorship to a subservient "democracy". Specialists on the Middle East dismissed the endeavor as sheer fantasy. The only positive achievement was the elimination of a brutal dictator – to the satisfaction of Israel, and the possible benefit of the Iraqi people. The consequences for the US were adverse. The consequences for the Middle East were impossible to predict.

Motivation – Government habitually relies on pretext to hide its real motives – from the electorate, and sometimes from itself. The professed rationale for the invasion of Iraq was particularly implausible:

"WMD's" - In late 2002, Bush told Americans that Iraq, having expelled the IAEA inspectors, would soon have nuclear weapons that it might well pass on to its Islamist allies in Al Qa'idah. He was wrong on three counts: 1) The inspectors had been pulled out in 1998 because Clinton was about to bomb targets in Iraq; 2) Iraq had suspended its nuclear-weapons program after its war with Iran. Saddam declined to let the IAEA in on the secret because he wanted Iran to think Iraq was about to become a nuclear power (Duelfer Report of 2004). Bush may have known his accusation was unwarranted; some analysts have cited persuasive evidence that Bush pressured the CIA to produce alarmist intelligence. 3) There was no alliance between secularist Iraq and Islamist Al Qa'idah, although Washington persuaded many Americans to the contrary. The absence of confirmation of any Saddam-bin Ladin tie was reported to Congress by CIA Director George Tenet and to the NSC by Richard Clarke.

Bush also cited alleged Iraqi possession of biological weapons. He did not mention that the United States had authorized sales of biological precursors to Iraq in the 1980's – in violation of an international convention ratified by Washington in 1972.

After the war, CIA official Tyler Drumheller said that the Bush administration had knowingly put out fabricated reports of an Iraqi arsenal of biological weapons, and was aware that there was no stockpile of weapons of mass destruction in Iraq: *Times*, 8/10/15.

"Democratization" – After the American forces failed to find the hypothetical WMD's, Washington switched signals – asserting that its basic motive was to liberate Iraq, in keeping with the persistent myth that America had a special mission to relieve the victims of tyranny: *Times*: 10/9/16, Max Fisher and Amanda Taub. Saddam's tyranny was not in question, but the liberation claim was:

1) Sacrificing American lives for good government overseas is not in the President's job description. 2) Washington reportedly rejected an opportunity to support a palace coup against Saddam. 3) Washington's preference for dealing with complaisant autocracies rather than capricious democracies is a matter of public record. America financed the overthrow of an elected Iranian Prime Minister in 1953. Deputy Defense Secretary Wolfowitz faulted the Turkish military in 2003 for not intervening to overrule the Parliament's refusal to allow the passage of American ground troops for deployment in Iraq.

What were the Bush Administration's real motives? Copious evidence supports the following elements:

190

Supremacism - "The National Security Strategy of the United States", issued by George W. Bush 43 on 9/17/02, heralded the towering ambition that imbued Bush 43 foreign policy. It may have reflected a sense that America was emasculated by its failure to oust Saddam in 1991. This attitude was crudely expressed by a neoconservative in 2003: "Every ten years or so, the United States needs to pick up some crappy little country and throw it against the wall, just to show the world we mean business." There was an ancillary intent to rekindle the morale of the armed forces.

Domestication of the Iraqi Government - A sign in an occupation office in Baghdad listed three objectives: durable peace, representative government, and an Iraq that no longer poses a threat to its neighbors. According to Naomi Klein, American objectives were even more ambitious, in that they envisaged Iraq as a showroom for laissez-faire economics.

Oil – In the area of foreign commerce, recent American administrations have been uncomfortable with the conventional strategy of relying on the process of supply and demand. Roosevelt set the precedent of the special relationship – assurance of American access to Saudi oil in return for a guarantee of Saudi security. Many Middle Easterners concluded that oil was Washington's prime motive in invading Iraq. They were probably wrong; even the fantasists in the hawk camp had the means to realize the repercussions of an invasion on the price of oil. In 2007 *McClatchy* reported that the 6000 aircraft of the USAF were burning seven million gallons of fuel a day – over half of total US Government consumption.

Military Base - Iraq's central location made it (in the view of many commentators) a base from which the Bush administration intended to control events in the region. The most sardonic articulation of this thesis came from novelist John le Carré: "… an old colonial war launched by a clique of war-hungry Judeo-Christian geopolitical fantasists … who exploited America's post-9/11 psychopathy."

Israel - For the United States, Saddam Husayn posed no serious threat, even as ruler of Iraq and Kuwait combined. For Israel, he was Public Enemy number one: paymaster for the families of Palestinian

191

suicide bombers; the only Arab ruler to have exploded missiles on Israeli soil.

For Israel, the results of the Kuwait War were incomplete. In the prosecution of the US-Iraq War, to minimize domestic opposition, Washington had to avoid any suggestion of joint planning with Israel. However, as noted later by Colin Powell, Anthony Zinni, and professors Mearsheimer and Walt, the circumstantial evidence was formidable:

1. Israel's people and government had long favored the ouster of Saddam.

2. The Bush administration was simultaneously driven by strategic reliance on Israel, by pressure from the Israeli Government, by pressure from major American Jewish organizations, by the expectation that the pacification of Iraq would open the way to Arab-Israeli peace on Israel's terms, by hope of reducing the Democrats' traditional lock on a big majority of the Jewish vote, and by the ostensible conviction of Bush 43 and many of his fundamentalist Christian supporters that, since a resurgent Israel would be the precursor of Judgment Day, striking down Israel's enemies was God's work.

3. Many well-known advocates, planners, and principals of the invasion were reported believers that the national interest of the United States and that of Israel are identical. Prominent in their ranks were Undersecretary of State for Arms Control John Bolton, Vice President Cheney, evangelist Jerry Falwell, Undersecretary of Defense for Policy Douglas Feith, David Frum, ORHA Chief Jay Garner, *Weekly Standard* Editor William Kristol, columnist Charles Krauthammer, Richard Perle, former *Commentary* editor Norman Podhoretz, evangelist Pat Robertson, Defense Secretary Donald Rumsfeld, and Deputy Secretary of Defense Paul Wolfowitz. In December 2007 the Krauthammer column made the extravagant claim that, by deposing Saddam, the US had eliminated the risk that his dynasty would "rearm and threaten the world." Wolfowitz, ultra-Zionist, was a major advocate of invasion of Iraq (*NYR*, 12/14/13, Mark Danner).

For Israeli dove Uri Avnery, Wolfowitz was "the father of the Iraq war".

Reelection - For every regime, Middle Eastern or American, the primary motivation behind policy is the compulsion to stay in power. The Bush clique seemed excited by their confidence in obtaining a victory more acclaimed than Bush 41's rescue of Kuwait. The ultimate architect of American policy in Iraq was Karl Rove. He is credited with the impressive Republican victory in the election of 2004, and his shrewd guidance is widely inferred in the sequential attenuation of the Administration's goals in Iraq, as they were increasingly impeded by Sunni resistance and Shiite recalcitrance.

Chaos? - Maureen Dowd suggested that the leaders of Israel and their closest allies in America had so sophisticated an understanding of the Arab World that they could not possibly have swallowed the Bush Administration's democratization fantasy – so they must have anticipated chaos and hoped Israel would profit from it. Potential benefits would be the neutralization of Arab military effectiveness such as two Arab states had mustered in the Yom Kippur war, or the emergence of a pro-Israel state of Iraqi Kurdistan, or better cover for more ethnic cleansing of the West Bank. This hypothesis is plausible, but in the absence of corroborative data, it fails the test of Ockham's razor. The 1982 invasion of Lebanon demonstrated that Israeli readings of Arab politics are not infallible.

The Run-up to Invasion

1991-2003 – The twelve years between the second Kuwait War of 1991 and the US-Iraq War of 2003-11 were pockmarked by recurrent American sanctions, provocations, air attacks, and attempts at subversion, directed against the Saddam regime, but calamitous for the general population of Iraq.

1995 – The US was maintaining 20,000 military personnel in the Gulf area, many on the 20 ships of the 5th Fleet, whose command center was in Bahrain. The US had no formal relations with Iraq or Iran. Iraq was subject to the Northern No-Fly Zone – instituted by the Allies in October 1991, serving as an unplanned umbrella for the evolution of the Kurdish Autonomous Region (KAR) – and to the Southern No-Fly Zone, proclaimed in August 1992. The Northern Zone was policed by the US European Command from Incirlik Air Base in Turkey, the Southern Zone by the US Central Command from Bahrain, and later from the new American air base at Al 'Udayd in Qatar.

Iraq was being quietly victimized by the economic sanctions, including a worldwide trade ban, intended to disable the Iraqi military establishment, imposed under UNSC Resolution 661 of August 6, 1990. Every member of its 15-person Sanctions Committee, sitting in New York, had veto power over any Iraqi request for an import license. The American member exercised that power stringently, citing possible dual use – military application of an ostensibly commercial product, although the regime in Baghdad continued to prosper, primarily from proceeds of smuggling oil to neighboring states. The consequences of the sanctions for the Iraqi economy were ruinous, and for public health lethal. On "Sixty Minutes" in 1996, Lesley Stahl asked Secretary of State Albright if the deaths of 500,000 children (from ruined public health facilities) were justified; Albright's reply: "... we think the price is worth it." Joy Gordon noted that the American member of the 661 Committee held up some import licenses for years – even on items like vaccines and yogurt makers. In 1999 Washington relented, and the UN lifted the embargo on Iraqi oil sales, but specified that the proceeds would be collected in Paris under UN oversight.

In the early years of the sanctions, Washington regarded them as a means to hold Iraq to UNSC Resolutions 687 (no WMD's) and 688 (no repression of Kurds and Shiites). Later on, Washington began to look at them as devices for ousting Saddam. In 1998, Clinton signed The Iraq Liberation Act, which embodied that specific objective.

1996 – A lethal bombing of the quarters of US military personnel at Khawbar Towers intimidated Saudi Arabia into giving US planes the right to raid Iraq from Saudi territory.

1996 – A CIA plan to mount an anti-Saddam coup from the KAR ended in fiasco when the ancient Barzani-Talabani feud led the Barzanis to collude in an Iraqi foray that repelled the Talabani advance and rolled up a four-year CIA operation. In reaction, the US reduced its presence in the KAR (Kurdish Autonomous Region).

1997 – Israel was promoting the movement for an independent Kurdish state in northern Iraq, to the distress of Turkey.

1998 – In December, Clinton notified the UN to withdraw its weapons inspectors from Iraq. Within hours, the United States and the UK subjected Iraqi targets to three days of heavy air strikes ("Desert Fox"). The rationale was Saddam's noncooperation with the inspectors. The real objective was to reduce Saddam's security structure, and if possible to kill him. Critics described the enterprise as disarmament by tantrum, and questioned its justification under the UN Charter. Its only significant consequence was Saddam's formal exclusion of the inspections regime. It also damaged American relations with the Arab states and Turkey. Clinton did not obtain congressional clearance for the operation under the War Powers Act.

1998 – In protest against Desert Fox, France withdrew from patrolling the Southern No-Fly Zone. The UN inspectors never went back to Iraq, allowing Washington's neocons to promote war with Iraq by resuscitating the canard that Saddam still wanted to go nuclear.

2000 – Turkey was troubled by Clinton's long-standing policy of "Dual Containment" of Iran and Iraq. It ran counter to Turkey's interest in promoting normal commercial relations in the region.

2001 – George Bush 43 seems to have come into office resolved to overthrow Saddam Husayn, if only to dispose of the man who allegedly schemed to assassinate Bush the father. The chronology was abrupt:

2001 – On 1/20/01, Bush was sworn in as the 43rd President. According to former Treasury Secretary Paul O'Neill, the decision to invade Iraq was made at Bush's first cabinet meeting.

2001 – In February, the media reported that the Bush administration had approved a plan, drafted by the Clinton administration, to fund Iraqi dissident organizations to collect evidence that Saddam was a war criminal.

2001 – In May, the White House released a report from the Vice President that the invasion of Iraq was essential to insure access to Middle East oil and block the threat of WMD's.

2001– The Al Qa'idah attack on New York and Washington on 9/11/01 had no known Iraqi participation, but it created a climate of outrage that enabled the Administration to convince most Americans, including irresolute Democratic leaders who should have known better, that the regimes in Kabul and Baghdad should be eliminated.

2001 – Bush reportedly told British Prime Minister Blair on 9/20/01 that he intended to invade Iraq.

2001 – American media reported in November that, under pressure from Cheney, Bush had ordered Rumsfeld to prepare for war with Iraq, and the administration was drawing up plans to privatize Iraqi industry.

2001 – Late in the year, Bush had Defense Secretary Rumsfeld update the standing plan for invasion of Iraq. By year-end, the Administration was drawing up occupation plans.

2002 – State of the Union address on 1/29/02: Bush warned of an "axis of evil" – North Korea, Iran, and Iraq. There was no compact to justify Bush's claim.

2002 – General Tommy Franks reportedly told Senator Bob Graham in February that military resources needed in Afghanistan were being shifted for use in invading Iraq.

2002 – In June, Cheney spoke to the Veterans of Foreign Wars about the benefits that would accrue from the ouster of Saddam.

2002 – According to Jonathan Freedland, in July National Security Adviser Rice told the State Department's Richard Haass "The President has made up his mind."

2002 – Kurdish leaders Mas'ud Barzani and Jalal Talabani were brought to Washington to plan military training of Kurds in the KAR. Kirkuk was in Ta'mim Province, outside the KAR, but in Kurdish eyes it was their Jerusalem, and Kirkuk oil was their Holy Grail. Kirkuk had 800,000 residents (Arabs – 70 percent, Kurds – 20 percent, Turkmens – 7 percent). The Turkmens enjoyed Turkish protection, reinforced by the deep-seated Turkish opposition to any expression of Kurdish identity in Turkey, or Kurdish nationalism in Iraq. The embryonic state of

Kurdistan had an income from tariffs on trade between Iraq and Turkey, plus an agreed 13 percent of Iraq's receipts under the Oil-for-Food Program, plus subsidies from the CIA. The power structure was an uneasy combination of the Barzanis' KDP and the Talabanis' PUK. (The Savichi Kurds were still close to the Saddam regime.)

2002 – On 7/23/02, at a meeting of British officials in London (summarized in "the Downing Street Memo"), the head of British intelligence said US intelligence on Iraqi intentions was being "fixed around" Bush 43's decision to oust Saddam: *Vanity Fair*, February 2009.

2002 – In August, Douglas Feith of DOD, close to Israel's Likud, set up his own office to look for anti-Saddam intelligence the Intelligence Community might have missed.

2002 – On 9/12/02, Bush alerted the UN Security Council to Washington's intention to act alone if the Council did not move to insure Iraq had no WMD's.

2002 - On 10/10-11/02, Congress authorized Bush 43 to attack Iraq (by 77 votes in the Senate, 296 in the House). The vote was predicated on erroneous intelligence reporting on the status of Iraq's WMD program.

2002 – On 11/8/02, UNSC Resolution 1441 declared Iraq in material breach of the Council's prior resolutions, set up a new WMD inspection regime, and warned of "serious consequences" if Iraq did not prove it had disarmed. By authorizing UNMOVIC (UN Monitoring, Verification, and Inspection Commission) (for chemical and biological inspections), and the IAEA (for nuclear inspections) to establish zones off limits to Iraqi military action, the Council took a step toward legalizing the two No-Fly Zones imposed by America and Britain (Chapter 9). Bush interpreted 1441 as an authorization to go to war.

2002 – On 11/13/02, Iraq agreed to comply with Resolution 1441, and denied it had WMD's.

2003 – On 1/20/03, Bush signed National Security Presidential Directive 24 setting up the Office for Reconstruction and Humanitarian Assistance (ORHA) in the Department of Defense to run post-invasion Iraq, under the direction of retired Lieutenant General Jay Garner.

2003 – On 1/31/03, Bush and British Prime Minister Blair agreed on March 10 as the date to initiate the attack: *Vanity Fair*.

2003 – On 2/26/03, Washington sponsored the first meeting of Iraqi Arab dissidents on Iraqi soil (the KAR) in nearly ten years.

2003 – The US had made pre-invasion arrangements for stationing troops in Qatar, and staging the invasion from Kuwait, with support operations in Jordan, the UAE, Oman, and Saudi Arabia. Secretary of Defense Rumsfeld and Joint Chiefs Chairman Myers had briefed Saudi Ambassador Bandar Al Sa'ud on invasion planning. The Saudis had authorized American overflights, and restricted access to the air control facilities at Prince Sultan Air Base.

2003 – The Supreme Council of the Islamic Revolution in Iraq (SCIRI) was reportedly infiltrating activists from Iran into Iraq weeks before the Americans invaded.

Invasion

2003 – On 3/19/03, the United States launched Operation Freedom with air attacks on Baghdad.

2003 – On 3/21/03, American ground troops invaded Iraq from Kuwait.

2003 – In March, KRG militia (Peshmerga) rose in the north, and in combination with US Special Forces overran villages controlled by *Ansar al Islam* along the Iranian border. According to Vali Nasr, Grand Ayatallah 'Ali al Sistani instructed his following not to resist the American invasion. His farseeing goal was to seize the opportunity for a historic transfer of power from the Sunnis to the Shia – making Iraq the first Arab state in modern times to be under mainstream Shiite rule. During the occupation, he never met with the Americans, leaving that function to his son.

2003 – On 3/28/03, the UNSC authorized the UN Secretary General to take over the management of the Iraqi Oil-for-Food Program.

2003 – The fall of Baghdad on 4/9/03 precipitated two months of unrestrained looting, arson, and theft of irreplaceable antiquities, undermining the Iraqis' confidence in the competence of the occupation forces. (In 2007, *The Nation* cited Ambassador Barbara Bodine as its source for the report that the American forces in Iraq were instructed by Washington not to interfere with the looters.) The turmoil may have been exacerbated by a highly organized resistance operation to seize especially valuable equipment.

2003 – On 4/9/03, US officers in Baghdad from DOD and the CIA were meeting to discuss reconstitution of the Iraqi Army, which was facing thousands of defections: Mark Danner.

2003 – In April, American forces blew up the pipeline linking northern Iraqi oilfields to Syrian ports.

2003 – In April, Ayatallah 'Abd al Majid al Khu'i, flown into Iraq by the Americans, was hacked to death in Najaf.

2003 – On 4/10/03, the US Army and the Peshmerga captured Kirkuk. Arabs fled, as Kurds looted.

2003 – On 4/13/03, Washington announced that retired Lieutenant General Jay Garner was the head of ORHA (Organization for Reconstruction and Humanitarian Assistance), whose mission was to guide Iraq to self-rule.

2003 – On 4/14/03, Coalition Forces declared victory, after 26 days of combat.

2003 – General Franks outlawed the Baath Party of Iraq (BPI), through Order No. 1, issued by the British-American Coalition Provisional Authority (CPA) on 4/16/03.

2003 – On 4/20/03, despite the widespread Iraqi desire for early withdrawal of the Coalition Forces, Washington was planning to establish four permanent military bases.

2003 – Disinvited by Saudi Arabia from basing its Middle East air operations at Prince Sultan Air Base, south of Al Riyadh, in April the US began the transfer of its squadrons to the new base at Al 'Udayd in Qatar. The Saudi demurral was a reaction to Islamist pressure.

2003 – Press report on 4/21/03: Garner was to be replaced by L. Paul Bremer, who would head a Coalition Provisional Authority (CPA) – the interim government of Iraq.

2003 – On 4/27/03, there were skirmishes in Mawsil between Arabs and Kurds. US forces were disarming Turkmen militia in Kirkuk.

2003 – In April, there was a mass flight of Iraqi refugees to Jordan.

2003 – In late April, US troops fired on demonstrators in Fallujah, killing thirteen.

2003 – On 5/1/03, outfitted in incongruous combat pilot gear, Bush 43 emerged from a small USN plane to the deck of a US carrier to announce "one victory in a war on terrorism". Also on the plane, which was emblazoned "Navy One" and "George W. Bush, Commander-in-Chief", were two US Navy pilots and a Secret Service agent. The dramaturgical setting projected the image of someone who, despite never having seen combat, took pride in the role of war President.

2003 – On 5/6/03, Bush designated Bremer a Presidential Envoy. As a retired Foreign Service Officer, he would be a civilian administrator, but he would supervise ORHA Chief Garner (sic) and report to the Secretary of Defense. Bremer had been a consultant to Kissinger Associates, which continued to exert great influence on the foreign policy establishment from behind the scenes. Bremer was close to Rumsfeld, Wolfowitz, and other neoconservatives.

2003 – The criminal courts in Baghdad resumed operation on 5/8/03.

2003 – On 5/11/03, American-sponsored exiles organized an Interim Iraqi National Assembly.

2003 – **US Proconsul Arrives** – On 5/12/03, Bremer arrived in Iraq. Garner and the ORHA team prepared to leave. The impromptu transfer of authority was tacit recognition of the Coalition's failure to replace the defunct Saddam regime with an effective civil administration; public services were shattered; security was breaking down. The Bremer appointment had been the compromise product of bitter infighting between the Departments of State and Defense.

2003 – On 5/16/03, a Bremer directive banned higher-level members of the BPI from positions in the new Iraqi government.

2003 – On 5/16/03, Bremer ordered that a pro-Iranian Shiite militia force, the Badr Brigade, be disarmed. (The directive was not implemented.) The Kurdish militia was not to be disarmed.

2003 – On 5/22/03, UNSC Resolution 1483 lifted the sanctions on Iraq and assigned the United States and Britain responsibility for running Iraqi affairs, subject to consultation with the Secretary General's Special Representative (Algerian diplomat Lakhdar Brahimi). The Oil-for-Food Program was to be phased out over six months. Iraq's foreign debt was to be rescheduled. Under 1483, the British-American CPA was to administer oil revenues for the benefit of the people of Iraq.

2003 – On 5/22/03, Bremer informed Bush he planned to dissolve Saddam's military and intelligence structures.

2003 – On 5/23/03, by CPA Order No. 2, in consultation with Wolfowitz and Feith, but against Garner's recommendation, Bremer disbanded the Iraqi army and cancelled its pensions, throwing hundreds of thousands of soldiers out of work. He also expelled the top four levels of BPI membership from government service, and dissolved the Republican Guard and the Ministries of Information and Defense.

2003 – The Iraqi oil infrastructure had been so badly damaged that production was down from the prewar two million barrels a day to 300,000. The American military was trucking product from Kuwait.

2003 – On 5/29/03, the Coalition Forces had held municipal elections in a few Iraqi cities. The result in the disputed city of Kirkuk was a Kurdish mayor and a city council with a Kurdish majority.

2003 – In the seven weeks since the capture of Baghdad, Iraq had become a free-trade zone, with immediate termination of the protective tariffs on which Iraqi industry had depended.

2003 – In June, mass Shiite protests foiled a British effort to set up an interim governing council in southern Iraq. SCIRI promised to boycott any council appointed by Bremer. Sistani and Mas'ud Barzani (Kurd) called for the election of a constituent assembly.

2003 – In June, General John Abizaid took over command of CENTCOM.

2003 – Recognizing that disbandment of the army had been a costly error, on 6/24/03 the CPA offered to resume paying 370,000 conscripts and 250,000 officers. Not all those eligible accepted the offer. Many had joined the resistance.

2003 – On 6/26/03, Sistani issued a fatwa demanding general elections for a constituent assembly and a referendum on the draft constitution.

2003 – On 7/2/03, Bush challenged Iraqi insurgents to "bring 'em on".

2003 – Bremer and Sistani having finally reached an accord, the Iraq Interim Governing Council (IGC) held its inaugural meeting on 7/13/03. Of its 25 members, 13 were Shia, representing all the major Shiite factions except that of Muqtada al Sadr. All had been handpicked by the CPA. In *The Middle East Journal* of Spring 2008, Adeed Dawisha noted that, up until the first American invasion in 1991, most Iraqi political parties had taken an Iraqi nationalist stance, but the anti-Baath uprising incited by Bush 41 in 1991 had compelled Saddam to enhance the Sunni character of his regime. In 2003 the CPA had reversed the sectarian mix in the Shiites' favor by its assignments of slots in the IGC. Of the 275 seats in the National Assembly filled by the election of December 2005, 250 were on the basis of ethnicity.

2003 – On 7/22/03, US forces killed Saddam's sons, Uday and Qusay.

2003 – Although the CPA principals had included the leader of SCIRI in the IGC, they feared that SCIRI was too close to the government of Iran. In July, they cancelled plans for an election in Najaf for fear SCIRI would win, and they raided SCIRI headquarters and carted off its files.

2003 – On 7/30/03, the IGC agreed to rotate its presidency monthly among its 25 members.

2003 – In July, the *Times* reported that the US Air Force was using alleged Iraqi violations of the No-Fly Zones as a pretext for conducting attacks on Iraqi defenses.

2003 – In August, Bremer undertook to create a National Defense Force, a Civil Defense Corps, and ancillary security services, and to reactivate the Iraqi police force.

2003 – On 8/7/03, the Jordanian Embassy in Baghdad was bombed (by Al Qa'idah's Abu Mus'ab al Zarqawi?).

2003 – On 8/14/03, UNSC Resolution 1500 welcomed the formation of the IGC.

2003 – On 8/18/03, UN Headquarters in Baghdad was car-bombed (by Zarqawi?). UN Special Representative Vieira De Mello was killed.

2003 – On 8/29/03, Ayatallah Muhammad Baqir al Hakim, Khomeini's choice for leader of an Islamic Republic of Iraq (*Middle East Policy*), like Sistani a supporter of the IGC and an advocate of staying out of the battle between the resistance and the CPA, died in a bombing (Zarqawi?) near the Shrine of Imam 'Ali, one of the two holiest sites in Shiite Islam. Christopher de Bellaigue cited Muhammad Baqir's faction (SCIRI) as the CPA's principal interlocutor in Iraq. He was succeeded by his brother, 'Abd al 'Aziz al Hakim, a member of the IGC.

2003 – On 9/1/03, the IGC appointed an interim cabinet of 25, whose ethnic distribution matched that of the IGC.

2003 – On 9/19/03, the CPA privatized 200 state companies. Foreign firms began moving into Iraq.

2003 – On 9/21/03, the Iraqi Interim Minister of Finance announced a law (drafted by the CPA) allowing foreign investors to own up to 100 percent of any asset except oil enterprises and real estate. (The law would threaten some Iraqi industries.)

2003 – On 10/16/03, UNSC Resolution 1511 conferred a mandate on the CPA to rule Iraq until an indigenous government was formed, but no later than December 31, 2005. It set a December 15, 2003, deadline for the IGC to lay out a timetable for drafting a constitution and setting up a democratic government in Iraq.

2003 – Although the CPA was constrained by Washington's quixotic promise to democratize Iraq, reaffirmed by Resolution 1511, its more pragmatic concern was to block a Shiite theocracy. To this end, in the fall, it announced a plan to select the members of an interim government via regional caucuses (an American contrivance never tried in the Middle East). Sistani rejected the scheme.

2003 – On 11/1/03, an AP report on mistreatment of detainees at Abu Ghurayb Prison in Iraq generated little reaction in the US media.

2003 – On 11/2/03, a SAM shot down a US Chinook helicopter, killing 16 US soldiers.

2003 – On 11/12/03, a suicide truck bombed the Italian troops' headquarters, killing 19 Italians.

2003 – On 11/15/03, as reported by Thomas Ricks, after consultations in Washington with Rumsfeld, Rice, and Bush, Bremer announced that the US would hand over power to the Iraqi authorities by the end of June 2004. (The elaborate plans for an American occupation of several years had been abandoned. Apparently, Washington had realized that, since the neocon ideologues were losing control in Iraq, the time had come for radical lowering of the American profile, to avoid adverse consequences to the Republican ticket in November 2004.)

2003 – By 11/29/03, the CPA had set up 88 neighborhood councils, nine district councils, and one city council, whose members were modestly compensated by the CPA but had no authority and no budgets.

2003 – On 12/13/03, US forces captured Saddam near his hometown of Tikrit.

2003 – On 12/29/03, the IGC replaced the Baathist civil code with one based on Islamic law, to be administered by Shia and Sunni clerics. Women's rights were attenuated.

2004 – In January, by staging huge Shiite demonstrations, Sistani intimidated the CPA into accepting his fatwa blocking plans for CPA appointment of an interim government.

2004 – In February, the Association of Muslim Clerics (Sunni) came out against a proposed election.

2004 – On 2/1/04, two suicide bombers killed 117 in Kurdish political offices in Arbil, KAR.

2004 – On 3/2/04, bombings in Baghdad and Karbala' on 'Ashurah holiday killed nearly 200.

2004 – On 3/8/04, the IGC endorsed the Transitional Administrative Law (TAL), an interim constitution drafted by the CPA. It guarded Kurdish autonomy and restricted Shiite ambitions, by setting up a Presidential Council of three (one Kurd) and stipulating that any three provinces could veto a final constitution by two-thirds majority of the popular vote. The KAR encompassed three of Iraq's eighteen provinces. The Shia delegates to the IGC signed under protest. Bremer tried to get around the Geneva-Convention prohibition against changing the law of an occupied territory by inserting into the TAL a legal booby trap – Article 26, which stated that the CPA's edicts would remain in force after the transfer of authority. The TAL provided for the general election of a constituent assembly by January 31, 2005. Sistani had compromised on the postponement of the general elections, for fear of a civil war.

2004 – On 3/24/04, US Marines took over control of the Fallujah area from the 82nd Airborne.

2004 – On 3/26/04, Bremer issued an executive order specifying that, after the transfer of sovereignty, operational control of the Iraqi armed forces would rest with the American Commander in Iraq, Lt. General Ricardo Sanchez, in accordance with UNSC Resolution 1511. Bremer granted Americans employed by private contractors immunity from Iraqi law: *Times*, 11/11/09. (Blackwater personnel on trial later for the Nisur Square shooting of 9/16/07 cited this exemption.)

2004 – The nom de guerre, Abu Mus'ab al Zarqawi, surfaced. A tape recording attributed to Usamah bin Ladin described Zarqawi as Al Qa'idah's leader in Iraq. The Zarqawi group and another calling itself *Ansar al Sunnah* were held responsible for 2004's wave of abductions and occasional beheadings of foreigners, and of suicide bombings, possibly including a particularly lethal attack on an American mess tent near Mawsil in December 2004. The Islamist wing of the resistance was believed to be receiving subsidies from sympathizers in the Middle East and beyond.

2004 – On 3/26/04, armed resistance erupted in Al Fallujah. On 3/31, four men from Blackwater (military contractor), trying to drive through the insurgent city, were killed and their bodies burned. US Marines fired on a crowd, killed 17 Iraqis, then withdrew.

2004 – Muqtada al Sadr, scion of a revered Shiite family, had been agitating behind the scenes. By closing his newspaper, *Al Hawzah*, the CPA precipitated a resistance effort by Muqtada's JAM (*Jaysh al Mahdi* – Army of the Mahdi). Under American attack, Sadr's forces took cover in the holy cities of Najaf and Karbala'. After heavy fighting and considerable damage to the neighborhoods of the shrines, Sistani arranged mutual withdrawal of the two opposing forces – the JAM still carrying its weapons. Sistani had reaffirmed his status as the leader of the Shiite sect. Sadr had burnished his image as the warrior who had challenged the occupiers and condemned their Iraqi representatives, the CPA-appointed government.

2004 – On 4/5/04, Marines launched an attack on Fallujah, but aborted it on 4/28 after allied Iraqi forces had disengaged.

2004 – On 4/16/04, Bush and Blair accepted the plan of Secretary General Annan's Representative, Lakhdar Brahimi, for the transfer of sovereignty to an Iraqi caretaker government on June 30. The Sistani faction was looking to the general election of January 2005 to defeat the Kurds' campaign for autonomy.

2004 – In May, Zarqawi's AQI (Al Qa'idah in Iraq) beheaded Nicholas Berg, an abducted American contractor.

2004 – Robert Woodward's *Plan of Attack* (2008) revealed that American foreign policy during the occupation of Iraq was being directed by Cheney, Wolfowitz, and Feith.

2004 – The Interim President of the new Iraq was to be Ghazi al Yawar, Sunni, a member of the influential Shammar tribe. Sistani had blocked Bremer's unimaginative choice, 'Adnan Pachachi, whose last official position had been with the British-backed monarchy in 1958.

2004 – On 5/17/04, a suicide attack killed 'Izz al Din Salim, head of the IGC.

2004 – On 5/24/04, the CPA introduced a flat income tax.

2004 – In *The New Yorker* of 5/25/15, Seymour Hersh summarized reports of crimes committed against detainees at Abu Ghurayb Prison. The crimes were condemned by the *Times* of 2/5/15, and later summarized in the media as rape, mistreatment, starvation, deprivation of sleep, sodomy, and one case of murder.

2004 – The CPA announced that the Interim Prime Minister would be Iyad al 'Allawi, Shiite, one-time Baathist and associate of Saddam, later head of the Iraqi National Accord, a secularist Arab exile group long financed by the CIA.

2004 – Bush 43 announced at a press conference on 6/1/04 that Iraqi Prime Minister Iyad al 'Allawi had announced formation of an interim government that would assume sovereignty on 6/30/04, in a major step toward the emergence of a free Iraq. It would include President Ghazi al Yawar, two Deputy Presidents (one Shiite, one Kurd), Prime Minister 'Allawi, five ministers of state, and twenty-six ministers of portfolio. The IGC was to expire at time of transfer of authority.

2004 – On 6/8/04, UNSC Resolution 1546 authorized the transfer of "full sovereignty" by June 30. 1546 had been meticulously drafted to downplay two awkward facts: 1) The invasion of Iraq had been an unauthorized, unilateral American action. Two months had elapsed before Washington had brought the conflicted Security Council on board (its Resolution 1483 of May 22, 2003). 2) The "sovereign Interim Government of Iraq" was to be the creature of the CPA. Responsibility for the physical security of its Prime Minister was to be assigned to American bodyguards, and its survival was to depend on American military suppression of the resistance. Under 1546, the UNSC agreed that the UN Assistance Mission for Iraq (established August 14, 2003; cut back sharply after the bombing of UN headquarters in Baghdad August 18, 2003) would play a leading role in facilitating the emergence of "a federal, democratic, pluralist and unified Iraq." Under pressure from Sistani, Washington had drafted 1546 to omit any mention of the TAL. To mollify the Kurds, 'Allawi agreed to keep the TAL in force, pending a ruling by the government to be elected in 2005. The Coalition Forces, identified in 1546 as the "multinational force", were to remain in Iraq (under American command) for an unspecified time.

2004 – On 6/27/04, Bremer's Executive Order Number 9 authorized the Coalition Forces to appropriate property as needed, notably for American headquarters and embassy in Baghdad's "Green Zone".

2004 – **The Proconsul Departs** – A new provisional constitution set a goal of 25 percent of Parliament to be women. A police pickup fired on the car of three CPA civilian employees, who were killed. One was Fern Holland, largely responsible for the 25 percent minimum for women: *Times*, 8/15/16.

2004 – During the year, Sadr unleashed his militia (JAM), which caused the abandonment of a CPA compound.

2004 – On 6/28/04, two days ahead of the Resolution 1546 deadline (a security precaution), the CPA transferred pro forma sovereignty to the Interim Government, and then dissolved itself. Bremer left Iraq. The Interim Government was a handpicked regime headed by Iyad 'Allawi. Saddam's former "Republican Palace" was to become the American Embassy. Bremer had prevailed on 'Allawi to honor CPA edicts favoring foreign investment, but the concession was academic: The resistance had destroyed the investment climate.

2004 – In June, Muqtada al Sadr arranged a prisoner exchange with 'Allawi's security forces and ordered his militia to go home. They remained the de facto government and police force in Sadr City (a Baghdad quarter where Muqtada had a massive cult following). Sadr adopted a more conciliatory tone vis-à-vis the Interim Government.

2004 – Israel had been sending military and intelligence operatives into the KAR: NY, 6/28/04, Seymour Hersh.

2004 – On 6/29/04, Ambassador John Negroponte presented his credentials to the leaders of the Interim Government (Yawar and 'Allawi).

2004 – On 7/1/04, General George Casey replaced Lt. General Ricardo Sanchez as commander of the Coalition Forces. By this time, the American effort to stabilize, pacify, and democratize Iraq had been blocked by the automatic resentment that all people feel for alien rule, exacerbated by the innate perversity of the country's demographic make-up: In the center, the occupiers were wrestling with a recalcitrant Sunni-Shia mix; in the south, the British were trying to keep the lid on Shiite factionalism; in the north, the Kurds were moving fast to exploit their sudden autonomy.

2004 – In July, an uneasy partnership of two rival Kurdish factions took advantage of US preoccupation with Arab Iraq to set up the basics of a Kurdish Regional Government (KRG) on 17,000 square miles of the Zagros Mountains in northeast Iraq between the Tigris River in the west, the Turkish frontier in the north, the Iranian border in the east, and Iraq proper in the south. After centuries of subjugation to rival communities, 3,500,000 Kurds had acquired a de facto state, comprising the three Iraqi provinces of Dahuq, Arbil, and Sulaymaniyyah. The KRG had its own president, parliament, flag, currency, passports, constitution, and a redoubtable militia, the Peshmerga. The Barzani headquarters was in Arbil; the Talabani headquarters was in Sulaymaniyyah.

2004 – On 7/6/04, 'Allawi signed the National Security Law, which gave him emergency powers.

2004 – In July, the CPA set up an Iraqi Special Tribunal under the direction of a nephew of Ahmad Chalabi.

2004 – In August, there was a second clash in Najaf between US and Sadrist forces.

2004 – In August, with CPA help, the Interim Government convened a National Conference of 100 and a Consultative Conference of 1000. Neither produced operational results.

2004 – On 9/30/04, a car bomb killed 35 children waiting for candy from US soldiers.

2004 – In October, General David Petraeus published an op-ed claiming that "tangible progress" had been made in Iraq. Paul Krugman suggested the piece was timed to help the administration in the November election.

2004 – On 11/3/04, the day after his reelection, Bush 43 reportedly issued an intemperate, illegal order for US forces in Iraq to lead an attack on the city of Fallujah, in reprisal for its killing of four American contract security personnel on 3/31/04: *Philadelphia Inquirer*, John A. Nagl.

2004 – From 11/8/04 to 11/18/04, coalition forces (American with some help from Kurd and Shiite forces of the Interim Government) conducted a massive offensive against Fallujah, leaving it a shambles, depopulated except for a few hundred resisters hiding out in the rubble. Sistani stood aside (as if defense of Sunnis is not a Shiite concern). Naomi Klein has noted that the Fallujah operation contributed to the alienation of the Sunni community, whose general abstention from the January 2005 election was to leave the Transitional Government under the control of the Shia and the Kurds.

2004 – On 11/22/04, Western states cancelled 80 percent of the 39 billion dollar debt they were owed by Iraq. Debts totaling over 100 billion dollars to Middle East states were still outstanding.

2004 – On 12/14/04, Bush awarded the nation's highest civilian decoration, the Medal of Freedom, to three dubious recipients: Paul Bremer, Tommy Franks, and George Tenet.

2004 – On 12/21/04, a bombing killed 18 Americans.

2004 – On 12/26/04, 31 US soldiers died in a helicopter crash.

2005 – On 1/30/05, per Resolution 1546, the election for a 275-member Transitional National Assembly (TNA) was held, under extreme security. In the words of Mark Danner, it was an "ethnic census", not a democratic procedure. The results were unrepresentative, because most Sunnis and many Sadrists had boycotted it, allowing SCIRI to win 40 percent of the vote in Baghdad and take control of six of the eight Shia-majority provinces in the south. The Assembly elected Jalal Talabani (Kurd) as President. Ibrahim al Ja'fari became Prime Minister: *World Almanac*, 2016.

2005 – In February, Iraq was beset by the first of a wave of Shiite revenge killings of BPI leaders.

2005 – In April, the CPA abandoned its campaign to privatize Iraqi industry.

2005 – On 4/7-8/05, after two months of altercation, the TNA elected – per the TAL of March 8, 2004 – the leaders of the Transitional Government: Prime Minister Ibrahim al Ja'fari (Shiite Arab), President Jalal Talabani (Sunni Kurd), Vice President Ghazi al Yawar (Sunni Arab), Vice President 'Adil 'Abd al Mahdi (Shiite Arab), and Speaker Hajim al Hasani (Sunni Turkmen). The TNA took no action on basic constitutional issues. Election of a permanent government was scheduled by December 31, 2005.

2005 – **Shiite Death Squads** – The designation in April of Bayan Sulagh (Bayan Jabr), Shiite Turkmen, former officer of the Badr Brigade, as Minister of the Interior coincided with the emergence of anti-Sunni death squads: Ken Silverstein.

2005 – In May, the Transitional Government of Prime Minister Ibrahim al Ja'fari was sworn in. Basic constitutional issues continued to divide the three main ethnic factions.

2005 – **American Death Squads** – In May, in an unsuccessful attempt to end the Iraqi resistance, the American occupation forces instituted the Israeli practice of targeted assassination of resistance leaders: *Newsweek,* Michael Hirsch and John Barry, 5/14/05, cited in *Middle East Policy* of Fall 2008.

2005 – On 6/13/05, the Kurdish "National Assembly" elected Mas'ud Barzani President of Kurdistan and Commander in Chief of its armed forces.

2005 – In July, in Tehran, Ja'fari signed an agreement for major Iranian military and economic aid.

2005 – On 7/19/05, nearly 100 Shia died in a bombing.

2005 – In August, the new Iraqi army was being organized by sect: 60 Shiite battalions, 50 Sunni, 10 Kurd (in addition to the Peshmerga?).

2005 – In August, US prisons in Iraq, holding 40,000 Islamist, Sunni, and Sadrist militants, had become anti-American resistance schools.

2005 – In August, the media began to report on a draft constitution. It reportedly required a two-thirds vote in Parliament to form a government. According to *The Middle East Report* of Winter 2005, most Sunni factions, including the Iraqi Islamic Party and the Association of Muslim Scholars, were distressed that the draft called for de-Baathification and federalism, and omitted reference to non-Arab Iraqis in the specification that "the Arab people of Iraq are part of the Arab nation." Defenders of the draft said it protected Sunni interests by providing for per-capita division of oil revenues. In *The New York Review of Books* of 10/6/05, Peter Galbraith reported that Condoleeza Rice had required the Shia and Kurds to accept Sunnis in the drafting process, but the views of the Sunni team, dominated by Baathists chosen by Salih al Mutlaq, an ally of 'Allawi, had been overruled in favor of a draft slanted to produce three autonomous entities – one Sunni, one Kurdish, and one Shia (under Iranian influence). A federal regime would control foreign affairs, defense, and economic affairs other than taxation, but other matters, including newly discovered oil, would be reserved for the regional governments. According to the *Times* of 12/29/05, the draft constitution provided for a referendum on whether Kirkuk's province should come under the administration of Baghdad or the KRG. The May 2007 *Atlantic* reported that, if 10 percent of residents of any of the three provinces adjoining the KAR (Ninawah, Ta'mim, Diyala) should petition to join the KAR, a referendum would be held to decide the issue.

2005 – On 8/31/05, rumors of a suicide bomber set off a stampede in northern Baghdad in which 1000 died.

2005 – In September, Zarqawi "declared war" against "collaborators" – meaning Shiites, excepting Sadrists.

9/14/05 – On 9/14/05, bombings in Baghdad killed 160, injured over 500.

2005 – **Resistance Escalating into a Three-Way Ethnic War** – In October, a war between Sunni and Shiite death squads was breaking out in Baghdad: Peter Galbraith; Mark Danner. The Sunni Islamist aim was to spark sectarian war that would draw in Sunni forces from neighboring countries. Killings were also reported in Basrah. Kurdish participation was in the cards.

2005 – In *Current History* of January 2006, Phoebe Marr reported that the TNA had ratified the draft constitution on 10/15/05. Formation of a government would require a two-thirds majority vote in Parliament. Vali Nasr detected the influence of Sistani in the provision that no law should contradict the tenets of Islamic jurisprudence, although in Nasr's view the Shia revivalists were open to democratic change. In Joost Hilterman's opinion, the constitution gutted the power of the central government.

2005 – On 11/8/05, at the request of Prime Minister Ja'fari, the UNSC extended the mandate of the multilateral force until 12/31/06.

2005 – On 11/19/05, in reported retribution for the combat death of an American soldier, US Marines reportedly killed 24 unarmed Iraqis. Prosecution of eight Marines dragged on for six years, after which one Marine was reduced in rank for dereliction of duty. Three supervisory officers had been reprimanded for failure to investigate.

2005 – On 12/15/05, the United Iraqi Alliance (SCIRI, Al Da'wah, Sadrists) won a near majority of the 275 seats in the new Parliament. Peter Galbraith reported in *The New Yorker* that the Kurds had won the right to their own oil, their own army, and their own law. Muqtada Sadr failed to win Sunnis over to an anti-American Shia-Sunni bloc: Juan Cole. According to Nasr, American Ambassador Khalilzad warned the

Alliance that exclusion of Sunnis from the next government could mean loss of American financial aid.

2006 – Early in the year, the American attempt to pacify Iraq by conventional patrols, vehicle or foot, had been frustrated by a stubborn guerrilla resistance whose most lethal weapon was the IED (Improvised Explosive Device). In the turbulent environment of Iraq, incidental expenditure on upgrading the school system, the CIA's takeover of Iraqi intelligence, and the construction of an immense network of military bases, were not compelling issues. On February 22, 2006, the bombing of the Golden Dome threw the Americans into the middle of a sectarian civil conflict, with the Shiites resisting Ambassador Khalilzad's futile efforts to bring Sunnis into the government, and the Sunnis raging at the Americans for failing to protect them from Shiite death squads.

2006 – In January, there were clashes in northern Iraq between Kurds and a combine of Arab and Turkmen forces.

2006 – On 1/7/06, the *Times* reported clashes between AQI (Al Qa'idah in Iraq) and Sunni resisters, alienated by AQI's strategy of ethnic cleansing of Shiites.

2006 – On 2/16/06, Parliament confirmed Ibrahim al Ja'fari as Prime Minister after he promised Sadr he would oppose a federal system and Kurdish takeover of Kirkuk, and support a timetable for the withdrawal of American troops.

2006 – On 2/22/06, by destroying the Golden Dome (a legendary feature of the 'Askariyyah Mosque in Samarra'), site of the tombs of the tenth and eleventh Imams, AQI finally achieved its objective of sectarian civil war. In the ensuing religious frenzy, Sadr lost control of many of his Shite militants, who revere their shrines as devoutly as Salafists hate them.

2006 – On 4/6/06, Patrick Cockburn reported in *The London Review of Books* that Article 140 of the new Iraqi constitution provided for returning Kirkuk to its demographic status before Saddam's expulsion of over 100,000 Kurds and their replacement with Arab settlers from south Iraq.

2006 – In April, thousands of Iraqis were fleeing from homes in ethnically mixed neighborhoods.

213

2006 – In May, American forces began a campaign to suppress the fighting in Baghdad.

2006 – In May, Nuri al Maliki replaced Ja'fari as Prime Minister. Maliki had spent most of his exile, not in Iran, but as director of the SCIRI office in Damascus. He was a follower of pro-Hizballah Lebanese cleric Muhammad Husayn Fadlallah (not Ayatallah Sistani who, according to Juan Cole, was closer to the tamer Amal). At Sunni insistence, Bayan Sulagh lost the ministry of interior and went to the ministry of finance.

2006 – On 5/20/06, Iraq swore in a new cabinet of 37 under Prime Minister Nuri al Maliki (Shia): 20 Shiites, 8 Sunni Arabs, 8 Kurds, 1 Christian. Three of the 37 were women.

2006 – On 6/8/06, the US military killed AQI leader Abu Mus'ab al Zarqawi and some of his aides.

2006 – In June, sabotage of the oil pipelines from Iraq to Turkey came to a stop. Sectarian violence was still escalating. The Tigris was clogged with human corpses: *The Atlantic*, September 2015, Peter Beinart.

2006 – On 7/9/06, Shia militias killed 40 Sunnis.

2006 – On 7/11/06, militiamen in black were roaming some Baghdad neighborhoods, killing Sunnis on the spot.

2006 – According to Michael Schwartz, by August the sectarian fighting had spiraled out of control. The American forces, which had entered that conflict in Baghdad in May, with heavy ground and air shelling, had done serious damage to buildings and public services, and by enclosing neighborhoods with concrete blast walls had ghettoized the city, from which 800,000 had taken flight.

2006 – On 8/11/06, there were clashes in Basrah between followers of Ayatallah Mustafa al Ya'qubi of Najaf and those of Sayyid Mahmud al Sarkhi of Karbala'. The pro-Sarkhi faction reacted to criticism of their leader in the Iranian press by burning the Iranian consulate: Juan Cole Blog.

2006 – On 8/19/06, the Jordanian ambassador, first Arab envoy to post-invasion Iraq, presented his credentials, but no embassy was opened (?). An Egyptian ambassador was abducted and killed a month after his arrival: *MEP*, Winter 2009, Gawdat Bahgat.

2006 – In August, to reduce the risk of US confrontation with Turkey over Kurdish autonomy, the State Department appointed General Joseph Ralston as a special envoy to assist Iraq and Turkey in suppressing PKK activity in the KAR.

2006 – **Rise of the Awakening** – In the summer, the non-Iraqi Arabs leading the AQI, which had been in league with the Mashhadani tribe, made a fatal error of trying to impose a reign of terror, marked by torture, imprisonment, summary executions, beheadings, and fanatic Islamism (veils, no smoking) in viscerally tribal 'Anbar Province. As reported by Patrick Cockburn in *Muqtada*, by Ahmed Hashim in *Current History*, and by Pepe Escobar in *Asia Times Online*, the AQI's proclamation of an "Islamic State of Iraq" was the last straw. Caught between the Shia and the AQI, Sunni tribes joined in formation of the 'Anbar Sovereignty Council (later called *Al Sahwah*, The Awakening, by the Anbaris; "Concerned Local Citizens" by the Americans). The organization's aim was to shut down the AQI (and later to deal with the Shia leadership in Baghdad).

2006 – In the summer, the sectarian battle of Baghdad ended with three-fourths of the city under Shiite control.

2006 – In September, Al Sahwah approached US Marines and offered to change sides. Following past British and Iraqi example, Petraeus picked up the option. By agreeing to pay recruits, both Shiite and Sunni, some 300 dollars a month, he bought a quieter Iraq.

2006 – On 9/9/06, the first audio message was received from Abu Hamzah al Muhajir (Abu Ayyub al Masri), reputed successor to Zarqawi as head of the AQI. He was thought to be an Egyptian explosives expert trained by Al Qa'idah in Afghanistan.

2006 – On 10/11/06, over the objections of Sunnis and some Shiites, Parliament adopted a law providing for each of Iraq's provinces to hold a referendum offering two choices: a unified state or a federation of autonomous regions.

2006 – On 10/16/06, the US military was reportedly building two bases in the KAR.

215

2006 – *Reuters* reported on 10/18/06 that Iraq had an unemployment rate of 60 percent and inflation of 70 percent.

2006 – Battle of 'Amarah between the Shiite JAM and the Shiite Badr Organization on 10/19/06.

2006 – In November, suspecting that Prime Minister Maliki had become an American puppet, thirty Sadrist MP's walked out, leaving Parliament unable to muster a quorum. (They were back by June 2007.)

2006 – The administration's failure to pacify Iraq produced a Democratic victory in the Congressional elections in November. Bush replaced Rumsfeld with Robert Gates.

2006 – The US had hoped to keep Saddam's December trial under strict control – in part to exclude any mention of Washington's authorization of the sale of anthrax and botulinum to Iraq for use against Iran in the 1980's (*The New York Times Magazine*), but Saddam was hanged on 12/30/06 by the embittered Shiite government in a manner more like a revenge killing than a judicial procedure.

2006 – On 12/6/06, the Iraq Study Group (ISG) (Baker and Hamilton) issued a gloomy estimate of the prospects of the US occupation of Iraq, which was in the throes of intense sectarian warfare, with some neighborhoods of Baghdad, per Juan Cole's blog, already depopulated of Sunnis. The Baker/Hamilton report was a thinly veiled indictment of Bush's foreign policy.

2006 – Writing in *Harper's*, George McGovern and Bill Polk argued that the US should reimburse Iraq for the nearly 200 billion dollars the CPA had overcharged Iraq in oil-concession negotiations.

2006 – By the end of the year, American forces and those of the Maliki regime were under attack by Sunni mujahideen and Muqtada's Shiite nationalists – who were probably responsible for most of the shells falling on the Green Zone, sanctuary of the American command and Maliki's government. America's Provincial Reconstruction Teams were blocked from pursuing their designated mission by their restriction to base, or to armored convoys. Baghdad had disintegrated into sectarian fragments, and countrywide sabotage of the infrastructure was making normal life an impossibility. Suicide bombings, new to Iraq, from 2003 to the end of 2007 exceeded 750. Nir Rosen cited castration and torture by electric drills as signature practices of the Shiite militias.

2007 – Early in the year, American forces (140,000, backed by 160,000 civilian contractors, including 25,000 armed guards, mostly Americans) were taking casualties from more sophisticated IED's – Explosively Formed Projectiles (EFP), which in the view of US Intelligence were being made in Iran, and supplied to Shiite militants by the Quds Force of the Islamic Revolutionary Guard. In the cynical words of an American soldier, "Our basic mission is to drive around until we get blown up." In Basrah Province, the British occupiers were under constant fire, whether on base or out on patrol. Retired General Barry McCaffrey came home in April from a visit to Iraq with an estimate that, despite having killed 20,000 militants and imprisoned another 27,000 (exclusive of 37,000 in GOI custody), the Americans and their poorly equipped Iraqi allies were confronted by 100,000 Sunni and Shia militants.

2007 –Iraqi labor unions were blocking the CPA's effort to impose an inequitable oil law on the Maliki Government: *MER*, Spring 2007.

2007 –The Transitional Administrative Law promoted by the occupation authority enshrined ethnic divisions, including a "Shiastan" of the nine southern provinces: *MER*, Spring 2007.

2007 – On 1/10/07, US troops switched their focus from killing insurgents to protecting civilians. Bush elevated the number of troops in Iraq from 132 thousand to 171 thousand – known in the US media as "the Surge": *World Almanac*, 2016.

2007 – On 1/20/07, the US blamed Iran for the killing of five US soldiers.

2007 – On 1/28/07, the "Battle of Najaf" engaged Shiite militias; nearly 300 died.

2007 – In February, the heaviest casualties among AQI militants were being inflicted by Iran-sponsored Shiite militias.

2007 – On 2/3/07, a bomb in Baghdad killed 135.

2007 – In February, Muqtada withdrew his JAM from action. Two Sadrists, former officials of the Ministry of Health, were arrested on charges of organizing the murders of hundreds of Sunni staff, patients, and visiting relatives in Baghdad hospitals.

2007 – On 3/6/07, bombings in Al Hillah killed 120 Shia.

2007 – On 3/27/07, a bomb in Tall 'Afar killed 132. Shia retaliated, killing 70 Sunnis.

2007 – On 3/28/07, at the 19th Arab League summit, King 'Abdallah of Saudi Arabia pronounced the occupation of Iraq illegal.

2007 – On 3/29/07, suicide bombings in Baghdad killed 82 Shia.

2007 – On 4/16/07, Sadr withdrew his six ministers from the government in protest against Maliki's failure to set a date for withdrawal of the American troops.

2007 – On 4/18/07, bombings in Baghdad killed nearly 200.

2007 – May was the third deadliest month to that time for American soldiers. The first battle of Fallujah had brought 147 deaths. The second battle of Fallujah brought deaths in November 2004 to 140. Deaths in May 2007 were 120. However, the overall situation was about to change. First, in February 2007, against the advice of his military chiefs, Bush instituted the "surge". Second, the American command had recruited thousands of Awakening militants, many of whom had previously been active in the resistance.

2007 – In May, according to Pepe Escobar, control of 'Anbar Province was split between the ASC, headed by Shaykh 'Abd al Sattar Abu Rishah, and the AQI, headed by Abu 'Umar al Baghdadi and Abu Hamzah al Muhajir.

2007 – In May, amid emerging confrontation between Iraqi unionists and federalists, Muqtada appealed for a united Shia-Sunni front.

2007 – In May, the oil pipelines from Kirkuk to the Mediterranean were inoperative (sabotaged by the resistance).

2007 – In June, SCIRI changed its name to the Islamic Supreme Iraqi Council (ISCI).

2007 – During the four-month period of June-September, four associates of Sistani were shot.

2007 – In July, in a video appearance, Zawahiri (Al Qa'idah) warned the AQI to work for Sunni unity.

2007 – On 7/10/07, the Green Zone, hideout of the American leadership and the Iraqi Government, was hit by projectiles – probably fired from Sadr City – that killed three, including one American and one member of Parliament, and wounded 22 MP's: *Times*, 2/26/09.

2007 – On 7/16/07, bombings in Kirkuk killed 86.

2007 – On 7/17/07, bombing in Amirli killed 156.

2007 – On 7/26/07, bombing in Baghdad killed 92.

2007 – On 8/14/07, four bombings of Yazidi communities killed 746.

2007 – In August, Tawafuq, the main Sunni bloc in Parliament, withdrew its fifteen ministers from the Maliki Government. (*Tawafuq* is variously translated in the media as Accord, Consensus, or Dialogue.)

2007 – On 8/20/07, clashes between Sadr's JAM and the Badr Force led to 51 deaths in Karbala'. Two ISCI provincial governors had also been killed.

2007 – On 8/28/07, Maliki announced agreement for the reinstatement of all but senior Baathists in jobs they had held in the Saddam Government.

2007 – On 8/29/07, Sadr ordered his JAM to freeze its activities for six months. Outside observers inferred that casualties inflicted on the JAM by ISCI's Badr Force, and/or by Maliki's "governmental" forces, with American air support, had decided Sadr to wait out the anticipated departure of the American forces. The freeze had the added advantage of dissociating the JAM from the expulsion of Sunnis from most of Baghdad.

2007 – On 9/13/07, Shaykh 'Abd al Sattar Abu Rishah, leader of the Awakening forces in 'Anbar Province, was killed – presumably by the AQI.

2007 – On 9/16/07, in Baghdad's Nisur Square, 17 civilians died when Blackwater contractors guarding an American convoy opened fire, which was later defended by Blackwater as an appropriate response to the circumstances, but denounced by Iraqi officials as lethal irresponsibility. The occurrence cost Blackwater its license to operate in Iraq. An article in the 2/1/09 *Times* suggested that this tragedy was the

219

tipping point between acceptance and rejection of the American military presence.

2007 – In October, Nir Rosen concluded that Iraq had broken up into city-states, loosely associated in sectarian cantons.

2007 – On 10/6/07, Nechirvan Barzani, KRG Prime Minister, wrote in *The Wall Street Journal* that the KRG's oil law followed the central government's formula for division of oil revenues: 83 percent for Baghdad, 17 percent for the KRG. So far the KRG had signed on its own eight production-sharing contracts. It hoped for continuation of the American presence.

2007 – On 10/13/07, British forces in Iraq were transferred from Basrah to a nearby air base.

2007 – On 10/29/07, the Americans' impending transfer of authority in Karbala' Province would bring the number of provinces under direct Iraqi control to 8 of 18.

2007 – On 11/12/07, near the Basrah oil terminal, the US Navy was building a military installation as a link in America's defense structure in the Gulf.

2007 – A dramatic drop in bombings and murders in Iraq in November, especially in Baghdad, was due to the 2006-07 "surge" in the number of American forces, to ethnic cleansing – including the Shiites' concurrent expulsion of nearly a million Sunnis from Baghdad (reported by Juan Cole in *The Nation* of 1/12/09), to compartmentalization of major cities by checkpoints and blast walls, to American recruitment of the Awakening forces, to tighter Syrian and Saudi restrictions on entry of foreign militants into Iraq, and to the JAM's stand-down.

2007 – In November, Tawafuq was boycotting Parliament in protest against the alleged arrest of its leader, 'Adnan al Dulaymi.

2007 – On 12/17/07, the UK reportedly transferred control of Basrah to the Maliki Government.

2007 – On 12/19/07, the UNSC extended the Multinational Force's mandate to 12/31/08.

2008 – In January, Parliament ruled that all but the most senior members of Saddam's BPI (Baath Party of Iraq) could return to their previous positions in the Iraqi Government (see 8/28/07 entry).

2008 – In February, when the American force in Iraq was back up to 157,000, Thomas Ricks wrote that the US was fighting three wars in Iraq: The action against the AQI was going fairly well (thanks to the rift between the AQI and The Awakening); the action against the mainstream Sunnis was dormant (by virtue of the new strategy of cooptation); the heaviest American casualties (down to 36 in February) were coming from the conflict with Shiite militants who were believed to be receiving arms, training, and funding from Iran. Lt. General Raymond Odierno told the *Times* US casualties were coming half from the AQI, half from the Shiites. According to *The Nation*, the American forces were still relying on massive air attacks.

2008 – In February, since the evacuation of British forces from Basrah, the city had become the arena of a Shiite power struggle.

2008 – On 2/21/08, Turkey launched an offensive against PKK rebels in northern Iraq.

2008 – In March, the Sunni resistance to the Baghdad regime was intensifying in Mawsil, whose officials were primarily Kurdish, but whose 1.8 million residents were mostly Arab.

2008 – Three major Shiite factions maintained militias in Iraq: ISCI (Badr Brigade), the Sadrists (JAM), and Fadilah. Maliki deployed the new Iraqi army against restive JAM forces in Baghdad, Basrah, and Maysan provinces (presumably hoping to consolidate his regime's position while the American forces were still around to help). In reaction to initial JAM successes (*Times* of April 7), US air units, Special Forces, and Awakening allies intervened in decisive force (*Times* of June 21), and sealed off Sadr City. Muqtada again shut down the JAM's military operations, even those in Sadr City, and called on his forces to cooperate with the regime.

2008 – In April, US and GOI forces occupied the southern quarter of Sadr City to inhibit the firing of rockets into the Green Zone. In June, the US command was recruiting Sadr City Shiites as "neighborhood guards".

2008 – On 4/10/08, the *Monitor Online* reported that the AQI, defeated in 'Anbar, had moved north to Diyala, Salah al Din, and Ninawah Provinces (http://www.csmonitor.com/).

2008 – Since January, the pro-Baghdad authorities in Mawsil had arrested 1100 Sunni militants, most of them former Baathists.

2008 – The AQI was blamed for several bombings in 'Anbar, Baghdad, and Ninawah Provinces in June, killing many Iraqis and several American soldiers.

2008 – On 7/19/08, Tawafuq cancelled its walkout of almost a year after Sunnis were guaranteed five ministries and one deputy premiership. The Sadrist bloc was still boycotting.

2008 – According to Robert Dreyfuss, writing in *The Nation* of 3/9/09, twelve Iraqi nationalist (unionist) factions had founded the "7/22 Gathering" on 7/22/08 to denounce the assignment of political position by ethnic community. They blamed the Coalition, in its emphasis on ethnicity (as exemplified in the language of the Constitution and in the election of 2005), for Iraq's having set up a government they considered unrepresentative and incompetent.

2008 – On 7/28/08, there were clashes between Kurds and Turkmens in Kirkuk.

2008 – On 7/30/08, *AP* reported that over the preceding year nearly 40 Sadrist leaders had been killed and over 60 detained by Maliki's forces. Muqtada was studying Islamic theology in Qom, Iran.

2008 – In August, Patrick Cockburn commented that the Americans had gotten themselves into the position of subsidizing two rival factions (Sunnis and Shia), but the only pro-American community in Iraq was the Kurds. According to *The Washington Post Weekly*, the US was practicing "Saddam-style politics".

2008 – In August, Kurdish forces under the command of Masrur Mas'ud Barzani controlled the key city of Kirkuk (population 900,000).

2008 – In August, The Awakening was challenging the traditional dominance of the Iraqi Islamic Party in 'Anbar Province.

2008 – In August, Iran had taken an active role in the construction of a new international airport for the Shiite pilgrimage center of Najaf: Kristian Ulrichsen.

2008 – On 8/22/08, pro-Baghdad authorities were arresting Awakening leaders in Diyala Province – a harbinger of post-occupation hostility between Shiite leaders in Baghdad and Sunnis in 'Anbar and points north.

2008 – On 8/25/08, *The Washington Post Weekly* reported that many units of the Iraqi army were unisectarian.

2008 – In September, Iraq's South Oil Company signed a 51-49 deal with Royal Dutch Shell to recover natural gas.

2008 – On 10/23/08, Peter Galbraith wrote that the Kurds, alienated from their former Iraqi allies, were striking out on their own. Kurdish officials affirmed their intention to retain control of the government of Ninawah Province, and reiterated their claim to its eastern districts.

2008 – On 10/28/08, Baathist and nationalist Sunnis in Ninawah, resentful of the Kurdish presence and of the support given it by the Americans, formed *Al Hadbah* (name of the leaning minaret of Mawsil's Al Nuri Grand Mosque: *Times*, 6/30/17) to contest provincial elections. The minaret was toppled by the IS in June 2017: *NYTM*, 7/23/17.

2008 – In November, the Maliki Government took over responsibility for paying Awakening's militants.

2008 – On 11/17/08, US Ambassador Crocker and Iraqi Foreign Minister Hishyar Zebari (Sunni Kurd) signed a status-of-forces agreement (SOFA) effective for three years, subject to one year's notice of cancellation. US forces – excluding trainers and support teams – would leave most Iraqi cities by 6/30/09 and the country by 12/31/11. The Iraqi Islamic Party, a member of Tawafuq, the Sunni bloc, demanded that the agreement be subjected to a referendum.

2008 – On 11/27/08, Parliament adopted a Status of Forces Agreement (SOFA) 149-35(including 30 Sadrists); of 275 MP's, 198 were present. Either signatory wanting to disengage from the SOFA had to give one year's notice. As of 1/1/09, the government of Iraq was to take military responsibility for the Green Zone, the US would conduct no military operations in Iraq without Baghdad's consent, and its civilian security contractors would be subject to Iraqi law. Maliki said America's 58 bases in Iraq would revert to Iraq. The agreement fell far short of Washington's invasion objective of making Iraq America's primary military base in the Arab World: Tomgram of 7/9/09

, Michael Schwartz. According to Patrick Cockburn (*The London Review of Books*), the agreement had rendered the invasion a failure. Juan Cole reported in *The Nation* that the Shiite opposition (Sadrists and Virtue Party) opposed the agreement as too liberal; its endorsement by the national referendum scheduled for July 2009 was not assured.

2008 – In December, the Kuwaiti Ambassador presented his credentials. Kuwait was holding out for full payment of Iraq's war debt.

2008 – On 12/4/08, the Presidential Council of three approved the SOFA, subject to referenda on it and on other key political issues.

2008 – On 12/23/08, Parliament extended until 12/31/09 Iraq's exemption from civil suits for damages inflicted by the Saddam Government.

2008 – On 12/24/08, Parliament approved the stay of non-American foreign troops beyond 12/31/08.

2008 – Iraq signed a twenty-year 3.5-billion-dollar contract with China to develop oil and gas production in Wasit Province, and a partnership with Royal Dutch Shell to recover natural gas.

2008 – Pepe Escobar took the position that Iraq's conclusion of oil production-sharing agreements with several Western oil companies proved that oil had been the primary British and American motive for invading Iraq. Michael Klare shared that view.

2008-09 – After the failure of two prime ministers, Washington had settled on a third, Nuri al Maliki, as its protégé in Iraq. Maliki was torn between his dependence on the support of the American occupation forces, and Iraqi expectations that the post-occupation government would demonstrate freedom from foreign influence – particularly on the Palestine issue. Maliki began a campaign of harassing Sunnis by arrest and intimidation: Peter Beinart.

2009 – In January, with the new administration in Washington committed to early withdrawal of "combat" troops, troop strength in Iraq was 145,000; Iraqis in American custody numbered 16,000 (plus 24,000 held by the Maliki regime). The American fortress/embassy, sitting on 104 acres, had a staff of a thousand plus a maintenance staff of several thousand, and was self-sufficient in water and electric power. The few thousand remaining Brits would be gone by the end of the year.

2009 – On 1/1/09, the SOFA replaced the UN mandate over foreign military operations in Iraq. The US transferred to Iraq responsibility for The Green Zone and all 18 provinces. Britain turned over control of the Basrah airport.

2009 – The Kirkuk police force was largely staffed with Kurds, and the KRG was taking every opportunity to expel Arabs from Mawsil and other parts of northern Iraq with the same brutality the Arabs had once inflicted on the Kurds. So far, Kurdish expansionism had not been inhibited by warnings of American intervention, or by the more sobering threat of Turkish intervention. Claiming an obligation to protect the interests of the Turkmen minority, numerous in the Kirkuk area, the Turks were obsessed by the contingency that a Kurdish state in Iraq could galvanize Kurdish nationalism in southeastern Turkey.

2009 – On 1/26/09, the Naqshabandi Army shot down two US helicopters, killing four soldiers. This organization was an underground Sufi Baathist militia formally known as the Army of the Men of the Naqshabandi Path. Its clandestine leader was said to be former Iraqi officer 'Izzat Ibrahim al Duri.

2009 – The resistance had not conceded. Iraq had a sovereign government, but no heavy weapons, no air force, and no navy, and its constitution had been honored mainly in the breach.

2009 – On 1/31/09, Iraq held elections for the provincial councils of 14 provinces, deferring the process in the three provinces that comprise the KAR and in a fourth province (Ta'mim) claimed by the KRG. Religious symbols were banned. Turnout was low, partly because ethnic cleansing had converted millions of eligible voters to DP's; those abroad had lost eligibility, and those in Iraq were separated from their precincts. Parliamentary elections were to be held by 1/30/10 (per schedule change of May 2009).

2009 – In the analysis of Robert Dreyfuss, writing in *The Nation* of 3/9/09, the election of 1/31/09 was a decisive victory for nationalism and secularism, and a defeat for separatism. ISCI and Al Da'wah were crippled, their coalition (the UIA) was defunct, and the Sunni Arabs,

225

who had boycotted the election of 1/31/05, had taken control of four provinces, and crushed the Kurds in those provinces outside the KAR where Kurds still held positions of leadership. The Maliki Bloc, benefiting from its position of power, American support, and Maliki's success in projecting an image of nationalism that overshadowed his affiliation with Shiite Al Da'wah, won a plurality in Baghdad, Basrah, and several other provinces. Opposition parties cried fraud. The Awakening captured 'Anbar Province from the Iraqi Islamic Party (a component of Tawafuq). The Sunnis' Al Hadbah won big in Mawsil. An Awakening/Tawafuq/'Allawi alliance carried Salah al Din Province – a Baathist stronghold in the Saddam era.

2009 – On 2/9/09, in the costliest incident for Americans since 5/2/08, four soldiers were killed in Mawsil by a suicide bomber – presumably provided by the AQI, whose forces had been driven north by Awakening forces.

2009 – On 2/10/09, French President Nicolas Sarkozy made a state visit to Iraq. It was seen as an early move by Maliki to end his government's client status – something of a challenge while that government was still heavily dependent on the support of the American forces. Dead set against arming an anti-Israeli regime, Washington had resisted Baghdad's requests for modern weapons.

2009 – On 2/12/09, the *Times* reported that Iraq had sold development rights on two southern oil fields to a combine of Royal Dutch Shell and Petronas (Malaysia), and a consortium headed by the China National Petroleum Company.

2009 – The Mujahedeen e-Khalq (MEK), founded in the 1960's, had committed numerous subversive actions against the Iranian regime. On 3/13/09, members of the MEK were detained at Camp Ashraf in Iraq, which was surrounded by Iraqi Government forces.

2009 – On 3/24/09, the *Times* reported that, of 94,000 Awakening Council militants (stipend 300 dollars a month), 84,000 had been transferred to Iraqi control, but only 5,000 had gotten appointments to the army (750 dollars a month) or the police (600 dollars a month). According to a later *AP* report, none of the transferees were being paid. Iraq's unemployed/underemployed rate was 38 percent.

2009 – The members of the Maliki Government voted themselves enormous pay raises: *Times*, 3/30/09.

2009 – On 4/7/09, on the anniversary of the founding of the Baath Party, "The National Islamist Pan-Arab Front" sent the *Times* the text of an audiotape message from 'Izzat Ibrahim al Duri, who had been Deputy Chairman of Saddam's Revolutionary Command Council. The message called on Iraqis to topple Maliki's "puppet regime".

2009 – In April, the new Iraq was still in a state of confusion. The provinces were just beginning to form the councils provided for by the January elections. Parliament had finally elected a speaker – Iyad al Samarra'i, head of the Iraqi Islamic Party. While the Kurds were besting the Sunni Arabs in a contest for control of the northern oil fields, the Shiites held the huge Rumaylah field in the south. April was punctuated by a rash of deadly bombings, some claimed by the "Islamic State of Iraq", a Sunni organization that included the AQI, now said to be led by Abu 'Umar al Baghdadi.

2009 – On 5/25/09, American media carried an *AP* report that funds allocated by Washington for the reconstruction of Iraq now totaled 50 billion dollars, but there was no accurate accounting of how they had been spent.

2009 – On 5/27/09, the KRG had begun exporting crude to Turkey. Baghdad planned to apportion the revenue from KRG shipments among Iraqi provinces and "regions".

2009 – On 5/28/09, UK combat troops withdrew from Iraq.

2009 – By June, the American casualty rate had diminished, but military and civilian Iraqis were taking fairly steady casualties from vehicle and suicide bombing. *The Christian Science Monitor*'s report that "low-level insurgency is expected to continue for years" contradicted the American presumption that the Maliki regime was the established government of Iraq, rather than one of several competing factions – the one that happened to enjoy US support at the moment (cf. South Vietnam).

2009 – On 6/10/09, further to the Parliamentary decision of 11/27/08, Baghdad and Washington agreed on the terms of the Status of Forces Agreement (SOFA), subject to a subsequent Iraqi referendum.

If the SOFA should be voted down, the American forces would have to complete withdrawal from Iraq within a year from the date the referendum had been held.

2009 – On 6/12/09, Tawafuq leader Harith al 'Ubaydi was shot dead at Friday prayers in Baghdad.

2009 – On 6/22/09, a new Iraqi contingent, the Special Operations Forces, had been conducting attacks on insurgents in the Baghdad area. They reported to Prime Minister Maliki, but were in effect a branch of the American armed forces.

2009 – On 6/24/09, came the third massive bombing of Shiite crowds in two weeks. Presumed objectives: to discredit the Maliki government, possibly to reignite sectarian war. At least some of the violence was claimed by the AQI and two new groups using the titles The Mujahidin Army and The Islamic Army of Iraq.

2009 – In anticipation of the June 30 deadline specified in the SOFA, most of the 130,000 American troops in Iraq had evacuated the cities, with the exception of huge Camp Victory on the western edge of Baghdad. After the total withdrawal deadline of 12/31/11, the US was expected to leave 35-50,000 trainers/advisers. Those already in country were living in compounds fortified against the risk of fragging by infiltrators into the Iraqi forces under training: *Times*, 6/26/09, quoting an Iraqi official.

2009 – On 6/29/09, Iraq put up for bids twenty-year service contracts on six oil fields – four in the south and two near Kirkuk. Iraq needed advances from contracting companies to finance reparation of infrastructure and restaffing of management, in hopes of achieving a radical rise in the annual production rate – now averaging only 2.4 million barrels a day, most of it produced by the government's South Oil Company. Most of the foreign contractors previously disqualified by the nationalization of Iraq's oil industry in 1972 were expected to bid, despite Iraq's unsettled security situation. The thirty contracts awarded by the Kurdish Regional Government were not recognized by the central government.

2009 – On 6/30/09, the response to Iraq's service-contract auction was disappointing – one deal with a joint venture of BP and the China

National Petroleum Corporation. Most foreign companies preferred the more lucrative production-sharing agreements, and guessed that Iraq's production capacity had been so badly depleted by sanctions, mismanagement, and deterioration of infrastructure that its need for foreign financial and technical assistance would force it to capitulate on the issue.

2009 – On 6/30/09, Iraqis celebrated the Americans' evacuation from the cities.

2009 – In June, the KRG Parliament approved a new constitution that accorded the KRG President extraordinary powers and endorsed Kurdish claims to a large segment of northern Iraq and to the oil and gas beneath it. This language was condemned by the Maliki Government, the KRG's opposition (*Gorran*), and Vice President Biden (on a visit to Iraq): *Times*, 7/10/09.

2009 – In June, Iraq signed a development contract for the vast Rumaylah field with British Petroleum: *Times*, 9/6/09.

2009 – On 7/1/09, 'Izzat al Duri and The Association of Muslim Scholars hailed the withdrawal of American forces from urban areas, and adjured Iraqis to fight Americans, not other Iraqis. Muqtada al Sadr (studying in Iran?) condemned the withdrawal as insufficient.

2009 – The February visit by French President Sarkozy and the July visit by Prime Minister Fillon to Iraq had helped Baghdad reestablish the close political and economic ties that linked Iraq and France in the Saddam era.

2009 – In July, the relative quiet in Iraq was still being interrupted by sporadic but lethal snipings, bombings, and assassinations of factional leaders and civilian and security officials of the Maliki Government. The *McClatchy* news agency reported that agricultural production had been crippled by drought, decline in river flow, three wars since 1980, UN sanctions, and official incompetence and corruption. The primary subject of debate was whether US adherence to the SOFA schedule would jeopardize the rebirth of an independent Iraq. No referendum on the SOFA had been held.

229

2009 – In August, the AQI and the Islamic State of Iraq, having joined forces, were responsible for much of the violence in northern Iraq, including two gigantic bombings.

2009 – *Al Zaman* reported that Sadrists, the ISCI, Fadilah, and Ibrahim al Ja'fari's Islah Party, in association with some Sunnis, had formed The Iraqi National Alliance (INA). The INA and Maliki's State of Law Party were the two main electoral blocs in Iraq: *Times*; *NYR*, Joost Hilterman; Juan Cole Blog, 8/25/09.

2009 – In October, reports came in that Baghdad, not recognizing the KRG's oil contracts, had closed the pipelines to Turkey, forcing the KRG to stop pumping. With the infrastructure devastated, the economy hostage to local warlords, and no functioning banking system, Iraq's oil production was stalled out at 2.5 million barrels per day, versus 2.8 million before the American invasion: *Times*; *Middle East Report*, Pete Moore.

2009 – In November, Vice President Tariq al Hashimi had left Tawafuq to form his own party: *Intervest*, Reidar Visser.

2009 – On 12/1/09, the *Times* reported that Iraq was shunning production-sharing agreements (more lucrative to the concessionaire) in favor of fee-per-barrel service contracts – including the Rumaylah deal with the British and Chinese.

2009 – Iraq's prize contract – development of the West Qurna field – had gone to Russia's Lukoil: Times, 12/12/09

2007-2009 – In three years, Iraq's annual number of violent civilian deaths fell from 26,000 to 5,000: Beinart.

2010 – In January, plans to hold Parliamentary elections in March had been blasted by an unexpected Parliamentary decision to ban over 500 candidates, most of them Sunnis, including Salih al Mutlaq and Dhafir al 'Ani, allies of Iyad al 'Allawi and Tariq al Hashimi (*'Iraqiyyah* Party).

2010 – Baghdad blacklisted the oil companies operating in the KAR: *Times*, 2/1/10.

2010 – On 2/26/10, a pre-election maneuver by the Maliki government was the reinstatement of 20,000 officers who had been dismissed from the army after the invasion.

2010 – On 3/7/10, under heavy American and Iraqi security, and despite continued bombings, Iraqis turned out in good numbers to elect an Iraqi Parliament of 325. The Sunni-Shia bloc, 'Iraqiyyah, won two more seats than Maliki's pro-Iraq bloc, but the Obama administration made an error of judgement – helping Maliki retain power: Beinart.

2010 – On 3/26/10, the results of the March 7 election were announced: Former Prime Minister Iyad 'Allawi's 'Iraqiyyah coalition (with large Sunni support) – 91 seats; sitting Prime Minister Nuri al Maliki's State of Law coalition – 89 seats; United Iraqi Alliance of Sadrists, ISCI, and other Shiite groups (all close to Iran) – 70 seats; Kurdish coalition – 43 seats; Kurdish opposition (Gorran) – 8 seats.

2010 – On 4/19/10, two AQI leaders were reported killed by US and Iraqi forces near Tikrit: Abu 'Umar al Baghdadi (Hamid al Zawi) and Abu Hamza al Muhajir (AKA Abu Ayyub al Masri). They had lately proclaimed the establishment of the Islamic State of Iraq: *MEP*, Winter 2014, Ahmed Hashim.

2010 – **End of the Occupation** – On 8/18/10, the last American combat brigade left Iraq via Kuwait. The neocons' faith in the conversion of military force into useful political results had been exploded: Beinart.

2010 – On 8/31/10, Obama declared an end to the American combat role: *World Almanac*, 2016.

2010 – On 12/21/10, Nuri al Maliki was sworn in for a second term as Prime Minister: *World Almanac*, 2016.

2011 – On 12/15/11, US troops completed their withdrawal: *World Almanac*, 2016.

2014 – On 4/30/14, parliamentary elections were won by the Maliki faction. On 7/24/14, Parliament elected Fu'ad Masum (Kurd) President of Iraq.

2014 – On 8/11/14, Masum named Haydar al 'Abadi (Shia) Prime Minister.

The Selection of an American Proconsul – Strong leadership is crucial to the success of any political organization, whether a nation or a short-time possession. For occupied Iraq, Bush 43 sent to Baghdad an officer of proven ability. Paul Bremer had a dream resume: Education –

231

Phillips Andover, Yale, MBA from Harvard (where Kissinger was a professor); Certificate of Political Studies from *L'Institut d'Études Politiques de Paris*. Career – Foreign Service Officer, 1968-89; staff assistant to Henry Kissinger (National Security Adviser and Secretary of State), 1973-6; Executive Secretary of the Department of State, 1981; Ambassador to The Netherlands, 1983 (age 42); Ambassador-at-Large for Counterterrorism, 1986-9; Medal of Honor (along with General Tommy Franks and George Tenet), 12/14/04. (These dubious awards may have been part of the Bush 43 campaign to defend his failed Iraqi policy.) Second Career – 1989, Managing Director of Kissinger and Associates; 1999, Chairman of the National Commission on Terrorism; 5/9/03, Presidential Envoy to Iraq, reporting nominally to Secretary of Defense Rumsfeld, more often to neocons Paul Wolfowitz and Douglas Feith in the State Department. On 6/28/04, limited sovereignty was transferred to the Iraqi Interim Government. Bremer left Iraq.

Washington was sending one of their top officers for that tricky job in Baghdad. What went wrong? First, Washington saddled him with a lunatic policy and an impossible assignment. Second, he accepted it. Third, he was getting bad guidance from people in Washington who knew almost as little about Iraq as he did. Washington was operating under the cavalier assumption that the costs of ruling Iraq would be met by its nonexistent government and bankrupt exchequer. Fourth, he had no control over the US military in Iraq, and negligible military experience of his own. Fifth, he overrated his own judgement. He rejected the warning of his predecessor, Lt. General Jay Garner, who did have some military experience, against disbanding the Iraqi Army. After a dreadful year in Iraq, he came home to give speeches in defense of his decisions. The speeches were not well received. At Clark University in April 2005, some students in his audience challenged his presentation, and the University's decision to pay an honorarium of $40,000: Rand Corporation; Worcester Indymedia, 4/19/05, 4/28/05; *The Modesto Bee*, 12/10/07.

The Anatomy of the Opposition to the Occupation – In their patriotic habit of following Washington's lead, the American media referred to Iraq's armed opposition as the <u>insurgency</u>, which carries the connotation of illegal violence against constituted authority. However, as UN Secretary General Kofi Annan publicly stated, the American invasion of Iraq, as a violation of the UN Charter, was itself illegal. Therefore, any Iraqi counteraction to it – at least at the outset – deserved the appellation of <u>resistance</u> (an "organization engaged in a struggle for national liberation in a country under military … occupation").

Some lawyers will take the position that Security Council Resolution 1483 of May 22, 2003, put to rest the legality issue. Others will dismiss 1483 as the "fruit of a poisoned tree." As of this writing, the juridical jury was still out.

Since the Baathist regime of Saddam Husayn was rooted in the Sunni community, the invasion was tacitly welcomed by mainstream Shiites and Kurds, and the resistance was largely based on the "Sunni Triangle", which roughly corresponds to the territory between the Tigris and the Euphrates, from the Baghdad area to the Syrian border. It included the Sunni segment of Baghdad, Mawsil (Iraq's third largest city), and several other populous cities along the two rivers. Greatly outnumbered by the quiescent Shia, the Sunnis fought an uphill battle against American armor, planes, and artillery. They had no allies of note in the Kurdish community except *Ansar al Islam*, an Islamist splinter group. In the Shia community, Muqtada al Sadr condemned the American invasion of Fallujah, but his spasmodic resistance efforts were not coordinated with the Sunnis; they were a backhanded challenge to Sistani's leadership of the Shia. In 2009, after the Americans inflicted heavy casualties on JAM forces in Najaf, Sadr joined Sistani in the background and suspended his paramilitary campaign.

Early Start - Like the other communities, the Sunni resistance was fragmented, with no overall leader. However, there were factors operating in its favor:

American officials concluded that, by staffing his administration with officials who had served his father in Gulf War I, Bush 43 alerted Saddam to make preinvasion arrangements for himself and his sons to go into hiding (those arrangements failed), and to set up the machinery for an underground resistance. The post-invasion orgy of looting may have been intentionally abetted by resistance strategy.

233

The BPI wing of the resistance was believed to be well financed by party funds banked in Syria. American intelligence initially estimated its numbers at over 2000 hard-core Baathists, plus several thousand part-time operatives motivated less by party discipline than by financial compensation. In early 2005, the Sunni resistance was estimated to be half BPI, a quarter Iraqi Islamists under the leadership of Jordanian Abu Mus'ab al Zarqawi, and a quarter foreign Islamists – for a total of 40,000, plus 160,000 part-time auxiliaries. The BPI wing seemed to have an intelligence net deep inside the interim government. The violent campaign to undermine law, public services, and Coalition authority, not visibly set back by the capture of Saddam, was holding its own in the Sunni Triangle and adjoining areas.

Coalition intelligence suspected that the BPI was running its operation from Aleppo, which was conveniently situated and politically congenial – since Syria, despite its Alawite leadership, is a Sunni country. The resistance was "a monster with its head in Syria and its body in Iraq". The role of voice of the resistance had been appropriated by The Association of Muslim Scholars, an ad hoc organization which claimed to represent 3000 Sunni mosques, and condemned Interim Prime Minister Iyad 'Allawi as an "American lackey".

Foreign Islamists - Although prewar accusations of collaboration between Baathists and Islamists have never been verified, the invasion converted canard to reality. Sunni volunteers from Syria, Lebanon, Saudi Arabia, Turkey, Yemen, Tunisia, and Morocco entered Iraq via Syria in numbers sufficient to play a significant role. For six months in 2004, Fallujah was under the control of a combine of Iraqi and foreign Islamists. In December 2004, some diehard defenders were still hanging on in the rubble, despite the American assault's having demolished many of its buildings, devastated its public services, emptied the city of its 250,000 residents, and converted it to a ghost town.

'Abdallah II, less solicitous of Jordan's neutrality than his father had been in Gulf War I, had angered the Iraqi resistance by letting American units deploy along the Iraqi border, but he may have hedged his bets by providing clandestine assistance to his Sunni coreligionists in Iraq.

BPI-Islamist Coordination - Whereas the Baathist wing of the resistance relied on conventional ambushes, furtive use of artillery, and the placement of camouflaged remote-control explosives (IED's) along roadsides, the Islamist factions were considered responsible for introduction of the suicide car bomb. In mid-2003 infiltrators carried out three devastating bombings (the Jordanian Embassy, UN headquarters, and the Shiite shrine of Imam 'Ali). In 2004, there were over 450 suicide bombings against the interim regime.

UN-US Coordination – UN Special Representative Sergio Vieira De Mello died in the bombing of his office. By choosing to operate outside the Green Zone, he had facilitated contact with Iraqis; Shiites who shunned Bremer would see Vieira De Mello. However, his neutrality was suspect in the eyes of the resistance. The UN had been the vehicle for America's harrowing interwar sanctions, and Vieira De Mello himself had become Bremer's invaluable adviser. He had been the only non-Iraqi to speak at the inauguration of the IGC, which he had helped the Americans concoct, and – as noted by Phyllis Bennis of the Institute for Policy Studies – his mission was deemed to operate under the auspices of the CPA.

Suspicion Between Kurds and Shia - Viewed as a voting bloc, Shia and Kurds far outnumbered their Sunni rivals, and they were united by their resolve to terminate 450 years of Sunni Arab rule of Mesopotamia/Iraq. However, as the haggling over the interim constitution revealed, they had incompatible agendas: The Shia favored early general elections as a crude means of establishing Shiite rule over an integrated Iraq. The Kurds in the KAR wanted a high degree of autonomy – if not outright independence.

The Shiite Campaign to Make History – If the Shiites' dream is realized, Iraq will become the first-ever mainstream Shiite Arab state. (The Egyptian Fatimids, Yemeni Zaydis, and Syrian Alawites paid allegiance to heterodox branches of Shiism.) Under Shiite rule, Kurds and Arab Sunnis could become disempowered minorities, like the Azeris in Iran, the Alevis in Turkey, the Copts in Egypt, the Shia in Saudi Arabia and Bahrain, and the Arabs in Israel.

However, as pointed out by Christopher de Bellaigue, the Iraqi Shiites are no less fractionated than their rivals. In 2003, he discerned three main factions: the Sadrists, led by Muqtada al Sadr; SCIRI (The Supreme Council of the Islamic Revolution in Iraq) led by the Sadrs' ancient enemies, the Hakims; and Al Da'wah (The Call), relic of the group assembled in Saddam's time by the revered Muhammad al Sadr, Muqtada's father. Above their worldly altercations sat Ayatallah 'Ali al Sistani, primary cleric in the Shiite world.

The Quietism of 'Ali Sistani - Cosmopolites like Iyad 'Allawi and Ahmad Chalabi functioned effectively in international milieus like the corridors of power in Washington and the Green Zone in Baghdad, but they did not produce evidence of significant following in Iraq. The Shiite masses looked to their sectarian leaders – the five surviving Grand Ayatallahs, headed by the reclusive 'Ali al Sistani.

As a "quietist" (an opponent of direct clerical participation in politics), Sistani escaped elimination by Saddam, and he took no positions in the IGC, the Interim Government, or any Shiite political party. From behind the scenes, he aimed at neutrality in factional disputes, but exerted decisive influence in the wrangling between the Americans and their Iraqi protégés.

In principle, Sistani opposed American Middle East policy, particularly Bush's inclusion of Iran in the "Axis of Evil", and the American occupation. Within days of the invasion, he issued a fatwa calling on Muslims to defend Iraq. He avoided meeting with CPA authorities, but he took no part in the armed resistance. His apparent strategy was to hang back while the Americans whittled down the Sunnis and the activist Shiites.

On the political front, however, Sistani exerted constant pressure on the CPA and the Interim Government for holding a nationwide election, on a proportional basis, for a transitional government and a constituent assembly. Impressed by early indications of Sistani's power to mobilize the Shiite street, the Americans tended to comply; hence UNSC Resolution 1546, and the election held in January 2005 – although analysts concluded that the Americans had managed to block outright Shiite control of the Transitional National Assembly by imposing the requirement for a two-thirds majority, and by assuring the Kurds a disproportionate number of seats.

The Challenger - To the surprise of the neophyte Americans, and perhaps even Sistani, the occupation activated a new contender for power – Muqtada al Sadr. Young and unschooled, he held the modest rank of *Hujjat al Islam*, far below an *ayatallah* in Shiite hierarchy. However, he derived vicarious charisma from his late father and uncle, both ayatallahs, and both presumed victims of Saddamist police. Martyrdom is a central theme in Shiite tradition. Muqtada also received a valuable endorsement from Grand *Ayatollah* (Persian spelling) Kazim al Ha'iri, resident in Qom, Iran.

In April 2003, the American invaders returned an exiled cleric, 'Abd al Majid al Khu'i, to Najaf, where he was murdered. The motivation (anti-occupation? anti-Sistani?) has not been established, but the four suspects picked up by the Americans were followers of Muqtada Sadr. From then on, relations between Sadr and the occupiers deteriorated. The absence of any member of the Sadr faction from the IGC was consistent with Sadr's demand in July 2003 for the Americans' withdrawal, his condemnation of anyone (Sistani?) who tolerated their presence, and his recruitment of an untrained but large and impassioned militia, the *Jaysh al Mahdi* (The Army of the Rightly Guided One, JAM). In August 2003, his militia went underground to evade an American order that all militias disband. In September 2003, a police station in "Sadr City" (the sprawling Shiite section of Baghdad) was the target of a suicide bombing, two Americans died in a clash there, and a Sadrist imam preached an anti-occupation sermon. More violent clashes followed.

In March 2004, the CPA closed Sadr's newspaper, *Al Hawzah*, on a charge of inciting violence, and arrested a Sadr associate for suspected complicity in the Khu'i killing. Sadr unleashed his militia. Under American attack, the JAM took refuge in the holy sites of Najaf and Karbala', cities in which Sadr had a large following. As the Americans began to take casualties, their solicitude for the sanctity of Shiite shrines dissipated, and some 1500 of Sadr's soldiers were killed.

Although Sadr was maintaining a façade of solidarity with Sistani, the ayatallah had to be hugely embarrassed by Sadr's resistance, which

237

complicated Sistani's strategy of extracting American agreement for a general election, posed a sharp contrast to the quietists' inaction, and reminded the faithful which Shiite faction had stood up to Saddam. The CPA wanted Sadr in prison and his soldiers disarmed, but Sistani demurred. Wary of alienating the Shiites as well as the Sunnis, the CPA capitulated. JAM evacuated the holy cities with its weapons, the Americans withdrew, and Najaf and Karbala' reverted to Baghdad's control. Sistani got credit for defusing the crisis. Sadr emerged chastened, but with his prestige as defender of the faith enhanced.

The next four years were beset by intermittent violence between the occupiers and JAM, even after Muqtada made the strategic decision to stand his forces down, while he reportedly moved to Qom to pursue clerical studies aimed at achieving elevation to ayatallah. In the summer of 2008 he reportedly split the JAM into a social service wing, the *Muhammadun*, and an elite militia, *Al Yawm al Maw'ud* (The Promised Day). Many Shiites believe the return of the Hidden Imam is near.

Ancient Rivalry - When the Americans arrived, the Sadrs and the Hakims were separated by an ancient Shiite feud. During the occupation, Muqtada joined the resistance, and the Hakims sat it out. In 2009, as the Americans began to leave, there were reports that Muqtada al Sadr and 'Abd al 'Aziz al Hakim had found the rise of the latest American protégé, Nuri al Maliki, ominous enough for them to set their historic enmity aside.

Cost-Benefit Analysis of the Invasion and the Occupation: 2009

According to a retired US military intelligence officer, if the occupation of Iraq is evaluated in accordance with the goals set forth by America's military leadership, it ended in utter defeat: *Atlantic*, January 2015.

Benefits

Saddam Ousted - Saddam gave the country basic services (the most efficient food-distribution system in the Middle East), secularism,

238

women's rights, economic development, and the Middle Eastern version of law and order. He cannot be faulted for having been a widely hated dictator – ethnicity-ridden Iraq can expect nothing else – but he exacerbated the hatred by brutality, extortion, barbarity (uncaring ruination of ecology in Kuwait and the Iraqi marshes), and recklessness (three disastrous wars against Iran, Kuwait, and the US – although Washington took his side in the first one). On balance, he was a bad dictator, but the case for condemning Iraq to the horror of war to get rid of him is demolished in advance by America's inability to insure that his successors are any better.

Reconstruction - After the devastation America inflicted on Iraq by the Kuwait War, sanctions, intermittent air attack, the US-Iraq War, and the anarchy that followed, it was only fitting that the CPA help Iraq recover. The bright spot was the renovation and resupply of many schools, and pay raises for teachers.

Costs

It seems self-evident that the incidental benefits of the invasion were overwhelmingly outweighed by its appalling costs. The ouster of Saddam gratified Iran (the end of Sunni dominance over Iraq) and Israel (elimination of an enemy regime), but its bloody means did grave disservice to the national interests of Iraq and the United States. No American can plausibly defend going to war just to replace one foreign dictator with another.

For many observers, the language of the Status of Forces Agreement, by providing no authorization for a permanent American military presence in Iraq, marked the failure of the invasion.

Casualties - 4486 American soldiers and 1100 auxiliaries lost their lives in Iraq: *Harper's*, October 2014. According to *Foreign Policy* of March 2008 and *The Nation* of 5/12/08, 31 percent of the 1.6 million American personnel deployed to Iraq and Afghanistan returned with physical and/or psychological injury. Washington kept no records on Iraqi deaths (an insensitive omission for avowed liberators), but the *Times* reported 1/10/08 that WHO and Government of Iraq estimates indicated that

151,000 Iraqis had died, most of them violently, between March 2003 and July 2006. *The Nation* of 2/16/09 carried an estimate that 100,000 Iraqi civilians had died since 2006.

Expenditure - The *Times* of 3/1/09 carried an estimate that the Iraq War had cost the American budget 860 billion dollars. American contribution to reconstruction had been minuscule – that amount of Congressional allocations of some 50 billion dollars not squandered by overhead or by profligate American contractors. No system of accountability had been set up. In September 2008 Joseph Stiglitz said the Iraq War, fought on credit, was the central cause of America's three trillion-dollar deficit.

The Nation of 7/7/08 concluded that the invasion of Iraq exacerbated America's financial stresses by spiking the price of oil in three ways: reducing Iraqi production, conjuring up the specter of terrorism, and empowering Iran as a threat to Arabian oil supply.

Infrastructure Devastated - War with Iran, sanctions, invasion, and occupation inflicted massive damage on Iraq's power, water, and sewage systems. Until 2006, resistance sabotage of oil pipelines was ongoing. A public-health system that had been one of the best in the Middle East was unable to meet demands – least of all in Fallujah. As of July 2004, the Tigris was an "open sewer." As of November, mortality rates were still rising because of insufficient drinking water. As of January 2005, provision of electric power in Baghdad and Basrah had fallen to a new low.

By 2009, Iraqi annual production of electricity was reportedly up to 6000 megawatts *(Times, 6/18/09)*, 150 percent of the prewar level, but *Newsweek* of 6/12/09 reported that in Al Mahmudiyyah, 40 miles south of Baghdad, public services were almost nonexistent.

Mawsil Dam – After the Iraqis had built a dam on the Tigris, north of Mawsil, they learned that the site was unstable. To guard against flooding out sections of Mawsil and Baghdad, they instituted a regimen of constant grouting, which required heavy machinery. During the hostilities in Kuwait, Saddam transferred the machinery to the front, where it was a casualty of US bombing. It has not been adequately replaced. The dam is a hazard for downstream communities: *NY,*

240

1/2/17, Dexter Filkins. The US has spent billions to rectify the damage it did to the Iraqi infrastructure. Upgrading the Mawsil Dam was not included.

Breakdown of Iraqi Society - In the words of Bill Polk, America shredded the social fabric of Iraq. The educational and healthcare systems had been devastated by mass exodus of professionals. Ten percent of the population had fled the country for their lives, most of them to Syria and Jordan, where they were trying to survive with no ration cards, and no prospect of return to Iraq: The sectarian menace still existed, and their homes had been usurped.

Iraq's Shiite clerics no longer had a secular power structure to inhibit them. Indulged by a deferential CPA, they set out to reverse liberal trends (women's rights) promoted by Baathist ideology. Policewomen who had been on street patrols were reassigned to desk jobs. Tribalism was reinvigorated by Petraeus's strategy of recruiting tribal levies, 20 percent of whose salaries went direct to the tribal leaders. Pepe Escobar reported that the killing or flight of most Western-educated professors had crippled the University of Baghdad and even the Mustansiriyyah, founded as a school of Islamic law in 1233 by al Mustansir, Caliph under the Seljuqs (Glasse: *Encyclopedia of Islam*), restored in modern times as a museum and a university.

Economy Shattered - Insecurity, power shortages, smuggling, and neocon revisions of Iraqi law had combined to hobble industry, cripple authority, and deny employment to half the adult population. State-owned companies were working at half capacity. Many factories were in shambles. Finance was stagnant. In 1996, under pressure from American-imposed sanctions, Saddam had established a state system for monthly distribution of rations. That system had broken down, especially for DP's. In 2007 Oxfam diagnosed a humanitarian crisis: four million Iraqi refugees in dire need of food assistance; two million of them still in Iraq, but driven from their homes, ignored by the "government", the occupation authorities, and the UN; 70 percent of Iraqis denied access to adequate water supply; most hospitals lacking basic medical necessities.

Democratic Claims Compromised - There was no evidence that democracy was the objective of the invasion of Iraq. By invading without due cause, condemning an anti-invasion decision by the Turkish Parliament, trespassing on the Geneva Conventions, maneuvering to prevent Iraq from electing a theocracy, and setting up a hand-picked interim government, Washington projected an image of classic imperialist opportunism.

Security Vacuum - Even before the invasion, Bush's "war on terror" had been widely interpreted as an assault, on Israel's behalf, on the Arab and Islamic worlds. Washington represented the invasion as having made Iraqis and Americans safer. This was a minority view – overseas, and from 2005 on even in the United States. Anti-Americanism had risen, and American relations with traditional allies had been shaken.

In 2005, Washington had presumed to impose four prohibitions on the future Iraqi government: 1) It should not be under Iranian influence; 2) It should not set a date for American withdrawal; 3) It should not make Iraq an Islamic state; 4) Iraq should not be partitioned. Later on, the US had to swallow all four injunctions.

No state should have expected to invade Iraq without inflaming endemic communalism. The mayhem was widely predicted. Political rivalry was exacerbated by standing militias: Maliki's "Iraqi Armed Forces", Kurdistan's Peshmerga, SCIRI's Badr Brigade, Sadr's JAM, the Baathist resistance's Army of Muhammad, the Iraqi Hizballah, and the self-styled Islamic State.

By late 2004, Muslim attacks on Christians had mounted, and the violence was beginning to take on the shape of an ethnic civil war. Sunnis were manning the resistance, and Shia and Kurds were doing the fighting for the 'Allawi Government – except in Najaf and the north, where Kurds and Shia sometimes fought each other. The Kirkuk/Mawsil area was the arena of a four-way dispute among Sunni Arabs, Shia Arabs, Kurds, and Turkmens. Most of the Arab beneficiaries of Saddam's ethnic transfers in Kirkuk had been Shiites, some of whom (followers of Muqtada al Sadr) condemned the secularist-minded Kurds as apostates (from Islam). Whereas Saddam had forbidden Kurds to buy or build in Kirkuk, the US had let it fall under KRG control.

242

In 2007 there was heavy fighting between the JAM and Maliki's forces (backed by the British) in Nasiriyyah. In 2008, according to Patrick Cockburn in *The Independent*, many of Baghdad's ghettoes were flying one of three flags: Sunnis displayed the old three-star flag, Shia a new Iraqi flag, Kurds the KRG flag. In February 2009 American media reported "ferocious enmity" between Baghdad's Nuri al Maliki and the KRG's Mas'ud Barzani. In the summer of 2008, there had been a face-off between their forces at Khanaqin, a town on the Iranian border in Diyala Province, at the outer edge of the KRG's area of control. Reports suggest that a clash was averted only by the intervention of American soldiers.

As of 2009, Iraq was the latest candidate for the mournful category of failed states. Six blood-soaked years of confrontation between the occupation, relying on its domination of the air, and the resistance, relying on its familiarity with the land, had denied a decisive victory to either side, but it had made Iraq "the most dangerous place in the world" (*LRB*, November 2008). Across wide areas of the country, responsibility for law and order had increasingly fallen on local militias.

Inhabitants of Iraq were compelled to adapt to a whole new environment – riven by ethnic cleansing, ghettoized in urban areas by the blast walls set up by a desperate occupation force. As of June 2007, Juan Cole noted that tens of thousands of former residents of devastated Fallujah were living in tent cities in the desert. In February 2008 Michael Schwartz reported that most of the 200 Baghdad neighborhoods that had been ethnically mixed were now homogeneous. According to The UN High Commissioner for Refugees, in April 2008 there were nearly 2.5 million displaced Iraqis in-country. Few had received financial aid from the Maliki regime. According to *The Nation*, Syria, Jordan, and even eleven of Iraq's eighteen governorates had closed their borders to Iraqi DP's.

In 1990, according to *The Washington Post Weekly* of 4/28/08, northern Iraq was the home of 1.35 million Christians (most of them Chaldean Catholics, affiliated with the Church of Rome). By 2008 their archbishop, based in Mawsil, had been killed, and their community had been reduced by death and flight to 5-600,000. Their nemesis, according to the *Times,* was the AQI. Driven out of Fallujah by US Marines, the AQI had moved to Ninawah Province and attacked the Christians as American allies. The American forces were unwilling to come to their defense, for fear of adverse propaganda. The Peshmerga welcomed the pretext to take over the five districts of Ninawah claimed by the KRG.

In 2009, the occupation forces were collaborating with an organization which was styled the Iraqi Army, but which was turning out to be the private militia of current Prime Minister Nuri al Maliki. In 2008 Washington had taken comfort in the subsidence of ethnic warfare, but the sporadic but persistent clandestine bombings of 2009-10 revealed that the Iraqi power struggle was yet to be resolved.

2006-? – Israel-Hizballah War

___

Phase I: Hizballah in the Israel-Lebanon War

1983 – On 4/18/83, a Hizballah bombing destroyed the front of the American Embassy in Beirut, killing 63, 17 of them Americans, including an outstanding Middle East expert for the CIA, Bob Ames.

1983 – On 10/23/83, a Hizballah truck bomb destroyed the US Marine barracks in Beirut, killing 241. A simultaneous bombing of the Beirut barracks of a French paratrooper unit killed 58.

1985 – Hizballah abducted Beirut station chief William Buckley and killed him by slow torture.

1985 – Hizballah hijacked a TWA plane.

1985 – To exact revenge for the Marine barracks bombing of 10/23/83, CIA Director William Casey colluded with Saudi Arabia in an operation to kill *Hujjat al Islam* Shaykh Muhammad Fadlallah, revered as a spiritual guide by Hizballah. On 3/8/85 a bomb exploded a few yards from Fadlallah's residence, as worshippers were leaving Friday services. The explosion missed Fadlallah, but killed 80 other Lebanese and wounded 256. After this fiasco, Reagan rescinded an anti-terrorist order he had issued 11/13/84: Fisk; *Washington Post Weekly*, 10/10/88, 10/29/01; *Veil: The Secret Wars of the CIA*, Bob Woodward.

1985 – By December the USSR had set up, under its own operation, SAM-5 defenses of Damascus and Aleppo, and Syria had deployed SAM-2's, SAM-6's, and SAM-8's close to the Israeli border. Syria had taken delivery of several naval ships from the USSR.

1985 – On 12/30/85, in retaliation for an attack on IDF forces by residents of Kunin (at the eastern end of the Security Zone), the IDF expelled its 2000 inhabitants (Lebanese). In Beirut, Shia militants "retaliated" by killing a Lebanese hostage of Jewish origin.

1986 – Muhammad Fadlallah denounced the UN presence in Lebanon on 7/13/86. His sermon was followed by attacks on the French contingent of UNIFIL.

1986 – On 11/14/86, the White House announced imposition of a variety of sanctions on Syria, in reprisal for a Syrian attack of April 1985 on an El Al plane.

1987 – In February, 23 militants of Hizballah were killed by Syrian troops in the course of their quasi-police action to end the civil war.

1988 – On 2/17/88, Hizballah abducted retired Marine Lt. Col. William Robin Higgins, who was serving in south Lebanon on a UN peacekeeping mission, at the request of Secretary of Defense Weinberger. His body was found later. After five years as an aide to Weinberger, he had full knowledge of clandestine US operations in the Middle East. National Security Adviser Robert McFarlane said after Higgins's disappearance his assignment to the Middle East had been a case of gross mismanagement: *National Enquirer*, Frank Greve. A group affiliated with Hizballah claimed that it hanged Lt. Col. Higgins in retaliation for the Israeli abduction of Shaykh 'Abd al Karim 'Ubayd: *Times*, 8/1/89, Ihsan al Hijazi.

1989 – On 3/14/89, General Michel 'Awn, new Prime Minister and Acting President of Lebanon, declared a war to liberate Lebanon from Syria (*MER*, Fall 2005), attacked Lebanese troops in east Beirut, and shelled west Beirut: *EB*, 14:845.

1989 – Rene Mu'awwad, elected President in November, refused Syria's demand that he dismiss Prime Minister 'Awn. After 17 days in office, Mu'awwad was assassinated. 'Awn reverted to the acting Presidency.

1990's – Hizballah carried out the abductions and sometime murders of several American civilians resident in Beirut.

1990 – On 10/13/90, Syrian forces ousted 'Awn from the Presidential Palace: *MER*, Fall 2005. 'Awn chose 15 years of exile in France. (He returned to Lebanon in May 2005.)

1991 – Syrian hegemony over Lebanon was institutionalized by two bilateral agreements: The Treaty of Brotherhood, and the Defense and Security Agreement. However, anti-Syrian factions were gathering force. The Shiite Hizballah, natural ally of the Alawite regime in Damascus, was under constant attack from Israeli intelligence, which managed to assassinate two successive Hizballah leaders in the 1990's. In Washington, credit for Asad's unexpected adherence to the anti-Iraq coalition in the Gulf War of 1991 faded soon after that short engagement had run its course. For the pro-West faction in Lebanon, Syrian control of Lebanon was intolerable. For the Israeli-American diarchy, it was a geopolitical threat. It facilitated the transit of Iranian arms to Hizballah, Iran's protégé, Israel's looming nemesis.

1992 – In February, Israeli agents assassinated Hizballah leader 'Abbas Musawi and family. His able successor was Hasan Nasrallah.

1992 – Hizballah operatives have been suspected in the 3/17/92 bombing of the Israeli Embassy in Buenos Aires.

1992 – Hizballah began running candidates for election to the Lebanese Parliament.

1994 – The Jewish Community Center in Buenos Aires was bombed. Hizballah was suspected.

1996 – Hizballah was believed to be responsible for the bombing of the Khawbar Towers, quarters for US military personnel posted in Saudi Arabia.

1997 – The US declared Hizballah a terrorist organization.

1997 – On 9/3/97, eleven members of Flotilla 13, a crack Israeli special operations squad, were killed by Amal and Hizballah fighters, possibly with help from Lebanese forces: *Times*, 9/6/97.

2000 – **End of the Israel-Lebanon War**.

Phase II: Israel-Hizballah Action Between the Wars

2000-2006 – Not much happened along the Israel-Lebanon border for the first six years after the Israeli evacuation of Lebanon, but the relative quiet was misleading. It masked intense military planning on both sides. Hizballah had set a priority on recovering Arab detainees held in Israel – 15 Lebanese abducted in violation of the Geneva Conventions, and 9000 Palestinian political prisoners. Hizballah was also engrossed in the construction of a formidable network of bunkers effectively concealed in the mountains of south Lebanon. Israel, smarting from the expulsion of its troops in 2000, had set its sights on extermination of the deadly enemy across the border.

2000 – Syria had been controlling Lebanese affairs through a succession of proconsuls, until President Bashar al Asad himself took over. Syria's primary asset in Lebanon was Hizballah, but that organization paid greater allegiance to its founder, the Supreme Leader of Iran, and sent soldiers there for religious instruction and military training. Since the expulsion of the Palestinian forces from Lebanon in 1982, Hizballah had been the mainstay of the Lebanese defense against Israeli expansion. Avoiding the PLO's mistake of trying to face Israel with a conventional army, Hizballah was training, arming, and fortifying a highly effective guerrilla force well adapted to clandestine operations in the mountainous terrain of south Lebanon.

2000 – Hizballah had 13 of the 27 Shiite seats in the Lebanese Parliament. (Amal had 8; its leader, Nabih Barri, was Speaker.) Hizballah had a social-service net, a TV station (*Al Manar*), a training program for its youth ("Boy Scouts"), an army of several thousand, satellite cells in some Arab states, and a hundred-million-dollar budget, financed by Iran, by private donations, and – per a Khomeini directive – by tithes from Lebanese Shiites.

2004 – UNSC Resolution 1559 of 9/2/04 issued another call for withdrawal of foreign troops (Syrian?) from Lebanon, and disarmament of Hizballah (still no takers).

2004 – The Lebanese Shia were focused on consolidating their base in quadripartite Lebanon (Maronites dominant in the high northern

248

range, Druze in the southern range, Sunnis in the coastal cities, and Shiites in the south and the *Biqa'* – the fertile plain between the Lebanon and Anti-Lebanon Ranges.) Lebanon was still supervised by Syrians, enforced by 20,000 troops in the Biqa'.

2004 – On 9/2/04, UNSC Resolution 1559 reaffirmed the terms of the Ta'if Accord (Syrian withdrawal, Lebanese militias disbanded). With Iranian support, Syria countered by extending the term of President Amil Lahhud by three years, to 2007.

2005 – On 2/14/05 former Lebanese Prime Minister Rafiq al Hariri (pro-West) died in a Beirut bombing that killed 21 others. A Lebanese special tribunal found compelling cell phone evidence of Hizballah complicity. Hizballah leader Hasan Nasrallah blamed Israel.

2005 – Under UNSC Resolution 1595, a European team investigated the Hariri killing. Its report of 10/20/05 implicated certain Syrian and Lebanese officials. As of 2015, there had been no further judicial action – in part because of a series of attacks on the lives of anti-Syrian figures in Lebanon.

2005 – Under international pressure, largely inspired by suspicion of Syrian involvement in the Hariri killing, the 20,000 Syrian troops in Lebanon were finally forced to withdraw – leaving Lebanon under the hegemony of Hizballah: *Times*, 1/15/11.

2006 – In May, two officials of Hizballah's Islamic Jihad were reported killed in Sidon by Israel's Mossad.

2006 – In June, Hizballah broke up an Israeli spy ring in Lebanon.

2008 – Juan Cole reported close ties between Hizballah and Iraqi principals Muqtada al Sadr and Prime Minister Maliki.

Phase III: Outbreak of the Israel-Hizballah War

The following analysis by Andrew Cordesman appeared in the *Asia Times* of 10/12/06 (and also in *Haaretz*):

In reaction to Ariel Sharon's refusal to release Israel's last three Hizballah prisoners, Hasan Nasrallah had signaled Hizballah's intent to kidnap IDF personnel. On 7/12/06, Hizballah rocket fire on Israeli villages lured an Israeli border patrol into violating standard procedures by exiting its vehicles while it was out of contact with its superiors and out of sight of covering fire. This mistake enabled Hizballah to abduct two soldiers. The patrol then made its second mistake by cross-border pursuit by two tanks that were put out of action by mines. In those and subsequent actions, eight IDF personnel were killed.

This was the provocation Israel was looking for. On July 13, Hizballah installations, Shiite neighborhoods, and Lebanese infrastructure came under "catastrophic" (Amnesty International) assault by the air and ground forces of the IDF. The assault had the full support of the Bush administration, which according to a *New Yorker* article by Seymour Hersh regarded Hizballah's missiles as a Damoclesian threat to Israel in the event of an American attack on Iran's nuclear sites. Hizballah's narrow objective was to exchange prisoners. Israel's broad objective was to wipe out Hizballah. After the failure of a three-day onslaught to penetrate Hizballah's defenses, against punishing resistance from militiamen armed with Iranian-made rockets and Russian-made antitank and anti-helicopter weapons, Israel supplemented its operations in the south with a massive air attack on Tyre, Sidon, and Beirut in an effort to depopulate south Lebanon, raze Shiite communities, and turn the other communities against Hizballah. Hizballah responded with a rain of primitive Katyusha rocket fire on northern Israel, plus an Iranian C-802 cruise missile that damaged an Israeli warship and killed four crewmen: *Times*, 7/16/06. Along the front, Hizballah was taking out Israeli armored vehicles, tanks, and helicopters: *JPS*, Autumn 2006, Norton.

2006 – On 7/15/06 the Israeli Air Force made an effort to attack the Hizballah leadership in Beirut, but they were well hidden. Israeli demands to Lebanese and UN authorities received no compliance: There was no evidence that the two missing Israeli soldiers had survived their abduction; there was no organization willing and able to disarm Hizballah; deployment of Lebanese troops in south Lebanon would have been irrelevant, since they were staying out of combat: *McClatchy*, 7/18/06.

2006 –Israeli ground forces were mounting tentative forays against Hizballah's bunkers, the Israeli Air Force was insisting that victory was at hand, and Hizballah was still holding out at the first ridge line: *Counterpunch*, 10/13/06, Alastair Crooke/Mark Perry.

2006 – By 7/22/06, Israel's frustrated command had added schools and mosques to its air targets, called up the reserves (who arrived at the front poorly equipped for combat), opened a second air front against Gaza, and received ready compliance from Washington with their request for replacement munitions.

2006 – Israel deployed cluster munitions, reportedly old-style, single-fused, indiscriminately lethal.

2006 – As of 7/28/06, Hizballah had upgraded the performance of the missiles striking Israel.

2006 – The culmination of Israeli frustration was realized when one of its air strikes collapsed an apartment building in Qana (ten miles southeast of Tyre), killing 28 Lebanese civilians. The strike was singled out as the most egregious example of the collective punishment meted out by Israel to its Lebanese neighbors: *The Guardian*, 7/31/06, David Clark.

2006 – For a number of days, the Israeli Air Force had been including the UN's Khiyam observation post in its withering attacks on Hizballah's front line. On 8/6/06 the post was destroyed, and its four neutral occupants killed: Internet: UN News Service. They were Du Zhaoyu (China), Hans Peter Lang (Austria), Paeta Hess-von Kruedener (Canada), and Jarno Makinen (Finland). After their deaths, the UN withdrew the surviving observers – Israel's presumed objective from the start. (Israelis suspected UNIFIL of leaking intelligence to Hizballah.)

2006 – On 8/11/06, UNSC Resolution 1701 called for a ceasefire, a buffer zone between the border and the Litani River free of armed personnel, and the deployment of Lebanese forces and an enlarged UNIFIL contingent in south Lebanon. The ceasefire was accepted by Lebanon on August 12, by Israel on August 13, and also by Syria and Iran. In its close coordination with the Israelis, Washington was resisting a ceasefire, but finally succumbed to pressure from its European allies.

Aftermath – Casualties on each side had been approximately equal. Iran spent 2-3 billion dollars on repair of the destruction from Israeli bombs: *NY*, 2/25/13. Through Hizballah, Iran awarded each homeless family $12,000 to start rebuilding Harat Hurayk: *Wall Street Journal*, 9/17/07. Hizballah won political credit for its efficient oversight of a massive project from which families of all sects benefitted. Lebanese aid came more slowly. As of a year after the fighting, aid promised by Western governments hadn't arrived.

In September 2006, as UNIFIL moved in, Israel lifted its air and sea blockade against arms shipments to Hizballah: *Los Angeles Times*, 9/7/06. Withdrawal of Israeli troops from south Lebanon was completed in the fall: *AP*, 10/1/06. The bodies of the two Israeli soldiers abducted July 12, 2006, were exchanged for five of Israel's prisoners on 7/16/08, a date proclaimed a Lebanese national holiday. One of the five was Samir Kuntar, a Druze operative of the PFLP who was reviled in Israel as having caused the deaths of three Israeli civilians, including an infant inadvertently smothered by its terrified mother: *Times*, 7/17/08.

In the analyses of Augustus Richard Norton and Abbas William Samii, Hasan Nasrallah demonstrated after the Israeli evacuations of 2000 and 2006 the leadership to rein in retaliation against Christian collaborators, to show respect for the Lebanese Army, and to direct reconstruction with probity and intersectarian harmony.

Combat Assessment – The Hizballah defense included snipers (usually operating at a distance of 1500 feet or more from their targets) and rockets (fired singly or from truck-launchers), all supplied from arsenals hidden along the battle lines: *Christian Science Monitor*, 8/11/06, Nicholas Blanford. Hizballah's resilience against Israeli attack was the reward of years of study of IDF doctrine and capabilities, study of guerrilla warfare, and shrewd long-range planning: Blanford. Unable to secure south Lebanon, to capture Marun al Ras or Bint Jubayl, or even to shut down Al Manar TV, Israel settled for an effort to set up a security zone: Blanford.

An IDF officer characterized Hizballah's forces as the best trained and most highly motivated Arab fighters the Israelis had ever faced: Blanford. Timur Goksel, a long-standing official of UNIFIL, noted the striking superiority of Hizballah organization to that of most groups in the Palestinian Resistance Movement: *JPS*, Spring 2007. Sagacious planning had enabled Hizballah to hold off the IDF with one brigade of

3000 men, backed up by 12,000 (?) irregulars, and a few thousand of the 18,000 Katyushas and Sagger (also Russian) anti-tank rockets in its arsenal: www.AsiaTimes.com, Crooke/Perry. Mines on all roads leading from the border, and Hizballah's honeycomb of secret bunkers and tunnels, had forced Israel's formidable Merkeva tanks to venture cross-country. Ubiquitous shoulder-fired rockets had stopped enough tanks to shatter the myth of Israeli invincibility born in the Six-Day War of 1967: *The Observer*, 8/13/06, Peter Beaumont.

Israel could have gone all-out against Hizballah in 2006, but full mobilization after so minor an incident could have been condemned by the electorate as over-reaction. The abortive conclusion of three previous forays into Arab territory (Sinai in 1956-7 and 1967-79, southern Lebanon 1978-2000) gave warning that permanent expansion beyond Israel's de facto frontier is infeasible.

This consideration presumably militated in favor of the decision of the Olmert Government in 2006 to deal with Hizballah by remote control – a combination of calibrated forays by ground troops, backed by carpet bombing from the air. In the event, Israel reconciled itself to an asymmetric war, wherein air action creates more enemies than it kills, and guerrillas have the key advantage of operating on their home ground. Unified by the decisive leadership of Hasan Nasrallah, fighting from defenses reportedly designed under the gifted direction of 'Imad Mughniyah, Hizballah managed to keep its own casualties on a par with those of the IDF, while neutralizing Israel's basic objectives: *Harper's*, March 2007, Charles Glass. The Israeli command made three basic errors of judgment: Exaggeration of the effect of air power; underestimation of Hizballah's defenses; misreading of the impact of invasion on Lebanese opinion: *JPS*, Autumn 2006, Norton. Hizballah had won mass acclaim as Lebanon's essential security force, whereas the other Arab states, inanimate throughout, were seen as a gaggle of timorous onlookers: *NPR*, 8/16/06. Hizballah stood alone as the first Arab force to go to war on behalf of the Palestinian cause as well as its own. (This spark of Arab nationalist fervor couldn't last. By 2012, Hizballah's reliance on financial and logistic support from Iran had forced it into the Shiite camp, as the Middle East collapsed into all-consuming sectarian war. In previous centuries, tribalism had been trumped by sectarianism, and sectarianism by language group. Then came the alchemy of the Arab Spring. By 2015, the determinant of political affiliation was no longer language. It was sect, as armies aligned themselves between the poles of Sunni and Shia.) The only benefit to Israel from the 1982 invasion was the third Palestinian exile, from Lebanon to Tunisia and divers Arab states. It was overshadowed in the regional power equation by the emergence of Hizballah.

Casualties – Property Damage: To the Lebanese infrastructure – 3.5 billion dollars, in south Lebanon and up the coast as far north as Beirut; 15,000 Lebanese residences; 900 Lebanese businesses and farms. To Israeli communities, from rockets, considerable loss of property, including 6000 residences. Displaced Persons: In Lebanon, 1,000,000. In Israel, 400,000. Deaths: Lebanese civilians, 743. Lebanese soldiers: 34. Hizballah militants, 68. Israeli IDF, 118. Israeli civilians, 39. Sources: *AP*, 8/18/06; www.*AsiaTimes.com*; *NYR*, 9/21/06, Max Rodenbeck.

Israeli Overkill – Amnesty International found both sides in Round Two guilty of war crimes and violations of international law: *Times*, 9/14/06. Both Israel and Hizballah unleashed flights of bombs and/or missiles indiscriminately at enemy territory. Israel alone violated the criterion of disproportionate damage. In the Six-Day War, Israel had scored a strategic point by summarily crushing the armed forces of three Arab states. In Lebanon, Israel went over the line in the view of many observers by punishing Lebanese communities that were not participants in the fighting. Israel wanted them to be won over by its demonstration of awesome power. Instead they were enraged to find themselves equal victims of Israeli vindictiveness. Adversaries and noncombatants alike were targets of Israeli excesses:

– Carpet-bombing of the ethnically mixed neighborhood of Harat Hurayk, a suburb of Beirut, far from the ground war: *MER*, Spring 2007.

– Seizure of thousands of civilian prisoners: *Times*, 7/21/07.

– Sowing south Lebanon with land mines, but providing no postwar map of their location.

– Devastating the Lebanese economy by taking out key elements of infrastructure, such as the oil depot at Jiyyah: Juan Cole Blog, 8/14/06.

– Preempting the ceasefire by saturating south Lebanon with old-style single-fused cluster bombs of lasting lethality.

– Targeting hospitals and a refugee convoy: *The Nation*, 10/2/06, Falk.

– Repetition of air strikes on UNIFIL's Khiyam observation post until all four observers were dead.

– Lethal use of white phosphorus: *LRB*, 8/17/06, Michael Byers.

– Slaughter of Lebanese civilians on the unproven grounds that they had voluntarily shielded Hizballah units: *MIT*, "Middle East", Lara Deeb, 8/23/06; *JPS*, Autumn 2006, Norton.

America's Favoritism, America's Loss – Washington's robotic endorsement of Israel's policies forces the US to share in Israel's failures and misdeeds. The Israel-Hizballah War was Israel's worst setback in its 60-year history. Washington's support for the misbegotten invasion was blatant from the outset. In the words of Turkish observer Timur Goksel, with Israel's "best friend", Bush 43, in the White House, Israel launched an air campaign intended to depopulate south Lebanon: *JPS*, Spring 2007, Goksel. According to Seymour Hersh, the primary objective of the Bush Administration in the Middle East was the destruction of Hizballah's capacity to shower northern Israel with missiles in the event of a future clash between Iran and the US or Israel: *NY*, Seymour Hersh. On July 18, 2006, House of Representatives Resolution 921 endorsed 410-8 Israel's invasion of Lebanon. The resolution cited Israeli hostages in Lebanon, but not the thousands of Palestinians held in Israel. On July 22, 2006, the US sent Israel a shipment of precision-guided munitions.

On 8/18/06, as the invasion was losing steam, and the US was under pressure from its European allies, Washington gave in to UNSC Resolution 1701's call for a ceasefire. The Israeli-Lebanese proxy war for the potential US-Iran War had been stalemated. Washington's slavish support for Israel's strategic aberration had undermined America's position in the Middle East, notably its pose as a valid mediator in the Arab-Israeli dispute. Hizballah, emerging from Round Two with its command and control systems intact, embodied a basic principle of asymmetric war: to succeed, the weaker party doesn't have to win; it just has to avoid defeat. Instead of mobilizing Sunni Arab states against Iran,

255

Washington had to deal with a Saudi appeal for an early ceasefire in Lebanon, while Shaykh Hasan Nasrallah was being hailed as an Arab hero.

Result: Military defeat for Israel, political defeat for the US.

Hizballah Action Since the Ceasefire of 8/13/06

2006 – On 9/22/06, hundreds of thousands of Beirutis came out for the first public appearance in Beirut of Hizballah leader Hasan Nasrallah: *Times*, 9/23/06.

2007 – According to Seymour Hersh, Hasan Nasrallah was under death sentence from Israel, Jordan, and Al Qa'idah (although Al Qa'idah leader Zawahiri reportedly praised the prowess of "our brothers").

2008 – On 1/25/08, Lebanese Captain Wisam 'Id, assigned to the Hariri case, was assassinated.

2008 – On 2/12/08, 'Imad Mughniyah was killed by a car bomb in Damascus. He had been a devout Shiite and a youthful member of Fatah. He was believed to have had a separate association with the office of Iran's Supreme Leader Khamenei: *NY*, 10/28/02, Jeffrey Goldberg. US and Israeli intelligence considered Mughniyah to have been a principal in many of Hizballah's major operations. The US had put a price on his head. His assassination is generally ascribed to Israeli intelligence.

2008 – In May, Hizballah occupied areas of Beirut, without resistance. By this action it acquired veto power over the Lebanese Government.

2008 – On 7/16/08, a prisoner exchange between Hizballah and Israel included the bodies of the two Israeli soldiers abducted by Hizballah 7/12/06.

In early 2009, Hizballah regarded Iran's Supreme Leader, Ali Khamenei, as its own leader, but in Lebanon it was headed by Nasrallah. Its unofficial spiritual mentor, Ayatallah Muhammad Husayn Fadlallah, had condemned suicide bombing and Al Qa'idah's attacks of 9/11, and taken the position that no Shia leader has a monopoly on truth. Augustus Richard Norton characterized him as the second most respected cleric in the Shiite world (Sistani being the first). Vali Nasr classified him with the moderates.

Syria's inclusion on Washington's list of states sponsoring terrorism was charged to Syrian support of Hizballah and tolerance of Hamas and Islamic Jihad offices – even though all three organizations were independent of Syrian control, participated in elections, did not call for restoration of the Caliphate, and were not known to have carried out operations in the US: *Current History*, Emile Nakhlah.

2009 – Four pro-Syrian Lebanese generals, who had been charged with complicity in the killing of Lebanese Prime Minister Rafiq Hariri, were released because of insufficient evidence.

2010 – Hasan Nasrallah called on the Lebanese government to boycott the UN tribunal investigating the Hariri assassination.

2011 – In January, Hizballah withdrew from the Lebanese Government, which collapsed.

2011 – In June Prime Minister Miqati formed a cabinet dominated by Hizballah.

2011 – In July the UN tribunal issued warrants for the arrest of four members of Hizballah.

2012 – Lebanese Major General Wisam Hasan, assigned to the Hariri case, was assassinated.

2013 – Israeli agents killed Hizballah principal Hasan Lakkis.

2013 – Hizballah forces, which were members of the March 8 Coalition, entered the Syrian Civil War on the side of Asad's Alawite regime. The March 14 Coalition sided with the rebels: *Current History*, December 2015.

2013 – By taking the Syrian town of Qusayr, Hizballah forces cut off the main supply lines of the rebels trying to defend Homs, which subsequently fell to the Damascus regime: *MEP*, Winter 2015.

2014 – On 11/5/14 the Lebanese Parliament voted to extend its members' terms in office by three years automatically – as it had in 2013 – on the grounds that no new electoral law had been adopted: *Times*, 11/6/14.

2015 – The IS and Nusrah viewed Shia as apostates. The Shia viewed the IS and Nusrah as takfiris (*takfiri* – one who condemns a non-Sunni as a nonbeliever, hence liable to execution): *Times*, 1/9/15.

2015 – The flood of Syrian refugees was replacing Shia with Sunnis as the largest sectarian community in Lebanon: *Times*, 1/14/15.

2015 – On 1/15/15 an Israeli helicopter strike in Syria killed 5 members of Hizballah, including Jihad Mughniyah, son of 'Imad Mughniyah. The action breached a tacit Israel-Hizballah agreement not to escalate their own conflict in the midst of the larger war: *Times*, 1/18/15.

2015 – From the Syrian front: Reports that the Free Syrian Army (FSA) had taken a major Damascus regime military base in southern Syria, and west of Damascus Hizballah had had its first clash with IS forces, and won that engagement. The FSA had received some help from the CIA, and also cooperated with Nusrah: *Times*, 6/10/15.

2015 – Druze Arabs have traditionally been loyal to the government of the country they inhabit: Syria, Israel, or Lebanon: *AP*, 6/25/15, Aron Heller. In Lebanon, after jihadists had moved into a Druze province, Druze MP Walid Junblat advised his community in Syria to reconcile with their Sunni neighbors: *Times*, 6/12/15.

2015 – Lebanon was so crowded with Syrian refugees (1.5 million) that it had closed its border to most new applicants, but not to Christians fleeing attack by the IS: *NYTM*, 7/26/15.

2015 – The Maronite community in Lebanon was split between pro-Saudis (under Samir Ja'ja') and a pro-Hizballah group (under General Michel 'Awn, who was back in Lebanon after a long stay in Paris): *NYTM*, 7/26/15. The general population of Lebanon was divided between the March 14 Movement (anti-Syrian) and the March 8 Movement (pro-Syrian): *Times*, 8/30/15.

2015 – On 11/15/15, two suicide bombings in Burj al Barajna, a suburb of Beirut, killed 43. The Lebanese authorities concluded from interrogation of a failed suicide bomber that a large IS cell was responsible: http://www.dailystar.com.lb/, 3/16/16; *Current History*, 11/12/15.

2015 – On 12/20/15, an Israeli air strike near Damascus killed Samir Kuntar, who had been high on Mossad's hit list. At the time of his death, he was affiliated with the Syrian National Defense Force: *FT*, 12/21/15.

2015 – In The Hague, the Special Tribunal for Lebanon began prosecuting five members of Hizballah. Lebanon, the US, and France were financing the trial. The court had no direct evidence, but circumstantial evidence from cell phone records.

2016 – Latest political lineup in Lebanon: Pro-Damascus regime – Samir Ja'ja's Lebanese Forces (Maronite Christian), Michel 'Awn's Free Patriotic Movement, Hizballah; Pro-Saudi – Sa'd Hariri's Future Movement: *Times*, 1/19/16.

2016 – With help from the Russian Air Force and Hizballah, forces of the Damascus regime recaptured Palmyra: *FT*, 3/28/16.

2016 – Lebanon was still operating on the basis of a 1996 agreement for power sharing along sectarian lines. There had been no President for the previous two years, and no Parliamentary elections. Parliament was voting term extensions on its own: *Times*, 5/11/16.

2016 – A huge explosion near the Damascus Airport killed Mustafa Badr al Din, brother-in-law of the assassinated 'Imad Mughniyah, longtime leader of Hizballah military and clandestine operations: *Times*, 5/14/16.

2016 – Lebanon now had six million residents – a million and a half of them refugees from Syria et al: *Times*, 7/5/16.

2011-? – Saudi-Yemeni War

———

Statistically speaking, Yemen and Saudi Arabia are the two major states of the Arabian Peninsula ("Arabia" in this text). Saudi Arabia has an area of 830,000 square miles (eleventh biggest in the world) and a population of 27,000,000. Yemen has an area of 204,000 square miles and a population of 25,000,000.

Financially and developmentally, they are poles apart: Saudi Arabia's per capita GDP, according to the 2017 *World Almanac*, is 53,600 dollars a year; in 2009, Yemen's was 2500 dollars a year. Yemen exports some oil, and its central massif with elevations of 10-12,000 feet brings rain, but population growth is outstripping water supply, and Yemen couldn't afford desalination facilities like those the Saudis rely on. Their current war is a case of an inexperienced Saudi Air Force wreaking death and destruction on the hapless Yemenis for no valid purpose.

When the war began, Yemen was a stormy combine of two long-separate entities. It had made little progress in reconciling the incompatibilities between them. The south had some oil. It had acquired a veneer of Westernization from years of British tutelage. Most of its inhabitants are Shafi'i Sunnis. Most of the northerners are Zaydi Shiites who have ruled northern Yemen for centuries, and trace their lineage to the Prophet: *The Week*, 2016.

1978-2012 – For twelve years, 'Ali 'Abdallah Salih (Zaydi) was President of North Yemen. From 1990 to 2012, he was nominal

President of a united Yemen, which combined the two previously independent states of North Yemen and South Yemen.

1990's – AQ operatives set up shop in southern Yemen: *Harper's*, September 2016, Patrick Cockburn.

1994 – In May, troops from north Yemen entered Aden and shut down south Yemen's bid to secede.

1997 – President Salih caused Husayn al Huthi to lose his seat in the Yemeni Parliament.

1999 – On 9/23/99, in Yemen's first vote under universal suffrage, 'Ali 'Abdallah Salih was reelected President of Yemen.

2000 – On 10/12/00, the USS Cole, a guided-missile destroyer, in Aden harbor for refueling, was damaged by a bomb placed by AQ operatives from a small boat. Seventeen crewmen died.

2001 – After Al Qa'idah's 9/11 attack on the US, Washington asked President Salih of Yemen to join the war against the Al Qa'idah fighters in Yemen. Salih countered by asking for help in suppressing the unruly Huthi tribe: *Harper's*, September 2016, Andrew Cockburn.

2004 – The Huthis, under the name *Ansar Allah* (Followers of God), ignited a multi-tribal rebellion against the Salih regime. Tribal leader Husayn al Huthi described Salih as a puppet of the US. A Huthi slogan called for "Death to America, death to the Jews": *The Week*, 2016.

2004 – Yemeni forces killed Husayn al Huthi on September 10.

2006 – In September, President Salih was reelected.

2007-11 – Yemen was disrupted by clashes involving the Huthis, the secessionists, affiliates of Al Qa'idah, and government forces.

2008-9 – The AQ militants in Saudi Arabia and Yemen merged as Al Qa'idah in the Arabian Peninsula (AQAP): *Times*, 4/15/15. AQAP bands hiding among Yemeni tribes carried out several attacks. They were the ones who claimed they had bombed the US Embassy in San'a'.

2008 – On 9/17/08, the American Embassy was attacked by six militants armed with rocket-propelled grenades, automatic rifles, and car bombs. In a brief battle between the attackers and Embassy security personnel, the six attackers, six Yemeni police, and six civilians died. No one on the Embassy staff was injured.

2009 – In December, at the request of Salih, the US began air strikes against suspected AQAP sites.

2009 – Overpopulation and shortage of oil and water supply had caused serious deterioration in the lifestyle of the Yemeni people: Kristian Ulrichsen.

2011 – A massacre of anti-regime protestors in north Yemen on 3/18/11 led to intensification of the tribal insurgency. Sunni Islamists and southern separatists joined forces with the Huthis against Yemen's armed forces, who were commanded by President Salih. The Huthi forces battled the 'Abdin tribes (pro-Salih) for the town of Sa'dah (elevation: one mile). By 3/27/11, the Huthis were in control.

2011 – On 3/31/11, AQAP militiamen took control of three cities in Abyan (a coastal governorate just east of Aden), including Zinjibar, the capital, and proclaimed Abyan an Al Qa'idah emirate in Yemen.

2011 – On 6/3/11, President Salih was severely wounded in the rocketing of the Presidential Compound in Sana'a'. Vice President 'Abdu Rabbuh Hadi took over as Acting President: *The Week*, 3/6/15.

2011 – On 11/3/11, in Riyadh, Salih signed a GCC-sponsored agreement under which he agreed to resign as President in favor of his Vice President, 'Abdu Rabbuh Mansur Hadi. The Huthis rejected the agreement on the ground that it did not provide for adequate reforms: *Harper's*, September 2016, Cockburn.

2012 – On 2/21/12, in an uncontested election, Hadi was elected President of the Republic of Yemen.

2012 – In the summer, the Yemen Army and tribal allies forced the AQAP contingent out of Abyan. The occupiers had alienated the population by trying to impose their strict doctrines – notably a ban on *qat*, the deleterious national addiction.

2013 – **Musical Chairs** – Hadi abolished the Republican Guard, which had been the personal militia of President Salih. Salih retaliated by forming an alliance of convenience with the Huthis against the government he used to head; *The Week*, 11/10/14.

2014 – As the Huthis fanned out across the country, several forces moved to confront them, plunging Yemen into carnage. Iran was lending political support to the Huthis. Saudi Arabia and the UAE were aligned with Hadi and Yemen's Sunnis against the Huthis. A mainstay on the Sunni side was Islah, a Sunni Islamist organization loyal to the Hadi faction.

2014 – The Saudis believed their enemy, Iran, was provoking the Yemeni Shiites against the Sunnis. The Saudis were forming a GCC coalition to support the Huthi-Salih faction.

2014 – On 9/9/14, 'Abd al Malik, who had succeeded his brother Husayn as leader of the Huthis, launched an attack against Sana'a', the capital of Yemen. On 9/21/14, they captured the city. As the new rulers of Yemen, they set up a Supreme Revolutionary Council: *Times*, 9/22/14, 11/27/14; *LRB*, 5/21/15.

2014 – The AQAP was operating on its own, although the Huthis were condemning the ongoing US drone campaign against the AQAP. The US, an automatic partisan of the Saudi/UAE alliance, had imposed sanctions on 'Ali 'Abdallah Salih and two Huthi leaders: *Times*, 11/10/14.

2014 – The IS sent militiamen into Yemen to exploit the disorder – in competition against the AQAP: *The Week*, 3/6/15.

2015 – Around 40 died in a car bombing at the Yemen Police Academy: *Times*, 1/9/15.

2015 – On 1/22/15, Huthi militia besieged the residence of President Hadi, who resigned. As Sunnis, the AQAP opposed Hadi's ouster.

2015 – At a cost to the US of hundreds of millions of dollars, Hadi's government had been encouraged to support the US drone war in Yemen. This subsidy ended with the Huthi takeover: *FT*, 1/26/15.

2015 – On 2/6/15, the tribal insurgents dissolved the Yemeni Parliament and installed a five-man Presidential Council.

2015 – AQAP forces and Sunni tribesmen were deploying to oppose the Huthi advance on Aden: *Times*, 2/21/15.

2015 – In March, Hadi escaped from Huthi detention in San'a' and fled to Aden.

2015 – In Yemen, the IS was recruiting fighters from the AQAP.

2015 – The GCC was asking for UN action versus the Huthi expansion: *The Week*, 3/6/15.

2015 – There was heavy fighting in the Aden area between pro-Hadi forces (including southern separatists) and forces of the Huthi/Salih faction: *Times*, 3/20/15.

2015 – The Huthis took segments of Ta'izz, with weapons flown in to San'a' by Iran: *FT*, 3/22/15; *Times*, 3/23/15. The GCC states were backing the pro-Hadi forces: *Times*, 3/20/15.

2015 – Four militias were fighting the civil war: Huthis and allies held Yemen from San'a' north; the pro-Hadi forces were based in Aden; the AQAP was based in southern Yemen.

2015 – On 3/20/15, the IS claimed suicide attacks on two mosques in Yemen. 142 were killed: *AP*, 3/26/15, Gwynne Dyer.

2015 – **War** – On 3/26/15, Saudi Arabia announced it was launching an air campaign (on behalf of the Hadi faction) against Yemen, starting in the Sana'a' area. According to the announcement, Egypt, Jordan, Morocco, Sudan, and all the GCC states would participate. In fact, Oman has not participated. The Saudis also imposed naval and air blockades around Yemen. The US would help with planning, logistics, and intelligence: The Jamestown Foundation (http://www.jamestown.org), 2/9/16.

2015 – To salvage Hadi's presidency, the Saudi Air Force went into haphazard action against targets in Yemen: *Harper's,* September 2016, Cockburn.

2015 – The Huthis in San'a' were under fire from Saudi aircraft. Misdirected Saudi strikes were causing extensive casualties among the Yemeni populace: *Times*, 3/31/15. Egyptian warships were patrolling the Yemen coast.

2015 – There was more heavy fighting in Aden between Huthis and forces of their several adversaries: *Times*, 4/1/15.

2015 – On 4/2/15, claiming to be acting on behalf of the Hadi faction, AQAP militiamen in the Hadramawt took over Mukalla, its capital, from soldiers of the Yemen Army, released hundreds from the central prison (including two senior AQAP officials), looted a large sum from the central bank, and claimed the city for the Al Qa'idah Emirate in Yemen: www.aljazeera.com, 9/16/16; *Times*, 4/3/15.

2015 – In north Yemen, the Huthis had abducted members of the Islah, an offshoot of the Muslim Brotherhood, funded by Saudi Arabia: *Times*, 4/7/15.

2015 – Hadi did not have a large following in Yemen. The north was infuriated by the murderous incompetence of the Saudi air campaign he had requested. The south favored secession; Hadi was a unionist: *FT*, 4/8/15.

2015 – The Huthis had overrun 'Ataq, capital of Shabwah Province, between Aden and Mukalla: *AP*, 4/10/15.

2015 – The AQAP, already in control of Mukalla's seaport and oil terminal, took its airport (*AP*, 4/17/15), and neutralized its defenders, a pro-Salih unit of the Yemen Army. The officers fled. The soldiers left unharmed: *Times*, 4/17/15.

2015 – There were reports of organizational and strategic links between the Huthis in Yemen, and the Islamic Revolutionary Guard Corps (IRGC) and Hizballah: *FT*, 5/11/15.

2015 – The national free-for-all among Hadi's forces, the Huthi/Salih forces, the AQAP, and the IS went on. Hadi's one-time cabinet, largely from Al Islah, was in exile in Riyadh: *LRB*, 5/21/15. Yemen, faced with grave shortages of food and fuel, was in despair. Ta'izz and Aden were being devastated by the fighting: *Times*, 5/3/15.

2015 – On 5/7/15, a US drone killed a gathering of AQAP members including Nasir al 'Ansi, a leader from the Hadramawt: www.cnn.com.

2015 – In Mukalla, the AQAP was angering its subjects by burning qat: *Times*, 5/15/15. (It was an admirable enterprise.)

2015 – To destabilize Yemen, Iran was providing arms to the Huthis: PBS Newshour, statement by US secretary of State Kerry.

2015 – In June, clashes between the Huthis and the Yemen Army cost 200 deaths: *WRMEA*, June 2015, Jason Ditz.

2015 – A Saudi Patriot missile shot down a Scud fired from Yemen toward Khamis Mushayt in Saudi Arabia. The missile had probably originated from the army of President Salih, which had acquired Scuds from North Korea in 2002: *Times*, 6/6/15.

2015 – A US drone in Mukalla killed Nasir al Wuhayshi, the leader of the AQAP in Yemen and deputy head of the AQAP's central organization: *McClatchy*, 6/12/15.

2015 – Many former Yemeni soldiers had followed 'Ali 'Abdallah Salih into the forces backing the Huthis: *Times*, 6/23/15.

2015 – The GCC air campaign against the Huthis included bombing residential areas, inflicting immense damage and casualties. It was having no visible effect on the actions of the Huthi forces. The Saudis considered the Huthis a proxy force for Iran: *Times*, 6/25/15.

2015 – With armored vehicles supplied by the UAE, Saudi-trained Separatist fighters recaptured most of Aden from the Huthis, but the city was not yet secured: *Times*, 7/15/15, 7/18/15.

2015 – The forces that had lately reversed the Huthi advance into southern Yemen included ground troops from the UAE and Saudi Arabia: *Times*, 8/4/15. The Huthi forces had been losing ground in southern and central Yemen since July: *Times*, 8/16/15.

2015 – In September, the AQAP occupiers formed the Hadramawt National Council to rule Mukalla until law and order had been restored in Yemen. The occupiers then retreated into the background, but promised to protect the city from Huthi attack. From Riyadh, Hadi endorsed the council: www.aljazeera.com, Saeed al Batati.

2015 – The Huthis captured the city of Ma'rib. The Huthis were gaining support by providing security to areas neglected by the previous Yemen government: *AP*, Ahmad al Hajj.

2015 – In San'a', the Huthis released six hostages – two Americans, one Briton, three Saudis: *Times*, 9/21/15.

2015 – Four suicide bombings in Aden and San'a' killed 15 or more: *Times*, 10/7/15; *FT*, 10/7/15.

2015 – On 12/2/15, AQAP forces took the Abyan cities of Zinjibar and Ja'r for a second time. Missiles were fired against them by the US, but not by the Saudi-UAE alliance: *Times*, 12/3/15.

2015 – On 12/6/15, Major General Ja'far Muhammad Sa'd, ally of ex-President Hadi, was killed by a car bomb in Aden. Five bodyguards died with him. The IS claimed the operation: *Times*, 12/7/15.

2016 – The Arab-Iranian cultural divide was driving a Saudi-Iranian proxy war in Yemen, Bahrain, and the Fertile Crescent: *LRB*, 2/4/16.

2016 – In February, the AQAP fought alongside the Hadi forces defending the city of Ta'izz: *Harper's*, September, 2016, Cockburn.

2016 – In February, a Western warship seized from an Iranian dhow thousands of weapons intended for the Huthis: *Times*, 1/11/17. From early 2015 to October 2016, US ships intercepted five such shipments: www.cnn.com, 10/28/16.

2016 – By February, Huthi/Salih forces were crossing the border to attack Saudi forces: *MEP*, Summer 2016, Legrenzi/Lawson.

2016 – In February, Hizballah shipped surface-to-surface missiles to the Huthis: Legrenzi/Lawson.

2016 – On 2/29/16, a Saudi-owned TV station lampooned Hizballah's Hasan Nasrallah as an Iranian agent, and accused Hizballah of being a threat to the people of the Gulf: *MEP*, Summer 2016, Legrenzi/Lawson.

2016 – On 3/1/16, Nasrallah broadcast a vituperative rebuttal to his Saudi critics. In mid-March, the Saudis penalized Lebanon for its deference to Hizballah by cancelling a promised 4-billion-dollar grant to fund the purchase of arms for the army and police: Legrenzi/Lawson.

2016 – The Huthi forces were fighting to recover areas in south Yemen lately taken by forces of the AQAP and the IS: *AP*, 3/1/16. In Aden, the AQAP was forcing the Gulf coalition (Saudi Arabia, UAE, and Hadi's forces [?]) to evacuate the city: *Times*, 3/14/16.

2016 – A US air strike killed 50 or more in an AQAP training camp on 3/23/16.

2016 – Pro-Hadi troops from Yemen and the UAE expelled AQAP forces from the Lahij Governorate, adjoining Aden: *Times*, 4/25/16.

2016 – Yemeni recruits under guidance from UAE special forces took over Mukalla, just evacuated by the AQAP: *Times*, 4/25/16.

2016 – In May, the Huthi/Salih forces were continuing: 1) a long siege of Ta'izz, which was defended by forces from the Shafi'i community and the AQAP; 2) clashes with Saudi forces along the Yemeni-Saudi border: *Times*, 5/11/16.

2016 – The GCC branded Hizballah as a terrorist organization: *MEP*, Summer 2016.

2016 – The flight of AQAP forces from their previous positions in Lahij and Hadramawt should allow the resumption of oil and gas export: *Times*, 8/17/16.

2016 – After their evacuation from Mukalla, capital of the Hadramawt, AQAP operatives began a round of clandestine bombings: Cockburn.

2016 – The AQAP was carrying out sporadic attacks against coalition forces in southern and eastern Yemen. IS suicide bombers were attacking Huthi/Salih positions in Aden and Lahij: *MEP*, Summer 2016.

2016 – With Iranian permission, Salih had sent into Saudi territory a small Huthi force that scored a humiliating victory over Saudi defenders. Saudi Arabia ordered massive quantities of arms from the US. The stated Saudi objective was to "eliminate traces of Iran in Yemen". In view of strong Saudi and Israeli opposition to the nuclear production deal between the West and Iran, Obama saw political necessity in supporting the Saudi operations against the Huthis, despite the sloppy performance of the Saudi Air Force, and reports that the operation was targeting Yemeni civilians. According to WHO, as of June 2016, nearly 6500 Yemenis had been killed. The Huthi forces had shelled areas held by the GCC coalition. The US was providing the neophyte Saudi Air Force with help in identifying critical targets: *Harper's*, September 2016, Cockburn.

2016 – The Huthi/Salih faction controlled most of north Yemen. The Yemen Army was backing the Huthi/Salih side in the Yemen civil war: *Harper's*, September 2016.

2016 – Yemenis opposed to the Huthi/Salih side remembered Salih's long rule as cruel and dictatorial. Salih had endorsed the American drone campaign against the AQAP and the IS: *Harper's*, September 2016.

2016 – On 10/1/16, a cruise missile fired from Yemen's coastal defense disabled a UAE military logistics ship: *Times*, 10/13/16.

2016 – After coalition planes had struck several of its medical sites, Doctors Without Borders announced it was withdrawing from helping six hospitals in Yemen.

2016 – A Saudi air strike against a funeral assembly in San'a' killed over one hundred: *Times*, 10/8/16.

2016 – On 10/14/16, in retaliation for two missile attacks on USN ships, US cruise missiles took out three radar sites in rebel-held territory. The earlier ground fire had severely damaged a commercial ship flagged by the UAE: *FT*, 10/14/16.

2016 – The US was supporting the Saudi war effort by providing intelligence and air-to-air refueling: *Times*, 10/15/16.

2016 – The Saudi air offensive was destroying, *inter alia*, hospitals, funeral parlors, and water-bottling factories. The Saudi blockade was bringing Yemenis to the brink of starvation: *The Week*, 10/28/16, Zack Beauchamp.

2016 – At the end of the year, the Huthi/Salih faction controlled most of north Yemen.

Section II: The Middle East Power Struggle

From Regional Turmoil to Sectarian Conflict

Our planet has a surface area of almost 200,000,000 square miles. 50 million of that is land. 40 million of that is habitable. Each newborn comes into the world with a hypothetical claim to nine-tenths of an acre – where you come out by dividing 7250 million people into 6560 million habitable acres.

On this planet, claim doesn't mean ownership. Mankind is hardwired to appropriate territory by force – of demography, immigration, arms, or invasion. Our colonists used these methods to take the center of North America from its previous owners. The Zionists used them to convert Palestine to Israel.

Geopolitics tells us the world has evolved into ten or fifteen regions, distinguished from each other by unique homelands, histories, and cultures. History suggests a trend in every region from anarchy toward union. If so, the region closest to union may be China. Under American hegemony (control), our own region, North America, may not be far behind.

The first challenge for every geopolitical hegemony is to dispel communalism – reconcile ethnic diversities, whether racial or sectarian. Down through history, the standard means was inter-ethnic war: Assyrians versus Egyptians, Parthians versus Romans, Christians versus Muslims, Mongols versus Westerners, European settlers versus

271

American Indians, Protestants versus Catholics, French versus Germans – the list is a long one.

From 1562 to 1648, France, Spain, Germany, Sweden, and the Netherlands were convulsed by the Wars of Religion, which centered on sectarian conflict among Catholics, Lutherans, and Calvinists, and burned out in the Peace of Westphalia: *EB*: 18:656. This achievement resolved several territorial disputes, and won a place in history by stressing the concept of nationhood: *EB*: 19:479. The Europeans were beginning to realize that capitulation to the straitjacket of random ethnicity was a primitive aberration. A more sophisticated determinant of political allegiance would be the nation. Ethnic rivalry should be removed from the realm of military action to that of civil debate. The probability that this step forward will take centuries does not alter the case.

In this text, the region under observation is the Middle East. It was the cradle of civilization, but its location at the junction of three continents is so vulnerable that it has periodically lapsed back toward anarchy. The latest such lapse took gradual effect as the region was being battered by a series of adventitious shocks:

1736 – End of the Safavid Dynasty in Iran.

1800's – Decline of the Ottoman Empire.

1840 – Suppression of the imperialist expectations of Egypt's Muhammad 'Ali by Britain and allies.

1882 – British forces assumed control of Egypt.

1914 – World War I: Allied imposition of hegemony over key areas of the Middle East.

1918 – Britain took Iraq, Jordan, and Palestine. France took Syria. Russia took the southern Caucasus. England and France took advantage of the Middle East's ancient communal divisions – suppressing the solidarity of all the communities under imperialist jurisdiction by encasing them in a superficial overlay of Westphalian "states". The objective was a region in perpetual disunity. If no single European power could take over the whole region, all of them working together – not by design but by coincidence – could inhibit the emergence of an

272

indigenous force able to fill the power vacuum left by the collapse of the Safavid and Ottoman Empires.

1939 – World War II: Consolidation of European hegemony, with America's unwitting participation from 1941.

1948 – Arbitrary insertion of a Jewish state in the center of the eastern Arab World.

1956 – Suez War: Replacement of Europe by the US as the imperialist power in the Middle East.

1973 – The Yom Kippur War established Israel as the preeminent military power in the Middle East.

1980-88 – The statehood system seemed to be catching on: the Iraq-Iran War aligned Iranians of all ethnic communities against most Arab Iraqis, both Sunni and Shiite.

1990-91 – And again in the two Kuwait wars, when the US fought multi-ethnic Iraq – until the Shiites and Kurds struck out on paths of their own.

2001 – The Americans' mindless overreaction to the 9/11 attacks was the proclamation of a Global War on Terrorism, which materialized into the invasions of Afghanistan and Iraq, and a region-wide drone war against anti-American activists.

2003 – With the occupation of Iraq, US strategy in the Middle East switched from military dalliance and political maneuver to the wholesale use of armed force.

The Arab Spring

In the early years of the 21st century, the Arab World was the setting for a mounting wave of fury against the inadequacies of its rulers.

The original protests were non-violent. The catalyst for violence was the report of the 1/4/11 death of Muhammad Bu'azizi, a Tunisian vendor driven by official persecution to a fiery suicide. In Syria, one of the most vicious civil wars in history was ignited by the arrest of a group of children in Dar'a. Their offense was writing anti-regime graffiti. Their punishment was administered by security forces of Bashar al Asad's regime, an Alawite clique whose constant stress from its minority status

273

had been intensified by the region's growing climate of instability. Reportedly, the maltreatment of the youngsters went as far as pulling fingernails.

Happenstance became legend as the Arab Spring. By March 2012, rulers in Tunisia, Libya, Yemen, and Egypt had been ousted: *Aljazeera*, 1/15/11; *Times*, 1/28/11; *The Daily Telegraph*, 2/23/11; *CSM*, 7/28/11, Scott Peterson.

The Arab Spring was widely misinterpreted as a first step toward democracy. Juan Cole saw it more accurately as a revolt by millions of young Arabs passed over by, or overeducated for, the backward economies they lived in: *MEP*, Winter 2015, *The New Arabs*, Juan Cole.

These tensions had already contributed to the outbreak of various local wars. They have imperceptibly fused into an ethnic power struggle that has absorbed many of the states in the region. As noted in *The New Arab Wars* by Marc Lynch, and discussed in the 6/23/16 *New York Review*, all the disparate factions perceive themselves to be contenders in a unified regional conflict. The 200-year struggle for a new hegemony over the Middle East had crystallized along ethnic lines.

Lynch suggests that "the transformation of the Arab uprisings… into a regional proxy war" was triggered by the intrusions of NATO states.

This analysis starts with backgrounders on the principal contenders. They comprise six Middle Eastern states (Turkey, Iran, Saudi Arabia, Egypt, Jordan, and Israel), two Middle Eastern rump regimes (Baghdad and Damascus), four autonomous militias (The Islamic State, Al Qa'idah/Nusrah, Hizballah, and the Yemeni Huthis), two international movements (The Muslim Brotherhood and the Kurds), and two great powers (Russia and the United States), for a total of sixteen.

Meet the Contenders

Revolutionaries (Protagonists of millennial change)

The Islamic State – The IS is dedicated to *jihad* (holy war). It aims at the conversion of twelve states (at least) in the eastern Arab world (Lebanon, Syria, Iraq, Israel, Jordan, Saudi Arabia, Yemen, Kuwait, Bahrain, Qatar, the UAE, and Oman) into a Sunni Arab nation and Caliphate. This bold policy, intensified by religious zeal, put the IS into confrontation against all other contenders.

On 9/11/01, the American people were introduced to Al Qa'idah, when it committed mass murder in an effort to dislodge the Americans from their military commitments and bases in the Middle East. According to a persuasive article ("The Mystery of ISIS") by "Anonymous", carried in *The New York Review* of 8/13/15, the Arab Sunni jihad of the second millennium of the Common Era derived its inspiration from Usamah bin Ladin, founder of Al Qa'idah, but there was an intermediate link. Its founder was a fierce activist, a Jordanian of Palestinian parentage, born in Al Zarqah. His birth name was reported to be Ahmad al Khalaylah, His nom de guerre was Abu Mus'ab al Zarqawi. In 1989, he went to Afghanistan to join the fight against the Soviet invaders, but they were on their way out, so he became a reporter. He met Usamah bin Ladin.

Back in Jordan, he was jailed in 1992 for storing weapons. He was released in the general amnesty of 1999. Exposed in Jordan as an incorrigible subversive, he fled back to Afghanistan via Pakistan, and obtained from bin Ladin funding to set up a camp to train guerrillas. In 2001, he was injured – possibly in combat against the American invaders – and went to Iran and Iraq for therapy. US forces razed his training camp.

On 10/28/02, USAID Administrator Lawrence Foley was shot to death outside his home in Amman. According to the Jordanian

275

government, the killers, a Jordanian and a Libyan, had been hired by Zarqawi. The two were executed.

On March 19, 2003, US forces invaded Iraq. Zarqawi's guerrillas were already there:

Timeline: 2003-2016 – In 2003, days after the invasion, the American command set up Camp Bucca to house suspected resisters. From 2003-9, over 100,000 Iraqi males came through the camp. It afforded an ideal opportunity for Abu Bakr al Baghdadi, subsequent claimant to leadership of a new Caliphate, to build the organization that became the Islamic State: Internet, *The New York Post*, 5/30/15; *ISIS: Inside the Army of Terror*, Michael Weiss/Hassan Hasan; "Anonymous". This process sparked the resurgence of Zarqawi's guerrillas: *FP*, March 2015, Cronin.

2003 – After American forces invaded Iraq, Zarqawi renamed his guerrilla outfit Al Qa'idah in Iraq (AQI). The AQI actively attacked US and Shiite targets: Internet: *The Guardian*, 7/12/08.

2003 – On 4/16/03, The Coalition Provisional Authority, by CPA-1, outlawed the Ba'th Party of Iraq (BPI). In so doing, it sealed the alienation of the Sunni minority from the incoming Shiite leadership: "Anonymous" citation of *The Unraveling*, Emma Sky.

2003 – On 5/23/03, US Proconsul Paul Bremer ordered the disbandment of the Iraqi Army – unleashing thousands of angry soldiers looking for employment. Many joined the Army of the Men of the Naqshabandi Order (*Jaysh Rijal al Tariqah al Naqshabandiyyah*) founded during the occupation by 'Izzat al Duri – Sufi, Baathist, former deputy to Iraqi dictator Saddam al Husayn. Unlike the Syrian branch of the Ba'th, the Iraqi branch had ambitious goals, which led to the establishment of pan-Islamic affiliates across the eastern Arab World. Although the Sunni-based AQI despised Shiites and deviant Sunnis as apostates from true Islam, it formed a working alliance with the Naqshabandis: *The Rise of the Islamic State*, Patrick Cockburn; *MEP*, Winter 2014, Ahmed Hashim; *MEP*, 2015, Stefan Rosiny.

2003 – In August, the AQI burst on the scene in Iraq. Escalating its operations from bombings and assassinations at the outset to guerrilla and conventional combat later on, it inflicted continuing casualties on

American and pro-American targets. The swarm of Iraqi soldiers released on the freebooter market by Bremer was a ready source of highly motivated recruits.

2003 – The truck bombing of the Jordanian Embassy on 8/7/03, killing 17, was ascribed to the AQI.

2003 – The 8/18/03 car bombing of the UN headquarters was ascribed to the AQI. UN Special Representative Sergio Vieira De Mello died in this action. His criticism of civilian deaths during forays by occupation troops may have had some connection with the absence of any US security detail at the UN site.

2003 – The AQI was blamed for the suicide car bombing on 8/29/03 near the hallowed shrine of Imam ʿAli in Najaf. (Takfiris despise the Shiite penchant for shrines.) The revered Ayatollah Muhammad Baqir al Hakim and some one hundred other Shia died in the blast. The suspected killers included two non-Iraqi Salafis (ultraconservatives) and two Baathist members of Zarqawi's AQI. The suicide bomber was thought to be the father of Zarqawi's brother-in-law. In the opinion of *The New York Review*'s "Anonymous", by deploying the AQI against Shia leaders and Shia holy sites, Zarqawi turned Iraq's anti-American insurgency into a sectarian civil war (which by 2015 was threatening to infect the entire Middle East).

2004 – In March, the AQI bombed Shiite shrines in Karbala' and Baghdad, killing a total of 180.

2004 – On 5/8/04, the decapitated body of Nicholas Berg (American) was found on a Baghdad street. According to unconfirmed reports, Berg had gone to Iraq in late 2003 seeking a business opportunity, was held some days by the American authorities, and released; then he was abducted by the AQI, and became the victim of the first jihadist beheading of a Western hostage. In May 2004, a video appeared that ostensibly showed the beheading of Nicholas Berg.

2004 – In October, Zarqawi, "prince of Al Qaʿidah operations in Mesopotamia", proffered his allegiance to Usamah bin Ladin. He condemned all enemies of monotheism as subject to excommunication (*takfir*) and death, proclaimed that all Sunnis constitute one nation, and denounced secularists (*'ulmaniyyin*), Baathists, tribalists, and nationalists as enemies of Islam.

2004 – In October, the AQI abducted a Japanese in Iraq. After Japan refused to withdraw a military unit it had stationed in Iraq, the prisoner was beheaded.

2004 – According to "Anonymous", the AQI also took part in pitched battles, including the armed resistance against the two American assaults on Fallujah: a brief assault in the Spring of 2004, a conclusive assault in November. Zarqawi "lost thousands of fighters trying to hold Fallujah." In Iraq, between 2003 and the American "surge" of 2006, 40,000 resistants were killed and 200,000 wounded: Larry Schweikart.

2004-5 – Zarqawi's strategy against the US occupation was to drag the leadership of Iraq's Shiite community into a civil war with the Sunnis, who were to turn en masse to the AQI for direction. An all-out civil war would attract volunteers from the neighboring Sunni majorities in Syria, Jordan, Turkey, and Saudi Arabia: *NYR*, 7/9/15, Malise Ruthven review of *Islamic State: The Digital Caliphate*, by Abdel Bari Atwan.

2004 – In December, the AQI exploded more bombs in Najaf and Karbala', killing 60.

2004 – A Jordanian court sentenced Zarqawi and eight confederates to death.

2005 – On 2/28/05, a car-bomb killed 125 in Hillah, Iraq.

2005 – February saw the onset of the first wave of Shiite revenge killings of BPI (Baath Party of Iraq) leaders who committed atrocities under the rule of Saddam.

2005 – The appointment in April of Bayan Sulagh as Iraqi Minister of Interior marked an escalation of Shiite death squads in Iraq.

2005 – In May the US forces in Iraq began assassinating resistance leaders. The Sunni resistance was ascribed 50 percent to BPI militants, 25 percent to AQI militants, and 25 percent to Islamist volunteers from abroad. The BPI was thought to have set up a headquarters in Aleppo. The voice of the resistance was the Association of Muslim Scholars.

2005 – On 5/7/05, the car-bombing of a US security convoy killed 22.

2005 – On 7/6/05, the new Egyptian ambassador was killed. The AQI reported his death as an "execution".

2005 – In September, Zarqawi declared war against "collaborators" (Shia). The Al Qa'idah leadership appreciated the publicity it gained from AQI's exploits, but Zarqawi's embrace of slaughter as a strategy alarmed them, including his Salafist mentor, Abu Muhammad al Maqdisi ('Isam Muhammad al Zarqawi). Ayman al Zawahiri, bin Ladin's deputy, challenged the practice in a letter reportedly intercepted by US Intelligence: *MEP*, Winter 2014. Zawahiri preferred the more moderate approach of Al Qa'idah's other affiliate, the Nusrah Front: *LRB*, 7/17/14.

2005 – From July through November, there were reports of a succession of AQI bombings of gatherings, hotels, and mosques in Baghdad and other cities of Iraq, that killed hundreds – mostly Shia. Peter Galbraith reported that the conflict between Sunni and Shia death squads was escalating into a civil war. Thousands of Iraqis were abandoning their homes.

2005-6 – Zarqawi changed the name of his organization again – from the AQI to the Organization of Monotheism and Holy War (*tanzim al tawhid wal jihad*).

2005 – US military prisons in Iraq, including Camp Bucca, were holding 40,000 resistants – Sunni and Sadrist (followers of Muqtada Sadr, a maverick Shiite).

2006 – *The Unraveling* by Emma Sky (cited by "Anonymous") reports the appearance on the streets of Baghdad of fifty bodies a day. The killers were Shiite militias, who had borrowed from Saddam's security personnel the execution method of trepanation by electric drill.

2006 – On 2/22/06, an AQI (?) bomb destroyed the revered 'Askariyyah Mosque in Samarra', serving the AQI intent to provoke an all-out sectarian war in Iraq.

2006 – On 6/8/06, with help from Iraqi and Jordanian intelligence, and after Zarqawi had posted pictures of himself on the Internet (*NYR*, 7/9/15, Malise Ruthven), the CIA tracked him down near Ba'qubah, and killed him and a few companions with an aerial bomb. Representative Mark Kirk of Illinois, who had arranged for a 25-million-dollar price on

Zarqawi's head, was quoted as saying that some reward money would be distributed. Al Qa'idah announced that the new leader of the AQI was Abu Hamzah al Muhajir (Abu Ayyub al Masri, former confidant of Zawahiri). In his elegy for Zarqawi, bin Ladin said: his "story will live forever with the stories of the nobles …": *NYR*, 8/13/15, "Anonymous".

2006 – The death of Zarqawi crippled the AQI: *FP*, March 2015, Cronin.

2006 – Just before Zarqawi's death, when the Sunni-Shia civil war in Iraq was at its height, some Iraqi followers of Al Qa'idah proclaimed the founding of the Islamic State of Iraq (*Dawlat al 'Iraq al Islamiyyah* – ISI): *Times*, 5/20/06. The proclamation was premature. Most of Al Qa'idah's militants denounced it, on the grounds that they wanted to fight America, not the rest of the Muslim World: *MEP*, Winter 2014, Ahmed Hashim.

2006 – In Baghdad, Shia death squads in black were roaming the streets in search of Sunni victims. In 'Anbar Province, the Sunni majority had formed a coalition, *Al Sahwah* (The Awakening), which had contracted to oust the AQI faction in return for compensation from the American occupation: Pepe Escobar.

2006 – On 6/16/06, three American soldiers died at the hands of the AQI (?). One was killed outright. Two were abducted and tortured before their deaths.

2006 – By December a million residents had taken flight from Baghdad, leaving some neighborhoods devoid of Sunnis: *The Nation*, 1/12/09, Juan Cole.

2006 – The Iraqi Special Tribunal convicted Saddam al Husayn of crimes against humanity, citing the murder of 148 Shiites in Dujayl, Iraq, in retaliation for an attempt to assassinate him. On 12/30/06, at Camp Justice in a Baghdad suburb, he was transferred from American custody to that of the Iraqi Government (sworn in on 5/20/06), and hanged in the presence of Iraqis only (no Sunnis reported). Saddam (whose visage alone was said to inspire fear) remained impassive but defiant. His reported last words were "Allahu Akbar. The Muslim Ummah will be victorious. Palestine is Arab", followed by the *Shahadah*, the Muslim profession of faith. As the rope was secured, his guards shouted "rebukes". Saddam asked "Do you consider this bravery?".

2007 – 'Abd al Sattar Abu Rishah, leader of Al Sahwah, was killed on 9/13/07.

2008 – In January a US-Iraqi campaign in Ninawah Province killed or captured 4000 resistants.

2008 – On 2/9/08 four American soldiers were killed by a suicide bomber.

2008 – In March, AQI forces, pressed by US Marines, began to decamp from 'Anbar Province to Ninawah Province, where they attacked Christians as US allies. In the first five years of the US occupation, Iraq's Christian community had dwindled from 1.35 million to 5-600,000: *Washington Post Weekly*, 4/28/08; *Monitor Online* (http://www.csmonitor.com/), Most Christians in Iraq were Chaldean Catholics, affiliated with the Church of Rome.

2008 – In June, the AQI perpetrated a wave of bombings in 'Anbar, Baghdad, and Ninawah Provinces.

2008 – In July, the AQI was eliminated from Diyala Province, and went underground in Iraq: *MEP*, Summer 2015.

2009 – In April, the "Islamic State of Iraq" (ISI, said to be led by Abu 'Umar al Baghdadi) claimed the deadly bombings afflicting Baghdad. On 6/24/09 a third massive bombing of a Shia crowd was claimed by AQI, and by "The Islamic Army of Iraq". A split between the ISI and Al Qa'idah seemed to be underway. No leader of the ISI or the IS had pledged allegiance to Al Qa'idah: *NYR*, 7/9/15, Malise Ruthven.

2009 – On 7/1/09 'Izzat al Duri and the Association of Muslim Scholars adjured Iraqis to fight Americans, not other Iraqis.

2009 – On the anniversary of the founding of the Baath Party, 'Izzat al Duri appealed in the *New York Times* to Iraqis to topple Prime Minister Nuri al Maliki's "puppet regime".

2009 – On 8/16/09 a coalition of the AQI and the "Islamic state of Iraq" was reported to be responsible for many of the snipings, bombings, and assassinations being committed in northern Iraq, including Baghdad: *MEP*, Winter 2014, Ahmed Hashim.

2009 – IS writers and spokesmen tended to rhapsodize about early Islamic practices like taking enemy women as slaves and later converting them. Their propaganda was triumphalist: *MEP*, Fall 2016, David Kibble.

2010 – **Abu Bakr al Baghdadi**: On 4/18/10, a US-Iraqi raid killed AQI/ISI leaders Abu 'Umar al Baghdadi and Abu Hamzah al Muhajir. By June, the organization was verging on extinction: *MEP*, Winter 2014, Ahmed Hashim. ISI's new leader, Ibrahim al Samarra'i, a member of AQI since 2006 (Gwynne Dyer, 5/15/15), chose a new name, Abu Bakr al Baghdadi, befitting the man who had fought the Americans in Iraq, who was born in Samarra' – seat of the Abbasid Caliphate from 836 to 892 – and had a vision of restoring the Caliphate. He gradually converted a catch-as-catch-can outfit into a disciplined militia, with councils for political affairs, military strategy, security, and intelligence – and a military commander for each of the Caliphate's two provinces, Iraq and Syria: Ahmed Hashim. For military expertise, he relied on Chechens and onetime officers of Saddam's army, still under the direction of General Duri. (The leadership of the movement, first Zarqawi and then Baghdadi, had no sympathy for Duri's Sufi mysticism or Baathist secularism. They had lived by their *shari'ah*. They sought the Sunni equivalent of Iran's Shiite state.)

The IS militia, an estimated force of 20,000, would be no match for one of the functioning national armies in the region. So far, however, its only adversaries on the ground were rival militias and the debilitated armies of Iraq and Syria. The IS had geopolitical advantage as the most active Sunni force in a region that had a Sunni majority of 250,000,000 out of a total of 420,000,000. By rough estimate, the arena of battle – northern Iraq, Syria, and southeastern Turkey – was populated by 30,000,000 Sunnis, 25,000,000 Shia, and 10,000,000 Kurds. Western politicians had learned to shun government by ethnicity, but the Middle East was a long way from separating church and state.

2011 – In March, ISI changed its title to ISIS (The Islamic State of Iraq and Syria). Abu Bakr was meticulously organizing his following – Arabs, Russians from the north Caucasus, and foreigners from all over – to emulate the era of the first Caliphate. ISIS had antagonized up to 60 governments, but as the most noteworthy Sunni Arab contender in the jihadist war, it enjoyed clandestine support from Qatar and Turkey. It had five primary sources of revenue: 1) the banks, companies, and oil wells it had taken over; 2) extortion and ransom; 3) donations from foreign sympathizers; 4) contributions from foreign recruits; 5) modern fundraising techniques.

2011 – The "foster parents" of the Sunni jihadist movements were Saudi Arabia, the Gulf monarchies, and Turkey: *LRB*, 8/21/14, Patrick Cockburn. Former Senator Bob Graham was quoted later as saying that the ISIS was "a product of Saudi ideals, Saudi money, and Saudi organizational support": *The Week*, 8/14/15.

2011 - In March, Syria exploded. Four years of drought had driven impoverished farmers into the cities. Syria's "Arab Spring" was erupting into civil war – a timely opportunity for jihadists.

2011 – In August, the ISIS sent a major force to join Syrian jihadists in their fight against the Asad regime and the secularist rebels (The Free Syrian Army – FSA): *NYR*, 8/13/15, "Anonymous". The switch of focus from Iraq, where the ISIS was losing to its American and Iraqi/Iranian Shiite opponents, to the power vacuum in Syria gave the ISIS a new lease on life: *Times*, 7/4/14.

2011 – Kayla Mueller, US aid worker, was abducted by the ISIS and "married" to Abu Bakr, who repeatedly raped her. She was killed in a Jordanian air strike: *Times*, 8/16/11.

2012 – In February, the ISIS ended its affiliation with Al Qa'idah and its offshoot, the Nusrah Front.

2013 – The ISIS was resurgent – energized by the decline of the AQI, by the leadership of Abu Bakr, by the Sunni resentment of Shiite rule in Iraq and Syria, and by the escalation of the Syrian Civil War: Ahmed Hashim. The ISIS's trademarks were ferocity and death to its enemies.

2013 – In April, Abu Bakr proclaimed a merger between the ISIS and Nusrah, but Nusrah's leader, Abu Muhammad al Jawlani, rejected it. Nusrah's fighters, most of them Syrians, were even more hostile than the ISIS toward the Asad regime: Ahmed Hashim; *MEP*, Summer 2015, Stephan Rosiny.

2013 – In August the ISIS established its de facto capital in Al Raqqah, a Syrian city on the upper Euphrates, and adopted a new title – the Islamic State (IS). Manned by Iraqis, Syrians, and foreign Muslims, the IS went on to establish control over areas of eastern Syria and northwestern Iraq inhabited by six to eight million people (mostly Sunni). Raqqah was large enough and sufficiently isolated from Damascus, Baghdad, and Turkey to serve as capital of an autonomous Sunni "state". Most of its leaders were Iraqis: *NYR*, 2/5/15, Sarah Birke.

2013 – In November, the IS captured Al Hajar al Aswad, a suburb of Damascus: *Times*, 7/3/16.

2013 – The IS was carrying out some 50 car bombings a month in Baghdad: *LRB*, 12/19/13.

2013 – Muslim fundamentalists, most from the region, some from far and wide, were moving into Syria. They were impelled by religious fervor, and enabled by arms and subsidies from sympathizers, particularly in Saudi Arabia and Qatar. The IS was clashing with forces of the Alawite state and rival revolutionaries, including Nusrah.

2013 – In July, a mass breakout from Abu Ghurayb Prison afforded the IS an influx of new recruits: *Times*, 7/4/14.

2013 – In late December, IS troops captured two major Iraqi cities – Ramadi and Fallujah: *Times*, 7/4/14. These conquests showed that the IS monopolized the support of the Sunni community: *FT*, 5/23/15. After Shiite militiamen defending Ramadi had run out of ammunition, the IS forces that took the city killed 25 Iraqi police and soldiers and 15 members of their families.

2014 – In January, the IS captured Jarabulus (Syria): *Times*, 7/3/16.

2014 – On 2/3/14, the general command of Al Qa'idah posted online a statement that it had disavowed the Islamic State in Iraq and the Levant (ISIL). It was an attempt by Ayman al Zawahiri to establish Nusrah as Al Qa'idah's official presence in Syria: www.aljazeera.com; Charles Lister.

2014 – Early in the year, the IS began seizing more towns along the Euphrates in Iraq's 'Anbar Province: *Times*, 7/4/14.

2014 – The IS regime in Raqqah was banning music, public smoking, drinking, and personal photos, and requiring women to wear gloves and

284

the *niqab* (veil) in public. Christians were taxed. The judiciary was headed by twelve Saudi judges: *The Economist*. Executions were carried out in the main square. All rival rebel organizations had been expelled: *AP*, 3/8/14.

2014 – In June, the IS lost an air base in Samarra' (Iraq): *Times*, 7/3/16.

2014 – In June, the IS made rapid advances in Syria and Iraq, capturing Manbij and Al Bu Kamal (Syria), and Rutbah, Tall 'Afar, and Mawsil, the third largest city in Iraq: *Times*, 7/3/16.

2014 – On 6/10/14, the IS routed four Iraqi divisions from Mawsil, Iraq's second largest city, and took over a large block of northwest Iraq. The sweep was facilitated for the IS by its congenial contacts with Sunni tribes in the Mawsil, Tikrit, and 'Anbar areas: *AP*, 8/9/15.

2014 – **Enter: Caliph Ibrahim** – On 6/29/14, an IS spokesman reported that the IS Shura Council had ruled that a Caliphate had been established under the rule of Abu Bakr al Baghdadi: *FT*, 6/29/14. Over 60 countries had claimed to be at war with IS, but the Sahwah had been cowed, and volunteers were joining the IS from all over the Arab World. The US Air Force was seriously engaged at the head of the anti-IS coalition.

2014 – In June, the IS killed 500 Iraqi soldiers near Tikrit: *AP*, Human Rights Watch.

2014 – During the first half of 2014, 6000 died in battles between the IS and opposing militias – Nusrah, the Islamist Front, the Free Syrian Army, and others: *MEP*, Summer 2015, Stephan Rosiny. An estimated 5000 Yazidis had been killed by the IS in Iraq: *Atlantic*, 7/5/14.

2014 – On 7/3/14, the IS captured much of Dayr al Zawr Province, including the *Al Bu Kamal-Qa'im* crossing (It was one of three between Syria and Iraq). Both the IS and the Syrian regime were allowing the Tabqah Dam on the Euphrates, 25 miles upstream from Raqqah, to supply power to eastern Syria: *Times*, 7/4/14.

2014 – On 7/4/14, Abu Bakr delivered an address in high Arabic, as Caliph Ibrahim. He was a descendant of the Quraysh Tribe – a requirement for a Caliph – and of the Bani Hashim, the Prophet's own clan. He was dressed in a black turban and cloak, as the Prophet was believed to have been dressed when he spoke after the capture of Mecca in 630: Rosiny.

2014 – On 7/5/14, Abu Bakr delivered a Ramadan sermon that sparked a steady flow of jihadists to IS territory: *Atlantic*, March 2015.

2014 – IS strategy was centered on the conviction that Judgment Day was near, and the IS would be a major factor in it. The IS considered the Muslim Brothers apostates. Al Qa'idah and IS strategies had been very different: Bin Ladin had no territorial claims; the IS needed a state in being. IS leaders respected bin Ladin, acknowledged the achievements of Zarqawi, and endorsed the views of Abu Muhammad al Maqdisi, spiritual guide of Al Qa'idah. They hated Ayman al Zawahiri. For followers of the IS, sinners, Shia, and resistant Christians were marked for death, but not Christians who paid the *jizyah* (head tax on free non-Muslims). Al Qa'idah and the IS both observed Salafi doctrine, meticulously following the prophecy and example of Muhammad. They also practiced beheading and crucifixion, which were not part of early Islam, and are not observed by Wahhabis: *Atlantic*, 7/5/14. IS followers respected Shaykh Muhammad 'Abd al Wahhab as a Salafi, and preached from a book he wrote, but didn't like to be called Wahhabiists.

Most adherents of the IS have been devout Muslims, but it appears that they have gone to war against the West for political reasons, not sectarian. They are trying to win recruits, not converts. They don't hate America for being Christian, but for trying to deny the right of the Middle Easterners to make their own decisions.

The viability of the IS is extended by its honesty, but abbreviated by its brutality and zealotry.

Its arguments for the strategy of brutality are weak – for example, that brutality intimidates opponents; that it reduces the access of foreign intriguers; that it impresses recruits; that there are precedents for the successful translation of brutality into power.

Zealotry also has its drawbacks. Martial fervor has a short half-life. When the warrior is recuperating from battle, he or she is likely to be less tolerant of prohibitions against creature comforts – music, smoking, socializing between the genders, or liberation from ancient shackles on attire, education, and expression of one's individuality.

2014 – The IS had cut the routes between Baghdad and Jordan/Syria: *McClatchy*, 7/8/14.

2014 – Defeating low-morale, poorly led Iraqi forces, the IS briefly held the Mawsil dam on the Tigris, 50 miles north of Baghdad. Iraq's stores of heavy military equipment from the US and NATO were serving the IS as a "mobile storefront": *FT*, 7/11/14.

2014 – The nucleus of the IS forces was the battle-hardened AQI: *LRB*, 7/17/14, Owen Bennett-Jones.

2014 – The forces of the Damascus regime were gaining in Aleppo. The IS was gaining in Dayr al Zawr: *FT*, 7/17/14.

2014 – In an apparent coincidence of convenience, Asad regime forces were withholding fire against the IS, and the IS was providing an opening for the Asad forces to attack the Syrian secularists: *McClatchy*, 7/19/14.

2014 – The IS had a strong following in Palestinian refugee camps in Syria: *FT*, 7/23/14.

2014 – The IS regime in Raqqah was ruthless, but more efficient and honest than its Alawite predecessor. It was bringing in foreign militants and technicians to supervise the bureaucracy – otherwise not much change in personnel from the Alawite era: *Times*, 7/24/14.

2014 – In Syria, IS forces had gained most of their territory from secularist rebels, but they had lately inflicted severe casualties on Damascus regime forces: *Times*, 7/26/14.

2014 – By July, the IS had routed forces of Nusrah and Free Men of Syria, leaving the IS in control of 100,000 square miles of eastern Syria and northwest Iraq, inhabited by 6,000,000 people. Most of them were Sunnis, glad to be free of Kurdish and Shiite attack. The IS was demanding that rival Syrian rebels swear allegiance to the "Caliphate" or give up their weapons: *NYR*, 8/21/14, Patrick Cockburn.

2014 – In the summer of 2014, the IS killed nearly 1700 Shia military personnel in Camp Speicher, near Tikrit: *Times*, 6/23/15. (In April of 2015, Iraqis were exhuming bodies of some 1700 Air Force cadets believed to have been killed by IS forces in the summer of 2014 in Tikrit: *The Week*, 4/17/15.)

2014 – The IS had gained influence in Syria and Iraq by making shrewd alliances with other militias. It was brutal to criminals and adversaries, but efficient in restoring order: *FT*, 7/28/14.

2014 – In August, the IS captured Tabqah (Syria): *Times*, 7/3/16.

2014 – Since August, the IS advance had been checked in Syria by Kurdish and Iraqi ground action and US air attacks, but defenses against the IS in Iraq had been undermined by the Sunni-Shiite feud: *Times*, 2/4/15, Kenneth Pollack.

2014 – In September, the CIA estimated the number of IS fighters at 20,000-31,000, including 15,000 foreigners from over 80 countries: Rosiny.

2014 – The IS, based on the eastern third of Syria, was advancing into the northwestern third of Iraq. It had adopted savagery as a strategy to undermine its opponents' morale. Jihadists were defecting from rival militias, attracted to the IS by its wealth, its copious stores of arms, and its battle-hardened troops: *Times*, 8/7/14

2014 – The IS declared a jihad against the US: *Times*, 8/10/14.

2014 – The IS considered Kurds, Sunni or not, as too secular: *Times*, 8/12/14.

2014 – The IS was profiting from its possession of most of the oil wells in Syria and five oil fields in Iraq. Its revenue from Iraqi and Syrian oil sales in 2014 was estimated at one to three million dollars a day. Its troop formations were small and mobile enough to be difficult targets from the air. US support for the Shiite regime in Baghdad had reinforced the support given the IS by the Sunni community: *FT*, 8/15/14, Borzou Daragahi.

2014 – As the most formidable Sunni force on the jihadist side, the IS was the Sunnis' best hope: *Times*, 8/17/14, Ali Khederi.

2014 – Combat attrition of the IS's top leaders had taught them to decentralize its organization: *Times*, 8/22/14.

2014 – The IS was effective at long-range planning. If an adversary posed a challenge, the reaction from the IS might come months later, when the timing was more propitious: *Times*, 8/22/14. The IS projected messianic fervor for a "transcendent cause", served by hundreds of would-be suicide bombers. On 8/24/14, the IS completed the conquest of Raqqah Province.

2014 – Navi Pillay, UN Commissioner for Human Rights, reported the IS had murdered hundreds or thousands of males from minority communities in northern Iraq: *Times*, 8/26/14. The IS had taken responsibility for the beheading of British aid worker David Haines. Also for the beheading of journalist James Foley, after ransom demands were not met. Ten to twelve European hostages had been released after ransom payment: Peter Galbraith; "Anonymous".

2014 – In August, the IS lost the Mawsil dam: *Times*, 7/3/16.

2014 – On 8/24/14, after two weeks of heavy fighting, the IS captured from the Damascus forces the airbase adjoining the Tabqah Dam on the Euphrates. It reportedly executed 160 soldiers it had taken prisoner.

2014 – On 8/27/14, after seven weeks of fighting that left 2200 dead, Israel and its Gazan adversaries, Hamas and Islamic Jihad, concluded a truce. The IS condemned all ceasefires and truces with an enemy as collaboration.

2014 – In August, IS forces opened a new front against the KRG: "Anonymous".

2014 – The IS was disciplined and highly centralized, with a sophisticated security apparatus. Its militia had a management structure of experienced Syrians, Saudis, and Iraqis. Many of the Iraqis had been former officers under Saddam. They included his later deputies, former BPI officers Abu Muslim al Turkmani and Abu 'Ali al 'Anbari. Abu Bakr had gotten to know them all in the US detention center at Camp Bucca: *Times*, 8/28/14. Abu Bakr's cabinet included a Sharia Council, a Sharia police force, and a court system. The IS school curriculum was strict Salafi, close to that in Saudi Arabia. The IS had built solid militia cadres in the Sunni provinces of Iraq (Salah al Din, 'Anbar, Diyala). Its Chechen personnel were particularly effective and fearless; they had spearheaded the takeover of Mawsil. The new Islamic "Caliphate", led by jihadists of the Salafi creed, dedicated to the suppression of the alleged conspiracy of the Christian-Jewish alliance to destroy Islam, regarded Shia, Sufis, and liberal Muslims as heretics, and members of Hamas as apostates, and claimed a religious sanction to kill the erring. With Al Qaʿidah in eclipse, and Sahwah disbanded, devotees of the IS felt a strong sense of divine mission. The IS published an online periodical, *Dabbik*, named in commemoration of the Islamic prophecy that the village by that name northeast of Aleppo is the site where in the legendary End-Times Battle of Armageddon the armies of Rome and Islam shall meet: Stephan Rosiny. The IS flag was described as a black field with a central white circle carrying the Seal of Mohammad under the Arabic inscription "There is no God but Allah".

2014 – In July, conflict arose between the IS and the Shuʿaytat tribe, numbering 80,000, centered in Dayr al Zawr Governorate of Syria, along the Euphrates near the border with Iraq. In August, IS forces ended the fighting in a three-day battle. Nine hundred tribesmen were reportedly shot, beheaded, or crucified.

2014 – Many world governments had accused the IS of ethnic cleansing. A UN spokesman charged it with grave abuses of human rights.

2014 – IS released a video that allegedly showed the beheading of a hostage, journalist Steven S. Satloff: *Times*, 9/2/14.

2014 – In June, the IS killed 500 or more Iraqi soldiers near Tikrit: *AP*, Human Rights Watch.

2014 – Most Sunni states were claiming to be at war with the IS, but none had announced any major commitment of troops. Most Sunnis were more intent on ousting Syrian leader Bashar al Asad, arch-genocidist. Syria's principal ally, Iran, was the bitterest enemy of the IS. It had been excluded from Washington's anti-IS "coalition": *Times*, 9/12/14.

2014 – A British scholar had estimated the number of IS militiamen from outside the Middle East at 12,000, most of them from Libya, Morocco, and Tunisia: *Times*, 9/13/14.

2014 – The IS had adopted overt brutality as a strategy – intended to dramatize its role as the champion of the Sunni cause: *FT*, 9/16/14, Borzou Daragahi. The IS was resorting to suicide attacks on a regular basis: *FT*, 9/16/14. It had beheaded scores of Shiites as apostates: *Times*, 9/22/14.

2014 – The revenue of the IS – a few million dollars a day – relied largely on a long-time oil-smuggling network that had evolved via Turkey as an evasion of US/UN sanctions imposed on Iraq after the expulsion of its forces from Kuwait in 1991. Washington had encountered great difficulty in shutting the smugglers down. The IS was controlling six of Syria's 10 oilfields, and four small fields in Iraq. Its buyers were Turkey, Iraq, and Jordan.

2014 – Abu Bakr had based his organization's creed of brutality on the Wahhabiism of the 1900's, on the ground that only brutality could save the Muslims from modernity's wicked ways. Brutality won recruits and shook the Western imperialists. It posed a stark contrast to imperialism's tame Arab regimes. The IS was citing Saudi textbooks. It had stressed that even Hamas had embraced apostasy by accepting ceasefires with Israel: *Times*, 9/25/14, from Bernard Haykel via David Kirkpatrick.

2014 – The stronghold of the IS was in Iraq: NYR, 9/25/14, Elizabeth Drew, from Bruce Riedel.

2014 – Baghdad's Shiite districts were suffering almost daily bombings, ascribed to the IS: *Times*, 9/29/14.

2014 – The IS was being directed by a council of former Iraqi generals, many of them one-time secularist Baathists, later converted to Islamism during detention in Iraqi or American prisons. IS operations were distributed among seven autonomous "vilayets". The IS's 10,000 soldiers in Iraq and 12,000 in Syria enjoyed broad support from the Sunni communities. The IS was earning 10 million dollars a month from ransoms and extortion, 150 million dollars a month from sale of oil. Unlike Al Qa'idah, it deployed conventional military forces, applying sophisticated methods: NY, 9/19/14, Dexter Filkins.

2014 – In September, the IS lost Ba'quba (Iraq): *Times*, 7/3/16.

2014 – In Homs, the IS had been killing Syrian soldiers at isolated bases, and carrying out a series of bombings: *Times*, 10/3/14.

2014 – A rebel offensive, mainly by the IS, had killed 5500 Iraqis since June. The IS had abducted hundreds of Yazidi women, and killed the many Yazidi men who refused to convert to Islam: *Times*, 10/3/14.

2014 – Although most Sunni tribesmen in Iraq sided with the IS, there were some who joined Baghdad's militia movement: *Times*, 10/4/14.

2014 – On 10/3/14 and 10/8/14, IS militiamen armed with Manpad shoulder-fired missiles downed two Iraqi helicopters.

2014 – Two of the most formidable ground forces in the Middle East, the militias of the IS and the PYD, were battling for Kobani ('Ayn al 'Arab in Arabic) on the Turk-Syrian border. The PYD consisted of Syrian Kurds affiliated with the PKK. Their objective was formation of an autonomous Kurdish zone in Syria: *Times*, 10/9/14.

2014 – IS militiamen were killing enemy fighters and "infidels", such as a female wearing pants: *Times*, 10/14/14.

2014 – In Sinai on 10/24/14, heavily armed Islamist militants attacked an Egyptian Army contingent, killing 28: *Times*, 10/25/14. The Army responded by demolition of homes along the Gazan border. Their occupants were relegated to the status of DP's: *Times*, 10/30/14.

2014 – **New IS Front in Libya** – Libya was at war between an internationally recognized faction based in Tubruq, led by retired General Khalifa Haftar, and the "National Salvation Government", or "Libya Dawn", based in Tripoli, led by former Prime Minister 'Umar al Hassi. Darnah was the base of various groups of militiamen, some of whom had sworn allegiance to the Islamic State: *FT*, 10/27/14.

2014 – The IS extracted 300 Libyans who had been fighting in its Syrian ranks, and sent them to Libya in support of IS affiliates there. Their commander was Abu Nabil al 'Anbari (Iraqi). Two hundred kilometers of Libyan coastline were under IS control.

2014 – The IS had killed hundreds of Shiites, Iraqi soldiers, and police. According to Human Rights Watch, it had killed 600, mostly Shia, who had been held in a prison near Mawsil: *Times*, 10/31/14.

2014 – Since the proclamation of the new Caliphate on 6/29/14, the Islamic State had been under attack by the Kurds, the Iraqi Army, Shia militias, secularist Syrian rebels, Hizballah, Iran, and the American Air

Force, but it had still gained territory in 'Anbar Province: *LRB*, 11/6/14, Patrick Cockburn.

2014 – US and Iraqi air attacks had forced the IS to cut back on conventional warfare in favor of sleeper cells. It was still massacring diehard opponents, such as 300 members of the Al Bu Nimr Tribe in 'Anbar Province near Hit (on the Euphrates, northwest of Ramadi): *Times*, 11/6/14. The IS was in a stronger position in Syria, where regime and rival rebels were exhausted by three and a half years of war.

2014 – **New IS Front in Sinai** – *Ansar Bayt al Maqdis* (Protectors of Jerusalem), founded in Sinai by Al Qa'idah, announced that on 11/10/14 it had switched allegiance to the Islamic State, and declared Sinai one of its provinces. The Egyptian Army had blamed the Muslim Brotherhood for a recent wave of simultaneous attacks that killed up to 30 Egyptian soldiers across Sinai, but the Ansar had claimed responsibility. They had killed hundreds of soldiers and police in reprisal for the ouster and arrest of former Prime Minister Mursi. Retaliatory raids by Egyptian forces were destroying whole neighborhoods along Egypt's border with Gaza to deny Ansar operatives hideouts: *Times*, 11/14/14, 11/29/14, 4/13/15; *AP*, 1/30/15.

2014 – Citizens of Raqqah disliked the extreme austerity imposed by the IS, but appreciated the return to law and order: *Times*, 11/14/14.

2014 – The IS had appropriated 5000 Yazidi females as slaves: *Times*, 11/15/14. (Slavery has been endorsed by Islam from the Qur'an on: *EB*, 27:88.)

2014 – Statement from the UN office in Geneva: Followers of the Islamic State have committed war crimes in Syria on a massive scale: *McClatchy*, 11/15/14.

2014 – The IS had consolidated its control over many areas of Sunni Iraq by remunerating cooperative tribesmen (as the US military did during its occupation). The Shiite regime in Baghdad was wary of arming Sunni tribes because of the high risk of later defection: *Times*, 11/16/14.

2014 – The IS released a videotape of its fifth beheading of a Western hostage: *Times*, 11/17/14.

2014 – In Syria, the IS was steadily converting Raqqah into the de facto capital of the new Caliphate. Late in the year, it completed the occupation of one fourth of Syria, along the upper Euphrates, and one-fourth of Iraq along the lower Euphrates. The new political structure appeased the long-suffering populace by its free schools and medical care and its unprecedented competence and honesty. It was attracting foreign recruits by sophisticated output over social media like Twitter and YouTube: *Harper's*, November 2014, James Harkins.

2014 – The IS lost control of the Bayji refinery in Iraq, but still held three others: *The Week*, 11/28/14.

2014 – The pro-IS militia based in Darnah, Libya, had taken over the city: *CNN*.

2014 – Foreign fighters with militias in Syria were paid seven dollars a day, plus three dollars for food, plus bonuses and the spoils of war: *FT*, 11/29/14.

2014 – The US aerial campaign against the IS was finding fewer targets, as IS militants decentralized, staged operations from dense urban areas, and travelled in smaller units: *Times*, 12/4/14.

2014 – The IS had begun attacking other rebel militias in Syria in bids for land they had already liberated from the Alawite regime: *NY*, 12/8/14, Robin Wright.

2014 – In the Syrian civil war, 200,000 Syrians had died and ten million had become DP's.

2014 – Public school teachers in Mawsil were being paid by the Baghdad government on condition that they continued teaching, even under IS rule: *Times*, 12/14/14. The same regimen applied to medical personnel. The University of Mawsil denied female students access to programs in fine arts, political science, law, and sports. Life in Mawsil was fairly quiet, but marked by confusion, deprivation, and fear. Electricity and drinkable water were in short supply: *Times*, 12/14/14. Residents resented the regimentation, and the inadequate public services: *Times*, 12/16/14.

2014 – A new unit of the IS military police in Raqqah was arresting fighters who refused to go into battle against the Kurds for Kobani: *MEP*, Summer 2015, citation from *Al Quds al 'Arabi*.

2014 – As Mawsil came under increasing air attack by the US and Iraq air forces, life there was becoming even more repressive and violent, although the IS had kept prices lower than in the KAR (Kurdish Autonomous Region). Mawsil's defenses against ground attack were mortar teams, snipers, suicide bombers, mines, and booby traps. The IS was hated by Shia, Kurds, Christians, and Yazidis, but grudgingly favored by Sunnis. The IS was honest. It paid four hundred dollars a month and up: *LRB*, 12/18/14, Cockburn.

2014 – The IS had arrested 400 fighters for trying to defect: *FT*, 12/19/14.

2014 – The IS was suffering reverses – in the battle for Kobani, where it had lost 1400 dead, on Mt. Sinjar, where on 12/19/14 Peshmerga troops from the KAR had broken the IS's siege of the Yazidis, and in general from losses inflicted by the air campaign, which was causing desertions: *FT*, 12/20/14.

2014 – A German correspondent allowed to spend ten days with the IS gave a presentation, heard on WUNC, Chapel Hill, that rated the IS as thriving, though stronger in Mawsil than in Raqqah. He reported that 70 percent of IS fighters in Syria were foreigners, 40 percent of them in Iraq: 12/24/14.

2014 – Following is a paraphrase of an article by orientalist Fawaz Gerges:

Al Qa'idah emerged from an alliance of Saudi Salafiism and radical Egyptian Islamism. The IS was an offshoot of Al Qa'idah, infused with viciousness from three sources: Baathist doctrine, rage against the American occupation of Iraq, and reaction to Alawite fanaticism. It was constantly reenergized by widening disgust for Arab autocracy and Western imperialism. The current breakdown of the eastern Arab political structure had allowed Abu Bakr to succeed where bin Ladin and Zawahiri failed – to build a formidable jihadist entity. In bin Ladin's time, the post-World War II political structure still had enough momentum to divert attack away from the "near enemy" and toward the "far enemy". AQI/IS had materialized at a time when attack against the flimsy Sykes-Picot structure in Iraq and Syria could be resumed, and perhaps later the way would be open for action against the opulent tribal structures in Arabia. In its formative years, the IS had absorbed an all-out sectarian ethos.

Gerges estimated IS troop strength at 18,000, plus 18,000 members of affiliated militias. All the members of the IS military council had served as army officers under Saddam. The AQI had been manned by Iraq's upper class. The IS had a large component from the rural masses, who operated by the law of the jungle.

The first meaning of *jihad* is striving for Islamic perfection. Today, the word is more often used by its adherents as Islamic holy war, by its detractors as Islamist rebellion. The concept of holy war was incorporated into the doctrines of the Muslim Brotherhood by its second leader, Sayyid Qutb, an Egyptian cleric who was hanged by Nasir in 1966. Qutb's writings strongly influenced the founders of Al Qa'idah, Usamah bin Ladin and Ayman al Zawahiri.

The historic Caliphate based its concept of the Islamic creed on law, as deduced from the Qur'an, and tradition. The new Caliphate was being established by the IS on the basis of the fiat of Abu Bakr, who was surrounded by ex-army officers, not by clerics (most of whom rejected IS claims). *Da'ish* is an acronym for *Dawlat al 'Arabiyyah al Islamiyyah* (the Islamic Arab State), used dismissively as an epithet for the IS by its critics: *Current History*, December 2014, Fawaz Gerges.

2014 – The year ended with the fate of the Islamic State in stark question.

On the negative side, the "suicidal attack" by the IS on the Syrian city of 'Ayn al 'Arab (Kobani in Kurdish) had been repulsed by Kurdish forces, supported by over six hundred US air strikes. The Islamic State had lost thousands of its fighters in that battle. Analysts were on the verge of concluding that it had been defeated by its own recklessness, brutality, and over-extension: "Anonymous". There were signs of the Islamic State's impending decline: *MEP*, Summer 2015, Stephan Rosiny. In Raqqah, militiamen had been penalized for refusing to fight: *Al Quds al 'Arabi*. Four hundred foreign jihadists had been arrested for trying to defect; one hundred had been killed: *FT*, December 2014.

There were also positive indicators, such as the income and respect the Islamic State was deriving from the honesty and efficiency displayed in its local governments in Raqqah and Mawsil: *Middle East Forum*, Aymenn al-Tamimi. In *The Digital Caliphate*, as cited by Malise Ruthven,

296

'Abd al Bari 'Atwan saw the Islamic state as "a well-run organization that combines bureaucratic efficiency and military expertise with a sophisticated use of information technology."

2014 – Over the year, the IS had killed 1000 Shia soldiers in Iraq: *Times*.

2015 – Clashes were breaking out between the surviving forces of the AQI and those of the Islamic State. Many AQI leaders had been eliminated: *Times*, 1/4/15.

2015 – In January, under heavy US air attack in Iraq, the IS Military Council made a low-key transfer to Syria: *NYR*, 7/9/15, Abd al Bari Atwan.

2015 – The IS had not built the infrastructure of a viable state. Its public services were inadequate. It was unrecognized, it didn't issue passports, it had to make do with three foreign currencies (Syrian, Iraqi, and American), and it was dependent on aid from foreign NGO's, and salaries still paid to civil servants by Baghdad and Damascus. Asad wanted to insure that the IS didn't blow up the infrastructure – especially the dams. The IS administrations were beginning to approximate normality in Raqqah and Dayr al Zawr, but not in the hinterlands. Its militiamen were well paid (from shaky sources); the general public was struggling with poverty and inflation. In Syria, the Damascus regime maintained the dams and the power plants, and the IS kept them in operation; agricultural machinery was deteriorating: *FT*, 1/6/15.

2015 – Most IS bombings in western cities were reactions to Western intervention in the Middle East. They were not a product of the Islamic mindset: Internet, Fareed Zakaria, citing *Cutting the Fuse*, Robert Pape/James Feldman.

2015 – Two gunmen who used small arms to kill staffers at the office of the satirical magazine *Charlie Hebdo* on 1/7/15 were brothers seeking martyrdom. The attack was the start of three days of terrorism in Paris. It may have been a reprisal for French air strikes against IS targets: www.bbc.com, 1/14/15; *Times*, 11/21/15.

2015 – IS beheadings of Western hostages were intended to trap the US and Saudi Arabia into a war violent enough to precipitate the fall of the Saudi monarchy: *LRB*, 1/22/15, Edward Luttwak. The IS leadership was largely Iraqi, but there was no secret about the debt Al Qaʻidah and the Islamic State owed to Saudi Arabia's underground rebels, and to the mystique of a Caliphate resurrected 1400 years since the founding of the first, inspired by 200 years of Middle Eastern subjugation to the enormities of Western imperialism.

2015 – An Iraqi delegate to the annual meeting of the World Economic Forum at Davos reported that the IS, already entrenched in Iraq and Syria, was emerging as a threat in Lebanon, Yemen, and Libya: *FT*, 1/24/15.

2015 – The IS claimed responsibility for the recent spate of bombings in Baghdad: *Times*, 1/26/15.

2015 – In the battle for Kobani, the IS had taken such heavy casualties from Kurdish ground action and US air action that it had withdrawn its forces: *Times*, 1/27/15.

2015 – In Egypt, *Ansar Bayt al Maqdis* had sought funds, arms, and advice from the Islamic State, and it had adopted medieval punishments, including beheading. However, it attacked only Egyptian security forces, not Christians or Westerners. An action of 1/29/15 killed 44 Egyptians – soldiers, police, and civilians: *Times*, February 2015.

2015 – On 2/3/15, a Jordanian pilot shot down by Islamic State forces was anesthetized and burned alive. Revulsion swept the Arab World: *Times*, 2/5/15. The *Financial Times* concluded that the Islamic State was trying to drive a wedge between Jordan's government and its tribes. Columnist Charles Krauthammer read the atrocity as an effort to destabilize Jordan by pulling it into the jihadist war; he noted that, since Obama had gone to war against the Islamic State, it had doubled the size of its Syrian domain, whereas the Syrian secular militias had been losing steam. The IS was using savage tactics to maintain order in its own ranks, and/or to terrorize its adversaries: *NYTBR*, 4/5/15.

2015 – In February, the IS publicized its expansion to Libya by video of the beheading of two Egyptian Copts. Entities that stood in the IS's way were coopted or crushed (the Shuʻaytat tribe in Syria, and the Farjan tribe in Libya): *FT*, 3/21/16.

2015 – The IS was the Salafist product of a serious attempt to recreate original Islam. Islam provides precedent for the violent practices of IS: smashing pagan images, taxing non-Muslims, enslaving captive women, executing enemy combatants: *Atlantic*, February 2015, Graeme Wood; *New Statesman*, Tom Holland.

2015 – The municipal government in Raqqah had been rebuilt as the headquarters of the IS militia. It had instituted price controls and graduated taxes, supplied limited electricity, controlled wheat production, and ensured food supply. Its discipline was brutal – torture, plus beheading for desertion and some other offenses. Its rule was effective and incorrupt.

2015 – IS rule was noteworthy for its honesty, culpable for its obscurantism and repression. School curricula were curtailed. All female employees had to work in full niqab. The IS was recruiting Syrians, many of whom had been alienated from the Asad regime by its wholesale bombing of residential neighborhoods. Militiamen received free housing. Widows were pensioned. The IS hierarchy was well disciplined. Every Syrian province under IS control had its own "amir". The Shari'ah was strictly enforced by two police forces – one male, one female: *NYR*, 2/5/15, Sarah Birke.

2015 – All IS employees, military and civilian, were paid around 400 dollars a month. The IS charged businesses the *zakat* (2.5 percent of revenue), alms, and a "fee" of $8.30 per month.

2015 – The IS had set up linkage with compatible paramilitary groups in Algeria, Libya, Egypt, and Afghanistan: *AP*, 2/15/15.

2015 – The IS issued a videotape that purported to show beheadings of Coptic hostages by a Tripolitanian (Libya) affiliate: *Times*, 2/16/15. Twenty-one Copts had been beheaded. Egypt had launched retaliatory air strikes: *Times*, 2/18/15.

2015 – Libya Dawn was affiliated with the IS, against the forces of former Libyan General Khalifa Haftar (recognized by Western powers): *Times*, 2/18/15.

2015 – Pro-IS militants from Surt and Darnah, Libya, had killed 40 by suicide bombings in Qubbah: *Times*, 2/21/15.

2015 – The IS had fallen on hard times: Loss of Kobani to Kurds and US planes; loss of Diyala Province to Iraqi troops and militias; Kurdish advance toward Mawsil; loss of oil revenue, from 2.4 million dollars a day down to 750,000 dollars a day: *The Week*, 2/20/15. Most Iraqi forces deployed against the IS were Shiite militias.

2015 – In northeast Syria, IS forces were capturing and enslaving Assyrians (Christians): *Times*, 2/27/15.

2015 – Air attacks on oil refineries had wiped out all but 300,000 dollars a day of IS revenue from oil. IS military expenses were 10,000,000 dollars a month, plus 4000 dollars to every wife and mother of an IS combatant lost in the war: *FT*, 2/28/15.

2015 – The Islamic State had recruited 15,000 foreign fighters: *FP*, March 2015, Cronin.

2015 – IS publicity claimed that the purpose of its savage strategy was to deter infidels from inviting bloody combat in the world's End Time. The IS condemned as polytheism national borders, secular governments, embassies, and the UN: *Atlantic*, March 2015.

2015 – In March, the IS lost Tikrit, Iraq: *Times*, 7/3/16.

2015 – Most Salafis were too non-activist or reformist to rally behind the IS. Even the Prophet said pay obedience in general to tolerable rules: *Atlantic*, March 2015.

2015 – According to news releases from the IS, a true Caliph is a Qurayshi, like Abu Bakr al Baghdadi. His obligations are to end dictatorship in Muslim lands, expel non-Muslims from the Arabian Peninsula, and abolish the state of Israel.

2015 – The IS was spending 10 million dollars a month to support 11,000 Arab fighters and 19,000 foreign fighters. It met that expense by exportation of oil, looting of banks, extortion from civilians, abduction for ransom, human trafficking, and donations from Islamist supporters: *Times*, 3/3/15.

2015 – Foreign fighters dominated the military and administrative bureaucracies of the IS. Stresses of combat, financial reverses, and the growing pains of a new Caliphate had elicited reports of dissension, imprisonment, and execution in the ranks of the IS: *Times*, 3/14/15.

2015 – Libya was in the throes of civil war between a democratically elected government, based in Tubruq, and an Islamist coalition, Libya Dawn, based in Misurata, and dominant in Tripoli. A third challenger was the faction that claimed allegiance to the IS.

2015 – The IS had reportedly sponsored public stonings to death for adultery: *Times*, 3/25/15.

2015 – Robert Ford, former US Ambassador to Syria, commented that since the US had started air strikes on IS targets, the IS had gained territory: *WRMEA*, March 2015.

2015 – The dwindling Palestinian refugee camp at Yarmuk, near Damascus, was long controlled by Hamas, but the IS was gaining support: *FT*, 4/2/15.

2015 – After review of *ISIS: Inside the Army of Terror*, Michael Weiss/Hassan Hasan, and *The Rise of the Islamic State* by Patrick Cockburn, the *New York Times Book Review* came to the following conclusion: Al Qa'idah tried to arouse the Arab masses by dramatic actions against Western imperialism, like the 9/11 attacks; the IS had recruited nearly 20,000 Arab and foreign volunteers in a much more challenging campaign to win control of the Arab east: *NYTBR*, 4/5/15.

2015 – The territorial expansion of the IS had been facilitated by a tacit understanding with the Damascus regime: *NYTBR*, Weiss/Hasan.

2015 – The IS rigidly enforced shari'ah law, but let its militants keep the proceeds of illegal activities: Weiss/Hasan.

2015 – Nineteen of the twenty ministers in the IS cabinet were former officials of the Baathist regime in Iraq: *MEP*, Spring 2015, Gunter.

2015 – While the IS was – in the words of UN Secretary General Ban Ki-Moon – turning residents of Yarmuk Refugee Camp into "human shields", the Asad regime was dropping 36 barrel bombs on the camp: *Times*, 4/11/15.

2015 – On 4/12/15, the *Ansar* killed 12 or more in three operations in Sinai: *Times*, 4/13/15.

2015 – In May, the IS captured Ramadi (Iraq) and Palmyra (Syria): *Times*, 7/3/16.

2015 – The best armed and organized fighters in Middle Eastern combat were those of the IS and Nusrah: *Times*, 5/8/15.

2015 – The IS was carrying out random decapitations at Mawsil checkpoints in an effort to provoke enemy regimes into cracking down on Salafis, thereby broadening the flow of recruits to the IS: *NYR*, 6/4/15, Nicholas Pelham.

2015 – In Afghanistan, hundreds of Afghan Taliban had defected to the IS: *Times*, 6/5/15.

2015 – In Syria, by dispersing, using small vehicles, and making their runs in daily traffic, IS operatives had reduced losses from US air strikes. The IS had had success in coopting Sunni locals. Asad's forces seemed terrified by the IS's reputation for savagery: *FT*, 6/9/15.

2015 – In June, the IS lost Tall Abyad (Syria): *Times*, 7/3/16.

2015 – The IS claimed to have affiliates in Afghanistan, Algeria, Egypt, Indonesia, Libya, Nigeria, Pakistan, Saudi Arabia, and Yemen: *Times*, 6/18/15; *FT*, 7/17/15.

2015 – When the IS took over an area, minorities, elites, and personnel of the defeated faction fled or died. The IS then revised the school system to help sell its message. In Syria, the IS was working hard to expunge hints of the previous regime – rewarding those who went along, eliminating those who didn't. There was a regular bus route between the IS's two main cities, Raqqah and Mawsil: *Times*, 6/17/15.

2015 – Northwestern Syria, ravaged by Asad's barrel bombs, acquired a new problem – dealing with an embargo by the IS on the sale of petroleum products to the Damascus regime. The IS had obtained great leverage from the area's dependence on diesel fuel for water supply, electricity generation, bakeries, agricultural machinery, and hospitals. The US was bombing oil refineries, but not oil wells, leaving the IS with the whip hand over the Syrian oil industry: *FT*, 6/19/15.

2015 – IS released a videotape of pro-American Arabs being burned to death, drowned, or blown up: *Times*, 6/14/15.

2015 – The tribes in 'Anbar Province, Iraq, were making no progress in their effort to revive Sahwah.

2015 – In June, IS forces tried to capture Al Hasakah, in northeast Syria at the center of a major agricultural area. Control of the town was divided between the Damascus regime (Alawite Arab) and the YPG (Kurdish). By the end of July, they had beaten back the IS offensive – presumably with US Air Force support: *NYR*, 12/3/15.

2015 – As assessed by Abdel Bari Atwan in his *Islamic State: The Digital Caliphate*, reviewed by Malise Ruthven in *The New York Review* of 7/9/15, the IS combined bureaucratic efficiency and military expertise with a sophisticated use of information technology. By judicious deployment of its forces in Iraq and Syria, it had doubled its area of control in Syria between August 2014 and January 2015. The IS was forward-looking in its politics but regressive in its ideology. The most powerful department in the IS administration was the Sharia Council, which oversaw draconian penalties, including amputation and execution, for violation of "God's limits". The police force had a branch to maintain law and order and another to enforce religious observance. An Education Council oversaw attention to a Salafi (ultra-orthodox) interpretation of the Koran and sharia law. In many situations, the Saudi curriculum had been adopted intact. The ban on teaching evolutionary biology was typical of the Salafi obscurantism to which the IS subscribed. After months of no salary, teachers were being paid. Gender segregation was mandatory, but women were allowed to drive. The IS salute was the right-hand index finger pointed toward Heaven.

The IS brand of terror was extreme, but disciplined. It systematically followed the injunctions of a treatise posted online in 2004 by Al Qa'idah ideologue Abu Bakr Naji, who saw savagery as a weapon in wearing down the "effeminate" Western powers, which were trying to perpetuate the imperialist rule but lacked the requisite resolve. He cited the War of Apostasy, fought between Caliph Abu Bakr (632-4) and backsliders, as grounds for directing institutionalized savagery versus the US and its allies.

The IS had reduced its reliance on preachers by its proficiency in exploiting the social media. For Atwan, one of the ranking figures in the IS hierarchy was the head of its media department, Abu Muhammad al Shami, a skilled dispenser of inflammatory propaganda.

Atwan estimated the number of the IS's fighters at well over 100,000, including at least 30,000 foreigners. The major foreign sources of recruits were Libya, Tunisia, Saudi Arabia, Jordan, Egypt, and Lebanon.

One reason for the early success of the IS was Abu Bakr al Baghdadi, its latest leader, known as the "shabah" (phantom). His given name was

Ibrahim bin 'Awwad bin Ibrahim al Badri al Qurayshi. His Bubadri tribe included the Quraysh, the Prophet's tribe. Abu Bakr was born in 1971 in Samarra', seat of the Abbasids from 750 to 1258. Atwan reported that, other than video appearances, he kept a very low profile – sound policy in a world where the US and Israel were committed to the extermination of every jihadist leader, whether Sunni or Shiite. Abu Bakr wore a mask when talking to his officers. He held a doctorate in Islamic jurisprudence from the Islamic University of Baghdad. He had extensive battlefield experience as a lieutenant to Zarqawi (*FT*, November 2014, George Packer) and a reputation as a shrewd tactician. His first deputy, Abu Muslim al Turkmani, came from Saddam's military intelligence. His second deputy, Abu 'Ali al 'Anbari, was an Iraqi major general.

2015 – The main foreign source of recruits to the IS was Tunisia: *FT*, 6/26/15. [*See:* supplement, p. 508.]

2015 – The AQI was fast losing members to the Islamic State, because the image projected by the Islamic State was more impressive than that of Al Qa'idah: *The Week*; www.NationalReview.com, 6/26/15.

2015 – On 6/29/15, Hisham Barakat, Egypt's chief prosecutor of leaders of the Muslim Brotherhood, was killed by a car bomb in Cairo: *AP*, 6/30/15. *Ansar Bayt al Maqdis* later claimed responsibility: *Times*, 7/18/15.

2015 – On 7/2/15, *Ansar Bayt al Maqdis* militiamen and suicide bombers staged violent attacks on Egyptian checkpoints. Nine Muslim Brothers were killed "resisting arrest". Seven others had been executed: *FT*, 7/2/15.

2015 – The IS controlled an area populated by 6 million people. It was conscripting all males over 16. It used foreign militiamen for suicide attacks, locals for armed combat: *LRB*, 7/2/15, Cockburn.

2015 – The British Air Force was attacking IS targets in Iraq, but not in Syria: *FT*, 7/3/15.

2015 – Most Christians had managed to flee IS rule to grim asylum in neighboring countries. Those who stayed had to pay the head tax, or be enslaved, or die. Christians were also subject to expropriation and abduction of their children. In Mawsil, a red "N" painted on a house meant *Nasrani* (Christian): *NYTM*, 7/6/15.

2015 – In Diyala Province, a bomb killed over 100 Iraqis: *AP*, 7/18/15.

2015 – The IS claimed responsibility for bombings in Kuwait and the Eastern Province of Saudi Arabia: *AP*, 7/18/15.

2015 – Two weeks after Turkey escalated arrests of suspected jihadists, a suicide bombing in Turkey, near Kobani, killed over 30. The bomber was a Turk suspected of ties with the IS: *Times*, 7/20/15.

2015 – The "citizens" of the IS were cowed by its brutality, but they preferred it to the corruption and caprice of the regimes that preceded it: *Times*, 7/22/15.

2015 –Many of the IS's religious posts were held by Tunisians and Saudis. To escape drone killings, which had whittled away AQAP's leadership, Abu Bakr was sending messages by furtive courier, or electronic but encrypted. His two top deputies were Abu 'Ala' al 'Afu (former deputy to Zarqawi) and Fadil al Hayali, AKA Abu Muslim al Turkmani, a former officer in the Iraqi Special Forces: *Times*, 7/21/15. (See Abdel Bari Atwan entry, page 300.)

2015 – The IS was mass-producing IED's (improvised explosive devices), detonated by cell phones: *Times*, 7/21/15.

2015 – In Syria, the IS consisted of Syrian Salafis who condemned Alawite (*Nusayri*) rule. It received donations from pious Muslims in the Arab monarchies. The IS was recruiting jihadists (*mujahidin*) from southeast Europe, North Africa, and Turkey. Their objective was liberation of the Levant as the nucleus of an Islamic empire. For them, Jerusalem and Damascus were holy cities: *MEP*, Summer 2015, "The Rise and Demise of the Islamic Caliphate", Stephan Rosiny.

2015 – The IS had probably peaked, headed for early downfall. It had made many enemies. Its income was declining. Its reliance on savagery provoked retaliation in kind. It had carried out two purges of rival leaderships – Al Qa'idah on 2/23/14, Free Men of Syria on 9/9/14: *MEP*, Summer 2015, Rosiny.

2015 – On 8/6/15, IS suicide bombers and ground troops took Qaryatayn on the Palmyra-Damascus road. Over 200 Christians disappeared: *Times*, 8/8/15.

2015 – Gunmen trained in Libya, linked to the IS, had staged lethal raids in Tunisia. A thousand Tunisians had joined jihadists in Libya, 4000 in Syria: *Times*, 8/10/15.

2015 - IS forces had killed dozens of secularist (?) rebels in the Aleppo theater: *FT*, 8/11/15.

2015 – The IS had recruited several thousand Chechens from Russia to fight in Syria: *Times*, 8/12/15.

2015 – The IS was incorrupt, non-exploitive, and efficient. Jessica Lewis's view: "incredible command and control". Most important, it was the closest thing Sunnis had to a militia that got results. As such, it had surprising ideological appeal, even to its opponents: *NYR*, 8/13/15, "Anonymous". The IS had created comprehensive civil service structures in occupied cities: Aymenn al Tamimi, cited in the *New York Review* of 8/13/15. Many Sunnis in Iraq and Syria felt that the IS was the only plausible guarantor of order and security in the civil wars: "Anonymous".

2015 – The IS claimed responsibility for a bomb that killed 60 in Baghdad on 8/13/15: *Times*, 8/14/15; *FT*, 8/14/15.

2015 – The IS had arranged for many of the women among the 5000 Yazidis abducted from Mt. Sinjar to become "wives" of IS fighters against the women's will: *Times*, 8/14/15.

2015 – In the Libyan power struggle between two rival factions, IS affiliates were participating in the fighting in Surt (Tripolitania) and Benghazi (Cyrenaica): *Times*, 8/16/15, 8/19/15; *FT*, 8/17/15.

2015 – The IS had called on Turkish Muslims to rebel against President Erdogan: *Times*, 8/19/15.

2015 – On 8/22/15, IS forces killed 50 opponents in 'Anbar Province, Iraq: *AP*, 8/23/15.

2015 – The IS in Syria was not a state but several cities and many towns and villages, all under brutal occupation. The IS was quite competent on the battlefield but its civilian administration was primitive. Its major challenge was paying and managing its 30,000 fighters. Its current income was one million dollars a day. (*Times* estimate: three million dollars a day.) Morality police patrolled the streets. Punishment for violating IS laws could be flogging, amputation, or execution. It had released videos showing gay men being thrown off high buildings. It had decreed that girls could be married at nine, and should be married by seventeen. It was feared and loathed by many of its subjects, but they were ambivalent because Asad's dictatorship and Baghdad's corruption and favoritism for Shia were equally repellent. Now inflation was taking its toll in IS territory. Question: Could any contemporary government in these chaotic times do better?: *The Week*, 8/28/15.

2015 – The *Ansar* had killed a random Croatian hostage in retaliation for Croatia's joining the coalition against the Islamic State: *Times*, 8/13/15.

2015 – UK operatives had attacked three IS suspects in Syria. France had delivered 200 air strikes against IS targets in Iraq: *Times*, 9/8/15.

2015 – The Jihadist-Coalition War had slowed down in Iraq, and was stalemated in Syria. Over the previous year, the Iraqi forces and the Iran-backed Shiite militia had recaptured Tikrit from the IS, but the IS had captured Ramadi and Fallujah. The IS was digging in. The conflict seemed to have divided the two arenas along communalist lines – Iraqi Shiite forces were controlling central and southern Iraq; Kurds were controlling the KAR and a strip along the Syrian side of the Syrian-Turkish border; the IS was controlling northwest Iraq and central and southern Syria. US air forces were operating from carriers in the Gulf and the Mediterranean and out of Incirlik in Turkey: *FT*, 9/19/15.

2015 – Over the past two years, 20,000 foreigners had signed up with the forces of the jihad – most of them with the IS. Many of the European recruits didn't stay long. A number had cited dissatisfaction with the IS as the reason for their defection: *Times*, 9/21/15.

2015 – IS principal Abu Bakr al Turkmani (Fadil al Hayali) died in combat in early September: *Times*, 9/23/15.

2015 – Since 2011, 30,000 foreign recruits had poured into Syria to join the IS.

2015 – The French Air Force, which had been operating in Iraq, bombed a jihadist training camp in Syria: *Times*, 9/28/15.

2015 – The IS had cells in Turkey, Jordan, Lebanon, and Saudi Arabia, and growing militias in Sinai and Libya: *FT*, 9/28/15.

2015 – The IS was using sulphur mustard bombs that cause great pain, and injuries that require months of convalescence: *Times*, 10/7/15.

2015 – The IS took advantage of its jihadist rivals' preoccupation with Russian attacks to seize a string of villages just north of Aleppo: *FT*, 10/8/15, 10/10/15.

2015 – The Russian intervention of October 2015, by initially concentrating on Nusrah, strengthened the positions of the IS and the FSA (Free Syrian Army): *FT*, 1/27/16.

2015 – In October, IS forces were driven out of Bayji City and refinery in Iraq: *Times*, 12/23/15.

2015 – Despite intensive bombing by Coalition aircraft of refineries and pipelines controlled by the IS, it was still earning 1.5 million dollars a day from selling petroleum products in a good local market. Syria runs on diesel fuel. No one wanted to destroy the production of crude. IS refineries were small, makeshift, inconspicuous facilities that were easily repaired. Product was moved by unmarked trucks resembling those used for general purposes. Washington had ruled out indiscriminate bombing of traffic in general. Oil trucks were driven by civilians, hard to locate, and politically inadvisable to bomb: *FT*, 10/15/15. Nor could the Coalition bomb the 6,000,000 civilians under IS control. The local administration of IS territory was highly decentralized among local governors, except for the oil industry, the media, and military operations.

2015 – Many Syrians, especially Christians, were fleeing Syria to escape the IS's draconian rule, but it was importing foreign experts in key fields: *FT*, 10/16/15.

2015 – The IS had a growing group of supporters in Afghanistan: *Times*, 10/16/15.

2015 – On 10/31/15, a Russian airliner leaving Sharm al Shaykh, a tourist Mecca in southern Sinai, exploded in midair shortly after takeoff.

2015 – In the early 2000's, a group of Sinai Bedouins began attacking government targets in Sinai. Many were jailed. After the ouster of Mubarak, some who had been released formed *Ansar Bayt al Maqdis* (Soldiers of Jerusalem) in collaboration with some anti-Hamas Gazans and extremist Egyptians. They began a campaign of sabotage of infrastructure in Sinai and northern Egypt. In late 2014, some of them broke away and joined the IS. Their campaign was more sophisticated and more savage. In November 2015, this organization announced that, in honor of the IS, it had taken the name *Wilayat Sina* (Sinai Province), and that it was the agent of the Russian airliner's destruction: *FT*, 11/6/15.

2015 – Sinai Province claimed responsibility for a bomb that killed four Egyptian police officers: *Times*, 11/4/15.

2015 – In Sinai, most of the membership of the former *Ansar Bayt al Maqdis* were operating under the new title of Sinai Province. The holdouts were still operating under the original name: *FT*, 11/6/15.

2015 – The IS claimed suicide bombings on 11/12/15 that killed over 40 Shia in Beirut: *Times*, 11/13/15.

2015 – On 11/13/15, suicide attacks on random targets in Paris killed 120. A concurrent item on Twitter criticized French military operations against the IS: *AP*, 11/13/15. On 11/14/15, the IS claimed responsibility for the 11/13 suicide attacks: *Post*, 11/15/15.

2015 – Russia revealed that the airliner lost on October 31 had been destroyed by a bomb: *Times*, 11/18/15.

2015 – The IS relied on acquisition of territory and unspeakable cruelty. Its emblems were the black flag and the severed head: *Times*, 11/19/15, Ian Fisher.

2015 – A surge in US air strikes on oil wells and tanker trucks sharply cut IS production and delivery of crude (at greater risk to the US military operations and Syria's economic future): *FT*, 11/19/15.

2015 – Millions of Sunni Arabs were turning to the IS out of resentment for the offenses committed by the Shiite regimes in Baghdad and Damascus. Obama, unwilling to admit that American forces in the region were surviving on borrowed time, was making pitiful efforts to stem the tide: *FT*, 11/23/15.

2015 – French President Hollande, at a meeting with Obama in Washington, urged closer alliance with Russia against the IS. Obama countered that Asad (Russia's ally) was an accomplice of the IS: *Times*, 11/25/15.

2015 – The IS had arranged an affiliation with a Libyan faction that had a 2000-man militia, controlled 150 miles of seafront based on Surt, and had engaged the forces of the two main contenders for control of Libya – the Tripoli/Misurata faction and the Benghazi faction. The IS had sent a team to take over the affiliate, which had come under US air attack: *Times*, 11/25/15. The IS had been sending fighters from Iraq and Syria to Surt for R and R: *FT*, 12/9/15.

2015 – In Iraq and Syria, the US air campaign had reversed the advance of IS troops. They lost Tall Abyad in June, Sinjar in November, Ramadi in December: *Times*, 12/23/15.

2015 – The IS theology was almost identical to Wahhabiism, but the IS had introduced modern methods that had brought in 20,000 recruits from abroad: *FA*, November 2015, Hisham Melhem review of *The ISIS Apocalypse*, William McCants.

2015 – According to defectors, the IS bureaucracy was weakening from loss of technicians: *Times*, 11/2/15, Ben Hubbard.

2015 – The IS had lost control of all the Syria/Turkey crossings except Jarabulus. To evade US air strikes, it had suspended conventional military tactics in favor of guerrilla war – hit-and-run and suicide attacks: *NYR*, 12/3/15, Steele.

2015 – On 12/2/15, Syed Rizwan Farook and his wife, Tashfin Malik, religious fanatics, fired on a party in San Bernardino, California, killing 14. Just before the attack, Malik had placed on Facebook a message addressed to the leader of the IS. They were Pakistani immigrants, apparently inflamed by the sermons of Anwar 'Awlaqi. They were killed by the police pursuing them. There was no report of any communication between them and the IS: *NY*, 2/22/16.

2015 – US, Russian, and Damascus regime air strikes were causing casualties in Raqqah. The IS was preventing people from moving out: *FT*, 12/5/15. US air strikes were turning residents against the US.

2015 – It was estimated that IS revenue from oil in 2015 was 450 million dollars, and that IS earnings from taxes, fees, and confiscations in its Iraqi and Syrian territories were roughly equivalent to earnings from oil: *FT*, 12/15/15.

2015 – The IS was attacking Kurdish lines north and east of Mawsil: *NY*, 12/16/15, Mogelson.

2015 – The IS had sworn to destroy the Saudi monarchy: *Times*, 12/19/15.

2015 – Over the previous 18 months, the flow of foreign fighters to Iraq and Syria had increased. IS forces included 27-31,000 foreigners: *The Week*, 12/25/15.

2016 – French President Hollande maintained that IS subversion in Europe was intended to undermine public support for fighting the IS: *NYT*, 2016, Stephen Erlanger.

2016 – An assembly of police, Iraqi army, local Sunni tribesmen, and Iraq's Counterterrorism Force retook the devastated city of Ramadi from the IS on 1/3/16: *Aljazeera*.

2016 – Affiliates of the IS controlled 300 kilometers of Libyan coastline, centered on Surt. The two main contenders for Libyan hegemony were deadlocked: the moderate-Islamist Libya Dawn, based in Misurata, supporting the government in Tripoli; and Operation Dignity, based in Tubruq: *Times*, 1/13/16; *FT*, 1/6/16.

2016 – On 1/4/16, IS affiliates in Libya blew up seven giant oil tanks in Libya's two main oil ports, al Sidr and Ras Lanuf, on the Gulf of Sidra: *FT*, 3/21/16.

2016 – With Turkey shutting down the flow of recruits to the IS, it seemed to have fixed on Libya as an emergency base of operations in case it was expelled from Iraq and Syria: *FT*, 1/8/16.

2016 – IS fighters who abandoned the defense of Ramadi were burned alive in the Mawsil town square: Fox News, 1/12/16. [This report was not seen from any other news source.]

2016 – In retaliation for Turkey's closure of its border with Syria, an IS suicide bomber killed ten tourists in Istanbul: *Times*, 1/13/16.

2016 – Sinai militants founded a jihadist group in Gaza: *NYR*, 1/14/16.

2016 – The IS was paying its militants 200-500 dollars a month: *Times*, 1/15/16.

2016 – IS forces attacked Dayr al Zawr neighborhoods long held by the Damascus regime. Deaths: 135, most of them from the regime: *AP*, 1/16/16.

2016 – The IS still held Tall 'Afar in Iraq, but it had lost the Raqqah-Mawsil highway to the Kurds: *NY*, 1/18/16, Luke Mogelson.

2016 – The collapse of the global price of oil, plus US air strikes on the oil infrastructure of the IS, had forced the IS to cut the monthly pay of its militiamen to 200 dollars a month: *The Week*, 1/29/16.

2016 – A UN report cited an estimate that 19,000 Iraqi civilians had been killed in the fighting between the IS and Iraqi forces from January 2014 to November 2015. The UN thought the IS may have committed genocide: *The Week*, 1/29/16.

2016 – As many as fifty Syrians died in the simultaneous detonation of three IS bombs in the Sayyidah Zaynab suburb (Shiite) of Damascus: *AP*, 2/1/16.

2016 – The IS released a training video to prove that it was the perpetrator of the violence that killed 130 in Paris in November 2015: *The Week*, 2/5/16.

2016 – As long as Iran was acting as a rogue state in the Arab World, the Sunni Arab states would not destroy the IS: *Times*, 2/10/16, Thomas Friedman.

2016 – The UN had designated the IS and Nusrah as terrorist organizations: *Times*, 2/12/16.

2016 – The number of Libyan militiamen loyal to the IS had risen to 6300: *Times*, 2/20/16.

2016 – The bombing in Ankara in October 2015, which Turkey had ascribed to Kurds, had been an IS operation: *FT*, 2/20/16.

2016 – Most of the contenders in the Syrian civil war were in Paris to discuss the terms of a ceasefire. The IS and Nusrah had been excluded: *FT*, 2/26/16.

2016 – Recent territorial losses by the IS in Syria included an oil field, but it was still delivering enough product through the USAF barrage to keep the local price down to 40-45 dollars a barrel: *FT*, 2/27/16.

2016 – In February, the IS lost the Bayji Refinery, which it had captured in the grand sweep of June 2014: *Harper's*, February 2016.

2016 – The IS claimed responsibility for a suicide bomb that killed 33 on 3/6/16 in Hillah (60 miles south of Baghdad): *Times*, 3/6/16.

2016 – On 3/13/16, Baghdad issued a charge that the IS had staged chemical attacks in Iraq on 3/9/16 and 3/12/16.

2016 – On 3/17/16, Secretary Kerry accused the IS of genocide against Christians, Kurds, Shia, and Yazidis: *Times*, 3/18/16.

2016 – Turkey announced that the suicide bombing of 3/19/16 in Istanbul was perpetrated by a Turkish follower of the IS: *Times*, 3/21/16.

2016 – There were further signs that, if the IS should lose its main bases of Raqqah and Mawsil, it would seek a sanctuary in Libya.

2016 – On 3/22/16, a European cell of the IS detonated in Brussels two bombs that killed 38. The IS claimed responsibility: *AP*, 3/22/16.

2016 – On 3/25/16, the IS claimed responsibility for a bomb that killed several leaders of a Shiite militia, *'Asa'ib Ahl al Haqq* (League of the Followers of Truth) in Babil Province of Iraq: *Times*, 3/26/16.

2016 – An IS suicide bombing in Istanbul killed three Israeli tourists and an Iranian: *Times*, 4/1/16.

2016 – The IS bombing campaign was meant to attract recruits by demonstrating paramilitary effectivity: *FT*, 4/7/16, Fawaz Gerges.

2016 – US air strikes had reduced IS oil revenue by one-third. The US had prevailed on Baghdad to stop paying civil servants who were working in areas under IS control: *Times*, 4/13/16. The IS had been forced to abandon Sinjar (Yazidi town between Raqqah and Mawsil) and the Bayji Refinery: *Times*, 4/13/16.

2016 – In April, the IS lost Hit (Iraq): *Times*, 7/3/16.

2016 – The Libyan coastal town of Surt was under the control of 6,000 IS troops: *The Week*, 5/3/16.

2016 – Both jihadism and the Arab Nationalism of the Ba'th, Nasir, and Saddam had the same objective: unification: *FT*, 5/3/16, Edward Luce.

2016 – The IS claimed responsibility for an ambush of a Cairo minibus in which eight policemen died: *Times*, 5/9/16.

2016 – IS car bombs north of Ramadi killed twenty members of Baghdad security teams: *Times*, 5/12/16.

2016 – The IS forces in Iraq and Syria totaled 19-25,000: *Times*, 5/16/16.

2016 – In an audio message of 5/21/16, IS spokesman Abu Muhammad al 'Adnani spoke in implicit recognition of the possible loss of the territory it held in Syria and Iraq. The IS might have to revert to guerrilla tactics. In April, Director of National Intelligence James Clapper Jr. had said the IS had clandestine cells in Britain, Germany, Italy, and Turkey. The IS militia had fallen from 33,000 men in 2015 to 20,000: *Times*, 7/3/16, Eric Schmitt.

2016 – In Baghdad, the IS staged a deadly streak of bombings from May 11 to May 23: *Times*, 5/19/16; *FT*, 5/27/16.

2016 – In May, the IS lost Rutbah: *Times*, 7/3/16.

2016 – Action by troops loyal to Libya's Government of National Accord had reduced the coastline under IS control to 40 miles, centering on Surt: *Times*, 6/10/16.

2016 – "There are more reports these days of Western jihadists trying to get out of IS territory than of people wanting to join the group": *FT*, 6/16/16, Roula Khalaf.

2016 – The IS lost Fallujah on 6/27/16.

2016 – In June, three IS bombers, a Russian, an Uzbek, and a Kyrgyz, killed 44. The IS's best fighters had come from the Soviet Federation: *Times*, 7/1/16.

2016 – On 6/30/16, Sinai Province operatives killed a Coptic Minister in Egypt: *Times*, 7/1/16.

2016 – On 7/3/16, a vehicle bomb killed over 140, most of them Shiites, in Baghdad. As the IS lost territory, it resorted more to guerilla action: *Times*, 7/3/16.

2016 – In Saudi Arabia on 7/4/16, the IS was suspected of three suicide bombings – one near the US Consulate in Jiddah, one near the Prophet's Mosque in Medina, one near a Shiite mosque. The bombing in Medina killed four security guards. The one in Jiddah wounded two guards: *The Week*, 7/15/16.

2016 – Three IS suicide bombers killed 45 at Istanbul's international airport: *The Week*, 7/15/16.

2016 – In Nice, the third bomb attack in 19 weeks was considered IS retaliation for France's active participation in the coalition's air war in Iraq and Syria: *FT*, 7/16/16.

2016 – The IS claimed a suicide bombing that killed 80 in Kabul: *AP*, 7/23/16.

2016 – Two IS operatives killed civilians in France: *Times*, 7/26/16.

2016 – Surt (Libya), defended by IS forces, fell on 8/10/16: *Times*, 8/14/16.

2016 – A suicide bomber killed over 50 at a Kurdish wedding in Gaziantep, Turkey. It was suspected to be IS retaliation for Kurdish advances, under US air cover, in Iraq and Syria: *FT*, 8/20/16.

2016 – Between January and August, IS operatives staged 25 attacks in Saudi Arabia: *Times*, 8/26/16.

2016 – On 8/24/16, a massive Turkish foray into Syria took Jarabulus, ousting IS forces from their last border crossing between Syria and Turkey. FSA forces followed the Turks into the city: *Post*, 8/29/16; *AP*, 9/6/16.

2016 – Abu Muhammad 'Adnani, chief strategist of the IS and Deputy to Abu Bakr, was killed in Aleppo Province by a US Reaper drone: *BBC Online*, 8/31/16, citing a DOD release; *Times*, 8/30/16.

2016 – In Aden, an IS suicide bomber killed 54 recruits from Hadi's army. They were to have been trained in Eritrea and Djibouti: *AP*, 8/29/16.

2016 – "Citizens" of the Caliphate had been turned off by its violence and oppression, and its failure to establish essential services. IS morale was slipping. The flow of new recruits was down to a trickle: *FT*, 9/5/16, John Sawers.

2016 – A foray into Syria by the Turkish/FSA force took the last 13 miles of frontier that had been held by the IS. They lost four lives to the retreating IS forces: *AP*, 9/6/16.

2016 – The IS was flying model-aircraft size drones for recon. One exploded under examination, killing two of the Kurdish examiners: *Times*, 10/12/16.

2016 – The monthly flow of recruits to jihadist organizations in Syria had fallen from 2000 to 200. The number of foreign fighters in Syria had dropped from 33,000 to 20,000: *Times*, 10/11/16.

2016 – Most residents of Mawsil, disillusioned by the harsh rule of the IS, wanted to escape. This report came from actual escapees. The

315

city was in crisis. IS revenues had been sliced by the loss of oil fields in the Raqqah region in Syria and the Qayyarah region in Iraq. There was no funding for teachers. The schools had closed. IS militants' pay had been cut to 100 dollars a month. The water supply to Mawsil residences had shut down. Since Kurdish forces had recaptured the Mawsil Dam, the electricity system was operating two hours a day: *Times*, 10/17/16, Rod Norland.

2016 – Syrian rebels claimed that 2000 militiamen, backed by Turkish tanks and planes, had retaken from the IS the legendary village of Dabiq.

2016 – Eighty died from a suicide attack in Kirkuk by an IS sleeper cell: *FT*, 10/21/16.

2016 – An IS spokesman had stated that if the IS lost its bases in Iraq and Syria, it would disappear into the desert of "Wilayat al Furat" (State of the Euphrates) and bide its time: *Times*, 10/24/16, Hasan.

2016 – Eighty pilgrims, most of them Iranians, died in a bombing in Iraq: *Times*, 11/25/16.

2016 – On 12/31/16 and 1/1/17, an IS attack on an Istanbul nightclub killed 390. For all of 2016, IS operations had killed 6870 in Baghdad: *The Week*, 1/13/17.

Al Qa'idah/Nusrah – The Al Qa'idah of Ayman al Zawahiri was a direct descendant of the organization Usamah bin Ladin founded, but its jihadist aspect had been subdued by Zawahiri's low-profile style, and by the more impressive geopolitical swath cut by Abu Bakr's IS. The current objectives of the new Al Qa'idah were less millennial than those of the IS. They were: 1) To subjugate rival contenders in the Arab East; 2) To expunge the American and Russian military presences from the region.

The new Al Qa'idah and the IS shared the same theology – a combination of Salafi Islam and latter-day Islamist activism, which rejected democracy as apostasy because it placed the caprice of the crowd above the will of God. "Salafi" is generally translated as ultraconservative.

During the Reagan administration, the CIA supplied funds, and possibly training, to bin Ladin's anti-Russian forces in Afghanistan via

316

Pakistani Intelligence. CIA director Casey built up the station in Islamabad to become the biggest in the world. Saudi Arabia participated in the mujahideen program primarily as a means of opposing the Shiite theocracy in Iran.

1981 – Zawahiri was one of the hundreds arrested after the assassination of Sadat, in retaliation for Sadat's conclusion of the 1979 treaty of peace with Israel. Under torture, Zawahiri reportedly gave up the name of an accomplice, who was executed.

1989 – The Soviet withdrawal from Afghanistan left Al Qa'idah with the services of a formidable force of battle-hardened devotees. Christiane Amanpur reported that bin Ladin was now a *mujahid*, but his offer to help Saudi Arabia expel Iraq from Kuwait was rejected. The Saudis, who have long managed to avoid hazardous involvement in foreign wars, had an ideal alternative – the combative United States. For Usamah this recourse was an intolerable profanation of sacred soil, and a violation of the Islamic tradition: "Let here be no two religions in Arabia."

1989 – On 6/30/89, Lt. General 'Umar al Bashir set up in Khartoum a regime loyal to the National Islamic Front, the political party of the Sudanese branch of the Muslim Brotherhood. Bin Ladin accepted its invitation to transfer Al Qa'idah's base from chaotic Afghanistan to Sudan. The timing was opportune, since his own country had ordered that he be restrained for having smuggled in arms from Yemen. Frustrated in his wish to overthrow the Saudi "near enemy", he set up training camps in Sudan to attack the royal family's protector, the American "far enemy".

Switch: From Anti-Russian to Anti-American – On 11/8/90, the FBI raided the New York home of a bin Ladin associate, Al Sayyid Nusayr, and found evidence of plotting to bomb buildings in New York City. Washington ended its relationship with Al Qa'idah.

1992 – Bin Ladin and Zawahiri issued their first call for jihad (neither of them is an imam) against the American military presence in Saudi Arabia and East Africa. Bin Ladin's pronouncements were having great impact in the Muslim world for their content, for his command of classical Arabic, and for the hypnotic effect of his voice.

1992 – On 12/29/92 came the failure of an Al Qaʻidah attempt to bomb the quarters used in Aden by US soldiers in transit to Somalia.

1993 – Al Sayyid Nusayr, Ramzi Yusuf, and Khalid Shaykh Muhammad were the principals in Al Qaʻidah's 2/26/93 truck bombing of the World Trade Center. On this first attempt, Al Qaʻidah failed to topple the towers, but it killed six people and injured a thousand. The avowed motive was revenge for US support for Israel. Bin Ladin had been particularly disaffected by the adoption of the devious Israeli-Palestinian Oslo Accord, and his own country's endorsement of it.

1993 – From Nairobi, Al Qaʻidah issued a claim of responsibility for the 10/4/93 downing of two US Black Hawk helicopters during the Somali civil war.

1993 – The Lebanese Hizballah was training Al Qaʻidah personnel in bombing technique.

1994 – In reaction to bin Ladin's vilification of the Saudi regime, and his support for the unionists against the Saudi-backed secessionists in the Yemeni civil war, the Saudis revoked bin Ladin's citizenship, froze his Saudi assets, and forced his relatives to cut off the stipend he had been receiving from the family.

1995 – Ayman Zawahiri became leader of Egyptian Islamic Jihad.

1995 – Zawahiri directed an attack on the Egyptian Embassy in Pakistan. Bin Ladin disapproved of it.

1995 – Ramzi Yusuf, involved in a Manila-based plot to destroy twelve airliners in flight, was arrested in Pakistan.

1995 – ʻUmar ʻAbd al Rahman, "the blind shaykh", was convicted by a US court of complicity in the 1993 bombing of the World Trade Center, and sentenced in 1996 to life in solitary confinement with no eligibility for parole. In the 1980's, he had been spiritual guide for the Egyptian Islamist Group and The Egyptian Islamic Jihad. His teaching was blamed for the 10/6/81 assassination of Anwar Sadat. Released from Egyptian prison in the late 80's, Shaykh ʻUmar had taken refuge in Jersey City.

1995 – In June, operatives of Zawahiri's Egyptian Islamic Jihad made an attempt on the life of Egyptian dictator Husni Mubarak.

1995 – A building of the Saudi National Guard housing military and civilian personnel of an American training mission was destroyed by a bomb, which killed five Americans and wounded 60 people: *CNN*, 11/13/95. Four Saudis were later beheaded for the operation. Al Qaʻidah claimed it: *Atlantic*, March 2016, Peter Beinart.

1996 – In May, under pressure from Washington, Sudan expelled bin Ladin. Uninvited, he moved back to Afghanistan, where the Afghan Taliban had captured Kabul and imposed an Islamist society. Bin Ladin earned the confidence of Mullah Omar, and reestablished his base in Afghanistan, operating like a state inside the Afghan Taliban's domain.

1996 – In June, bombing of the Khawbar Towers, a residence of US Air Force personnel in Saudi Arabia, killed 19 and wounded 372. Bin Ladin told Robert Fisk (*The Great War for Civilization*) Khawbar Towers had been an Al Qaʻidah operation.

1996 – In August, bin Ladin issued a second call to jihad – a "Declaration of War Against the United States". Couched in Salafi phraseology, it rejected the legitimacy of the Saudi monarchy, and adjured Muslims to drive the American troops out of Saudi Arabia.

1996 – Khalid Shaykh Muhammad, later known in Washington as KSM, presented to bin Ladin an intricate scheme that would shock America on 9/11/01. From 1999 until he went into hiding on 9/11/01, KSM was director of propaganda for Al Qaʻidah. He was a Baluchi from Pakistan, grew up in Palestinian circles in Kuwait, graduated in mechanical engineering from North Carolina A & T State University, fought in Bosnia, and served as a project engineer for the government of Qatar. He spoke Baluchi, Arabic, English, and Urdu. Ramzi Yusuf was his nephew.

1997 – An Egyptian court sentenced Ayman Zawahiri to death in absentia on a charge of participating with members of the Islamic Group in the massacre on 4/17/97 of 58 tourists and 4 Egyptians near Luxor.

1998 – On 2/23/98, in association with Zawahiri and other Islamists, bin Ladin issued a fatwa condemning American "occupation" and "plundering" of Islamic lands, and proclaiming the formation of The World Islamic Front for Holy War Against the Jews and the Crusaders.

The manifesto's injunction to kill Americans cost Al Qa'idah the loss of those members opposed to killing civilians.

1998 – In May, bin Ladin told PBS that Al Qa'idah was committed to restoration of the pride of those who had been victims of foreign masters. If American injustice persisted, Al Qa'idah would move the battle to the US.

1998 – In August, Al Qa'idah's suicide bombings at the American embassies in Kenya and Tanzania killed 223 people, probably in retaliation for American "extraordinary rendition" of Egyptian Islamists to Egypt. Clinton's retaliatory cruise-missile attacks of 8/20/98 against questionable targets in Sudan and Afghanistan seemed to have no consequence except more publicity for bin Ladin, who was reported to be receiving financial and political support from sympathetic officials in Pakistan, Qatar, the UAE, Yemen, and Saudi Arabia (whose government was apprehensive of revelations about his ties with some members of the royal family). He had consolidated his alliance with the Taliban by taking a daughter of Afghan Taliban leader Mullah Omar as one of his wives.

1998 – Zawahiri was indicted by a US court for complicity in the East African bombings.

1998 – Zawahiri merged his Egyptian Islamic Jihad into Al Qa'idah.

1999 – The four 9/11 hijack pilots spent the year training for 9/11 – fitness and military training in Afghanistan and Pakistan, flight training in the US. The 16 muscle hijackers trained in Pakistan. Bin Ladin had selected all 20 after a brief interview with each one. All had agreed to participate in a suicide mission – presumably anticipating their rewards in the hereafter.

1999 – In retaliation for the failure of the Afghan Taliban in Kabul to extradite bin Ladin, Washington imposed sanctions on their regime on 11/14/99.

2000 – On October 23, Al Qa'idah operatives bombed the USS Cole (destroyer) in Aden harbor, killing 17 sailors. Bin Ladin had become an Arab hero. With characteristic lack of finesse, Washington had stumbled into the picture by treating bin Ladin as a common criminal and putting a price of ten million dollars on his head.

2000 – The four hijack pilots obtained their licenses in the US – at least two of them commercial licenses. Their profiles during pilot training were eccentric; this was the vulnerable phase of the conspiracy, when the FBI and/or the CIA should have spotted it. One of the four muscle hijackers scheduled to take UA 93 had been deemed an implausible applicant for an entry visa by an immigration inspector in Orlando, but no one saw him as a potential hijacker. From 8/25/01 to 9/5/01, the other 19 operatives were in the US, where they bought air tickets. The four pilots took familiarity flights around the country: *The 9/11 Commission Report.*

2001 – On 8/6/01, the President's Daily Brief carried a reminder of Al Qaʻidah's continuing threat to the United States proper.

The 9/11 Hijackings

On September 11, 2001, 19 operatives (fifteen Saudis, the other four from the UAE, Lebanon, and Egypt) carried out the meticulous hijacking of four American jetliners. Two demolished the World Trade Center in New York. A third blew up a side of the Pentagon. The fourth was flown into the ground as a result of intervention by heroic passengers. Al Qaʻidah's goal was revenge for US impairment of Arab self-determination, as in the disfranchisement of the Palestinians and the Saudi people. The operation was reportedly arranged in Germany and the US, not in Afghanistan. The early financing came from Saʻid Bahaji, a German member of an Al Qaʻidah cell in Hamburg that provided three of the pilots. One them, Muhammad ʻAtta, had headed the cell: *Times*, 10/31/09. *Newsweek* noted the disturbing fact that the planners and the operatives of the 9/11 attacks were from countries whose governments were allied with the US. The attacks took the lives of 2996 people: 2606 in and around the World Trade Center, 125 at the Pentagon, 246 passengers and crew on the four commercial flights – plus the 19 hijackers.

The following details are from *The 9/11 Commission Report* (undated). (Arab names have been converted to standard Arabic-English transliteration):

321

American Airlines Flight 11, Boston-LA, took off at 07:59, and was hijacked at 08:14 by Muhammad 'Atta (Egyptian) and his team of four. At 08:46, they flew it into the North Tower of the WTC.

United Airlines Flight 175, Boston-LA, took off at 08:14, and was hijacked at 08:42 by Marwan al Shahhi (UAE) and his team of four. At 09:03 they flew it into the South Tower of the WTC.

American Airlines Flight 77, Dulles-LA, took off at 08:20, and was hijacked at 08:51 by Hani Hanjur (Saudi) and his team of four. At 09:37 they flew it into a side of the Pentagon.

United Airlines Flight 93, Newark-San Francisco, took off at 08:42, and was hijacked at 09:28 by Ziyad Jarrah (Lebanon) and his team of three. Just after 10:00, the plane was crashed in Pennsylvania after the intervention of passengers who had learned from their cell phones of earlier hijackings and crashes. By leaving the hijackers no other recourse consistent with their mission except flying the plane into the ground, the self-appointed vigilantes probably spared the nation the destruction of the White House or the Capitol.

US Government Against a Stacked Deck – The 9/11 operation was meticulously planned, overseen by a resourceful team (KSM, bin Ladin, Ramzi bin al Shibh, Abu Turab al Urduni, and Muhammad 'Atif, working from Afghanistan, Malaysia, Germany, and Pakistan), and financed early on by Sa'id Bahaji. The operation was implemented by competent and dedicated personnel in almost total secrecy. All the preparations generated a flood of warnings, but taken separately they were too vague to be spotted by an uncoordinated US intelligence community. No American official was focusing on the elementary concept of using airliners as missiles. Westerners don't think in terms of mission-oriented collective suicide. NORAD (the Canadian-American North American Aerospace Command) had standing orders to shoot down foreign sneak attackers, but not hijacked American planes. As long as the hijackers' identities didn't leak, all systems were go.

2001 – **A Failure of Crisis Management**

08:14 – Hijacking of AA 11 (the first)

08:19 – Start of flight attendant Betty Ong's blow-by-blow account on the cell phone to American Airlines (in Cary, NC) of the hijacking of AA 11.

08:25 – FAA's (Federal Aviation Administration) Boston Air Traffic Control Center inferred the AA 11 hijacking from a mistaken radio transmission by the hijackers.

08:28 – Boston Center to the national Air Traffic Control system in Herndon, VA: Has AA 11 been hijacked?

08:29 – American Airlines confirmed the AA 11 hijacking to FAA's Boston Center.

08:32 – Herndon notified the FAA Operations Center of the AA 11 hijacking.

08:38 – The Boston Center reported the AA 11 hijacking to NORAD's New England Air Defense Sector (NEADS) – this was the first time that any sector of the military had heard of it. NEADS scrambled F-15's from Otis Airbase in Falmouth, MA (airborne 08:53, but no target was supplied).

08:42 – Hijacking of UAL 175 (the second).

08:46 – AA 11 hits the WTC North Tower.

08:51 – AA 77 hijacked (the third).

08:52 – Passenger Peter Hanson phoned his father a request to notify United Airlines of the hijacking of UAL 175.

08:56 – FAA radar began to track AA 77, but FAA did not keep its controllers informed.

09:03 – UAL 175 hit the South Tower of the World Trade Center (WTC).

09:03 – New York Center informed NEADS of the second hijacking.

09:07 – Boston Center asked Herndon to elevate cockpit security, nationwide. There was no report that Herndon complied.

09:10 – Boston Center to its controllers: Elevate cockpit security.

09:12 – Passenger Renee May phoned to inform her mother that AA 77 had been hijacked.

323

09:20 – Teleconference of DOD, FAA, and other agencies. DOD withdrew after the Pentagon was hit, 09:37.

09:24 – NEADS ordered jets at Langley Airbase to scramble (airborne 09:30; jets from Otis still circling over New York City).

09:28 – Hijacking of UAL 93 (fourth).

09:29 – The National Military Command Center (NMCC) convened a teleconference. The FAA representative was almost an hour late. It turned out that he was of little help, not having been briefed on the hijackings. Rumsfeld was an hour late.

09:34 – Washington Center informed NEADS that AA 77 was missing.

09:36 – Boston Center informed NEADS that a hijacked aircraft was in the vicinity of the White House. The reference was probably to AA 77.

09:37 – AA 77 hit a side of the Pentagon. The jets from Langley were off on a wild-goose chase.

09:37 – The NMCC convened a second teleconference on the crisis.

09:42 – Herndon learned from press reports (!) of the AA 77 crash into the Pentagon, and issued an order to all aircraft in US airspace to land immediately at the nearest airport. The unprecedented procedure was carried out without a hitch.

09:57 – The hijackers of UAL 93 were assaulted by some of the passengers.

10:03 – UAL 93 was flown into the ground by its hijackers.

10:20 – The President authorized the defense planes to shoot down the hijacked airliners.

10:31 – NORAD transmitted a cryptic order from the Vice President to NORAD's regional divisions to shoot down "tracks of interest", but the commander of the New England zone later reported that he had not acted on the order because he was "unaware of its ramifications".

10:39 – Cheney told Rumsfeld he understood NORAD's defense pilots, on instructions, had downed two hijacked planes. Cheney was mistaken. No orders had reached the NORAD pilots. Pilots of the DC Air National Guard had acted on a request of the Secret Service: At 10:38, they had taken off from Andrews Air Force Base with authorization to fly "weapons free" – i.e., to attack any aircraft they thought needed shooting down. This authorization had not been coordinated with NORAD. The Air National Guard's order to the pilots had been too fragmentary to produce any results.

Observations – During boarding of AA 77, something in a hijacker's pocket set off a metal detector. That incident was never resolved. During the takeovers of the four cockpits, knives and box cutters were brandished. At that time, the FAA guidelines allowed passengers to carry short knives and box cutters: *Atlantic*, September 2016, Steven Brill; the airlines did the screening. (At this writing, screening is more exacting, and most screeners are federally trained.) The FAA informed NEADS that AA 11 was on its way toward Washington; this message was sent after AA 11 had hit the Pentagon. The *9/11 Commission Report* stated that the protocol for communication between FAA and NORAD was unsuited for a crisis of this magnitude; there was no record of any exchange between them, or between FAA and DOD's National Military Command Center. The President kept losing phone contact with key officials. Before the crisis, excessive compartmentalization blocked exchange of information among FBI, NSA, CIA, CAA, and British Intelligence. Intelligence expert James Bamford believed that the Intelligence Community had accumulated enough real-time data to abort the 9/11 attacks, if the data had not been buried by FBI-CIA rivalry. According to Steven Brill, the CIA knew two suspected terrorists who had been in the US for months, but didn't pass that information on to the FBI. (Now, all security agencies circulate a single watch list for all security agencies.) US intelligence agencies had collected incriminating messages exchanged between the 9/11 hijackers and their superiors, but the agencies were so submerged in intercepts and other data that they didn't realize the messages' import: *Times*, 11/22/15 Zeynep Tufecci.

Conclusion – The US air control system is so immense and intricate that it will always be vulnerable to subversion, especially by cyber-attack. The one judicious decision during the whole imbroglio was the nationwide grounding of all aircraft. This order came at 09:42, 88 minutes after the first hijacking. If mass grounding had been ordered at 08:32, when the system became aware of the first hijacking, before AL 93 had taken off, the savings in life and property might have been well worth the national inconvenience.

The 9/11 disaster was a predictable consequence of America's outrageous Middle East policy. The *9/11 Commission Report* makes no allusion to the heavy responsibility that weighs on the architects of that policy.

Aftermath of the 9/11 Attacks – In Afghanistan, the Afghan Taliban rejected the Bush 43 demand that it deliver bin Ladin and company.

2001 – On 9/14/01, Congress authorized the use of military force against "terrorism". Bush 43 signed the bill on 9/18/01. Pronouncing the Geneva Convention inapplicable, Bush issued the grandiose National Security Directive 9, calling for the death of bin Ladin, the destruction of his organization, and the global elimination of terrorism!

2001 – On September 17, according to Lisa Hajjar (*MER*), Bush authorized the CIA to carry out secret detentions and interrogations of terrorist suspects in foreign countries. In Hajjar's words, the renditions of the Clinton era (abduction of suspects to the US for trial on criminal charges, as in the case of Adolph Eichmann, who was abducted from Argentina by Mossad, tried in Israel, and hanged 5/31/62) were ramped up to extraordinary renditions (as described by Scott Horton in *Harper's*, illegal detention and torture in secret prisons of the CIA or allied regimes). CIA "black sites" had been operating in countries known to use torture for their own purposes.

326

2001 – UNSC Resolution 1373 of 9/28/01 condemned terrorism.

2001 – On October 7 a new bin Ladin manifesto focused for the first time on the plight of the Palestinians (occupation) and the Iraqis (sanctions).

2001 – **War with the Taliban** – On 10/7/01, US and UK planes attacked sites in Afghanistan.

2001 – On 11/13/01, with US air support, a coalition headed by the CIA-funded Northern Alliance ousted the Afghan Taliban regime from Kabul. The defeated forces took refuge in Pakistan, as did most of Al Qa'idah's forces. Some Al Qa'idah leaders were thought to be hiding out in the Tora Bora caves, close to the Pakistan border, but the allied forces found the caves empty. Bin Ladin had taken refuge in Pakistan with his staff, except for Muhammad 'Atif, who was killed in Kabul 11/15/01.

2002 – In April Al Qa'idah admitted its responsibility for the attacks of 9/11, and rationalized the operation as an obligatory response to American support for apostate regimes in Saudi Arabia and other Muslim states. By this time, Al Qa'idah had operatives in 65 countries, headed by Afghanistan, Pakistan, Iran, Syria, Yemen, and Saudi Arabia, and possible sleeper cells in the United States. Under relentless pursuit by Washington, it had transferred much of its recruiting and publicity efforts to the Internet. The capture of major figures like KSM would be undercut by evidence of continuing recruitment, and the fact that bin Ladin and Zawahiri were still at large.

From 2003 to 2007, a number of bombings in several Western countries, plus Turkey, bore the fingerprints of Al Qa'idah – notably the Madrid train attacks that led to the withdrawal of the Spanish contingent in Iraq. Just before Secretary of State Powell visited Saudi Arabia in May 2003, 20 people – eight of them American civilians – died in suicide bombings of four compounds in Saudi Arabia. The subsequent bombing of a residential area for foreign residents (mainly Arab) in Riyadh killed seventeen.

2003 – On 8/29/03, two car bombs outside the hallowed Imam 'Ali Mosque in Najaf, Iraq, killed 95, including the Ayatallah Muhammad Baqir al Hakim, spiritual leader of the Supreme Council of the Islamic Revolution in Iraq.

327

2003 – Pakistan's ISI captured KSM in Rawalpindi, Pakistan, and turned him over to the US. He was waterboarded over 100 times by the CIA in at least five sessions, but was not broken.

2003 – The Iraqi branch of Al Qaʻidah sprang from an insurgency of Sunni soldiers angry about being cashiered by the "amateurish" and "vainglorious" viceroy, Paul Bremer: *Times*, 2/22/15, Maureen Dowd.

The Internet carried a video in which Zawahiri denounced the leaders of Egypt, Iraq, Jordan, and Saudi Arabia as traitors. According to Robert Leiken and Steven Brooke, his faction also despised moderate Islamists like Hamas, some Muslim Brothers, and the new Shiite leaders in Iraq – all for embracing elections instead of violence.

2004 – In October, bin Ladin publicized a videotape stating that Al Qaʻidah had attacked the WTC towers to avenge Israel's destruction of towers in Beirut in 1982. The 9/11 Commission Report already contained an exhaustive report on Al Qaʻidah as the presumed agency behind the 9/11 operation.

2006 – On 9/6/06, Bush 43 confirmed that the CIA had held terrorist suspects in secret prisons in many countries.

2007 – The surviving assets of Al Qaʻidah (Arabs, Paks, and Afghans) were thought to be hiding in North Waziristan – territory of a valued US ally, Pakistan. In September, when bin Ladin made his first video for TV in three years, the media reported that Al Qaʻidah's rebuilt organization in the Peshawar area of Pakistan was dominated by former members of Zawahiri's Egyptian Islamic Jihad, and directed by a council that reported to bin Ladin.

2007 – Al Qaʻidah claimed responsibility for the Najaf bombing of 8/29/03: *New York Sun*. Iraq hanged an Al Qaʻidah militant for complicity.

2008 – A *Times* article of May 2008 featured Abu Yahya al Libi, an Islamic scholar who had escaped from an American prison in Afghanistan in 2005, as a new member of the Al Qaʻidah high command.

2009 – In January, Al Qaʻidah in the Arabian Peninsula (AQAP) was formed by the merger of Al Qaʻidah's branches in Saudi Arabia and Yemen: *MEP*, Fall 2016, Farhad Rezaʻi. (Herein, subsequent references to AQAP are contained under "Saudi-Yemeni War".)

2009 – Al Qa'idah was filling vacancies (many of them caused by US Predator drones) by volunteers from across the Muslim World. It was still close to the Afghan Taliban. Al Qa'idah's new spokesman on the Internet was Adam Gadahn, an American convert to Islam. Al Qa'idah was supporting the anti-American operations of Mohamed Aideed in Somalia. It still provided guidance and inspiration to the Afghan Taliban.

2009 – December press reports: The CIA, US Special Forces, and units from the Blackwater contractors were perpetrating abductions and killings of Islamists in Afghanistan, Pakistan, Yemen, and Somalia: *Time*; *The Nation*, Jeremy Scahill.

2009 – On 12/30/09, at a US base near Khost, on the Afghan-Pak border, seven CIA operatives and an Afghan employee were killed by Jordanian Humam al Balawi, who attended a secret meeting wearing a suicide vest. Reportedly, he had been exempted from search on the strength of his promise to act as a mole against his militant associates.

2010-11 – The absence of reporting on Al Qa'idah during this period suggested that, with bin Ladin's whereabouts unknown, his organization may have gone dormant.

The Death of Usamah bin Ladin – On May 2, 2011, the CIA launched from Afghanistan an operation, covert at the start, by operatives from the US Navy Seals, the US Army Special Operations Command, and the CIA, who raided the Abbottabad hideout of Al Qa'idah leader Usamah bin Ladin, killed him, and buried his body at sea. Amnesty International questioned the killing of an unarmed man. Intelligence collected during the raid revealed that bin Ladin was still the active leader of Al Qa'idah: *FA*, September 2011, William McCants; US Government statements.

2011 – Ayman al Zawahiri, member of the Muslim Brotherhood at 14, former leader of the Egyptian Islamic Jihad, longtime Deputy Leader of Al Qa'idah, succeeded Usamah bin Ladin as leader of an etiolated Al Qa'idah.

2011 – In midyear, IS leader Abu Bakr al Baghdadi sent a party of AQI militants under Muhammad al Jawlani to Syria to set up another jihadist offshoot of Al Qa'idah central: *MEP*, Summer 2015, Stephan Rosiny; *Carnegie Endowment*.

2011 – Late in the year, several Islamist militias coalesced into the Islamic Movement of the Free Men of Syria (*Harakat Ahrar al Sham al Islamiyyah*) to intensify the rebellion against the Damascus regime. (In this text, the movement is identified as Free Men of Syria.) With 10-20,000 fighters, it was the second largest rebel unit in Syria after the Free Syrian Army (FSA) until the entry of the IS.

2012 – On 1/23/12 came the announcement of the formation of Guardian of the People of Syria (*Jabhat al Nusrah li Ahl al Sham*), a branch of Al Qa'idah. (Herein, this branch is identified as Nusrah.) Its goal was to convert Syria to an Islamist state. In December, Washington put Nusrah on its list of terrorist organizations.

2012 – In the summer and fall, Nusrah was reported to have carried out random bombings in Damascus and Aleppo.

2012 – In November, Nusrah was fighting Syrian troops in Idlib and Hamah Provinces in coordination with the secularist forces of the FSA. Nusrah was described as a disciplined, effective force of 6-10,000: *Washington Post*, *McClatchy*, 4/28/13. The Army of Islam (*Jaysh al Islam*), which was denying the IS direct access to the Damascus front, included Free Men of Syria, Nusrah, and the Syrian Legion (*Faylaq al Sham*). On 12/12/12, the Army of Islam killed 15 Alawite and Druze civilians: *MER*, Winter 2015.

2013 – Nusrah forces were also fighting in the Aleppo area, relying extensively on suicide bombers.

2013 – In August, Free Men of Syria was driven out of Raqqah by the IS, and moved its base to Idlib Province, where it would carry out a number of joint operations with Nusrah. For Syria, the UAE, Russia, Iran, and Egypt, Free Men of Syria was a terrorist organization.

2013 – On 8/13/13, Abu Bakr announced that the IS and Nusrah would merge. The next day Nusrah leader Muhammad al Jawlani denied Abu Bakr's assertion, stating that Nusrah was the representative in Syria of Al Qa'idah. Zawahiri corroborated that assertion.

2013 – The recovery of Al Qusayr (20 miles south of Homs) by Damascus forces, with the help of thousands of Iranian, Iraqi, and Hizballah forces, was a major victory for the Damascus regime.

2014 – Nusrah was a highly effective force: *FT*, 1/16/14. It was more hostile than the IS to the Damascus regime: Ahmed Hashim. The Islamist forces – the IS, Nusrah, Free Men of Syria, and splinter groups – had eclipsed the secularist FSA in the metrics of the Syrian civil war. Nusrah was directed by an Advisory Council (*Majlis al Shura*), whose strategy of moderation and cooperation with like-minded militias suggested that its long-run prospects were better than those of the IS.

2014 – On 2/2/14, Al Qa'idah formally cut its ties with ISI's successor, the Islamic State (IS), in reaction to the Islamic State's overt adoption of tactics of brutality, such as massacre of Shia militiamen, beheading of hostages, and killing a senior emissary from Al Qa'idah: *Times*, 2/4/14.

2014 – In the spring, Jawlani reportedly resisted an offer of financial support, posed by Qatar on behalf of itself and some other Sunni states, if Nusrah would transfer allegiance from Al Qa'idah to the bidders.

2014 – On 4/1/14, rebel forces captured the Nasib crossing between Syria and Jordan: *MER*, Winter 2015.

2014 – In May, there was heavy fighting in the Governorate of Dayr al Zawr between Nusrah and the IS. By July, a defeated Nusrah had decamped to western Syria, minus those militants who had defected to the IS. Six thousand had died in the Nusrah-IS conflict: *MEP*, Summer 2015, Stephan Rosiny.

2014 – Asad's forces were targeting secularist rebels. He had managed to induce the US to concentrate its air attacks against IS targets. However, the US campaign was inhibited by casuistic politics: The US was at war against the IS, but not against those IS forces that were in actual combat with Asad's forces – for fear of Sunni complaints that the US was helping to keep Asad in power: *LRB*, 11/5/15, Patrick Cockburn.

2014 – In July, the forces of Nusrah and Free Men of Syria were being pressed by the Damascus regime from the south and west, and by the IS from the east, to the point of demoralization. More and more Syrian rebels were defecting to the IS: *LRB*, 8/21/14, Patrick Cockburn.

2014 – In western Syria, the FSA was stalled, but Nusrah was gaining ground in Idlib Province – also in the Dar'a sector along the Jordan border: *FT*, 7/17/14.

2014 – On 9/9/14, an IS (?) bombing of a secret meeting almost wiped out the leadership of Free Men of Syria: *MEP*, Summer 2015, Rosiny; *Times*, 9/10/14.

2014 – Nusrah seized Syria's ghost town, Al Qunaytirah. Rebels – jihadist and secularist – had gained control of most of the Syrian side of the frontier with Israeli-controlled Golan: *FT*, 9/15/14.

2014 – Tripoli, Lebanon, had become the arena of a battle between Nusrah and an alliance of pro-Asad forces and the Lebanese Army, presumably co-opted by Hizballah: *Times*, 10/27/14. In reaction, Islamist militias fired rockets from Syria against Lebanese Army units near Arsal: *Times*, 10/28/14.

2014 – In October, Nusrah was attacking units of the FSA, its former ally, in the Province of Idlib.

2014 – In November, Nusrah defeated two US-backed secularist rebel groups in Idlib Province. Determined to make the ouster of Bashar al Asad their signal accomplishment, most Syrian rebels rejected the US campaign to persuade them to switch their focus to defeating the IS: *The Week*, 11/14/14. Claiming that the US Air Force was sparing the Asad regime, Syrian rebels had shut down their campaign against the IS. Four rebel militias had formed an alliance against Damascus: the IS, Al Qa'idah, Nusrah (affiliate of Al Qa'idah), and The Mujahidin Army.

2014 – In Syria, Nusrah was avoiding the brutish strategy chosen by the IS, in favor of building ties with other rebel militias, and marrying some of its fighters to Syrian women: *ISIS: Inside the Army of Terror*, Weiss/Hasan.

2014 – With Nusrah's capture of the Wadi al Dayf army base in Idlib Province, insurgents controlled an area that included parts of Homs and Aleppo governorates. No FSA force could operate in northwest Syria without Nusrah permission. In southern Syria, FSA forces were dependent on help from suicide bombers supplied by Nusrah.

2014 – In December, Nusrah controlled most of Idlib Province. The Syrian forces were holding on to Idlib City.

2015 – Nusrah had been described as a partnership of an anti-Asad faction and an anti-US faction: *Times*, 3/7/15.

2015 – With arms and financing from Saudi Arabia, Qatar, and Turkey, Nusrah forces had shouldered FSA forces aside and captured Idlib City from the forces of the Damascus regime. Nusrah's forces consisted of Syrians and a few non-Arabs. It was close to Free Men of Syria and loyal to Al Qa'idah: *FT*, 3/31/15; *Times*, 3/31/15.

2015 – In Pakistan, the leadership of Al Qa'idah was being weakened by losses to US drone strikes: *Times*, 4/25/15.

2015 – Qatar was still trying to buy out Nusrah. As insurance against defeat by the IS, Nusrah was clinging to Al Qa'idah: *Times*, March 2015, May 2015.

2015 – Nusrah claimed the Damascus bombings of March and May: *Times*, 5/17/15.

2015 – As the rebels advanced in Idlib Province, Alawite residents of the Damascus area were looking for permanent refuge on the Syrian coast: *Times*, 5/20/15.

2015 – Sources in Syrian-occupied Golan, including members of UNDOF (UN Disengagement Observer Force), were reporting incidents of Israeli support for Nusrah operations against the Damascus regime: air support, and hospitalization for wounded militiamen. As explained to the *Wall Street Journal* by retired Israeli General Amos Yadlin, the best outcome for Israel in Syria would be perpetual chaos. However, if the Alawite rulers were to be replaced, Sunnis would be better, in view of the likelihood that they would cut the supply line from Iran to Hizballah – Israel's direst enemy. If the replacements were Sunni rebels, the best option would be Nusrah, which had not echoed the extremist goals of the IS: *Electronic Intifadah*, 6/16/15, Rania Khalak.

2015 – Military pressure from Nusrah on the small Druze community on the Syrian side of the Syria-Golan border had enraged the Druzes of Israel, and posed a dilemma for Israel on how to respond: *FT*, 6/20/15. Nusrah was killing some of the Syrian Druze who refused to convert to Islam: *LRB*, 7/2/15.

2015 – In June and July, Nusrah was advancing in Idlib Province and the Damascus area. Nusrah was a faction of the Army of Islam or the

Army of Conquest (*Jaysh al Fath*) (?). On 6/10/15, in Qalb Lawzah in northern Idlib Province, a Tunisian commander with Nusrah moved to confiscate the house of a Druze suspected of loyalty to Damascus. In an exchange of fire, a villager and a Nusrah militiaman were killed. The Nusrah commander responded by killing some 20 Druze villagers of varying ages. His superiors ended the fighting. The leader of Al Nusrah, Abu Muhammad al Jawlani, had announced in May that Nusrah would not target Druze. However, there was a report from Idlib that several hundred Druze had been forced to convert to Sunni Islam: www.bbc.com, 6/11/15; *LRB*, 4/21/16.

2015 – Nusrah had announced its withdrawal from the anti-IS front in northern Syria on the grounds that the US and Turkey had agreed to set up a buffer zone in defense of Turkey, not in opposition to the regime in Damascus: *Times*, 8/11/15; *FT*, 8/11/15.

2015 – Nusrah was rounding up gays. Some of them had been killed: *Times*, 8/23/15.

2015 – Zawahiri had advised Nusrah to attack the forces of the Damascus regime, not those of the US, and to coordinate with other rebel organizations. Nusrah was operating overtly in Aleppo, underground in Damascus: *Times*, 2015.

2015 – On 8/13/15, Ayman al Zawahiri, leader of Al Qa'idah, broke a year of radio silence to pledge allegiance to the new leader of the Afghan Taliban, Mullah Akhtar Muhammad Mansur. Some had interpreted Zawahiri's long silence as evidence that he was inactive or dead: *Times*, 8/14/15.

2015 – After a two-year siege, on 9/9/15 Nusrah captured Damascus's last military base in Idlib Province, Abu Dabur: *WRMEA*, November 2015.

2015 – Columnist Gwynne Dyer reported force estimates for major active rebel organizations in Syria: The IS – 35 percent; Nusrah – 35 percent; Free Men of Syria – 20 percent. These three were Islamist. The secular militias were in eclipse: *Raleigh News and Observer*, 10/8/15. The secular militias were in tactical alliance with Nusrah. The most immediate threat to Damascus was the anti-IS Army of Conquest, which included Nusrah: *Times*, 10/13/15.

2015 – The DOD had announced that US and Afghan troops had raided Al Qa'idah training camps in southern Afghanistan. Al Qa'idah was reportedly reemerging under new leadership: *Times*, 10/21/15.

2015 – Nusrah was the leading component of the rebel Army of Conquest, whose possession of American TOW missiles had enabled them to wrest Idlib Province from the Damascus forces.

2015 – On 12/25/15, rockets fired by Russian or Damascus forces killed Muhammad Zahran 'Allush, leader of the Army of Islam based in the Damascus Ghutah (oasis), a major component of the Islamic Front. Several members of the Syrian Legion were killed in the same strike: Arun Lund, in "Syria Comment", Joshua Landis blog.

2015 – The only noteworthy part of Syria under control of secularist rebels was a strip along the Jordanian border. The Damascus regime held Damascus, Homs, and Hamah. Nusrah held patches of land between Damascus and Palmyra. The IS held Raqqah and Dayr al Zawr Province, and west almost to Aleppo. The Kurds held most of Syria along the Turkish border.

2016 – Many of the rebel militias in North Africa and the Sahara were affiliates of Al Qa'idah: *Times*, 1/2/16.

2016 – Ayman Zawahiri was operating from sanctuary in Pakistan: *Times*, 2/7/16, Carlotta Gall.

2016 – A Russian/Damascus offensive was driving FSA fighters north toward the western end of the Turkish border, which was closed. Kurdish forces were exploiting their retreat: *Times*, 2/16/16.

2016 – Nusrah was still entrenched in Idlib Province. It was gaining popularity among the secularist militias as they came to the conclusion that support from the US was failing them: *FT*, 2/26/16.

2016 – The new leader of the Army of Islam was Muhammad 'Allush, chief rebel negotiator at the Geneva Talks in April. The Army of Islam and the IS were bitter enemies: http://www.bbc.com/.

2016 – US and Russian hopes that the ceasefire of 2/27/16 would split the forces of the IS and Nusrah (both excluded from the ceasefire) from all other rebels in Syria were dashed when a joint Nusrah/FSA offensive pushed Damascus forces back in the Aleppo area, and Free Men of Syria led a rebel advance in Latakia Province: *AP*, 4/3/16.

335

2016 – The San Bernardino killers (12/2/15) were just two of the many lost souls seeking to strike a blow for Islam, but having no known affiliation with any Islamist organization. These two had been pushed over the edge by an article in *Inspire*, an Al Qaʻidah publication, that advocated violence to strike terror in the hearts of enemies of Allah: *NY*, 2/20/16.

2016 – Al Qaʻidah's militiamen, numbering 5-10,000, were all in Syria. Al Qaʻidah's leaders in Pakistan had sent a team to Syria to look into possibilities of expanding operations there: *Times*, 5/16/16.

2016 – On 7/28/16, Nusrah changed its name to Syrian Conquest Front (*Jabhat Fath al Sham*) – still under the leadership of Abu Muhammad al Jawlani. The presumed objective of the name change was to lend plausibility to Nusrah's claim that it had cut its ties with the "terrorist" Al Qaʻidah – thus becoming more eligible for alliance with more secular militias, if not for US arms supply. An attractive candidate for alliance was Free Men of Syria (20,000 militants): *FT*, 8/22/16. Al Qaʻidah had endorsed the name change: www.al-monitor.com.

2016 – The Syrian Conquest Front was the spearhead of rebel forces in northwest Syria: *FT*, 8/22/16.

2016 – The two most formidable anti-Asad militias were Islamist. Al Qaʻidah was controlling both: *The Week*, 9/2/16.

2016 – For the long run, Al Qaʻidah was more viable than the IS: *FT*, 9/3/16.

2016 – In September, under great pressure from ferocious Russian air attack and Damascus ground attack, the secularist rebels holding east Aleppo turned to the Islamist rebels for help: *Times*, 9/25/16, Max Fisher.

2016 – Asad's forces had suffered so much attrition that the odds on his survival in office were under 50 percent.

2016 – The AQAP was responsible for the *Charlie Hebdo* massacre. The future for the AQAP had rarely looked brighter: *The Week*: www.VOANews.com, Barbara Slavin.

2016 – The fighters of Nusrah were estimated to number 10,000: *Times*, 11/18/16.

The Muslim Brotherhood – In 1928, in reaction to Turkey's dissolution of the Caliphate, the break-up of the Ottoman Empire, and the shock of Kemalist secularism, Egyptian schoolteacher Hasan al Banna founded the Muslim Brotherhood (MB) as an organization dedicated to eliminating Western secularism and British imperialism; the UK had been de facto ruler of Egypt since 1882.

The theme of the MB was "Martyrdom for the sake of God". Its slogan was "Islam is the solution": *LRB*, 3/3/16. Its chapters spread steadily across the Arab World. Membership was by invitation, after the unwitting candidate had been studied for suitability: Citation from Hazem Kandil in Malise Ruthven's article in the *NYR*, 4/7/16.

The MB has not deployed a standing militia, but it has been an agent of insurrection in several Arab states. It was active in the Palestinian Revolt of 1936-9, and it sent volunteers to the Palestine-Israel war of 1948. On 12/28/48, an MB member assassinated Egyptian Prime Minister Mahmud Nuqrashi for outlawing the MB (on suspicion of conspiracy against the monarchy). Banna condemned Nuqrashi's killing, but on 2/12/49 Banna was assassinated by agents of British puppet King Faruq.

1952 – On July 23, a group of midlevel officers, headed by Colonel Jamal 'Abd al Nasir, disaffected by British rule and Egyptian impotence – as demonstrated in Israel's War of Independence – ousted Faruq and ended sixty years of humiliation by taking Egypt out of the British Empire.

1954 – On 10/26/54, an attempt by an MB member to assassinate Nasir (for signing the conciliatory Anglo-Egyptian Treaty of 1954) led to the mass jailing of Muslim Brothers, the torture of Banna's successor, Sayyid Qutb, and his hanging in 1966.

1964 – Syrian dictator Amin al Hafiz banned the Brotherhood, which staged an insurrection that was centered in Hamah. The regime responded by tank and artillery fire that killed 70 residents of the city and crushed the uprising, although damage done to a mosque caused a nationwide reaction that forced Hafiz to resign: *The Syrian Jihad*, Charles Lister.

1971 – The MB struck a deal with Sadat for recognition in return for the MB's renunciation of force, and its formation of a conventional political party: *MEP*, Fall 2015, Sherifa Zuhur/Marlyn Tadros.

1979 – Subsequent MB unrest in Syria culminated on 6/16/79 in an assault on the Aleppo Artillery School – in which 83 cadets died – and an armed insurgency against the regime of Hafiz al Asad.

1980 – In March, pitched battles broke out in Syria between Islamists and security forces. In April, the Syrian Army killed hundreds of insurgents and arrested 8000. The insurgency was still smoldering in Hamah. On 6/26/80, dictator Hafiz al Asad escaped an assassination attempt.

1980 – On 7/7/80, Syrian Law 49 made MB membership a capital offense. The Brotherhood was outraged on political and religious counts: As Alawites, the regime claimed to be Shiite; the Brotherhood challenged the claim; even if it was true, for hardline Sunnis, Shiites were infidels.

1981 – In April, the Syrian army arbitrarily extracted 400 males from Hamah and killed them. August, September, and November 1981 were interrupted by three vehicle-bombs, deployed by the Muslim Brothers, causing hundreds of deaths.

1981 – In Egypt, a member of the Egyptian Islamic Jihad assassinated Anwar al Sadat on 10/6/81 for his conclusion of a peace treaty with Israel: Zuhur/Tadros.

1982 – On 2/2/82, the MB took over the Syrian city of Hamah. Asad surrounded it with troops, which for 27 days bombarded its residents as if they were an invasion force – which in a cultural sense they were. Between 10,000 and 30,000 civilians were killed. The Syrian branch of the Brotherhood had been crushed. Its leadership went into exile. It was dormant for years thereafter.

1984 – The MB elected its first members of the Egyptian Parliament.

1990's – The Egyptian branch of the Brotherhood renounced violence – four months before the horrific Luxor massacre of 11/17/97.

2011 – On 1/25/11, the Arab Spring upheaval hit Egypt. The MB stayed off the streets.

2011 – In April, secular groups in Syria rose against the regime of Bashar al Asad, son and successor of Hafiz ad Asad.

2011 – In Yemen, Al Islah, a political party close to the MB, became the center of the pro-democracy opposition to the dictatorship: *MEP*, Spring 2016.

2012 – On 3/25/12, the latent Syrian branch of the Brotherhood called for conversion of the country to a modern democratic state: *Carnegie Endowment.*

2012 – In Egypt, the failure of the repressive Mubarak government to deal with Egypt's serious problems, domestic and foreign, had been fostering the steady Islamization of public opinion: *Current History.* In a troubled Egypt, the MB formed the Freedom and Justice Party. Muhammad Mursi of the Egyptian chapter of the Muslim Brotherhood was elected President. He took office 6/30/12. The military command retreated into the background. Many experts on Egypt concluded that the Brotherhood had staged a coup d'état by election, ending 60 years of army rule. However, the alacrity with which the army resumed control a year later suggested the equal likelihood that the high command had always been in control. Confident of its ultimate dominion, it had chosen to play it cool and give the inexperienced Mursi enough rope to hang himself.

2012 – To avoid divisive argument, the MB had maintained an anti-intellectual approach that discouraged scientific inquiry. Members were allowed to cling to beliefs that defied reason – e.g., success was a sign of God's approval: *NYR*, 4/7/16, Malise Ruthven.

2012 – While Mursi was President of Egypt, the police force (under Army control?) refused to function: *LRB*, 3/3/16, Carol Berger.

2012 – On 7/9/12, Egypt's Supreme Constitutional Court blocked Mursi's attempt to call back into session the Parliament that SCAF (the Supreme Command of the Armed Forces) had dissolved.

2012 – On 7/10/12, the MB staged a large demonstration in Cairo in Mursi's support.

2012 – Mursi's first cabinet was sworn in on 8/2/12.

2012 – On 8/12/12, Mursi purged the leadership of SCAF, replacing Muhammad Husayn Tantawi with 'Abd al Fattah al Sisi, promoted from chief of military intelligence. Apparently Mursi lacked the resources to vet Sisi, whose promotion turned out to be a huge mistake. Mursi issued a decree awarding himself full legislative powers, and assumed charge of drafting a new constitution.

2012 – On 9/11/12, Egyptian Salafis raided the US Embassy.

2012 – On 10/11/12, Mursi attempted to dismiss Egypt's Prosecutor General, an illegal action from which he soon backed down.

2012 – Mursi took the extreme step of issuing a decree intended to award himself unlimited powers. Qatar reportedly gave President Mursi four billion dollars: *MEP*, Fall 2015, Zuhur/Tadros.

2012 – Qatar was backing the MB in Gaza and the West Bank.

2013 – On 6/30/13, vast crowds assembled to demand Mursi's resignation.

2013 – On 7/3/13, Sisi unleashed the army, outlawed the MB, arrested Mursi, declared his ouster from the Presidency, suspended the Constitution, called for new Presidential and Parliamentary elections, named an interim President, and issued warrants for the arrest of hundreds of MB leaders: Internet citation from *The Guardian*.

2013 – After Mursi's ouster, the military regime declared the MB a terrorist organization: *NY*, 3/7/16, Peter Hessler.

2013 – The MB's persistent harassment of writers and other intellectuals had engendered so much hatred that they had welcomed Mursi's ouster and the attendant killings. This reaction dissipated after Sisi proved to be much more dictatorial than Mursi had been: *Nation*, 3/21/16, Ursula Lindsey.

2013 – On 8/14/13, Egyptian police raided two camps of Islamist protesters, at Al Nahda and Al Rab'ah Squares in Cairo. Over 1000 were killed at Al Rab'ah Camp: *Nation*, 3/21/16. The Nur Party (Salafi), a frequent opponent of the MB in the Egyptian Parliament, had favored Mursi's ouster, but switched to his support after the massacre of the camps: *NY*, 3/7/16.

2013 – On 6/15/13, Muhammad Mursi told a Syrian crowd he was committed to the liberation of Syria.

2013 – In disapproval of the massacres of protestors in Cairo on 8/14/13, the US suspended military aid payments to the Sisi regime: *Times*, 8/3/15.

2014 – On 3/5/14, Saudi Arabia, Bahrain, and the UAE withdrew their ambassadors from Qatar to protest its support for the Brotherhood: *MEP*, Spring 2015. On 3/7/14, Saudi Arabia's King 'Abdallah issued a decree equating the Muslim Brotherhood with organizations banned in Saudi Arabia, such as Hizballah, Al Qa'idah, the IS, and Nusrah. The MB released a statement that it never judges state governments. The MB had ties with Hamas, Qatar, Turkey, and the Syrian rebels: *McClatchy*, 3/7/14; *Times*, 3/7/14.

2014 – On 3/24/14, an Egyptian court sentenced 529 members of the MB to death. Over 16,000 had been jailed.

2014 – Egyptian officials were blaming Hamas (an offshoot of the MB) for the Palestinian deaths in the ongoing war with Israel. Some Egyptian media personalities were praising the Israeli campaign: *FT*, 7/21/14.

2014 – In the feud between the Sisi regime and the MB, Saudi Arabia and the UAE sided with Sisi. Qatar and Turkey supported the MB.

2014 – The Shia-Sunni confrontation in the Middle East intensified the rivalry for leadership of fundamentalist Sunni Islam among the Wahhabis, the MB, and the IS. Saudi Arabia was financing mosques, schools, and congenial governments (Lebanon and Egypt). The MB was competing in elections. The IS was fighting a territorial war: *FT*, 8/8/14, Gardner.

2014 – The deputy leader of the Jordan branch of the MB, Zaki Bani Rushayd, accused the UAE of being America's cop, and a cancer in the body of the Arab World. Jordan jailed him for harming its foreign relations. It did not ban the MB: *Times*, 12/8/14.

2014 – The Islah Party in Yemen was affiliated with the MB: *Current History*, December 2014, Wehrey.

2015 – The effectiveness of the anti-IS coalition had been impaired by the factional rift between Saudi Arabia (anti-MB) and Turkey and Qatar (both pro-MB): *FT*, 4/14/15.

2015 – Yusuf al Qaradawi, a Muslim scholar who had memorized the Qur'an at the age of ten, was born in Egypt but moved to the more fundamentalist climate of Qatar, where he had been on the faculty of Qatar University. Bitterly anti-Israel and anti-US imperialism, he was a highly influential spiritual leader of the MB. On 5/18/15, he was one of over a hundred members of the MB sentenced to death by the Sisi regime: "Discover the Networks" website; *Al 'Arabi al Jadid*.

2015 – In June, after some months of closure, Egypt reopened the crossing between Egypt and Gaza. Egypt may have been influenced by signs of IS recruiting in Gaza: *Times*.

2015 – The membership of the Egyptian MB was in ferment, as a youth movement condemned the leadership for a strategy that had resulted in the seizure of MB assets, the imprisonment of thousands, the death of over a thousand, and the issuance of hundreds of death sentences. The Sisi regime considered every Muslim Brother a terrorist. The names of the Egyptian MB's new executive committee, elected in February 2014, were secret: *Times*, 8/6/15.

2015 – In Saudi Arabia, the MB joined hardline clerics in urging the government to mount a jihad against the Russian intervention on the regime side in the Syrian civil war.

2015 – In the role of Syrian dissidents, the MB had been replaced by new contenders like Nusrah and Army of Syria. There was no overall command. Kurdish operations in Syria (YPG) were much better coordinated than Arab operations: *MER*, Winter 2015, Ali Nehme Hamdan. Turkey, the former backer of the Islamist faction, was now watching from the wings.

2015 – After Hizballah militiamen had cut all Homs's supply lines, the Damascus regime had recovered the city. In December, it recovered Hamah: *MER*, Winter 2015, Hamdan.

2016 – In Jordan, the MB had lost its party registration for failing to meet governmental requirements. Its headquarters had been closed. It seems King 'Abdallah II had decided regional alignments were convenient for Jordan to follow the anti-MB stance of Saudi Arabia, the UAE, and Egypt. However, The MB Society, a rival offshoot, was registered: *Times*, 4/14/16, 9/22/16.

2016 – The MB condemned the attack of 1/7/15 on the periodical *Charlie Hebdo*. The MB had declared itself nonviolent.

2016 – As President of Egypt, Mursi had left the blockade of Gaza untouched: *FA*, November 2016, Steven Cook.

2016 – Mursi was serving a life sentence. Egypt had overturned his death penalty: *Times*, 11/16/16.

Turkey – Democracy Manqué – The modern history of the Middle East has generally revolved around three centers of population: Iran; Egypt; and Anatolia – as augmented by the storied European metropolis of Byzantium/Constantinople/Istanbul. Today, they are the sites of the region's three keystone states: Iran – the link with Asia; Egypt – the link with Africa; and Turkey – the link with Europe and the US.

After World War I, Turkey was abruptly downgraded from the majesty of the Ottoman Empire to the degradation of a defeated, put-upon state. It was saved from the impositions of its European conquerors by the military and political genius of Mustafa "Kemal", whose benign dictatorship subjected his country to a uniquely radical course of secularization, modernization, and Westernization. In 1950, it began the long progression from military dictatorship to democracy by holding its first election for a new president.

Built-In Ambivalence – Since 1950, Turkish policymakers have had to function under the constraints of three frustrating polarities: between the subdued Kemalist (secularist) faction and the ascendant Islamist faction of Prime Minister Recep Erdogan and his AKP; between Turkish nationalism and the diehard Kurdish minority in the southeast; and between Turkey's treaty obligations to imperialistic NATO and Turkey's geopolitical obligations to Middle East liberation.

Turkey's role as a protégé of the US began in 1947, when Congress designated it under the Truman Doctrine a recipient of economic and military assistance to hold off the Russians – the Turks' nemesis for the past 400 years. Turkey contributed acclaimed troops to the Korean War (1950-3), joined NATO (North Atlantic Treaty Organization), and in 1955 became a founding member of CENTO (Central Treaty Organization) and "the bulwark of NATO's southeastern flank". By the

343

end of the century, Turkey was the cornerstone of the American security structure in the Persian Gulf.

After World War II, as the US escalated its intrusion into Middle East affairs, it clashed with Turkey's fundamental interest in ultimate regional autonomy, and Turkey's ongoing communal interest in cultivating Arab Sunnis – even those at war with the US and Turkey. A major issue has been US access to the Turkish Air Base at Incirlik, strategically located near Adana, 60 miles west of the Syrian border. The US Army Corps of Engineers built the base in the 1950's, and the Air Force has always based personnel there, but operational access to the base has been periodically cut off: in 1975, during the Turkish invasion of northern Cyprus; in 1993, from US attacks on Iraq; in 2014, from American air operations against the Islamic State (IS) – until 2015, when Turkey gave in to US pressure.

The Alevis – Turkey's 10-15 million Alevis have a shadowy Shiite history, but they don't make a big issue of it. They revere Shiite Imam 'Ali, but drink alcohol, worship on Thursday, and doubt the existence of heaven and hell. Men and women worship together. "Alevi" seems to correspond semantically with the Arabic term *'Alawi* (Alawite).

In some respects, Alevis are second-class citizens. Sunni imams are on salary from the state; Alevi places of worship have no official recognition. Alevis usually vote for the Kemalist RPP. A recent check revealed that, among Turkey's 81 provincial governors, there were no Alevis. In 1937-8, an Alevi uprising in Dersim Province was suppressed by the killing of thousands of rioters and the resettlement of thousands more. The Alevis were the victims of the "Maras Massacre" of 1978 and the "Corum Massacre" of 1980. More recently, the Alevis have confined their campaigns against inequality to demonstrations and occasional rioting, but they do not blend in to mainstream Islam – or are not allowed to.

Turkey and the EU – On 12/12/99, the European Union (EU) recognized Turkey as a "candidate for full membership," but the candidacy faced serious obstacles: The partition of Cyprus between an independent segment (aligned with Greece) and a segment under the de facto control of Turkey; since 1999, public opinion of the EU states had

344

seemed opposed; on 6/20/13, Germany blocked the start of new accession talks; France has lately opposed accession.

Under Prime Minister Erdogan, Ankara has sidelined its application for membership in the EU. Instead, Erdogan launched a campaign to rebuild the regional leadership role it lost in the declining years of the Ottoman Empire.

The Turkish Political Kaleidoscope Since 2007 – On 2/23/96, Turkey signed with Israel a military cooperation agreement under which Turkey bought arms from Israel, and the Israeli Air Force was allowed to stage training flights in Turkey: *JPS*, Fall 1997. In July 2007, the decisive victory of the moderate Islamist AKP (Justice and Development Party) over the military's RPP (Republican People's Party) boosted Turkey's slow climb toward democracy under the leadership of Recep Erdogan, who then was getting strong support from the Kurds. The Kemalists were wary of all Kurdish factions, but under Erdogan, Turkey and the KRG in northeastern Iraq moved toward strategic alliance, based mainly on the KRG's reliance on oil export independent of Iraq, and Turkey's interest in reducing its dependence on oil from Iran and Russia: *MEP*, Spring 2015.

2007 – Turkey was on good terms with Iran, Syria, and Hamas. Hamas principal Khalid Mish'al visited Turkey after the first Palestinian election: *Third World Quarterly* (online), Winter 2007.

2010 – On May 31, the right-wing administration in Jerusalem characteristically overreacted against the latest attempt at running the Israeli blockade – the "Gaza Freedom Flotilla" – by staging a boarding operation by commandos who, in the process of detaining six ships and their several hundred passengers (most of them unarmed), managed to kill nine Turks on the lead ship.

2010 – Enraged by Israel's assaults on Gaza in 2008 and on the Freedom Flotilla in 2010, Erdogan suspended Israeli training flights in Turkish airspace, downgraded Turkey's diplomatic representation in Tel Aviv, added a corvette to its navy (first naval ship built largely in Turkey), and, as the (pro-Israel) PKK escalated its operations against Turkish rule, responded in kind against the PKK.

345

2011 – In June, the AKP won its third consecutive general-election victory, while dozens of military officers were detained on a charge of plotting to seize power: *The World Almanac, 2014*. As the prospects of an invitation to Turkey to join the EU fell into decline, Erdogan turned his attention to promoting closer relations with its Asian neighbors, and in 2013 concluded a truce with PKK leader Abdullah Ocalan, then in prison. These initiatives ran afoul of the seismic shock that convulsed the Arab World in 2011 – "The Arab Spring".

2011 – Erdogan called on Bashar al Asad to step down. Turkey was allowing anti-Asad recruits to cross into Syria: *Times*, 6/30/16, Max Fisher.

2011 – On 8/23/11, a group of Syrian Army officers, angered by Asad's genocidal retaliation against peaceful public protests, met under Muslim Brotherhood sponsorship in Antalia, Turkey, and set up a Syrian National Council, to be based in Istanbul. In October, Turkey authorized another group of dissident Syrian officers to situate the headquarters of the Free Syrian Army (FSA) in Hatay Province: *LRB*, Summer 2015, review of *From Deep State to Islamic State*, Jean-Pierre Filiu.

2012 – By allowing passage of Islamic rebel traffic through Turkish territory, Erdogan revealed Turkey's basic interest in maintaining constructive relations with every major Sunni faction, however controversial: *MEP*, Spring 2015, Gunter.

2013 – In December, followers of Fethullah Gulen with positions in the Turkish police arrested dozens of government officials as corrupt: *Times*, 7/22/16, Mustafa Akyal. At that time, Gulen was an ally of Erdogan.

2014 – In June, the IS abducted 49 officials from the Turkish Consulate General in Mawsil. They were eventually released: *MEP*, Winter 2015, Kilic Kanat and Kadir Ustun.

2014 – On 7/18/14, Erdogan accused Israel of practicing systematic genocide against Gazans: *FT*, 7/21/14.

2014 – According to the *Financial Times* of June 28, an AKP spokesman said that Turkey was ready to deal with an independent Kurdish state. If this report was accurate, the spokesman must have had only the KRG in mind. Past indications suggest that super-nationalistic

Turkey would never tolerate cession of any Turkish territory. The report may have been a trial balloon lofted by Israel, since the same news item alleged that Avigdor Lieberman, Foreign Minister of Israel – the Kurds' closest ally – told John Kerry the emergence of a Kurdish state was a foregone conclusion. Turkey would welcome statehood for the KRG, insofar as it provided a buffer against the persistent turmoil in Iraq: *The Week*, 7/25/14.

2014 – The Alevi community in Turkey were wary of Recep Erdogan because he was a devout Sunni: *FT*, 7/28/14.

2014 – Turkey had rendered great service to the IS by keeping the 500-mile border with Syria open: *LRB*, 8/21/14, Patrick Cockburn.

2014 – On 8/28/14, Erdogan rose from Prime Minister to President of Turkey.

2014 – Turkey had saved many Syrian lives by setting up camps for 600,000 refugees. Neither the Turks nor their government wanted to join the fight in Syria.

2014 – In the fall, Erdogan wanted to swing the battle for Kobani in the IS's favor, but his alliance with the US wouldn't let him: *NYR*, 12/17/15, Bellaigue.

2014 – Turkey was not blocking the flow of jihadist recruits to Iraq and Syria, nor the IS exportation of oil worth a million dollars a day: *Times*, 9/14/14.

2014 – As an Islamist, Erdogan supported all Islamist adversaries of his bête noire, Asad: *The Week*: *Today's Zaman*, 9/26/14.

2014 – *Gumhuriyet* reported that Turkish intelligence was shipping a truckload of arms to its Turkmen allies in Syria. The government denied the report: *FT*, 1/28/16.

2014 – Erdogan had been moving Turkey away from secularism toward a mild form of Sunni sectarianism. This effort had been set back by the fall of Egypt's Mursi government in 2013, and the continuing failure of the Syrian rebels to oust Asad. Turkey was at odds with Saudi Arabia in the Egyptian case, and at odds with Iran in the Syrian case. Turkey and the IS had a common cause – checking Kurdish expansionism and overthrowing Asad: *FT*, 10/3/14, 10/8/14.

2014 – Turkey's NATO connection inclined it to let the US fly drones against the IS from Incirlik Air Base. The US wanted Turkey to sign up with the anti-IS coalition. Turkey wanted the US to create a buffer zone in northern Syria against Asad's air force: *Times*, 10/9/14.

2014 – Turkey resumed air strikes against PKK targets: *FT*, 10/15/14.

2014 – Erdogan had commented that the American air campaign against the IS was not for peace, but for oil: *FT*, 10/17/14. Erdogan was resisting US pressure to join the fight against the IS, since Asad was his real enemy: *Times*, 11/1/14.

2014 – The US pressured Erdogan to allow PKK units into the battle for Kobani, even though he saw the PKK as an enemy, and the IS and Nusrah as allies: *LRB*, 10/24/14, Patrick Cockburn.

2014 – The US was sending relief supplies worth three billion dollars into Syria via Turkey. Syrian refugees in Turkey now numbered 1.6 million: *NY*, 12/8/14, Robin Wright.

2014 – Erdogan was quoted as saying birth control is treason.

2015 – In January, the IS withdrew its forces from Kobani: *NYR*, 12/3/15, Jonathan Steele.

2015 – Erdogan, a member of the Muslim Brotherhood, was keeping the border open for the IS supply line into Syria: *CNN*, 2/5/15.

2015 – The political situation in Turkey was polarizing in two ways: 1) Erdogan's bid for increased presidential powers, against a large bloc of citizens who feared for Turkish democracy; 2) Turkey's ambivalence between making peace with PKK leader Abdullah Ocalan, and building subtle ties with Sunni enemies of the Kurds, such as the IS: *Times*, 3/22/15.

2015 – On March 31, two gunmen of the banned Revolutionary People's Liberation Party/Front took as hostage a Turkish prosecutor who had handled a case that had arisen during anti-government riots in 2013. All three were killed in a shoot-out with Turkish police. The hostage operation was seen as an attempt to disrupt the upcoming parliamentary elections: *BBC*, 3/31/15; *The Week*, 4/17/15.

2015 – The Erdogan government strongly opposed Kurdish autonomy in Syria: *MEP*, Spring 2015, Gunter.

2015 – Turkish investment in, and trade with, the KAR was creating a pattern of bypassing Baghdad: *MEP*, Spring 2015, Romano.

2015 – When Syrian planes attacked units of Nusrah in the spring, Turkey jammed the Syrian radio: *News and Observer*, 11/27/15, Gwynne Dyer.

2015 – According to a Turkish official, Turkey supported Free Men of Syria, but not Nusrah.

2015 – The US was pressing Turkey (Erdogan?) for permission to launch drones against the IS from Turkish territory. Turkey (Erdogan?) condemned the American campaign against the IS for being motivated by "oil greed": *FT*, 5/12/15.

2015 – Many Kurds believed the suicide bombing of a Kurdish cultural center had collusion from the Erdogan government, to justify its reaction to the bombing: arrest and aerial bombing of Kurds: *FT*, June 2015.

2015 – Turkey resented the American air support for the YPG's campaign to take 'Ayn al 'Arab and Tall Abyad. In a reference to the YPG, militia of the Syrian Kurdish party PYD, Erdogan said Turkey would never allow the creation of a state between Turkey and Syria: *Times*, 6/30/15; *The Week*, 6/26/15.

2015 – The Turk-PKK truce of Spring 2013 collapsed in July 2015 after Kurdish militants claimed they had killed 42 Turkish policemen – two by execution: *FT*, 8/17/15.

2015 – In June elections, the Kurdish HDP won its first cabinet positions, upsetting the parliamentary majority the AKP had held since 2002, and disrupting Erdogan's political strategy to the point that he switched from truce talks with Ocalan to renewed military operations against the PKK: *FT*, 7/27/15.

2015 – Under pressure from the US and the EU powers, Turkey claimed to have arrested 21 IS suspects, barred passage to Syria to 14,000 applicants, and deported 1500: *Times*, 7/11/15.

2015 – On 7/20/15, the IS massacred 33 Kurdish activists. The PKK blamed the Turkish government for the deaths and resumed its past attacks on Turkish police and soldiers. The first victims were two Turkish security officers. The Turkey-PKK ceasefire of 2013 ended.

Although Turkey had given in to US pressure to join the anti-IS coalition, it had carried out only one air strike against IS forces (in Syria), against scores of strikes against PKK forces in Iraq. The PKK controlled parts of several towns in southeastern Turkey. The PKK had escalated its anti-Turkey operations from raids on military outposts to assassinations and roadside bombings. Turkey responded by offensives against the PKK and the KAR: *FT*, 7/20/15, 8/27/15; *MEP*, Winter 2015, Kilic Kanat/Kadir Ustun.

2015 – In July, Turkey gave the US permission to stage air attacks on IS forces in north Syria from Incirlik: *Times*, 12/16/15.

2015 – The IS condemned the Turkish government as an apostate regime. Under US pressure, Turkey allowed the forces of the KRG and the FSA to defend Kobani against the IS attack, and supported the sectarian rebels that retook Manbij from the IS: *Times*, Mustafa Akyal.

2015 – On 7/20/15, a suicide bomb killed 33 Kurds in Suruc District of Turkey. The IS claimed it. Turkey retaliated against the IS in north Syria by air strikes: *MEP*, Winter 2015.

2015 – On 7/23/15, Turkey directed artillery and air attacks against IS installations, and yielded to the American request for permission to bomb the IS from Turkey: *FT*, 7/25/15; *Times*, 7/24/15.

2015 – On 7/24/15, Turkish and IS units clashed in Kilis, on the Turkey-Syria border. Turkey also resumed air strikes against the PKK: *Times*, 7/24/15; *FT*, 8/17/15; *NYR*, 12/17/15, Bellaigue.

2015 – Turkey and the US agreed to create a safe zone in northern Syria for the "moderate" rebels, for protection from the forces of the IS and Asad: *FT*, 7/27/15.

2015 – In July, the IS was defending the Euphrates Valley against the Kurds, while Turkey was bombing Kurdish installations in northern Iraq: *FT*, 7/28/15, Gardner.

2015 – The US and Turkey agreed to cooperate in cleansing IS forces from a 60-mile strip along the Turkish-Syrian border. The YPG (Kurdish) was not a party to the agreement. Turkey wanted to exclude forces of the Asad regime from the strip by making it a No-Fly Zone. The US wanted to ensure that, in the event of collapse of the Asad regime, Islamists did not take over. Turkey wanted to check Kurdish inroads into Syria: *Times*, 7/28/15.

2015 – The US began drone strikes against IS targets in northern Syria from Turkey: *FT*, 8/5/15.

2015 – There was a widespread view that Erdogan had switched his Kurdish policy from conciliation to militancy in the hope that the general public would be imbued with nationalistic sentiment that would benefit the AKP in a new election. Erdogan was reluctant to back the Kurds against the IS, out of fear of boosting the military power of the PKK. Turkey had released many IS detainees for lack of "incriminating evidence": *Times*, 8/6/15.

2015 – One reason that Erdogan followed US advice to join the fight against the IS was that it provided a pretext for bombing PKK targets in the KAR, and for setting up a zone in Syria that would be IS-free – and Kurd-free. US air strikes had enabled the Kurds to capture the key Syrian border areas of 'Ayn al 'Arab (Kobani), Tall Abyad, and Hasakah Province. The PKK was eager to link up in Syria with the 35,000 soldiers of its Syrian offshoot, the YPG, which controlled 11,000 square miles of Syria along the Turkish border: *Times*, 8/10/15.

2015 – With Aleppo and environs devastated, Turkey had provided a lifeline that was keeping the inhabitants alive and creating a zone of Turkish economic influence. Devaluation of the Syrian pound was forcing the conurbation to trade in dollars. The rebels who were running the city council wanted to switch officially to the dollar or the Turkish lira. Against the dollar, the lira had fallen 19 percent in 2015, but the pound had fallen 80 percent: *FT*, 8/19/15.

2015 – Although Turkey had caved to US pressure, as by launching air strikes against the IS, it was staging a much more robust campaign against the PKK. The strategy was meant to help Erdogan regain the governmental control he had lost with the electoral triumph of Selahattin Demirtas and his HDP in June, and to divert the PKK from its conflict with the IS. Erdogan considered the IS, or a less radical successor, as the likeliest candidate to replace the Alawite regime in Damascus with a Sunni regime of the MB stripe: *Times*, 8/27/15, 8/28/15.

2015 – Turkey lifted its ban on US air strikes against IS targets from Incirlik: *Times*, 8/27/15.

2015 – Turkey was tolerant of the IS, supportive of Nusrah: *Times*, 8/27/15.

2015 – Since fighting between the PKK and Turkish forces had resumed in July, 200 combatants had died, including 70 Turkish police and soldiers: *Times*, 9/7/15.

2015 – The PKK believed that Erdogan was cultivating the IS as a weapon against the Kurds: *The Week*, 9/25/15.

2015 – Russian planes were targeting forces of Free Men of Syria, which had Turkish support: *FT*, 10/6/15. Erdogan told the press the Russian air campaign in Syria was unacceptable to Turkey: *Times*, 10/6/15.

2015 – The death toll from the fighting between Turkey and the PKK was rising. Turkey was challenging the cooperation between the PYD and the American coalition against the IS: *FT*, 10/7/15.

2015 – Follow-up to the July 20 Suruc bombing: On 10/10/15 two suicide bombings of an HDP rally in Ankara killed 100, most of them Kurds. Most Turks blamed the IS. Hours later, the PKK announced a ceasefire with Turkish forces, and pledged to suspend offensive operations at least until the parliamentary election of 11/1/15: *Times*, 10/11/15; *NYR*, 12/17/15, Bellaigue; *FT*, 10/12/15, 10/20/15.

2015 – Observers feared that, after thirteen years of friction between Erdogan's AKP and the HDP, Turkey was dangerously polarized. In the past three years, the AKP had drifted toward support for Sunni supremacy in the region. Erdogan had started bidding for the vote of the MHP (Turkish Nationalist), which was nationalist and Turkish irredentist. The AKP and the IS shared a formidable common enemy in the Kurds. Another enemy of the AKP was the organization of Fethullah Gulen, which was combing the civil service for evidence of AKP corruption. In reaction, Erdogan had had thousands of prosecutors and police sacked. Journalists had been jailed. Two TV stations had been shut down. Turkey had complained to the US and Russia about their support for the Kurdish expansion into Syria. Erdogan's ultimate objective was a new constitution that provided for a powerful Presidency: *Times*, 10/11/15; *FT*, 10/14/15; *NYR*, 12/17/15.

2015 – On a visit to Turkey, German Chancellor Merkel renewed talk of Turkish accession to the EU, and suggested Turkey agree to hold Syrian refugees in its territory in return for 3,000,000,000 Euros: *FT*, 10/20/15, Gardner.

2015 – Rebels backed by Turkey had surrounded Aleppo. Turkey was using its professed campaign against the IS to camouflage its war against the Kurds: *NYR*, 10/22/15.

2015 – Turkey confirmed that it had machine-gunned two YPG units in northern Syria: *Times*, 10/28/15.

2015 – In the election of 11/1/15, Erdogan regained his solid majority in Parliament: *Times*, 11/1/15.

2015 – Turkey had been horrified by the YPG's sudden takeover of patches of northern Syria: *LRB*, 11/5/15, Cockburn.

2015 – Turkey was sending via Haifa exports it used to truck across Syria before the Syrian civil war: *LRB*, Thrall.

2015 – In November, the EU had agreed to pay Turkey three billion Euros to hold Syrian refugees in Turkey: *NYTM*, 12/20/15.

2015 – The fact that Turkey and the IS have a common enemy in the Kurds has had a regrettable consequence – Turkey's benign neglect of the reprehensible IS: *Times*, 11/8/15, Roger Cohen.

2015 – On 11/24/15, Turkish jets shot down a Russian SU-24 bomber. The pilots bailed out. One was hit by ground fire. Turkey claimed that after repeated warnings the plane had violated Turkish air space. Russia denied that claim. Putin called the action a stab in the back, demanded an apology, banned importation from Turkey of some fruits and vegetables, and stopped the lucrative traffic of tourists to Turkey. Turkey's primary concern may have been Russian fire on the Turkmen Brigade. Turkey viewed the defense of the 100,000 Turkmen residents of coastal Syria as a strategic obligation: *FT*, 11/25/15.

2015 – Turkey was limiting shipment into Kobani of supplies needed by its Kurdish administration to rebuild the ruined city: *Times*, 11/24/15.

2015 – Turkey called an emergency meeting of NATO, but did not invoke the security agreement: *Post*. On 11/29/15, Turkey issued a tentative apology to Russia.

2015 – Since Russia deployed SAM's in Syria, Turkey had stopped overflying it: *FT*, 12/10/15.

2015 – Turkish Prime Minister Davutoglu: Russian forces were charged with eliminating anti-Asad rebels from Latakia: *FT*, 12/10/15.

2015 – Iraq had protested Turkish training of Peshmerga militiamen at a camp near Mawsil: *FT*, 12/10/15.

2015 – Whereas Turkish forces had observed the IS-Kurdish battle for Kobani without intervening, Turkish planes were now striking Kurdish bases in Iraq. The US was backing the Kurds in their opposition to Turkey's interest in setting up a No-Fly Zone in northern Syria. The Kurds saw the project as a pretext for bombing Kurds. It was only under US pressure that in October Erdogan had allowed entry into Kobani of the Kurdish reinforcements that sealed the Kurdish victory there. To facilitate the Kurdish campaign against the IS, Asad had cannily helped them take Kobani by disengaging his own forces in northern Syria: *NYR*, 12/17/15, Bellaigue.

2015 – The Syrian rebellion was being fought by up to 500 autonomous militias, variously backed by a number of states. Gaziantep, Turkey, was a favored refuge for anti-regime Syrians. Many claimed to be planning the operations of rebel militias in Syria, but none could prove the claim: *MER*, Winter 2015.

2016 – Turkey was bombing YPG sites in Syria and fighting the PKK in Turkey, but it had excellent political relations with the KRG: *FT*, 2/26/16, citing Henri Barkey of the Wilson Center. (See previous report on Turkish training of Peshmerga troops.)

2016 – The Turkey-PKK War was turning many urban districts in southeast Turkey into bloody battlefields: *Times*, 1/1/16.

2016 – Turkey was supporting the Saudi air campaign in Yemen: *Times*, 1/9/16.

2016 – On 1/12/16, a bomb killed 33 in Istanbul.

2016 – Turkey considered its worst enemy to be the PKK, whose depredations were far more of a threat than the IS's suicide bombings: *FT*, 1/14/16.

2016 – In February 2016, Turkey fired on PYG forces north of Aleppo: *Times*, 2/16/16.

2016 – On 2/17/16, a car bomb destroyed a Turkish military vehicle in Ankara, killing 28. Turkey demanded that the YPG, ally of the US, be branded as terrorist for the bombing, which it admitted. US pressure was preventing Turkey from opening a front against the IS in Syria: *Times*, 2/17/16, 2/19/16, 3/14/16.

2016 – On 3/13/16, a bomb in Ankara killed 34, wounded 125: *Times*, 3/14/16. Turkey blamed the PKK: *Times*, 3/15/16.

2016 – Turkey was now at war against the PKK/YPG, the IS, and the Asad regime in Damascus: *FT*, 3/15/16.

2016 – Since December 2015, the Kurdistan Freedom Falcons (TAK) had claimed three bombings in Istanbul and Ankara. Observers theorized that the IS was hitting Kurdish targets in Turkey to escalate the Turkey-PKK war, and divert the PKK from action versus the IS: *FT*, 3/21/16.

2016 – On 3/25/16, bombings of two Istanbul synagogues killed 23 and wounded 300.

2016 – Since July 2015, over 1000 had died in the Kurd-Turkey fighting. Young Kurdish Turks were joining the PKK: *FT*, 4/1/16.

2016 – Russia had informed the UN Security Council that Turkey was supplying arms and military equipment to the IS: *AP*, 4/2/16.

2016 – A refugee camp in Turkey was populated with former Syrian military officers and their families: *NY*, 4/18/16.

2016 – In his isolation, Erdogan was wooing old adversaries Israel and Russia, condemning some democratic institutions, and cracking down on respected journalists: *Times*, 5/7/16.

2016 – Turkish Prime Minister Davutoglu was stepping down, lost in a power struggle with his former mentor: *Times*, 5/6/16.

2016 – In Erdogan's effort to acquire despotic powers, he had perverted Turkey's judicial and political systems: *FT*, 5/18/16, Marin Wolf.

2016 – Turkey was building a military base north of Mawsil, aimed at the Kurds: *FT*, 5/24/16.

2016 – A car bomb aimed at police in Istanbul on 6/7/16 killed eleven. Suspicion was likely to fall on the PKK: *FT*, 6/18/16.

2016 – On 6/26/16, after six years, Israel and Turkey agreed to resume full diplomatic relations: *Times*, 6/27/16.

2016 – Under international pressure, Turkey had stepped up action against the IS: *Times*, 6/28/16.

2016 – In dealing with political problems at home and abroad, Erdogan's primary objective is to create an executive Presidency: *FT*, 6/29/16. Erdogan had gone into alliance with Gulen in order to exploit Gulenists in the government in Erdogan's power struggle with the military. The Gulenist probe of corruption in Erdogan's inner circle sparked confrontation between Gulen and Erdogan.

2016 – Between June 2015 and June 2016, Turkey suffered at least fourteen bombings, causing some 270 deaths. Four had been attributed to the IS, eight to Kurdish organizations. Friction between Turkey and the IS had begun to escalate in March 2015. Most of the IS attacks had been directed against Kurdish targets. The IS had never claimed any attack in Turkey. Fighting between security forces and the PKK was reducing Kurdish towns to rubble. The Kurdistan Freedom Falcons were using car bombs against military targets: *Times*, 6/30/16; *FT*, 6/30/16.

2016 – In June, Erdogan apologized to Putin for the downing of the Russian bomber.

2016 – On June 15, upper-grade military officers attempted a coup against the Erdogan government. Erdogan managed to broadcast an appeal to the Turkish people to "take to the streets". They complied in great numbers, forcing the malefactors to capitulate. Erdogan accused the Gulen organization, which had thousands of followers in the military and the civil service, of masterminding the venture. When Erdogan and Gulen had split in 2007, Gulen had been granted permanent residence in the US. He settled in the Poconos, and continued his effort to build a world-wide network of schools, and infiltrate the Turkish government, in the service of Islam. Gulen, born in 1938, was a reclusive cleric who, after 20 years in the US, spoke little English, but was widely revered in Turkey as the Mahdi. Gulen claimed to have meetings with the Prophet: *Times*, 7/22/16, Mustafa Akyal. There had been complaints from the military that Erdogan was undermining Ataturk's secular society. Over 100 officers had participated in the uprising, but the generals stayed loyal to Erdogan. Lives lost numbered 265. F-16's bombed the Parliament building. The police played a central role in putting the rebels down: *Times*, 7/17/16; *FT*, 7/18/16; *NY*, 10/17/16, Dexter Filkins.

2016 – Erdogan was empowering the Islamist underclass, but he was getting more autocratic, his coterie was getting richer, and his new residence was colossal: *Times*, 5/7/16, 7/12/16, Sabrina Tavernese.

2016 – Turkey suspended US anti-IS flights from Incirlik. The alternative for the DOD was long bombing flights from the Gulf: *Times*, 7/18/16.

2016 – Putin offered to help Turkey: *Times*.

2016 – Turkey had not yet sealed its border with Syria from passage by followers of the IS: *The Week*, 7/15/16.

2016 – Erdogan launched an operation to place 50,000 adversaries under detention. An editorial in the *Times* charged him with "indiscriminate retribution": *Times*, 7/20/16; *FT*, 7/22/16.

2016 – Turkey's fence-mending with Israel and Russia was evidence that Erdogan had backed away from his effort to win over successor states of the Ottoman Empire: *FT*, 7/26/16, Gardner.

2016 – A purge of 3000 officers had caused the implosion of the armed forces: *FT*, 8/3/16.

2016 – 70,000 Turkish officers and officials, including 150 generals and 3,000 from the judiciary, had been dismissed. Erdogan valued his drive for Presidential power more than Turkish democracy: *FT*, 8/7/16.

2016 – Reacting to Western leaders' failure to denounce the coup attempt, and their charges that he was violating human rights, Erdogan made a visit to Russia: *The Week*, 8/19/16.

2016 – On 8/24/16, Turkey sent into Syria planes, 30 tanks, and 5000 militiamen that enabled the FSA to take Jarabulus, closing the IS's last remaining access route to Turkey. The IS put up little resistance: *Times*, 8/24/16; *AP*, 9/4/16.

357

2016 – The evidence indicates that Gulenist officers were behind the coup attempt: *FT*, 8/26/15, Gardner.

2016 – The Turkish foray against Jarabulus was meant to push the Kurds back east of the Euphrates. The foray had US support: *Times*, 8/26/16.

2016 – Until its foray into Syria in alliance with Turkish forces, the FSA had had little battlefield success: *FT*, 9/7/16.

2016 – Washington had brushed off Erdogan's request for approval of a No-Fly Zone in northern Syria: *Times*, 9/8/16.

2016 – A small US Special Operations team had entered Syria to support Turkish military intervention: *AP*, 9/17/16.

2016 – At a conference in Istanbul, Putin reopened a pipeline that, before suspension, had supplied natural gas to Turkey and Greece: *Times*, 10/11/16.

2016 – Erdogan was demanding Iraqi permission for Turkish troops to take part in the battle for Mawsil. The objective would be to keep the PKK forces out, and protect Turkmens and Sunni Arabs. Baghdad already resented Turkey's forward base at Bashiqa, and its training of Peshmerga and Sunni Arab forces. Prime Minister 'Abadi wanted to reserve the drive against Mawsil to Iraqi Sunnis and the Peshmerga. He had stated that any Turkish intervention in the battle for Mawsil would be met with force: *Times*, 10/24/16, Michael Gordon/Tim Arango.

2016 – Erdogan had arrested many leaders of the HDP, the main Kurdish party in Turkey: *Times*, 11/8/16.

2016 – The Kurdistan Freedom Falcons claimed two bombings that killed 38 in Istanbul: *AP*, 12/12/16.

2016 – The Nineveh Guards had been founded by Athil al Nujayfi (Al Hadbah Party), exiled governor of Nineveh Province in Iraq. Numbering 2500, they had been trained by Turkey: *FT*, 11/8/16.

2016 – Russia and Turkey reached a compromise whereby Turkey could move against the YPG, and Turkey would be more tolerant of Russian policy, especially in favor of Russia's support for Turkey's enemy, Bashar al Asad: *Times*, 2/10/17.

Revisionists (Opportunistic, Restricted by Circumstances)

In the regional context, Sunnis outnumber Shiites 250,000,000 to 140,000,000. In normal circumstances, this imbalance would favor a geographic division between Shiite hegemony in Iran and southern Iraq, and Sunni hegemony elsewhere in the region – as was roughly the case during the coexistence of the Safavid and Ottoman Empires. As of 2016, circumstances were abnormal. Egypt, Turkey, and Arabia had been hamstrung by their own problems, leaving 30 million Sunnis on their own against 100 million Shiites. The Shiites – and the YPG Kurds – had been waging a campaign of opportunism. They could not expect to rule the whole region, but they had seized the moment to expand their sphere of influence into areas long controlled by Sunni regimes. If and when Turkey, Egypt, and Arabia were freed from their current preoccupations, regional hegemony would be likely to correspond with the overall sectarian division.

Iran – Since the death of the Prophet Muhammad in 632 CE, Islam has been haunted by a dynastic/doctrinal dispute between the Sunnis and the Shiites. To the Sunni *Shahadah*, "There is no God but God; Muhammad is the Prophet of God." Shiites add "'Ali, Muhammad's companion, is the vicar of God." For Shiites, an Imam is infallible. The Sunnis recognize the first four Caliphs – Abu Bakr, 'Umar I, 'Uthman, and 'Ali – but not 'Ali's descendants. The Shiites revere 'Ali, the Prophet's son-in-law, as the only true successor to the Prophet. 'Uthman and 'Ali were murdered. Mu'awiyah, a kinsman of 'Uthman, and governor of Syria, imposed himself as 'Ali's successor. Sunnis accept that succession. Shiites hold that the true succession went from 'Ali to his son Hasan, and then to his second son Husayn, whose fight for the Caliphate ended in his death in Karbala', Iraq, in 680. For Shiites, 680 CE is a crucial date: Sandra Mackey.

From these events evolved the Shiite faith – conceived in the mystique of martyrdom. The faith first acquired political gravitas in 1502, when the Safavid rulers of Iran proclaimed it the state religion, and faith and nationalism joined language as the factors that have sharply distinguished Iran from its neighbors, with the exception of Shiite Afghanistan and, since 2010, the de facto Shiite state of South Iraq.

Over the centuries, the dynastic and doctrinal disputes between Sunnis and Shiites reinforced both communities. Analysts speculate that Shiite doctrine may be influencing the political strategies of the Twelver Shiites who rule the Iranian theocracy. Some Muslims believe that a Mahdi will appear on Earth to establish a reign of righteousness for the few more years until the world ends. Many Sunnis have doubts, based on the paucity of definitive references to a Mahdi in the *Hadith* (sayings of the Prophet), and the total absence of mention in the Qur'an: *EB*: 7:697. A central tenet of Twelver Shiism is that the line of legitimate caliphs ended with the twelfth, Muhammad al Mahdi, who in 874, as a child, was supernaturally occulted to an unknown place, and will return – possibly very soon – to win the Battle of Armageddon against the forces of Satan and establish a righteous Islamic state for the few years until the Second Coming of Jesus, the Messiah, and the advent of *Yawm al Qiyamah* – Resurrection Day.

From American Patronage to Dogmatic Theocracy – The Shah was an incompetent leader who survived by dint of Savak's torture and/or killing of dissidents, plus British/American machination. In 1953, they saved the Shah from the reformers by neutralizing the elected Prime Minister, Mohammed Mossadeq. They couldn't save the Shah from the Shiite clerics in 1979. The clerics brought Ayatollah Rohallah Khomeini back from Europe to be Chief of State. He appropriated the title of Imam – a potent honorific for Shiites.

1979 – On April 1, Khomeini proclaimed Iran an Islamic Republic. Its constitution was based on the Koranic pronouncement of an absolute God, and it confirmed the laws of Islam as the base of a regime headed by a Supreme Leader who derived his authority from the word of God: R. K. Ramazani. Khomeini sold the Iranians on a radical break with the monarchy's separation of religion and state. He reconfirmed a doctrine that had long been incorporated into Shiite theology – the Zoroastrian (pre-Islamic) thesis of a world eternally divided between pure believers and decadent infidels.

In the intricate architecture of the theocracy's political infrastructure, the Supreme Leader appoints the members of the Expediency Council, which is meant to be the overall arbiter of the regime: *Atlantic*, July/August 2017, Alex Vatanka.

Foreign Policy – Theocracy Style – In ancient times, Persian troops marched twice into the western reaches of the Middle East. From 550 to 330 BCE, the Persian Empire often held sway in Mesopotamia, Anatolia, the Levant, Egypt, and even Libya and Thrace. In the early 600's, the Sassanian dynasty ruled most of Anatolia, plus the Levant, Egypt, and Yemen. The Safavid dynasty controlled Mesopotamia in the early 1600's, and Bahrain from 1602 to 1783. Khomeini came to power with ambitious foreign objectives: reconciliation of the Shiites and Sunnis in a pan-Islamic community, elimination of the Jewish state, and elimination of the American military presence. PLO leader Yasir 'Arafat made an early visit and was offered the Israeli embassy building as his Tehran office. Khomeini anticipated taking the lead of the activist Islamist movement that shared these objectives.

1980-81 – Abolhassan Bani-sadr was President of Iran.

1981 – Mohammed-Ali Rajai was President of Iran.

1981-89 – Ali Khamenei was President of Iran.

1982 – Khomeini responded rapidly and effectively to the Israeli invasion of Lebanon. He assigned the response to his own security force, the Islamic Revolutionary Guard Corps (IRGC), which operated through several subsidiaries, including the Quds Force. The Quds Force set up in the Biqa' a training program for Lebanese Shiite activists. The product was the redoubtable *Hizballah* (Party of God).

1980-8 – The ruinous eight-year war with Iraq brought home to the Iranians the essentiality of their permanent subjugation of Iraq. It also forced them to realize that they could not afford the luxuries of total support for the secularist Palestinians, or absolute hostility to Israel. When 'Arafat requested permission to amend his image in America by bringing the Embassy hostages home, Khomeini saw need to hold onto them for Iranian exploitation. When the Iraqi invasion pointed up Iran's

361

desperate shortage of high-tech weapons, the Israelis – recipients of inside information from Iran's Jewish community, and confident Iraq couldn't win – were on the spot to ship arms to Iran, and to bring the Pentagon into the procedure. Also, Iran and Israel shared a visceral horror of Arab Nationalism and Sunni expansionism: *WRMEA*, April 1988, Bahram Alavi (pseudonym).

1980's – Tension was building between two opposing Iranian camps – the moderates, who saw advantage in promoting ties with other states, and the hardliners, who were suspicious of exposure to deleterious foreign influence. Meanwhile, the commoners were developing a vibrant subculture that was engrossed by impious presentations on inconspicuous satellite TV dishes. Khomeini had two rival protégés – Akbar Hashami Rafsanjani, a moderate, and Ali Hosseini Khamenei, a hardliner. Rafsanjani let Khamenei succeed Khomeini as Supreme Leader in 1989. Two of the next four Presidents were Rafsanjani and his ally, Hassan Rouhani: *LRB*, 2/4/16, Hilterman: Razoux.

1989 – Death of Khomeini. Ayatollah Ali Khamenei succeeded him as Supreme Leader.

1989-97 – Akbar Rafsanjani was President of Iran.

1990's – In sharp contrast with practice in Iran's arch-rival, Saudi Arabia, Iranian women could drive cars, hold jobs, vote, and win seats in Parliament. Reform was still not moving fast enough for the students, who were gaining political impact.

1997-2005 – Mohammed Khatami was President of Iran.

2003 – Early in the year, several leaders of Iraq's exile community went to Iran to consult with Muhammad Baqir al Hakim, leader of Iraq's SCIRI Party (later ISCI), on how to exploit the upcoming American invasion of Iraq. US intelligence initiated cooperation with agents sent into Iraq by Iran. The agents included members of SCIRI's militia, the Badr Brigade.

2003-10 – The Quds Force reportedly conducted a clandestine campaign against US soldiers in Iraq, and supplied arms and financing to the Asad regime in Damascus. According to David Ignatius, Iran's top foreign policy strategist was Brigadier General Qassem Suleimani, commander of the Quds Force. Under his shrewd direction, Iran had practiced extreme caution toward the imponderable situation in Iraq, allowing for the Iraqis' opposition to theocracy and their wariness of growing Iranian power, and hedging its bets by collaborating with all major Shiite factions and even on occasion with Sunni factions. Iran's vision of Iraq is a state that is orderly and unified (to block the emergence of a Kurdish state) but not so strong as to challenge the new Iranian leadership in the Gulf area. Press reports of 2008 suggested that Iran would favor ISCI's reputed plan for a federalized Iraq in which the nine southern provinces would be a semi-autonomous unit.

2005-13 – Mahmoud Ahmadinejad was President of Iran.

2005 – Iran was troubled by corruption among the clergy, and by a distressed economy, two-thirds of which was encumbered by state ownership: Bellaigue.

2005 – Members of the Badr Brigade had preempted top positions in the administration of Iraq's Al Basrah Province: *Times*.

2006 – The Quds Force was reportedly providing arms and financing to the Shiite wing of the Iraqi resistance to the American invasion. The main beneficiary was Muqtada Sadr's Mahdi Army (JAM).

2007 – UNSC Resolution 1747, sponsored by Washington, banned further financial aid to the government of Iran.

2007 – Iran was a quasi-democracy that was executing more people than any other country but China.

2007 – In January, during a failed attempt to seize two high-ranking Iranian guests of Jalal Talabani in Arbil, US forces mistakenly abducted five Iranian officials of the Iran-KRG liaison office: Patrick Cockburn.

2007 – The economies of Iran and Iraq were moving toward integration. Iraq desperately needed help in rebuilding its infrastructure, ravaged by American sanctions and two American invasions. Iran was scheduled to build two small power plants in Iraq. Many Iraqis were going to Iran for medical treatment: *Times*, March 2007.

2007 – Iran's main goal in the Caucasus was to prevent the emergence of oil-rich Azerbaijan as a powerful state: *MEP*, Summer 2007.

2008 – Iran was not self-sufficient in gasoline or food: *MEP*, Barbara Baktiari.

2008 – Inflation in Iran had risen to 25 percent, because of: 1) state monopoly of the economy; 2) American-imposed sanctions, which had forced Iran to turn to China for spare parts: *Washington Post Weekly*.

2008 – The regime had been trying to keep up Khomeini's tradition of downplaying Iran's Shiite identity in favor of projecting support for pan-Islamism. This effort was overtaken by the rise of sectarianism in Iraq, and the consequent partisan requirement that Iran lead the Shiite bloc in the momentous battle between Shiites and Sunnis for hegemony in the Middle East: *MEP*, Fall 2015.

2008 – In March, bloody clashes in Karbala' between the JAM and the Badr Brigade during pilgrimage season were a collective Shiite embarrassment. Qassem Suleimani, Commander of the Quds Force, and Iran's proconsul in Iraq, upstaged Iraqi Prime Minister Maliki by brokering a truce.

2008 – Encirclement of Iran by US military bases, and harassment of Iran by US-inspired UN sanctions, had forced Tehran to cultivate ties with Pakistan, India, and China. The Iranian leadership saw a strong Iranian state as essential to the ascendancy of a pan-Islamic *Ummah* (nation): Tomgram of 5/1/08 (www.tomdispatch.com), Pepe Escobar.

2008 – In a speech on the Israeli-Palestinian conflict, Ahmadinejad had said "The regime occupying Jerusalem must vanish from the pages of time.": Escobar.

2009 – Iran was emerging as the major beneficiary of the American invasion of Iraq. Iran was the first country to recognize the new government in Baghdad: *FA*, July 2009, Mohsen Milani. Iraq's post-invasion leadership included ISCI, Al Da'wah, and Jalal Talabani – all long-time allies of Iran.

2013 – On 6/14/13, in a first-round landslide, liberal Hassan Rouhani was elected to replace hardliner President Ahmadinejad.

2014 – Since 1/1/14, rebel pressure on the forces of the Damascus regime had forced Iran to contribute 20 billion dollars to Damascus when Iran was afflicted by forty-dollar oil: *FT* 5/13/15, 7/21/15.

2014 – In June, after IS forces overran northwestern Iraq, Iran sent Shiite militiamen into Iraq. Their violent sectarian tactics alienated most Iraqi Sunnis: *FT*, 5/23/15.

2014 – For years, Israel had been trying to sabotage Iran's nuclear program. One tactic was to kill Iran's nuclear scientists. Since 2007, Israeli agents had killed seven – one ballistic-missile expert, one cybernetic expert, five nuclear experts. The preferred method was for a motorcyclist, passing a vehicle in slow traffic, to arm it with a magnetic bomb. Some of the agents were members of the *Mujahedeen-e Khalq* (MEK), an organization of Iranian dissidents that was founded in the 1960's by Iranian Massoud Rajavi, and had a long record of subversion in Iran under the monarchy and the theocracy. The MEK denied the charge that it had collaborated in the murder of Iranian scientists. On 3/2/14, Obama pressed Israel to desist from that practice.

2014 – Hamas was obliged by its Sunni Islamist identity to endorse the Islamist rebel groups in Iraq and Syria, but the endorsement cost it the 240-million-dollar subsidy it had been receiving from Iran: (Raleigh) *News and Observer*, 7/15/14, Gwynne Dyer.

2014 – An American official who had served in Iraq said that, through Quds Commander Major General Qassem Suleimani, Khamenei was ruling Iraq, Syria, Lebanon, and Yemen. Iran was supplying Iraq with military equipment, flying drones from a Baghdad airfield, and bombing sites of adversaries of the Baghdad regime: *Times*, 12/4/14.

2015 – On 3/2/15, a joint Iraqi-Iranian offensive recaptured Tikrit from the Islamic State. Now conspicuous in Iraq's Sunni Triangle were replicas of the flag of the Sunnis' nemesis, the Badr Organization, and photographs of Iran's Supreme Leader, Khamenei: *Times*, 3/6/15.

2015 – There was evidence that officers of the Iranian Al Quds were fighting alongside Asad's forces. However, mobilizing Shiite fighters against Sunnis was like trying to douse a fire with gasoline: *NY*, 4/6/15, Steve Coll.

2015 – Iran was much more culturally advanced than most of the eastern Arab World. The three arms of power of the Khamenei regime were the bazaar, the clergy, and the armed forces. In the era of President Ahmadinejad (2005-13), hardliners dominated Iranian foreign policy. Under the subsequent president, Hassan Rouhani, Iranian foreign policy had swung back to the center between revolution and reform.

Khomeini's fifteen grandchildren supported the reformers: *NY*, 7/27/15, Robin Wright. Whereas Rouhani had been elected by the youth vote, most of the 86 members of the Assembly of Religious Experts were hardliners: *FT*, 12/17/15, Roula Khalaf. The Assembly, elected by the people, determines who is Iran's Supreme Leader: Escobar.

2015 – On 7/14/15, Iran and a coalition of the US and European powers signed the Joint Comprehensive Plan of Action – a precarious agreement on Iran's nuclear program. The US and Israel favored preservation of Israel's Middle East monopoly of nuclear weaponry. Iran had apparently concluded from analysis of American strategy that Washington had no compunctions in invading a country (Iraq) that did not have nuclear weapons, but avoided hostilities with countries (North Korea) that did: Ergo, Iran had to have a nuclear weapon to eliminate the risk of an American invasion. The issue was not negotiable. Israel wanted to preempt by taking on the dubious task of destroying facilities hidden under distances of solid rock. Obama persuaded hothead Netanyahu to hold off, while Western powers tried the inferior but time-tested strategy of postponement. The Treaty sets a term of ten years between Adoption Day (10/18/15) and Termination Day. In those ten years, circumstances might well change.

2015 – The sanctions on Iran would be lifted, but not the arms embargo. Israel and the Gulf shaykhdoms remained opposed to the agreement: *Times*, 7/15/15.

2015 – Iran's major military decisions for Syria were being made by General Qassem Suleimani. He commanded Shiite militiamen from Iran, Iraq, Afghanistan, and Lebanon: *NYR*, 10/22/15. Iran's Revolutionary Guard Corps (to which Suleimani was attached) had a wing of Iraqi Shiite torture squads: *FT*, 7/23/15.

2015 – On 10/7/15, a ranking Iranian general, Hossein Hamedani, was killed by IS forces (?) near Dabiq in Aleppo Province, Syria: *Times*, 10/10/15; *FT*, 10/10/15. Dabiq (rhymes with syllabic) had past and future significance for Muslims. It was cited in the *Hadith*. It was the site of the historic defeat of the Egyptian Mamelukes by the Ottomans at Marj Dabiq in 1516. In Islamic lore, it might be the site of an epic battle in which Muslim defenders were destined to defeat invading Christians, in the opening phase of the End of the World. *Dabiq* was the Arabic name of an English-language monthly published by the IS.

2015 – By September, Iran had established critical influence over the Baghdad regime, while staving off collapse of the Damascus regime. At this point, Damascus got a new lease on life from the surprise entry of Russian aircraft.

2015 – As the fighting in Iraq and Syria had coalesced along ethnic lines, Iran had had to sideline Khomeini's vision of a pan-Islamic regime in Iran and assume leadership of a coalition of Shiite forces in Iraq, Syria, and Lebanon, and support for more distant Shiite communities in Bahrain, Yemen, and Saudi Arabia: *MEP*, Fall 2015.

2015 – Iran was more interested in organizing Alawites into a Shiite militia than in trying, like Russia, to prop up the Asad regime in Damascus: *FT*, 11/21/15.

2015 – Hardliner Khamenei had allowed moderate Rouhani to sign the nuclear agreement, for fear of a popular uprising. The agreement had been opposed by the armed forces, the Revolutionary Guard Corps, and the Guardian Council: *The Week*, 12/11/15.

2015 – Iran was relying on its Fordow underground nuclear installation as the best defense against IS or Israeli attack. Secretary of State Kerry had made public mention of a putative American countermeasure, the Massive Ordnance Penetrator: *NY*, 12/21-28/15, David Remnick.

2015 – In the course of 2015, Iran executed nearly 1000 convicted criminals: *FT*, 1/5/16.

2016 – On 1/16/16, Iran's compliance with the international agreement on its nuclear industry was endorsed by the IAEA, and went into effect.

2016 – The execution of Shiite Shaykh Nimr al Nimr in Saudi Arabia precipitated anti-Saudi riots in Iran, and the burning of the Saudi Embassy: *FT*, 4/5/16. Saudi Arabia expelled Iranian diplomats: *The Week*. Supreme Leader Khamenei and Foreign Minister Zarif condemned the Embassy attack: *Times*, 1/20/16.

2016 – The Revolutionary Guard Corps was suspected in a cyber-attack of November 2015: *FT*, 1/13/16.

2016 – In recognition of Iran's signing of the nuclear agreement of 7/14/15, the West ended anti-Iran sanctions on 1/16/16. The IAEA would monitor Iranian nuclear operations: *Washington Post*, 1/16/16.

2016 – On 1/18/16, Iran "stormed back" into the global oil market, ordering a sharp increase in production. Brent crude, the international benchmark, fell below $28 a barrel for the first time since 2003: *FT*, 1/19/16.

2016 – As the sanctions had escalated, Iran had dismantled much of its nuclear project, and shipped out 95 percent of its nuclear fuel: *Times*, 1/20/16.

2016 – The acceptance of the nuclear agreement had been a victory for the Iranian moderates, but Khamenei seemed to have kept to his hard line in the political arena by backing the hardline stance of the Guardian Council. Voting for the 86 members of the next Assembly and the 290 members of the next Parliament was scheduled for February: *FT*, 1/27/16.

2016 – Iran was bidding for regional hegemony: *The Week*: *Beirut Daily Star*, 2/12/16.

2016 – The elections of 2/26/16 produced a Parliament almost equally divided among hardliners and moderates. Hardliners still dominated the IRGC and the judiciary: *FT*, 3/9/16. The election put President Rouhani on a cautious path to reform: *Guardian*, 2/29/16. The moderates under the leadership of Rafsanjani and Rouhani scored a "historic victory" – 59 percent of the membership of the Assembly, versus 25 percent of the previous Assembly.

2016 – The US developed the Stuxnet computer virus that sabotaged Iran's nuclear program. Iran had used another virus to wipe out the hard drives on 306 Saudi Aramco computers: *NYTBR*: 3/6/16, P. W. Singer citation from *Dark Territory: The Secret History of the Cyber War*, Fred Kaplan.

2016 – In a conference on Saudi-Iranian rivalry, a participant stated that Iran had perpetrated assassinations of diplomats of Middle East states, especially those of Saudi Arabia: *MEP*, Summer 2016.

2016 – Under the nuclear agreement, some restrictions of the arms embargo on Iran will be removed in five years. In ten years, if Iran still wants a nuclear bomb, it will have it: *FA*, July 2016, Ayelet Shaked.

2016 – The Quds Force was training a large body of military recruits in Syria: *Times*, 9/17/16.

2016 – Hizballah was crucial to Iranian defense against Israeli attack. Syria was crucial as Iran's route for shipment of arms to Hizballah: *Times*, 9/21/16, Fisher.

2016 – Iran had allowed American cell phones to accept calls in Iran: *Times*, 10/9/16.

The Baghdad Regime – Picture 167,000 square miles of desert and uninviting mountain. This would be Iraq, but for the crucial alleviation provided by two modest rivers – the Tigris and the Euphrates – which rise in the mountains of southern Turkey, and meet 120 miles north of their outflow into the Persian Gulf.

At latitude 33 north (the latitude of Atlanta, Georgia), the twin rivers are only 30 miles apart. This favored site has seen the capitals of a series of dynasties going back to prehistory. Baghdad was founded there in 762 by al Mansur, second Caliph of the Abbasid Dynasty of Islam.

Baghdad reached its zenith, economic and intellectual, under Caliphs al Mahdi, Harun al Rashid, and al Ma'mun from 775 to 833, when its wharves were lined with ships from East Africa, India, and China: *EB*, 14:589.

However, the land of Mesopotamia (Greek for "between the rivers") paid a terrible price for its location athwart the routes between the Middle East and the rest of Asia. The worst episode was the invasion in 1250 by Hulegu's Mongols, who sacked the city, killed the Caliph, massacred hundreds of thousands of Baghdadis, and ravaged the local irrigation system beyond repair.

After World War I, Britain and France resumed their favorite sideline, imperialism, in the former Ottoman territories. In the Fertile Crescent, five new countries emerged. They were advertised as "states", but they were still dependencies, and their people had become chattels of governments that were not even Middle Eastern. Syria and Lebanon went to France. Palestine, Jordan, and Iraq went to Britain.

In a brutal coup by the Iraqi military in 1958, King Faysal II, his family, and Britain's political mainstay, Nuri al Sa'id, were killed, and British-Iraqi ties were severed. Iraq came under the rule of the Baath Party, which was promoting a progressive program in Syria and Iraq. They learned the Middle East is decades away from real progress, but Saddam managed to make Iraq the most modern state in the Arab World until 1980, when he went off the rails – a victim of regional chaos, American opportunism, and his own despotism.

Saddam's invasion of Iran mushroomed into eight years of futile war, which allowed three million northern Kurds to defect to the Iranian side, and led feckless policymakers in Washington into going so far overboard in their support of Iraq, as a way of pursuing their petty feud with Iran, that they infused Saddam with the wild idea that he could get away with the annexation of Kuwait. That mistake sparked a vindictive scheme by Washington's neocons to destroy Saddam and Iraq. The vehicle was the Pentagon's Desert Storm.

The scheme was a smashing success for the neocons, who measure success in Israeli terms. For the Middle East and its well-wishers, it was a disaster. From 1/17/91 to 2/28/91, at the head of a nominal coalition, the US ousted the Iraqi troops from Kuwait in a campaign that seemed designed to punish Iraq for all its offenses – invasion of Kuwait, promotion of Arab Nationalism, and hostility to Israel.

On 2/24/91, the CIA's Voice of Free Iraq Radio urged the Iraqi people to rise up against Saddam. Apparently, the Bush 41 administration was unaware of King Faysal II's belated realization that "there is no Iraqi people": FA, November 2015, Ali Khedery. By mid-March, the Shia were in full rebellion in the south, and the Kurds in the northeast. Saddam had kept his elite troops home during the expulsion of Iraqi forces that had been in Kuwait. Now he unleashed his Republican Guard in a genocidal repression of the two rebellions.

Bush 41 recognized his responsibility for the carnage. In April 1991, he ordered the US Air Force to exclude Iraqi aircraft from a No-Fly Zone over Iraqi Kurdistan, thereby consolidating Kurdish rebel control of its cities, plus Kirkuk. Shiite rebels in south Iraq were given their own No-Fly Zone in August.

Between Desert Storm and the next US-Iraq war, Iraq was subjected to an equally vindictive US/UN array of sanctions. Bush 43 completed the reduction of Iraq to the shattered remnant of statehood by ordering the invasion of 2003. This action has been widely condemned as the worst foreign policy blunder in the history of the US: *Times*, 7/3/16, review of *Bush*, Jean Edward Smith. The blunder was compounded by egregious mistakes in execution, including the disbandment of the Iraq Army and the appointment on 5/20/06 of Nuri al Maliki as Prime Minister.

None of the invasion's predicted benefits materialized. Instead, Iraq, the US, and the Middle East were all losers. The only winners were Iran and the Kurds. Under American occupation, Iraq shifted from secularism (the Baath) to sectarianism, in the form of a Shiite political bloc subtly led by Ayatallah 'Ali al Sistani. The post-Baathist Prime Minister, Nuri al Maliki, was a hyper-partisan of Shiite rule: *FA*, Ali Khedery. The members of his cabinet were chosen by Iranian generals: *Times*, 8/17/10.

This outcome left no room for Iraq's Sunni minority. The American invasion began as a war between Americans and Iraqis. In 2011, when the Americans went home, they left behind them a feud between Sunni and Shiite death squads, which had metastasized to Syria: *Atlantic*, May 2016. In Iraq, Christians had tended to look to non-Muslim communities for protection against Muslim discrimination, Sunni and Shiite: *LRB*, 12/18/14, Patrick Cockburn.

On 8/28/16, in the *National Interest*, Tom Cooper told a story, unconfirmed, of a Mossad triumph, the alleged defection of Munir Radfa, an Assyrian Christian pilot in the Iraqi Air Force, who on 8/16/66 defected to Israel in his MiG-20 D.

Other sources, including the *Jewish Virtual Library*, have reported that Radfa's award was cash and the right to permanent residence in Israel (or the US) for him and his extended family, who were smuggled by Mossad from Iraq via Iran to Israel. Most versions of this story hold that

Israel received the plane in time to learn the plane's characteristics before the Six-Day War.

Timeline: 2014-2016 – The US invasion force completed its withdrawal from Iraq in 2010. By 2014, American destruction of Iraq's infrastructure and its secular society had plunged the country into sectarian civil war:

2014 – On 1/4/14, the Sunni IS captured Fallujah.

2014 – On 6/6/14, 4-5,000 IS militiamen invaded Iraq's third largest city, Mawsil. Thirty thousand Iraqi soldiers and policemen fled in panic. After eight years of Maliki rule, the IS invasion was made easy by Sunni hatred of the partisan and corrupt Iraqi army, which was terrified by the specter of a mass Sunni uprising: *LRB*, 6/10/15, Cockburn; *NY*, 1/18/16, Mogelson; *NYTM*, 8/14/16.

2014 – By 6/11/14, the IS had taken Baiji and Tikrit. In Tikrit, IS gunmen killed 1700 cadets training at Camp Speicher: *LRB*, 6/10/15, Patrick Cockburn.

2014 – Within days of the Mawsil occupation, the KRG's Peshmerga had taken control of Kirkuk and nearby oil fields.

2014 – Maliki's blatant discrimination was motivating Sunnis to join the IS: *NYR*, 2014, Max Rodenbeck.

2014 – Maliki reduced to 20,000 the number of tribesmen on salary from the government. The departing US authorities had been paying 100,000: *Times*, 7/13/14; *Current History*, December 2015, Norton.

2014 – In lieu of the disgraced Iraqi Army, Al Quds was training thousands of Iraqi Shiite militiamen from Muqtada Sadr's Mahdi Army (*Jaysh al Mahdi*) and its affiliate, League of the Righteous (*'Asa'ib Ahl al Haqq*): *FT*, 7/24/14.

2014 – By July, the IS had taken over much of northwestern Iraq, and it had declared a Caliphate over its new territories: *MEP*, Spring 2015, Philippe Le Billon.

2014 – On 8/14/14, Nuri al Maliki, having alienated Sunni and Kurdish Iraqis, was forced to resign as Prime Minister, but he was still one of three Iraqi Vice Presidents. He refused to give up his office in the Green Zone, and he continued to wield influence.

2014 – Iran had long financed the Al Da'wah party/militia, bitter enemies of Saddam. Sunnis and secular Shia looked down on its members as puppets of Iran. Maliki's security forces were mostly Shiite. They were allied with militias trained in Iran: *Times*, 8/17/14, Ali Khedery.

2014 – In retaliation for a suspected Sunni attack on a Shia tribal leader, Shia militiamen attacked a Sunni mosque in Diyala, killing 60: *Times*, 8/22/14.

2014 – Iraqi Sunnis wanted amnesty for the tens of thousands of Sunni political prisoners, and a voice in the government: *FT*, 8/18/14.

2014 – As the Islamic State was taking over the Mawsil area, Shiite militias retaliated by killing Sunnis by air and ground action, alienating neutral Sunnis from the regime in Baghdad: *Times*, 9/11/14.

2014 – The Baghdad regime's principal militias were the League of the Righteous, Battalions of Hizballah (*Kata'ib Hizballah*), and the Badr Corps: *Times*, 9/17/14.

2014 – Baghdad's Shiite militias intimidated Sunnis and even Shia: *Times*, 9/29/14.

2014 – There were two standing armies in Iraq. The Iraqi Army was nugatory. The Kurdish Peshmerga was formidable, but fought only for territory with a substantial Kurdish community: *NY*, 9/29/14, Dexter Filkins.

2014 – Former Prime Minister Maliki, still active in the government, replaced many qualified Sunni officers with Shia loyalists: *AP*, 10/8/14.

2014 – New Prime Minister Haydar al 'Abadi held a PhD in engineering from the UK and was fluent in English. Two of his brothers had been executed by Saddam. 'Abadi admitted the Iraqi armed forces had collapsed, and would need two or three years of overhaul. After 35 years of nearly continuous war, dispersal by the American invaders, and the loss of Mawsil, their morale was abysmal: *FT*, 10/2/14.

2014 – IS forces took the Iraqi towns of Hit and Zuwayyah in October, killing or expelling Iraqi police. Many Sunnis fled from the IS advance, only to be further dispersed, or killed by Iraqi Shiites: *Atlantic*, May 2016, Screenivasan Gopal.

2014 – Late in 2014, Iraqi forces expelled the residents and the IS garrison from Jurf al Sakhar, a Sunni city thirty miles south of Baghdad, in the largely Shiite province of Babil. Two Sunni leaders were shot dead, and the city was left a wasteland: *Times*, 12/6/14.

2014 – Under persecution by the IS, the Mandean minority was disappearing from Iraq. For Salafis, the Mandean creed was quintessentially infidel. It rejected Judaism, Christianity, and Islam, and held that the material world is not ruled by the supreme, unknowable God, but by a fallible deity: *Inter-Press Service*, 11/5/14.

2014 – In Baghdad's sphere of influence, Shiite militias were abducting and killing Sunnis: *LRB*, 11/6/14, Patrick Cockburn.

2014 – The officer corps of the Iraqi Army was shot through with nepotism and other forms of corruption: *Times*, 11/24/14.

2014 – Prime Minister 'Abadi was making a start in moderating the anti-Sunni prejudices promoted by his predecessor, Nuri al Maliki, among the Iraqi judiciary and armed forces. Specific corrective efforts: Cancelling a biased death sentence, and curtailing the common practice among military officers of adding fictitious names to the rolls and cashing their "salaries". Maliki was still operating out of his own office in the Green Zone: *Times*, 12/16/14.

2015 – Shiite militias killed 72 Sunnis in a revenge operation in Diyala Province, as Baghdad took the province back from the IS: *Times*, 1/30/15.

2015 – Under the leadership of Hadi al 'Amiri, the Badr Brigade had pushed IS forces back from Diyala Province. The Brigade was being accused of barbarity toward Sunnis, and subservience to Iran: *Times*, 2/8/15.

2015 – Shiite militiamen killed an Iraqi Sunni leader, his son, and nine bodyguards: *Times*, 2/14/15.

2015 – In the spring, the 50,000 men of the Iraqi People's Militia (*Al Hashd al Sha'bi*) retook from the IS a large area of northwest Iraq: *NYR*, 11/10/16, Joshua Hammer. Most of their roster were Shiite, many of them linked to Iran.

2015 – The Shiite advance toward Mawsil had given rise to reports of looting and revenge killings of Sunnis: *Times*, 3/19/15.

374

2015 – The Baghdad Regime had a pro-Shia bias so strong that it was losing Iraq's Sunni northwest: *FA*, March 2015.

2015 – The Iraqi government was running a large budget deficit: *Times*, 4/15/15.

2015 – On 4/4/15, 20-30,000 of Baghdad's fighters recaptured Tikrit. The outcome was determined more by militiamen than by soldiers: *Times*, 4/18/15. The militiamen looted and killed Sunni civilians in the streets: *FT*, 5/19/15.

2015 – In Ramadi, pro-Sahwah tribesmen blamed sectarian bias on the part of the Baghdad regime for its failure to mobilize Sunni support: *FT*, 5/19/15.

2015 – Ayatallah Sistani called for jihad against the IS. The mobilization of Shiite militias depended on recruiting poor young men from the Shiite south. Sunnis were being forced out of central and southern Iraq: *NYR*, 6/4/15, Pelham.

2015 – With the number of Iraqi DP's up to three million (85 percent Sunni), the KRG was blocking the entry of Sunni DP's into the KAR, and the Baghdad regime was blocking Sunni entry into territory under its control. Thousands of Sunni DP's already in Baghdad were crammed into 32 mosques: *Times*, 5/28/15, 7/26/15.

2015 – The Badr Organization was the biggest and most openly pro-Iranian Shiite militia in Iraq: *NYR*, 6/4/15, Pelham.

2015 – There was little interest anywhere in Iraq, among Sunnis or Shiites, for sectarian reconciliation. The Sahwah had been disillusioned when the Baghdad regime failed to continue the stipends they had been receiving from the US military: *Times*, 6/4/15.

2015 – The Shiite regime installed in Baghdad by the US occupation had settled in. The Shia forces that had retaken Tikrit had prevented most of its Sunni residents from returning: *FT*, 6/9/15.

2015 – To escape persecution by the Islamic State, most Christian residents of Mawsil had fled. The Kurds had denied them arms, but some of them had formed small militias that fought alongside Kurds and Shia: *NYTM*, 7/6/15, 7/26/15.

2015 – The Baghdad regime and the KRG were economic rivals (competing exporters of Iraqi oil), but military allies against the Islamic State: *FT*, 7/18/15.

2015 – In August, Sistani had 'Abadi try to prune the government of excess deputy prime ministers and vice presidents. Maliki refused to leave: Ali Khedery.

2015 – Three hundred IS militiamen drove thousands of trained and heavily equipped Iraqi soldiers out of Ramadi: *NYR*, 8/13/15.

2015 – Iraqi resistance to the IS incursion had been undermined by endemic corruption, and by the global collapse of oil prices: *AP*, 9/6/15.

2015 – Many Iraqi Shiites were evading the Iraqi draft by escaping to Europe. Shiites in Iraq were losing interest in regaining Sunni-populated areas like Mawsil and 'Anbar Province. Thanks to Iranian military leadership, the Baghdadis were feeling less threatened by IS attack. They felt the IS was a Sunni problem. 'Anbar Sunnis who had asked Baghdad for military assistance now regretted it, having learned that the Shiite regime looked on 'Anbar Province more as a buffer zone than as Iraqi territory: *Times*, 10/4/15, Vali Nasr.

2015 – After a month of US air strikes, Iraqi troops and Shiite militias retook Bayji Refinery from the IS: *Times*, 10/16/15.

2015 – In recent weeks, Sunni-Shia feuding had intensified. Although Washington was still nursing the myth of "moderate" Shia, both communities were in a fight to the finish: *LRB*, 11/5/15, Cockburn.

2015 – In November, Peshmerga forces, backed by US air support, were slowly recapturing the Sinjar area of Iraq: *NYR*, 11/10/16, Hammer.

2015 – Two explosions in Baghdad killed 26 Shiites: *Times*, 11/13/15.

2015 – The Baghdad regime was in crisis because Vice President Maliki and Ayatallah Sistani were opposed to Prime Minister 'Abadi's economy drive, including civil service pay cuts: *FT*, 11/24/15. The regime had also been undermined by Maliki's sectarian bias.

2016 – Vice President Biden congratulated the Iraqi Security Forces on their liberation of Ramadi from the IS. The operation had followed

600 air strikes by US planes since July 2015, wreaking wide destruction. The major participant on the ground was Iraq's Special Anti-Terrorism Forces (SATF): *FT*, 1/2/16.

2016 – Civilians were dying in Iraq at a staggering rate. Three million Iraqis were displaced. A UN report accused the IS of genocide: *The Week*, 1/29/16.

2016 – Thirty-five-dollar oil was crippling the economies of the Baghdad Regime and the KRG. Government salaries were not being paid: *Times*, 2/1/16.

2016 – By February, the People's Militia had driven IS forces out of 'Anbar Province.

2016 – Since Iraq was now controlled by Iran, 'Abadi's efforts to reconcile rivals in his government were hopeless: *Times*, 2/13/16. 'Abadi's rival, Nuri al Maliki, had welshed on his promise to incorporate the Sahwah alliance into the Iraqi Security Forces: *Times*, 2/13/16. His cabinet was hiding out in the Green Zone: *FA*, September 2015, Ali Khederi.

2016 – The influence on Iraq of the Shiite militias, especially the Badr Organization, led by Hadi al 'Amiri, former Iraqi Minister of Transportation, was rising. 'Amiri was saying that most Iraqi political leaders had their private militias. He had fought the Saddam regime, and then with Iranian funding had led the Badr force against the American occupation.

2016 – As the Shiite forces recovered territory from the IS, Iraqis were returning to the homes they had evacuated during the IS advance. In Tikrit (Salah al Din Province), ninety percent of the original residents were back. However, most of them were Sunnis, and the Sunni-Shia rift was still unresolved. In Diyala Province, between Baghdad and Iraqi Kurdistan, the People's Militia was close to the pro-Iranian Badr Organization. Iraq was still in political and economic crisis: *FT*, 4/13/16.

2016 – A chain of assassinations in Baghdad was seen as the IS's revenge for its recent defeats: *Times*, 1/16/16.

2016 – The Western coalition opposed the participation of the People's Militia in the war against the IS, because they had a penchant for sectarian killing: *FT*, 3/30/16.

2016 – The trial of Saddam had been corrupt. His defense lawyers had been killed: *NY*, 4/18/16.

2016 – The Baghdad regime was in turmoil. The political situation had been disrupted by Iraq's three-way ethnic split, which Maliki had exacerbated, and which 'Abadi was failing to alleviate. Muqtada Sadr was leading protests against official corruption: *Times*, 4/23/16.

2016 – The Iraqi political system was barely operative. Shiite and Kurdish militias had clashed. Ali Khedery had advised Washington to abandon its futile effort to salvage Iraq: *Times*, 4/24/16, Tim Arango.

2016 – Nuri al Maliki, Prime Minister from 2006 to 2014, had exploited the US effort to reestablish a centralized Iraqi government as a tool to consolidate his personal control over the cabinet in Baghdad. He had disbanded the Sahwah in 2008, with Washington's concurrence. The Baghdad Regime's army was still demoralized. 'Abadi had concluded a truce with the KRG: *MEP*, Spring 2016, Dylan O'Driscoll.

2016 – Muqtada Sadr sent followers into the Green Zone to protest 'Abadi's failure to eliminate corruption and sectarianism in the government: *FT*, 5/2/16.

2016 – Iraq was a failed state: *Times*, 5/3/16, Arango.

2016 – The IS claimed the largest of three bombs that killed nearly 100 citizens of Baghdad – most of them Shiites: *Times*, 5/11/16.

2016 – On 5/20/16, followers of Muqtada staged a second wave of protests against 'Abadi in the Green Zone.

2016 – Pro-regime Kurds and Sunnis were pressing 'Abadi to renounce the People's Militia: *FT*, 5/24/16.

2016 – In May, the US Air Force and Iraqi ground troops pushed IS forces out of Rutbah: *Times*, 5/21/16.

2016 – Iraq's sectarian split had been caused by Saddam's misrule and defective US policy. The deadliest Shiite militia was The League of the Righteous, which had been trained by Iran's Al Quds force: *Atlantic*, May 2016, Gopal.

2016 – Since the IS had overrun Mawsil in 2014, the Baghdad Regime had relied on its own Special Anti-Terrorism Forces (SATF) and the People's Militia. These two organizations were under Baghdad's nominal control, but they ran their own military campaigns. The SATF had been trained by US soldiers. In the siege of Fallujah, the People's Militia was assigned to securing the outskirts of the city, SATF to secure the city itself. There was little coordination between the two commands: *AP*, 6/8/16, Susannah George.

2016 – The SATF was holding 80 percent of what was left of Ramadi. It had been largely destroyed by US air strikes. IS forces had been driven out by US saturation bombing. Many IS soldiers chose suicide to capture: *Times*, 6/8/16.

2016 – In 2003, the US had made the mistake of disbanding the Iraqi Army. By June 2016, the US had spent over 25 billion dollars to build a new one. Many of its divisions were still ineffective. A new counterterrorism force was leading the 2016 offensive against the IS. Logistics were still a weak link. An Iraqi unit deployed east of Ramadi ran out of water. In their need for supplies, or wish for promotions, commanders often had to pay bribes. The army was dependent on the People's Militia, which included Iran-backed militias known to torture and kill Sunnis. The Iraqi Minister of Interior, Muhammad al Ghabban, was a member of the Iranian-backed Badr Organization: *FT*, 6/24/16.

2016 – Iraq announced the recapture of (devastated) Fallujah on 6/27/16. When the IS took Fallujah in 2014, 80,000 residents had stayed on, while 100,000 had fled. Recaptured Fallujah was not ready for business as usual. The water and electricity systems were not in operation. 80,000 refugees from IS occupation were camped in the desert with primitive facilities. The Iraqi Shiites were suspicious of the residents who had never left. There were reports that Shiite militias that had participated in the recapture were torturing Sunni detainees: *FT*, 6/30/16.

2016 – The US had advised 'Abadi to set up escape routes for Sunnis from besieged Fallujah, but he had allowed two Shiite militias, The League of the Righteous and battalions of Hizballah, to surround the city. Some of their militiamen were killing Sunni males: *NYR*, 11/10/16, Hammer.

2016 – Demonstrators in Baghdad pelted Prime Minister 'Abadi with rocks and shoes (grave insult) in protest of the government's failure to stop IS bombing: *Times*, 7/3/16.

2016 – Muqtada al Sadr ordered his JAM to attack the US troops deploying to participate in the battle for Mawsil. US troops in Iraq were expected to increase to 4600.

2016 – In July, an IS bomb killed over 300 in Baghdad: *Times*, July 2016.

2016 – In Iraq, as in the rest of the Middle East, government jobs were often assigned by tribal leaders. Many officials in the Iraqi civil service had been Baathist in name only: *Times*, 8/14/16.

2016 – A *Financial Times* review of the economy in Basrah, Iraq's only large port, found that, since 2014, the efforts of local leaders to maintain subsidies for fuel and food were failing. The major employer was the People's Militia. Addiction to crystal meth was rising.

2016 – Iraq's unity was crumbling – among its three ethnic communities, and also within each one. A major irritant was domestic politics. Prime Minister 'Abadi was trying to reduce Iraq's traditional corruption. Former PM Maliki was trying to make a comeback. In September, the 'Abadi faction had voted out of office the Sunni defense minister and the Kurdish finance minister, Hushyar Zebari, whose KDP Party still dominated the KAR, even as Kurdish rivals voted against him: *FT*, 10/7/16.

2016 – The population of Mawsil had fallen from 2 to 1.2 million: *Times*, 10/8/16.

2016 – Baghdad's battle plan for the recapture of Mawsil was to exclude Kurdish forces and Shiite militias. As the attack began, civilians who managed to escape the city waved white flags and promised to provide information on IS defense positions: *Times*, 11/2/16; *NYR*, 11/10/16, Hammer.

2016 – Many Sunni residents of Mawsil had welcomed the IS occupation of 2014 as a respite from the tyranny of Maliki's security forces: *NY*, 1/10/16, Mogelson. In 2016, the overriding emotion of Mawsil residents as the Iraqi forces reached the city was relief at the prospective liberation from IS asceticism (no tobacco, no shaving, no cell phones): *Times*, 11/3/16.

2016 – By 11/2/16, Mawsil was under attack by 4000 Peshmerga, 22,000 Iraqi soldiers, 6000 Iraqi tribesmen (most of them Sunni), and

560 US advisers. Mawsil was defended by 5000 IS militiamen, who were leaning heavily on suicide vehicle-bombers: *The Week*, 11/28/16: *Commentary Magazine*, Max Boot. In Tuz Khurmatu, Iraqi militiamen attacked Peshmerga militiamen. All residents of Mawsil opposed entry of either Shiites or Kurds: *NYR*, 11/10/16.

2016 – Fighters from Peshmerga, the People's Militia, and the Iraqi army were advancing on Mawsil. Baghdad wanted to block the Peshmerga from entering Mawsil: *NYR*, 11/11/16, Hammer.

The following discussion relies heavily on Nasser Rabbat's "Anatomy of the Syrian Regime" in *The London Review of Books* of 7/14/16:

The Damascus Regime – Syria/Lebanon has long been hyper-politicized. In 1916, 33 Arabs – Muslims and Christians – were tortured and hanged in Beirut by their Ottoman rulers for having appealed to France to support Arab independence from Turkey: *The Great War for Civilization*, Robert Fisk.

After World War I, the hapless Syrians got the support they asked for – in the form of French imperialism, and its standard practice of divide-and-rule. Paris tore Lebanon out of Syria as an independent state, and partitioned the rest of Syria into four statelets – Damascus, Aleppo, the lands of the Druze, and the lands of the Alawites. This arrangement pleased the Alawites, who had survived in Syria for centuries as an inferior class, demeaned and mistreated by the Sunni majority.

In 1936, the French administrators formed the 10,000-man *Troupes Spéciales du Levant*, and rigged its recruiting to ensure that one third of the roster were Alawites. The young men of the impoverished Alawite mountains that paralleled the Syrian coast welcomed the opportunity of lucrative and respected military service. The Troupes became the nucleus of the Syrian Army.

The Ba'th (Renaissance) Party of Syria (BPS), founded in 1947, promoted minority membership in its own ranks. By the mid-50's, the BPS had learned that the most effective way to build a power structure was to infiltrate the army, which had been toppling Syrian governments since 1948.

The price Syria paid for Nasir's concurrence in the formation of the United Arab Republic (UAR) in 1958 was dissolution of Syrian political parties. In 1961, after a conservative-oriented unit of the Syrian Army dissolved the UAR, and resuscitated the Syrian Arab Republic (SAR), six ex-Baathist officers who had been stationed together in Cairo formed a cabal to restore the Syrian Ba'th to power. Three of the six, as Alawites, would have a decisive advantage in the upcoming power struggle for Syrian rule.

In the SAR, every time a Sunni coup group ousted the members of the previous Sunni coup group, the Alawite officers imperceptibly gained a little more influence over military affairs. On March 8, 1963, the Syrians awoke to the realization that the Baathists not only controlled the Syrian army, they had taken command of the country. The three conspirators from Cairo were leading members of the coup group. One of them was Hafiz al Asad.

Over the next several years, the Baathist leadership had two preoccupations: first, forcing Sunni officers to retire and replacing them with Alawites; second, competing in an intra-Ba'th power struggle. Under these handicaps, the Syrian Army was in no condition to stand up to an army as professional as the IDF. In 1967, Syria lost Golan.

After the Six-Day War, Asad kept a low profile among his colleagues, and became Commander of the Air Force. The ostensible leader of Syria then was Salah Jadid, who met his downfall in Jordan. During the civil war between King Husayn and the PLO, Jadid sent a force into Jordan to support the Palestinians. Husayn ordered his troops and his small air force into battle against the invaders, and secretly appealed to his western sponsors for help. Israel put its air force on alert. Asad withheld his air force. Jadid had to call for a humiliating withdrawal.

On 9/13/70, Hafiz al Asad became President of Syria. Salah Jadid spent the last 23 years of his life in jail. Asad spent the next 30 years of his life performing the remarkable feat of keeping tumultuous Syria on an even keel – aside from the Hamah massacre of 1982, when Asad's cannons put an end to a violent uprising of the Muslim Brotherhood.

Asad's regime maintained a pervasive sectarian structure, based on Alawite solidarity and Sunni intimidation, that long enabled the Alawite minority of two million (12 percent of all Syrians) to control a country with a Sunni majority of 74 percent: *Inheriting Syria*, Flynt Leverett. The Kurdish minority was also placed at 12 percent; most Kurds were Sunni. Asad took out extra insurance by constructing two elite divisions, The Republican Guard and the Fourth Armored Division, with Alawite majorities. He arranged for Musa Sadr, the charismatic Shiite Imam in Lebanon, to pronounce that Alawites are genuine Shiites. Syrian Alawites began moving from their mountains to the cities and taking places in the business sector. Syria's rulers, families, and friends were accumulating fortunes. Many non-Alawite professionals, alarmed by regional instability, clung to the regime as a guarantor of security. In 1994, after the death of his older brother in a car crash, Bashar had been called back from studying ophthalmology in London to become the heir apparent. His handlers had given him a crash course in dictatorship, but in 2011 when insurrection loomed, it seems all he remembered was the ruthless part.

After Bashar succeeded to the dictatorship in October 2000, the Syrian situation began to go downhill. Bashar made an effort to consolidate ties with the Christians and other minorities, and with the upper-class Sunnis who had stuck with the Alawite regime, but that effort was frustrated by corruption in the government, particularly in the secret police (*Mukhabarat*): *The Syrian Jihad*, Charles Lister. Bashar could not match his father's shrewdness in keeping Syrians safe. In ten years, he undid what had taken his father thirty years to build. He replaced his father's associates with his own coterie. Cronyism took on the appearance of state policy. Rash and conceited statements clouded Bashar's image.

Hafiz had taken advantage of Lebanon's civil war to subtly bring Lebanon under his de facto jurisdiction. Bashar's regime was openly linked to the 2005 assassination of Lebanese Prime Minister Rafiq Hariri. International pressure compelled Syria to withdraw its garrison from Lebanon. Hafiz had dealt with Iran on a basis of equality. Under Bashar, Syria joined Iraq as one of Iran's client states.

2007-8 – Syrian agriculture was blighted by an intense drought. Over half the villages in the Hasakah and Dayr al Zawr Governorates were depopulated by a flight to the already overcrowded cities: Lister.

2008-11 – Successive years of drought put the regime under intense political pressure: *MER*, Winter 2014, Brent Eng/Jose Ciro Martinez; *NY*, 12/7/15. The conjunction of Syrian economic distress and the Arab Spring was too much for Damascus to cope with.

2011 – The initial collision occurred in Dar'a, a modest Sunni city on the Syria-Jordan border, 30 miles east of Israel's Lake Tiberias. It was the capital of the Governorate of Dar'a. In March 2011, fifteen schoolboys were picked up for scrawling anti-regime slogans. They were soon released, but it was said that some came back missing a fingernail.

The consequence was a <u>real</u> protest – a march by leading citizens of the community. The regime faced its moment of decision – conciliation or repression?

Hafiz al Asad had done his best to project a mood of deep concern for the welfare of his 22 million constituents, but his office was not one that he could campaign for every four years. When protest flared, both Asads revealed a deeper concern for the welfare of the regime. From the Asad point of view, it seems, Syria's 17 million Sunnis were just another obstreperous tribe.

Both Hafiz and Bashar had all the military advantages except manpower. However, their circumstances were different. Hafiz's challenger, the Muslim Brotherhood, was just one of many rival factions, and its offenses were much greater than Dar'a's peaceful protest. Bashar faced millions of underprivileged, stifled Sunnis (*FA*: *Current History*, December 2015, Samer Abboud), and Bashar was no Hafiz.

Bashar's response was an overreaction. Security forces opened fire on the Dar'a protesters. Violence escalated. Within days, the roof of the Dar'a hospital was a nest of snipers charged with blocking rebel admission: *NY*, 6/27/16.

2011 – On 4/25/11, the Fourth Armored Division, led by Bashar's brother, Mahir, deployed tanks in a massive attack on Dar'a. Over the next eleven days, citizens resisted, defecting Syrian soldiers joined them, and over 200 residents died. The Syrian Civil War had begun: *NYTM*,

8/14/16. In its sectarian panic, the Asad regime was about to inflict on its constituents genocidal atrocities that vitiated any claim to the legitimacy of their regime. By the summer of 2011, the regime's security forces were beating suspected rebels to death: *NY*, 4/18/16, Ben Taub.

2011 – During the summer, as the fighting intensified, appalled army officers met in small groups in Qatar and Turkey to discuss remedial options. On October 11, Turkey gave approval for a Free Syrian Army (FSA) to set up headquarters in Hatay Province: *LRB*, review of *From Deep State to Islamic State*, Jean-Pierre Filiu. From the outset, organized rebellion was ruled out by the failure to reach consensus among a jungle of political factions. The Muslim Brotherhood wanted to help, but it had not recovered from the punishment wreaked by Hafiz al Asad in 1982. Instead, a number of new militias emerged to fight Damascus and each other, and Syria dissolved into internecine war.

2011 – In August, the Islamic State sent forces into Syria from Iraq.

2011 – In November, Syria suffered an eruption of sectarian abductions and murders: *NYTM*, 8/14/16: *Aljazeera*.

2012 – Mahir al Asad, Bashar's brother, was directing the suppression of demonstrators. There had been a sharp rise in high-level defections to the FSA, but its troops were inferior to the jihadist rebels: *NY*, 4/18/16, Taub.

2012 – On 7/18/12, a blast, allegedly the work of the FSA, killed the chairman of the Damascus regime's Crisis Cell, the head of the Bureau of National Security, the Minister of Defense, and Asif Shawkat, Bashar's brother-in-law and a key official of the Regime: *NY*, 4/18/16, Taub.

2012 – In July, Syrian combat troops were withdrawn from Kurdish-populated areas. There had been no Syrian air strikes there. The Kurds had let SARG units stay in Qamishli and Hasakah so that SARG could claim it was holding those territories. Damascus was paying civil service salaries in Kurdish-held areas: *NYR*, 12/3/15, Steele.

2012-13 – In its military weakness, the Asad regime resorted to a campaign to starve its rebel citizens out. Between August 2012 and January 2013, Asad's planes hit 80 bakeries in rebel territory. Grain silos were also hit. The inept FSA was unable to combat the starvation campaign, but in Aleppo Province the rebels had greater success. In 2014, the IS seized Iraqi government wheat silos, but for its own purposes. The recipients of food supplied by the UN were unknown, since the UN felt obligated to let Damascus decide who they were: *MER*, Winter 2014.

2012 – Iran's Islamic Revolutionary Guard Corps and Hizballah had come to the support of Asad's forces: *Times*.

2014 – In May, all rebels escaped from Homs during a ceasefire. In three years of siege, many had died of starvation. The survivors had lived on leaves and weeds: *NYTM*, 8/14/16.

2014 – By summer, the results of the fighting had partitioned Syria into autonomous zones: <u>Kurdish</u> – along the Syria-Turkey border; <u>IS</u> – both banks of the upper Euphrates; <u>Nusrah</u> – in and around Idlib Province; <u>FSA</u> – along the Syria-Jordan border; <u>Damascus regime</u> – one-third of prewar Syria, including Damascus, west Aleppo, Homs, Hamah, and the Mediterranean coast, excluding rebel enclaves along the Golan frontier and in suburbs of Damascus. The Damascus regime's territory was being defended by its army (down to 50,000 men), its air force, the undisciplined Shabihah militia, and several thousand fighters from Hizballah: Robin Wright.

2014 – A UNSC initiative to end the fighting in Syria was undercut by four Russian vetoes: *Times*, 7/14/14.

2014 – The IS capital, Raqqah, was under nagging air attack by US planes on the outskirts, by Syrian planes against the city center.

2014 – By copious use of weapons of mass lethality, including barrel bombs and chemical weapons, the Damascus regime was delaying the rebel advance, killing 25,000 civilians a month: *FT*, 10/22/14; *Times*, 11/20/14.

2014 – In October, Russia and China blocked a UN resolution to grant the ICC (International Criminal Court) jurisdiction over war crimes committed in Syria: *NY*, 4/18/16.

2014 – A photographer had assembled photos of 10,000 Syrians tortured to death by Asad's security forces: *Times*, 11/1/14.

2014 – By the end of the year, there were 6,000,000 displaced Syrians in Syria, and 3,000,000 outside Syria. 200,000 Syrians had died: *Current*

History, December 2014, Max Weiss. As of 10/9/14, the Jordan border was closed to most Syrian refugees: *Times*, 10/9/14.

2015 – Satellite photos showed vast devastation in Aleppo, Homs, 'Ayn al 'Arab (Kobani), and Dayr al Zawr. Many of Aleppo's two million prewar residents had fled. Its ruins were divided between secularist rebels in the eastern half and regimist forces in the west: *Times*, 2/15/15.

2015 – The death toll of the civil war had risen to 220,000: *Times*, 3/13/15. Since it opened for business in 2002, the ICC has secured just four convictions. The viability of the court is in question: Times, 11/3/16, editorial.

2015 – The morale of the Damascus regime's forces was sinking: *McClatchy*, 4/28/15.

2015 – The Damascus forces were continuing their use of illegal weapons against illegal targets. Aleppo's pharmaceutical industry had collapsed in 2012. Doctors practicing in rebel-held areas were treated by the regime as terrorists; many had been executed. In the realm of disease control, the Syrians had been plunged back into the Dark Ages: *NYR*, 5/7/15.

2015 – After the US Air Force took over the air battle against the IS, the Damascus regime focused its military effort against units of the secularist FSA, in the expectation that the US would continue to direct its air attacks against the IS forces: *Times*, 6/3/15.

2015 – Update of displaced Syrians: In-country – 7.6 million; outside – 4 million. Of Syria's prewar Christian community of 1.5 million, 600,000 had fled the country: *NYTM*, 7/26/15.

2015 – Since the civil war broke out, the Alawite forces of the Damascus regime had been reduced by casualties and desertion from 300,000 to 100,000: *The Week*, 8/7/15.

2015 – Bashar al Asad would accept the destruction of anti-regime Syria as long as he could salvage a rump state: *Times*, 8/12/15.

2015 – Free Men of Syria, a Syrian rebel militia nearly wiped out by the IS in 2014, had regrouped under Hashim al Shaykh, and was collaborating with Nusrah. They both tended toward an exclusively Syrian outlook: *Times*, 8/26/15. Free Men of Syria was supported by Turkey.

387

2015 – The Druze community in Syria had tried to stay neutral in the civil war, but the Jabal al Duruz was inflamed by a vehicular bombing that killed a Druze cleric who had supported refusals to serve in the Syrian army, and by a bombing of the hospital to which Druze wounded had been taken. The Damascus regime was suspected of responsibility for both: *Times*, 9/6/15.

2015 – The Asad regime was bombing markets, hospitals, and schools in territory held by mainstream rebels. Territory held by the IS was not under attack. UN agencies were being forced to cut food rations and medical assistance in the territories being bombed. Most of the Syrian refugees had been driven out by Asad's bombs. Refugees in states neighboring Syria were jammed into contaminated camps with no education for their children and not enough food. Palestinians got monthly assistance from UNRWA. Other refugees had only the impecunious facilities of the UN Refugee Commission. Refugees in Lebanon owed the government 200 dollars a year, but they were denied employment: *FT*, 9/9/15.

2015 – A report that Moscow was sending soldiers and weapons to Syria was followed by a rumor that Russia had plans to build a military base in Latakia. Russia was pro-Asad and the US was anti-Asad, but both opposed the jihadist movement. Russian quote: Russia had no reason to save Syria, since Syria no longer existed; the goal should be to end the civil war: *FT*, 9/12/15.

2015 – The UN had a report that Asad's forces were destroying hospitals in rebel-held areas: *Times*, 9/27/15.

2015 – The toll of Syrian war-dead had risen to 320,000. DP's in Damascus had raised its current population from 2 to 10 million: *NYR*, 10/22/15.

2015 – Russia and Iran were concentrating their attacks on rebel factions in northwestern Syria, not against the IS: *FT*, 10/30/15, Gardner.

2015 – The main cause of the Syrians' flight from their country was the Damascus regime's barrel bombing: Gardner.

2015 – Turkey and Saudi Arabia were insisting that Asad had to go, but Western powers were beginning to suggest that he could stay on for a while: *FT*, 10/30/15, Gardner.

2015 – In areas held by the Damascus regime, civilians were beginning to starve: *Times*, 11/1/15.

2015 – Many observers suspected a secret truce between Damascus and the IS: *Times*, 11/19/15, Ian Fisher.

2015 – Damascus was under daily mortar attack from the Ghuta neighborhood. The battle lines seemed to coincide with communal boundaries. The FSA had been rescued in 2014 by Turkey, Qatar, and Saudi Arabia. The Damascus regime had been rescued in 2015 by Iran, Hizballah, and Russia: *LRB*, 11/5/15, Cockburn.

2015 – Physicians for Human Rights accused Asad's air force of killing health workers and bombing hospitals and ambulances in Aleppo: *Times*, 11/18/15.

2015 – After Hizballah militiamen had cut all Homs's supply lines, the Damascus regime had recovered the city. In December, it recovered Hamah: *MER*, Winter 2015, Hamdan.

2015 – The efforts of Syrian rebels to set up municipal services in cities under their control, notably in Dar'a and parts of Aleppo, had been frustrated by Damascus's barrel bombs: *MER*, Winter 2015.

2016 – In January, Damascus regime forces retook the Marj al Sultan air base in the eastern Ghuta: Landis blog.

2016 – The UN considered IS forces responsible for depriving 200,000 civilians of food and medicine, the Damascus regime forces for 180,000: *Times*, 1/19/16.

2016 – The Damascus regime and the IS were interdependent. The two most powerful independent militias in Syria were the Army of Islam and Free Men of Syria. Both were focused only on the overthrow of the regime, making a total of 150,000 rebels fixed on that objective: *MEP*, Spring 2016, Lister.

2016 – Secretary Kerry accused the Damascus regime of using mass starvation as a tactic: *Times*, 2/3/16.

2016 – With support from Iraqi, Iranian, and Hizballah ground troops and Russian air action, Damascus forces had made major advances in the Darʿa, Latakia, and Aleppo sectors: *Times*, 2/5/16.

2016 – In five years of war, 470,000 Syrians had died. The US was backing the Revolutionary Army, which was part of the Syrian Democratic Forces: *Times*, 2/12/16.

2016 – On 2/9/16, a UN commission charged the Damascus regime with a crime against humanity: killing thousands by beating and torture: *The Week*, 2/19/16. Human Rights Watch accused Russia and the Damascus regime of using cluster bombs in Syria.

2016 – In the Aleppo theater, four hospitals had been struck by Russian and/or Damascus regime aircraft: *Times*, 2/17/16.

2016 – Damascus regime forces were not engaging IS forces unless they were threatening the regime's supply lines: *FT*, 2/26/16.

2016 – In northwest Syria, the Russian and Damascus air forces were believed to be conducting a campaign to deny medical services to rebels: *Times*, 2/26/16.

2016 – Behind Russian air strikes, forces of the Damascus regime had lately captured 4,000 square miles of territory from rebels: *Times*, 3/16/16.

2016 – Russian efforts to reshape the rump Syrian army had been frustrated by its chronic manpower shortage after five years of war. According to Lebanese analyst Mohammed Ballout, the Russians were also frustrated by Bashar's holdout for recapture of all prewar Syria: *FT*, 3/18/16.

2016 – Aided by Hizballah and by Russian air support, forces of the Damascus regime retook Palmyra from the IS: *Times*, 3/27/16.

2016 – The Committee for International Justice and Accountability, an independent investigative body founded in 2012 in reaction to the Syrian civil war, issued a legal brief incriminating Bashar and his regime of the torture and murder of tens of thousands of Syrians: *NY*, 4/18/16, Ben Taub.

2016 – Dozens of shoppers and shop owners died in an attack on the market in Maʿarrat al Nuʿman: *Times*, 4/19/16.

2016 – Control of Aleppo was still divided between the Damascus regime on the west side and rebels on the east side. Strikes by aircraft of the Damascus regime had pulverized a rebel hospital, killing 25-30: *AP*, 4/29/16.

2016 – Eighty percent of the people still in Syria were living below the poverty line. Inflation was rising: *FT*, 5/12/16.

2016 – International humanitarian groups were accusing Damascus of trying to starve out besieged rebels: *The Week*, 5/27/16.

2016 – A UN affiliate had accused forces of the Damascus regime of "deliberately [targeting] medical personnel to gain military advantage". It was trying to eliminate emergency hospitals being set up by *Médecins Sans Frontières*. The Regime was also committing massacres by barrel bombs, and by sarin gas (1400 killed in Damascus in 2013). Russian aircraft were also attacking rebel hospitals: *NY*, 6/27/16, Ben Taub.

2016 – The Asad regime, a pervasively sectarian structure, exploited its Baathist label to pass as secularist. The new Alawite upperclass was clinging to the Damascus regime: *LRB*, 7/14/16, Nasser Rabbat.

2016 – With help from Iran, Hizballah, and Russia, Damascus forces were closing in on rebel positions in east Aleppo: *Times*, 7/16/16, Anne Barnard/Kamal Shammali.

2016 – With Russian endorsement, Damascus offered safe corridors out of east Damascus for residents and rebels who would turn over their arms. They were too distrustful of Damascus and Moscow to accept: *AP*, 7/28/16.

2016 – On 8/6/16, a rebel combine under Nusrah leadership temporarily broke the siege of east Aleppo. The Damascus regime controlled west Aleppo (population two million). The rebels controlled east Aleppo (population 250,000): *Times*, 8/14/16.

2016 – Nusrah leader Jawlani was trying to unite all Syrian jihadis under one command: *FT*, 8/8/16.

2016 – Nusrah was credited with masterminding the recent rebel advance in the Aleppo sector, on the strength of their receipt via Turkey of escalated shipments of arms, ammunition, and cash: *FT*, 8/9/16.

2016 – Bashar relied heavily on the actions of the motley Shabihah crowd: *Times*, 8/14/16.

2016 – The people of Darayya, a suburb of Damascus, had been miraculously holding out against the Damascus regime. After four years of siege, deprivation, and starvation, they capitulated. Rebel militiamen were to hand over their arms and leave: *The Guardian*, 8/25/16, Emmy Graham-Harrison; *Times*, 8/26/16.

2016 – An office of the UN reported that Damascus was continuing to spread chlorine gas from the air: *Times*, 8/27/16.

2016 – The Damascus forces had been targeting all medical centers in rebel territory since the civil war began: *NY*, 9/5/16, Steve Coll.

2016 – Damascus and Russian forces resumed the siege of Aleppo: *Times*, 9/6/16.

2016 – Over 100 Syrians were being treated in surviving Aleppo hospitals for the effects of chlorine: *Times*, 9/8/16.

2016 – In September, the US and the UK accused Russia of barbarism for directing the most ferocious aerial bombardment of the war against Aleppo, targeting operations of rescue organizations and hospitals, using bunker busters: *Times*, 9/26/16; *The Week*, 10/7/16.

2016 – Rebel forces headed by Nusrah launched a second offensive to break the siege of east Aleppo. Participating were twenty rebel groups – eleven of which had been supplied arms by the CIA: *Times*, 10/29/16.

2016 – Bombing by Damascus planes shut down three rebel-operated hospitals, leaving Aleppo with none: *Times*, 11/21/16.

2016 – Wartime inflation had reduced the Syrian lira to one-tenth of its prewar value. The US and the EU had established a sanctions program against Syria for its violations of human rights: *Times*, 11/22/16, Anne Barnard.

2016 – By September, the strength of the forces of the Damascus regime had fallen from 270,000 to 65,000.

2016 – According to a report from Amnesty International, between 2011 and December 2015, 17,700 political prisoners had died from maltreatment in Syrian prisons. Several thousand political suspects had been hanged after trials that lasted one to three minutes each: *FT*, 2/7/17.

2016 – Damascus forces recaptured Palmyra in December: *Times*, 2/7/17.

2016 – Human Rights Watch issued a report that Syrian military helicopters had dropped canisters of chlorine gas on civilian neighborhoods at least eight times: *The Week*, 2/24/17.

Hizballah – Of the four autonomous militias in the eastern Arab World, two (the Islamic State and Al Qaʻidah – including Al Qaʻidah in the Arabian Peninsula) are unaffiliated with any recognized government. The Huthis have occupied the capital of Yemen, but they are locked in a struggle for Yemeni hegemony. Only Hizballah has achieved unchallenged domination of an Arab state:

Aimless Lebanon – By drawing frontiers that included a population divided between Christian and Muslim communities of roughly equal size, Lebanon's unimaginative founders created a state immobilized by ethnic stalemate. Lebanon can say no – as it does to the Palestinian refugees' appeal for more human rights, such as ownership of property (*Economist*, 6/2/07) – but it hardly ever says yes. The price its citizens pay is a heavy one – civil war from 1975 to 1990, intermittent governmental paralysis like the situation in 2015-16, when the citizens of Beirut were trying to deal with rising mountains of trash. The Middle East needed to shrug off its obsession with communalism. Lebanon looks to be the last locale in the region to join that movement.

Competent Hizballah – *Amal* (Hope) was Lebanon's first Shiite communal organization, but *Hizballah* (Party of God) had much more impact on Shiism, on Lebanon, and on Arab prestige. Hizballah is the only Arab force that has fought Israel to a draw (asymmetric). Its violence has been unspeakably costly to Americans and American interests; *NY*, 10/14-21/2002. Its survival seems to derive from the gifted leadership of Hasan Nasrallah, the inspiration of Ayatallah Muhammad Fadlallah, the dedication of its Iranian sponsors, and the resolve of its fighters. In Lebanon, with the army deadlocked between its Christian and Muslim wings, Hizballah was the center of power.

Syria/Lebanon – The endemic turmoil in the cultural entity of Syria/Lebanon is a product of a long series of foreign initiatives and local disruptions:

393

Shiite Connection – Looking for allies against Maronite and Sunni dominance, Lebanon's Shiite community has had ties with Iran since 1502, when Iran's Shiite dynasty proclaimed Shiite Islam the state religion. The Shia of Lebanon, Iran, and Iraq became culturally interlinked by intermarriage, and by Lebanese study at the seminaries of Najaf (Iraq) and Qom (Iran).

Vali Nasr tells us that in 1959 Iraqi Ayatallah Muhsin al Hakim sent a charismatic Iranian cleric, Musa al Sadr, to Lebanon as Hakim's resident representative. In 1974, Sadr founded *Amal* (Hope), an association/militia to rescue the Lebanese Shia from their traditional subjection to class discrimination. "Amal" is an Arabic acronym for *Afwaj al Muqawamah al Lubnaniyyah* (Lebanese Resistance Battalions).

French Intervention – In 1920, the officials of the French Mandate in Syria followed imperialism's venal practice of creating gratuitous political divisions. An extreme example was the bipartition of the French share of former Ottoman territory: Many of the inhabitants of three Ottoman provinces – Aleppo, Syria, and Beirut – found themselves reclassified from citizens of the Empire to citizens of two new sovereign states, "Muslim" Syria, with a large Christian minority, and "Christian" Lebanon with a large Muslim minority. Lebanon was blatantly encumbered by a political system rigged to perpetuate its domination by the Francophile Maronite (Catholic) community. Consequences included three civil wars – Lebanon in 1958 and 1975-90, Syria from 2011.

In drawing the dividing line so as to award the synthetic Lebanese state as many recalcitrant Muslim subjects as was politically feasible, the French failed to factor in the higher Muslim birthrate and the greater Christian inclination to emigrate. Lebanon has never dared to take a census, but a growing Muslim majority has been a longstanding assumption.

Palestinian Intervention – In 1970, civil war erupted in Jordan between the Hashemite regime and Fatah, the nucleus of the Palestinian Resistance Movement. After a military alert in Israel deterred Salah Jadid's initial impulse to intervene in Jordan, King Husayn's army expelled the Palestinians to south Lebanon. The Lebanese government was too beset to object, but the Shia were not.

The PLO was determined to convert south Lebanon into a military base. The Shia chose resistance to the PLO over war with Israel. Their modest efforts were ineffective – particularly after 1978, when Amal lost its leader. On a visit to Libya, Musa Sadr mysteriously disappeared. Vali Nasr cites a report that Sadr was killed on orders from the Sunnis' erratic champion, Mu'ammar al Qadhafi. In 1982, when Israel invaded Lebanon proper, the Shia followed their instincts by mounting no immediate resistance to the IDF. Instead, according to Nasr, Amal fought a short but bitter war against the Palestinian refugee camps that adjoined Shiite neighborhoods in south Beirut.

In 1981, as exchanges between Palestinian artillery and Israeli aircraft intensified, Reagan's special representative, Philip Habib, arranged an understanding between Israel and the PLO that called for a ceasefire, brought Syria back into the realm of international diplomacy after four years in the wilderness, and gave political status to the PLO – even though Habib was prohibited from direct contact with 'Arafat by a blanket commitment that Kissinger had made to Israel in the aftermath of the Yom Kippur War.

The Habib arrangement required the PLO to abandon its second exile in south Lebanon for its own diaspora. 'Arafat and aides went to Tunisia. The militants scattered among various Arab states. No state would grant exile to all the Palestinian "brothers". 'Arafat left Lebanon for Tunisia on 8/30/82: *Times*, 8/31/82.

Syrian Intervention – The outbreak of Lebanon's grinding civil war in 1975 afforded Syria an opportunity, and an obligation, to intervene. For the next fifteen years, Syria wielded its military superiority – primarily in the interest of restoring the unity violated by France in 1920, but in the process Syria lent material assistance to the Lebanese effort to restore order.

An unimaginative dictator would have used the meat-axe approach – as the US President did later in Iraq. Control of Lebanon was being disputed between a pro-West faction and a pro-Arab faction. Hafiz al Asad sensibly realized that promoting a tandem regime that balanced both factions would minimize the constant risk of Israeli interference. Over the next fifteen years, he tweaked the exercise of Syrian power until 1990, when a Syrian-Lebanese force commanded by Lebanese Colonel Amil Lahhud imposed the "neutral" but pro-Syrian regime Asad wanted, and the civil war petered out.

A large Syrian garrison that worked with new President Amil Lahhud ensured Syrian hegemony. A 1991 treaty of coordination was followed up by recognition of a Syrian voice in the internal affairs of its Lebanese "region" (*qutr*). Asad wisely excluded any hint of annexation from his talks with the Lebanese, most of whom were still partial to the meretricious attractions of local autonomy.

In 1991, Asad appeased Washington by signing up Syria on the Coalition side in the second Kuwait War.

Lebanon's Muslim communities, Sunni and Shia, were steadily gaining an increasing majority over the Christian (largely pro-West) community. The Saudi-sponsored Ta'if Accord of 10/22/89 eased the tension by changing the prescribed sectarian ratio in Parliament from six to five (from 54 Christians/45 Muslims to all even – 64 each). Under the Lebanese Compromise of 1943, the Presidency has been reserved for a Maronite, the Premiership for a Sunni, and the speakership for a Shiite.

However, the power of decision has rested with whichever political/military faction was strongest. That reading has been volatile: From 1943 to 1952, it was the Maronite community. From 1952 to 1958, it was Pierre Jumayyil's ultra-Maronite militia, the Phalange. In 1958, the Muslims challenged Maronite leadership in Lebanon's first civil war. Fu'ad Shihab, Maronite commander of the Lebanese Army, shrewdly kept the army neutral, and negotiated a compromise under which he became President. He was succeeded in 1964 by Charles Hilu, who was succeeded by Ilyas Sarkis in 1976.

The Sarkis Presidency was blighted by Lebanon's second civil war, which broke out in 1975. The election of Phalangist Bashir Jumayyil as President in August 1982 was the Maronites' last gasp. Bashir was assassinated in September 1982, before taking office. His killer was suspected to have been a Syrian agent.

The Israeli invasion of Lebanon in June 1982, countered by Lebanese, Palestinian, and Syrian forces, threw the issue of Lebanese hegemony into confusion. In June 1985, the Israeli forces evacuated Lebanon, allowing Syrian forces to take over.

The Ta'if Accord had endorsed Syrian hegemony in Lebanon by authorizing Syrian forces to remain until September 1992. Lebanese disorder allowed the Syrians to delay their departure.

In the longer run, Syria had to deal with Washington's determination to rectify Syria's hostility to Israel. As a refuge of Palestinian resistance leaders, Syria had long been on Washington's blacklist of "terrorist" states. In 2003, Bush 43 signed the Syrian Accountability and Lebanese Sovereignty Restoration Act, which would impose minor economic sanctions on Syria until it terminated its support for the Palestinian resistance, closed its border with Iraq, and withdrew its troops from Lebanon. In 2004, Washington managed to promote UNSC Resolution 1559, which called for the dismantling of all militias in Lebanon and the withdrawal of foreign forces. (Russia and China abstained.)

By these two initiatives, Washington posed a threat to vital Syrian interests. Lebanon employed hundreds of thousands of Syrian workers, its free-enterprise economy was Syria's main source of hard currency, and Beirut was Damascus' natural entrepot (as Latakia was for Aleppo). Lebanon's southern border was a major avenue of Israeli encroachment.

In September 2004, Bashar al Asad met the separatist challenge from Lebanon head-on by persuading the Lebanese Parliament to revise the Constitution and extend the tenure of President Lahhud for another three years, but in 2005 Syria succumbed to pressures from Washington and elsewhere, and withdrew its forces from Lebanon.

Israeli Intervention – In 1978, Israeli troops occupied Lebanon south of the Litani River. This was not enough for Israel's new Defense Minister, Ariel Sharon. The life-long Arab fighter found his pretext in June 1982, when a pro-Iraqi Palestinian splinter group attacked the Israeli Ambassador to Britain. Three days later, on 6/6/82, Israel launched a massive invasion of Lebanon proper.

Prime Minister Begin wanted to strike a blow for Zionism in Israel, and for Israeli hegemony in Occupied Palestine, by bolstering the

Maronites, Israel's clandestine allies, and undermining the PLO. Sharon seemed to have more ambitious objectives: 1) annihilation of the PLO, which had discomfited Israel by accepting the principle of a two-state solution; 2) establishment of a puppet government in Beirut; 3) destruction of the Syrian armed forces; 4) demonstration for Reagan that Israel was a strategic asset in the Cold War; 5) expulsion of Palestinian refugees from Lebanon back to Jordan, in the interest of the conversion of the Hashemite monarchy into a Palestinian state.

Habib had tried to insure the safety of the Palestinian noncombatants left behind in Lebanon. His plans were overridden by the Phalange and the IDF. On 9/14/82, a member of the Syrian Social Nationalist Party (SSNP) killed Lebanon's new President, Bashir al Jumayyil. Phalange official Elie Hubaykah, already admired by Phalangists for having led a massacre of some 80 Lebanese citizens and PLO militiamen in Yarun in south Lebanon, staged an operation on his own initiative. He had the mistaken idea that Bashir had been killed by Palestinians, but reportedly he also had a personal motivation – Palestinians had just killed his fiancée and her family.

Hubaykah had reportedly been authorized by the IDF to search the Shatila Refugee Camp and the adjoining Sabra neighborhood for PLO fighters in hiding. Under the Habib agreement, those sites had been protected by the MNF (the UN's Multinational Force, sent to Lebanon to help keep the peace). The MNF had been prematurely withdrawn from Lebanon on 9/11/82. The IDF had moved in and impounded the Sabra-Shatila residents.

On 9/16/82, Hubaykah led a gang of Maronite misfits into the two neighborhoods and – under the eyes of impassive IDF onlookers – spent the next day and a half killing every resident they met. No PLO fugitives were found. After dark, the attackers had the convenience of Israeli flares. Two thousand (?) Palestinian and Shiite noncombatants died.

In 1983, Israel's Kahan Commission found the IDF personnel on the scene indirectly guilty of the Sabra-Shatila massacre because they had not intervened. The Commission suggested that Sharon had been directly responsible.

1948-2000 – Among the regional powers in the Middle East, Israel established its preeminence by winning four of five successive wars against the neighboring Arab states: 1948, 1956, 1967, 1970, and 1973. It has always had the capacity to penetrate alien territory – as in Sinai in 1956-7, again from 1967 to 1969, and in Lebanon from 1978 to 2000.

End of the Israeli Intervention – However, every power has its limits. The defensive coalition of Lebanese, Syrian, Palestinian, and Hizballah forces exposed Israel's limits in May 2000. Most of the credit flowed to Hizballah, which had avoided the Palestinian mistake of challenging Israel in conventional warfare. Instead, Hizballah resorted to the traditional strategy of the weak – asymmetric warfare. Eighteen years after Israel invaded Lebanon proper, the Israel-Lebanon War was officially ended in June by UNSC endorsement of the Secretary General's certification that the withdrawal of Israeli forces from Lebanon had met the terms of a ceasefire drawn up by Secretary of State Warren Christopher in 1996. (Minute exception: Israel still occupied Shab'ah Farms, a ten-square-mile enclave that by UN decision is part of the Syrian Golan, hence subject to UNSC Resolution 242; but also claimed by Lebanon.)

The ceasefire of 2006 gave Hizballah a plausible right to claim it was the first Arab force to defeat the Israeli juggernaut.

Iranian Intervention – In 1979, Ayatollah Ruhollah Khomeini returned from exile to be hailed the Supreme Leader of the world's only theocracy. Amal proclaimed him Imam of <u>all</u> Muslims. Khomeini had introduced this pan-Islamic theme by his early emphatic espousal of a Sunni cause – Palestinian independence.

In Lebanon, the IDF was antagonizing the Shia by its perpetration of the standard offenses of military occupation – notably depredation of communities that obstructed its advance. Thousands of Shia fled north. More combative Shiites rallied to the dynamic program of Khomeini's personal security force, The Revolutionary Guard Corps. In 1982, it posted 1500 of its fighters in the Lebanese Biqa' to train militiamen. The result was Hizballah, The Party of God, which emerged in 1982 as an activist rival to Amal. Hizballah recognized Khomeini as its *marji' al taqlid* (source of emulation), and hewed to his rigidly anti-Western, militaristic

399

approach. The militants of Hizballah had a pipeline for transit of arms and financing from Iran by way of Syria.

The Rise of Hizballah – In its early years, Hizballah was distrusted in Beirut and repressed in Syria. However, the longer the IDF held out in Lebanon, the more Lebanese Shiites switched from Amal to Hizballah: *JPS*, Autumn 2006, Augustus Richard Norton. By 1989, Hizballah was strong enough to overshadow the sect-ridden Lebanese Army, and to ignore the provision of the Ta'if Accord – seconded by UNSC Resolution 1559 of 9/2/04 – that all militia in Lebanon should be disarmed.

Hizballah's style of resistance to American imperialism was proactive and vicious. It had been influenced by Ayatollah Khomeini's endorsement of suicide bombing: *Wall Street Journal*, 8/3/06. Track one would introduce the vehicular suicide bomb. Track two would include aircraft hijacking and abduction, torture, and killing of Western victims in the Middle East and overseas.

At the same time, Hizballah was becoming a political force in Lebanon – strong enough to disregard UNSC Resolution 425 of 3/19/78, which established UNIFIL (The UN Interim Force in Lebanon), and called for the disarmament of all militias in Lebanon. From 2005, Hizballah has dictated Lebanese policy.

Timeline: 1982-2016 – In reaction to the Israeli invasion of Lebanon proper, Iran created the anti-Israel Party of God (*Hizballah*), which came to supplant *Amal* as Lebanon's leading Shiite party, and become the preeminent political force in the country, overshadowing the traditional sectarian balance and switching Lebanon from pro-US to pro-Iran.

1983 – Hizballah bombed the American Embassy in Beirut, killing 63, and destroyed the US Marine barracks there, killing 241.

1984 – As a precaution after the Marine barracks bombing, Reagan removed the US expeditionary force from Lebanon – without fanfare.

1985-1990's – Hizballah committed abductions and killings of American civilians and officials in Lebanon.

1992 – Hizballah began running candidates for the Lebanese Parliament.

1997 – The US declared Hizballah a terrorist organization.

2000 – Hizballah had 13 of the 27 Shiite seats in Parliament.

2000 – Israel withdrew the forces that had been holding out in south Lebanon. Israel had abandoned the campaign for Lebanon, but its war with Hizballah had just begun.

2004 – Two rival political coalitions emerged in Lebanon: The March 14 Coalition (Sunni/Christian) and the March 8 Coalition (Shiite/Hizballah): *Current History*, December 2015.

2005 – On 2/14/05, a truck bomb killed former Lebanese Prime Minister Rafiq Hariri, leader of the pro-Western faction in Lebanon. An investigatory commission was set up by the UN.

2005 – In April, under international pressure, Syria removed its troops from Lebanon, leaving it deadlocked between The March 14 Coalition (pro-West) and the March 8 Coalition (pro-Arab): *MEP*, Spring 2016, Szekely.

2005 – As of 10/31/05, the UN Commission on the Hariri killing had no conclusive findings, but the UNSC endorsed them anyway.

2006 – On 8/18/06, Israel accepted a ceasefire in its asymmetric war with Hizballah – the first Arab force to stalemate a conflict with Israel. The result was deadlock.

2006 – The 24 portfolios in the Lebanese cabinet were equally divided among The March 8 Coalition, The March 14 Coalition, and the various neutrals.

2008 – 1/28/08 was the date of the unsolved killing of Lebanese security officer Wisam 'Id, believed to have discovered key cell phone data in the UN's Hariri investigation: *NOW*, 8/27/11.

2008 – Hizballah ended Lebanon's political deadlock by occupying government buildings in a decisive show of force. The quarters of the principal Sunni newspaper were burned. In four days of clashes, 17 died. Sunni leader Sa'd al Hariri and Druze leader Walid Junblat were confined to their homes. As the Hizballah militiamen left, they turned the government sites over to the Lebanese Army, which has generally maintained a neutral position in domestic political disputes: *AP*, 5/9/08.

2010 – A Lebanese police officer and UN investigators had unearthed cell phone conversations that implicated Hizballah in the

Hariri killing, according to an investigation conducted by the Canadian Broadcasting Corporation. The mandate of the UN Commission on the Hariri killing had expired. Its task had been assigned to the UN Special Tribunal for Lebanon: www.washingtonpost.com, 11/21/10.

2013 – During the Syrian rebels' siege of Al Qusayr, close to the northern border of Lebanon, Hizballah announced its involvement in the Syrian civil war as an ally of Asad: *Aljazeera*, 6/1/16, Chafic Chouceir. The organization that had won a reputation as the champion of all the Arabs had narrowed its image to the champion of the Shiites.

2014 – On 1/23/14, four operatives of Hizballah went on trial by the UN's Special Tribunal for Lebanon. The charge was the assassination of Lebanese Prime Minister and 22 others on 2/14/05.

2016 – Unable to come to terms, the tribal factions in Lebanon had agreed on two extensions of the Parliament. The Presidency had been vacant for two years: *WRMEA*: *Agence Globale*, October 2016, Rani Khoury (by permission).

2016 – Latest political lineup in Lebanon: Pro-Damascus Regime – The Lebanese Forces (Maronite Christian) of Samir Ja'ja', Michel 'Awn's Free Patriotic Movement, Hizballah; Pro-Saudi – Sa'd Hariri's Future Movement: *Times*, 1/19/16.

2016 – According to the Saudi government, in February Hizballah shipped surface-to-surface missiles to the Huthis.

2016 – On 3/6/16, Hasan Nasrallah confirmed armed intervention by Hizballah in Syria: *MEP*, Summer 2016, Legrenzi/Lawson.

2016 – Lebanon was still operating on the basis of a 1996 agreement for power sharing along sectarian lines. There had been no President for the previous two years, and no Parliamentary elections. Parliament was voting term extensions on its own: *Times*, 5/11/16.

2016 – There was a confrontation between the March 14 Alliance (anti-Syrian) and the March 8 Alliance (pro-Syrian). In May, Michel Sulayman, President of Lebanon, resigned. The battle over his successor was deadlocked. Saudi Arabia backed Sulayman Franjiyyah. Hizballah backed Michel 'Awn: *MEP*, Summer 2016, Legrenzi/Lawson.

2016 – A huge explosion near the Damascus Airport killed Mustafa Badr al Din, brother-in-law of the assassinated 'Imad Mughniyah, longtime leader of Hizballah military and clandestine operations: *Times*, 5/14/16.

2016 – Lebanon now had six million residents – a million and a half of them refugees from Syria et al: *Times*, 7/5/16.

2016 – On 10/31/16, Lebanon elected General Michel 'Awn as President. Once a Maronite leader, he went into exile in France in 1990. He returned to Lebanon in 2005 and founded what became Lebanon's dominant Christian political party. In 2006, he made an abrupt switch to the pro-Syrian side and in Damascus signed an alliance with Hizballah. His election to the Presidency was supported by Hizballah and the Sunni Future Party of Sa'd Hariri, son of the murdered Rafiq Hariri: *FT*, 11/3/16.

The Huthis – In modern Arabia, the dominant subject is oil. In ancient Yemen, it was myrrh and frankincense. On their exportation rested the wealth and renown of a series of empires hailed throughout the Mediterranean World.

Early in the Christian era, Christianity and Judaism found converts in Yemen. Late in the 200's, the Himyarite dynasty from southwest Arabia expanded their rule to all of Yemen (also known as Saba, or Sheba).

Around 520, a Himyarite ruler of the Jewish faith, colloquially known as Dhu Nuwas, massacred Ethiopian residents on the Red Sea coast, Christians in Najran, and Byzantine merchants. The Emperor of Byzantium requested help from the Aksumite King of Ethiopia, which had accepted Monophysite (Eastern Orthodox) Christianity around 450. The Ethiopian king sailed across the Red Sea, killed Dhu Nuwas in battle, replaced him with a Christian Viceroy, and sailed home. The dethroned Himyarites prevailed on the Sassanian Emperor of Persia to expel the Ethiopian governors and establish Persian rule in Yemen. The last Persian Governor of Yemen converted from Zoroastrianism (?) to Islam in 628. His Arab successor was the son-in-law of The Prophet: *EB*, 13:848.

From 893 until 897, the Imam Al Hadi Ilah al Haqq Yahya, grandson of the Prophet, made two visits to Yemen at the invitation of the highland tribes. He was unable to establish his own state, but he inculcated among his followers policies and practices that were to evolve into Yemen's unique brand of Shiite doctrine – Zaydiism. From his descendants came a Zaydi tradition that bonded with the mountaineer spirit of independence that resisted foreign rule – even that of the Caliphate – and survived in the highlands for a thousand years. A unified Yemen was precluded by hostility between the Zaydis of northern Yemen and the Sunnis to the south and east. Yemen's imams have based their legitimacy on descent from the Prophet, through Al Qasim al Rassi, whose descendants were known as Rassids, or Qasimids.

The following timeline is largely based on *Encyclopaedia Britannica*:

600's – Yemen became a province of the Islamic Empire.

897 – Imam Yahya bin Husayn founded a Zaydi religious structure that gave rise to the Qasimid Dynasty (1597-1872), and inspired Yemen's long succession of sectarian regimes until 1962.

1171 – The Fatimid Caliphate, based in Cairo, adherent of the Isma'ili sect of Shiite Islam, was ruling Egypt, most of North Africa, the Levant, and the Hijaz. After the death of the Caliph in 1171, the Fatimid regime was abolished by "the most famous Kurd in history", Salah al Din Ibn Ayyub. At age 33, he replaced the Caliphate with the Ayyubid Dynasty, which paid allegiance to the Abbasid Caliphate (Sunni) in Baghdad.

1173 – Salah al Din annexed Yemen to his realm. In later years, his successors had difficulty holding on to that obdurate country.

1229 – The Turkmen Rasulids succeeded the Ayyubids until 1454.

1517 – The Ottoman Empire recaptured Aden.

1600 – The Ottomans established a base in the Yemeni highlands.

1618 – British traders set up a trading post in Yemen's coastal city of Mocha (*Al Mukha*), historic center for the export of Arabian coffee.

1785 – At Mocha, Americans overtook the British as the main exporters of Arabian coffee.

1800 – The UK established a garrison in Aden, a key point on the Lifeline to India: *EB* 1:95.

1802 – The UK signed a treaty with the Sultan of Lahij. His domain included Aden.

1839 – In response to the plundering of a British merchant ship, a British sea captain forced the Sultan of Lahij to accept British protection.

1848 – The Ottomans came back to Yemen again.

1849 – Yemenis massacred an Ottoman force sent to occupy San'a'.

1872 – Ottoman forces were back in Yemen again.

1904 – Imam Yahya succeeded his father as ruler of Yemen in the Hamid al Din line.

1911 – An Ottoman force, sent from Libya to pacify 'Asir (now a district of Saudi Arabia) and Yemen, suffered heavy losses. Neighboring principalities and the Ottomans persuaded the Imam of Yemen to sign the Treaty of Da'n, which allowed Ottoman troops to be stationed on the coast of Yemen.

1918 – The defeat of the Ottomans in World War I enabled the Qasimids, descendants of the first Yemeni Imam, to found the Mutawakkil Kingdom of Yemen.

1937 – Aden became a British crown colony.

1946 – President Truman recognized the Kingdom of Yemen.

1948 – Military opponents of feudal rule assassinated Imam Yahya. His son Ahmad rallied the supporters of the Hamid al Din's.

1955 – Imam Ahmad defeated a second military coup attempt.

1958 – On 3/8/58, with Nasir in the political ascendancy in the Arab World, Imam Ahmad joined the United Arab States, a federation of Yemen and the UAR. It was a nonstarter.

1962 – Imam Ahmad died, and was succeeded by his son Badr on 9/18/62.

1962 – On 9/26/62, an uprising of junior army officers, inspirited by the proclamation of Syrian-Egyptian unity, proclaimed the founding of the Yemen Arab Republic (YAR). Civil war broke out between the followers of deposed Imam Badr, backed by Saudi Arabia, and revolutionaries, backed by an expeditionary force sent from Egypt by Jamal 'Abd al Nasir. The rebels named 'Abdallah al Sallal President of the YAR.

1963 – The UK united south Yemen (Aden and the Aden Protectorate territories) in the Federation of South Arabia.

1963 – Two rebel factions in south Yemen, one backed by Egypt, the other Marxist, resorted to violence against British rule and each other.

1966 – On 9/18/66, Sallal was ousted by a bloodless coup led by 'Abd al Rahman al Iryani, an inveterate activist who had spent fifteen years in a Yemeni jail. Iryani became President in 1967.

1967 – The UK gave up in south Yemen, which became an independent state. Aden was named capital in 1968.

1970 – President Iryani concluded a national conciliation agreement with the Royalists. Yemeni-Saudi relations were restored.

1974 – Another military coup sent Iryani into exile in Syria.

1978 – 'Ali 'Abdallah Salih, backed by Egypt, became President of Yemen.

1990 – On 5/22/90, north and south Yemen united as the country of Yemen, with the capital at San'a'.

1990 – In August, Yemen abstained from UNSC resolutions authorizing military action versus Iraq for having occupied Kuwait. In retaliation, Kuwait and Saudi Arabia expelled their Yemeni guest workers, numbering 800,000. The Yemen economy took a hit.

1990's – In North Yemen, the contentious Huthi tribe (Zaydi) emerged as a political force in the Sa'dah Governorate of northwestern Yemen.

1992 – Husayn al Huthi, son of the Huthis' leader, founded "The Believing Youth" to promote a Zaydi revival. The movement was pro-Iranian and hostile to Salafis, Saudi Arabia, the US, and Zionism.

1994 – From May to July, north Yemen forces occupied Aden and forced south Yemen to rescind its decision to secede from Yemen.

1999 – On 9/23/99, in Yemen's first vote by universal suffrage, it elected 'Ali 'Abdallah Salih (Zaydi) President.

2000 – In Aden harbor, guided-missile destroyer USS Cole was damaged by a bomb placed by an AQAP operative. Seventeen crewmen died.

2003 – The Huthis were infuriated by the American invasion of Iraq.

2004 – The Huthi tribe ignited a multi-tribal rebellion against the regime of President Salih, who ordered the army to take countermeasures.

2008 – The AQAP claimed the bombing of the US Embassy in San'a'.

2009 – In December, at the request of Salih, the US began air strikes at suspected AQAP sites.

2009 – Overpopulation and shortage of oil and water supply had caused serious deterioration in the lifestyle of the Yemeni people: Kristian Ulrichsen.

2011 – The massacre of anti-regime protestors in north Yemen on 3/18/11 led to intensification of the tribal insurgency.

2011 – On 11/3/11, in Riyadh, Salih signed a GCC-sponsored agreement under which he agreed to resign as President in favor of his Vice President, 'Abdu Rabbuh Mansur Hadi. Yemen was being sectarianized (*Times*, 11/20/11), but the regime was military, not clerical.

2012 – On 2/21/12, in an uncontested election, Hadi was elected President of the Yemen Arab Republic (YAR). One third of the Yemenis were Zaydis.

2015 – On 1/22/15, Huthi militiamen besieged the residence of President Hadi, who resigned. The AQAP opposed the action.

2015 – On 2/6/15, the tribal insurgents dissolved the Yemeni Parliament and installed a five-man Presidential Council.

2015 – On 3/20/15, ISIL claimed suicide attacks on two mosques in Yemen. 142 were killed. (See entry of 2/3/14 about Al Qa'idah's disavowal of the ISIL.)

2015 – On 3/25/15, Saudi Arabia announced a campaign of air strikes in the San'a' area. Egypt, Jordan, Morocco, Sudan, and all the GCC states except Oman would participate. The US would help with planning, logistics, and intelligence.

NB: The Huthi story is continued in the section on the Saudi-Yemeni War.

The Kurds – Every language learned is a key to opportunity, but only a native language leaves indelible imprints on a person's lifelong outlook.

The international languages – English most of all – open doors worldwide. The hundreds of localized languages, like Georgian, or Hebrew, or Kurdish – to cite examples from the Middle East – can have vibrant literatures and a multitude of applications, but too often they condemn their speakers to a sterile dedication of life and limb to a false patriotism that blocks avenues of assimilation with the rest of humanity.

So it is with the twenty-five million Kurds of Turkey, Iraq, and Syria, who belong to more than one religious sect, speak widely variant dialects, and have trouble getting along with each other, and yet are obsessed with the substantively irrelevant happenstance that the "Kurds" have never had a state of their own. This obsession compels them to interpose one more obstacle to the ultimate unification of the Middle East – and apparently to forget that the history of a multi-ethnic state like the Ottoman Empire can be forever illuminated by "outsiders" like Salah al Din al Ayyubi, the "Kurd", and Muhammad 'Ali, the "Albanian".

In 2016, the Kurds were estimated to number 14,000,000 in Turkey, 5,000,000 in each of Iraq and Iran, and 2,000,000 in Syria.

The Kurds may be descendants of the Medes. Their Indo-European language is akin to Persian. They have been centered in the Taurus Mountains of Turkey and the Zagros Mountains of Iran for millennia. They were early converts to Islam. Most Kurds are Sunnis, but there are Shia, Alawite, and Yazidi Kurds as well.

The Kurds have been agitating for statehood for centuries. Two huge obstacles stand in their way: 1) The four competing post-Ottoman states are dead set against the emergence of a fifth, which would have to make territorial demands on the other four; Ataturk stressed his personal opposition to the Kurdish homeland provision in the abortive Treaty of Sèvres; 2) Kurdish tribalism has been exacerbated by the same rugged terrain that has helped them resist assimilation by Turks, Persians, or Arabs. Since the early 1900's, Kurdish leadership in Iraq has been contested between two rival confederations – one led by the Barzani clan, the other by the Talabanis – that wear distinguishing scarves (*NYTM*, 6/14/16) and speak very different dialects (Kurmanji and Sorani) of their Indo-European language. As late as 2016, the Kurds had no common front.

2000's – The UN Charter denies UN membership to stateless peoples. The Kurds were not even accorded the observer status held by the Palestine Liberation Organization. Nevertheless, under American protection they had made impressive strides toward the acquisition of all the tangible institutions of a sovereign state. As for recognition, America, the adjoining states, and the UN are committed to the preservation of a sovereign Iraq within its present borders.

In their common antipathy to Kurdish nationalism, Turkey and Iraq used to be natural allies, and their concord was reinforced by Turkish reliance on Iraqi oil and the revenues from pipeline transit. Interruption of these revenues by the Kuwait Wars cost Turkey billions. In 1998, John Tirman perceived a de facto alliance of Turkey, Iraq, and the Barzani Kurds (whose territory was transited by the pipeline) against the Talabani Kurds (who were closer to the PKK and Iran). Turkey was also suffering financial losses from UN sanctions against Iraq. By 2002, trade between Turkey and Iraq was back up to a billion dollars a year.

From the Arab point of view, the Kurds have never been good citizens of Iraq. They fought on the Ottoman side in World War I, the Iranian side in the 1980's, the Coalition side in 1991, and the American side in 2003-04. Their only ally – and clandestine arms supplier – is Israel. CPA efforts to divert the KAR from its insistence on autonomy were unsuccessful. Kurdish nationalism promises to be an issue of mounting international concern, inasmuch as it impinges on the status of Kurds in Turkey, control of Iraq's northern oil fields, allocation of the flow of the Tigris and the Euphrates, boundary disputes, the Arab-Israeli conflict, and nuclear proliferation.

In 2003, the American invasion of Iraq plunged Iraq, Turkey, and their whole neighborhood into a new era of unremitting chaos.

In 2009, two Kurdish militias (Peshmerga and the YPG) had begun exploiting a new source of recruits – women: *FP*, November 2014, Packer.

The Drive for Kurdish Statehood in Turkey

Mid-1800's – Ottoman armies dismantled a series of Kurdish principalities.

1920's – Ataturk established Turkey's tradition of fierce loyalty to the borders he established after World War I, and of intolerance of any hint of political or cultural expression on the part of any ethnic minority. The Kurdish identity was smothered: *NYTM*, 5/29/16, Robert W. Worth.

1925 – The Kemalist government crushed the first Kurdish uprising, executed 47 "bandit" leaders, and stripped the Kurds of any legal identity.

1930's – Turkish law required mass Kurdish dispersal, to ensure that no district had a Kurdish population exceeding five percent of the district total.

1978 – Abdullah Ocalan founded the Kurdish Workers' Party (PKK), which assumed leadership of the Kurdish insurgency in Turkey. The PKK began as a Marxist organization of male and female militants: *MEP*, Winter 2008, Robert Pape. Its objective was to convert part of the territory of Turkey into a Kurdish state: *MEP*, Spring 2015, Till Paasche. Turkey imposed martial law.

1978-98 – Turkey suffered through two decades of mass arrests, torture, killing, deportation of Kurds, destruction of Kurdish villages by actions of both sides, and the dispersal of hordes of Kurds to the cities – over a million to Istanbul.

1978-98 – The Baathist regime in Damascus allowed the PKK to site its base in Syria, and to project its message of statehood to Kurds in Turkey – but not to Kurds in Syria. The Baathists welcomed the opportunity to apply moderate pressure on the government in Ankara, which had been oblivious to Syrian and Iraqi complaints about Turkish diversion of water to its ambitious power and irrigation projects: *NYR*.

1984 – Outbreak of the PKK rebellion: Worth. Ankara imposed a state of emergency in ten southeastern provinces. Many Kurds have emigrated from this sector to western Turkey or Europe.

1990's – In Turkey, violence between its security forces and the PKK reached a peak (*MER*, 12/17/15), although the rebellion was largely confined to the mountains and countryside: Worth.

Mid-90's – Turkey concluded an alliance with the Iraqi Kurdish KDP against the PKK.

The sudden appearance in 1992 of a Kurdish Regional Government (KRG) – even a "parliament" – in Iraq's KAR caused Ankara considerable distress. At that early stage, the Barzanis' KDP and the Talabanis' PUK were collaborating against the PKK, to the point of resisting units that sought refuge in Iraq. However, the forces of the PKK (and those of its Iranian affiliate, PEJAK) had long relied on hideouts in the KAR's Kandil Mountains.

Also in 1992, PKK leader Abdullah Ocalan, an egocentric who was inclined to have his Kurdish rivals killed, was in Syria operating a boot camp and orchestrating infiltration into Turkey. Ankara was trying to balance its conflicting interests by restricting the flow of Euphrates water into Syria, and allowing US flights from Incirlik to defend the enclave being set up by Iraqi Kurds in northeastern Iraq, even though Ankara detested the northern No-Fly Zone because it reduced Turkish revenue from trade with Iraq, afforded sanctuary for Turkish Kurds, and its Kurdish sector was beginning to take on the attributes of an independent state.

In the 1990's, hostilities caused the razing of 3000 of Turkey's Kurdish villages.

1996 – Despite Ankara's scorched-earth strategy, its conscription of a Kurdish force that fought for the regime, the proscription of the PKK, the ban on Kurds' return to their ancestral home unless they signed a document that blamed the PKK for the destruction of Kurdish villages, and the consequent assimilation of millions of Kurds into Turkish society, the PKK had managed by 1996 to nullify government control of ten southeastern provinces.

1998 – Turkey made history by allowing the election to Parliament of Kurds who implicitly represented the PKK. Turkey's pursuit of insurgent Kurds continued.

1998 – Turkey lost patience with Syria. It warned Damascus to expel Ocalan or get ready for war. Hafiz al Asad expelled Ocalan and his guerrillas: *Out of Nowhere*, Michael Gunter (cited by Jonathan Steele in the *NYR*, 12/3/15). Syria and Turkey confirmed their accord in the Adana Agreement. The PKK's deal with Syria came to an end.

1998 – To preserve US base rights at Incirlik, Washington tolerated Turkey's repression of its Kurds, while Washington was involuntarily abetting a Kurdish quasi-state in Iraq's KAR.

1998 – The CIA mitigated this offense to the Turks by helping them chase Ocalan down in Kenya. He was brought back to Turkey and imprisoned for life. His associates took refuge in the KAR. The PKK declared a five-year ceasefire, and the Turkish Parliament lifted the ban on teaching and broadcasting in Kurdish. Imprisonment turned out to be a strategic advantage for Ocalan: Now he could work for a peace process with Turkey. He proposed a new strategy of Democratic Confederalism, under which the PKK would seek autonomy <u>within</u> the existing boundaries of Turkey. Kurds who had suffered in the battle for their own state were supposed to abandon that objective: *MEP*, Spring 2015, Till F. Paasche.

1999 – Ocalan's confinement brought a lull in the insurgency. The Turkish State of Emergency, in effect since 1984, was lifted. As a gesture to the European Union, Ankara announced that the state broadcasting authority would allow limited programs in Kurdish.

2000 – From its outset, the PKK insurgency had cost the razing of thousands of Turkey's Kurdish villages, and the loss of 30,000 Turkish and Kurdish lives. Both sides had committed atrocities. At least 5000 Kurdish activists had disappeared – probably eliminated by police death squads. Two million Kurds had left their mountain homes for the cities.

2000 – Recep Tayyip Erdogan became Prime Minister of Turkey.

2004 – Still hoping that Turkey would join the EU, Erdogan banned torture of Kurds and released many PKK prisoners. Private schools began teaching some classes in Kurdish. State TV aired its first Kurdish-language program. The rebellion lapsed: Worth.

2006 – Most of the PKK's 5000 militants, operating from the KAR under the leadership of Murat Karayilan, were still killing Turkish soldiers. The PKK units there were protected from Turkish attack by the American occupiers of Iraq, and were using new tactics learned from the Iraqi resistance against the American occupiers: Stephen Kinzer.

2006 – In March, the killing of fourteen PKK militants (in Turkey?) precipitated violent Kurdish protests, especially in Diyarbakir, a largely Kurdish city of a million with 70 percent unemployment. The US and the European Union were urging a receptive Erdogan to proclaim a general amnesty for the PKK. Since the American invasion of Iraq, the PKK and the KDP had built close ties, but Ankara was cultivating President Talabani (PUK). In Turkey, the anti-tribal PKK had had lethal clashes with the pro-tribal "Kurdish Hizballah": *MEP*, Spring 2006 and 2007. Although thousands of the fundamentalist faction had been jailed, some 20,000 were still active. In August, a group thought to be the urban wing of the PKK claimed responsibility for a string of lethal bombings.

2006 – In the fall, while Ocalan's PKK was calling for a ceasefire, a new Kurdish resistance force, The Kurdistan Freedom Falcons (TAK), were carrying out lethal bombings of tourism sites in Turkish cities. The PKK condemned these operations.

2006 – Turkey initiated F-16 strikes on PKK sites in the KAR. Ankara was refusing to deal with Jalal Talabani or KRG President Mas'ud Barzani.

2007 – Turkey's new Chief of Staff opposed amnesty for the PKK, but expected that over time the Kurdish problem would solve itself: Half of Turkey's Kurds, including Ocalan, still spoke Kurmanji at home, but millions had been assimilated into Turkish society, and the conciliatory strategy of Erdogan's AKP was having good effect: Bellaigue.

2007 – In December, Ocalan was directing PKK operations from prison: *Wall Street Journal*, Michael Rubin.

2007 – Erdogan had switched to a more pragmatic posture. Ankara was supporting Turkish investment in the KAR (80 percent of total foreign investment there), had reopened its consulate in Mawsil, and was allowing charter flights to the KAR. The Turkish military, which had maintained a force of 1500 in the KAR since the conclusion of the alliance with the KDP, was opposed to Erdogan's détente: Peter Galbraith.

413

2007 – In December, out of frustration with Iraq's failure to extradite PKK leaders, Turkey mounted heavy air strikes on PKK targets in the mountains of Iraq. Although the Turkish military disclaimed any role in the tripartite dispute, a Turkish official alleged that the strikes had benefitted from Turkish receipt of American intelligence. The heavy dependence of the American occupation force in Iraq on supply lines from Turkey may have figured in the political equation: Peter Galbraith.

2009 – In December, the Democratic Society Party (DSP) (Kurdish) was disbanded by Ankara on a charge of cooperating with the PKK.

2013 – In March Erdogan announced a ceasefire with the PKK, and the withdrawal of all elements of the PKK to the KAR. Turkey reduced its troop deployment in the southeast: Worth.

2013 – On 4/25/13, as a result of peace talks between Erdogan and Ocalan, the PKK confirmed that its forces in Turkey were being transferred to the KAR. Although Turkish Kurds speak either Turkish or their own dialect of Kurdish, the commonality of the Kurdish label was winning them the political support of Iraqi Kurds.

2015 – In July, a PKK killing of two Turkish officers in a private home ended the two-year ceasefire between Turkey and the PKK. The PKK escalated its attacks from raids on security outposts to assassinations and roadside bombings. Turkey resumed anti-PKK military operations in Turkey and the KAR: *MEP*, Winter 2015. The DSP's Democratic Confederalism became a dead letter.

2015 – A PKK attack killed 37 Turkish soldiers. The Turkish Air Force retaliated strongly: *Times*, 9/8/15; *FT*, 8/17/15.

2015 – Turkish mobs had raided 180 buildings of the PDR, a political party suspected of collaboration with the PKK: *Times*, 9/15/15.

2015 – Erdogan's prediction that the IS would capture Kobani put a damper on Turkey-PKK conciliation. (Some weeks later, under international pressure, Erdogan allowed a Kurdish military convoy from Iraq to bring more troops for the Kobani battle: Worth.)

2015 – The Kurdish insurgents in Turkey were getting younger. Kurd-Turk clashes were moving from the mountains into the cities: *FT*, 12/24/16.

2016 – Kurdish insurgents had taken the battle into three cities in southeastern Turkey. Several hundred combatants and civilians had died in those encounters: *FT*, 1/12/16.

2016 – The detonation of a bomb in Ankara on 3/13/16 was a message that, after 30 years of war in the mountains, the PKK had moved its attacks into the heart of the Turkish state – if Prime Minister Davitoglu was correct in his conclusion that the bombing was a PKK operation: *FT*, 3/15/16, Firat Keyman.

2016 – The TAK had no ties to the PKK. Its operations were more extreme, and included suicide bombings: *FT*, 3/21/16.

2016 – The TAK claimed the 3/13/16 bombing in Ankara: *Times*, 3/17/16. The bombing had caused 37 deaths, mostly soldiers: *Times*, 4/1/16.

2016 – On 3/31/16, a car bomb killed seven policemen in Diyarbakir: *Times*, 4/1/16.

2016 – Since the full-scale resumption of the civil war in Turkey, 350 security personnel and thousands of Kurdish militants had died: *Times*, 4/1/16.

2016 – Southeastern Turkey had come to resemble a war zone: *Times*, 6/30/16, Max Fisher.

2016 – Since the end of the ceasefire of July, 500 Turkish soldiers had died in the renewed fighting: Worth.

The Drive for Kurdish Statehood in Iraq

In 1926, the Iraqi monarchy accorded its Kurds certain special rights, but no hint of autonomy.

During World War II, Mustafa Barzani's effort to establish a Kurdish state in Iraq was crushed, and he fled to the Soviet Union. After the fall of the Iraqi monarchy in 1958, he returned with 800 tribesmen and concluded with Prime Minister 'Abd al Karim Qasim an agreement under which Qasim legalized Barzani's Kurdish Democratic Party (KDP) as a counterweight to Qasim's Arab Nationalist rivals. The deal paid off for Baghdad in 1959, when the Barzani Kurds crushed a mutiny by Iraqi army units in Mawsil. At this point, the leadership of Barzani,

415

whose following was largely based in the countryside of the northwestern half of Iraqi Kurdistan, was challenged by Jalal Talabani, who commanded more support among the urban Kurds in the cities of the southeastern half.

The 1960's were disrupted by intermittent Barzani violence against the Iraqi regime, and several abortive efforts by Baghdad to negotiate a compromise between Arab hegemony and Kurdish autonomy. In 1970, the Saddam regime mollified the Iraqi Kurds by promulgating a constitution that described Iraq as a country of two nationalities—Arab and Kurd. This formula failed to resolve the issue of the division of oil revenues. In 1974, the Barzanis, emboldened by clandestine support from Iran and Israel, in collusion with the United States, went back on the warpath in a bid for control of the Kirkuk oil fields. Secretary of State Kissinger was believed to favor backing Kurdish activism as a means of diverting Iraq from providing military support to adversaries of Israel, like Syria during the Yom Kippur War.

In 1975, Barzani and Kissinger were simultaneously challenged from an unexpected quarter. At an OPEC summit in Algiers, Saddam and the Shah of Iran buried their own hatchet. Iraq renounced its claims to Khuzistan (the Iranian area populated by people of Arab extraction) and ceded control of the Shatt al 'Arab (the channel in which the twin rivers merge and flow into the Gulf). In return, the Shah closed the border, terminating the financial and logistic support the Barzanis had been receiving from Iran, Israel, and America. Baghdad took advantage of this situation to hit the Kurds with a major offensive. Mustafa Barzani fled to Iran and died in exile.

New York Times columnist William Safire viewed the 1975 Algiers transaction as Iranian betrayal of the Kurds in return for Iraqi participation in OPEC. British writer Patrick Seale reached a different conclusion: In collusion with Israel and the Shah, Kissinger had lured the Barzanis into a rebellion they were not intended to win, but which would prevent Iraq from aiding Syria against Israel, as it had in the 1973 war. Seale felt this cynical strategy had produced a backlash, in that one of Saddam's motives in invading Iran in 1980 was to tear up the 1975 Algiers Agreement.

416

In 1976, Barzani's ancient rival, Jalal Talabani, formed a second Kurdish party, the Patriotic Union of Kurdistan (PUK): *MER,* Summer 2008, Joost Hilterman. The Talabani Kurds enjoyed the political support of Iran and the Asad regime in Syria, but neither was of any utility in 1975, when Saddam instituted a cold-blooded expulsion of Kurdish, Turkmen, and Christian residents from Kirkuk's oil-field area to southern Iraq, their replacement with Arabs from the south, and the execution of some Kurdish leaders. The United States sat silent through these events. 1978 witnessed another roundup of Kurdish opponents of the Saddam regime.

The Iraq-Iran war of 1980-88 afforded the Iraqi Kurds a new opportunity to pursue their campaign for self-rule. The KDP and the PUK papered over their differences and built up a formidable militia (*Peshmerga*) with weapons from Iran. However, the Kurds continued to pay the price of their incorrigible tribalism. In 1983, Baghdad exploited the PUK's bid for negotiation by attacking the forces of the KDP and abducting several thousand males who were never seen again. In the ensuing years Baghdad punished the Kurds for their alliance with Iran by a brutal series of mass detentions, executions, and episodes of chemical warfare; it was characteristic of Iraqi and Kurdish politics that some Kurdish tribes still sided with Baghdad. During the fighting, some 3800 Kurdish villages were emptied, and upwards of 200,000 Kurds killed. (In the interest of balance, it should be noted that – as reported by Nicholas Kristof of the *Times* in 2003 – the Kurds of Turkey, who did not make common cause with any enemy state, have been treated even more brutally than the Kurds of Baathist Iraq.) The Iraqi Kurds avoided conflict with Turkish forces, and did not interpose resistance to Turkey's periodic intrusions into northern Iraq in pursuit of PKK fighters from Turkey.

1988 featured Baghdad's infamous *Anfal* campaign against rebellious Iraqi Kurds. In the village of Halabjah, suspected of having sided with Iran in the bitter Iraq-Iran border war that had been raging for eight years, hundreds of residents died from napalm and chemical-weapon attacks. Over 100,000 rebel Kurds lost their lives during Anfal from action by Iraqi forces and their Kurdish allies.

417

After Iraq's expulsion from Kuwait in 1991 and Bush 41's ill-considered call for an Iraqi uprising, the Iraqi Kurds revolted in sync – but not in coordination – with the Shia in south Iraq. Within weeks, they had captured three northern provinces (Dahuk, Arbil, Sulaymaniyyah). As in the south, the United States chose not to obstruct Baghdad's repression of the insurrection – until the plight of a million or two Kurds fleeing north from Iraqi attack, but blocked at the Turkish border, became so grave that Washington, London, and Paris felt compelled (in apparent violation of Iraqi sovereignty) to designate that part of Iraq north of the 36th parallel as a No-Fly Zone – off limits to Iraqi military air operations – and to enforce it by an Allied air umbrella based at Incirlik Air Base in Turkey. Washington even felt an obligation to set up a program to feed the 700,000 Iraqi Kurdish refugees in the Kurdish Autonomous Region (KAR) – but not the million who had taken refuge in Iran.

That fall Baghdad evacuated its forces and cut off all government services to the three Kurdish provinces. The Kurds set about establishing all the essential machinery of local government – army, police force, civil service, and a school system that taught in Kurdish. In 1992 the KDP founded the Kurdish Regional Government (KRG) in Arbil (*NYTM*, 8/14/16), and the KDP and the PUK collaborated in the election of a figurehead KRG parliament, although Kurdish leadership was still contested between the Barzanis, based in Arbil, and the Talabanis, based in Sulaymaniyyah. A meeting of Iraqi Kurdish dissidents, convened in Washington by the US Government in the interest of Kurdish reconciliation, was attended by Jalal Talabani, but Mas'ud Barzani declined.

1994 witnessed another violent falling-out between Iraq's two Kurdish factions – this time over the division of customs revenue, notably from tolls paid by trucks carrying diesel fuel through Zakhu to Turkey. The route ran through KDP (Barzani) territory.

In 1996, backed by its Iranian neighbors, the PUK was on the point of winning, when the battered KDP turned to Baghdad, whose ground forces reentered the Kurdish zone, drove PUK forces out of Arbil and Sulaymaniyyah, rolled up the CIA's assets in the area, and reinstated

KDP control of the disputed customs revenue. The PKK, stronger than the two Iraqi factions, but much weaker than Baghdad, did not intervene. Later in the year, the PUK retook Arbil and Sulaymaniyyah with help from Islamic Revolutionary Guards. In *The Nation*, Dilip Hiro reported that the Zakhu customs arrangement was a breach of the UN sanctions on Iraq, but that Washington let it go, being averse to assuming responsibility for financing the Kurdish entity it had just created.

In the eyes of many Iraqi Kurds, the US had now betrayed their cause three times: 1975, 1991, and 1996. On the other hand, the Kurds continued to betray each other. In 1997, the KDP, in compact with Turkey, drove PUK forces out of Arbil and PKK forces out of the KAR. In 1998, the US mediated a truce between the KDP and the PUK. In Washington, they signed an agreement to coordinate with Turkey's campaign to suppress the "terrorist" PKK. The KAR enclave remained partitioned between them.

2002 – Mas'ud Barzani and Jalal Talabani came to Washington to plan US military training of Kurds in the KAR.

2003 – When the American forces invaded Iraq, its Kurdish citizens, like those in Turkey, were widely dispersed. 800,000 were living in Baghdad. In Iraq's Ta'mim Province, Kurdish officials included the Governor and most members of the Provincial Council. Kirkuk, which sits on one of Iraq's two richest oil fields (the other is in the Basrah area), had been victimized by population transfers imposed by Saddam; Kurds had been dispossessed, and Arabs (mainly Shia) had been brought in from southern Iraq.

2003 – The US invasion of Iraq afforded the Iraqi Kurds major benefits, including the opportunity (in 2005) to institute their own oil laws: *MEP*, Spring 2015, Philippe le Billon. The Turkish Parliament had gone along with public opinion, rather than the preference of the Turkish military, by denying the invaders access to Iraq via Turkey.

2003 – On 3/19/03, US air attacks on Baghdad launched the invasion of Iraq. In the KAR, in combination with US Special Forces, the Peshmerga attacked villages held by *Ansar al Islam* along the Iranian border. (*Ansar al Islam* was a pro-Qa'idah Kurdish Salafi militia established in the KAR in 2001 by Mala Krekar and Abu Mus'ab al Zarqawi.)

2003 – On 4/10/03, forces of the US army and the Peshmerga captured Kirkuk. Arabs fled as Kurds looted.

2003 – On 4/27/03, US forces disarmed Turkmen militia in Kirkuk, while Arabs and Kurds skirmished in Mawsil.

2003 – On 5/1/03 Bush 43 announced the end of major combat in Iraq, "one victory in a war on terrorism."

2003 – On 5/22/03, UNSC Resolution 1483 lifted the UN sanctions imposed on Iraq after the Kuwait Wars and assigned responsibility to the US and the UK for running Iraqi affairs, subject to consultation with Lakhdar Brahimi, Special Representative of the UN Secretary General: https://www.un.suborg/en/sanctions.

2003 – After the invasion, Turkey and Iran were preoccupied with denying Kirkuk to Kurdish forces based in the KAR. Within weeks of the invasion, the Kurds' expansionist campaign, undeterred by Coalition disapproval, was well underway. By late May, the Kirkuk police force was largely manned by Kurds.

2004 – In December, five Turks died in the ambush of a Turkish military convoy in Mawsil.

2005 – The Iraqi Kurds instituted their own oil laws.

2005 – Condoleezza Rice, US National Security Adviser, called on Iraqi Shia and Kurds to accept Sunnis in the drafting of an Iraqi constitution, but the views of the Sunnis had been overruled in favor of a draft favoring the establishment of three autonomous entities – one Sunni, one Kurdish, and one Shia (under Iranian influence): *NYR*, 10/6/05, Peter Galbraith.

2005 – The draft would provide for a referendum on whether Ta'mim Province, site of Kirkuk, should come under the administration of Baghdad or the KRG: *Times*, 12/29/05.

2006 – The KRG, operating through the "Parliament" in Arbil, had combined the administrations of the KDP and the PUK, trenched its southern boundary, posted Peshmerga units to guard it, prohibited the entry of forces of the Government of Iraq, installed a "President of the Kurdistan Region" (Mas'ud Barzani), hoisted its own flags in place of

Iraqi flags, and concluded oil agreements with several foreign companies. It had not yet corrected the communications problem caused by inheritance of two incompatible cell phone systems – one based in Arbil (KDP territory), the other in Sulaymaniyyah (PUK).

2006 – The new power structure in the KAR was offering more latitude for PKK operatives and receiving less cooperation from Washington. Iraq's President Talabani (a Kurd) was infuriated by the visit to Turkey by Iraqi Prime Minister Ja'fari. Bush 43 was still stewing about Turkey's denial of transit rights for US troops on their way to invade Iraq: Bellaigue. Some Turks theorized that Washington had eased its opposition to Kurdish nationalism in hopes that PEJAK (the Kurdish insurgent group in Iran) could divert Iran from its campaign to undermine the US occupation of Iraq. PEJAK was basing its anti-Iran operations in southeast KAR.

2006 – On 9/1/06, KRG President Mas'ud Barzani ordered that the Kurdish flag be flown in place of the Iraqi flag. New international airports in Arbil and Sulaymaniyyah offered direct flights to foreign destinations.

2006 – Late in the year, the US and Israel were jointly providing PEJAK with intelligence on the situation in northwest Iran: Seymour Hersh.

2007 – The KRG initiated the establishment of an American University of Iraq in Sulaymaniyyah. The regional economy was booming, with investment flowing in from Turkey and the US. On 8/6/2007 the Kurdish Parliament adopted a KAR oil law that endorsed the formula for the division of oil revenues laid down in the Iraqi Constitution. *The Wall Street Journal* reported that, since the KAR law had not been recognized by the regime in Baghdad, the major companies had stayed away from the KAR. Hunt Oil had signed a contract, and shipments to Turkey began in June 2009: Thomas Friedman.

2007 – In August, the KRG Parliament enacted a law that apportioned revenues from Iraqi sale of oil – 83 percent for Iraq, 17 percent for the KRG.

2008 – In February, Turkey staged a small incursion into the KAR to discipline the Peshmerga. In March, Iraqi President Talabani went to Turkey for meetings with President Gul and Prime Minister Erdogan.

2008 – In March, resistance in Mawsil to the Iraqi regime in Baghdad was intensifying. The administration in Mawsil was Kurdish, but its 1.8 million residents included an Arab majority and a Turkish minority: *Harper's*, February 2016, Glass.

2008 – In July, Kurds and Turkmens clashed in Kirkuk.

2008 – In July, Erdogan made the first Turkish state visit to Iraq in eighteen years.

2008 – The KAR was requiring all immigrants from other parts of Iraq to carry ID cards that had to be renewed every three months.

2008 – **The Iraq-KAR Boundary Dispute** – The KRG was claiming parts of Ninawah, Ta'mim, and Diyala provinces that adjoined the KAR. In Ninawah Province, the city of Mawsil was largely inhabited by Sunni Arabs west of the Tigris and by Turkmens and Christians east of the Tigris. Kurdish forces dominated the eastern section. By 2008, law and order had given way to Arab-Kurd clashes and assassinations. In Ta'mim Province, the governor, most members of the Provincial Council, and most of the police were now Kurds.

2008 – The Iraqi Kurds were striking out on their own in the Iraqi power struggle: Peter Galbraith. Kurdish forces under the command of Masrur Mas'ud Barzani controlled Kirkuk (population: 900,000).

2009 – In May, the KRG was exporting crude to Turkey.

2009 – The Iraqi elections for provincial councils bypassed the three KAR provinces (Dahuk, Arbil, Sulaymaniyyah) and a contested province (Ta'mim).

2009 – The KDP and the PUK finally came together in a loose coalition. In a direct election, Mas'ud Barzani was chosen President of the KRG.

2009 – The KRG had largely taken over the Kirkuk police force, and was taking every opportunity to expel Arabs from northern Iraq with the same brutality Saddam had once inflicted on the Kurds. Kurdish expansionism had not been inhibited by warnings of American intervention. The Turks were obsessed by the contingency that a

Kurdish state in Iraq could galvanize Kurdish nationalism in southeastern Turkey. Claiming an obligation to protect their Turkmen kindred, the Turks were supplying arms and military training to centers of Turkmen population, especially Kirkuk and Tall 'Afar. American forces had acted against Turkish arms supplies and commando squads.

2009 – On 7/25/09, the KAR electorate reelected President Mas'ud Barzani, and selected the members of a 111-seat Parliament.

2009 – In October, to prevent the KRG from honoring its oil contracts with foreign customers, Iraq had closed the pipelines to Turkey.

2010 – Baghdad had blacklisted the oil companies operating in the KAR.

2010 – The Kurdish Autonomous Region – an unplanned consequence of America's deranged Iraqi policy – was emerging as a de facto state. It controlled three of Iraq's 18 governorates (Dahuk, Arbil, and Sulaymaniyyah), and claimed the oil center, Kirkuk, which is in a fourth (Ta'mim). It had taken shape with about 17,000 square miles, 3,500,000 residents, a "capital" (Arbil), a constitution, a government, a flag, a police force that maintained a respectable level of law and order, an airport at Dahuk, a school system, and the most formidable indigenous militia in Iraq, the Peshmerga. The KAR had held no recent elections, but its structure seemed to have submerged the ancient Barzani-Talabani feud. It had all the attributes of sovereignty except international recognition and a delineated frontier. It paid no Iraqi taxes, and had adopted legislation claiming control of all oil produced within its territory.

2014 – In the summer of 2014, two formidable fighting forces burst on the Iraqi-Syrian scene. The Islamic State (IS), otherwise known as the Islamic State of Iraq and Syria (ISIS), captured a quarter of Iraq from the Iraqi army, and a third of Syria from the Syrian army and from the forces of two rival Islamist militias – The Nusrah Front and Free Men of Syria. From its base in the KAR, the Peshmerga of the KRG took advantage of the Iraqi flight from Mawsil to seize Iraqi territories adjoining the KAR.

2014 – The Peshmerga took Kirkuk in June: *Times*, 12/2/14.

2014 – The Peshmerga had seized two oil production sites in Iraq's Kirkuk Province: *Times*, 7/11/14.

2014 – The three Kurdish ministers in the cabinet of Iraqi Prime Minister Maliki would boycott its meetings until Maliki resigned: *Times*, 7/10/14.

2014 – The YPG (militia of the PYD – the Democratic Union Party of Rojava) joined the Peshmerga in action against IS forces in northern Iraq: *McClatchy*, 8/6/14. [*See* **Rojava**, page 428]

2014 – After 15 US air strikes on IS forces guarding the Mawsil Dam, Kurdish forces retook the dam: *FT*, 8/18/14.

2014 – Since IS forces had invaded Iraq, the KRG was closer to autonomy, but it did not have the financial resources to meet the expenses of an independent state: *Times*, 8/30/14. It had not received the heavy weapons expected from the US.

2014 – The KRG needed crude from the IS to produce gasoline at a convenient price: *FT*, 9/22/14.

2014 – Kurdish forces had recovered key territory from the IS: *NY*, 9/29/14, Dexter Filkins.

2014 – The KRG was unable to meet its payroll. Baghdad, still feuding with the KRG over division of oil revenues, had suspended payment of KRG's share of joint oil revenues, and by legal action blocked KRG's sale of its own oil: *NY*, 9/29/14, Dexter Filkins.

2014 – The Peshmerga took advantage of the IS invasion of Iraq to consolidate their control of Kirkuk: *FT*, 10/21/16.

2014 – KRG tankers loaded with crude were cruising aimlessly – blocked by Iraqi and US legal action. Some of their oil was being sold on the black market: *Times*, 10/26/14.

2014 – In the KAR, the Peshmerga was the essential channel of patronage and power: *NYR*, 11/6/14, Rory Stewart.

2014 – The Iraq-KRG feud was resolved. Iraq was again paying Peshmerga salaries and approving the flow of weapons to the KRG from the US. The KRG would provide 550,000 b/d of crude for sale, with the proceeds to be divided equally with Iraq: *Times*, 12/2/14. The KRG was pumping over 300,000 b/d through the pipeline from Kirkuk to Turkey: *FT*, 12/2/14.

2015 – Continuing disunity between the KDP and the PUK had obstructed KRG efforts to centralize its operations. The KRG's installation of its own pipeline to Turkey had strengthened its negotiating position with Baghdad: *MEP*, Spring 2015, Le Billon.

2015 – The Peshmerga, militia of the KRG, was now a well-trained force of 160,000: *Times*, 6/13/15.

2015 – Iraq's Ninawah Plain, lately populated by Christians, was coming under control of the KRG: *NYTM*, 7/26/15.

2015 – The KRG was shipping KAR oil via Ceyhan, Turkey. Customers included Italy, France, Greece, and Israel. Israel was importing almost three-fourths of its oil from the KAR: *FT*, 8/24/15.

2015 – Under US air cover, Kurdish forces had advanced westward to a point only 20 miles north of Raqqah: *FT*, 10/9/15.

2015 – The KRG was running low on funding. It was three months late in paying the salaries of the Peshmerga: *Times*, 11/13/15.

2015 – Masrur Barzani, head of the KRG Security Council, stated that Sinjar, a city recently captured by Kurdish forces, was part of "Kurdistan": *FT*, 11/18/15. Sinjar is in the Iraqi Governorate of Ninawah, on the main road between Mawsil and Raqqah, the two main bases of the IS. When captured by IS forces, it had a population of 100,000, mostly Kurdish Yazidis, whom the IS holds in particular enmity, because most of them cling to a modern form of Zoroastrianism: *NYTM*, 8/14/16. After the IS capture, the Kurds' recapture, and the escape of survivors into nearby mountains, Sinjar was a ghost town: *NY*, 1/18/16, Luke Mogelson.

2015 – Kurdish forces in Iraq and Syria were concentrating on trying to capture all regions populated by Kurdish majorities. Wherever they reached the fringes of these regions, they stopped: *Times*, 12/8/15.

2015 – In past years, the KRG's Peshmerga had had occasion to fight against the PKK forces for lands in Iraq.

2016 – The decline in the price of oil had impoverished Baghdad and the KRG. Baghdad had suspended paying the KRG its share of Iraqi oil revenues: *Times*, 1/14/16.

2016 – Since the Peshmerga's occupation of Kirkuk in 2014, it had demolished thousands of Arab homes, forcing out their occupants:

Times, 1/20/16. The population of Kirkuk was half Kurdish, half Arab Muslim/Turkmen/Christian: *Harper's*, February 2016, Glass. Both KRG forces (the Peshmerga) and the Shiite militias of the Baghdad regime were exacerbating the sectarian feud by razing homes in Arab villages: *FT*, 1/28/16, Roula Khalaf.

2016 – Baghdad's army was still ineffective, but its People's Militia was not: *Harper's*, February 2016, Glass.

2016 – Shia members of the Turkmen community were supportive of the Shia side in the Arab sectarian dispute. Sunni Turkmens were split on this issue: *Harper's*, Glass.

2016 – The KRG had two armed forces – the competent Peshmerga, and civilian volunteers, who were underpaid, underequipped, and unreliable: *Harper's*, Glass.

2016 – Both the Baghdad Regime and the KRG were at war with the IS, but there was no coordination between their forces.

2016 – On 7/9/16, Baghdad's forces had captured Al Qayyarah Air Base, which they valued as a jumping-off base for the recapture of Mawsil: *FT*, 7/12/16.

2016 – With US help, Kurds chased the IS out of Manbij (Syria): *FT*, 8/22/16.

The Drive for Kurdish Statehood in Syria

1957 – The Iraqi KDP founded a Syrian branch: *MEP*, Spring 2015, Till Paasche.

1962 – There were half a million Kurds in Syria. In 1962 Hafiz al Asad arbitrarily stripped 120,000 Kurds of their Syrian citizenship: *The Syrian Jihad*, Charles Lister.

1978 – Asad granted refuge in Syria to the Kurds, as a lever in the Syrian-Turkish negotiations on the flow of Euphrates water. Syrian citizenship was accorded to 250,000 Kurds: *Current History*, December 2014, Max Weiss.

1998 – Under threat of Turkish invasion, Asad terminated PKK access to Syria, and expelled Abdullah Ocalan.

2002-3 – Pro-Ocalan Kurds in Syria founded the PYD (the Democratic Union Party). Its stated objective was a federal relationship between a Kurdish enclave and the Damascus regime: *MEP*, Spring 2015, Till Paasche; *NYR*, 12/3/15, Jonathan Steele (citing *Out of Nowhere*, Michael Gunter). The YPG was formed later as the PYD's militia.

2003 – A long-term objective of the two million Syrian Kurds was the creation of an autonomous enclave in Syria along the Turkish border. It was to be named Rojava, divided into three cantons: Afrin in the west, Kobani in the center, and Jazira in the east.

2011 – The Iraqi KDP founded the KNC (the Kurdish National Council) to stand in opposition to the PYD. Since the KNC was not based in Syria, little had been heard from it since.

2011 – The Syrian Kurds took advantage of the Syrian civil war by staging a campaign whose ultimate objective was a Kurdish autonomous region in Syria: *MEP*, Spring 2015, Gunter.

2011 – The Sunni uprising in Syria would later destabilize the sectarian balance of power in Iraq: *LRB*, 8/21/14.

2012 – YPG forces, the militia of the PYD, deployed in Kurdish-populated areas along the Syria-Turkey border, went into battle against forces of the Syrian regime.

2013 – In July, Saleh Muslim, co-President of the PYD, assured Turkish officials in Istanbul that the PYD was not seeking independence from Syria: *NYR*, 12/3/15, Jonathan Steele; *MEP*, Spring 2015, Gunter. Later in the year, intense combat arose between forces of the YPG and the IS over the Syrian border town of 'Ayn al 'Arab (Kobani to the Kurds).

2014 – Along Syria's Turkish border, PKK affiliate YPG was blazing a trail toward a second Kurdish autonomous region.

2014 – The YPG joined the Peshmerga in action against IS forces in northern Iraq: *McClatchy*, 8/6/14.

2014 – The YPG had been at war with the IS for two years. It was reportedly collaborating with the forces of the Asad regime: *FT*, 9/18/14.

2014 – Late in the year, the enclaves of Syria under Kurdish control became an effective military adversary of the IS, and a plausible political

427

alternative to the IS and the regime in Damascus: *MEP*, Spring 2015, Paasche.

2015 – In June, IS forces attacked the Damascus regime's garrison in Hasakah. When the IS tried to move into Kurdish-held neighborhoods, the YPG pushed them out of Hasakah. The YPG had significant help from US and Damascus air force units: *NYR*, 12/3/15, Steele.

Rojava

2012 – The Kurdish YPG, the militia of the PYD, set out to occupy Syrian territory, along the Turkish border, that had been evacuated by the forces of Bashar al Asad's Damascus regime. The YPG conceived of that territory as a Kurdish autonomous area, to be known as Rojava. Extending from Turkey's Hatay Province across the Euphrates River to Iraqi Kurdistan, it would consist of three cantons: 'Afrin at the west end, Euphrates in the center, and Jazira at the east end. It would include the cities of 'Afrin, Jarabulus, 'Ayn al 'Arab (Kobani), Tall al Abyad, Ra's al 'Ayn, and Al Qamishli. On 3/17/16, the Rojava leadership introduced their Democratic Federation of Rojava. Damascus denounced it.

2015 – On 6/16/15, YPG forces advanced the Rojava project by the capture of Tall al Abyad, located at the center of the frontier: *Times*, 6/17/15. The Kurds were expelling Arab Sunnis from the disputed territory, and not allowing them to return: *LRB*, 7/2/15, Cockburn; *Al Arabia*, 5/2/16.

2015 – In the summer, after a long, bitter battle between Kurdish forces and the IS, both of whom stressed the ethic of martyrdom, a devastated Kobani fell to the Kurds. Strong support for the Kurds from US aircraft may have been the deciding factor: *MEP*, Summer 2015, Rosiny.

2015 – IS forces had checked the westward advance of the YPG at the Euphrates: *FT*, 9/23/15.

2015 – In July, Turkey-PYD relations had soured, but Turkey was allowing forces from the Kurdish KRG and Arab FSA to defend Kobani against the IS assault: *MEP*, Winter 2015.

2015 – The PKK and its affiliate, the YPG, were rivals of the KDP, the Barzani faction that was in control of the KRG: *FT*, 11/13/15.

2015 – The de facto capital of Rojava was Qamishli: *NYTM*, 11/29/15.

2015 – The US considered the PKK terrorist, but supported the PYD, which under the leadership of Saleh Muslim had become a political and military force. Muslim was confident that the US would block Turkish intervention against the Kurds. There was some military cooperation between the leftist PYD and the center-right KRG, but Saleh Muslim asserted that all Peshmerga troops helping the PYD in Syria were under YPG command. Syrian Arab and Turkmen refugees in Turkey alleged that the PYD was committing ethnic cleansing in Syria. Syrian Kurds were not as religious as they were nationalistic. Most Kurdish clerics were Sufi Sunnis: *NYR*, 12/3/15, Jonathan Steele.

2015 – In northeastern Syria, the Kurdish advance had stopped because they had taken over all Kurd-majority territory: *Times*, 12/8/15.

2015 – Some secular Syrian rebels, including the FSA, handicapped by shortage of equipment and incoherent chains of command, were fighting alongside PYD forces: *MEP*, Winter 2015, Ali Nehme Hamdan.

2015 – The PYD viewed forces loyal to Mas'ud Barzani, leader of the KDP and President of the KRG, as a threat to its control of Rojava. Both the PKK and the YPG paid allegiance to Ocalan, still in Turkish prison: *NY*, 1/18/16, Luke Mogelson.

2016 – The People's Militia took an oil refinery from the IS at Bayji, halfway between Baghdad and Mawsil: Glass.

2016 – Kurdish forces in Syria were receiving direct support from the US, indirect support from Russia. Kurds were advancing on Aleppo under the title "Syrian Democratic Forces". It was a front for the YPG: *FT*, 2/18/16.

2016 – The "Syrian Democratic Forces" included Kurds, Arabs, and Turkmens: *Times*, 3/17/16.

2016 – According to Saleh Muslim, Syria might become a federal state "like Iraq": *LRB*, 4/21/16.

2016 – Damascus would allow the YPG to claim autonomy if it accepted a ceasefire, but the two forces were clashing in Qamishli on 4/21/16: *Times*, 4/22/16.

2016 – After days of heavy fighting against the Damascus forces, the YPG occupied most of Hasakah Province. Damascus signed a generous ceasefire: *Times*, 8/24/16.

2016 – An Arab force backed by Turkey took 14 Syrian villages, of which 10 had been held by the YPG, four by Damascus. The action was a major setback for the Kurds.

2016 – The men of the Syrian Democratic Forces, an arm of the YPG, were Kurds and a few Arabs: *Post*, 8/29/16.

2016 – The YPG's interest in the creation of an autonomous regime in Syria would hinge on closing the gap between the Afrin and Kobani sectors. Turkey was dead set against it. The Turkish takeover of Jarabulus from the IS had been a crushing blow to the Kurds. To avoid provoking Turkey, the US was avoiding contact with the Democratic Union, the political party of the YPG: *Times*, 9/2/16.

2016 – A force of 32,000 Kurds and 13,000 Arabs, covered by US planes, was moving on Raqqah. Over the past month, US planes had destroyed almost 200 tanker-trucks: *Times*, 12/11/16.

2016 – Three thousand Kurds who had split off from the YPG were receiving military training from the KRG's Peshmerga: *Times*, 1/18/17.

2016 – Kurds chased the IS out of Manbij, Syria.

Russia – The Russians tried for centuries to establish a foothold in the Middle East. Their methods were crude – military pressure along the Turkish border, and more recently along the Georgian border – and political intrigue, especially among the Armenian and Kurdish communities: *The Middle East in World Affairs*, 3rd edition, George Lenczowski.

In the early 1800's, Russia took over the southern Caucasus. After the disbandment of the USSR in 1991, the southern Caucasus became the three independent states of Georgia, Armenia, and Azerbaijan.

In the Arab-Israeli conflict, Moscow started out by supporting the Arab side, but the sequence of Israeli victories seemed to chill Russian interest in competing with the US for influence in the Middle East.

On 6/18/15, the *Financial Times* reported that the advance of rebel forces in Syria had led Russia to reduce its presence in that country.

Russian Bombshell – In July, General Qassem Soleimani, in Moscow, warned that Russia's naval base in Tartus, Syria, was in jeopardy. Bashar al Asad asked for Russian air support.

By steering clear of engagement in the Syrian civil war, Obama had left an opening. Vladimir Putin, President of the Russian Federation since 2012, decided to rush in where Obama feared to tread. On 8/26/15, Russia and Syria agreed to Russian access to Khmaymim Air Base, near Latakia: MEP, Winter 2016, Williams/Souza. On 9/22/15, Russia sent 50 strike aircraft to Syria. Two days later, the upper house of the Russian Federal Assembly authorized deployment of aircraft to Syria.

Motivation – Review of the profuse speculation in the media suggests that Russia saw in intervention several potential opportunities:

Exploit Russia's Special Situation in Syria – Russia and Syria had had an army-to-army relationship ever since Hafiz al Asad took over Syria. Most Syrian generals, including Hafiz, had received training in Russia: *FT*, 7/9/15; *MEP*, Winter 2016. At Tartus, under an agreement concluded in 1971, Russia had a floating facility for supply and maintenance of Russian warships. It was too small to serve newer ships, but a Russian squadron had been deployed there. It was Russia's only overseas "base".

Russia was owed millions by Syria. The Russian military-industrial complex was keenly interested in maintaining its close ties with Syria, its best customer in the Middle East. From 2007 to 2010, Russia's sales to Iran had fallen sharply, but sales to Syria had risen to 4.7 billion dollars: *Times*, 2/19/12.

Take the Chechens Down a Peg – The 20,000,000 Russian Muslims are Sunnis – natural adversaries of Shiite regimes. In Russia, the Chechens were a persistent threat to state security. In Syria, 7,000 Chechen volunteers, graduates of the insurgency in Russia, were mainstays of the Islamic State. By this time, the forces of the Islamic

431

State were in retreat. The prospective winners of the Syrian civil war were the Shiite Bloc, Russia's tailor-made allies.

To prevent a break with Middle Eastern Sunnis in general, Russia would continue to support basic Sunni causes, like the liberation of Gaza.

Keep Turkey in Its Place – Russia dominated the Black Sea. Russian preeminence in Syria should further inhibit Turkish initiative on behalf of NATO.

Steal a March on the US – By projecting the image of a decisive Russia against that of a dithering US, Russia might end the century-long preeminence of the US in the Middle East, and relieve Russia's global isolation. Washington would have to revise its foreign policy, which Putin despised: *FA*, January 2016, Angela Stent. Any US inclination to comply with the standing rebel request for No-Fly Zones would be checked.

Divert Global Attention from Crimea and Ukraine – Projection of Russian power overseas might diminish the global condemnation of Russian expansionism.

Timeline of the Intervention: 2015-16 – In 2015, Russia was sending modern tanks to a new base south of Latakia, Syria, near the ancestral home of the Asads. Russia's air supply route transited Iran and Iraq: *Times*, 9/14/15.

2015 – On September 27, the Iraqi military announced an agreement among Russia, Baghdad, Damascus, and Iran to share intelligence on the IS: *Times*, 9/27/15.

2015 – October 1, the second day of the Russian air offensive, featured attacks on a loose rebel coalition of Nusrah, Ahrar, and FSA forces, which cooperated on objectives but not on operations. The strikes were occurring in adjoining areas of Homs and Idlib provinces, close to Russian positions in Latakia. Ammunition for the strikes was stored at the Russian base in Tartus: *Times*, 10/2/15.

2015 – After months of planning, Russia, Iran, Hizballah, and the Asad regime had embarked on a coordinated campaign against the Sunni revolutionaries. The campaign included Russia's firing cruise missiles across Iran and Iraq from its Caspian fleet: *Times*, 10/7/15.

2015 – So far, Russian forces in Syria had concentrated their fire against Nusrah and FSA forces that were threatening Latakia from Hamah and Idlib Provinces: *Times*, 10/10/15.

2015 – From 9/30/15 to 10/12/15, Russian planes struck targets of Nusrah, the IS, and the FSA in northwest Syria: *Times*. Although Russian spokespersons claimed the attacks were focused on IS targets, in fact rebels in western Syria received the brunt of the attacks, which brought the Syrian civil war to a dramatic turning point: *Guardian*, 3/14/16.

2015 – Russian attacks on the Sunni rebels (who included Chechens) were enraging Russia's 20 million Muslim residents: *FT*, 10/14/15.

2015 – Russia's construction of three bases, one at Damascus and two near Latakia, had snuffed out any possibility of US establishment of a No-Fly Zone in Syria: *FT*, 10/15/15.

2015 – On 10/18/15, Russian planes wiped out an IS convoy near Raqqah: *LRB*, 11/5/15, Cockburn.

2015 – Putin said Russia was trying to promote a peace process in Syria, and asked the US to participate. Washington declined: *FT*, 10/23/15.

2015 – Bashar visited Moscow, in his first absence from Syria since 2011: *FT*, 10/23/15, Gardner.

2015 – On October 31, a Russian airliner bound from Sinai to Russia crashed shortly after takeoff. All 224 aboard died: *Bloomberg*, 10/31/15. Russia later stated the plane had been bombed by the IS affiliate in Sinai.

2015 – Ninety percent of the bombs dropped from Russian planes over Syria had been aimed at "moderate" rebel groups, few at IS troops: *FT*, 11/7/15.

2015 – Russia had established a joint command center in Baghdad for the coalition of Russia, Baghdad, and Damascus: *Times*, 11/14/15.

2015 – On 11/24/15, Turkish jets shot down a Russian aircraft that had allegedly entered Turkish air space.

2015 – Russia had bolstered the Asad regime by stationing 2000 troops at three bases near Latakia, Syria. The deployment had reduced the freedom of action of the Israeli Air Force versus the operations of its northern adversaries.

2015 – Russia had entered the Syrian civil war on the regime side because it feared that, if the Alawites lost, the IS's Chechen militiamen would resume their insurgency in Russia: *WRMEA*, November 2015, Patrick Buchanan.

2015 – Russia was basing 30 jets and 15 helicopters at Latakia, and was setting up a second airbase near Homs: *The Week*, 12/11/15.

2015 – Russia had required Bashar to dispose of Syria's main stockpile of chemical armament. The US had decided to let the Asad faction stay in power for a while longer: *NY*, 12/21-28/15, David Remnick.

2015 – Amnesty International: Since September 15, 2015, Russian aircraft had killed over 200 Syrians by releasing unguided missiles and cluster bombs in densely populated areas. These actions might be declared war crimes: *FT*, 12/23/15.

2015 – The receipt of anti-tank missiles from Saudi Arabia and the US had enabled the Syrian rebels to push the Damascus forces back – until September, when supplies from the CIA were drying up, and the deployment of Russian aircraft had turned the military tide: *Times*, 8/7/16.

2016 - Russia was sending in enough ground troops to defend Russian bases, but not to fight in the civil war. By mid-2016, there were 4000 Russian ground troops in Syria: *Times*, 3/7/16.

2016 – Thirty-one-dollar oil was forcing Russia to economize: *FT*, 1/13/16.

2016 – Like their Syrian allies, the Russian pilots were not distinguishing civilian targets from military targets: *Times*, 1/15/16.

2016 – Escalation of the Russian offensive in northwestern Syria had created an opportunity for YPG forces to advance closer to Aleppo. Moscow had asked the UN to condemn Turkish attacks on advancing Kurds. Turkey denied the Russian charge that it was allowing passage to Syria for IS recruits, and out of Syria for IS wounded: *FT*, 1/16/16.

2016 – Russia had expanded its bombing runs to include targets south of Damascus. It was building a base in eastern Syria at Qamishli: *FT*, 1/23/16.

2016 – The Russian intervention in Syria had strengthened the jihadists over the moderates: *FT*, 1/27/16.

2016 – In January, forces of the Damascus regime were making gains in the Latakia area.

2016 – Putin feared that chaos in the Middle East could exacerbate anti-Russian Islamism in or near Russia. Disagreement between Russia and the US, notably over Russian attacks on US-backed rebel groups, had increased tension between the two powers. Why hadn't Russia been more aggressive against the IS?: *FA*, January 2016, Angela Stent.

2016 – The Russian air forces had angered the populace of Al Shaykh Miskin, a town between Damascus and Darʻa. They were killing mainstream rebels supported by the West, and hundreds of Syrian civilians.

2016 – Russian bombing in the Homs and Aleppo areas was unprecedented in its intensity: *Times*, 2/3/16. It was enabling Damascus regime forces to advance toward Aleppo, the last stronghold of the Syrian rebels: *FT*, 2/5/16; *Times*, 2/6/16.

2016 – Thomas Friedman believed Putin was bombing Syrian rebels to increase refugee flow to Europe: *Times*, 2/10/16.

2016 – The Russian/Damascus offensive against secular rebels in the Aleppo area suggested Putin's strategy was to reduce the contenders in the Syrian civil war to two: Damascus regime versus the IS: *FT*, 2/12/16, Geoff Dyer.

2016 – Five years of war in Syria had left 470,000 people dead: *Times*, 2/12/16.

2016 – The main cause of deaths in the Syrian civil war in 2016 was Russian air strikes: *Times*, 2/16/16. Putin's chief objective in Syria was a political triumph in Syria that would overshadow America's triumph in the Arab-Israeli wars of the 1960's and 1970's: *FT*, 2/17/16.

2016 – In northwestern Syria, Russian planes were targeting bakeries, schools, and hospitals: *FT*, 2/20/16.

2016 – Russia had set up an S-400 air defense system to protect its access to Syria's Khumaymim airbase near Latakia: *Times*, 3/16/16. Putin was exasperated by Asad's declaration that the Damascus regime would fight until Syria had been reunited. Putin would favor an early election to determine who should be President of Syria: *Times*, 3/16/16.

2016 – Some of the Russian jets that had been stationed in Syria were on their way back to Russia. At its peak, the Russian force in Syria had 40 jet fighters, eight Su34 strike aircraft, 12 Su24 strike aircraft, 12 Su25 ground attack aircraft, four Su30SM fighters, four Su35S fighters, and a surface-to-air missile system. Russian soldiers in Syria numbered 3-6000: *FT*, 3/16/16.

2016 – Damascus's recapture of Palmyra was enabled by Russian air support: *Times*, 3/24/16. US aircraft also helped: *LRB*, 4/21/16.

2016 – Syrian deaths inflicted in six months of Russian bombing were estimated at 5000: *LRB*, 4/21/16.

2016 – In Iraq, rebels shot down a helicopter, killing five Russian airmen. Retaliatory Russian air strikes killed twelve: *TASS*, 8/1/16.

2016 – Russian air attacks on Syria by bombers too big for its base in Syria had been originating in Russia. In August, these flights began originating in Iran, a thousand miles closer to Syria. Russian air strikes on Aleppo were fiercer than ever: *Times*, 8/16/16.

2016 – Cruise missiles were being fired into Syria by Russian warships off the Syrian coast: *Times*, 8/20/16.

2016 – After Russian use of Iranian bases to bomb Syrian targets was revealed in Russian propaganda broadcasts, Iran cancelled its permit for these operations: *Times*, 8/23/16.

2016 – Russia was shipping SAM's to Iran, and sharing intelligence on Syria: *Times*, 9/17/16, Vali Nasr.

2016 – In an air attack on a UN convoy in the Aleppo area, described by UN Secretary General Ban Ki-Moon as "apparently deliberate", a Russian plane destroyed most of the convoy's cargo and killed 20. The convoy was manned by the Red Cross, and escorted by the Syrian Red Crescent: *Times*, 9/19/16.

2016 – On 9/23/16, Russian and Damascus aircraft carried out another ferocious attack on rebel sites in east Aleppo, killing 70-100.

2016 – Putin had transferred Russia's Northern Fleet (seven ships) to the Mediterranean. The corridor from Aleppo to Dar'a was the area of Russian air action: *MEP*, Winter 2016.

2016 – The Russians were using bigger bombs than ever in support of the Damascus effort to take east Aleppo. One year after the Russian intervention, there had not been much change in the battle lines. Outside of Aleppo, the war had been stalemated. Russian air action in Syria had caused worldwide outrage, and was helping rebel factions to unite: *Times*, 9/25/16, Max Fisher.

2016 – In east Aleppo, hundreds had died in the most ferocious air bombardment of the civil war. Targets had included vehicles and offices of rescue organizations. Bunker busters were being used.

2016 – On 10/5/16, Secretary Kerry stated in a speech that Russia had turned a blind eye toward Damascus's use of chlorine gas and barrel bombs.

2016 – Russia had shipped new anti-aircraft systems to Syria: *Times*, 10/6/16.

2016 – Damascus and Russian planes were carpet-bombing east Aleppo, including two hospitals: *The Week*, 10/7/16. They systematically targeted aid workers and doctors: *Wall Street Journal*, 10/7/16.

2016 – Putin was moving aggressively in Syria to exploit the White House hiatus between the 11/8/16 election and the 1/2/17 inauguration. The bombing of Aleppo was one of the modern world's most egregious war crimes: *NYR*, 11/10/16, George Soros.

Reversionaries (Resuscitate Sykes-Picot – Plus Israel)

Saudi Arabia/UAE – Arabia (the Arabian Peninsula) is a rectangular plateau of one million square miles, punishingly arid except in the southwest corner, where the nameless mountain range in Yemen rises to 12,000 feet, and in the southeast corner, where the Hajar Mountains of Oman rise to 10,000 feet. One-fourth of the rectangle, centered in the south, is the Empty Quarter (*Al Rub' al Khali*), the world's largest sea of sand. At ground level, it is forbidding; from the air, it is a mesmerizing etching by nature's hand of the symmetrical tree-forms of age-old wadi courses.

Saudi Arabia is the hard-won reward for the victory of the Saudi clan in three hundred years of tribal warfare, accentuated in 1744 by the conclusion of an enduring alliance between Amir Muhammad Ibn Sa'ud and Shaykh Muhammad Ibn 'Abd al Wahhab, founder of the severe, obscurantist Wahhabi movement of Islam. The exchange of political endorsement from a government in exchange for religious endorsement from a sect has been adopted elsewhere – notably in Israel. Wahhabiism demonizes Shiites, Christians, Jews, and the "dissolute" culture of the West: *The Week*, 5/3/16. The Wahhabi family are the descendants of the marriage of the Amir's son to the cleric's daughter: *The Week*, 8/14/15.

On 1/15/1902, at the age of 21, 'Abd al 'Aziz ibn 'Abd al Rahman (widely known as Ibn Sa'ud) and forty cronies captured from the Saudis' ancient rivals, the Rashidis, the settlement of Riyadh (then a village, now a city of six million). For the next twenty-five years, Ibn Sa'ud inexorably expanded the frontiers of his domain by the dual strategy of plural marriage and military conquest.

On the marital side, he built ties with other tribes by adjusting his household of the permissible four wives in order to build ties with neighboring tribal leaders by marrying their daughters. On the military side, he had the requisite charisma and organizational ability. He set the pattern early on:

In 1904, the Ottoman Sultan responded to an appeal from the Rashidis by sending troops to enforce the sovereignty over Arabia the Ottomans claimed. After two years of Saudi guerrilla attacks on Ottoman supply lines, the Sultan capitulated and withdrew his troops from Saudi territory.

Ibn Sa'ud's greater challenge was indigence. In Arabia before oil, pilgrimage to Mecca and Medina was the most lucrative enterprise. (The *Hajj* takes two forms: <u>annual</u>, during the Islamic month of *Dhu al Hijjah*; *'Umrah*, applied to "lesser pilgrimage" undertaken at other times of the year: *Concise Encyclopedia of Islam*, Cyril Glassé.) In 1908, with British approval, the Ottoman Sultan declared Sharif Husayn Ibn 'Ali al

Hashimi Amir of Mecca. During World War I, the Allies recognized him as King of the Hejaz – site of both holy cities.

In 1922, as part of Britain's postwar consolidation of its position in the Middle East, British High Commissioner to Iraq Percy Cox proclaimed the "Treaty" of 'Uqayr, which fixed the boundaries between Iraq and its two Arabian neighbors, Kuwait and the Sultanate of Najd (Saudi Arabia), plus two neutral zones to allow for future alteration. The document cited British recognition of most of Ibn Sa'ud's territorial gains, and Saudi recognition of British territorial claims along Arabia's Gulf coast to shelter vital coaling stations.

On 3/3/24, the Turkish National Assembly abolished the Islamic Caliphate, whereupon the Sharif, like Ibn Sa'ud a professed descendant of the Prophet, proclaimed himself the new Caliph, but he had no troops able to stand up to the "Ikhwan" – Wahhabi zealots – who did the fighting for Ibn Sa'ud. They moved out of the Najd toward the Hijaz, bloodily routing the Sharif's garrison in Ta'if on the way. The Sharif abdicated as King and Caliph. On 12/23/25, having declared holy war and occupied Mecca, Ibn Sa'ud entered Jiddah. Not in any mood to go back to war, Britain resigned itself to the unceremonious derailment of its plans for Arabia. On 5/20/27, Britain signed the Treaty of Jiddah, by which it recognized Ibn Sa'ud as King of the Hijaz and the Najd, and Ibn Sa'ud – unlike the Sharif – recognized Britain's mandates over Iraq, Transjordan, and Palestine: *Muddle of the Middle East*, Nikshoi C. Chatterji.

Saudi Arabia's indigence problem had been resolved, pro tem. On 9/23/32, Ibn Sa'ud consolidated his regime as the Kingdom of Saudi Arabia – the third state in Saudi history – and reenergized the ancient alliance with the Wahhabi clerisy: *The Kingdom*, Robert Lacey.

Meanwhile, the world depression that struck in 1929 had cut the annual flow of pilgrims from 130,000 in the best year to 40,000 in 1931. Again Providence intervened – in the form of American enterprise. On 5/9/30, Ibn Sa'ud awarded an exploration contract to Standard Oil of California. On 3/16/38, SOCAL brought in its first well.

From the 1970's, they have presided over a campaign to export the Wahhabi ("purist") version of Salafiism: NYR, 4/7/16, Ruthven.

Ibn Sa'ud lived until 11/9/53. He has been succeeded by a series of six of his sons. The latest was King Salman who ascended the throne on 1/23/2015. Crown Prince Muhammad bin Nayif was his nephew, educated in the US. The Second Prime Minister and Minister of Defense was his son, Muhammad bin Salman, born 8/13/85, educated in Saudi Arabia: *The Week*. He is widely regarded as the power behind the throne. There is an unconfirmed report suggesting that Muhammad bin Salman's early rise to that elevated status derived from concern that King Salman might have shown early signs of cognitive decline: *Harper's*, September 2016, Cockburn.

In 1979, 500 (?) radical clerics who saw the infiltration of American attitudes as cultural contamination invaded the Grand Mosque in Mecca. The panic-stricken royal family turned the clock back thirty years, closed movie theaters and record shops, gave more power to the religious police, and intensified across the Muslim World their campaign of Wahhabi proselytization, proliferation of mosques and schools, and financing of resistance to wicked interlopers like the Russians in Afghanistan: *The Week*, 8/14/15.

The Royal Family – The royal family consists of the descendants of Muhammad bin Sa'ud, founder of the Emirate of Dir'iyyah (1818-91) and his brothers. Their estimated number in 2016 was 25-30,000 princes and princesses: *Times*, 12/27/16, Nicholas Kulish/Mark Mazzetti.

Saudi Arabia's traditional reliance on the financial lever began with its own progeny – the extended Royal Family. The operative word is cornucopia. Subsidies to ordinary citizens have been generous, but far exceeded by stipends to the royal relatives. The details of the monthly stipends were a state secret, but in 1996, an American Embassy official in Riyadh saw evidence that the sons of Ibn Sa'ud were receiving 270,000 dollars per month, and stipends for more distant relatives ranged down to 800 dollars per month. The Embassy guessed that the stipends totaled two billion dollars of the annual budget of forty billion: *Green Left Weekly*, 10/9/11, Timothy Lawton.

Oil – As the planet's richest state in reserves of crude oil, Saudi Arabia is the cynosure of the oil world, which lives by the global price per barrel. The Saudis' power to influence that price is unique but not omnipotent: *FT*, 2/25/16, Philip Verleger.

In the 1980's, the coming on stream of fields in the North Sea was a major factor in the shocking collapse of the price per barrel from 35.50 dollars in 1980 to 13.50 in 1986. It went up again to 28.50 in 1990, and down to 12.50 in 1998. (According to one source, these shocks put the Soviet economy into a tailspin that was a central cause of the dissolution of the USSR in 1991.)

Saudi Arabia went along with what it thought was universal resignation to the collapse in the 1980's, only to conclude that some major producers had taken advantage of it to raise their output to gain market share from producers who didn't: *FT*, 2/27/16.

From 2011-14, the price (not adjusted for inflation) held at well over 100 dollars. In 2014-15, it fell below 30 dollars, possibly in reaction to greater world attention to the climate-change crisis. With the lesson of the 1980's in mind, and its budget 85 percent dependent on oil revenues, Saudi Arabia made clear that it would raise its production as high as the market would bear.

The Saudis had three strong motives for keeping the global price of oil low: 1) <u>Wealth</u> – Few countries matched Saudi Arabia's financial depth per capita; 2) <u>Competition</u> – The bargain-basement price of oil was an opportunity to eliminate Johnny-come-latelies – notably high-end frackers in North America; *Financial Times* reported on 3/9/16 that US production of shale oil had risen from 5.5 million barrels a day in 2010 to ten million in 2015; 3) <u>Economic Warfare</u> – Three political adversaries of Saudi Arabia were highly vulnerable to any downturn in the oil market: The Kurdish enclave in Iraq (adventitious ally of the Asad regime in Damascus); Russia, champion of the Asad regime; Iran: *Forbes*, 12/4/15, 1/12/16; *FT*, 1/12/16, 2/12/16, Philip Stephens; *LRB*, 2/4/16, Joost Hilterman.

By 2015, the toll of cheap oil on high-cost producers was beginning to tell in Russia, around the North Sea, and in the US: *FT*, 9/12/15. At higher price levels, half the Russian government's revenue had come from sale of oil and gas. Its sovereign wealth fund had been depleted, factories were closing, and inflation was rising.

Saudi Political Alignments – Under the autocratic leadership of the Saudi family, Saudi foreign policy is a known quantity. The royals have suffered from some gyrations of American Middle East policy – support for the ouster of Egyptian dictator Husni Mubarak, indecision vis-à-vis the Asad regime in Damascus, and, traumatically, Obama's unavoidable opening to Iran as the only hope of postponing the looming nuclear crisis in the Middle East: *FT*, 2/19/16. Nevertheless, there has been no hint of Saudi defection from the unwritten 1945 agreement between FDR and Ibn Sa'ud to exchange privileged American access to Saudi oil in return for an American security guarantee.

Of Saudi Arabia's 5.5 million workforce, 3 million worked in the government: *Times*, 2/20/15. Saudi Arabia has admitted 9 million guest workers to serve its 18 million citizens: *The Week*, 2/5/16.

Eighty-five percent of the Saudi workforce are expatriates from Muslim countries. Although many of them have been exploited by Saudi employers, the outflow of foreign currency seems to have inhibited any serious friction between Saudi Arabia and the countries of origin.

The Saudis' 1744 alliance with the Wahhabis requires Saudi allegiance to bastions of conventional Sunniism – four Gulf shaykhdoms (Oman is 'Ibadi), Egypt, Jordan, the Sunni faction in Yemen, and the moderate Islamist rebels in Syria: *Harper's*, February 2016, Glass; *Times*, 6/17/15. Even the Islamic State, which openly calls for the overthrow of the Saudi regime, benefits from official Saudi ambivalence in recognition of the Wahhabi antecedents of IS doctrine, the pro-IS sentiment harbored by an unknown cohort of Saudi citizens, and the fact that, despite reverses, the IS still was the strongest Sunni militia – the only Sunni faction at war on the ground against Iran. According to a former British intelligence official, the IS takeover of northern Iraq in 2014 was financed by private donations from Qatar and Saudi Arabia: *LRB*, 8/21/14.

In the 1980's, the Saudi regime released the leader of the 1979 invasion of the Grand Mosque, Muqbil al Wadi', and sent him to found a Wahhabi school in Yemen. The Huthis countered by inviting Iran to send Shiite teachers to Yemen: *Harper's*, September 2016, Cockburn.

The Saudis' claim to leadership of the Muslim world, as "Guardian of the Two Holy Shrines", is shaken by IS publicity on the royal family's profligacy. *The New York Review of Books* carried a report on the desecration of Mecca by the construction of the world's largest hotel, with 10,000 deluxe bedrooms and forty-five stories, five of which are set aside for the use of the royal family: *NYR*, 7/9/15, Malise Ruthven.

Saudi Arabia, Turkey, and the Sunni shaykhdoms on the Gulf are committed to the permanent elimination of the Alawite regime in Damascus. The Saudis were even more closely welded to Bahrain by their joint effort to suppress their respective Shiite communities, as demonstrated by the deployment at Bahrain's request of 1000 Saudi National Guardsmen to Bahrain from 2011 to 2014 to participate in the brutal suppression of a massive Shiite uprising: *Aljazeera*, 3/29/14. For conservative Sunnis, Shiites are apostates (*rawafid*), and must be subjugated.

Saudi foreign policy reflects a major domestic problem – controlling its 2,000,000 restless Shiites, who are numerous in the Eastern Province, along the upper Gulf coast, and the 'Asir Region, north of Yemen on the Red Sea coast: *Times*, 1/5/15. Their protests were not in support of the Khamenei regime, but to condemn Saudi repression of Shiites. Riyadh was mishandling the problem: *FT*, 1/6/16.

Second to the Saudi reliance on the US is the longstanding alliance between the Saudi regime and the Egyptian military dictatorship. Both sides have seen Saudi affluence and Egypt's overgrown military establishment as an ideal basis for partnership. For the Saudis, the dynastic dispute between 'Abd al Fattah al Sisi and Muhammad Mursi switched the Muslim Brotherhood from associate to enemy.

In theory, the state that detached Palestine from the Muslim World should be Saudi Arabia's bitterest enemy, but Israel poses no visible threat to Saudi Arabia. The Saudis are obsessed by the threat they sense from Iran. They and the Israelis have reportedly been exchanging intelligence on that common enemy. Riyadh's suspicions of Iranian intentions are exacerbated by past history: The Safavids were the nominal rulers of Bahrain from 1602 to 1717. Rumors that the Iranian legislature is saving two seats for Bahrain do not help: *MEP*, Spring 2015.

Political differences between Qatar and Saudi Arabia have been construed by some as consequences of difference of interests between a producer of oil and a producer of natural gas.

Saudi Military Posture – Saudi Arabia has the third largest arms procurement program in the world: *FT*, 5/10/16. As the ruling structure gets more top heavy, and the price of oil stays low, the inequity between the family oligarchy and the general public becomes more blatant. The power base of the regime seems too narrow for it to risk the installation of a modern armed force. Saudi Arabia has taken an active political and financial part in the metastatic Middle East power struggle. It is stuck in a destructive but inconclusive air campaign that by March 2015 had killed nearly 2000 Yemenis: *FA*, Goldenberg/Dalton. Nevertheless, it has never been a significant participant in any ground war. The primary missions of the Saudi Army and the National Guard seem to be to keep an eye on each other. Saudi Arabia's only effective weapon is the American dollar. It was only after suffering the indignity of Pakistan's refusal to fight the Saudis' war against the Zaydi (Shia) Huthi tribesmen in Yemen that Saudi Arabia and the UAE sent attack planes and a few ground troops against the Huthi takeover of most of Yemen.

The Gulf States – On the map, Arabia is partitioned between two states of average size and population – Saudi Arabia and Yemen, which occupy the Arabian hinterland and the western and southwestern coasts – and five mini-states perched along the Gulf and southeastern coasts. Yemen and Saudi Arabia have pulled themselves up by their own bootstraps. Kuwait, Bahrain, Qatar, the UAE, and Oman are the fortuitous by-products of imperialism's myopic penchant for dividing and ruling. They have survived by clinging close enough to the coast to reside within the range of the naval guns that used to be the mainstay of a British Empire, and of the aircraft that now undergird the Americans' hypertrophied presence in the region. The Gulf States' imbalance between oil wealth and military weakness condemns them to precarious satellite status.

Of the five Gulf Shaykhdoms, the only one to have a substantial military role in the regional power struggle is the UAE, which in 2014 sent aircraft to attack Islamist positions in Libya (*FA*, Gold/Dalton), and since 2015 has had ground troops in southern Yemen.

The Gulf Cooperation Council - On 5/25/81, with Western encouragement, six peninsular states founded the Cooperation Council of the States of the Arab Gulf (*Majlis al Ta'awun li Duwal al Khalij al 'Arabi*). On 1/1/15, the GCC proclaimed a customs union. It has an annual GDP of over one trillion dollars. As a unit, it would be the world's major producer of petroleum products. As of now, it consists of six tribal monarchies – each one jealous of its independence. The UAE itself is a loose composite of seven tribal entities, each with its own emir, but one is dominant: Abu Dhabi has enough petroleum income to exert influence over the other six – Dubai, 'Ajman, Sharjah (*Al Shariqah*), Umm al Qaiwain, Ra's al Khaimah, and Fujairah.

The GCC is riven by political rivalries. Saudi Arabia has managed to enlist Bahrain and the UAE in its sphere of influence. Saudi Arabia and the Island of Bahrain are linked by a causeway. Abu Dhabi is a short flight from the Saudi capital, Riyadh. The turbulent politics of Kuwait, whose political system has moved slightly beyond tribalism, obstructs ready agreement with its tribal neighbors. As far back as 1988, Kuwait's investments were more remunerative than its dwindling oil reserve: Elaine Sciolino. After the US and Russia, Qatar is the world's third leading producer of natural gas, which finances the keen interest of the Al Thani dynasty in playing an active role in Middle Eastern affairs.

Unique Oman – Doctrinal schism first befell the Muslims in 657, when the murder of the fourth Caliph, 'Ali, split them into three factions: pro-'Ali and heirs; pro-Mu'awiyah, who succeeded 'Ali; and the Kharijites, as they were later known, who rejected both of the above. Before the Kharijite sect expired, it gave birth to the 'Ibadi subsect, which has survived as the state religion of Oman: *EB*, 6:833. Because of its unique history, the reserved disposition of its ruler, Sultan Qaboos, and geography, Oman has the most aloof policies of all the Arabian states. The 70-mile sea route across the Strait of Hormuz, from Khasab on the Musandam Peninsula to Bandar Abbas, makes Oman Iran's second nearest Arab neighbor, after Iraq. Iran simultaneously presents to Oman the sobering proximity of an unpredictable superior, and the invitation to profit as the logical Arab-Iranian intermediary. Oman stayed neutral in the Iraq-Iran War: *MEP*, Winter 2015, Richard Schmierer.

In August 2013, Sultan Qaboos was the first foreign head of state to visit Iranian President Hassan Rouhani. Rouhani's first trip to Arabia was a visit to Qaboos. Otherwise, Qaboos is a staunch ally of the US: *NYR*, 8/14/14, Hugh Eakin. Oman is neutral between the Damascus regime and the Syrian rebels. In December 2013, Qaboos denounced a Saudi proposal to turn the GCC into a political union. Oman has a large community of Baluchis, who play a prominent role in the army. Qaboos is trying to replace Oman's large population of foreign workers with its own citizens.

Oman is the GCC state that, as of this writing, has not joined the coalition against the Huthis: *Times*, 8/7/15.

Arabia Timeline – In 2009, President Salih obtained Saudi permission to send Yemeni troops across the border to repel Huthi infractions. Huthi troops moved across the border, and were met by Saudi air and ground forces, which they defeated.

2013 – Saudi Arabia supported General Sisi's takeover in Egypt: *FT*, 8/31/15.

2014 – The Grand Mufti of Saudi Arabia identified the primary enemies of Islam as Al Qa'idah and the IS: *MEP*, Summer 2014, Stephan Rosiny.

2014 – Saudi Arabia earmarked one billion dollars to help Lebanon repel attacks by the IS: *FT*, 8/7/14.

2014 – Qatar was sponsoring the religious programs of Shaykh Yusuf al Qaradawi, spiritual leader of the Muslim Brotherhood, resident in Qatar (*FT*, 3/10/14, Roula Khalaf), but Saudi Arabia, Kuwait, and the UAE had histories of animosity toward the MB: *Harper's*, August 2014, Negar Azimi.

2014 – In the round of 2014 in the Israel-Gaza conflict, Saudi Arabia, Oman, and the UAE took the Israeli side. Qatar was working openly with Israel in the rebuilding of demolished Gaza: *LRB*, 11/5/15, Nathan Thrall.

2014 – The US had helped the UAE develop one of the more effective air forces in the Arab World. It had launched air strikes against jihadist militias in Libya from Egyptian bases – an action Cairo did not admit. The UAE supported Libyan tribal militias. Qatar supported Libyan jihadists: *Times*, 8/26/14, 9/14/14.

2014 – The UAE had rejected the retrogressive creed of the Islamic State: *Times*, 9/6/14, UAE Ambassador to the US.

2014 – Qatar backed the Muslim Brotherhood, but not financially. Saudi Arabia, Bahrain, and the UAE opposed it. After the fall of the Brotherhood in Egypt, three Arab states (Egypt, the UAE, and Saudi Arabia) withdrew their ambassadors from Qatar: *Times*, 9/7/14, 9/8/14; *FT*, 12/1/14.

2014 – Qatar was denying permission for the US to launch air attacks against the Islamic State from Al 'Udayd Air Base: *Times*, 9/15/14.

2014 – A treaty of 1868 between the UK and the tribes of Qatar set the course for the independence of Qatar under the rule of the Al Thani dynasty: *EB*. Since 1950, Qatar was a sanctuary for Arab political refugees: Palestinians – Mahmud 'Abbas, Muhammad al Najjar, 'Azmi Bishara; Muslim Brothers – Hasan al Banna, Yusuf al Qaradawi, Khalid Mish'al. Banna and Qaradawi helped Qatar build an educational system based on the Egyptian model, not the Saudi. Ever since, Qatar had backed the Brotherhood, although its official creed (Salafi) was too undemocratic for the Brotherhood to be operative there: *MEP*, Fall 2014.

2014 – In Kuwait, government control of oil revenues subordinated individual freedom to universal dependence on government largesse: *MER*, Fall 2014.

2014 – With a foreign exchange reserve of 750 billion dollars, Saudi Arabia could ride out years of cheap oil. Iran, burdened by its commitment to subsidies to Iraq and Syria, would be financially constrained until the international sanctions against it were lifted: *FT*, 12/10/14.

2015 – Saudi Arabia was erecting an elaborate barrier of razor wire, trenches, turrets and sensors along its 500-mile border with Iraq: *Gizmodo*, 1/14/15.

2015 – The Saudi leadership strongly supported the Sisi dictatorship in Egypt, and opposed Sisi's nemesis, the MB. Saudi Arabia, Kuwait, and the UAE had promised Sisi a subsidy of twelve billion dollars. However, many individual Saudis, as Salafis, shared doctrine with the MB: *Current History*, December 2014, Frederic Wehrey; *Times*, 1/24/15.

2015 – In Syria, the Saudis had joined Jordan, Qatar, Bahrain, and the UAE in contributing flights to the American air war against the IS. Saudi Arabia had condemned Hizballah, Nusrah, Al Qa'idah, and the IS as terrorist organizations, whereas the Saudi public empathized with the IS. The Saudi regime had agreed with Turkey and Qatar on a joint anti-Asad policy. The Saudi leadership feared that Washington had decided to suspend operations against the Asad regime, and support for the secularist Syrian rebels, in a gesture that might win greater Iranian support for the pending nuclear treaty: Wehrey.

2015 – The new Saudi King, Salman bin 'Abd al 'Aziz, crowned on 1/23/15, named his nephew, Muhammad bin Nayif, as his heir, and his 30-year-old son Muhammad as Minister of Defense.

2015 – In the US Congress, pressure was rising to declassify Part 4 of the *9/11 Commission Report*, which was said to charge that some Saudis, possibly some government officials, had provided financing for the Al Qa'idah operation of 9/11/01: *Times*, 2/5/15.

2015 – The collapse of the price of oil from a hundred dollars a barrel to the fifty-dollar range had inflicted severe economic problems on Russia. The Saudis hoped that promoting the lower price by producing at previous high levels would serve as leverage to induce Russia to abandon its support for the Asad regime in Damascus – at some cost to the well-padded Saudi economy: *Times*, 2/4/15.

2015 – Qatar faulted Egypt for its air strike in Darnah, Libya. *Aljazeera*, financed by Qatar's Al Thani dynasty, condemned Sisi's violent suppression of demonstrations in Egypt: *Times*, 2/20/15.

2015 – Saudi morale was boosted when Salman declared a (one-time) bonus of 32 billion dollars, although the fall of the price of oil had caused a large deficit in the 2015 budget.

2015 – On 3/26/15, Saudi Arabia and allies shocked Yemen by launching an air war, a blockade, and an embargo. They were intended to reverse the Huthi expansion, and reinstate the Hadi regime: *Harper's*, September 2016, Cockburn.

2015 – In March, US-made jets from Saudi Arabia dropped US-made cluster bombs that were aimed at Huthi soldiers, but killed hundreds of other Yemenis in homes, schools, and refugee camps: *NY*, 5/25/15.

2015 – Under US pressure, Saudi Arabia and the UAE announced the temporary suspension of their air campaign in Yemen. A Saudi blockade and embargo had been starving Yemenis of food, water, fuel, and medicine: *Times*, 4/22/15.

2015 – The replacement of the MB government in Cairo by a military regime was a political victory for the Saudi Government: *FT*, 4/30/15.

2015 – Whereas Saudi King 'Abdallah had branded the MB as terrorist, King Salman was collaborating with Al Islah, the pro-MB party in Yemen: *Times*, 5/12/15.

2015 – Over the past twenty years, Saudi Arabia had spent 500 billion dollars on its military forces – three-fourths for purchases from the US. The Saudis had also financed Pakistan's nuclear program and the Mubarak and Sisi regimes in Egypt: *Times*, 5/12/15, Jean-Francois Seznec.

2015 – In the Saudis' bitterness against Iran, they were prepared to destroy Yemen: *LRB*, 5/21/15.

2015 – The IS claimed responsibility for the bombing of a Shiite mosque on 5/22/15: *MEP*, Summer 2016.

2015 – UAE Special Forces and Yemenis who had been trained in the UAE and Saudi Arabia recaptured most of Aden from the Huthis: *FT*, 7/15/15. President Hadi set up his base of operations there.

2015 – Riyadh announced the arrest of 400 Saudis suspected of affiliation with the IS: *AP*, 7/18/15.

2015 – In another indication of a thaw between Saudi Arabia and the MB, on 7/17/15 King Salman met in Mecca with Khalid Mish'al and other leaders of Hamas (an offshoot of the MB). Hamas had lost its Iranian support when it backed the Syrian rebellion against the Asad regime: *Times*, 7/18/15.

2015 – The UAE had been upgrading its armed forces. In Yemen, the UAE contingent was the spearhead of the coalition's ground attack, in which Saudi forces and Saudi-trained Yemenis from Islah, Yemen's Islamist party, also participated. In the summer of 2015, they achieved a quick occupation of Aden and, with assistance from local adherents of the IS, parts of the adjoining governorates of Lahij and Abyan. They were checked at that point by forces of the opposition (Huthi tribesmen, known as *Ansar 'Abdallah* – Followers of 'Abdallah), and pro-Salih units of the Yemeni army: *MEP*, Summer 2016, Legrenzi/Lawson.

2015 – Qatar was now the leading exporter of LNG (liquid natural gas). Its current annual sales totalled 180 billion dollars: *Times*, 8/6/15.

2015 – The Huthi forces had been losing ground in southern and central Yemen since July: *Times*, 8/16/15.

2015 – In the analysis of British columnist Gwynne Dyer, Saudi Arabia was maintaining its usual oil production level in an effort to put the American frackers out of business. The strategy had led the Saudis to begin drawing on their financial reserve (the Saudi Arabian Monetary Agency) and to sell government bonds: *AP*, 8/21/15.

2015 – Saudi Arabia and Bahrain joined the UAE in deploying ground troops against the Huthis in southern Yemen: *AP*, 9/6/15.

2015 – In revenge for the GCC's devastating air attacks, Huthi forces – with alleged Iranian help – fired a missile into an ammunition dump whose explosion killed some 60 soldiers from Bahrain, Saudi Arabia, and the UAE: *FT*, 9/12/15.

2015 – New King Salman, cognitively impaired, had transferred the reins of government to his son, Muhammad: *Harper's*, September 2016.

2015 – Salman had severely intensified political repression. Saudi security forces were torturing suspects on an industrial scale: *NYR*, 10/22/15.

2015 – The deficit in the 2015 Saudi budget was approaching 20 percent of GNP: *FT*, 11/9/15.

2015 – The UAE had imported hundreds of mercenary troops from Latin America to Yemen. Saudi Arabia had brought in Sudanis: *Times*, 11/26/15.

2015 – Deputy Crown Prince Muhammad bin Salman was also Minister of Defense, head of the Security Council, director of the Public Investment Fund, head of the team restructuring the economy, CEO of

Saudi Aramco, and overseer of the operations of the Royal Court, Saudi Arabia's most powerful body: *FT*, 11/30/15.

2015 – In a letter to the *Washington Post*, the UN High Commissioner on Human Rights had reported a humanitarian crisis in Yemen as a result of the war with Saudi Arabia and its allies. In the latest six months, 2355 Yemenis had died and 4862 had been wounded: *WRMEA*, November 2015.

2015 – Lukewarm American and European support for the anti-Asad rebellion had led many moderate rebel factions to reject their help. Saudi Arabia's hostility to the Damascus regime was intense enough to tip it in the rebels' favor, even though an IS victory could lead to the ultimate overthrow of the Saudi regime: *FA*, November 2015, Steven Simon/Jonathan Stevenson.

2015 – Saudi propagation of Wahhabi doctrine had contributed to the rise of the jihadist movement in Syria and Iraq: *Nation*, 12/7/15.

2015 – A large number of Saudi citizens were favorably disposed toward the IS: *Times*, 12/9/15, Thomas Friedman.

2015 – Seventy-five combatants had just died in an air and ground battle on the Saudi-Yemen frontier: *AP*, 12/20/15.

2015 – US support for the Saudi air offensive in Yemen included intelligence exchange, refueling assistance, and a 129-million-dollar arms deal with Saudi Arabia: *Times*, 12/23/15.

2015 – Since March, the Saudi bombing of targets in Yemen had crippled its public health system and left 80 percent of its 24,000,000 citizens in need of aid. Children were dying of starvation: *The Week*, 12/25/15.

2015 – A drain of 98 billion dollars from the Saudi budget was forcing Saudi Arabia to cut back its air attacks against the Huthis in Yemen and the Asad regime in Syria: *Times*, 12/29/15.

2015 – Saudi executions of political activists in 2015 had totaled 158: *Times*, 1/4/16.

2015 – The State Department asked Riyadh about its objectives in Yemen. Answer: Elimination of all traces of Iranian influence in Yemen. According to a State Department official, Saudi Arabia's only war plan was to destroy every suspect site in Yemen: *Harper's*, September 2016, Cockburn.

2016 – On 1/2/16, Saudi Arabia executed 47 political activists, including many AQAP operatives from the Sunni faction, and Shaykh Nimr al Nimr from the Shiite faction. Nimr had condemned violence but called openly for the ouster of the Saudi regime. The 47 executions were meant to counter the pro-IS trend in Saudi Arabia: *FT*, 1/6/16. The startling execution of a man as moderate and influential as Nimr was variously explained. According to *The Week* of 1/2/16, it was meant to distract the Saudis from the recent cutbacks in their lavish welfare subsidies. For Roula Khalaf of the *Financial Times* of 1/7/16, it was intended to convince the Saudi public that the regime was just as loyal to Wahhabi doctrine as the IS was.

2016 – A strike by planes of the Damascus regime killed leaders of the Army of Islam, which was backed by Saudi Arabia: *FT*.

2016 – The Shiite protestors in Saudi Arabia did not support the diehard regime of Khamenei in Iran. They advocated relaxation of Saudi repression. Riyadh mishandled the problem by crying heresy: *FT*, 1/6/16.

2016 – Muhammad bin Nayif, Saudi Minister of the Interior, was responsible for national security and for Saudi policy for Syria: *FT*, 1/9/16. The power behind the throne was the King's son, Muhammad bin Salman. The King's nephew was educated in the US, the King's son in Saudi Arabia: *The Week*, 2/5/16.

2016 – On 1/15/16, in retaliation for the execution of Shaykh Nimr, a Tehran mob burned the Saudi Embassy. Saudi Arabia, Bahrain, Kuwait, the UAE, and Sudan broke diplomatic relations with Iran. After Lebanon failed to condemn the Tehran riots, Riyadh cancelled a four-billion-dollar grant to Lebanon for its armed forces, and closed the Beirut office of *Al Arabia*, a property of the Saudi royal family: *FT*, 4/5/16; *MEP*, Summer 2016. Another Lebanese offense was its deference to Hizballah: *Times*, 4/19/16.

2016 – Planes from the anti-Yemen coalition struck a market in northern Yemen, killing some 90 Yemenis: *Times*, 3/16/16.

2016 – Saudi Arabia had a long way to go in modernizing its educational system. In the 1920's, the faculty at the Mosque of the Prophet in Medina were still teaching that the earth is flat. In 1999, the highest religious authority in the kingdom proclaimed that any Muslim who endorsed heliocentrism deserved to die: *NYR*, 4/7/16, Ruthven.

2016 – Saudi confidence in the US had been undermined by the American failure to stand by Mubarak in Egypt, by its failure to punish Bashar al Asad for his use of chemical weapons in Syria, by hints in the American media of official Saudi culpability in the 9/11 attacks, and by the détente with Iran: *Times*, 4/8/16.

2016 – Aside from devastating Yemen, driving it to the brink of famine, and killing over 6000 Yemenis (June estimate by WHO, cited in *Harper's* of September 2016), the Saudi air war had had little political effect. The Saudi economy was depressed by cheap oil and the Huthi war. The Saudi regime was struggling to pay its bills: *Times*, 4/19/16.

2016 – A meeting of OPEC representatives in Doha was surprised when Saudi Arabia rejected a proposal for an oil production freeze – apparently on the basis of a ruling from Muhammad bin Salman in his role as head of the Saudi Economic Council: *FT*, 4/19/16.

2016 – Bahrain suspended *Wifaq*, a predominantly Shiite political organization: *FT*, 6/15/16.

2016 – The original printing of the *9/11 Commission Report* of 2002 omitted 29 pages, which were released in 2016. They reported that some of the hijackers received assistance from Saudis who "may be connected to the Saudi government". Saudi officials stated that there was no proof and the matter was finished: *The Week*, 7/29/16; *FP*, Simon Henderson.

2016 – The sharp decline in Saudi oil revenue had caused borderline Saudi companies to lay off workers. Layoffs were particularly hard on foreign workers whose passports, held by the companies, were difficult to retrieve. Without passports, they could not get back home. Many of the 3,000,000 Indian workers had found themselves in this situation: *Times*, 8/3/16.

2016 – Since the Saudi-led coalition had opened an air war against the Huthis in Yemen, four Yemeni hospitals had taken direct hits: *Times*, 8/16/16.

2016 – Another attack on a hospital in Yemen's Al Hajjah Governorate on the Red Sea coast killed 19, belying the coalition's promise to stop bombing hospitals. Doctors Without Borders was evacuating its staff from six hospitals in north Yemen. The Yemeni staffers were staying on: *Times*, 8/19/16.

2016 – Egypt felt that it could take anti-Saudi positions, because a stable Egypt was an overriding Saudi interest: *Times*, 11/2/16.

2016 – The coalition's bombing of Yemen had demolished much of the infrastructure of one of the world's most impoverished countries. The blockade had cut supplies of food, fuel, and medicine. The air strikes had been frequent and constant. Many were "double-tap" – bomb, wait for the crowd to gather, then bomb again. The bombers seemed to hold a particular grudge against shoppers. Human Rights Watch documented a dozen attacks on crowded markets, causing casualties in each attack as high as 100.

2016 – A retired Major General led a Saudi delegation to Israel for discussions on their shared disapproval of US policy for Syria and Iran: *Times* editorial, 8/28/16.

2016 – In reaction to the Huthi occupation of San'a', Deputy Crown Prince Muhammad had ordered a counterattack without consultation with other Saudi officials – even the commander of the National Guard. The Crown Prince, who is diabetic, had spent early 2016 in his family's villa in Algeria: *Times*, 10/16/16.

2016 – At the UN, Egypt supported a Russian-sponsored resolution that was opposed by Saudi Arabia. The Saudis halted fuel shipments to Egypt: *Times*, 10/25/16, Peter Baker.

2016 – Saudi Arabia was waging a war to achieve political goals by destroying the Yemen economy: Jamie McGoldrick, UN Humanitarian Coordinator for Yemen. The Saudi air attacks had suspended government air traffic from and to San'a', and destroyed key bridges, government buildings, and factories. Before the war, Yemen was importing 90 percent of its food. In 2016, food shipments were being delayed by destruction of cranes in the port of Hudaydah: *Times*, 11/14/16, Ben Hubbard.

Egypt – The Middle Eastern countries most scarred by Western imperialism – British and American – were Palestine and Egypt. From 1882 to 1952, Egypt was under exploitive British rule. In 1952 Lieutenant Col. 'Abd al Nasir headed a military coup. The British puppet King Faruq was ousted, and Egypt had a few Camelot years. The first free Egyptian government in seventy years (*EB*, 18:138) undertook the monumental task of building a nation – only to be sidetracked by collision with an American creation, the combative new state of Israel.

In 1948, Nasir had fought in Egypt's first defeat by Israel. As President of Egypt, he had to preside over the ordeals of 1956, 1967, and 1969-70. In 1970, he died in ignominy.

In 1973 his successor, Anwar Sadat, launched the Yom Kippur War, a yeoman effort by Egypt and Syria to turn the tables. Failure revealed that the Arabs' military cause was hopeless: Arab-Soviet military power was overshadowed by Israeli-US military power. Sadat took the loser's way out – switching sides from the Soviets to the Americans. The 1979 Treaty of Peace with Israel came at a heavy price for Egypt: Arab scorn; abandonment of the Palestinian cause; worst of all, the country long regarded as the leading military power in the Arab east could no longer even deploy troops there. As a military contender in the Middle East Power Struggle, Egypt had been neutralized in theory and in practice. The theory was dictated by the peace treaty. The practice was dictated by geography: Israel is a territorial buffer between Egypt and the heart of the Arab world. There is no way by land for Egypt to move forces east of a security-conscious Israel.

Egypt won five benefits: Arms supply from the US, recovery of Sinai, access to Gaza, a US policy of preventing any more Israeli expansion, and a chance to deal with looming domestic problems – for which the common key words in Washington have been "basket case". A country whose 88 million people (as of 2016) were trying to eke out a living from a small strip of irrigated land (12,000 square miles in 2010, and shrinking) needs imaginative programs. They are hard to sell to an electorate that is 25 percent illiterate, and largely controlled through extended families whose members vote as ordered by opinionated male elders: *NY*, 3/17/16, Peter Hessler. The probability that these orders are communicated by Facebook does not make Egypt a developed country.

Imagination was also hard to find in a military regime based on an army that had forgotten its purpose. Since the armed forces lost their job, the Supreme Command of the armed forces had allowed them to deteriorate into a corrupt financial empire (*FT*, 11/7/15), and SCAF had converted itself into a despotism. Human rights were being flagrantly and systematically abused: *WRMEA*, August 2015, Dale Sprusanski quoting Joe Stork; *Current History*, December 2015. Political opposition had been criminalized: *NYTBR*, 7/2/15, Wendell Steavenson. Resources had been diverted from building infrastructure and financing scientific progress to providing creative comforts to those in uniform, and to their entrepreneurial allies: *LRB*, 3/3/16, Owen Bennett-Jones.

Overpopulation was undermining the Egyptian economy. Tourism, a traditional source of foreign currency, had been crippled by anti-regime subversion. In these circumstances, the subsidies from Saudi Arabia and the US took on even greater importance.

By 2005, Mubarak had been in office long enough to win the contempt of Egyptians at large. Their main grievances were corruption, the use of thugs to bully dissidents into submission, and the peace treaty with Israel: *Times*, February 2005, Scott Anderson.

Egypt Timeline – On 1/25/11, Egypt's April 6 movement (founded in the early years of the century) reacted to the "Arab Spring" uprising of December 2010 by staging large demonstrations that challenged security forces with brickbats, and took over Tahrir Square in Cairo.

2011 – On 1/29/11, dictator Husni Mubarak dismissed his government. Riots broke out.

2011 – On 2/2/11, The Muslim Brothers assumed leadership of the rioters.

2011 – On 2/3/11, thousands of scabs mobilized by the regime fired on demonstrators, killing and wounding around 50 before the scabs were dispersed by warning machine-gun fire from an army tank force.

2011 – On 2/10/11, Mubarak resigned, transferring Presidential power to the SCAF (Supreme Command of the Armed Forces), which was commanded by General Muhammad Tantawi. Tantawi took over the country and dissolved Parliament. During the eighteen days of protests, over 800 civilians had been killed. The civilian protests were suppressed. Mubarak went to jail. The SCAF held power until June 2012: *Current History*, December 2015.

2011 – On 3/4/11, a civilian was named Prime Minister, and a referendum called on the SCAF to suspend Mubarak's state of emergency and oversee the establishment of democratic institutions and the drafting of a new Constitution. The SCAF did not comply. Observers concluded that the SCAF had favored the ouster of Mubarak because it distrusted his son and heir, Jamal, but that it shared Mubarak's opposition to democracy, as well as his penchant for jailing dissenters.

2011 – By October, the SCAF's failure to reactivate the security police had plunged Egypt into a crime wave, featuring Salafi attacks on members of the Coptic community of five million. Soldiers shared responsibility for the rash of Coptic deaths.

2012 – The Muslim Brotherhood won 350 of 498 seats in elections for Parliament. Egypt's first democratically elected President, Muhammad Mursi, took office on 6/30/12. Other MB candidates for President, perhaps more experienced, had been rejected by the courts, possibly under SCAF influence.

2012 – In June, the SCAF transferred most presidential powers to the Supreme Constitutional Court.

2012 – On 7/9/12, the Supreme Constitutional Court, a holdover from the Mubarak era, endorsed Tantawi's dissolution of Parliament.

2012 – Mursi was losing popular support because of SCAF sabotage, and his own clumsy overreaching – notably by decreeing that, until the adoption of a new constitution, his Presidential decisions would be immune to judicial oversight: *Times*, 4/22/15; *NYTM*, 8/14/16.

2012-13 – During Mursi's Presidency, there was a continuing struggle between Islamists and secularists over Article 2 of the 1971 Constitution, which had declared the Islamic sharia the basis of all legislation. By denigrating Mursi in the media, and blocking Mursi's initiatives, the SCAF managed by 2013 to polarize Egypt between Islamists and secularists, while the Egyptian military continued to enjoy the public support it had won in Nasir's time: *NYTM*, 8/24/16, Scott Anderson.

2013 – On 6/30/13, large anti-Mursi demonstrations set the scene for the SCAF to make its move.

2013 – On 7/1/13, General 'Abd al Fattah al Sisi emerged as leader of the Egyptian military, and decreed that, if Mursi did not respect the people's demands, the military would intervene: *NYTM*, 8/14/16.

2013 – On 7/3/13, after a year under Mursi, the Egyptian military stepped out of the shadows and resumed overt control of Egypt. This event was widely reported in the Western media as a coup d'état. That term would be inappropriate if, as some observers including this writer read the sequence of events, the SCAF had retained ultimate control through the courts, and was biding its time until Mursi brought on his own downfall. "The military faction never lost control": *WRMEA*, Marina Ottaway. The military used the courts and the security forces to "regain" power: Thanassis Cambanis.

2013 – Sisi took over rule of Egypt from Mubarak, who was still on trial, and decreed trial for Mursi, who was subsequently sentenced to death. Sisi suspended the Constitution, declared Chief Justice 'Adli Mansur interim president, and exploited the military's privileged position (acquired in 1952) to initiate a despotism of a severity new even to Egypt: *Times*, 11/7/14; *FT*, 2016, Roula Khalaf. Over the next three years, the Sisi regime concentrated on one objective: destroy the Muslim Brotherhood and its Gazan offshoot, Hamas. To this end, Sisi arrested 40,000 and killed hundreds: *FA*, November 16, Steven A. Cook.

2013 – On 8/14/13, by firing on a massive Islamist sit-in at Al 'Adawiyyah Square in Cairo, Egyptian police (subordinate to the military) killed 5-700 protestors and destroyed the adjoining mosque: *Times*, 7/18/15.

2013 – The Muslim Brotherhood still held to its customary stance of conciliation, but Sinai had become the base of a more militant group, Protectors of Jerusalem (*Ansar Bayt al Maqdis*), which opened a campaign of bombings, some by suicide: *Times*, 10/28/13.

2013 – In November, the regime promulgated a law that cancelled the right to assemble. Economic slump was contributing to the decline of law and order: *Current History*, December 2015.

2013 – On 12/24/13, a bomb at the Directorate of Security in Mansura, Egypt, badly damaged the building, killed 16 or more, and wounded over 100. Protectors of Jerusalem announced that it had joined Al Qa'idah, and claimed responsibility, but the authorities ascribed responsibility to the Muslim Brotherhood and pronounced it a terrorist organization. There were 16,000 Islamists in Egyptian jails: *Harper's*, Negar Azimi.

2014 – On 3/8/14, Egypt's interim President issued a law providing for an election for a new President.

2014 – In the election of 5/26-28/14, SCAF Commander Sisi won the Presidency with 97 percent of the vote. MB members had been disqualified from running in the election. Sisi's summary disposal of Mursi and the MB had won him a temporary wave of popularity.

2014 – In June Sisi cracked down on all the SCAF's rivals.

2014 – Sisi suspected Hamas to be the provocateur of the Islamist insurgency in Sinai: *FT*, 7/17/14. Hamas's major grievance against Egypt was its collaboration with Israel in keeping the border tunnels closed.

2014 – In August, Egyptian and UAE aircraft struck jihadist targets in Libya.

2014 – Categories of Islamic dissenters in Egypt: Salafi Front – In favor of demonstrations; Muslim Brotherhood, Party of Light (*Nur*), and The Islamic Association (*Al Jama'ah al Islamiyyah*), opposed to violent demonstrations; Protectors of Jerusalem – Insurrectionist. The largest dissenting faction, the Muslim Brotherhood, had been subdued by withering police fire and mass arrests: *Times*, 11/29/14.

2014 – Most charges against Mubarak, including that of ordering the murder of protestors on 1/25/11, had been dropped: *Times*, 11/30/14. Sisi had surrounded himself with former officials of the Mubarak regime: *Times*, 12/1/14.

2014 – On 12/2/14, Mubarak, his two sons, and his former security chiefs were acquitted of the charge of ordering 900 dissenters' deaths in

2011: *FT*, 12/2/14. A Sisi decree of October 2014 had elevated the arbitrary powers of military tribunals to new heights.

2014 – Egyptian courts had been condemning protesters on the charges of rioting and causing deaths of police officers. No one had been executed on these charges so far: *Times*, 12/2/14.

2015 – Arab countries in Africa were still accessible to Egyptian forces. On 2/16/15, Egyptian planes attacked targets in Libya in retaliation for the beheading of 21 Copts in the Tripoli sector. The beheadings were a jihadist idea of how to recruit: Gwynne Dyer.

2015 – Sisi was grooming Egypt, not for return to its former leadership of the Arabs, but as an arena for the enrichment of the military. For Sarah Chayes, the Sisi regime was an example of the military-kleptocratic complex: *Times*, 2/22/15.

2015 – Muhammad Mursi and 14 associates were sentenced to twenty years for inciting violence during his Presidency: *AP*, 4/21/15.

2015 – In the previous twenty-two months, Egypt had received 42 billion dollars in subsidies from Kuwait, the UAE, and Saudi Arabia via the Gulf Cooperation Council: *Times*, 5/3/15.

2015 – In June, Egypt's Prosecutor General, Hisham Barakat, was assassinated by a car bomb in Cairo: *Current History*. Sisi was making a brutal effort to eliminate opposition, filling the prisons as never before: *FT*, 6/23/15. The regime had killed 2500 dissidents, and imprisoned 40,000: *FT*, 11/7/15. Intimidation and welfare programs had reconciled the public to military rule: *Current History*.

2015 – Sisi introduced an anti-terrorism law with language that could be used to sentence members of the Muslim Brothers to death: *FT*, 8/18/15.

2015 – Israel reopened its Embassy in Cairo on 9/9/15, four years after demonstrators had stormed it and brought about its closure: *Times*, 9/10/15.

2015 – Egyptian recon aircraft were looking for subversives in the western desert. One of their helicopters misidentified a four-vehicle convoy of tourists in the Bahariyyah Oasis, 230 miles southwest of Cairo. Twelve in the convoy died – six Egyptians and six foreign tourists: *BBC Online*; *The Guardian*, 9/14/15.

2015 – With dynamite, poison gas, and flooding, Egypt had closed 230 tunnels from Gaza, with 20 more to be dealt with: *Times*, 10/8/15.

2015 – Egypt endorsed the Russian campaign against the Syrian rebels: *FT*, 10/8/15.

2015 – Egypt's ultra-Islamist Nur Party broke with the MB in favor of Sisi: *AP*, 10/18/15.

2015 – At a Washington conference of 10/20/15 on Egypt, some participants suggested that the Saudi subsidy to Egypt was all that kept the Sisi regime in power.

2015 – Turnout for the October Parliamentary elections was very low. MB candidates were banned: *FT*, 10/29-30/15.

2015 – On 10/31/15, the crash of a Russian airliner carrying Russian vacationers out of Sharm al Shaykh (in southern Sinai) crippled Egyptian tourism.

2015 – While the Egyptian military was expanding its business empire, the brutality of Sisi's security forces was converting mainstream Muslims into jihadists: *FT*, 11/4/15.

2015 – Egypt had moved closer to Israel than ever before: *FA*, November 2015, Michael Waheed Hanna. Sisi and Israel were joined in an all-out campaign to destroy the failing Gazan aquifer: *WRMEA*, November 2015.

2016 – Since 2013, hundreds of Egyptians had been abducted and tortured in secret detention centers as suspects of membership in the MB. jihadists had killed hundreds of Egyptian soldiers and police: *Nation*, 3/21/16, Ursula Lindsey.

2016 – French President Hollande visited Egypt and signed a billion-dollar arms deal: *Times*, 5/20/16.

2016 – An Egyptian airliner on a flight from Paris to Cairo went into the Mediterranean: *Times*, 5/20/16.

2016 – "A sense of gloom" hung over Egypt, which was politically marginalized, unable to play any effective role in the Syria crisis, except as the fulcrum of American influence in the Arab world: *Times*, 8/3/16.

2016 – Light was shed on the status of Egyptian morale by a report that, in a country afflicted by mass obesity and chain smoking, the young people had been electrified by a fitness craze. All classes, both male and female, were outdoors walking, running, exercising, cycling, and kayaking. Sociologists interpreted the phenomenon as an instinctive reaction to the repression of political expression. In the arena of athletics, the military government was supportive: *Times*, 8/24/16.

2016 – In July, Egypt's foreign currency reserve had fallen to 16 billion dollars, the Egyptian pound was collapsing, tourism had withered, the infrastructure was crumbling, and education and public health were deteriorating: *FA*, November 2016, Cook. Egypt was still receiving 1.3 billion dollars a year in aid from the US: *FA*, November 2015, Hanna.

2016 – Former Egyptian Foreign Minister Samih Shukri was the first Egyptian leader in nine years to visit Israel.

2016 – The regime depopulated Rafah, on the Gaza border, and created along the border a buffer zone, including a moat of seawater that was polluting Gazan farmland: *FA*, November 2016, Cook. Sisi supported the Bashar al Asad regime.

2016 – Mubarak was still under detention. His sons were free.

2016 – Like Sadat and Mubarak, Sisi operated through a political front, the National Democratic Party: *NY*, 1/2/17, Peter Hessler.

2016 – In August, the IMF granted Egypt a loan. To relieve Egypt's 15 percent inflation, it was required to devalue the pound by one-third: *FT*, 11/4/16.

2016 – A new Egyptian law allowed the military to partner with private companies. Inflation was 20 percent. The pound was floating. Unemployment was severe. Tens of thousands of political prisoners filled the jails: *FT*, 12/20/16.

Jordan – Most of the countries that materialized from the fragmentation of the Asian wing of the Ottoman Empire had some reason for being. Turkey insured its arrival into the community of nations by armed force. Iraq was the Land of the Two Rivers. Syria was the heart of the Arab world. Lebanon was the paradise created by the Lebanon-Anti-Lebanon Range. Palestine was the land of the three great religions.

Jordan was an afterthought. From 1916 to 1918, 'Abdallah, elder of the two sons of Sharif Husayn by his first wife, played a key role as planner of T. E. Lawrence's Arab Revolt against Ottoman troops in

Arabia. On 7/24/20, in the Battle of Maysalun (15 miles west of Damascus), French troops defeated troops of Faysal, younger of the Sharif's two sons, who with British sponsorship had been ruling Syria. 'Abdallah moved Arab troops north to engage French troops on behalf of Faysal. Winston Churchill talked him out of it. Faysal was expelled from Syria, but on 8/23/21 Britain found him another royal posting in Iraq.

Britain was arranging for the terms of its Palestine Mandate to include a provisional division between the Palestinian and Transjordanian sectors of the Mandate. The Palestinian sector was reserved for implementation of Balfour's Jewish national home. The Transjordanian sector, with 200,000 inhabitants, including 100,000 nomads, would go ahead on its own. This sector would have no Jewish residents. The frontier between the sectors ran from the Gulf of 'Aqabah north to the Dead Sea, and then up the Jordan River to the Syrian line.

The emergence of the new enclave afforded Britain the opportunity to reward 'Abdallah for his wartime contributions by making him Amir of the brand-new country of Transjordan. In May, 1923, Amir 'Abdallah was given royal powers, subject to British supervision. The Arab Legion, Transjordan's army, was trained and led by a British officer, John Bagot Glubb ("Glubb Pasha") from 1939 to 1956.

Under British hegemony, Transjordan played a brief but major part in the 1948 War, when the Arab Legion defeated Israeli forces in Jerusalem and enabled Transjordan to occupy an enclave of Palestine ("The West Bank") for the next 19 years. On 7/20/51, King 'Abdallah was assassinated in Jerusalem by a young man reportedly under direction of a group close to Hajj Amin al Husayni, a protagonist of the conversion of Palestine into an independent Arab state, and a bitter critic of 'Abdallah's annexation of the West Bank: *The Guardian*, 7/21/51. After a brief interregnum under 'Abdallah's son Talal, who had mental problems, his grandson Husayn succeeded to the throne of Jordan in 1953: *EB*.

From 1948 on, the Jordanian monarchy was the constant victim of subversion from various regional protagonists of Arab Nationalism.

In 1954, clumsy British pressure for Jordanian membership in the abortive Baghdad Pact led to the dismissal of General Glubb and his British officers. Husayn made up temporarily with Nasir. The monarchy survived.

By 1967, the next Arab-Israel war was inevitable. On May 30, 1967, to appease public opinion and insure against a military coup in Jordan, Husayn brushed off Nasir's recent denunciations of the "lackey of imperialism" and signed a defense agreement with Egypt, even though he expected the Arabs to lose.

On June 5, Husayn responded to Israel's air attacks on Egypt and Syria by ordering the strafing of an Israeli airfield. It was all the justification Israel needed to destroy the Jordanian Air Force (with Washington's approval) and seize the West Bank. Jordan's Palestinian refugees from 1948 were joined by another 150-200,000. Jordan became the base of the PLO.

In 1970, the friction between Palestinian interests and Hashemite interests erupted in the Jordan-PLO War. The Salah Jadid faction of the Baathist regime in Syria sent ground troops into Jordan in tentative support of the PLO's war effort, but the rival Hafiz al Asad faction withheld air support, putting the expedition at some risk from King Husayn's pickup air force.

There was a greater risk. After Husayn's secret appeal for Western help, Israel began conspicuous preparations to alert its air force. The Syrians abruptly withdrew their forces from Jordan. Jordan sealed its victory over the PLO by expelling 'Arafat and all his forces to Lebanon.

Since that revealing sequence of events, Jordan has been an unadvertised protectorate of Israel.

In the Yom Kippur War of 1973, the myth of Arab solidarity required Husayn to send two armored brigades and three artillery units to Syria. They were not heavily involved in the fighting. While keeping up appearances, Husayn reportedly conducted a secret campaign to insure clandestine cooperation with Israel: On 9/25/73, he met with Golda Meir to warn her that Syrian forces were deployed for early attack. He later apologized to Israel for the obligatory deployment of Jordanian forces to Syria: *Haaretz*, 9/8/13, Amir Oren; 9/12/13, Ofer Adent; The History Learning Site, 5/26/15, 3/3/16.

In the Israeli invasion of Lebanon in the late 70's and 80's, Jordan played a hypothetical role. Sharon expected to subdue Lebanon, and he saw Jordan as the ideal territory to become the new Palestine, where the troublesome Arab subjects of Lebanon and Israel could be parked.

Ever since Jordan and Iraq had started out under the rule of two Hashimite brothers, the two states had been bonded by a sense of kinship. On 1/28/82, Iraq announced that it would accept Jordanian enlistments to fight for the armed forces of Iraq – then locked in a desperate struggle with Iran. Whenever Iraq lost maritime access to the Gulf, its fallback solution had been the Jordanian seaport at 'Aqabah. Their connection ended in 2003 with the American invasion of Iraq, and its subsequent transition from Sunni to Shiite domination.

On 9/9/05, the bombings of three Amman hotels took a heavy toll in lives. Al Qa'idah was held responsible: *FT*, 9/10/15.

2014 – There were US troops in Jordan to defend it against Syrian attack: *FT*. On 2/3/15, the US and Jordan signed a three-year memorandum of understanding. The US was to provide Jordan one billion dollars a year, subject to the approval of Congress.

On 9/9/15, the tenth anniversary of the Amman hotel bombings, there came a shooting at a training facility of the Jordanian police: *FT*, 9/10/15.

2016 – In September elections for Parliament, Islamists, including the MB, won 15 seats.

Jordan has experienced three traumatic inundations of refugees: Palestinians exiled by the 1948 War, Palestinians exiled by the 1967 War, and 650,000 Syrians exiled by its civil war: *Times*, 9/22/16. Jordan has not allowed the Syrians to take jobs, but they have received some food from the office of the UN High Commissioner for Refugees and from the World Food Program. Many have had to survive on bread and tea: *MER*, Fall 2014.

By 2014, Jordan had put its airfields and military training centers at the service of the coalition formed to destroy the Islamic State: *FT*, 10/6/14; *Times*, 11/20/14.

On 2/3/15, reportedly after his total anesthetization, the IS burned alive Mu'adh al Kasasbah, a Jordanian F-16 pilot, and broadcast videotapes of the atrocity. Most Jordanians dreaded the IS and favored the Damascus Regime in the civil war: *LRB*, Patrick Cockburn.

From 1953 to this writing, Hashimite rulers Husayn and his son 'Abdallah II (1999-) have coped successfully with the administrative and political complexities attendant on running a government of Beduin East-Bankers in a country with a presumed anti-Hashimite majority.

Israel – Since the Middle East Power Struggle erupted in 2011, Israel has stayed on the fringes, and yet has been a major contender. Israel's five devastating encounters with Arab armies (1948-73) sealed its image of military preeminence, which has awarded it a respite from having to prove itself in armed conflict. It has standing influence over the policies of its neighbors by just being there. This doesn't mean that the IDF can be idle. It is still taxed with responsibility for dealing with constant parochial dissention: Arab unrest in Greater Israel (Israel and the Occupied Territories); the Gazan fight for breathing room; and ongoing border clashes with Hizballah, which is committed to the ultimate termination of Jewish rule over Arab subjects – just as Zionists are committed to the ultimate reconciliation of their neighbors with their version of Israel.

Israel's obsession with militancy is an understandable consequence of past tribulation.

Anti-Semitism – In the Muslim World of the past, aside from a few years under Caliph 'Umar, and a few more years under Mongol rule, the worst that Jews experienced was discrimination. In Baghdad of the later Ottoman period, the Jewish community won admiration for its intellectual attainments.

In the Christian world, the Jews faced persecution – magnified by the canard that held all Jews responsible for a crucifixion perpetrated by Jewish priests and Roman soldiers centuries before. There are allegations that even into the 1900's, some Catholics in their rituals were singling out "the Jews" as the killers of Christ: www.yahoo.com, 1/22/07.

The persecution was intensified by the stubborn survival of the Jews as a community throughout the centuries of foreign diaspora and European subjugation, by the widespread failure of Christians to practice the precepts of their own faith, and by the pall of superstition that permeated unschooled society.

The timeline of anti-Semitic actions includes the expulsion of the Jews from England in 1290, expulsion from Castile in 1492, pogroms in the Russian Empire in the 1800's, and American failure to open its doors to Jewish survivors of Holocaust in the 1940's. The world has had to grapple with the paradox that in the enlightened state of Germany, whose Jews seemed well on their way to assimilation, the Nazi apostles of depravity managed to channel the resources of the state into the methodical annihilation of six million Jews, and the condemnation of the world's six million Jewish survivors to unremitting grief, to the corrosive sin of undying hatred, and to lifelong distrust of other peoples.

The Lisbon Massacre – In 1495, the throne of Portugal passed to Manuel I, who married Isabella, daughter of Ferdinand and Isabella of Castile, on condition that Manuel "purify" Portugal of Jews. During most of his reign, Manuel was protective of Jews, but in 1497, under his marriage contract, he ordered all Jews to convert to Catholicism or leave. Converts became known as "new Christians". Many of them were killed in a Lisbon riot in 1506: *EB*, 25:1055.

There is a story that, on 4/19/1506, in the Convent of São Domingos de Lisboa, prayers for an end to a drought and an epidemic were electrified by an outcry that a congregant had just viewed at the altar a vision of the face of Christ. A New Christian ventured that it could have been a trick of the candlelight. He was beaten to death, and three Dominican friars promised the assembly that killers of children of Israel would receive absolution. A town magistrate was forced to hide in his house for three days while mobs circled the city, pulling New Christians from their homes. Some were killed in the streets; many were burned in the courtyard of the convent and in the Lisbon town square. Before authority intervened, nineteen hundred died. Two of the errant friars were burned at the stake. The third friar escaped and left Portugal. King Manuel imposed harsh punishment on the populace of the town,

467

confiscating the property of some and hanging others. Thirty years later, the Portuguese Inquisition used the convent and the Lisbon town square as sites for autos-da-fe: *Massacre of the Jews*, Susana Bastos Mateos/Paulo Mendes Pinto.

The Future of Zionism? – Israel is an ungainly combination of state-of-the-art technology and anachronistic policies. The world's most promising exemplar of nationhood, the United States, has been making tortuous progress toward stamping out ethnicity as a basis for political affiliation. Israel claims to be a democracy, but it shatters that claim by insisting on recognition as a Jewish state. Israel's "Arabs" are genetically close to Israelis who came from Europe and Africa (Almut Nebel, Hebrew University), but they are systematically restricted to second-class citizenship. From the dawn of the Israeli state, the regime has made a meticulous effort to exclude "Arabs" from the policy-making process. The "Jewish" members of the Knesset rig its voting to keep "Arabs" on the periphery: *FA*, July 2016, Aluf Benn; As'ad Ghanem. Ninety percent of "Arabs" (1,900,000 – 20 percent of the total) live in all-Arab towns and villages, attend separate inferior schools, and are routinely penalized by discrimination in confiscation of land and allocation of housing: *FA*, July 2016, Ghanem.

The first Israeli Prime Minister, David Ben-Gurion, set the state on a course of total reliance on brute force. That mentality persists even in the nuclear age, which has rendered ultimate force obsolete. Netanyahu seems to have been dead set on war with Iran, until Obama, the faltering pacifist, excluded that eventuality from the list of strategic options. In the realm of conventional war, Israel's military advantage still suffices for warding off direct attack by any Middle East state, and for deferring a solution of Israel's Gazan dilemma: The Gaza Strip is an integral part of geographic Palestine, but its incorporation into Greater Israel would saddle the "Jewish" state with a non-Jewish majority, while liberation of Gaza would add one more anti-Israeli player to the list of hostile neighbors. Israel's chosen recourse for Gaza's inconvenient subjects was lockdown. Lockdown can't be permanent, and in the suspicion of this writer would already have been found to violate international law but for the undue influence of a partisan superstate over an irresolute UN. The Israeli-American view that repression of the Gazans' struggle for liberation is self-defense against "terrorism" clashes with the international consensus that Israel has no legal claim to Gaza or any other part of Occupied Palestine.

Meanwhile, Israel calibrates its Gaza policy. Allowing 800-1000 truckloads a day of supplies saves Gaza from strangulation by the Egyptian blockade: *FA*, November/December 2016, Cook.

The issue of further Israeli expansion seems to have been resolved by the fortunes of war. As of now, Israel is in control of the territory of the former Palestinian Mandate, plus Golan, lately part of Syria. Israeli abandonment of a military presence in Lebanon, after years of setback in an asymmetrical confrontation with Hizballah, seems to have established that Israel can expand no further – that it has reached its ultimate borders.

Inside this geopolitical frontier, Israel has reduced Arab dissension to manageable levels by trademark imperialism – fragmentation of the occupied territories into tiny, discontinuous, fenced-in enclaves: *NYR*, 4/7/16, David Shulman (an associate of Coexistence [*Ta'ayush*] a partnership of Israeli and Palestinian volunteers).

The battle for Palestine is zero-sum. The polarization between Arabism and Zionism is so extreme that no compromise plan, whether unitary or binary, has ever gained a foothold. The only recourse has been war. So far, war has strongly favored the Zionist side. Zionist preeminence has rested on three keystones: 1) military superiority, which derives from Israel's relentless drive for effective strategy and state-of-the-art technology; 2) the medieval attitudes and practices that prevail among Israel's antagonists; 3) great-power support.

From 1916 to 1947, the great-power support came from Britain – first in the form of official endorsement of the nebulous concept of a Jewish national home in Palestine, later by subtle favoritism for that concept in the administration of the mandate, and in its authorities' dereliction of their obligation to prepare the territory for an orderly transition to independence.

From 1947 on, the great-power support has come from the US, the alchemist whose UN Resolution 181 transmuted a small chunk of the

469

Ottoman Empire into a haven – however precarious – for Jewish refugees from extermination, and the protector of that haven by all requisite succor – political, economic, or military.

Israel-Palestine Timeline – On 1/3/16, Britain and France concluded a super-secret accord that has come down in history as the Sykes-Picot Agreement. Mark Sykes (British) and Georges Picot (French), working in London, did the spadework. Their instructions were transmitted to Sykes every evening from the office of Lord Horatio Herbert Kitchener, Secretary of State for war, who had acquired his immense prestige by being at Khartoum in lucky circumstances. Sykes-Picot foreshadowed the Allies' 1919 establishment of control over the Fertile Crescent – France in Syria and Lebanon, Britain in Iraq, Jordan, and Palestine: *A Peace to End All Peace*, David Fromkin.

1917 – Ze'ev Jabotinski, a pillar of early Zionism, founded and served in the Jewish Legion, which fought in the Middle East beside UK troops in World War I: (JVL).

1917 – On 11/2/17, a letter from British Foreign Secretary Arthur Balfour to Baron Walter Rothschild ("The Balfour Declaration") contained the contradictory assertions that Britain favored the establishment in Palestine of a National Home for the Jewish people, but it would not prejudice the rights of non-Jews! The British objectives were to win Jewish support for American entry into the European war, ingratiate Britain with German Jews, and smooth the way for the establishment in postwar Palestine of a defensive base along the maritime Lifeline between England and India ("the jewel in the crown"). At a time when Arabs in Palestine outnumbered Jews 600,000 to 55,000, the Balfour letter made no mention of Arabs: *Fallen Pillars*, Donald Neff, the rapporteur laureate of the Arab-Israeli wars. Balfour had presumably been acting on instruction from Prime Minister David Lloyd George, who had been the lawyer for Theodore Herzl (the founder of political Zionism: *EB*: 5: 895) and British Zionists in the early 1900's, and was himself a Christian Zionist.

1920 – The founding of *Haganah* (Defense), which in 1948 was the core of the Israel Defense Forces: *JVL*.

470

1922 – In June the League of Nations awarded the UK a mandate to rule Palestine until it was able to rule itself. "Mandate" was a euphemism for <u>possession</u>. As the creation of the Allied powers, the League was responsive to the Allies' requests, including the implementation of the Sykes-Picot compact.

1923 – Jabotinski founded the Betar Youth Movement. He was an inspiring writer and a spell-binding orator in several languages: *JVL*.

1925 – Jabotinski was a founder of the Union of Zionists/Revisionists, which called for a Jewish state (to be achieved by violence): *JVL*. He was a close friend of Ben-Gurion. He had the insight to embrace the UK as the likely winner of World War I: *NYR*, 11/6/14, Avishai Margalit.

1931 – Jabotinski was a founder of the National Military Organization (*Irgun Tsvai Leumi*), the military arm of the Jabotinski Movement. It fought the Palestine Arabs from 1931 to 1939 and the Arabs and the British thereafter.

1936 – The Irgun became the instrument of the Revisionist Party, a right-wing rival of Haganah. Haganah was to become the core of the IDF.

1944 – On 9/20/44, the British War Office authorized the incorporation of a Jewish Brigade into the British armed forces.

1947 – Intense US pressure on individual members of the UNGA ensured its passage of Resolution 181, requiring partition of Palestine between Arabs and Jews. It was adopted by the required two-thirds vote (33-13, with 10 abstentions and one absence). It included a map that proposed the preposterous division of Palestine into six segments – three each for the Arab and Jewish states. These details were ignored, and Arabs rejected the Resolution altogether, but it has survived as the legal basis of the Israeli state.

1947 – Civil war between Arabs and Jews erupted in Palestine. The British security forces began to break down. On 12/16/47, the Palestine police turned over to the Jewish police authority over the conurbation around Tel Aviv. London refused to order its 100,000 troops and police to impose partition: Neff.

471

1948 – The emergence of a Jewish state on 5/14/48, and the subsequent war of independence, reduced the Palestinian Arabs to a diaspora of three communities isolated and alienated from each other. The Arabs who had stayed in Israel became citizens of Israel; Arabs who had stayed in the West Bank were stateless; most of the Arabs in Jerusalem became <u>residents</u>.

1948 – David Ben-Gurion, father of the Jewish state (*medina*) and the Palestinian disaster (*nakbah*), became its Prime Minister.

1948 – In the summer, the US and the UK agreed in secret talks that any part of Palestine not annexed by Israel would be absorbed by Jordan and possibly other Arab states: Neff.

1948 – The US had given the Zionists crucial political support. The Soviet Bloc had sold the Zionists crucial arms. Unready to choose whose sponsorship it preferred, American or Russian, Israel adopted a temporary policy of "non-identification". In the 1950's, Israel finally sided with the US stance on Korea, and looked for access to American arms: Neff.

1949 – UNGA Resolution 302 (IV) established the UN Refugee and Works Agency (UNRWA), which ever since has provided impecunious but caring support for the well-being and education of Palestinian refugees. Lately registered with UNRWA: West Bank – 760,000; Gaza – 1,260,000; Lebanon – 450,000; Syria – 525,000; Jordan – 2,100,000; total registered with UNRWA: 5,095,000. Most of them were living in 59 refugee camps – a far cry from the homes they left behind. However, of all the refugees in the Middle East, the Palestinians are still the only ones favored with their own dedicated refugee organization.

1950 – On 5/5/50, Britain, France, and the US issued the Tripartite Declaration, which opposed an Arab-Israeli arms race, and incorporated a quixotic commitment to counter any aggression from either side or both (?) across the 1949 armistice lines: *The Iron Wall*, Avi Shlaim. The Declaration was later allowed to lapse.

Israel Timeline – In 1954, Moshe Sharett replaced Ben-Gurion as Prime Minister in 1954.

1955 – Ben-Gurion returned as Prime Minister.

1956 – In Kuwait, Yasir 'Arafat (born in Gaza or Cairo on 8/4/29) cofounded Fatah (an offshoot of the Muslim Brotherhood). Fatah is a colloquial form of *Fath*, meaning victory. It is a reverse acronym of *Harakat al Tahrir al Watani al Filastini* (The National Palestinian Liberation Movement).

1956 – The Suez War was the product of collusion among England, France, and Israel. In 1957, France pursued the link with Israel by beginning a secret program to build a nuclear reactor and a plutonium processor in Israel. France detonated its own nuclear test weapon in 1960. Israel's Dimona reactor went critical in 1963: *Exploiting the Bomb*, Matthew Kroenig; *Nuclear Weapons Frequently Asked Questions*, Carey Sublette; *Israel and the Bomb*, Avner Cohen (www.NTI.org).

1963 – Levi Eshkol replaced Ben-Gurion as Prime Minister.

1967 – Six-Day War: Israel defeated Egypt, Syria, and Jordan.

1967 – In September, the Arab League issued a statement that none of its members would recognize, negotiate with, or make peace with (an expansionist) Israel. Israel took responsibility for the security of the Temple Mount, and gave all other responsibility to the Islamic *Waqf*, whose employees were paid salaries by Jordan: *Times*, 10/31/14.

1968 – The treaty on the non-proliferation of nuclear weapons was open for signature. Signers included the five permanent members of the UN Security Council. Israel, which was developing a nuclear weapons capability, declined to sign.

1969 – Golda Meir replaced Levi Eshkol as Prime Minister.

1969-70 – Israel and Egypt fought the War of Attrition.

1973 – Israel won the Yom Kippur War against Egypt and Syria. Israel called its first nuclear alert.

Radical Shift in the Arab-Israeli Military Pattern – In a series of five wars (1948, 1956, 1967, 1970, and 1973), Israel won four victories. That was enough for the Arabs. Twenty-five years of a fight for the survival of Israel have been succeeded by a cold peace. The IDF has been kept busy by border clashes with the militants of Hizballah in Lebanon and Hamas in Gaza. If diplomacy between the West and Iran should fail, the issue of Israel's survival could reemerge as a military issue.

1973 – Israel began stockpiling Jericho ballistic missiles capable of delivering nuclear weapons.

1974 – Yitzhak Rabin replaced Golda Meir as Prime Minister.

1977 – Menachem Begin replaced Rabin as prime minister. He put together a new right wing, headed by the Union (*Likud*) Party, and brought religious parties into the government, but left the left wing alone: *FA*, July 2016, Aluf Benn.

1979 – On 9/22/79, there was a flash of light off the east coast of South Africa. The flash has been construed as a joint atmospheric nuclear test by Israel and South Africa.

1981 – On 6/7/81, under the Begin doctrine of preemption of any nuclear threat, Israeli aircraft destroyed Iraq's Osirak reactor, under construction near Baghdad. Israel had assistance from France.

1983 – Yitzhak Shamir replaced Begin as Prime Minister.

1984 – Shimon Peres replaced Shamir as Prime Minister.

1986 – On 10/5/86, Mordechai Vanunu, former employee of the Israeli nuclear program, revealed classified details to the press in London, then spent 18 years in an Israeli jail.

1986 – Shamir replaced Peres as Prime Minister.

Outbreak of Intifadah I – 1987 was the first of six years of mass protests and stone-throwing.

1991 – On 1/18/91, during the second Kuwait War, the landing in Israel of Scud missiles from Iraq precipitated Israel's second nuclear alert.

1992 – Yitzhak Rabin replaced Shamir as Prime Minister of Israel.

End of Intifadah I: 1993

1995 – Yitzhak Rabin was assassinated on 11/4/95. Shimon Peres replaced him as acting Prime Minister.

1996 – Netanyahu replaced Peres as Prime Minister.

1996 – On 9/25/96, Israel signed the Comprehensive Test Ban Treaty.

1999 – Ehud Barak replaced Netanyahu as Prime Minister.

1999 – Israel was building submarines as its third nuclear delivery system.

Outbreak of Intifadah II – In 2000, the Palestinians introduced suicide bombing.

2001 – Ariel Sharon replaced Barak as Prime Minister.

2003 – Laborite Avraham Burg wrote: "the Israeli nation today rests … on foundations of oppression and injustice …: *MEP*, Fall 2015, Slater.

2003 – "We are running a military occupation regime in the territories that denies 3.5 million people their basic rights …": *Haaretz*, English-language edition: *MEP*, Fall 2015, Slater.

2005 – Large-scale security measures in Israel against Palestinian activists caused thousands of casualties.

End of Intifadah II – Since the murder of Yitzhak Rabin in 2005, Israeli society had become more religious, conservative, and messianic: *NY*, 10/26/05, Dexter Filkins.

2006 – Ehud Olmert replaced Sharon as Prime Minister.

2006 – In democratic elections, the Islamist Hamas came to power in Gaza. Israel resorted to economic and military warfare against the resistance in Gaza: *MEP*, Fall 2015, Slater.

2007 – On 9/6/07, Israeli aircraft destroyed the site of a suspected reactor under construction with North Korean help at Kibar, Syria.

2008-09 – Operation Cast Lead, a major attack on Gaza.

2009 – Benjamin Netanyahu replaced Olmert as Prime Minister. To insure against antagonizing Obama, Netanyahu was leaning to the left: *FA*, July 2016, Aluf Benn.

2010 – In mid-July, the Free Gaza Movement and a Turkish humanitarian foundation formed a volunteer flotilla of small ships to carry humanitarian aid and construction materials through the Israeli blockade of Gaza. On 5/31/10, Israeli security personnel boarded the ships and fired on unarmed defenders, killing nine.

2011 – On 10/23/11, Palestine became a member of UNESCO.

2012 – On 11/29/12, exactly 65 years after the adoption of the Palestine Partition resolution, by a vote of 138-9, the UNGA designated Palestine as a non-member observer state: UN press release.

2014 – Operation Protective Edge, a major attack on Gaza.

2014 – Some leaders of Likud criticized Operation Protective Edge as too feeble, and vowed: 1) to compel Israel's Arab citizens to take loyalty oaths to the Jewish State; 2) to build a new temple on Temple Mount. The new President of Israel, Likudist Reuven Rivlin, was the benign face of his party. He spoke sympathetically of Palestinian problems, and encouraged Palestinians to accept the "Jewish Democratic State": *NY*, 11/17/14, Editor David Remnick. Remnick endorsed Israeli policy, and criticized Palestinian rejection of Ehud Barak's peace offer of 2000 and Ehud Olmert's peace offer of 2008.

2014 – Israel had become a sectarian project. In 1948, the only religious party in the Knesset had 16 members. In 2014, religious parties held one-fourth of the seats in the Knesset. Forty percent of Israelis were thinking of emigration: *Harper's*, September 2014, Eva Illouz.

2014 – The population of Jerusalem was 815,000. Ten percent of the city's budget was spent on the 300,000 Palestinians. The path of the Separation Wall (Security Barrier) had been plotted to maximize the number of Jews inside and the number of Arabs outside: *LRB*, 12/4/14, Nathan Thrall.

2015 – For the Knesset elections of 3/17/15, the four Arab parties had formed a joint list that produced a 63.5 percent election turnout by the Arabs. Netanyahu was behind in the pre-election polls, but he tacked right, ran a tendentious campaign, scored an unprecedented invitation from the US Republican leadership to address the US Congress, and pulled off a solid election victory. The biggest three winners were Netanyahu's Likud (30 seats), the center-left Zionist Union (24), and the Arab bloc, led by Ayman 'Awdah, (an unprecedented 13). Netanyahu's new allies were the long-ostracized Mizrahim (Sephardis) and the Religious Zionists, who had been gaining political clout, and championed continued expansion of Jewish settlement in the Occupied Territories: *FA*, July 2016, Aluf Benn. The Israeli peace camp had withered.

2015 – Estimated numbers of Arab residents: Israel – 1.5 million; West Bank – 2.7 million; Gaza – 1.8 million.

2015 – The number of Jewish settlers on the West Bank had risen to 389,000: *Washington Post*, 10/23/15, Steven Levitsky/Glen Weyh.

2015 – Israel's bitter feud with Hizballah was determining its Syrian policy, which was aimed at replacement of the Asad regime with Sunnis, who would be more likely to block the transit of arms from Iran to Lebanon. To this end, Israel was allowing wounded Nusrah militiamen to visit Israel for medical treatment: *WRMEA*, November 2015: Consortium News, Robert Parry.

2015 – A wave of solo Palestinian attacks on individuals in Israel had caused the deaths of over 200 Arabs. This new phase had been termed "The Loner's Intifadah": *FA*, July 2016.

2015 – Jewish society is said to have had universal male literacy 1700 years before any other society: *Times*, 10/11/15, Nicholas Kristoff.

2015 – Jordan had nominal responsibility for the protection of the Muslim holy places in Jerusalem: *LRB*, 11/5/15, Thrall.

2015 – Fatah, the onetime mainstay of the Palestine Liberation Movement, had been smothered in the embrace of the cowed PA: *LRB*, 11/5/15, Nathan Thrall.

2015 – Israel was a time bomb: Stephen Walt.

2016 – The *Times* carried a message from UN Secretary-General Ban Ki-Moon, who made the following points: Israel was continuing the expansion of illegal settlements in the occupied West Bank by declaring the land they occupied state territories, which typically were reserved for use by Israeli (Jewish) settlers; Palestinians were losing hope; history proves that people will always resist occupation: *Times*, 2/2/16.

2016 – Under the leadership of Netanyahu, the Israeli Government, members of the Knesset, right-wingers, and the Israeli media were behind a coordinated campaign to crush Israel's leftist faction. Minister of Justice Ayelet Shaked was a rightist fanatic. Netanyahu, *Haaretz* correspondent Ari Shavit, and many others had lately precipitated a witch-hunt against the ex-soldiers' organization, Breaking the Silence. Coexistence was also under rightist attack: *NYR*, 4/7/16, Shulman.

2016 – Cyberwar by Israel and/or the US had put 3000 of Iran's 8200 centrifuges out of operation since 2010: *Post*, 4/18/16; *Slate*, Fred Kaplan; George Will.

2016 – At the annual meeting of the Herzliya Conference (June 14-16), Israeli President Reuven Rivlin said the trend in Israeli society was division into four sectors: secular, Haredi/ultra-orthodox, National Religious Party, and Arabs. Two of these categories did not identify with Zionist doctrine: *WRMEA*, August 2016.

2016 – Two hundred retired Israeli security officials sent a message to Netanyahu recommending that he end the occupation of the West Bank, cede the West Bank to its Arab residents, freeze Jewish settlement there, and support the creation of a Palestinian state: *AP*, 6/29/16.

2016 – The Knesset passed a law providing for the ouster of any of its members who foster racial unrest or support armed struggle against Israel: *Times*, 7/20/16.

2016 – Aluf Benn, editor of *Haaretz*, contended in an article in *Foreign Affairs* that, since the election of March 2015, Israel had been moving rapidly toward becoming a state that served Jews only and discriminated against all other citizens. Tzipi Livni of the Zionist Union advocated Israeli progress toward a two-state solution: *FA*, July 2016.

2016 – In mid-July, the Knesset adopted the Israeli Expulsion Law, under which a three-fourths majority of the members can expel other members. The bill was aimed at Palestinian MK's, in particular at MK Hanin Zu'bi of the Balad Party. She had created a furor by terming the deaths of passengers on the Freedom Flotilla in July 2010 as murder. Netanyahu made two comments: "Those who support terrorism against Israel will not serve in the Israeli Knesset." "We need to secure the State of Israel from the wild beasts that surround us.": *WRMEA*, October 2016; *LRB*, 10/6/16.

2016 – Jewish settlers on the West Bank numbered 400,000: *Times*, 10/7/16.

2016 – Now that the jihadists seemed to have replaced Israel as the worst enemy of the Arab states, Netanyahu was launching a diplomatic push to enhance that view: *FT*, 8/8/16.

2016 – Israel was erecting high-tech anti-filtration fences along all its borders: *FT*, 6/30/16, John Reed.

The United States, from Wilson to Obama – In its formative years, the American democracy was preoccupied with nation-building at home. Its foreign concerns were largely confined to promoting ties with the

European powers, while keeping them out of the Americas (Monroe Doctrine). After the Civil War, humanitarian Americans found opportunity to help in the advancement of Third World countries. In the Middle East, American missionaries concentrated more on education than on proselytization, founded several outstanding schools, and built an image of America as a benevolent bystander.

As American power grew, the image of benevolence faded. America had always practiced imperialism on its own continent. World War II turned its attention to Europe and the Middle East. When it joined the Allies, it became a proxy imperialist, by virtue of its share in the consequences of the Europeans' conversion of their Middle Eastern possessions into a military base against the Axis.

European imperialism came out of the war too depleted to go on. The new superpower moved to fill the vacuum. In those days, Washington saw its vital interests in the Middle East as peace, access, and oil. In 1945, an ailing President Roosevelt marshaled his political genius for one last time. In a congenial meeting with the Saudi Arabian ruler Ibn Saud, Roosevelt concluded a verbal agreement: the exchange of privileged access to Saudi oil for an American guarantee of Saudi security. America had now become a Middle Eastern imperialist in its own right: Alliance with Saudi Arabia committed the US to monitoring the Saudis' enemies. Saudi Arabia had become a peripheral contender in the ongoing regional power shuffle.

In 1945, the US played a leading role in the creation of the UN, the vanguard of globalization, one more baby step toward stamping out the obsolete institution of war.

In 1947, Washington leaped headlong into the company of Middle East contenders by bulldozing through the neophyte UN General Assembly a resolution that proposed a bizarre scheme for the partition of the Palestine Mandate between its 1.3 million Arabs and its 650,000 Jews. The resolution was never implemented, and the Arabs rejected it, but it remains the basis for the legality of the Israeli state. Since the creation of Israel in 1948, it has been accorded American support almost equivalent to that accorded each of the fifty states. A major element of this support has been the deployment of permanent military forces in and around the Persian Gulf. At first the central mission of the US garrisons in the Middle East may have been seen in Washington as insuring access to Middle East oil.

Also in 1947, Harry Truman issued the Truman Doctrine as a commitment to the security of Turkey, especially against the USSR, and Congress created the National Security Council (NSC) and the Central Intelligence Agency (CIA), which under NSC direction collects data on foreign affairs. The secrecy required of the Agency gives it occasion to break international law. A current example is the maintenance of overseas "black sites" for the "enhanced interrogation" of abductees suspected of "terrorism" – notably in Afghanistan and Pakistan: *The Week*, 12/26/14. The extensive debate on what the constraints on interrogation should be produced the "torture memo" which argued that the Geneva Convention did not apply to American interrogators overseas. The Supreme Court rejected that argument.

The first public use of the term "Cold War", for the intense postwar rivalry between the US and the USSR, came in 1947 from Presidential Advisor Bernard Baruch in Congressional testimony.

In 1947-48, George Marshall's Marshall Plan for the reconstruction of postwar Europe blazed new trails in the evolution of enlightened foreign policy.

In 1950, Turkey became a member of NATO. Four years later, the US built a Turkish-American air base at Incirlik, strategically located near the Mediterranean Sea and the Syrian border.

Eisenhower was the President who did the best job of maintaining neutrality between the US and the Arabs.

In 1956, another ailing leader, Prime Minister Anthony Eden, made a futile stab at reversing the Anglo-Egyptian Treaty of 1954, under which the UK had started withdrawal of its garrison from the Suez Canal Zone. The UK had two co-conspirators – France and Israel. The military part of the plot began well, with the British and French taking over Port Said, and the Israelis occupying Gaza and Sinai, but the plotters had misread Eisenhower, who was appalled by the absurdity of the scheme, and enraged by the insult to his intelligence. He threatened to pull the rug out from under the Pound Sterling. The conspirators capitulated. In so doing, they signaled the end of an era. The new imperialist power in the Middle East was the United States.

In 1961, Congress adopted the Foreign Aid Act.

In 1967, Lyndon Johnson ended John Kennedy's policy of trying to do business with Nasir. Johnson terminated the sale of American wheat to Egypt under Public Law 480, which had allowed Egypt to pay for the wheat in its own currency.

In 1970, in the *London Review of Books*, Tariq Ali hailed the IT (Information Technology) revolution in the US as the most remarkable development of recent times (in contrast to America's failure to correct defects in its political system).

On Nixon's visit to Moscow in 1972, the two powers agreed on détente.

In Washington in 1975, the hawks took wing. As "Ignotus", Edward Luttwak wrote in the March *Harper's* that the Americans had discovered Arabian oil, so by rights it was "ours": *America's War for the Greater Middle East*, Andrew Bacevich.

The Carter Doctrine of 1980 (the US would act against any force that threatened to take control of the Persian Gulf) inaugurated America's war for the greater Middle East, as noted in Andrew Bacevich's book by that title.

To implement the doctrine, Washington proclaimed the creation of the Rapid Deployment Joint Task Force (RDF). Its organization was never completed: Bacevich.

The Reagan administration (1981-89) was an era of fast and loose American militancy.

In 1981, Reagan rephrased America's security guarantee to Saudi Arabia to include American defense of the Saudi regime against any internal threat!

On 6/6/82, Israeli troops who had invaded South Lebanon in 1978 moved north to Beirut. By June 15, they had put Beirut under siege, and were bombing PLO bases in West Beirut. Later in the month, under strong pressure from Reagan, Begin ordered the IDF to "end the attack", but they did not leave. Reagan sent Ambassador Philip Habib back to Lebanon for a second round of diplomacy to repair the damage done to

481

the understanding he had tried to build in his first round. On 8/12/82, after a day-long Israeli bombardment of targets in Beirut, Habib negotiated a truce calling for withdrawal of Israeli and PLO forces from Lebanon. To oversee the process, a new multilateral (international) peacekeeping force, again including US Marines, began to arrive in Beirut in August.

In July 1982, Reagan replaced Secretary of State Alexander Haig – who had failed to prevent Ariel Sharon's senseless invasion of Lebanon – with George Shultz, who tried to be realistic about the Middle East, but didn't know the territory. He didn't realize that the arbiter of Lebanon's immediate future was not Israel. It was Syria, backed by Iran and Hizballah. On April 18, 1983, a suicide bombing of the US Embassy, ascribed to Hizballah, killed 63.

On May 17, 1983, a conclave of American, Israeli, and Lebanese representatives – no Syrian – concluded an agreement that Israel and Syria would withdraw their troops from Lebanon. By August, there were no more Israeli troops in the Beirut area, but the way was open for re-escalation of Lebanon's ongoing civil war between pro-West and pro-Syrian factions, and for a campaign by the pro-Syrians to frustrate American designs on Lebanon. By August 1983, the Marines were taking lethal fire, and Lebanon's pro-West regime was asking for US support in repelling militia attacks on the Lebanon Army. Washington authorized return fire against the offending Muslim and Druze militias. From September 8 until December, the Marines maintained defense on the ground, and units of the Sixth Fleet shelled pro-Syrian positions in the hills east of Beirut. Naval aircraft attacked Syrian missile positions. Two US planes were shot down.

On October 23, 1983, in the midst of the conventional fighting, Hizballah (?) sent a gigantic truck bomb to destroy the Marine barracks. That operation killed 241, most of them American servicemen. It dampened American interest in involvement in intra-Arab combat. In early 1984, the Marines were quietly withdrawn from Lebanon.

By this time, mass defections of Muslims and Druze from the Lebanese Army to the pro-Syrian militias were altering the Lebanese balance of power. On March 5, 1984, Lebanon cancelled Shultz's

482

agreement of May 17, 1983. In the struggle for control of Lebanon, Syria and Iran had defeated Israel and the United States.

1983 – Reagan created the Central Command (CENTCOM) to defend the Persian Gulf. He announced Washington's over-ambitious decision to prevent closure of the Strait of Hormuz (connecting the Gulf with the Arabian Sea).

1987 – The Fifth Fleet destroyed a number of Iranian oil platforms and PT boats. The PT's were the mainstays of the Iranian Navy.

1991 – Mikhail Gorbachev won a place in history by keeping Russia quiet as the USSR dissolved.

1991 – The US led the forces of many other states in the Second Kuwait War, which accomplished the summary expulsion of the Iraqi force that had occupied Kuwait in 1990.

1991 – By joining the Western coalition to oust Iraq from Kuwait, Syrian dictator Hafiz al Asad won a reward – US approval for Syrian troop operations in Lebanon.

1992 – The Fifth Fleet was granted base rights for its headquarters in Bahrain.

1993 – Turkey denied permission for the US to stage air attacks on Iraq from Incirlik Air Base.

1993 – Clinton adopted a policy of "dual containment" intended to prevent any Iraqi or Iranian anti-West subversion or military action.

1993 – Egypt allowed the CIA to base its Middle East operations in Cairo.

1994 – The US began pre-positioning in Kuwait and Qatar military materiel to cover unexpected demands on US forces in the region. They numbered 20,000, including the crews of the Fifth Fleet's 20 warships.

1996 – US planes were policing the northern No-Fly Zone in Iraq from Gulf states, not from Saudi Arabia.

Early in the twenty-first century, members of the "realist" school in foreign affairs analysis, like Chalmers Johnson and John Mearsheimer, demanded that the US dismantle its foreign bases, and keep its armed forces in the US and Canada, ready to deal with threats to the national interest, but not to indulge in political adventurism or political bias: *LRB*, 4/9/15, Tariq Ali.

2001 – The US chose to attack Afghanistan in reprisal for Al Qaʻidah's attacks of 9/11/2001 – a scheme that seems to have been kept secret from the Taliban, then rulers of Afghanistan. The killing of an Afghan in October was the first lethal operation by a US drone (unmanned aerial vehicle): *FP*, October 2001, James Bamford.

2002 – The US lost access to Saudi Arabia's Prince Sultan Airbase, where the headquarters for the Middle East operations had been sited. The Pentagon was allowed to build a substitute base at Al ʻUdayd in Qatar.

2002 – The Arab Human Development Report asserted that the Arab world was far behind the West in the realm of technology, and that its elementary education systems were among the worst in the world.

The occupation of Iraq began in 2003, and terminated in 2011, amid mounting regional disorder. According to the Weiss/Hasan analysis, the US compounded the error of invasion by misreading the related events in Syria. Washington wrongly assumed that the Alawite regime in Damascus would collapse on its own. Washington failed to realize that a civil war in Syria would further destabilize Iraq: *NYTBR*, 4/5/15, review of the Weiss/Hasan book.

2006 – At the start of the Israel-Hizballah war, Secretary of State Condoleeza Rice told representatives of Lebanon's March 14 coalition (pro-West) that the time had come for a new Middle East.

2009 – The secret US Joint Special Operation Command (JSOC) met in the company of Blackwater personnel to plan drone operations, including the killing of Taliban and Qaʻidah operatives: *Nation*, 12/21/09, Jeremy Scahill. The JSOC is a component of the US Special Operations Command (USSOCOM).

2011 – As the CIA's funding for pro-Western factions in Afghanistan was being distributed by General Zia ul Haq's Pakistani Inter-Services Intelligence (ISI), the old order in the Arab World was collapsing. By 2015, the Middle East was in chaos. Iran was calling the tune in Iraq. The ranking military power in the region was Israel, with the blind support of the US. Iraq and Syria were wrecked. Syria's brutal military dictatorship was torturing and killing as if the Arab Spring had never happened: *LRB*, 4/9/15, Tariq Ali. The Sykes-Picot edifice was cracking along its ethnic seams. Local conflicts were being subsumed into a regional sectarian feud between Sunni and Shiite coalitions. Turkey was being ripped apart three ways – secular militants against Islamist politicians, Turkish nationalists against Kurdish insurrectionists, and NATO demands versus Middle Eastern obligations. Israel was detached from the worst of the fighting, unable to influence its outcome. The American commitment to Israel's survival was a major incentive for its gratuitous interferences in a conflict raging on the opposite side of the planet.

2011 – The US and Israel cut off their funding for UNESCO, which had just made Palestine a full member. The annual US contribution had been 80 million dollars – 22 percent of the UNESCO budget: *Post*, 10/31/11. In 2013, the US and Israel lost their voting rights in UNESCO: *AP*, 11/8/13.

2015 – The US invasion of Afghanistan was a misdirected war of revenge (for Al Qa'idah's 9/11 attack). The occupation of Iraq had been one of the most destructive acts in history. By handing over the rule of Iraq to Shiite parties, the US had destroyed Iraqi society and deepened the Shiite-Sunni split. The EU was under the thumb of the US: *LRB*, Tariq Ali.

2015 – In a battle for control of the CIA, Leon Panetta won out over Admiral Dennis Blair. The White House complied with Panetta's request for control of CIA funding, and the right to use drones in Pakistan: *FP*, May/June 2015, Yochi Dreazen/Sean Naylor.

2015 – The US had 800 military bases worldwide, backed by a military-industrial complex of defense contractors, arms dealers, lobbyists, and consultants. What media had challenged the justification for these bases?: *NYR*, 6/25/15, Michael Manning.

2015 – Arab refugees from the fighting in the Levant and Iraq were flooding Europe, but not Arab countries, because the refugees did not want to become third-class citizens of autocracies, and the autocracies were terrified of letting in revolutionaries: *The Week*, 9/18/15.

2015 – The US was maintaining heavy military presences in four of the Gulf shaykhdoms (not Oman). It had been engaged in conflict in the Middle East for the previous 25 years, including the Afghan and Iraqi wars – the two longest conventional wars in US history. It had spent more on Afghan reconstruction than on the Marshall Plan. Its actions had resulted in the enormous empowerment of Iran. Ninety percent of US spending abroad had gone to overuse of the military. Congress was the culprit because of its pandering to the military-industrial complex: *NYR*, 9/24/15, Jessica Mathews.

2015 – The US should bring the troops back home: *Superpower*, Ian Bremmer.

2015 – America's assertive foreign and security policies, supported by both political parties, were a costly mistake. So was their disregard in Middle East matters for international law: *Restraint*, Barry Posen.

2015 – *The Nation* cited a Hillary Clinton declaration: "The US can, must, and will lead in this new century."

2015 – There are challenges (in the Middle East) that require US action: *Nation*, 9/28/15, Katrina van den Heuvel.

2015 – The millions of Arabs who took to the street in 2011 were united by an intense desire to destroy the old political order – in which the US was deeply implicated. Washington was having trouble grasping this reality because it clashes with American illusions: Middle East reliance on US stewardship, the inviolability of Israel, and the necessity to indulge client states in their caprices. Example: US toleration of the Saudis' haphazard air campaign against Yemen, so as not to provoke Riyadh into wrecking the nuclear talks with Iran: *FA*, Fall 2015, Marc Lynch.

2015 – Clinton's insistence on dual containment of Iraq and Iran had necessitated a long-term military presence in the Gulf, which had triggered the rise of anti-Americanism, to which the US had responded by the invasions of Afghanistan and Iraq, which had already cost the US 6 trillion dollars: *WRMEA*, November 2015, Charles Freeman.

2015 – President Hollande was pursuing an oil campaign against the IS in concert with Russia, and in tacit alliance with the Damascus regime: *LRB*, 12/3/15, Adam Shatz.

2015 – From arms sales to rich states like Qatar, Saudi Arabia, and South Korea, the US was earning 36 billion dollars a year, and originating half of global arms sales: *Times*, 12/26/15.

2016 – Obama's inaction in Syria had made Putin the dominant actor there: *FT*, 2/17/16.

2016 – The US military build-up in the Middle East began in 1990-91, when Bush 41 sent 700,000 troops to expel the Iraqis from Kuwait, and many of those troops stayed on: *Atlantic*, March 2016, Peter Beinart.

2016 – The US was backing the Lebanese army against Hizballah: *Times*, 4/19/16.

2016 – An op-ed piece in the *New York Times* blamed the mess in Iraq on the American occupiers' endorsement of ultra-Shiite Maliki as Prime Minister. His ostracism of Iraq's Sunni community had led to the rise of the IS: *Times*, 4/23/16, Bernard Haykel/Steffen Hertog.

2016 – The Americans' main military objective in Syria and Iraq was to end IS control of Raqqah, Mawsil, and a Syrian border-crossing town, Manbij. Achievement of this objective had been obstructed by factional friction among Kurds, between Kurds and Arabs, and between the KRG and Baghdad: *FT*, 5/26/16.

2016 – The US was providing air support for the YPG troops moving toward Raqqah. Syrian rebels were resisting US pressure to join the YPG offensive: *FT*, 5/27/16.

2016 – The US-Turkey alliance was being strained, as the US treated the YPG as being independent of the PKK, while Turkey was shelling YPG targets: *Times*, 5/29/16, Worth.

2016 – Since 2013, the CIA and the Saudis had cooperated in training and arming Syrian rebels. The Jordanian security services were responsible for distribution of the arms to the rebels. Few rebels had received training. Most of the arms had been hijacked by the Jordanians: *Times*, 6/27/16.

2016 – An editorial in the *European Times* contended that Washington had been shockingly ineffectual in dealing with suspected war crimes. Washington had failed to distance the "moderate" rebels from Nusrah, whose cooperation they needed because its military operations had been more successful than theirs: *FT*, 8/4/16.

2016 – The US and Russia had been so fixated on pursuing their own strategies that both of them were failing Syria: *FT*, 8/5/16.

487

2016 – One hundred US troops had been deployed in the front lines of the advance into Mawsil: *AP*, 10/18/16.

US-Arabia – In 1939, the US and Saudi Arabia established diplomatic relations.

1943 – In February, Secretary of the Interior Harold Ickes arranged for Roosevelt to declare the welfare of Saudi Arabia vital to the defense of the US – making it eligible for US aid.

1945 – Although FDR was only two months from death, on his way back from Yalta he was able to muster his legendary empathy to have a profitable get-together on 2/14/45 with Saudi Arabian King Ibn Sa'ud and Beduin entourage on the deck of the US cruiser Quincy in the Suez Canal. Roosevelt wanted to confirm access to oil (via the American company Aramco), find a Middle East site for an American air base, and obtain Saudi help in resolving the Palestine dispute. While Ibn Sa'ud brooked no slight to his regality, he was looking for the most congenial partner in mitigating his country's poverty and underdevelopment. No written record of the meeting has surfaced. The fallback is the report by Marine Col. William A. Eddy, US diplomatic representative to Saudi Arabia, who was the interpreter between the two chiefs of state. In his words, Ibn Sa'ud was adamantly opposed to the creation of a Jewish state in the Middle East, but he accepted Roosevelt's proposal of a standing agreement on an American security guarantee for Saudi Arabia, in return for privileged access to Saudi oil: *The Link*, April/May 2005, Thomas W. Lippman.

1980 – Carter Doctrine: Any move to seize control of the Persian Gulf would be regarded as an assault on the vital interests of the US.

1983 – Reagan created a new military command, CENTCOM, to dispel any threat to American access to Persian Gulf oil

1992 – The US began construction in Bahrain of a naval base for headquartering the new Fifth Fleet.

2002 – The US gave Oman military assistance valued at 50 million dollars for access to military facilities on Masirah Island: *MEP*, September 2002.

2004 – The US transferred its garrison's headquarters from Saudi Arabia to Al 'Udayd Air Base in Doha, Qatar.

2011 – The CIA established a secret drone base in the southwestern desert of Saudi Arabia for attacks against AQAP targets in Yemen: *Harper's*, September 2016, Alexander Cockburn.

2013 – Saudi Arabia was contributing arms and money to a CIA program to arm Syrian rebels: *Times*, 1/24/16.

2014 – Four GCC states (Kuwait, Qatar, Saudi Arabia, and the UAE) were buying Patriot missile defense systems from the US. Qatar was buying Apache helicopters as well.

2015 – Saudi Arabia pursued its air attacks on Yemeni "terrorists". The death and destruction raining on Yemen from the air had led to greater cooperation between the AQAP and the Yemeni separatists: *Times*, 1/27/15.

2015 – Since 2002, US drones had killed 900 Yemenis. US soldiers were training Yemeni soldiers: *The Week*, 3/6/15.

2015 – In Yemen, IS affiliates were committing suicide attacks against Zaydi mosques in San'a'; over 100 of the victims had died. The US had withdrawn its special operations trainees from Yemen. Many Yemenis despised the US "counter-terrorism" campaigns, especially the drones: *Times*, 3/21/15.

2015 – Since 2009, US drone strikes against targets in Yemen amounted to over 900: *AP*, 3/22/15.

2015 – The US was providing logistic and intelligence support to GCC forces (due to be deployed in Yemen): *FT*, 3/27/15.

2015 – The US was expediting deliveries of arms to Saudi Arabia (engrossed in the Yemeni War): *Times*, 4/8/15.

2015 – The US-Saudi relationship was conflicted. For the US, Saudi Arabia was a lucrative client for sale of arms. For Saudi Arabia, Obama's nuclear negotiations with Iran and his failure to take effective action against Bashar al Asad were unacceptable: Tom Friedman, from conversation with the President: *NY*, 5/25/15, Steve Coll.

2015 – In Yemen, the US supported the Saudi air campaign against the Huthis, but attacked the Huthis' other enemy, the AQAP: *Times*, 6/17/15.

2015 – Former Senator Graham of Florida was calling for ending the classification of a portion of the *9/11 Commission Report*. The classified

489

section alleged that the 9/11 assault on US targets was a product of Saudi money, ideals, and organizational support: *The Week*, 8/14/15.

2015 – The US had backed the Saudi air strikes against the Huthis in Yemen, in which 2000 Yemenis had already died. Yemen was on the brink of famine: *FT*, 8/31/15.

2015 – Coalition bombs meant for Huthi targets in Yemeni cities were falling haphazardly, killing hundreds of innocents. Resentment of Saudi Arabia and the US was mounting. The US was peripherally involved in the action by supplying logistic and intelligence support, and selling the Saudis weapons, including the questionable cluster bombs: *Times*, 9/13/15.

2015 – DOD press releases on the Islamist-US conflict were being datelined "southwest Asia" to obscure the fact that the US forces were based in Kuwait. Congress had not authorized the war: *Times*, editorial, 9/17/15.

2015 – At first, Obama endorsed the Saudi bombing of Yemen in order to inhibit any Saudi disruption of US-Iranian nuclear negotiations: *FA*, September 2015.

2015 – The states of the GCC were very troubled by the US effort to persuade Iran to suspend its nuclear program in return for cancellation of the sanctions. They believed the Asad cabal should be ousted from Damascus first: *FA*, November 2015, Han Goldenberg, Melissa Dalton.

2015 – In 16 months, oil had dropped from 110 dollars a barrel to 38. Few US oil fields were making money: *Times*, 12/8/15.

2015 – US support for the Saudi air offensive in Yemen included intelligence exchange, air-to-air refueling, and a 129 million dollar arms deal with Saudi Arabia: *Times*, 12/23/15.

2016 – The Saudis had to live with the Western view that Saudi Arabia was an ally, but Iran was the wave of the future. For Riyadh, Iran was a greater enemy than Israel, with which Saudi Arabia was developing covert ties. This improbable linkage was troublesome for the West, as was the Saudi feud with the Huthis and with its own Shiites: *FT*, 1/8/16, Philip Stephens.

2016 – An American Major General, second in command of the Marines in the Middle East, was the head of a military planning group that was providing intelligence to its Arabian members – Bahrain, the UAE, and Saudi Arabia: *Times*, 3/14/16.

2016 – Saudi pilots fly too high to maintain bombing accuracy. Since the start of their war with the Huthis a year before, they had killed 3000 civilians: *Times*, 3/14/16.

2016 – After Obama mentioned Saudi Arabia in his criticism of US allies who were "free riders" in the war against "terrorism", Prince Turki al Faysal of Saudi intelligence complained that the US condemns Iran as a terrorist state, and then expects Saudi Arabia to share the Middle East with them: *Times*, 3/15/16. Saudi officials were accusing Obama of prolonging the Syrian civil war by denying the rebels effective anti-aircraft weaponry (on the grounds that it might fall into terrorist hands). The Saudis feared the days of close Saudi-US ties were over: *Times*, 4/19/16.

2016 – An editorial in the *Times* criticized Obama for his extensive involvement in Saudi Arabia's questionable air campaign against Yemen: wholesale provision of arms; supply of intelligence; inflight refueling: *Times*, 8/17/16.

2016 – As casualties from the Saudis' haphazard bombing mounted, condemnation of the Saudi air war, and US support for it, was growing in Congress: *Times*, 8/24/16.

2016 – The September issue of *Harper's* carried a wide-ranging analysis by Patrick Cockburn including the following observations:

- The US had obtained a UNSC resolution demanding, in effect, that the Huthis surrender.
- Metal fragments from a coalition air strike in Yemen were from GBU-31 satellite-guided bombs of US manufacture. A State Department official had contended that precision weapons kept collateral casualties to a minimum.
- Washington was pressing the Yemeni contingent in the coalition to attack AQAP targets.
- The value of the arms recently supplied Saudi Arabia by the US was 60 billion dollars. In Saudi Arabia, thousands of Americans were engaged in weapons maintenance, military training, naval

491

support for the blockade, and promoting the sale of the weapons that were keeping them busy. The US government received a commission on each sales contract. The sales included F-15 jet fighters, helicopters, and cluster bombs. Maintenance of the weapons in Saudi Arabia was a gold rush for American mechanics and engineers. Obama had become the enabler of the US military/industrial complex.

- There was no apparent justification for the war. It had no relevance to the security of the United States, except as it might be distracting Saudi Arabia from doing damage elsewhere – as by trying to abort the nuclear talks with Iran.

2016 – An editorial in the *Times* contended that the US should end its complicity in the humanitarian catastrophe being inflicted on Yemen: 10/11/16.

2016 – In appreciation for US support for the Saudis' operations against the Huthis, the Saudis had muted their opposition to the international nuclear deal with Iran: *Times*, 11/20/16.

US-Arab Levant (Syria, Lebanon, Jordan) – On 9/14/82, a Syrian (?) agent assassinated Lebanese president Bashir Jumayyil. The UN peacekeeping force, including US Marines, was sent back to bolster the pro-West government of his successor, Amin Jumayyil, his brother: *The Iron Wall*, Avi Shlaim.

1983 – In August, IDF forces began withdrawing from the Shuf, a district in the Lebanese Range east of Beirut, but not before being caught in Arab crossfire as the Lebanese civil war resumed where it had left off: Shlaim.

1983 – On 9/19/83, Reagan authorized the Marines to fire in defense of themselves and the regime of Amin Jumayyil against attack from pro-Syrian militias. Units of the Sixth Fleet shelled Druze positions in the town of Suq al Gharb, reportedly causing heavy civilian casualties. On 9/23/83, two Marine checkpoints came under heavy attack. The exchanges between militias and Marines, who were taking casualties, continued through October. Syrian ground-to-air missiles fired on USN recon planes, downing two. Fleet units shelled Syrian missile bases.

1983 – On 10/23/83, a Hizballah (?) suicide bomber drove a truck into the Marine compound in Beirut, destroying their barracks and killing 241 American servicemen.

1991 – Hafiz al Asad had joined the Western coalition against his bitter Baathist rival, Saddam Husayn. This perceived dedication to the American maintenance of law and order in the Middle East was rewarded by American recognition of the two treaties of 1991 between Syria and Lebanon (*See*: page 396).

2011 – Obama called on Bashar al Asad to resign as President of Syria: *FT*, 9/9/16.

2013 – The White House revealed that the Defense Department and CIA had recommended that the US arm the secularist rebels in Syria, but the suggestion was rejected, in part because of the risk that the arms could be taken over by enemies of Israel: *McClatchy*, 2/9/13.

2013 – A UN commission reported in August that Asad's forces had hit rebel sites near Damascus with missiles armed with sarin nerve gas. Obama warned Asad that use of chemical weapons would "cross a red line", but when Asad ignored the warning, Obama took no action: *NY*, 12/21/15, David Remnick. Many officials in the administration were highly critical of his decision not to take counteraction. The IS seized arms from FSA stores in December 2013: *McClatchy*, 9/2/14.

2013 – Obama authorized CIA arming of the moderate rebels in Syria. Saudi Arabia contributed arms and money to the project: *Times*, 1/24/16.

2013 – In August, Damascus attacked the east Ghutah, a suburb, with sarin gas, killing 1400: *The Syrian Jihad*, Charles Lister.

2015 – Asad's plausible survival argument: The fall of his regime would be a bonanza for Islamists thirsting for the blood of defenseless Alawites: *The Week*, 8/7/15.

2015 – Russia seemed to be bringing the US around to agreeing that Bashar al Asad should be salvaged. Arabs in Syria and Saudi Arabia were still set on the elimination of the ruler who for the past four years had been dropping barrel bombs on his own people. Asad would accept the destruction of most of Syria as long as he could salvage a rump Alawite state under his control in the rest of it. Most of Syria was lost – the east to the IS, the northwest to Nusrah. Several thousand Russians (Chechens) were fighting for the IS. Russia might give up its support for Asad, but not its support for the consolidation of an Alawite state: *Times*, 8/13/15.

2016 – In a Damascus prison, the regime was torturing terrorist suspects on behalf of the CIA: *LRB*, 1/7/16, Hersh.

2016 – The ceasefire brokered by the US and Russia, excluding the IS and Nusrah, was holding fairly well: *AP*, 3/27/16.

2016 – The CIA had been training Syrian rebels to "keep pressure on" the Damascus regime. The DOD had been training a force of Kurds and a few Arabs to repel the IS advance. Now Kurds and Arabs were fighting each other: *Tribune Newspapers*, 3/28/16.

2016 – Since late May, by the estimate of the Syrian Observatory of Human Rights, over 100 civilians in the Manbij area had been killed by US and/or French air strikes: *Times*, 7/22/16; *Saudi Arabia News Agency*.

2016 – The US signed with Jordan a three-year agreement for an annual payment to Jordan of one billion dollars: *Times*, 6/7/16.

US-Egypt – In 1993, President Mubarak let the CIA base its Middle East operations in Cairo.

2001 – The outbreak of Intifadah II sparked pro-Palestinian demonstrations in Egypt.

2003 – The US invasions of Afghanistan and Iraq exacerbated the Egyptian public's resentment of US policy in the Middle East.

2003 – Mubarak's regime condemned activist Sa'd al Din Ibrahim to seven years in jail for monitoring Egyptian elections. The US and the EU espoused his cause, but it took three years of pressure on Mubarak to effect Sa'd al Din's release: *Times*, 7/18/03.

2011 – Egyptian demonstrations led to the removal of Mubarak from office: Lister. The US had long supported him: *MEP*, Fall 2015, Zuhur/Tadros. Obama hated to lose a ruler who got along with Israel, but he had felt compelled on humanitarian grounds to warn Egypt that if Mubarak did not step down, the annual subsidy was not guaranteed.

2012-13 – During the administration of Egypt's elected President Muhammad Mursi, the US was open to dealing with it, and relatively cool to the Sisi administration that replaced it.

2014 – 'Abd al Fattah Sisi was even more autocratic than Mubarak. Nevertheless, the US allotted Egypt half a billion dollars: *Times*, 7/17/14. It could have been a reward to Egypt for its crackdown on Hamas.

2014 – After Sisi's cabal crushed the Brotherhood in Egypt, Obama suspended payment of part of Egypt's Camp David aid. Later on, as an incentive for Egypt to join the anti-IS "coalition", Obama restored the aid: *Times*, 10/8/14.

2015 – In surrender to the policy long favored by the US, reliance on Middle East autocrats, the World Economic Forum, meeting at Davos, gave Sisi a warm welcome. It may have been a reaction to the emergence of the IS: *FT*, 1/24/16.

2015 – Obama lifted the freeze on sales of F-16's, Harpoon missiles, and Abrams tanks to Egypt. The US-Egypt strategic dialog had been resumed: *Times*, 4/1/15; *FT*, 5/11/15.

2016 – The US General Accounting Office reported that Egypt was using US military aid funds to finance violations of human rights by Egyptian security forces: *Times*, 5/19/16.

2016 – Since June 2015, Egypt had received 25 billion dollars from Saudi Arabia, but its relations with the US had become stressed by the removal of Mursi, and by human rights abuses under Sisi: 8/3/16.

2016 – The US had stopped Damascus's air strikes against the Kurds, but was blocked from action against Damascus's attacks on rebels in east Aleppo because the Russians got there first: *Times*, 8/24/16.

US-Iran – In 1953, the US colluded with Britain in the ouster of Iran's elected Prime Minister, Mohammed Mossadeq, who had challenged British skimming from the proceeds of the Anglo-Iranian Oil Company.

1979 – The anti-Americanism of Khomeini's revolutionary regime was ascribed largely to the Western conspiracy of 1953 against Mossadeq.

1980-8 – The US intervened as necessary in the Iraq-Iran War to prevent an Iranian victory.

1996 – The Iran-Libya Sanctions Act (ILSA) authorized the US executive branch to impose trade sanctions on third-country firms that were heavily invested in Iran or Libya.

2001 – In May, the US vetoed "terrorist" Iran's membership in the World Trade Organization: *BBC*, 5/9/01.

2001 – US Government broadcasts were urging Iranians to change their form of governance: *FA*, January 2003.

2014 – By bombing IS emplacements around Amarliyyah (south of Kirkuk), while Iran-backed militias operated on the ground, the US acted in de facto alliance with its nominal enemy, Iran: *Times*, 9/1/14.

2015 – In the siege of Tikrit, the Iraqi forces had maintained communication between the Americans and the Iranians. Washington was trying to play down the reality of US-Iranian coordination: *Times*, 4/4/15.

2015 – Obama wanted to open Iran to the outside world – a development that Iranian hardliners would regard as a threat to the identity of the regime: *The Week*, 12/11/15.

2016 – The US lifted sanctions on Iran earlier than planned, to boost Rouhani in the Parliamentary elections: *FT*, 1/21/16.

2016 – Two joint Israeli-American cyber-attacks, by the viruses/worms Stuxnet and Flame, on Iran's uranium enrichment complex at Natanz had destroyed 1000 centrifuges and delayed the program one year: *Times*, 1/20/16, 2/17/16.

2016 – A US effort to cooperate with Iran against the IS had been obstructed by an Iranian effort to open a land route to Syria through Iraq's Anbar Province. The US and Iran were at swords' points over suits by Americans seeking compensation for losses caused by Iranian military action. The US Supreme Court had validated the suits. Iran sought redress from the International Court of Justice (ICJ): *Times*, 4/26/16.

US-Iraq (Baghdad Regime) – In 1991, US forces headed a multiple coalition in the brutal expulsion of Iraqi occupation forces from Kuwait. Washington followed up the aerial devastation of Iraq's infrastructure with twelve years of vindictive policing of a draconian set of trade sanctions on Iran.

2003 – The invasion and occupation of Iraq was the centerpiece of America's post-9/11 convulsion, although Iraq had no responsibility for 9/11. On the deck of the carrier Abraham Lincoln in the Pacific, Bush 43 landed on deck in a flight suit, and emerged from a Navy plane (flown by a Navy pilot?) to deliver his "Mission Accomplished" speech, in which he announced his intention to bring democracy to Iraq: *NYTBR*, 7/3/16, Review of *Bush* by Jean Edward Smith.

2003 – The American occupiers failed to guard Saddam's arms and ammo dumps, allowing resistance forces to help themselves: Anderson.

2004 – Shiite leader Muqtada Sadr launched his *Jaysh al Mahdi* (Army of the Mahdi) in a guerrilla campaign against the occupying forces.

2004 – A civilian contract employee for the US occupation forces in Iraq for three months resorted to subjecting Iraqi prisoners to "enhanced interrogation", as by keeping them nude in a cold cell: *NYR*, 3/20/16.

2008 – During the US occupation of Iraq, up to one million Christians fled the country: *NYTM*, 7/26/15.

2011 – On 12/15/11, US forces completed their withdrawal from Iraq. Obama had been prepared to leave a few thousand troops in Iraq after the withdrawal date if the Iraqi Parliament guaranteed their legal immunity. No such guarantee was offered: *FA*, November/December, 2014. Many sources were blaming the debacle of the Bush 43 administration's actions in Iraq for the emergence of Zarqawi's Islamic State in Iraq.

2014 – Obama had authorized the stationing of 3000 US soldiers to train Iraqi troops: *Times*, 12/4/14.

2015 – On 3/2/15, Iraq launched an operation to retake Tikrit. The US, doubting Iraq's readiness, regretting Iraq's failure to appease its Sunnis, and irritated by Iraq's reliance on Iran, provided no air support for the Tikrit operation. Washington had reports of entry of Iranian ground troops into Iraq. Qassem Suleimani, Commander of the Quds Force in the Islamic Revolutionary Guard, seemed to be an active participant in Iraq's military operations: *Times*, 3/2/15; *FT*, 3/3/15.

2015 – In Iraq, the US had found circumstances unfavorable for repetition of the pragmatic strategy practiced during the occupation of 2003-11 – buying off Sunni tribesmen. Maliki had let most of the "salaries" lapse, and Sunni-Shia relations were much worse. The recent experience with Baghdad's overbearing Shiites had been alarming: *FT*, 3/28/15, Erika Salomon; *Times*, 6/4/15.

2015 – Ignoring US advice, Iraqi Prime Minister 'Abadi ordered his Shiite militias to recapture Ramadi: *Times*, 5/20/15.

2015 – Obama didn't know, or wouldn't reveal, US objectives in Iraq. After admitting "We don't yet have a complete strategy" for military training of Iraqis, he was sending only 450 more trainers, who would be kept out of combat. US Apache helicopters would not be deployed in support of Iraqi ground operations. For Obama, the greatest evil for the US in Iraq would be another US invasion. For many tribal leaders in Sunni-populated 'Anbar Province, the greatest evil would be a Shiite invasion: *Raleigh News and Observer*, 6/13/15, Eugene Robinson.

2015 – The US was pressing the Baghdad government to bring more Sunnis into its security forces, while the US was also sharing a base in 'Anbar Province with Iranian units: *Times*, 9/14/15.

2016 – In Iraq, Fallujah was under siege by Shiite militants, and civilians were starving. Flight from the city was blocked by its IS occupiers. Elsewhere in 'Anbar Province, Shia militias backed by Iran were abducting and killing Sunni Iraqis: *Times*, 4/26/16, Tim Arango.

2016 – Having ordered the withdrawal of US troops from Iraq in 2011, Obama began to send troops back when IS forces took Mawsil. US troops in Iraq now totaled 4647: *Times*, 7/12/16.

2016 – Much of the heavy fighting for Fallujah was being done by Iraqi counter-terrorism troops trained by US servicemen: *Times*, 8/1/16.

US-Israel/Palestinians – On 9/11/22, a joint resolution of Congress echoed the Balfour letter in favoring a Jewish homeland in Palestine: Neff.

Two prominent Americans, Supreme Court Justice Louis Brandeis and Rabbi Stephen S. Wise, urged President Wilson to endorse Zionism. Wilson did so in his September 1928 letter of holiday greetings to the American Jewish community.

1942 – On 8/22/42, Abba Hillel Silver convened at the Hotel Biltmore in New York an extraordinary Zionist convention that was attended by the two greatest Zionists of the time – Chaim Weizmann (then head of the World Zionist Organization, later first president of Israel: *EB*, 12:565) and David Ben-Gurion (head of the Jewish Agency, the de facto Jewish government in Palestine). The "Biltmore

Declaration" called for the founding of a Jewish commonwealth in Palestine. The exhilarated delegates gave Silver a standing ovation, broke into *Hatikvah*, the Zionist anthem, and endorsed the Declaration 480 to 4: Neff. Silver went on to energize the powerful Zionist lobby, then dubbed AZEC, later AIPAC (The American Israel Public Affairs Committee).

1945 – On 3/16/45, President Roosevelt authorized Rabbi Wise to issue a public statement that FDR continued to support the establishment of a Jewish state. Neff.

1947 – The US State Department, Defense Department, and CIA prophetically warned that creation of Israel would be a dangerous source of future trouble: Neff.

1947-61 – The US embargoed the sale of arms to Israel and the Arabs from 11/14/47.

1947 – Four days before 11/29/47, when the UNGA was scheduled to vote on the recommendation of a UN special committee for partition of Palestine between an Arab and a Jewish state, Truman unleashed US embassies in a worldwide drive to build a majority for partition – over last-ditch opposition from the Department of State. Many countries succumbed to the pressure. Washington then exploited its postwar preeminence and the inexperience of the neophyte UN General Assembly to push through it UNGA Resolution 181, which called for a partition of Palestine in terms that favored Zionism. The resolution provided a legal basis for the arbitrary imposition of a Jewish state in an Arab country surrounded by other Arab countries. The result was a perpetual conflict between two alien communities for one 10,000-square-mile block of land. In the absence of any hint of compromise between the parties, this geopolitical deadlock has obstructed the conventional processes by which regions usually terminate a vacuum of power.

1948 – Israeli resolve and military superiority defeated Arab fecklessness in Israel's War of Liberation.

1956 – Dwight Eisenhower, seemingly the only President so far to be unbiased on the Arab-Israeli issue, quashed the 1956 invasion of Egypt. On 2/20/57, he took a political position available only to a

President who had just led the Allied forces in World War II and was immune to political attack from any quarter, even the Israeli lobby. He went on television to explain why he would require Israel to withdraw the forces that had occupied Gaza and Sinai during the Suez War. He reportedly informed Ben-Gurion privately that he would impose sanctions on Israel, and might cut off private American donations to Israel if it did not withdraw from Sinai. With great reluctance, Israel withdrew its troops from Sinai, and subsequently from Gaza.

1960 – Washington leaked evidence that Israel had begun a nuclear project. Ben-Gurion stated that any Israeli action in that field was for peaceful purposes.

1961-3 – The Kennedy administration tasked the State Department's Office of Near Eastern Affairs with writing the rationale for excluding Jordan from the American embargo on the provision of arms to Israel or its Arab adversaries. The assignment went to this writer. The only ostensible beneficiary would be Jordan. However, the obvious plan was to exploit the modest favor to Jordan as justification for a balancing favor to Israel, which needed newer weapons in the interest of hanging on to its territorial conquests in the Six-Day War. The writer made a pro forma effort to tell city hall why that ploy would be a mistake – and then found cover in a convenient reassignment to Aden.

1962 – Kennedy demanded access of American inspectors to view a site of major construction in Israel's Negev Desert. The inspectors were allowed in, but they were shown the mockup control room of a "manganese plant". The real controls were underground.

1967 – Lyndon Johnson, the most pro-Zionist President on record (Donald Neff), welcomed Israel's overwhelming victory in the June war, covered up the attempt by Israeli naval units to sink the USS Liberty, and supported UNSC Resolution 242 that exempted Israel from any requirement that Israel withdraw its troops from Palestinian territory occupied in the war.

1968 – In November, Johnson authorized the provision of Phantom jet fighters to Israel.

1969 – In September, Nixon and Meir agreed that Israel would not test a nuclear weapon, and that the US would abandon Dimona

500

inspections and stop pushing Israel to sign the NPT. Israel's public position: It would not be the first nation to introduce nuclear weapons into the Middle East.

1971 – After interviewing a number of Foreign Service Arabists (alumni of a course in spoken Arabic at the State Department's Foreign Service Institute), including this writer, columnist Joseph Kraft told readers of *The New York Times Magazine* of 11/7/71 that many of them were not just pro-Arabic, they were pro-Arab, but the electorate needn't worry, since the Department no longer assigned Arabists to policy-making positions.

1973 – On 10/6/73, Egypt and Syria launched surprise attacks on Israel – the start of the pivotal Yom Kippur War. Richard Nixon ordered an emergency airlift to Israel of state-of-the-art weapons, which began arriving on 10/14/73. According to Stephen Green, the JCS on its own initiative rushed informal arms shipments from US stocks in Germany. Israel may have received them by 10/6-7/73. On 10/9/73, under immense pressure on both fronts, Israel reportedly rolled out a nuclear weapon.

1973 – By 10/10/73, Israel had established complete control of the air, and was driving Egyptian and Syrian forces back.

1973 – The Symington and Glenn Amendments prohibited US aid to countries trafficking in nuclear weapons technology outside the provisions of the Nuclear Nonproliferation Treaty. Nixon adopted a policy of "strategic ambiguity" to avoid international accusations of Israeli violation of that treaty, and/or Zionist accusations of US disloyalty to Israel. Nixon and Meir agreed that their two countries would not admit that Israel had had a nuclear capability since 1968: Paul Pillar, 4/10/15.

1978 – At Camp David, Carter devised an agreement, signed by President Sadat of Egypt and Prime Minister Begin of Israel, that papered over the insoluble Palestinian issue.

1985 – On 10/8/85, in retaliation for PLO assassination of two Israeli intelligence agents on Cyprus, Israel staged a surprise raid against the PLO compound in Tunisia, killing 60 Palestinians and 12 Tunisians. The UNSC condemned the raid; the US abstained. Reportedly the US did not use its veto power for fear of Libyan intrigue against the Tunisian regime, or Libya's possibly breaking relations with the US. American failure to condemn the raid raised speculation about US complicity. Lingering Tunisian resentment of the raid was considered to be one motivation for Tunisian support for the Iraqi occupation of Kuwait in 1990. Columnist Joseph Harsch approved Reagan's position that the Israeli raid was a legitimate response to a terrorist attack. Reagan later said the raid could not be condoned: *The Iron Wall*, Shlaim.

2005 – Bush 43 denied Israel's request for assistance in development of a peaceful nuclear industry.

2006 – An article in the *London Review of Books* by Professors John Mearsheimer and Stephen Walt expressed the opinion that Washington had had occasion to subordinate the interests of the US to those of Israel, and that AIPAC (The American Israel Public Affairs Committee) was manipulating American media and academia: *Independent Global News: LRB*, 5/24/06.

2006 – A draft UNSC resolution charging Israel with disproportionate use of force in Gaza, in its reaction to the abduction of an Israeli soldier, failed 10-1 (US veto) - 4: *Times*, 7/14/06.

2006 – The Israeli strategy of closing the border crossings to Gaza from Israel and Egypt was meant to starve the Islamists out of office. Washington and its European allies went along. By mid-2006, Israel had cut off financial aid and public and private loans to the Palestinian Authority, while Israel was blocking Gazan exports and had suspended transfer of the Gazan tax and customs receipts Israel had been importunately collecting on behalf of the PA. The suspension prevented the PA from meeting the payrolls of its 138,000 employees. UN Human Rights investigator Richard Falk was barred from entry to the territory.

2007 – A new daily newspaper, *Israel Hayom* (Israel Today), appeared in Israel. It was financed by Sheldon Adelson, an American supporter of Netanyahu: *FA*, July 2016, Aluf Benn.

2009 – The dispute between Prime Minister Netanyahu and Obama over US efforts to steer Iran away from nuclear weapons had escalated into an Israeli-US power struggle, to be decided by the American electorate: *The Link*, April 2016. Obama reaffirmed Washington's denial of peaceful nuclear assistance to Israel.

2011 – Assistant Secretary of State for Political-Military Affairs Andrew Shapiro stated that America's alliances in the Middle East were critical to the maintenance of regional stability and the security of Israel: *Times*, 4/19/15.

2012 – The US and Israel were among the nine countries voting against the UNGA resolution that accepted Palestine as a non-member observer state.

2014 – A poll published in December 2014 found that 50 percent of Republicans wanted the US to lean toward Israel, as against 17 percent of Democrats: *Times*, 2/28/15, Nicholas Kristoff. In March 2015, Netanyahu spoke to Congress and brazenly tried to exploit America's partisan deadlock by attacking Obama's policy on Iran's nuclear planning.

2015 – On 4/10/15, at a full-bore conference in Washington on the Israeli lobby, former Republican Representative Paul Findlay said that the GOP had colluded in Netanyahu's recent disrespect to the Presidency, and that Obama should have blocked Netanyahu's entry to the US long enough to prevent his condemning US foreign policy before a fawning Congress.

2015 – Now that Israel and the Arab monarchies were de facto allies against the IS, the US did not have to be so rigorous in maintaining a qualitative advantage for Israel over the Arab states in arms sales. Also, the flow of Russian arms to Iran invited more extensive sales to the Arabs: *Times*, 4/19/15.

2015 – The F-35 Lockheed Stealth aircraft was the jet fighter of the future – for sale to Israel, not to the Arab states: *Times*, 5/11/15.

2015 – A US-Israel memorandum of understanding, signed in 2009, due to expire in 2018, was being renegotiated. It would award Israel three billion dollars a year, most of it to buy arms from the US: *Times*, 7/16/15.

2015 – In the US, religious convictions were locking the Christian right into support of Israel: *NYTM*, 7/26/15.

2015 – Obama denounced the lobbyists who were spending millions on false advertising that advocated the same hawkish alarmism that had trapped the US in Iraq. He made no mention of AIPAC – the clear target of his criticism. US-Israeli relations had fallen to a new low: *Times*, 8/8/15.

2015 – The Israeli lobby had made a monumental gamble against Obama's nuclear treaty with Iran, and lost. A Senate vote of 9/10/15 blocked a GOP bid to reject the treaty. The "stinging defeat" exposed the declining influence of the Israeli lobby: *Times*, 9/10/15.

2015 – Many Israeli Arabs despised the Palestinian (National) Authority (PA) for its Quisling links with the Israeli and American governments.

2015 – In a letter to the *Times*, a retired US intelligence officer wrote that Israel had traded data stolen by Jonathan Pollard to Russia for relaxation of its restriction on emigration of Jews to Israel: *Times*, August 2015.

2015 – On 9/10/15, the UNGA voted 119-8 (US, Israel, Canada, Australia) to allow the Palestinian flag to fly over UN Headquarters: *Times*, 9/10/15.

2015 – Israel denied a US request to freeze construction in new settlements: *FA*, November 2015, Natan Sachs.

2015 – *The Washington Report on Middle East Affairs* published a tabulation of estimated aid to Israel for the years 1949 through 2015. The total of grants and loans over 67 years was 137 billion dollars: *WRMEA*, October 2015, Shirl McArthur.

2015 – The collapse of Secretary Kerry's Israeli-Palestinian peace initiative had rendered Washington more sensitive to Israel's security concerns – leading to greater estrangement between the US and the Arab states: *MEP*, Fall 2015, Waleed Hazbun.

2016 – The IDF had admitted collaboration with the US in the development of two cyber-viruses, Stuxnet in 2009-10 and Flame in 2012. Both damaged the Iranian nuclear program. The IDF did not admit any involvement in these two cyber-attacks: *FT*, 1/20/16.

2016 – The US had denied an Israeli request for bunker-buster armament: *Times*, 1/20/16.

2016 – Hillary Clinton had pledged to fight the anti-Israel Boycott, Divestment, and Sanctions Program (BDS), an international movement to penalize Israel until it abides by international conventions: Alternet Organization, 2/22/16.

2016 – The ten-year US-Israeli agreement on military aid would expire in 2018. The agreement permits Israel to spend one-fourth of the proceeds outside the US: *Times*, 7/2/16.

US-Kurds – Up to early 1975, with arms from the US and training from Iran, the Iraqi Kurds' Peshmerga had fought the larger Iraqi Army to a standstill. In March, Iraq and Iran achieved détente. Kissinger cut off US aid to the Iraqi Kurds. Baghdad was free to exploit its gas reserves and its military superiority in its effort to subdue Kurdish dissension.

1979 – After Khomeini came to power in Iran, he enraged Washington by ousting the Shah, detaining the staff of the US Embassy, and taking a position of radical support for the Palestinian cause. Washington retaliated by switching its support from Iran to Iraq, even trying to place on Iran the blame for the Iraqi gassing of the village of Halabjah: *NYTM*, Anderson.

1991 – After the second Kuwait War, as the US forces were withdrawing from Iraq, Bush 41 called on the Iraqi people to rise against Saddam. Apparently neither Bush nor his advisers realized that the majority of the Iraqi people were Shiites. With unwarranted confidence in Washington, the Shiites and Kurds complied with Bush's suggestion, and ran head-on into Saddam's best troops, whom he had not risked in Kuwait. Their punishment of the insurgents was brutal. In remorse, Bush set up two No-Fly Zones in Iraq to protect the Shiites and the Kurds, respectively, from Saddam's helicopters. Ultimately, Saddam was hanged, Iraqi Kurdistan set up an autonomous regime, and the rest of Iraq, after 500 years of Sunni rule, became a Shiite state. None of these events had been contemplated by US policy-makers. US policy was and is supportive of a united Iraq: *MEP*, Spring 2015, Le Billon.

2003 – The US invaded Iraq on the false premise that Saddam was developing nuclear weaponry.

2006 – The American University of Iraq was founded in Sulaymaniyyah, Kurdistan. Kurds and Americans sat on the board. The language of instruction was English.

2000's – The UN Charter denies UN membership to stateless peoples. The Kurds were not even accorded the observer status held by the Palestine Liberation Organization. Nevertheless, under American protection they had made impressive strides toward the acquisition of all the tangible institutions of a sovereign state. As for recognition, America, the adjoining states, and the UN were committed to the preservation of a sovereign Iraq within its present borders.

2007 – The KRG was hostile to the PKK rebels in Turkey, but the Peshmerga was not strong enough to keep PKK militants out of the KAR. Both the PKK and the PEJAK in Iran paid allegiance to Abdullah Ocalan. The US considered the PKK a terrorist organization, but received PEJAK leader Rahman Hajj Ahmadi in Washington: *Times*, 10/23/07.

2014 – The CIA was supplying arms to the Peshmerga: *NY*, 8/25/14, George Packer.

2014 – The US was providing air support to the KRG's Peshmerga operations against the IS, although the US opposed Kurdish statehood: *NY*, 9/29/14, Dexter Filkins.

2014-15 – Since the occupation of Mawsil in 2014 by the IS, the Peshmerga had consolidated KRG control of the territory (Iraqi) between Mawsil and the KAR. The US had been the enabler, by providing the Kurdish forces with training, intelligence, arms, and air support: *Times*, 6/3/15.

2015 – In March, the US began attacking IS targets by piloted and drone aircraft: *Times*, 10/28/15.

2015 – In the Arab view, the only militias trusted by Washington were Kurdish (which were allies of Israel and the most effective enemies of the IS): *Times*, 10/10/15.

2015 – The American alliance with the Kurds was undermining the US effort to mobilize "moderate Arabs" against the IS: *FT*, 11/4/15.

2015 – In 1991, the US established a No-Fly Zone in northern Iraq to protect the Kurds. In 1992, the US proclaimed a second No-Fly Zone in southern Iraq to protect the Shiites. There was no such amenity to protect the Syrian Kurds from Asad's forces: *MER*, Winter 2015.

2016 – Russia tacitly backed the Syrian Kurds: *FT*, 2/18/16, 2/19/16.

2016 – In late July, the Syrian border town of Manbij was under siege by the Syrian Democratic Forces (SDF), which were 20 percent Arab, 80 percent Kurdish. Seventy-five civilians in the area of Manbij had been killed by air strikes, reportedly American: *Times*, 7/30/16.

US-Turkey – Syrian troops withdrew from Raqqah in the spring of 2013. The IS expelled Nusrah from Raqqah in January 2014.Turkey was providing arms and funds to Nusrah: *LRB*, 1/7/16, Seymour Hersh.

2014 – Conflict between the IS (secretly favored by Turkey) and the PKK (accused by Turkey of killing Turkish security personnel) had stalled Turkey-PKK peace talks: *FT*, 11/13/14.

2015 – The US and Turkey agreed on joint operations against the IS, but not against the PKK: *FT*, 7/27/15.

2015 – In an effort to reinstate himself as the unchallenged leader of Turkey, Erdogan had resumed attacks on PKK forces, in the hope that renewed hostility between Turkey and the Kurds would weaken the HDP of Selahattin Demirtas in the election which Erdogan intended to call. To placate Washington, he had given the USAF permission to bomb the IS from Incirlik Air Base, while Turkish forces concentrated their efforts against the Kurdish militias, forcing them to let up on their campaign against the IS. Survival of the IS would promote Erdogan's interest in the establishment in Damascus of a Sunni regime of the MB stripe. According to DOD Under Secretary of Defense Eric Edelman, Turkish policy had not helped matters: *Times*, 8/27/15.

2015 – The US was annoying Turkey by supporting the Kurdish PYD against the IS. Turkey was treating the PYD's wounded in Turkish hospitals, but it resented Kurdish encroachment into a strip of Syrian territory adjoining the Turkish border. Turkey did not share US determination to destroy the IS. Turkey's foreign enemy number one was the Asad regime in Damascus: *MEP*, Winter 2015.

2016 – The Turkish press, which is susceptible to government guidance, was characterizing the US as Turkey's primary enemy: *Times*, 2/3/16.

2016 – The US was disturbed by Turkey's claim that the YPG was linked with the PKK, and by Turkey's bombing and shelling of YPG targets: *Times*, 3/15/16.

2016 – On a conciliatory visit to Turkey, Vice President Biden stated that Kurdish forces would have to pull back east of the Euphrates in order to continue to receive US support. The US was supplying Turkey with intelligence obtained from drone flights: *FT*, 8/25/16.

2016 – Arab-Turkish militiamen, trained in Turkey, had done poorly against IS and Kurdish opponents: *FT*, 8/25/16.

2016 – FSA militiamen were part of a surprise foray by Turkish troops and tanks, supported by Turkish air cover, into northern Syria. They quickly took a key border city, Jarabulus, from its Kurdish occupiers: *FT*, 8/29/16. They had US support.

2016 – The US had provided arms to moderate rebel organizations in Syria, but not to hardliners, and not to the Kurds: *Times*, 9/22/16.

2016 – Obama would like to increase pressure on the IS by supplying the YPG with heavy weapons, but Turkey was so exercised by US support for the Kurds that it was delaying clearances for US air strikes from Incirlik: *Times*, 1/18/17.

Post-procedural supplement to page 304

2015 – On June 23, Abu Muhammad al 'Adnani aired a call to IS militants to attack enemies during Ramadan. On June 26, there were suicide bombings in France, Somalia, Tunisia, and Kuwait. In Kuwait City, a bombing killed 27 and wounded 227; 15 suspects were convicted: *Guardian*, 6/26/15; *MEP*, Summer 2018, Cinzia Bianco.

Section III: Chain of Causation

The Cascade Effect of Eighteen Wars

———

Each of the eighteen wars under review here had its own rationale and its own local impact, but each one generated changes that ricocheted against the causes and consequences of wars that followed. Taken together, all these wars determined the regional trend – ultimately toward a new hegemony.

The British Subjugation of Iraq – British imperialism in the Middle East evolved in two phases. Phase one began in 1615, when the British Navy took Bombay (later Mumbai) from the Portuguese. From 1615 on, British maritime preeminence over the Mediterranean, the Red Sea, the Persian Gulf, and the Arabian Sea enabled Britain to parlay the East India Company (chartered by Queen Elizabeth I in 1600) into an economic empire that controlled the trade in Asia's three major export commodities – sugar, tobacco, and tea. The Middle East challenge mounted by Napoleon was crushed in 1798 by Admiral Horatio Nelson's victory over the French fleet at Abu Qir, off the coast of Egypt. By the end of World War I, naval and economic power had made Britain protector of the five Arab shaykhdoms along the western shore of the Persian Gulf, preeminent in India, steward of the Suez Canal, and the de facto ruler of Egypt. As the heirs of the Ottoman Empire, Britain and France went on to dictate the postwar trajectories of Iraq, Syria, and Palestine.

The second phase began with London's decision to consolidate its postwar holdings by supplementing its naval operations with the

510

deployment of ground and air forces. Britain had already made an adventitious start by establishing a military base at Isma'iliyyah in the Suez Canal Zone.

After an initial defeat by the Ottomans, the British had taken Baghdad in 1917. After the war, they decided to stay. In 1920, the Iraqi uprising led to Britain's first serious collision with Arab ground forces. The British deployment was not large, but the rebels had no army, while Britain's primitive fleet of two-wing bombers gave it the same immunity from retaliation that drones were to give the Americans eighty years later. By 1922, the rebellion had been largely suppressed. However, by 1958 the Iraqis did have an army. A Baathist coup d'état wiped out the puppet leadership in Baghdad and sent the British home. The Iraqi resistance had heralded the rise of Arab Nationalism – as exemplified by the Nasirist coup in Egypt in 1952, and the Baathist takeover in Syria in 1958.

The British Subjugation of Palestine – As a mandatory power, Britain was charged with the reconciliation of Arabs and Jews, and guiding all Palestine toward independence. Imperialism was not cut out for so benevolent an assignment. Instead, it allowed politics back home to undermine its objectivity. By 1947, the mandatory authorities had lost control, the Palestinians had lost the initiative, and the Jewish community was on the road to statehood.

In the empire's happier days, London had envisioned a Jewish state in Palestine as a bastion in the defense of the Suez Canal. Since the creation of Israel in 1948, the Canal has been closed three times – during the Suez War, the Six-Day War, and the Yom Kippur War.

The War for Israeli Independence – The Jews had every military advantage over the Palestinians and their allies – more troops, better training, better organization, and superior morale. They fought by Ben-Gurion's rules: Build maximum military power, and use it. Many Jews were inspired by belief in the sanctity of their mission.

The Arabs had to control their own disunity, and then cope with crushing defeat at the hands of alien interlopers.

The war established Israel as a new member of the Middle Eastern community. Israel was heartened by the suspension of fedayeen

511

(*fida'iyyin*) raids from Gaza. The 1948 war was not conclusive. The Israelis still had to disabuse the Arabs of their conviction that Israel was a temporary phenomenon. Egypt, its most formidable adversary, was reinforced in that conviction in 1952, when Nasir's coup d'état put an end to British rule.

The Suez War – For the Middle East, 1956 was a momentous year. The Suez War was a turning point from European to American domination: Donald Neff. Britain and France had misread the new strategic situation in the region, and sent "invasion forces" into a trap from which there was no escape except humiliating withdrawal.

Credit for the conversion from military defeat to political victory projected Nasir to the zenith of his prestige in the Arab World. His version of Arab Nationalism (Arab unity) gained millions of adherents. Syria threw itself into union with Egypt. These political gains screened out the reality that no Arab state came to the assistance of Egypt.

Israel's impressive military action in Sinai was drowned out in the consternation at the showdown between the US and the Franco-British conspirators, but the war favored Israel with helpful changes: the armistice lines were "dead": Ben-Gurion. The Strait of Tiran was opened to Israeli ships: Neff. The fedayeen attacks ended. As a reward for Israeli participation in the enterprise, France built a secret plutonium production reactor at Dimona in the Negev Desert: *WRMEA*, May 2016, Dr. Roger Mattson.

On the central issue of Israeli-Arab confrontation, the Suez War was inconclusive. The great-power confrontation took the limelight. The Arab-Israeli conflict ground on.

The Six-Day War – Israel's summary disposal of three Arab air forces crowned it as the ruler of Arab-Israeli skies. After an air war, wrapped up with lightning speed, Israel had needed no rescue from Washington. Under Lyndon Johnson, Washington would have complied. Johnson went so far as to try to hush up Israel's apparent order to its armed forces to sink the US ship USS Liberty with all hands on board: *Assault on the Liberty*, James M. Ennes, Jr. Johnson reportedly cited his determination to spare Israel from embarrassment as the reason for his recall of a flight sent by the Sixth Fleet to rescue the Liberty. No

President has ventured to establish an investigation, along the lines of the 9/11 Commission, to throw light on the mystery. Under Johnson's aegis, Israel was allowed to keep the territories it occupied in 1967 – the Palestinian West Bank from Jordan, the strategic Golan Heights from Syria, Sinai from Egypt, and Gaza.

The War of Attrition – After the Six-Day War, Soviet resupply of weapons, plus political pressure on the Arab governments to redress losses in the conflict, moved Nasir to resume attacks on Israeli defenses on the east bank of the Canal. Israel instituted a campaign to subdue Arab furor. The campaign began with attacks against Egyptian positions on the west side of the Canal, went on to air attacks and commando raids against targets west of the Canal Zone, and ended in 1970 with air strikes against the Egyptian heartland – the Nile Valley.

In January 1970, Nasir made a secret visit to Moscow to appeal for direct support. In return for permission to build an air base near Alexandria, the USSR assumed direct responsibility for the defense of Egypt. By May, Soviet pilots were challenging Israel's domination of the skies over the Canal Zone. Soviet pilots in MiG's were no match for Israeli pilots in Phantoms, but Soviet SAM's along the west side of the Canal shot down enough Israeli planes to balance the two opposing forces – and also to alert Washington and Moscow to the apocalyptic threat of a Soviet-American confrontation. The great powers imposed a ceasefire on Egypt and Israel. The War of Attrition ended, but the SAM's along the west side of the Canal remained as an omen that the war to resolve the Israeli-Egyptian conflict was yet to be fought.

Jordan-PLO War – In principle, the PLO was created to fight Israel. In practice, it has fought many of its battles against other Arabs. The largest Palestinian community is in Greater Israel. The second largest is in Jordan. In 1970, Jordan was the main base of the PLO.

In February, King Husayn issued an edict that restricted the PLO's activities. By September, the PLO set up a government-in-exile in Irbid. 1970 was the year when Husayn escaped from several assassination attempts.

On 9/7/70, the PFLP – a rival of the PLO – hijacked Swissair and TWA airliners, landed them in Jordan, released the passengers, and blew them up. The objective was precipitation of a showdown between the Palestinians and King Husayn. The King declared martial law and sent troops to subdue the refugee camps and restore order.

On 9/18/70, the Baathist regime in Syria sent troops into Jordan to support the Palestinians. Husayn made a secret plea to the US, the UK, and Israel to help. When Israel put its air force on alert, the new dictator of Syria, Hafiz al Asad, withdrew his troops from Jordan. By 1971, Jordan's Arab Legion had routed the Palestinian forces and forced them to leave the country. The weak government in Beirut was unable to keep the Palestinians out of Lebanon, their last possible refuge in the Middle East.

On 11/28/71, Black September, a clandestine section of the PLO, killed Jordanian Prime Minister Wasfi Tall while he was on a visit to Cairo.

The Jordan-PLO scenario had thrown considerable illumination on Middle Eastern reality: 1) The PFLP hijackings, by forcing the PLO into an untimely showdown, had revealed the huge handicap inflicted on the Arabs by their strategic disunity; 2) Husayn had been pressed so hard that he had to expose the embarrassing fact that Jordan is a de facto protectorate of Israel; 3) Until the Middle East power struggle is resolved, it will contribute greatly to the security of Israel; 4) Israel had been supplied with a barely plausible case for its fallacious claim that it is a big help in America's (failing) effort to keep the peace in the Middle East; 5) If the Middle Eastern power struggle should be won by jihadists, the security of Israel would be thrown into great jeopardy; as long as Washington is sworn to protect Israel, the Islamic State – or its successor – will be America's main enemy in the Middle East.

The Yom Kippur War – The fifth and last Israeli victory over Egypt was decisive. Anwar Sadat had fooled the experts and the Israelis by super-secret marshalling of his armed forces, by super-secret recruitment of Syria, and by kickoff on 10/6/73 of joint surprise attacks. Egypt troops crossed the Canal, overran the supposedly impregnable Bar Lev Line, and alarmed Israel into wheeling out eight Phantoms carrying nuclear weapons.

514

After three days, the Syrian attack was halted. One day later, the IDF turned the tide in Egypt. On 10/18/73, Israeli forces crossed the Canal and began the dismantling of the Egyptian forces. They could have gone on to Cairo, except that Washington sensibly blew the whistle. Israel resisted a ceasefire in order to pursue the elimination of Egyptian positions west of the Canal, and the surrender of the Egyptian Third Army, marooned east of the Canal.

On 10/25/73, the UNSC demanded an immediate ceasefire. At long last, Israel complied – but only after that rarest of political phenomena, an ultimatum to Israel from Washington. The Yom Kippur War ended 10/28/73.

After the war, Secretary of State Kissinger negotiated the withdrawal of Israeli forces from the eastern fringe of Golan, and from Sinai and Gaza. Washington made a contribution to a peaceful solution of the Arab-Israel conflict when it restored all the territories Egypt had lost in the war. Sadat, ever the pragmatist, faced up to the reality of Israel-American supremacy in the Middle East by switching from the Soviet camp to the American, and setting the scene for the signature of an Israeli-Egyptian peace treaty in 1979.

On 6/5/75, the Suez Canal was reopened, eight years after the Six-Day War had shut it down.

The end of the Yom Kippur War marked the suspension of the Egyptian-Israeli conflict – but the issues that divide them show no evidence of abatement.

Israel-Lebanon War – The Palestinian exploitation of Lebanon for attacks on Israel was the proximate cause of the Israel-Lebanon War. From its new base in south Lebanon, the PLO resumed its forays into Israel. Thirty-eight Israelis died in a PLO incursion by sea into the Tel Aviv area. In 1978, Prime Minister Begin sent in a small occupying force that put a stop to the raids, until the UN posted in the area a peacekeeping force that required the Israelis to go back home. Israel continued to supply Lebanese Christian militias with arms, money, and ad hoc assistance to their anti-PLO campaign. All this took place in the south while the rest of Lebanon was fighting a bitter sectarian civil war that had begun in 1975.

515

On 7/17/81, in response to renewed attacks on Israel by the PLO, Begin sent aircraft north to Beirut to bomb PLO headquarters. On 6/6/82, he ordered a full-scale invasion of Lebanon. He and/or Defense Minister Sharon were intent on eliminating the PLO, imposing a peace treaty on Lebanon, and setting up a puppet government in Beirut. Maronite leaders, already in collusion with Israel, would be the puppets.

The invasion was challenged by Lebanese soldiers, by PLO fedayeen, and by Syrian forces already engaged in Lebanon's civil war. The IDF took Beirut in August, and linked up with Phalangist (Maronite) forces. The Israeli siege of Beirut had gone on for 70 days. West Beirut, a Palestinian center, had been largely destroyed by carpet bombing. Reagan had had enough. He bought the PLO evacuation, but not the puppet government. He replaced Secretary of State Alexander Haig, who had reputedly given Begin the green light to invade, with George Shultz. He ordered Israel to accept a ceasefire. The PLO was forced to leave Lebanon. Evacuation began 8/21/82.

During the war, the Sixth Fleet had stationed carriers off the Lebanese coast. On 8/25/82, US Marines set up camp in Beirut as part of an international peacekeeping force. They left after a stay of 16 days. They were sent back to Lebanon after a Syrian (?) agent assassinated Lebanon's new Phalangist President, and Phalangist militiamen retaliated by massacring over 1000 Palestinians and others who were in the Phalangists' way. The second MNF, with 1200 Marines, came back in October.

On 5/17/83, Shultz required Lebanon to sign a peace treaty with Syria and Israel. It was dead on arrival; Washington had overlooked the fact that the new hegemon of Lebanon was Syria.

In August, after the IDF had left the Beirut area, the Marines started taking lethal fire. In September, US destroyers shelled anti-West positions in the hills east of Beirut, and 2000 more Marines arrived. On 9/19/83, heavier units of the Sixth Fleet joined the barrages against invisible targets in the hills. On 10/23/83, a suicide bomber from Hizballah blew up the Marine barracks in Beirut, killing 241. The battleship New Jersey fired eleven 16-inch projectiles against Druze positions in the hills. US aircraft went into dogfights against Syrian planes. Both sides lost planes. On 2/8/84, in retaliation for renewed shelling of Beirut, Sixth Fleet units destroyed anti-West gun batteries in the hills. The evacuation of the Marines was completed a few days later.

The US intervention in the Israel-Lebanon War made no known contribution to America's national interest. On 12/28/83, the Long Commission concluded that the Marines' mission had been perverted from peacekeeping to irrelevance.

On 3/5/84, the successor President of Lebanon went to Damascus and scrapped the treaty George Shultz had arranged ten months before. The war had ended in a Syrian political victory over the Israeli-American diarchy. The Israeli invasion had exacerbated Arab hostility. Worst of all, it precipitated the founding of Hizballah, which was to become Israel's worst enemy.

The American error was the knee-jerk reflex in support of a reckless venture.

The war was a beneficial lesson for both Israel and America: The effort to perform the conversion of Lebanon was a flagrant case of overreaching. It suggested that the borders of Zionist Israel cannot include non-Jewish neighbors.

Iraq-Iran War – If there are necessary wars, this was not one of them. An eight-year conflict, in which a million (?) soldiers died, ended in stalemate.

It did have consequences: The principal one was the impoverishment of Iraq that impelled Saddam to invade Kuwait – the first war allegedly fought in the cause of Arab Nationalism.

The war's only beneficiaries were Israel (setbacks for its two worst enemies) and Turkey (the opportunity for a neutral state to continue trading with both sides): *MER*, October 2000.

America's effusive support for Saddam in the Iraq-Iran War misled Saddam into the impression that he could get away with the annexation of Kuwait.

Israel-Palestine War – The war without end between the Israelis and the Palestinians (Gaza is the extreme case) is for many observers evidence enough that Israel, to be accepted by its neighbors, will have to undergo revolutionary structural change, starting with the abolition of its

517

instinctive reliance on overwhelming force, whether in the conventional arena or the nuclear arena.

The Kuwait Wars – Both wars featured mistakes on both sides:

- Saddam's gamble destroyed relations with the US, and led to catastrophe for the people of Iraq.
- Ambassador April Glaspie's surprise prewar meeting with Saddam, on Iraqi grievances against Kuwait, dramatized America's failure to appreciate Iraqi reality. Glaspie was not authorized to impress on Saddam the likelihood of American intervention.
- Both the American expulsion of Iraqis from Kuwait and its postwar regimen of sanctions against Iraqi economy and society were unnecessarily severe: *George Bush's War*, Jean Edward Smith. The most powerful nation on earth is not always mindful how insidiously power corrupts. Even those Arab states that opposed Iraqi annexation of Kuwait resented America's display of facile lethality.
- The occupation of Kuwait in one day revealed how vulnerable any peaceable Arabian state would be to sophisticated attack without an altruistic protector like the United States.

Palestinian Power Struggle – This is a recent example of how readily a community can split into factions just as embittered against each other as they are against a common adversary. The Palestinian Arabs, the Kurds, even the pre-independence Zionists, have often failed to honor the axiom that success lies in unity.

The US-Taliban War – This is another textbook example of the costs of unnecessary war. The American war against Al Qa'idah, right or wrong, had its advocates. The war against the Afghan Taliban had no justification, particularly if the Taliban government had no prior knowledge of Al Qa'idah plans for 9/11. As of this writing, the Al Qa'idah leadership is thought to be anywhere but in Afghanistan, yet here is America still fighting a superfluous war there. As of 2016, Washington's interest in keeping up this charade seemed to be fading.

US-Jihadist War – This asymmetric conflict shows no signs of resolution. Its relevance lies in its longevity. There has been no harbinger of a conclusion.

There has been a strategic distinction between the two protagonists of jihadism. The IS seems to be faltering, partly because of its extremism – brutality for brutality's sake, an archaic brand of asceticism, challenges to all other contenders, and an unwarranted confidence that they are in tune with fate. Nusrah is recoiling under attack from the formidable coalition of Shiite expansionism and Russian Machiavellianism, but it may offer a sounder approach toward Sunni Arab leadership. Since the collapse of the secularist Arab nationalists, jihadism is all the Sunni Arabs have.

The Western powers view their enterprise as a noble conflict to purge the Middle East of troublemakers. The jihadists – and the countless victims of "collateral damage" – look on American drones as just one more curse to be endured until the Middle East gets back on its feet.

US-Iraq War – Unusual in its extent and its ferocity, this war unleashed a multitude of consequences.

Political Repercussions

1) Reinforcement of Iranian theocracy and Khomeini's leadership: Dilip Hiro.
2) Sunni fence-mending included the rehabilitation of Egypt from the disgrace of having signed a peace treaty with Israel: *Oil, Turmoil, and Islam in the Middle East*, Sheikh R. Ali.
3) Democracy suffered another blow. In the underdeveloped Middle East, the Americans' effort to democratize Iraq was ahead of its time. The attempt to take over where Saddam left off suggested that officials raised in a democracy are terrible at playing dictator.
4) Washington's only accomplishment, for better or worse, was the historic transfer of Iraq, after 500 years, from Sunni to Shia rule.

519

Damage Done

1) Subjection of Christians to Muslim persecution.
2) The invasion boosted the cause of a Kurdish state, but intensified the fight between the Kurds and the occupants of land that viable Kurdish statehood requires.
3) By destroying Iraqi unity, the US subverted its own interest in regional pacification: *FA*, November 2015, Goldenberg/Dalton. In a few short years, one war was to proliferate into three: Thomas Ricks.
4) The war aggravated the Arab-Israeli conflict, which had been quieted by the Yom Kippur War.
5) Iraq had been the most modern, secular, prosperous state in the Middle East: *Times*, ca. 1980, Yusuf Ibrahim; *NY*, 7/14/03, review of *The Modern History of Iraq*, Phoebe Marr. It came out of the war with Iran, the American occupation, and the American sanctions, a derelict relic.
6) The US acquired the legendary reputation as the catalyst to the sectarian tide engulfing the Middle East: *NY*, 4/6/15, Steve Coll. By destroying a force for regional unity (Arab-Nationalist Iraq), the US promoted sectarian fragmentation – in contrast to the Sykes-Picot version of unity the US still favors.

Israel-Hizballah War – The Israeli campaign of 2006 was intended to free two hostages, expel Hizballah's forces from south Lebanon, disarm them, and cut off their resupply from Iran and Syria. A later addition to the list was termination of the missile barrage against northern Israel.

Despite the deaths of 1200 Lebanese and the temporary displacement of a million Shiites from the south, none of these objectives was accomplished. Hizballah emerged with its command and control systems intact – even its TV station, *Al Manar* (The Minaret). In contrast with Israel's customary routs of the Palestinians, who tried to build a conventional army, Hizballah conducted a skilled guerrilla

520

operation. The Israeli offensive was poorly conceived and executed. Result: Military defeat for Israel, political defeat for the United States.

Hizballah's success in fighting Israel to a draw elevated it to the status of Israel's direst enemy.

Saudi-Yemeni War – The Saudi oligarchy has been too insecure to risk the founding of an effective army. Three other Arab governments have already been overthrown by their own armies. A primitive and capricious air force has been as far as the Saudis have gone. Yemeni society is too underdeveloped, and its economy too frail, to build a sophisticated military. Hence, the lamentable pattern of their current war – an ill-trained air force against an ill-equipped ground force. So far, this configuration has been calamitous to Yemen, but inconclusive for both sides.

Overview

The crucial date in the history of US relations with the Middle East was November 29, 1947, when the UN General Assembly adopted Resolution 181, which called for withdrawal of the British hierarchy from Palestine by 8/1/48, and the establishment of two successor states – one Arab, one Jewish – by 10/1/48.

The specifics of the UN plan were not implemented, but with the determined political support of its sponsor, the US, partition was. In the absence of consensus, the division was accomplished by war. There were several contenders: the Palestinians; the Zionists; several Arab states; and Jordan. The Zionists defeated the Palestinians and their Arab allies, but on the eastern front Jordan defeated Israel.

The result was tripartition. Jordan acquired the only land it wanted – the West Bank and most of Jerusalem. Thanks to dogged Egyptian support, Palestinians held out in the Gaza Strip. The Zionists captured the rest – 8000 square miles, over three-fourths of Palestine.

The succeeding 69 years have inundated the Middle East in violence. The Zionists used violence to expand the harried state of little Israel to the supreme state of Greater Israel.

521

Eighteen Wars Under the Microscope

War	Instance	Factors	Results
UK-Iraq	UK imperialism	Resistance inadequate	UK stayed 44 years
UK-Palestine	UK imperialism	Arab and Israeli resistances weak	UK stayed 31 years
Israel	Ethnic clash I over Palestine	Zionist army, Soviet arms, US control	Israeli statehood
Suez	Eur. imperialism; ethnic clash II over Palestine	Decisive US intervention	Invaders out in a few months
Six-Day	Ethnic clash III over Palestine	Arab resistance weak	Israel stayed 16 years in Sinai; kept Golan
Attrition	Ethnic clash IV over Palestine	Mutual attrition; Soviet entry	Draw between Israel & Egypt
Jordan-PLO	PLO uprising	Jordan defense; Israel warns Syria	1st PLO expulsion
Yom Kippur	Ethnic clash V over Palestine	Israel holds out, gets across Canal	Egypt, Jordan, Syria surrender
Israel-Lebanon	Israeli expansionism (US-backed)	Hizballah/Syria defense	Draw; 2nd PLO expulsion
Iraq-Iran	Border war	Gruelling 8 yrs.	Draw
Israel-Palestine	Israeli expansionism	Palestinian guerrilla war	Ongoing
Kuwait	Iraqi occupation	Kuwaiti resistance; US intervention	Iraq stayed 6 months
Palestinian struggle	Border war	PA submissive; Hamas at war	Ongoing
US-Taliban	9/11 shock	US intervention	Ongoing
US-Jihadist	9/11 shock	Endless drone war	Ongoing
US-Iraq	Saddam's Arab nationalism	US suppresses Iraq and Jihadists	US stayed 7 years
Israel-Hizballah	Hizballah provocations	Israeli defense	Ongoing
Saudi-Yemeni	Saudi/UAE attack	Yemen devastated; US on Saudi side	Ongoing

Section IV: The Taxonomy of Political Factions in the Middle East

Aspirants Lost in the Vacuum of Power

———

"Nothing endures but change": Heraclitus (ca. 540-ca. 480 B.C.). From the dawn of history, the Middle East has fluctuated between periods of unification and periods of fragmentation. Since 1800, the inhabitants have had to cope with the evils of fragmentation. The disintegration of the Safavid and Ottoman Empires had left a vacuum of power. Successor regimes, domestic and foreign, have tried to fill it. All have failed. Of the wars discussed in Section I, twelve are over, six still underway. All eighteen are part of the concomitant power struggle for regional hegemony. Each war will have made its mark on the ultimate outcome. Success awaits the emergence of viable contenders. This natural process has been delayed by ethnic and doctrinal discord, which has been exacerbated by the intrusion of British, French, and American imperialism.

At stake is the political architecture of a new Middle East: *Times*, 10/25/16, Peter Baker (citing Bassel Sallouch). The outcome will depend on a battle waged in all six of the arenas of power: geographic, demographic, political, economic, cultural, and <u>military</u>.

Sunni Arabs

The Islamic State (IS) – The IS is a lapsed offshoot of Al Qa'idah. It has gone through two reincarnations. The first sprang up in Iraq as a close-up enemy of the US invading forces. Their efforts to eradicate the IS nearly succeeded. Then, in an improbable alliance, the Salafi AQI (Al

Qa'idah in Iraq) was taken over by officers from Saddam's armed forces. Under this new leadership, the IS evolved from an underground militia to a standing army dedicated to conquering land as a base from which they could undertake to convert the Levant and Iraq into a new Islamic Caliphate. The chaos caused by the Arab Spring allowed the IS to establish a de facto regime over eastern Syria, based on Raqqah, and over northwest Iraq, based on Mawsil. In 2014, the IS was receiving subsidies and logistic support from Saudi Arabia and Qatar (Owen Bennett-Jones), and Turkey was providing an open border for the transit of troops and supplies. The 30,000 soldiers of the IS, including many resolute recruits from Russia's rebellious Caucasus, carried out sophisticated military operations: *MEP*, Spring 2016, Cronin. In 2014, Al Qa'idah disowned the IS as too aggressive and bloodthirsty: *NY*, 12/12/216, Robin Wright.

The IS is a sworn enemy of the Damascus regime, but the details of the relationship are obscure. On 7/9/15, the *New York Review* carried a report that the IS had been benefitting from the US/EU ban on Syrian exploitation of oil by selling directly to its enemy in Damascus. Observers suspected that the IS and Damascus were in collaboration in the oil arena. On 1/28/16, the *Financial Times* carried a report that Asad had agreed to help IS forces withdraw from Damascus and the area of Russian operations. There had been no major attacks on IS sites by the Damascus air force or by its Russian allies, aside from their recapture of Palmyra in the spring of 2016.

The IS shares with every other regime in the Middle East the handicap of overreliance on ethnic community. The IS seeks to emulate the Islamic Conquest, but it will never succeed until it can learn how to match the success of the Conquest in assimilating non-Muslim communities. The IS has clung to its own fanaticisms that threaten to bring its downfall. IS fanaticism repels prospective allies, invites new adversaries, and alienates subjects by banning common pleasures like smoking, drinking alcohol, and listening to music. It condemns Shiites as heretics, Christians as polytheists, Kurds as atheists, and Secularist Sunnis as apostates. The IS openly advocates and practices brutal tactics, like beheadings and massacres. On 8/14/16, the IS murdered 1000 Shiite cadets at Camp Speicher, an Iraqi training base. In June 2014, the IS revealed its intention to exterminate Christians, Shiites, Kurds, and Yazidis, and 5000 Yazidis died: *NYTM*, 8/14/16.

The IS is also congenitally retrogressive and obscurant. Case in point – no public schooling for females.

In January 2017, the two major cities controlled by the IS were under attack by a formidable coalition of Shiite, Kurdish, and American forces. The IS was falling back on those fronts. It still controlled most of Dayr al Zawr Province: *Times*, 1/10/17. The IS leadership and its 18,000 fighters in Iraq and Syria (*NY*, 12/12/16, Robin Wright) were said to be prepared to resort to years of underground existence if Allah so willed. Their organization seems unlikely to survive, but it could be progenitor of a Sunni movement with more pragmatic beliefs.

In southern Yemen, IS units have been competing with AQAP forces for relevance in the local power struggle.

In Libya, the Tripoli regime, after six months of US air support, expunged the IS occupation forces from Surt: *Times*, 12/7/16.

Al Qaʻidah/Nusrah – Before the outbreak of the Syrian and Iraqi civil wars, Al Qaʻidah, operating from outside the Middle East, pioneered the Islamists' anti-American campaign. Operating from afar, it carried out major subversive operations in the US. So far, the IS has confined its operations to challenging adversaries on the ground in the Middle East. As of 1/1/17, the Islamic State and Nusrah, Al Qaʻidah's branch in Syria, were the leading protagonists of the Sunni franchise in the Middle East power struggle.

The legacy of Usamah bin Ladin is presently incarnated in Syria's Nusrah Front. Its formation was announced in January 2012. In April 2013, the Amir of Nusrah, Abu Muhammad al Jawlani, rejected the claim of IS leader Abu Bakr that Nusrah was an affiliate of the IS, stating that Nusrah is an affiliate of Al Qaʻidah. Jawlani is a Syrian, born as Ahmad Husayn al Sharʻa. The rebel name Jawlani may be a challenge to Israel's hold on the Syrian Golan (*Jawlan*). In November 2013, Al Qaʻidah leader Zawahiri confirmed that Nusrah was Al Qaʻidah's affiliate in Syria, and ordered the disbandment of the ISIL (IS).

In the spring of 2014, Dayr al Zawr was being contested by several armed forces, including those of the Damascus regime, the IS, and Nusrah. Hundreds were killed in fighting between the IS and Nusrah. On April 16, 2014, IS operators killed Nusrah's chief in Idlib and his family. By 2014, the Nusrah forces had been largely expelled from Dayr al Zawr. They then joined their colleagues in Idlib Province, forming the main rebel force there. Less successful rebel militias, Islamist and secularist, joined the battle along with Nusrah forces.

Washington has classified both the IS and Al Qa'idah/Nusrah as terrorist. In 2016, in an effort to lose this indictment, Nusrah changed its name to Front for the Liberation of the Levant (*Jabhat Fath al Sham*), and disclaimed any link with Al Qa'idah (which endorsed the change). (For operations in Syria, this text continues to use "Nusrah".) In contrast with the millenary goals of the IS, Nusrah's 10,000 fighters were focusing on a less ambitious campaign to replace the Asad dynasty in Damascus, the government in Beirut, and the pro-Iran regime in Baghdad. In December 2016, Nusrah forces in Idlib Province came under intensified attack from Russian and Damascus forces.

Another offshoot of Al Qa'idah is Al Qa'idah in the Arabian Peninsula (AQAP), which is engaged, largely underground, as an outside contender in the Saudi-Yemeni War. Al Qa'idah has other transnational branches operative in Arabia, South Asia, and the horn of Africa: *NY*, 12/12/16, Robin Wright.

The Muslim Brotherhood/Qatar – In February 1982, the Syrian Army shelled the MB stronghold in Hamah for a month. The Syrian branch has been underground ever since. In Egypt, Muhammad Mursi was elected President in 2012, but failed to take advantage of the opportunity. A year later, the street turned against him, and he was jailed by the military, which had been watching events from the sidelines – and may have been masterminding them. Thousands of Muslim Brothers were jailed, hundreds died, and membership in it was declared a penal offense.

The Brotherhood is still recognized in Qatar. In 1995, when Shaykh Hamad Khalifa became the ruler of Qatar, a former client state of Saudi Arabia, the country adopted an independent stance: *Times*, 6/17/16.

527

The Shiite Bloc (Revisionist, pro-Russian)

The preponderance of Sunnis over Shiites in the Middle East (250,000,000 to 140,000,000) would normally militate for Sunni hegemony over Arabic-speaking areas. Present days are not normal. The three most populous Sunni states in the Middle East – Turkey, Egypt, and Saudi Arabia – have been prevented by circumstance from full participation in the fighting. In the four arena countries – Iran, Iraq, Syria, and Lebanon – Shiites outnumber Sunnis by 100,000,000 to 30,000,000.

The Shiite Bloc has other advantages:

1) Two Shiite militias – Iranian-trained Arabs in Iraq, and Hizballah in Lebanon and Syria – have high morale and proven competence.

2) The Russian Air Force units on site have provided the Damascus regime with decisive support.

3) The Sunni Arab rebels have been wildly disunited. In Syria, the Bloc has focused its attacks on militias in more direct conflict with Damascus forces: *LRB*, 12/3/15, Adam Shatz. That fact has enhanced speculation about the possibility of a secret understanding between Damascus and the IS.

Iran – The leader of the Shiite Bloc has been inspirited by its advance into traditionally Sunni territory – and perhaps by hope of expanding the Iranian sphere of influence to include the Levant.

Hizballah – Starting during the Israeli invasion of Lebanon, Iranian trainers created a Shiite militia that controls Lebanon from behind the scenes, has become a major adversary of Israel, and has given Damascus crucial support in the battle for Syria. Hizballah has broadened its relevance by creating a Christian wing: *NY*, 12/12/16, Robin Wright.

Iraq – The shaky regime in Baghdad is trying simultaneously to rebuild Iraq from the sorry state in which American invaders and politicians left it, to recover lands lost to the IS, to deny independence to the KRG, and to accept crucial support from Iran without allowing the conversion of rump Iraq from protectorate to possession.

Syria – Hizballah, Iran, and the Russians have helped Damascus regain territory, and may drive the Islamic State back underground, but they cannot resolve the basic problem of a Sunni country in the clutches of an Alawite minority. They cannot even give Bashar al Asad a viable country. Heedless of conscience and consequences, he devastated it by his paranoid war against his own people – and got over 400,000 of them killed. Any caprice of the international community to support Alawite rule in Syria would be another reminder of the folly of challenging the inexorable logic of demography: *MER*, Winter 2015.

In 2016, at the annual meeting of the Herzliya Conference, Israeli Chief of Military Intelligence Major General Herzi Halevi stated that Israel did not want the IS to lose in the civil war because an IS regime in Damascus would be preferable to the survival of the Asad regime. (Hizballah, a major ally of that regime, was Israel's bitterest enemy.): *WRMEA*, August 2016, Jason Ditz.

Palestinians (Sunni and Christian)

In the ongoing Israel-Palestine War, the Palestinian side is circumscribed: those in the diaspora, most of them dispersed in refugee camps in Lebanon, Syria, Jordan, and Occupied Palestine, are policed by governments that have troubles of their own. The abortive Oslo Accord of 1993 had extracted from the Palestinians the recognition of Israel (*Financial Times*, 1/24/16), but in the Arab-Israeli conflict, diplomacy is irrelevant. Some Palestinians in the West Bank still look for ways to undercut Israeli rule, but most are affiliated with the Palestinian Authority, whose only role is as docile intermediary between the Israeli authorities and PA constituents. The PA receives Israeli subsidies in return for undertaking to keep those constituents under control. The PA has been accused of corruption, incompetence, and harsh treatment of Palestinian Islamists: *NYR*, 4/17/16; *Return,* Ghada Karmi; *NY*, 12/12/16, Robin Wright.

In 2016, rivalry between a PA faction led by President 'Abbas, and another led by Muhammad Dahlan, escalated into an armed clash: *WRMEA*, October 2016, Ramzi Baroud.

Hamas – The inhabitants of Gaza have few freedoms. One of them is active resistance. In 2001, resistance got results: Israel traded a thousand Palestinian prisoners for one Israeli. Subsequently, Gaza has been repeatedly mauled by IDF air and ground forces. Palestinians in general condemn the PA's incongruous position, in contrast with Hamas's sacrifice. Hamas won the last election for leadership of Gaza, and would win election in the West Bank but for the thousands of Islamists in Israeli jails. Hamas might condemn the PA as a quisling organization except for the awkward fact that Hamas has lately had to live on whatever subsidy the PA is willing to contribute.

Turkey: Victim of Ambivalence

Recep Erdogan, Prime Minister of Turkey since 2003, was elevated to President in 2014. He was cooling toward Europe, which was dragging its feet on Turkey's application for membership in the European Union. He began tilting toward his Asian neighbors, convulsed since 2011 by the Arab Spring. Syria was in desperate need of foreign support against the despotism of Bashar al Asad's Alawite regime in Damascus. The Sunni rebels looked north. Turkey, in normal times the most formidable state in the Middle East, had a built-in affinity with the Sunni side in Syria. Erdogan switched his relationship with Asad from mentor to sworn enemy: www.consortiumnews.com, Graham Fuller, reprinted in the *WRMEA* of 8/17/16. Erdogan adopted a supportive stance on behalf of Syrian Arab and Turkmen rebels (*FT*, 11/13/15) and facilitated the passage of IS supplies, recruits, and personnel across the border with Syria.

After Putin caught the world's attention by deploying a small number of Russian aircraft in support of the faltering Damascus regime, Turkish planes shot down a Russian plane that had wandered close to, or into, Turkish airspace. Turks and Turkmens felt that shooting the plane down was justifiable reprisal for the deaths that Russia had inflicted on Turkmen civilians in Syria: *MEP*, October 2016.

Then Washington confronted Erdogan with a dilemma: It pressed him to join the coalition that had set out to eradicate the IS. US leverage

530

was strong. NATO, Turkey's traditional ally against Russian expansionism, had designated the IS as terrorist. Erdogan had little time to solve this riddle. His highest priority was ending the ugly battle in southeast Turkey between the government and the PKK insurgents. Many of Turkey's 15,000,000 Kurds were members of the main Kurdish political party, the HDP.

Erdogan stalled for time by allowing the US to base planes at Incirlik Air Base. Then IS fanaticism made his ultimate decision for him. IS operatives began bombing sites in Turkish cities. The targets were Kurdish, but the responsible government was in Ankara.

In 2016, the US, Russia, and Turkey were operating in an anti-IS coalition, but Turkey resisted a Russian request to close its border to insurgents, and Russia resisted the Turkish position that it should be assisting moderate rebel organizations: *Times*, 8/10/16.

Since July 2016, Erdogan has been forced to focus on the domestic front. On 7/15/16, a military faction attempted a coup against the Erdogan regime, citing erosion of secularism, and trend toward autocracy. After a brief period of violence, which caused the deaths of hundreds and the wounding of many more, the attempt was stringently suppressed, 40,000 suspects were detained, and thousands of civil servants were suspended or dismissed: *Post*, 7/16/16; *Times*, 8/17/16, 9/16/16.

In August 2016, Erdogan began dealing with still another critical problem by sending well-armed raiding parties into Syria to check Kurdish expansion along the border. To this end, he mended fences with Russia. The offense of shooting down a Russian plane was negotiated away, and Erdogan moderated his support for Syrian rebels and his insistence on the summary ouster of Asad, in return for Russian acceptance of Turkish action against the Kurdish forces in Syria: *FT*, 11/29/16; *Times*, 12/3/16.

Another element in the sudden re-Westernization of Turkish foreign policy was a shift in its relations with Israel. On 1/29/09, at the annual meeting of the World Economic Forum in Davos, Switzerland, a heated debate broke out between Erdogan and Israeli President Shimon Peres over Israel's bloody Operation Cast Lead against Gaza in the winter of

2008-9. Erdogan stormed out of the meeting. On 6/27/16, reconciliation between Turkey and Israel was codified in a joint agreement. The Palestinians were not forgotten. Turkey was to funnel aid to Gaza through the Israeli port of Ashdod, and to build a power plant/water distribution center in Gaza: *WRMEA*, August 2016, Jonathan Gorvett.

In 2016, the IS bombings of Kurdish neighborhoods had escalated to include Turkish neighborhoods. Erdogan started bombing IS sites in Syria. Later in the year, he began sending well-armed troops into Syria on missions to block westward expansion of the YPG, a Kurdish affiliate of the PKK. Turkish forces based northeast of Mawsil were participating in the grinding campaign to expel the IS defenders.

On 1/5/17, the *Financial Times* reported that Turkey had had its bloodiest period in years. In 2016, terrorists had killed 685 people. Erdogan's eventual goal was a buffer zone in Syria. Turkey was trying to shut down cross-border infiltration, but old smuggling routes were still operative. Anti-Americanism was growing. Erdogan was blaming the US for the "Gulen" coup attempt. Turkey was polarized between the Islamists (led by Erdogan) and their adversaries.

The Kurdish Bloc (Revisionist, pro-American)

PKK/YPG – By 2015, southeast Turkey was a battleground between the government and the PKK. Erdogan was berating the main Kurdish political party, the HDP, alleging that it was in collusion with the insurrectionists. Turkish mobs were burning HDP offices (*FT*, 9/11/15) and attacking Kurds in the streets. In Syria, Turkish forces had checked the westward advance of the YPG, the military arm of the PYD, the Kurdish political party in Syria, and the ally of the PKK. The YPG was an effective militia, which, with US air cover, had captured enclaves along the Syrian-Turkish border. It was a significant ally of the US in the war against the IS.

KRG – In the KAR, the KRG was consolidating an autonomous enclave. The Baghdad regime was too weak to stop it. The KRG was maintaining businesslike relations with Baghdad and Ankara, but it was on bad terms with the PKK and the PYD. It had not resisted Turkey's forays against PKK forces taking refuge in the KAR.

The KRG had a dual administration because tribal rivalry still persisted: *NYTM*, 8/14/16. The KRG's Peshmerga was participating in the Iraqi siege of Mawsil, and maneuvering to expand its sphere of influence in northeast Iraq. Oil-rich Kirkuk was of special interest, although most Kurds in Kirkuk were pro-PYD.

The Iraqi Kurds' only steadfast friend was Israel, which had been providing them financial and military assistance for over 40 years.

Russia

In 2015, Iran warned Prime Minister Vladimir Putin that the Asad regime was about to fall. In July, Qassem Soleimani, Commander of Iran's Quds Force, went to Moscow and warned the Russians that they might lose their "naval base" in Tartus, the only base they had abroad. On 8/26/15, Russia and Syria concluded an agreement according Russia access to Khmaymim Air Base, near Latakia, close to a Syrian commercial airport: *MEP*, Winter 2016, Williams/Souza.

In October 2015, Russian air cover for the forces of the Damascus regime reversed the military balance in the Syrian civil war. Russia supplemented its air action with cruise missiles, fired from planes and ships. To appease the US, Russian bulletins claimed their assault was directed at the forces of the IS. Actually, the Russians were operating in northwest Syria, where the most active rebel organizations were Nusrah and allied secularist rebels, some of whom were receiving support from the CIA: *MEP*, Winter 2016; *The Week* (from *National Review*), 12/9/16, Tom Rogan. When the Russians started losing Russian-made tanks to the rebels' US-made TOW missiles, the Russians switched their tactic to helicopters.

By December 2015, the Russian forces, now numbering 4000, were intensifying their offensive and using scorched-earth tactics. Indiscriminate bombing had killed 2000 Syrian civilians: *MEP*, Winter 2016.

In February 2016, Russian air attacks on Free Syrian Army (FSA) sites in Dar'a enabled Damascus forces to recapture the Damascus-Dar'a road. In the spring, Russian aircraft supported Damascus's recapture of Palmyra. Russian ground troops set up a base nearby.

At this point, Aleppo was divided between a large enclave on the west side controlled by Damascus, and a small sector on the east side controlled by rebels. In August 2016, Russian planes opened a stronger offensive against rebel defenders in east Aleppo. The Tartus base was supporting jet fighters, attack helicopters, and missiles – under the supervision of a sophisticated headquarters: *Times*, 4/16/16. In October, an editorial in the *Financial Times* condemned Russian forces for colluding with Damascus in the slaughter of rebels in east Aleppo by depraved tactics – using proscribed munitions, destroying water reserves and food supplies, bombing clinics and aid convoys – and rescuing a despot who had ruined his own country for years to come: *FT*, 10/10/16.

In late December of 2016, the Russian-Damascus air offensive overwhelmed the rebel sector in Aleppo. The fall of Aleppo (once Syria's largest city) was widely viewed as a milestone in the civil war, but not its end. The rebels were still in control of central and eastern Syria. Early in 2017, Russian bombing flights came to the aid of Turkish forces that were moving toward Al Bab, between Aleppo and Palmyra, but had been bogged down by IS resistance: *Times*, 1/9/17, 1/18/17.

The Reversionary Bloc (pro-American)

Saudi Arabia – Its government is a glaring anachronism. As a tribal regime, the Royal Family is painfully aware that pro-West governments in Syria, Egypt, and Iraq were eliminated by military coups. The main missions of the Saudi Army and National Guard seem to be keeping an eye on each other. Saudi infantry units fought well in two wars against Israel (1948 and 1973), but on a small scale. Saudi infantry has never been in a major action outside Arabia. In the Saudi-Yemeni War, the Saudis have not sent troops across their common border.

Saudi power is economic. In 2016, Lebanese authorities detained a Saudi prince on a charge of carrying amphetamines on his plane. In retaliation for this and other Lebanese (Hizballah) slights, Saudi Arabia cancelled its commitment to give Lebanon 4 billion dollars for the Lebanese Army and police.

As Iran has loomed in the Saudis' eyes as their worst enemy, they have quietly moved toward Israel, their former worst enemy. Saudi Arabia has two secondary enemies: its Shiite minority and Sunni jihadists. To impress its own subjects, Riyadh carried out the paranoid execution of Shiite Shaykh Nimr Nimr in January 2016. To promote the Sunni cause, the Saudis have been subsidizing jihadist militias in Syria. Here they come up against divided loyalties. Millenarians, led by the IS, condemn the regime in Riyadh as too dissolute to survive. Official Saudi reaction to this threat is tempered by realization that the IS, the paradigm of Wahhabiism, is admired by many Saudis.

Late in 2016, the new government in Saudi Arabia was becoming disenchanted with the Sisi regime in Egypt.

Egypt – After Israel had pounded Egypt into submission, the traditional leader of the Arabs signed a peace treaty with Israel, and opted out of the war for the Middle East. Egypt couldn't participate even if it wanted to. Israel is an impassable land barrier between Egypt and the other states of the eastern Arab world.

Theoretically, Egypt still has the capability to bypass Israel by air or by sea. Nasir considered intervening against the Syrian secessionists in 1961, but decided against taking on the risks. In the 1960's, Nasir sent troops down the Red Sea to rescue the revolutionary side in the Yemeni civil war. The alien terrain frustrated them.

In 2015, Egypt joined Saudi Arabia's coalition against the Huthis and sent 800 soldiers to Yemen. As the Egyptian economy sags, Cairo's dependence on American and Arabian financial assistance increases. If Sisi chose to send Egyptian troops to Yemen in force, Israel would not automatically intervene. It views inter-Arab combat as advantageous. However, there has been no sign of any Egyptian interest in another war.

Since Sisi took charge of Egypt, its annual subsidy from the US has fallen from 3 billion dollars to 1.3 billion: *NYTM*, 8/14/16.

As a secularist adversary of Islamist Hamas, Egypt has drifted into convenient but unadvertised cooperation with Israel against Hamas and Iran. These developments have given the Egyptian High Command more time to attend to the military's everyday interests, and to the suppression of Islamism in Egypt (MB) and Gaza (Hamas). In late 2016, Egypt was reportedly relaxing its hostility to the Asad regime in Damascus, in order to cultivate closer relations with Russia. Syrian security chief 'Ali Mamluk had been publicly hosted in Cairo: *Times*, 12/3/16.

As its guns fall silent, Egypt loses relevance in the Middle East power struggle.

Jordan – Arab politics have drawn Jordan into several Arab-Israeli wars. The Arab Legion distinguished itself in the first one. Since then, King Husayn was realistic enough to join most wars against Israel, but to calibrate actual participation in wars he knew the Arabs were bound to lose.

Israel – Although Prime Minister Netanyahu has barged into America's domestic politics on the Republican side, the Democrat administrations have been equally supportive of the Israeli state.

The US – Current relationships with the nineteen Middle Eastern states might be summarized as follows:

> Strained – Iran, Syria, Yemen
> Uneven – Egypt, Lebanon, Turkey
> Average – Azerbaijan, Bahrain, Cyprus, Georgia, Iraq, Kuwait, Oman, Qatar, UAE
> Positive – Armenia, Jordan, Saudi Arabia
> Special – Israel

Toward a New Hegemony

In the short term, war may be the prime mover of history. In a few recent years, it has propelled most of the Middle East into chaos. Over the centuries, war has to be evaluated in the wider context of all the forces of geopolitics, which can change history in even more fundamental ways:

Settlement – War was epitomized by the Mongol invasion of the Middle East in the 1200's. The first Mongol Empire ruled the Middle East for a century, and devastated Persia and Mesopotamia, but finally went home, leaving no permanent imprint on society. Conversely, the Arabs overran most of the Middle East, and Arabized it. The Central Asian Turks overran Anatolia and Turkified it. The difference was settlement.

The Middle East is still experiencing the trauma of settlement.

Since the 1940's, Jewish immigrants have replaced most of the pre-Israel inhabitants of Palestine. The Arab-Israeli wars of 1948 and 1967 caused the flight of a million Palestinians to nearby states. They have not been assimilated.

During the American occupation of Iraq, millions of Iraqi refugees made an unplanned exodus to nearby states. The US invasion preceded – and may have caused – a sectarian war. The Christian population of Iraq fell from 1.5 million in 2003 to 500,000 in 2015.

Since the outbreak of the Syrian civil war in 2011, Syrian refugees have flooded Europe. Refugees still in the Middle East were estimated in 2016 to number: Lebanon – 1.6 million (increasing its population by 40 percent); Jordan – .6 million; Turkey – 1 million; Iraq – .2 million; Egypt – .15 million. Syria had lost 4.4 million of its citizens, Iraq 3.1 million: *Times*, 7/27/15. In 2017, 6.5 million more Syrians were still holding out in their country, but displaced: *Times*, 8/29/14, from the UN High Commissioner for Human Rights.

Language – International friction is exacerbated by difference of language. The people of the Middle East fall into five major linguistic communities: Arabic and Hebrew (Semitic Language Family); Turkish (Altaic); Persian and Kurdish (Indo-European); *Atlas of Languages*; *EB*: 7:40.

Language can make all the difference. Around 1970, FSO Ed Djerijian, a product of the Foreign Service Institute's Arabic program, was walking back to Embassy Beirut when he was stopped by a group of angry protestors. As he told it, one of them accosted him: "*Inta Amrikani.*" The right answer saved him from a possible incident: "*Walaw,*

537

ana Lubnani!', which in Lebanese colloquial Arabic can be loosely translated as "The hell you say, I'm Lebanese."

The Middle East is one of the many areas of the world where English is evolving into the essential second language.

Tribalism – For centuries, governments have formed along genetic lines. In the Middle East, tribal government is family-oriented, traditionalist, intensely personal, and discriminatory toward females. Tribalism still prevails in the seven states of Arabia, Jordan, and in some communities of Israel ("chosen people"). The concept of the Jewish people as a "consecrated brotherhood … remains fundamental to Judaism in the Twentieth Century": *EB*: 3:268.

Six of the tribal-oriented Arab states are ruled by family oligarchies. In Yemen, hegemony is currently in dispute between a faction of the army and the Huthi tribe.

Tribalism is above sectarianism in that some tribes include members from different sects. All Arabian governments are based on Islam, and discriminate against adherents of other creeds. In Israel, the law reserves superior status for Jews. The government classifies its Jewish citizens on the basis of the affiliation of the mother, as corroborated by the matrilineal chain back for generations.

Sectarianism – The Middle East power struggle has lately evolved into a conflict between Sunnis and Shiites. (Most Kurds are Sunnis, but their community is distinguished from others by language.) The British imperialists used the term nationalism, as envisioned in the Peace of Westphalia, to camouflage the reality of British hegemony. Nationalism hung on for some years in independent Iraq. The Iraq-Iran War was more nationalistic than sectarian. The government of Iran was and is a Shiite theocracy, but the Sunni government of Iraq was a secular dictatorship with more Shiites than Sunnis in its army.

However, the culture of the greater Middle East has long been supremely devout – even to the point of commemorating their faith by naming many of its children after revered predecessors, or one of the 99 names of God. Unlike secular politics, religious doctrine tends to be absolute. Result: Middle Eastern governments offer no room for compromise, and many of their wars are sectarian – as now. The quintessential sectarian state is Lebanon, whose top three positions in the government are reserved for a Christian, a Sunni, and a Shiite, in that order.

Autocracy – All Middle Eastern governments are autocratic – dictatorial or sectarian – never democratic. Several governments are products of military coups d'état, as in Syria, Egypt, Iraq, and Yemen, or adventitious, as in Turkey (Mustafa Kemal) and Iran (Ruhollah Khomeini). Iran may be the only theocracy in the world. Turkey's progress toward democracy, however faltering, is an encouraging note for the rest of the region. President Erdogan has been accused of trying to revise the Turkish constitution to award autocratic powers to presidents of Turkey.

Revolution?

The Middle East is in dire need of political reform. Historians have spotted three past revolutions there – Iranian in 1905 (suppressed by Russian intervention in 1911); Turkish after World War I; Iranian in 1979. Nasir had revolution in mind (*Philosophy of the Revolution*), but for the past 65 years, Egypt has been stuck in successive variations of the military regime Nasir created. Middle East revolutionaries have been stifled by the forces of retrogression: the regimes in Baghdad and Damascus, Hizballah, Iran, Egypt, Russia, and the US. Crucial assistance from Turkey for the Syrian revolutionists is waning, as Turkey is overwhelmed by domestic furor, Kurdish insurgence, and great-power pressure.

The Arab Sunni governments are frozen in traditionalism. They have mastered the art of showboat patriotism, unalloyed by constructive action. The unknown quantity is the people they govern. There are faint indications that the people are beginning to appreciate that traditionalism is responsible for their travail.

Section V: Precautions for Policymakers

2017 – Problems Unresolved

———

Since 1956, when Washington commandeered control of the Middle East, it has had 60 years to settle things down. Instead, the region is more turbulent than ever.

US-Jihadist War

Of the 1500 rebel groups in Syria (*The Syrian Jihad*, Charles Lister), two were preeminent – the Islamic State and Nusrah. Both were too Islamist to suit Washington, which had condemned them as terrorist, and which was continuing its escalating campaign from the air versus IS positions and infrastructure: *Times*, 8/26/15. Nusrah and allied militias, supported by Turkey (*Financial Times*, 12/21/16), still controlled Idlib Province in western Syria.

In the IS campaign to combine Iraq and the Levant in an expanded Caliphate, the IS had resorted to violence against all other contenders – even its natural ally, Turkey. Nusrah, focused on the ouster of the Damascus regime, had been receptive to overtures from secularist rebels impressed by its record on the battlefield.

US military action had not extended to western Syria. The Russians got there first. The US had condemned the brutality of the Damascus regime from the outset of the civil war, but the regime had not been intentionally targeted by US forces. The CIA and DOD had supplied arms to "moderate" rebels, but that approach had gone sour because of Washington's profound allergy to Jihadist rebels. The US had denied the moderates' requests for ground-to-air missiles, for fear they would fall into Jihadist hands, and the CIA and DOD had made a bizarre effort to persuade the moderates to forget the reason why they went to war in the first place, sign up with the American war against the IS, and become de facto allies of the Damascus faction they despised.

Since the basic strategy of the IS was to acquire territory, and its primary source of revenue was taxation, the indicated counter-strategy was to retake territory: Lister. This required ground troops. The US had had remarkable success in picking off IS leaders from the air (*Times*, 12/14/16), but Obama's rejection of major ground deployment forced him to fall back on the Kurds. This strategy had three drawbacks: 1) The Kurds were also looking for territory, but they were not interested in fighting for land that lacked an active Kurdish community; 2) The YPG Kurds, active in Syria, were bitter enemies of America's NATO ally, Turkey; 3) The Kurds, the West's only reliable allies in the conflict, were suspect in Arab eyes. After the IS occupied Mawsil in June 2014, Washington complied with a request for help from KRG President Mas'ud Barzani. Since Washington was channeling its aid to Barzani's KDP, the PUK – the KDP's partner and rival – turned to Iran: *LRB*, 11/7/16, Joost Hilterman.

In Syria, US air action against IS forces had been instrumental in their retreat. In Libya, the expulsion of the defenders of the IS's fallback base in Surt had been expedited by weeks of US air attacks: *The Week*, 3/3/17.

Saudi-Yemeni War

The fighting was in a lull, with the Huthis in control of northwestern Yemen, and the anti-Huthi coalition (Saudi Arabia and the UAE) in control of Yemen's south and east: *Times*, 12/19/16.

The Syrian Civil War

On December 13, 2016, Russia announced that the rebel position in east Aleppo had fallen: *Times*, 12/14/16. The Damascus regime's recapture of Syria's major occupied city, after a four-year siege, was widely viewed as a game-changer – though not the end of the war. Some occupants of the recaptured area had been shot down in their homes or in the streets. Under a rebel-Russian agreement negotiated by Turkey, but not well observed, thousands of rebels and civilians managed to escape. Some of the rebels were adherents of Nusrah. Most were affiliates of secularist militias. The victory had been won by ground action by forces of Lebanon's Hizballah, Iran's Revolutionary Guard Corps, and affiliated Shiite militias, by indiscriminate Russian bombing, and by modest participation of the dwindling forces of the Damascus regime: *FT*, 12/16/16, Gardner.

So far, the only radical consequence of the Syrian Civil War had been the dismantling of Sykes-Picot Syria. The country had been partitioned into three enclaves. The Damascus regime held the populous west. The IS was holding out in the east. Syrian Kurds had put together a wide strip along the border with Turkey. Of 21,000,000 prewar Syrians, over 10,000,000 were DP's – 6,000,000 in Syria, 4,800,000 elsewhere. An estimated 470,000 were dead. Rump Syria was a coalition of <u>haves</u> – Alawites, other Shiites, and Christians. The rebels were a farrago of Sunni <u>have-nots</u>: *FT*, 9/17/16.

In addition to the fighting in Iraq and Syria, IS operatives were continuing isolated but lethal attacks overseas, including running a vehicle into a Berlin crowd, and a foray by a suicide team of commandos in Jordan: *Times*, 12/21/16.

The Iraqi Civil War

In reaction to mistreatment of Sunnis by the administration of Iraqi Prime Minister Maliki, the Sunnis of Mawsil had welcomed the IS takeover – until the IS began to impose its fanatical precepts and jail or execute those who resisted: LRB, 5/4/17, Jackson Lears.

The Baghdad regime was locked in a political battle to consolidate its hold on the capital, and a military battle against jihadists – with the help of Iranian-organized Shiite militias, the (all-Shiite) 100,000-man People's Militia (Mogelson), the KRG's Peshmerga, US advisors on the front lines, and US air support. Of 45,000 warriors bearing down on Mawsil, over half were Kurds: *Times*, 12/26/16.

As of December 2016, the siege of west Mawsil had settled into a grinding war of attrition: *Times*, 12/19/16. The US was playing a critical role. US Apache helicopters, armed drones, and warplanes, flown by Americans, were supporting action on the ground against the IS defenders, estimated to number fewer than 1000: *Times*, 5/5/17, Gordon.

Any attempt by Baghdad to counter the KRG's march toward statehood would come later, if ever.

Friction Between Turkey and the US

Turkey considered the PKK (operating in Turkey) and the YPG (operating in Syria) its bitterest enemies. Turkey's hostility toward the militants of the Islamic State was moderated by their basic linkage as Sunni communities.

For the Americans, the Islamic State was their nemesis, while the Syrian Kurds were their only Syrian allies. For years, Washington had pressured Ankara to go easy on the YPG.

In 2016, Erdogan lost patience. He threw down the gauntlet by starting a cautious process of occupying small areas of northern Syria, and expelling units of the YPG, even though this process brought Turkish forces ever closer to American soldiers embedded with units of the YPG, and the seizure of Syrian territory contradicted Russia's role as protector of the Damascus regime.

A demonstration at a Russian Consulate in Turkey, and the assassination of the Russian Ambassador, reflected some rank-and-file condemnation of Turkish rapprochement with the country that had had a central role in the fall of Aleppo. In the siege of Mawsil, the attackers were relying on attrition of weapons and militiamen to bring the stubborn IS resistance to an end, but it was reported that replacements of arms and personnel were still filtering into Syria via Turkey: *Times*, 12/19/16. In order to mute Russian opposition to

Turkish enclaves in Syria, Turkey had had to cut back its support for the jihadists: *FT*, 12/29/16, Gardner.

Interaction Between the US and Russia

The relationship between the US and Russia has been appropriately correct, but highly competitive.

In the Russian-American standoff, the US has practiced a double standard. The Clinton administration pressed for extension of NATO up to the Russian border – whereas the US flatly opposed any extension of Russian influence into the rest of Europe, let alone into the Middle East. The Obama administration had resisted the Russian absorption of territories that had been part of the USSR.

For years, Russia had seemed to resent the Americans' special access to the Middle East. In 2015, Middle East turmoil and American perplexity combined to open the door to Russian intervention. Putin responded with alacrity. It was an opportunity to turn the tables: *LRB*, 5/4/17, Lears.

"Russia is back as a key player in the Middle East": *FT*, 1/20/17. "Russia's action in Syria is not really about Syria, or even about the Middle East. It's about its global role – and eventually a coalition of equals with the US.": *FT*, 12/16/16, Gardner, quoting Dmitri Trenin of The Carnegie Moscow Center.

Of the 100,000 rebels in Syria and Iraq, 30,000 were foreigners from over 100 countries (Lister), perhaps in a Middle Eastern analogy to the Spanish Civil War. Many of them came from the rebellious provinces of the Russian Caucasus, where Moscow has learned to beware of Sunnis. Shiite Iran was an ideal partner for military operations in Syria – a partner that Russia could assist or ignore as its global policies dictated.

The US had its own allies on the Sunni side, but Russian support for the Shiite Bloc far exceeded America's half-hearted support for the Sunni rebels. US policy was preordained by the commitment to the security of Zionist Israel. The NATO tie with Turkey was undercut by Turkey's dependence on Russian gas and by its sectarian obligation to take the Arab side against Israel if the chips were ever down. At a time when the American role in the Middle East was waning (*FT*, 12/14/16), Russia and Iran shared the laurels of their grisly victory in Aleppo. The Russian intervention in Syria had shattered Obama's idea of a settlement negotiated in Damascus: *Times*, 2/11/16, David Sanger.

Both Russia and the US were trying to fit into tomorrow's Middle East with yesterday's policies.

The American Reaction: Discomfited but Determined

DOD Infrastructure in the Middle East – The US Department of Defense maintains six regional unified combat commands. The US Central Command (CENTCOM) was established in 1983, taking over the responsibilities of the Rapid Deployment Force (founded in 1980). CENTCOM's Headquarters are at MacDill Air Force Base in Tampa, Florida. Its forward headquarters were transferred in 2009 from Camp Al Sayliyyah (Qatar) to Al 'Udayd Air Base (Qatar). CENTCOM's primary troop deployments have been in Afghanistan, Iraq, and Syria.

Responsibility for super-secret commando forces, like the Army's Delta Force, falls on the Joint Special Operations Command (JSOC) based at Fort Bragg, North Carolina: *Times*, 1/23/05. The JSOC targets jihadists in dozens of countries, maintains clandestine centers for interrogation of suspects, and oversees US drone operations in Afghanistan, Pakistan, Africa, and the Middle East: *MEP*, Winter 2016, Brynjar Lia.

Riyadh is the site of a compound housing 2000 Americans deployed for the defense of Saudi Arabia: *Harper's*, September 2016. Deep in the Saudi desert, there is a CIA base for drone attacks on AQAP targets in Yemen. In Syria, the Syrian Democratic Forces (SDF) are receiving CIA support. The Kurdish YPG in northern Syria has been receiving DOD support.

US forces in Iraq, withdrawn in 2011, had lately risen to 5000 to support the Iraqi campaign to recover Mawsil: *Times*, 10/17/16.

US naval units in the eastern Mediterranean are commanded by the Sixth Fleet, based in Naples. US naval units in the Gulf and the

Arabian Sea constitute the Fifth Fleet, based in Bahrain. The US military presence has made the Persian Gulf an American lake: *MEP*, Fall 2013, Michael Klare.

Bremerton Naval Station, Washington, is the home port of the USS Carl Vinson, a Nimitz-class supercarrier, launched in 1980, that has been a critical launch pad for strikes in Syria and Iraq against the IS.

DOD's annual budget has been estimated at 720 billion dollars, 5.7 percent of the US GNP.

US Military Readiness – In the Middle East, war has become a normal condition: *FA*, 8/24/16, Bacevich. US commitments to defend Egypt, Jordan, Saudi Arabia, Gulf States, and Greater Israel (Israel plus Occupied Palestine and Golan), plus NATO commitments to Turkey, have resulted in the construction of a huge military infrastructure in the Middle East and the seas that surround it. Washington has honored its commitments by its expulsion of Iraqi forces from Kuwait in the Second Kuwait War, and by urgent political, economic, and military support, as needed, to Israel. Washington has exceeded its commitments in the Israel-Lebanon War, the Iraq-Iran War, the Israel-Palestine War, the US-Taliban War, the US-Iraq War, and the Saudi-Yemeni War.

The commitment to Israel has always had special significance. For the past 70 years, the Arabs and the Israelis have been frozen in a zero-sum conflict. Since there is no visible likelihood of a negotiated settlement between two claimants for the same territory, basic US policy for the Middle East has been locked in place since 1948.

Congress has formally declared war five times: War of 1812, Mexican War, Spanish-American War, World Wars I and II. The Congress's resolution endorsing US participation in the liberation of Kuwait was indirect authorization for US air defense of the No-Fly Zones in Iraq: *Times*, 8/24/02. Presidents unable to get action from Congress have fallen back on executive agreements, which are as binding as a treaty: *NYR*, 3/24/16, Jessica Mathews.

Combat in the Middle Eastern Environment

Middle East terrain falls into two zones – mountainous and arid. The semi-wooded mountains of south Lebanon, northeast Iraq, and Yemen shelter the forces of Hizballah, the Peshmerga, and the Huthis respectively. Elsewhere in the region, skies are usually cloudless, and ground cover is sparse, affording a significant military advantage to the side that controls the air – the UK in post-World War I Iraq; the Israelis against the Arabs; the Israeli lockdown of Gaza; the Americans against the IS; the Saudis against the Huthis; and American drones against jihadists in a number of Muslim states.

Human Rights: A Utopian View

The Rights of the Peoples of the Middle East

Liberty – Like gravity in physics, liberty is an irresistible force in human relationships. The Golden Rule governs all relationships – individual and collective. The Monroe Doctrine was an American codification of humanity's universal right to self-determination—though misused in later years.

Nasirism began as a young Nasir's reaction to British military overflights (*Ya 'Aziz, Dahiyyah takhud al Ingliz* – Allah, immolate the English: *Philosophy of the Revolution*, Nasir).

Unity – Liberty springs from an orderly society. Its guarantor is political unity. In earlier times, unity was the adventitious product of settlement or empire. Settlement has often led to metamorphosis, as accomplished by Arabs in North Africa and southwest Asia, by Turks in Anatolia, by Europeans in North America, and by Jews in Palestine. Imperialism is ephemeral. The British spheres of influence in India and the Middle East lasted 300 years. The American sphere of influence in the Middle East has lasted 70 years. It is on the way out.

In the modern Middle East, the first step toward regional unity is likely to be the separate unification of ethnic communities. Arab unity was the watchword of the Baath Party in Syria and Jamal 'Abd al Nasir's party in Egypt.

548

Rights of the US in the Middle East

Americans have the right to promote by peaceful means a Middle East of stable politics, conciliatory policies, and fair foreign access to routes and resources. Today's Middle East turmoil is the inevitable concomitant of a chronic vacuum of power. US security guarantees have massively contributed to both.

The right of foreign intervention exists in three circumstances: 1) Self-defense against attack; 2) Preemptive self-defense against a predictable attack – like the Nazi excrescence; 3) Response to a justifiable request for rescue from genocide. In the absence of a global police force, a foreign state or coalition should be allowed to comply with international consensus for a benevolent intervention. Without international opposition, the US has properly violated Syrian sovereignty by supplying arms to rebels against the genocidal regime in Damascus. The Western world seemed to favor more direct US intervention, which was contemplated in Washington, but not adopted. (The refugee problem confronted Europe with an even more pressing motive for intervening on its own behalf, but the EU is too young to take on so radical a venture.)

US Overreach

Small, modern homogeneous states are easy to govern – big heterogeneous states, desperately difficult. The United States is the greatest and – barring electoral accident – the most enlightened power the world has yet seen. The following views of how American policy may have gone astray are meant as a reminder to incoming administrations of how the corruptive influence of great power can overwhelm the best of intentions:

Problematic Alliances – The capricious politics of Washington on the rampage have dropped the American democracy into incongruous associations with Arab autocracy and Israeli sectarianism. In 2016, Washington saw the Sisi dictatorship in Cairo as its only reliable Arab ally against the Jihadist threat: *LRB*, 3/3/16.

Security Guarantee for Saudi Arabia – Perhaps the immediate circumstances required Franklin Roosevelt to guarantee Saudi security in return for favored Western access to Saudi oil. Allied supplies of fuel and Nazi lack of it had just accelerated the end of World War II. The ruler of the neophyte Saudi state welcomed the sponsorship of the new superpower. At some point, Washington should have loosened the bond. Instead, seventy years later, Washington reflexively got on board the Saudis' grotesque air offensive against Yemen. The US supported the invasion by selling Saudi Arabia massive quantities of arms, and providing mid-air refueling to Saudi bombers: *Times*, 11/14/16. Washington's lame justification was the alleged need to prevent Riyadh from trying to abort the 2016 nuclear understanding with Iran. The counter-argument is that the positive effect of US opposition to the Saudi-Yemeni War should have carried enough weight in Tehran to outweigh the negative effect of appeasing paranoia in Riyadh.

In bellicose Saudi Arabia, women have not been able to drive or to vote in national elections. They generally need official permission to travel alone: *Vanity Fair*, 7/27/10, Maureen Dowd. In victimized Yemen, women can drive, vote, and move freely: *Times*, July 1994, David Killian; *The Week*, 7/27/16.

Superiority Complex – In our own display of the corruptive influence of power, US belligerence abroad is defended by the US government and media. The US is represented as the benevolent superpower on a mission to boost less-favored states and save them from "extremism".

George Bush 43's "National Security Strategy" of September 2002 was the apogee of nationalistic hubris. He had the panache to denounce states that "display no regard for international law" – one year before US forces ran roughshod over international law in his incomprehensible invasion of Iraq.

His manifesto of 2002 reached its climax by the assertion that "Our forces will be strong enough to dissuade potential adversaries from … hopes of surpassing … the power of the United States". The denouement cites "a battle for the future of the Muslim world" as if their future is as much our business as theirs: *NYR*, 11/19/15, review of

American Foreign Policy and its Thinkers, Perry Anderson. Washington has taken on itself arbitrary responsibility for life and death. Usamah bin Ladin, unarmed, was shot down (and martyrized): *Harper's*, 5/2/11, David Bromwich.

"The United States is the sole guarantor of Gulf security": *MEP*, Fall 2004. Obama reportedly bought into Rumsfeld's view of the world as a perpetual battlefield, with the US as the referee: David Cole, 1/25/12. The Middle East is "desperate for American leadership": *Times*, 10/25/16. Romney's campaign rhetoric alleged "there is a longing for American leadership". The administration of liberal President Obama sought an American presence potent enough to exclude jihadists from the post-Asad Syrian government, and to guarantee Israel's nuclear monopoly in the region.

George Kennan warned of the impossible dream of determining the political realities in foreign countries. Vis-à-vis the US, the only Arab longing is for arms, money, and military support.

Overemphasis on Military Solutions

Washington deplores the absence of democratic regimes in the Middle East. It does not highlight its own readiness to join in the anti-democratic violence. Home-grown violence is probably an unavoidable phase of the evolutionary process, but violence by intruders is a digression. It only slows the process down.

Since 1945, the US has rung up a list of conflicts, ranging from skirmishes (Grenada) to utter devastation (Iraq). Perhaps American imperialism is no worse than the British variety, but the latter was mitigated by a dedicated Colonial Service: *Washington Post Weekly*, 3/15/04, review of *The Sorrows of Empire*, Chalmers Johnson.

1950 – Under the Tripartite Declaration, the US, Britain, and France made a quixotic commitment to counter any aggression from either side (or both?) in the Arab-Israeli conflict: Shlaim, *The Iron Wall*. The Declaration could not survive the 1956 War.

1955 – Secretary of State Dulles sparked the creation of the Baghdad Pact, under which Turkey, Iran, Iraq, Pakistan, and Britain were to mobilize Middle East regimes against Soviet infiltration, and ensure that the West had an inside track to Middle East oil. To reassure Israel that it was not being screened out, the US didn't join, but became an "observer". Pressure to recruit Jordan caused riots in Amman. By replacing Arab Legion Commander Glubb with an Arab, King Husayn won Arab acclaim. After the 1958 coup in Baghdad, Iraq withdrew from the Baghdad Pact, and it was renamed CENTO (The Central Treaty Organization). CENTO was dissolved in 1979.

1957 – The <u>Eisenhower Doctrine</u> was intended to unite Middle East states behind a US commitment to exclude Soviet influence from the region and to ensure Western access to the Persian Gulf, if necessary by force. The only state to join was Lebanon, then under Maronite control. Eisenhower sent an expeditionary force to deal with Lebanon's first civil war, but Army Commander Fu'ad Shihab negotiated a truce, and the American force went home.

1980 – In his State of the Union address, Carter proclaimed the <u>Carter Doctrine</u>: Any hostile move to gain control of the Persian Gulf would be quelled – if necessary by force. His police force would be the Rapid Deployment Force.

1980 – For no apparent reason except to spite Khomeini, who had just ousted the Shah and denounced Israel, the US Fifth Fleet became actively involved on the Iraqi side in the inconclusive but lethal eight-year war between Iraq and Iran. This action led to the burgeoning of America's provocative military presence in the Arab Gulf states: *MEP*, Summer 2015, Chas Freeman.

1981 – Reagan expanded the Carter Doctrine of 1980 by stating that the US should protect not only Saudi Arabia but also the Saudi regime: "Saudi Arabia must not be allowed to fall like Iran".

1983 – Secretary of State Alexander Haig broke one of America's own rules by allowing US ground, air, and naval forces to participate intermittently in the Israeli invasion of Lebanon.

1983 – Reagan created CENTCOM (The Central Command) to guard Persian Gulf oil. Carter's Rapid Deployment Force became part of it.

1989 – After eight years of Soviet occupation of Afghanistan, the Mujahidin force created by the US and Saudi Arabia forced the Russians out. The Mujahidin then turned against the US, under the initiative of Usamah bin Ladin's Al Qa'idah: *LRB*, 12/19/13, Owen Bennett-Jones.

1990 – The US began to step up military operations in the Middle East. US troops in the region began taking heavier casualties: Bacevich.

1991 – After a few days of deep thought, George Bush 41 mobilized a huge coalition to expel the Iraqi invaders from Kuwait. Many countries sent troops, but US forces did most of the fighting. The expulsion took four days, but the Americans inflated their mission to six weeks of "near apocalyptic" devastation of Iraq – carpeting it with a million tons of munitions, including uranium-tipped shells that may have bequeathed birth defects to the offspring of Iraqis and Americans alike: *Harper's*, James Bill. The action included leveling trenches with helpless conscripts still in them, strafing sitting-duck Iraqi convoys (Elaine Sciolino) whose mad effort to flee north was clear evidence that they had given up, and as late as March 1991 obliteration of an Iraqi unit deep in its own country. In 1995, former US Commander Schwarzkopf lamely "explained" the strafing of the escaping convoys by noting that he had orders to destroy as much Iraqi military equipment as possible, and that the victims were "a bunch of rapists, murderers, and thugs": *Stars and Stripes*, 2/23/03, Joseph Giordano.

A more sensitive assessment, delicately phrased, appeared in the autobiography of Colin Powell, Chairman of the Joint Chiefs at the time of Gulf War I: "TV coverage was starting to make it look as if we were engaged in slaughter for slaughter's sake …": *My American Journey*, Colin Powell.

The overkill by the US military painted a vindictive picture, which was amplified by the draconian implementation of UNSC Resolution 661 of August 16, 1990. It imposed on Iraq economic sanctions explicitly intended to disable Iraq's military establishment.

Why was Washington so severe?

Possible explanations: 1) resentment of Saddam's temerity in challenging American dominance of the Persian Gulf; 2) playing to the crowd. It is a tragic defect of the democratic system that the unstudied convictions of the electorate can lead governments to adopt erroneous policies: After the bloody American expulsion of the Iraqis from Kuwait in 1991, Bush 41's approval rating shot up to 83 percent; 3) DOD's obsession with power; 4) showing off for Israel: Bush had prevailed on Prime Minister Shamir not to retaliate on Israel's own account, which was considerable. Some 40 Scuds landed in Israel, killing one person, and leading Israel to declare its first nuclear alert. Saddam's Iraq was the first Arab state to evade Israel's vow of always taking responsibility for its own defense. More serious – the Iraqi bid for Kuwait had conjured up the nightmare specter of Arab union. The theme of Arab Manifest Destiny is anathema in Zionist circles.

Iraq posed a grave threat to Israel, but none to the security of the US. In fact, Iraqi annexation of Kuwait would have been in the ultimate interest of the US, insofar as it advanced the cause of Middle East unity.

1993 – The Clinton administration outbid its predecessor by endorsing the strategy of <u>Dual Containment</u> of <u>both</u> Iraq and Iran – although it had no visible consequences. For ten years thereafter, America exacerbated Iraq's misery by a series of coup attempts and destructive air strikes: 1993 – Missile attack in retaliation for an alleged assassination plot against Bush 41 while he was on a visit to Kuwait; Randolph Ryan opined in *The Boston Globe* that Pentagon politics had violated the Constitutional requirement that Congress decide on acts of war; 1994 – Clinton's instructions to the CIA to arrange Saddam's ouster; 1996 – support for a coup effort by Iyad 'Allawi, which ended in fiasco; 1998 – A four-day wave of air strikes, which redounded to Washington's disadvantage, since the UN's prior withdrawal of its arms inspectors denied the Americans an illegal intelligence channel and enabled Saddam to discard his inspection agreement with Secretary General Annan on the grounds that the withdrawal of the inspectors showed their job was done.

1998 – In the early years of the US/UN sanctions against Iraq, Washington regarded them as a means to hold Iraq to Security Council Resolutions 687 (no WMD's) and 688 (no repression of Kurds and Shiites). Later on, Washington began to look on them as devices for ousting Saddam. In 1998 Clinton signed the Iraq Liberation Act, which embodied that specific objective.

2001 – The severity of the 9/11 attacks on the US suggested that bin Ladin's intention was to goad the US into a radical response: Either a decision to back away from its 55-year intrusion into the Middle East, or – more likely – mindless overreaction. The Bush 43 administration fell into the trap: *NY*, 3/28/16, George Packer. The White House and Congress merged their outrage in the proclamation of the Global War on Terror, and the passage in October of the Patriot Act to enhance the powers of specified federal agencies to participate in that war.

Years later, *The Nation* condemned Karl Rove's "Orwellian use of language" as elevating common criminals to the status of legitimate combatants: *Nation*, 12/14/15, Juan Cole. The jihadists, despite their non-recognition, were genuine combatants in the regional power struggle, whereas the US had no justification for its participation.

2001 – In the process of dealing with Al Qaʿidah, perpetrator of the 9/11 attacks, the US got itself into a pointless war against the Afghan Taliban. Fifteen years later, Washington still stations troops there in an effort to avoid taking the rap for another lost war.

2001 – America's unending, all-purpose, illegal, insidious drone war against Islamist activists across the Middle East and East Africa was a byproduct of the Afghan War. Observers believe this exercise in Jovian vengeance is a major cause of anti-Americanism: *Times*, 4/14/15; *MEP*, Summer 2015, Chas Freeman; Jeremy Scahill; *Project Syndicate*, 12/22/15, Jeffrey D. Sachs.

2003 – As the protagonist of Arab Nationalism, and the only state to have dropped missiles on Israel, Iraq was already in Washington's sights. George Bush 43, who was said to share with Wilson and Carter the belief that he was an instrument of God's will, was confident that invasion of Iraq was a good way to advance his goal of a democratic Middle East: *NY*, 7/4/16, Thomas Mallon. The American invasion of Iraq has acquired a legendary reputation as the catalyst that plunged the region into an ethnic power struggle.

2004 – On 6/28/04, the US handed sovereignty over Iraq to the interim Iraqi government. The transfer deepened the Sunni-Shia split.

Steady support for US actions in the Middle East came from the EU, which was under the thumb of the US: *LRB*, Tariq Ali.

2006 – "The crimes of the US have been constant, vicious, remorseless": *Times*, 10/21/06, remarks in Harold Pinter's Nobel Prize acceptance speech.

2009 – Obama was elected President largely on his recognition that the invasion of Iraq was wrong. The chorus of neocons and pro-Zionist liberals intimidated him into agreeing that the invasion of Afghanistan was right. By early 2009, he knew better, but he never found a graceful way to say so – not even after November 2010, when Ambassador Karl Eikenberry, highly credentialed as the former commander of US troops in Afghanistan, cabled from Kabul that the US could never conquer the whole country: *Harper's*, June 2015, David Bromwich.

2009 – On June 4, Obama delivered in Cairo the conciliatory speech he had promised. "A New Beginning" quoted from the Qur'an, and gave a half-hearted defense of the invasion of Iraq. He defended the invasion of Afghanistan, but his promise to withdraw the troops by 2012 may have contained a hint that the invasion clashed with his liberal instincts: Tomgram of 8/27/09 (www.tomdispatch.com) citing Chalmers Johnson.

2009 – Late in the year, Obama escalated the US fighting in Afghanistan – perhaps in reaction to Hillary Clinton's campaign charge that he was unqualified to lead the US in an emergency. If so, "he paid Clinton back by making her Secretary of State, directly responsible for Afghanistan": *Harper's*, June 2015, Bromwich.

2009 – US hawks, conservative and liberal, have kept the US a national-security state for over 60 years: *Nation*, 12/21/09.

2011 – Having been denied diplomatic immunity for its troops by the new Iraqi authorities the US had helped install, the US agreed to withdraw from Iraq by the end of the year. It left behind a mangled infrastructure, a confused bureaucracy, and the simulation of a government, which had taken refuge from assassination in the Green Zone, the redoubt of a giant American Embassy.

2014 – Constant American bombing of Al Qa'idah operatives had killed some of its leaders, and dispersed the rest: *Times*, 6/1/14. In Syria,

556

US air strikes on installations of Nusrah may have tipped Idlib Province to Nusrah control.

2015 – The CIA was the tip of the spear in the US Drone War, from Yemen to Pakistan. The day-after-day hunt for Islamists was a grim process that had degraded the CIA into a torture chamber: *NYR*, 2/5/15, Mark Danner and Hugh Eakin. The DIA was reporting to DOD, the FBI to the Department of Justice, and INR to the State Department. The only intelligence agency that reported directly to the President was the CIA. Its Director was a Presidential appointee.

2015 – At the end of the year, there were 10,000 troops in Afghanistan. The Taliban were still advancing.

2016 – Some 5000 troops had returned to Iraq, and were taking casualties: *Times*, 4/12/16.

2016 – In his second term, Obama was sharply reducing the frequency of killer-drone attacks, and shut down CIA safe-houses overseas, but US Special Operations teams were operating in 70 countries: *NYR*, 9/29/16, Mark Danner.

2008-16 – Over his two terms in office, Obama approved 543 drone strikes that killed 3797 people. Congress has never updated the Authorization for the Use of Military Force it adopted on 9/11/01: *Times* (editorial), 3/16/17.

Exploitation – Overseas: How Did Our Oil Get Under Their Sand?

On the precedent of Disraeli's purchase of shares of the Suez Canal Company, Winston Churchill bought up 51 percent of shares in the Anglo-Persian Oil Co. (later the Anglo-Iranian Oil Co., AIOC, and then British Petroleum). World War I was looming and the Royal Navy needed oil: *Wall Street Journal*, Summer 2002. For a time, 84 percent of AIOC profits went to the British government: *LRB*, 6/28/12.

1953 – The worst case of US exploitation overseas was the CIA's first major operation of the Cold War, whereby Washington joined the UK in financing a coup against Iranian Prime Minister Mohammed Mossadeq: *LRB*, 6/28/12. London wanted him out because of his campaign to nationalize the AIOC. In Washington, President Eisenhower, new to the Middle East, was misinformed by the Dulles brothers (John Foster at State, Allen at the CIA) that Mossadeq wanted to sell out Iran to the Soviets: *Washington Post Weekly*, 12/22/86, John Prados. Another objective, at least for the Dulles brothers, was to make the Middle East safe for US oil companies: *Overthrow*, Stephen Kinzer.

Exploitation – Domestic

In his 1961 Farewell Address, President Eisenhower did the nation a vital service by reviving the term "Military-Industrial Complex" in a warning to the American people that the government's support for a state-of-the-art arms industry can serve the industry's interest in distorting that relationship from patriotism to greed. Political delicacy may have led Eisenhower to abbreviate the original version of the term – Military-Industrial-Congressional Complex – but it should be reinstated to spread awareness of the incestuous relationship that tempts the industry and members of Congress to collude in padding the military budget. Perhaps the dispersal of subsidiary arms-makers to most states, if not to all, is more than coincidence: *Atlantic*, January 2015, James Fallows review of *Self-Destruction*, Cecil Currey.

Double Standard

"Terrorism" is defined in the *American Heritage Dictionary* as "the use of violence … for political goals". Leaving war aside, it might be impossible to find a state that has never resorted to that offense. Nevertheless, Washington draws a casuistic distinction between the "terrorism" practiced by its adversaries and the "counter-terrorism" practiced by the US. Their suicide bombings may be more barbaric than our shooting down an unarmed bin Ladin without due process, but on the scale of legality or morality, both actions are equally indefensible. The Israeli construal of its lockdown of the inhabitants of Gaza as self-defense – with Washington's concurrence – is a flagrant case of sophistry. The lockdown is an exercise in sadism: *LRB*, 6/15/17, Sara Roy.

For most Americans, jihadists are terrorists. For many Arabs, they are patriots.

Due Process Flouted – By holding Jihadist suspects at Guantanamo, or torturing suspects without legal recourse, the US has desecrated the honored Anglo-American institution of habeas corpus – first regularized in the early 1500's, in the reign of Henry VII. Khalid Shaykh Muhammad, architect of the 9/11 operation, has been held for years without trial, and undergone 183 episodes of waterboarding. He might be found liable to execution under US law, but his case has not come up. If he were tried under military law as a soldier, perhaps he would receive a lighter sentence. After 9/11, Bush 43 elevated "terrorists" to the status of belligerents, though not combatants.

Security Guarantees – Guaranteeing the survival of a state sounds benign, but closer examination reveals that awarding a security ticket to a favored state automatically subverts the security of the neighboring states not so favored. The Tripartite Declaration's blanket commitment to police both sides in the Arab-Israeli dispute was fanciful. In a tumultuous environment, guaranteeing an obsolete political structure is retrogressive, and guaranteeing the security of a specific state is a devious way of taking sides. For any state that has no vital interest in a region, taking sides therein is incautious policy. The US has gone even further by using its power to bulldoze inconvenient regimes, factions, and movements out of the way: *JPS*, Spring 2000, Pascal Boniface; *LRB*, 3/3/16, Bennett-Jones. The US has no guarantee against sudden upsets. In 1979, the Shah's docile regime was abruptly replaced by a vehement critic of US policy – Ayatollah Khomeini. In 1990, Saddam abruptly switched from ally to enemy when he challenged the West by invading a sacrosanct source of Arab oil.

In 1988, Washington bailed Saddam out of the war with Iran. Four years later, Washington made the arrangements for his execution.

Inconsistency

Before World War II, the Middle East rarely came up on American radar. Washington trusted the UK to keep the region under control, as it had more or less for 200 years. After the war, imperceptibly at first, Washington drifted into the role of Britain's successor, but without the experience required to formulate a coherent overall policy. Instead, the US tried to deal with each new problem on the basis of trial and error. The result was a haphazard assortment of policies that were sometimes in conflict with each other. Washington's preoccupations were access to oil, the welfare of Israel, and an orderly environment in which to pursue them. Washington has never admitted that the interests of the Muslim states and Zionist Israel are irreconcilable.

1991 – After Kuwait had been rescued from the clutches of Iraq (whose claim to Kuwait is not all that weak), Washington congratulated itself on a job well done. It took a while for onlookers to realize that, in saving Kuwait, the US had wrecked Iraq. Aside from the pointless war damage, Washington had managed to break Iraq into three pieces, a Shiite south, a Sunni northwest, and a Kurdish northeast – all this caused by the superpower whose stated objective was to keep Iraq intact: Joshua Hammer, 11/10/16.

2003 – It seems the US hadn't done enough. The invasion of Iraq and the subsequent punitive sanctions finished the hatchet job. The eight-year occupation ended in Iraq's rapprochement with its recent enemy – and Washington's new enemy – Iran: *NYR*, 6/23/16, Ruthven and Lynch. The Iraqi chapter of the Global War on Terror ended in the unceremonious withdrawal of the American ground troops, but not American air cover. Iraq's attempt to regain Mawsil was dependent on intense American bombing, on help on the ground from Shiite militias mobilized by Iran, and on Kurdish troops – who would do their best to annex any territory they would choose to capture.

In the words of Patrick Cockburn, the assertion that the US and allies are sponsoring a third force of "moderate" rebels to fight both Asad and the IS is fantasy. No Sunni rebel had any interest in signing up with Washington's arbitrary inconsistency: *Times*, 4/18/16. The administration professed hostility to the Shiite regime in Damascus, but cooperated with the Shiite regime in Baghdad and took the Sunni side in Yemen: *Times*, 11/8/14. Of all the contenders in the Middle East power struggle, the IS had been the only one the US was eager to fight, until November 2016, when Obama announced a military effort versus Nusrah – although Nusrah was based in Idlib Province, in the Russian zone: *NYR*, 12/22/16, Roth.

2008 – The US maneuvered itself into subsidizing Iraq's two Arab factions, Sunni and Shia, whereas the only pro-US faction was the Kurds: Cockburn.

2014 – The US was shipping arms to one enemy of the US (Hizballah) for use against another enemy of the US (the IS).

2016 – In the Saudi-Yemeni War, the US was siding with Saudi Arabia against the Huthis, but with the Huthis against AQAP.

2011-16 – **The Longest Conventional War in US History** – The US invaded Afghanistan on 10/7/01. The war was unnecessary, but it has been as hard to end as the war in Vietnam. Once again Washington has fallen into the not-on-my-watch trap. We're in a war we can't win, but no administration dares to take the responsibility for losing it. Instead, we have seen fifteen years of fighting to save face. In 2010, US troop strength there was 100,000. As of 1/1/17, we had whittled that number down to 8400, but we're still there. Over that fifteen years, Washington, dogged by a war that won't stop, has issued a bewildering series of announcements of planned escalation or withdrawal that add up to a tale of utter frustration. As 2017 arrived, the 30,000 Taliban guerillas were holding their own against Afghanistan's 352,000 armed defenders, and an Afghan branch of the IS was taking shape. The Afghan government was receiving financial and military support from the US. Pakistan's Inter-Services Intelligence agency (ISI) participated in the founding of the Afghan Taliban. Ever since, the ISI had provided them covert assistance, including arms and safe haven in Pakistan: *Harper's*, February 2017, Mary Jeong.

1952-2016 – **Turkey Gets the Procrustean Treatment** – The US recruitment of Turkey into NATO in 1952 gave Turkey a sense of greater security against the expansionist instincts of Russia. In return,

Washington has sought Turkish support for American projects in the Middle East, but Turkey, as a Middle Eastern state, can't identify with those American objectives that clash with majority opinion in the region. Citizens of Turkey have been active in the campaign to end the Israeli blockade of Gaza. US pressure on Turkey to join the anti-IS coalition is distruptive. It clashes with Turkey's interest in the solidarity of the Sunni community in Turkey and the Arab states. The US has not complied with Turkey's request for the extradition of Fethullah Gulen and associates who are living in the US. After the 8/9/16 meeting of Erdogan in Moscow, some Turks saw the NATO-Turkish relationship in crisis: *Al-Monitor's Turkey Pulse*, 8/18/16, Metin Gurcan.

2011-2016 – **Indecision in Syria** – If any regime is deserving of obliteration, it is the Asad machine in Damascus. For the past six years, in the petty interest of its own survival, it has waged a vicious war against its own citizens. 470,000 Syrians are reported dead. 200,000 are in prison. Thousands of the prisoners will never be seen again. With Russian collusion, Damascus has adopted a deliberate strategy to depopulate rebel-held areas by genocidal means like barrel bombs. Legitimate air attack doesn't win wars, but carpet-bombing does – especially if it is supplemented by siege tactics to starve people out: *NYR*, 12/22/16, Kenneth Roth.

The Europeans have been indirect victims of the carnage, which has driven floods of desperate refugees north. On dual grounds of humanitarianism and self-interest, the Europeans could have responded, but the EU is not ready for collective action. The only capability of effective intervention rested with the US. President Obama couldn't ignore the crisis, but he could not bring himself to take the risks of direct intervention – such as setting up No-Fly Zones – so he equivocated. He called on Asad to abdicate, and warned him not to use poison gas, but sat back when Asad called his bluff. He authorized the CIA to provide weapons to rebels, but he excluded the most effective militias (the IS and Nusrah) because they were "terrorists" (jihadists), and he denied the "moderates" ground-to-air missiles for fear they would leak to the jihadists: *Current History*, December 2016, Faysal Itani; *Times*, 4/23/16, 9/22/16. Later on, Obama unleashed an air war against the IS.

Short-Range Thinking – The Vietnam War gave rise to the saying that "We had to destroy the city to save it". In the Middle East, that vision has come true. Iraq is a huge example, Fallujah a small one. Recapture from the IS left the city in ruins. There has been no sign of planning for its reconstruction. Imperialism is better qualified for destruction than for construction.

Retrogression

The Alawites want to turn the clock back to pre-civil-war Syria. The jihadists want to turn the clock ahead to a whole new Middle East. Washington has condemned Alawite brutality, but in a tolerant way – unlike the paranoia it feels about Jihadism. The White House has not explained the paradox, but perhaps no explanation is needed: 1) We know that Washington is on the side of retrogression; 2) We know that Washington is dead set against the Jihadist plan. By destroying the Jihadist community, Washington seeks to preserve the Zionist community.

So in the name of peace, Washington is making a contribution to the bloodshed. American use of force has boosted Jihadist recruitment, and augmented the millions of Middle Easterners who share Jihadist doctrine: *MEP*, Winter 2016, Lia. Americans who see change inscribed on the wall of history believe events have already exploded the facile thesis of the "Global War on Terrorism" that "it is better to fight them over there than over here."

Washington tries to mask its guilt by laying blame for Middle East violence on Islamic culture. Obama has spoken of "a violent, radical, fanatical, nihilistic interpretation of Islam by a … tiny faction … within the Muslim community …". Many Islamists are bigoted and fanatical, but that does not alter the fact that their grievances against the US are legitimate. What we call "terrorism" is resistance to US imperialism. That problem can be suppressed only by remediation of imperialistic offenses: *Washington Post*, 3/28/16, Arun Kundnani.

The American effort to resuscitate the contrived nationalism of the Sykes-Picot era has immersed the Middle East in a regional war of ethnic communalism. The likely consequence will be the demise of the American imperium in the evolution of a homegrown hegemonic system: *Times*, 9/27/15; *FA*, November 2015, Stephen Walt.

Political Deadlock in the Middle East

The last regional hegemony expired with the collapse of the empires of Muhammad 'Ali in Egypt, the Safavids in Persia, and the Ottomans in Anatolia. The rise of the next hegemony awaits resolution of the regional power struggle, which is undeclared but the operative composite of the ongoing welter of parochial conflicts.

Of all these conflicts, the most stubborn is that between Israel and Muslims over the 10,000-square-mile territory known to the Arabs as Palestine, but controlled since 1967 by Israel.

Israel expelled most Palestinian Arab occupants in the wars of 1948 and 1967. The agreement that Carter negotiated at Camp David with Israel's Begin and Egypt's Sadat was hailed as a diplomatic triumph, although the people most directly concerned, the Palestinian Arabs, were sold down the river: *LRB*, 11/5/15, Thrall. Most of them are penned up in futureless refugee camps in neighboring states. Nearly two million have been consigned to the unending ordeal of life in Gaza, which is stateless, hopeless, and unique in the history of communal abuse.

The Middle East may never see peace until this conflict is resolved.

Washington's Mistakes

The American assumption from the Europeans of leadership in the Middle East went astray from the start. In 1945, the world's leading democracy assumed in the Middle East quasi-imperialist powers. In 1948, this anomalous authority implanted an alien state at the geopolitical fulcrum of the Muslim world. The impetuous designation of Zionist Israel as a ward of American imperialism vested the US with ultimate leverage over the Israeli government, but Washington has studiously neglected the attendant responsibilities. It has intervened as needed to keep Israeli expansionism within viable borders, but not to check Israel's discrimination against the three Arab communities within those borders – 1.7 million second-class citizens in Israel, 2.7 million Arab subjects in the West Bank, and 1.9 million Arab prisoners in Gaza: *The World Almanac, 2017* (statistics).

The Freeze – So far, Washington's 70-year effort to tranquilize the Middle East has had no visible effect except the exacerbation of the regional power struggle. In 1946, Americans on the balcony of their Beirut Legation smiled as a gaggle of teenagers threw rocks – not realizing that they were witnesses to the genesis of anti-Americanism. In 2017, every American in the Middle East is looking over his or her shoulder. The US has been drawn, or trapped, into wars in Afghanistan and Syria, and three wars in Iraq. Of the eighteen wars reviewed herein, Israel has been a combatant in eight. By its support for Zionist Israel, democratic America has become the champion of the ethnic communalism that is fueling Middle Eastern bloodshed.

Israel has always been on the lookout for allies in the region. Its alliance with the Lebanese Maronites collapsed after the Syrians occupied Lebanon. Its understanding with Turkey is still valid, but it was shaken in 2003 by the Turkish Parliament's opposition to the invasion of Iraq, and in 2009 by Turkish outrage at the intensity of the Israel assault on the Gaza Strip.

Israel is not a democracy. US Middle East policy is not democratic. To make Israel safer, the US favors pliable Arab autocracies: *LRB*, Bennett-Jones.

Free Ride for Israel – From the day Israel was founded, it has had cast-iron insurance against financial collapse or military defeat. American foreign policy has been preempted by domestic politics, which has ordained that what's good for Israel is good for the US. This postulate liberates Israel from the normal responsibilities of an independent state. In time of Middle East crisis, the Israeli desk officer in Washington is the President. Edward Snowden reportedly uncovered documentation that the paramount goal of US Middle East policy is the survival of Israel: *WRMEA*, May 2016, Grant Smith.

Over half of America's total annual military aid goes to Israel: *LRB*, 11/5/15, Nathan Thrall. In 1967, the IDF routed the armies of Syria,

Jordan, and Egypt. In 2015, Israel was viewed in Washington as the most powerful state in the Middle East: *MEP*, Summer 2015.

The US has come to Israel's support in many ways:

1973 – Rush shipments of arms to help Israel repel the Syrian and Egyptian surprise attacks.

1980's – Encouragement of Israeli aggression against Lebanon.

1983-4 – Naval action against anti-Israeli forces in Lebanon.

1991 – Summary expulsion of Iraqi occupation forces from Kuwait.

1994 – Dual Containment: Clinton's effort to protect Israel from attack by either of its two worst enemies, Iraq and Iran: *MEP*, Summer 2015, Chas Freeman, Jr.

2001 – Start of the US Drone War against Islamist operatives from Al Qa'idah and the AQI (later the IS).

2003 – Overthrow of the Saddam regime in Iraq. One of the American goals in that war was to promote Arab-Israeli peace on Israeli terms: *MEP*, Spring 2003, Harlan Ullman. Concomitant to Israel's security guarantee is a tacit obligation to guard against any threat from another state: *MEP*, Summer 2015, Freeman. This means Washington's constant calibration of the military power of every conceivable enemy of Israel.

2011 – After UNESCO admitted Palestine to membership on 10/23/11, the US terminated its funding for UNESCO.

2016 – The US and Israel signed a Memorandum of Understanding. One of its provisions was 38 billion dollars' worth of military aid, 20 percent of which will finance the supply to Israel of two squadrons of F-35's: *LRB*, Daniel Soar.

American Sacrifices on Israel's Behalf – The price of American overreach in the Middle East is escalating anti-Americanism. Washington has been living a lie. It has made no effort to refute the pro-Zionist fictions that basic Israeli and American goals coincide, that Washington is neutral in the Arab-Israeli conflict, and that Israel is a strategic asset to the US. Reality is just the opposite, as events have repeatedly demonstrated.

Cover-Ups – The Foreign Assistance Act of 1961, as amended, bans US aid to states with a clandestine nuclear option. This subject is taboo in Washington: www.mondoweiss.net, 4/21/15, Freeman.

The Israeli claim of mystification about the USS Liberty doesn't fly. Its operations and function were no secret to the Israeli High Command, which may have ordered that it be sunk to eliminate any risk that Washington would intervene if it discovered Israel's determination to capture the Golan Heights at any cost: *The Passionate Attachment*, George Ball/Douglas Ball; *WRMEA*, June/July 2017, Ernest A. Gallo.

Johnson tried to hush up the attack. Reportedly, he ordered Admiral Isaac Kidd to interview every American survivor. During the interviews, the Admiral – minus his stars – reportedly ordered each man to say nothing about the attack. The DOD omitted from its subsequent comments the fact that the survivors had watched Israeli planes and boats fire on the ship and the lifeboats it had launched: Ennes; *WRMEA*.

In the absence of an official US/Israeli inquiry, we may never know the whole truth.

Nuclear Favoritism – The US saved itself and its allies in World War II by solving the nuclear riddle before the Nazis did. The only use of nuclear weapons was the two American bombs that blasted Hiroshima and Nagasaki. Ever since, nations have sought ways to ensure that nuclear weapons will never be used again. The Cold War was an era of tension between two nuclear powers, the US and the USSR. That experience suggests that the best way to guard against a future use of nuclear weapons is to avoid nuclear monopoly in hostile situations, in accordance with the theory of MAD, mutual assured destruction (the actuality, not the rejected strategy). The US violated this postulate three times: 1) by helping Israel acquire a nuclear monopoly in the Middle East; 2) by trying to prevent all other states in the Middle East from access to nuclear weapons; 3) by the agreement between Nixon and Meir to practice nuclear ambiguity: Never confirm the well-known fact that Israel has nuclear weapons: *WRMEA*, 3/18/16, Roger Mattson.

The nuclear agreement concluded between Iran and the joint Western powers attempts to defer the problem by dissuading Iran from trying to match Israel in the nuclear arena for at least ten years.

The Western powers are engaged in a joint effort to dissuade Iran from trying to match Israel in the nuclear arena, at least for the life of their agreement. This violation of the principle of equal opportunity for all individuals and all states is presumably defended on the arbitrary ground that the government of Iran is more fanatical than the government of Israel.

In any case, the Netanyahu administration rejects the agreement (*LRB*, 11/5/15, Thrall) on the ground that its wording would put Iran on the road to legitimation as a nuclear threshold state. Netanyahu took advantage of the chasm between the Democratic administration and the Republican Congress to accept an opportunity to deliver in Congress a speech challenging Obama's nuclear policy in his own capital.

US-Israeli Tension – On 12/23/16, Obama shocked Israel by abstaining on UNSC Resolution 2334, which condemned construction for prospective Jewish settlements in the West Bank. The relationship between the US and Israel had hit a new low in tenor, though not in practice.

For the last 70 years, the Zionists have joined the rest of the Middle East in its primitive failure to distinguish between random communal affiliations and reasoned national associations. An overall solution to the Palestine dispute is out of sight, but an attendant crisis cries out for respite. It dates from 2005, when Washington failed to prevent Sharon from bungling the exclusion of Gaza from the de facto Israeli state. After 13 years of gratuitous agony for 2 million catspaw Gazans, the UNGA is registering deep concern. On July 24, 1922, the League of Nations awarded Britain a temporary mandate over Palestine. The British failed in this benevolent mission. The UNGA is the League's more sophisticated successor – better equipped to initiate mentorial assignments for peace. The mission of a latterday mandate could be the restoration of the Gazans' despoiled right of self-determination. There must be impartial governments ready to introduce a new era of UN initiative – or to make amends for past mistakes.

The Jewish Legacy

Since the reign of the legendary King David 3000 years ago, the Jewish people have constructed their own religion, culture, and survival strategy.

Judaism was the first "religion of the Book". Christianity and Islam took different paths, but they borrowed from their predecessors.

The Jews are widely respected as the founders of the tradition of intellectual achievement. History suggests that from ancient times, when rabbis first championed education, literacy has facilitated the transformation of the Jews from herdsmen and farmers to craftsmen, merchants, scientists, and financiers: *Forward*, 8/28/12, Jonathan B. Kramer review of *How Education Shaped Jewish History, 70-1493*, Maristella Botticini and Zvi Eckstein.

Survival – Superpower support was probably a prerequisite for the founding of a Jewish state in the center of a Muslim region. However, grim experience has taught the tiny Jewish community in the Middle East that, in the final analysis, they must rely on their own devices. They have followed a precedent set by David Ben-Gurion before independence: maintain military superiority over all adversaries, and take every opportunity to exploit it.

In the Middle East, they regard nuclear preeminence as their last resort.

The Syndrome of Racism

The German plunge from a civilized society to demented Naziism may always be incomprehensible, but for those who grew up in the US before World War II, the elements of genteel racism were all too familiar. Humanity's universal rivalry for success and recognition has been eased for many by the existence of a community or class that could be looked down on – like statusless Blacks in the South and new immigrants in the North. Before World War II, fraternity houses were bastions of country-club racism. America's failure during the war to open its doors to all Jewish refugees from Naziism has been ascribed in part to an unacknowledged climate of racism.

In Europe, antisemitism has been sharpened by the Jews' emphasis on exclusivity: 1) strict criteria for determining who is a Jew; 2) relative disinterest of Judaism in proselytization; 3) divergence between the Jewish stress on the solidarity of every Jewish community (*Yishuv*) and the requirements of assimilation into a non-Jewish entity; 4) Marriage within the faith.

The more distinct the community, the more vulnerable it is to opprobrium.

Irresponsible regimes found that the fancied Jewish "schemers" were a convenient scapegoat for the regimes' misrule. In cases of organized hostility (general expulsion from some countries in medieval Europe, later pogroms in Eastern Europe, Holocaust in Germany), the assimilation option for Jews was preempted.

The Future of Israel

Successive Departments of State have spun their diplomatic wheels in a hopeless quest for Arab-Israeli compromise – apparently not realizing that compromise had been preempted by the American security guarantee. The American premise of a permanent Jewish state in the Muslim east is a non-starter. In disregarding this fact of life, Washington has tolerated the takeover of the Israeli government by a negativist clique that rejects compromise. Israel could not project this level of inflexibility without overdraft rights from its sponsor. Washington has not challenged Netanyahu's unilateral declaration that the Arab-Israeli conflict will never end: *FA*, July 2016, Aluf Benn. Washington has not even called Israel to account for its fraudulent claim that it is ready to compromise whenever the Arab side is ready to listen to reason. The "notion of peace negotiations ... has been little more than [an Israeli] device to perpetuate ... the occupation": *NYR*, 6/22/17, David Shulman, citing Nathan Thrall's *The Only Language They Understand*.

In one key respect, the generous American guarantee of Israel's security is a critical drawback. It encourages Israel's complacency in the magic of preeminent force. When they come to realize that six million

Jews cannot shoot their way to peace with 400 million Muslim neighbors, they will have to abandon the lure of absolute Zionism for the uncertainties of open negotiation. Associations of expediency with Islamic dictatorships can hardly compare with negotiated alliances based on lasting common interest.

Under the American umbrella, Israel has become the strongest and most advanced state in the Middle East, but the link between the US and Israel is not indelible. The US has never practiced colonization in Israel. The status of <u>protectorate</u> is transitional. Someday, unforeseen circumstances will close the American umbrella. Israel can avoid traumatization only by starting now to deal with autonomy. No one can predict what that new status would entail. It seems safe to cite some of the changes Israel will have to make:

Unite Israel – The idea of partition of Palestine has come up over and over, but it's a nonstarter. In its contentious neighborhood, an independent Palestine, whether Jewish or Arab, would be too small and hemmed in to be subdivided. Israel will have to erase the artificial borders separating "the West Bank" and "the Gaza Strip" from the rest of the country.

Democratize – To live in peace with its neighbors, Israel will have to do the US a service – and itself a priceless favor – by aiming for total democracy, instead of democracy for Jews only. Israel must free "settlement" from its invidious connotation.

Israelis: Join the Neighborhood – There are Israelis for whom Muslims killing Muslims is grounds for schadenfreude. They will have to learn that geography rules. Jews and Muslims are in the same boat.

Americans: Step Aside

If the United States had been a going concern in the 1600's, and had made a commitment to guarantee the survival of one of the contenders in the Thirty Years War between Catholics and Protestants, it would have been powerless to determine the outcome. In the Middle East 400 years later, there is an analogous sectarian war building between Sunnis

571

and Shiites, and Washington has bound itself to the survival of several contending states whose future no one could possibly predict.

America's Middle East policy is boxed in by its incautious obligations. They compel Washington to base its policies on the outlandish premise that Western imperialism's opportunistic arrangements for the Middle East are the norm, and that actions against them are temporary aberrations.

We Americans are no longer colonists. We are foreigners. We don't speak the languages. We're 9000 miles away. We should not presume to preempt their sovereign right of self-determination.

Envoi

As Americans were recovering from the world's worst war, they were consumed with patriotism inspired by their victory, rage as they learned of Nazi atrocities, and empathy as they heard of the horrors inflicted on anti-Nazis and Jews. There has been a powerful synergy between the American public's identification with the dramatic rise of Israel, and the flow of political contributions to members of Congress who approve. The American public has been too unschooled in the arcane world of foreign affairs to realize that the establishment of a Jewish state had to come at an excruciating price, which is being paid by all factions concerned, starting with the Palestinian victims.

The unruly peoples of the Middle East need to understand that the neutralization of the Palestinians was not only symbolic of the region's troubles, it was one of the causes. Equalization of the rights of every community is a prerequisite for the pacification of the region.

Seventy years later, Washington still doesn't admit this fact of life. The US government holds that the US and Israel are innocent victims of Islamic fanaticism. The media are happy to join in. For an op-ed in the *Washington Post Weekly* of 9/6/04, Arab union was a "leftist ideology". Too many Americans and Israelis are misled by chauvinistic folklore – call it warlore.

The rebel militias are destructive, disruptive, and brutal, but they are telltale symptoms of the necessity of reform. Those that can advance the basic needs of the region will survive. Those that can't adapt will vanish. The militias' immediate targets are foreign interference and domestic misrule. Their ultimate goal should be to replace the superstitions of outmoded communalism with the sovereign prescription – democracy.

2016 was a good year for imperialism. Russian air power enabled the Damascus regime to reconquer Aleppo; US air power enabled the Baghdad regime to reconquer Mawsil. Both Moscow and Washington seem to have suppressed recent experience with Afghanistan: Moscow gave up there after ten years; Washington is groping for a way to get out after 16 years. Whenever we leave an occupied country, its inhabitants will still be there to pave over most of what we left behind.

While trapped in the twisted logic of political expedience, Washington looks for military measures to bail us out of our political mistakes. The Founders would not approve. They fought the Revolutionary War for the right to issue the Declaration of Independence. They then drafted a Constitution that guards the nation against the poisons of communalism by stressing separation of church and state.

Global Escalation? – Arab states fought five wars for Palestine. They were crushed by the IDF. Washington waits for the losers to admit defeat. Some of the regimes out there would like to, but their citizens won't. Meanwhile, Israel has run into new enemies, and the US and Russia have incurred the ominous risks of rival intervention. Could there be a stronger argument for international arbitration?

What Next? – US diplomatic approaches to solving the Palestine dispute have always been clumsy, but that reality is irrelevant if – as the writer believes – the dispute is too stark to be resolved by negotiation. The only other option in present international circumstances is blatant coercion.

Index

576

American Airlines 322, 323
American Civil Liberties Union (ACLU) 169
American Embassy (Beirut) 400
American Embassy (Cairo) 34
American Embassy (Kenya) 320
American Embassy (Tanzania) 320
American International School (Gaza) 128
American Israel Public Affairs Committee (AIPAC) 499, 502, 503
American Jewish community 498
American Joint Chiefs 63
American University of Iraq 421
Ames, Robert 80, 245
'Amir, 'Abd al Hakim 38, 44, 57
'Amiri, Hadi 374
Amiriyyah bomb shelter 144
Amman hotel bombings 465
Amnesty International 129, 136, 137, 185, 250, 254, 329, 392, 434
'Anbar Sovereignty Council 215
'Anbari, Abu 'Ali al 289, 304
'Anbari, Abu Nabil al 292
Anderson, Jon 141
Anderson, Perry 551
Anderson, Scott 456, 458
Andrews Air Force Base 325
Andropov, Yuri 79
Anfal campaign 106-108, 417
Anglo-Egyptian Treaty of 1936 30
Anglo-Egyptian Treaty of 1954 37, 337, 480
Anglo-Iranian Oil Company (AIOC) 557, 558
'Ani, Dhafir al 230
Annan, Kofi 232, 554

"Anonymous" 275-280, 283, 289, 296, 306
Ansar al Islam 198, 233, 419
Ansar al Sunnah 205
Ansar Allah 261
Ansar Bayt al Maqdis 293, 298, 304, 308, 309, 458
'Ansi, Nasir al 265
Anti-Islamic State Coalition 308, 309
apostate 443
April 6 Movement 456
AQAP (*see* Al Qa'idah in the Arabian Peninsula)
'Aqal, 'Imad 148
AQI (*see* Al Qa'idah in Iraq)
Arab arms embargo 101
Arab bloc (Israel) 476
Arab Higher Committee 15
Arab Human Development Report 484
Arab League 20, 21, 32, 49, 53, 114, 116, 130, 140, 218, 473
Arab Legion (Jordan) 25, 27, 28, 32, 56, 463, 514, 536, 552
Arab Liberation Army 21, 23, 25, 29
Arab Nationalism, Pan-Arabism 11, 13, 26, 50, 91, 143, 313, 362, 370, 463, 511, 512, 517, 555
Arab Revolt (World War I) 11, 462
Arab Revolt (1936-39) 15, 16
Arab Spring 254, 273, 274, 283, 338, 346, 384, 456, 484, 525, 530
Arab Trade Union Congress 42
'Arafat, Yasir 53, 54, 73, 76, 78, 93, 114-116, 118-121, 123, 148, 361, 395, 464, 473

578

Ayyubid Dynasty 404
Azeris 235
Azimi, Negar 446, 459
'Aziz, Tariq 92, 103

Baathist (*Ba'th*) 77, 88, 91, 100,
  140-143, 200, 203, 204, 218,
  219, 221, 222, 229, 231, 237,
  239, 274, 275, 280, 293, 299,
  368, 377, 379-382, 370, 388,
  407, 414, 461, 489, 493, 508,
  511, 514
Babylonians 100
Bacevich, Andrew 481, 547, 553
Badr Brigade 100, 101, 178, 200,
  210, 215, 219, 221, 242, 362-
  365, 373-375, 377, 379
Badr al Din, Mustafa 259, 402
Baghdad College 141
Baghdad Pact 34, 464, 551
Baghdad regime President 421,
  422
Baghdad regime Prime Minister
  178, 421, 424
Baghdad regime's ground forces
  418
Baghdadi, Abu Bakr al (Ibrahim
  al Badri al Qurayshi) 176,
  186, 276, 282, 283, 285, 286,
  289, 291, 295, 296, 300, 303-
  305, 315, 329, 330, 526
Baghdadi, Abu 'Umar al 218,
  227, 231, 281
Bahaji, Sa'id 321, 322
Bahgat, Gawdat 214
Baker, James 143, 216
Baker, Peter 168, 454, 524
Baktiari, Barbara 363
Balad Party (Israel) 478
Balawi, Humam al 329

Balfour Declaration 8, 14, 470,
  498
Balfour, Arthur 14, 470
Bali', Muhammad 153
Ball, Douglas 567
Ball, George 40, 74, 567
Ballout, Mohammed 390
Baluchis 446
Bamford, James 42, 325, 484
Ban Ki-Moon 129, 301, 436, 477
Bani Hashim (Qurayshi) 285
Bani-Sadr, Abolhassan 97, 110,
  361
Bank of Palestine 152
Banna, Hasan al 337, 447
Bar Lev Line 51, 59, 62, 69, 514
Bar-Joseph, Uri 71
Barak, Ehud 117, 119, 474, 476
Barakat, Hisham 304, 460
Barghuti, Marwan 149
Barkey, Henri 354
Barnard, Anne 133, 154, 391,
  392
Barnet, Richard J. 68
Baroud, Ramzi 529
Barri, Nabih 248
Barry, John 210
Baruch, Bernard 480
Barzani, Mahmud 11
Barzani, Mas'ud 196, 201, 211,
  222, 242, 413, 418-423, 429,
  542
Barzani, Masrur 222, 422, 425
Barzani, Mustafa 93, 415
Barzani, Nechirvan 219
Barzani-Talabani feud 194, 423
Barzanji, Mahmud 9
Bashir, 'Umar al 317
Basij (Iran) 96, 99, 110
Batati, Saeed al 266
Batatu, Hanna 141

Brennan, John 170
Brezhnev, Leonid 67, 68
Brill, Steven 325
Britain-Iraq Alliance of 1924 11
Britain-Iraq Treaty of 1922 11
Britain-Iraq Treaty of 1930 12
Britannica 6-13, 72, 73, 86, 88,
    96, 156, 246, 272, 292, 360,
    369, 404, 445, 447, 455, 463,
    467, 470, 498, 537, 538
British Air Force 39, 146, 159,
    304, 510, 511
British Colonial Service 551
British ground forces 510
British Labor Party 19
British Mandate for Palestine
    463, 510
British Navy 14, 510
British Petroleum (BP) 228
British War Office 471
Bromwich, David 551, 556
Brooke, Steven 328
Brooks, David 83
B'Tselem (Israeli Information
    Center for Human Rights in
    the Occupied Territories) 127
Bu Nimr Tribe, Al 293
Bu'azizi, Muhammad 273
Bubadri tribe 304
Buchanan, Patrick 434
Buckley, William F. 111, 245
Bureau of Intelligence and
    Research (INR) 36, 66, 557
Burg, Avraham 475
Burr, Richard 170, 177
Busaysu, 'Atif 118
Bush 41, George 142-144, 193,
    202, 370, 418, 487, 505, 553,
    554
Bush 43, George 88, 94, 128,
    159, 176, 183, 185, 189, 191,
    193, 195, 197, 200, 206, 209,
    231, 233, 255, 326, 328, 371,
    397, 420, 421, 496, 497, 502,
    550, 555, 559
Byers, Michael 255
Byrne, Malcolm 104
Byzantine Empire 3, 403

Cairo Conference (UK) 11
Caliph Abu Bakr 359
Caliph 'Ali 445
Caliph Harun al Rashid 369
Caliph Ibrahim (projected)
    (Ibrahim al Samarra'i) 285
Caliph al Ma'mun 369
Caliph al Mahdi 369
Caliph al Mansur 369
Caliph al Mustansir 241
Caliph 'Umar I 359, 466
Caliph 'Uthman 359
Caliphate 3, 92, 282, 296, 305,
    337, 359, 439, 525, 541
Caliphate (Fatimid) 404
Caliphate (projected) 275, 278,
    282, 285, 289, 292, 293, 296-
    298, 300, 315, 372, 541
Calvinists (Europe) 272
Cambanis, Thanassis 458
Camp Al Sayliyyah 546
Camp Ashraf 226
Camp Bucca 276, 279, 289
Camp David 116, 119, 495, 501,
    564
Camp Justice 280
Camp Speicher 287, 372, 525
Camp Victory 228
Campbell, John 165
Canadian-American North
    American Aerospace
    Command NORAD 322, 325

Canadian Broadcasting
   Corporation 402
Carmeli Brigade (Israeli) 23
Carnegie Endowment 329, 339
Carnegie Moscow Center 545
carpet-bombing (Israel) 76, 89,
   253, 254, 516
carpet-bombing (Damascus)
   (Russia) 178, 183, 299, 392,
   437, 562
carpet-bombing (Saudi) 178
Carré, John le (David Cornwell)
   191, 425, 505
Carter Doctrine 481, 488, 552
Carter, Jimmy 93, 96, 97, 112,
   116, 141, 157, 501, 552, 555,
   564
Casey, George 208
Casey, William 83, 245, 317
Catholic 86, 272, 281, 392, 467,
   571
Cavendish, Richard 34
Central Asian Turks 537
Central Command (CENTCOM)
   146, 194, 201, 483, 488, 546,
   552
Central Powers 7
Central Treaty Organization
   (CENTO) 343, 552
Chalabi, Ahmad 209, 236
Chaldean Catholics 243, 281
Charlie Hebdo 182, 297, 336,
   343
Chatterji, Nikshoi C. 439
Chayes, Sarah 164, 460
Chechens 282, 289, 306, 431,
   433, 434, 494
chemical weapons 99-102, 108,
   147, 308, 386, 391, 392, 437,
   453, 493, 505, 562

Cheney, Richard 192, 196, 206,
   325
Chevron 105
China National Petroleum
   Corporation 226, 228
Chomsky, Noam 20
Chouceir, Chafic 402
Christian 72, 75, 79, 85-88, 135,
   191, 192, 214, 242, 243, 252,
   258, 271, 281, 284, 286, 289,
   295, 298, 300, 304, 305, 308,
   313, 366, 371, 374, 375, 381,
   383, 387, 393, 394, 396, 401,
   403, 417, 422, 425, 426, 438,
   466, 467, 470, 497, 503, 515,
   520, 537, 538, 543, 569
Christison, Kathleen and Bill 124
Christopher, Warren 399
Churchill, Winston 8-11, 463,
   557
Church of Rome 243
CIA (Central Intelligence
   Agency) 61, 66, 80, 96, 107,
   111, 112, 141, 143, 149, 150,
   157, 159, 160, 162, 168, 170,
   173-175, 177, 181, 186-188,
   190, 194, 195, 197, 199, 206,
   245, 258, 279, 288, 316, 317,
   321, 323, 326-329, 392, 412,
   434, 480, 483, 485, 487, 489,
   493, 494, 499, 506, 533, 541,
   542, 546, 554, 557, 558, 562
Circassians 22
civil war 21, 32, 43, 72, 74, 77,
   79, 87-89, 97, 136, 148, 156,
   157, 159, 162, 170, 176, 205,
   213, 242, 246, 264, 268, 277-
   280, 283, 294, 300, 312, 318,
   331, 342, 353, 372, 382, 383,
   387, 388, 390, 392-396, 402,

584

Gadahn, Adam 162, 329
Gaitskell, Hugh 40
Galbraith, Peter 108, 211, 212, 222, 279, 289, 413, 414, 420, 422
Gall, Carlotta 335
Gallipoli debacle 8
Gallo, Ernest A. 567
Gardner, David 183, 341, 350, 353, 354, 357, 358, 388, 389, 433, 543, 545
Garner, Jay 192, 197, 199, 232
Gates, Robert 216
Gaza Freedom Flotilla 130, 131, 136, 345, 472, 475
Gaza lockdown 33, 126, 468, 558, 568
Gaza tunnels 127, 129, 135, 137, 152, 153, 459, 461
GCC (*see* Gulf Cooperation Council)
George, Susannah 379
Geraghty, Timothy 82
Gerges, Fawaz 295, 296, 317
Geneva Conventions 48, 124, 204, 241, 248, 293, 326, 480
Ghabban, Muhammad al 379
Ghanem, As'ad 468
Ghani, Ashraf 163, 165
Ghazi bin Faysal 12
Ging, John 128
Ginor, Isabella 42
Giordano, Joseph 553
Gizmodo 447
Gladstone, Rick 136
Glaspie, April 142, 518
Glass, Charles 253, 422, 426, 429, 442
Glassé, Cyril 241, 438
Glenn Amendment 501

Global War on Terrorism 273, 555, 560, 563
Glubb, Sir John 21, 25, 26, 34, 463, 464, 552
Goksel, Timur 252, 255
Golan Heights (annexation) 97
Golan Heights Law 48, 49
Goldberg, Jeffrey 186, 256
Golden Dome 213
Goldenberg, Han 444, 490, 520
Goldstone Report 129
Goldstone, Justice Richard 129
Gopal, Screenivasan 373, 378
Gorbachev, Mikhail 107, 483
Gordon, Joy 194
Gordon, Michael 358, 544
Gorenberg, Gershom 48
Gorran 229, 231
Gorvett, Jonathan 532
Graham-Harrison, Emmy 392
Graham, Bob 196, 283, 489
Great Mosque of Mecca 95, 106, 440, 442
Green Left Weekly 440
Green Zone 180, 207, 216, 218, 221, 223, 224, 235, 236, 372, 374, 377, 378, 556
Green, Stephen 45, 50, 51, 60, 62-65, 70, 73, 78, 98, 501
Greider, William 64
Greve, Frank 246
Guantanamo (Guantanamo Bay Naval Base, including detention camp) 170, 559
Guardian Council (Iranian) 367, 368
Guardian of the People of Syria 330
Guardian of the Two Holy Shrines 443
Gubser, Peter 149

Harsch, Joseph 85, 502
Harvard 231
Hasan, Hassan 276, 301, 316, 332
Hasan, Wisam 257
Hasanayn, Ahmad 152
Hasani, Hajim al 210
Hashim, Ahmed 108, 215, 231, 276, 280-283, 331
Hashimi, 'Abd al Ilah al 12
Hashimi, Husayn bin 'Ali al (Sherif Husayn) 8, 11, 439
Hashimi, Tariq al 230
Hassi, 'Umar al 292
Hatikvah 499
Hayali, Fadil al (*see* Turkmani, Abu Muslim)
Haykal, Muhammad 43
Haykel, Bernard 291, 487
Hazbun, Waleed 504
HDP (*see* Peoples' Democratic Party)
Heller, Aron 258
Henderson, Simon 453
Heraclitus 524
Hersh, Seymour 98, 174, 206, 208, 250, 255, 256, 421, 494, 507
Hertog, Steffen 487
Herzl, Theodore 470
Herzliya Conference 477, 529
Herzog, Chaim 16, 18, 20, 21, 23-25, 28-32, 37, 38, 41, 42, 45-47, 50, 60-67, 70-72, 75, 78, 79
Hess-von Kruedener, Paeta 251
Hessler, Peter 340, 456, 462
Higgins, William Robin 246
High Dam 35, 36
Hijazi, Ihsan al 246

Hilterman, Joost 103, 106-108, 212, 229, 362, 417, 441, 542
Hilu, Charles 396
Himyarite 403
Hiram of Tyre 88
Hiro, Dilip 95, 100, 103, 107, 112, 139, 145, 419, 519
Hirsch, Michael 210
Hish (*see* Field Guard)
Histadrut 15, 18
History Today 34
Hitchens, Christopher 123
Hizballah (Iraq) 242
Hizballah (Party of God) (Islamic Jihad) 80, 83, 84, 88-90, 104, 110, 111, 115, 125, 140, 151, 170, 171, 182, 213, 242-259, 265, 267, 268, 274, 292, 318, 330, 332, 333, 341, 342, 361, 369, 373, 379, 386, 389-391, 393, 399-403, 413, 432, 448, 452, 466, 469, 473, 476, 482, 484, 487, 493, 516, 517, 520-522, 528, 529, 534, 539, 541, 543, 548, 561
Hizballah Battalions (*Kata'ib*) 373, 379
Hizballah entry into the Syrian civil war 402
Hobson, John 6
Holland, Fern 207
Holland, Tom 299
Hollande, Francois 181, 309, 461, 486
Holocaust 89, 467, 570
Horowitz, Dan 19
Horton, Scott 326
House Foreign Affairs Committee 100
House of Commons 40
Hubaykah, Elie 77, 398

590

International Criminal Court
(ICC) 121, 136, 152, 154, 386
International Monetary Fund
(IMF) 40, 462
International Security Assistance
Force (ISAF) 160
International Solidarity
Movement 121
Intervest 230
Inter-Press Service 374
intidab 11
Intifadah I 116-118, 474
Intifadah II 119, 123, 149, 474,
475, 494
Iran-Iraq Agreement of 1937 92
Iran-Libya Sanctions Act (ILSA)
495
Iranian air force 102-104, 106,
365
Iranian Air Lines 108
Iranian Army 99, 103
Iranian Navy 105, 107, 109, 141,
479
Iranian Parliament 368
Iranian revolutions 93
Iraq: from Sunni to Shia rule 519
Iraq Interim Governing Council
(IGC) 202-204, 206, 207,
235-237
Iraq Liberation Act 194, 555
Iraq Study Group 216
Iraqi air force 97, 102-106, 108,
144, 371
Iraqi army 11, 13, 28, 103, 187,
199, 201, 211, 221, 222, 232,
243, 276, 292, 311, 372-274,
379, 381, 415, 423, 505
Iraqi Constitution 204, 211, 213,
22, 420, 421
Iraqi Interim Governing Council
202

Iraqi Islamic Party 211, 222, 223,
225, 227
Iraqi National Accord 206
Iraqi National Assembly 200,
202
Iraqi National Alliance 229
Iraqi Parliament 207, 213, 215,
220, 223, 497
Iraqi Special Tribunal 209, 280
'Iraqiyyah Party 230
IRGC (*see* Islamic Revolutionary
Guard Corps)
Irgun 14-19, 21-25, 28, 29
Iryani, 'Abd al Rahman al 406
IS (*see* Islamic State)
IS Militia 282, 294, 314
IS Shura Council 285
Isaacson, Walter 58, 68
Isabella, daughter of Ferdinand
and Isabella (Castile) 467
ISAF (*see* International Security
Assistance Force)
ISCI (*see* Islamic Supreme
Council of Iraq)
ISI (*see* Pakistani Inter-Services
Intelligence)
ISIS (*see* Islamic State of Iraq
and Syria)
Islah (Iraq) 229, 263
Islah (Yemen) 229, 263, 265,
339, 341, 449, 450
Islamic Association, The 459
Islamic Conquest 525, 537
Islamic Jihad (Egypt) 318, 319,
328, 329, 338
Islamic Jihad (Gaza) 119, 126,
149
Islamic Jihad (Lebanon) (*see*
Hizballah)
Islamic Movement of the Free
Men of Syria 330

Jesus of Nazareth 135, 360
Jett, Dennis 159
Jewish Agency 15, 20, 22, 25, 26, 499
Jewish Brigade 19, 471
Jewish community (Baghdad) 466
Jewish communitiy (Iran) 362
Jewish Community Center (Buenos Aires) 247
Jewish expulsion (Castile) (England) 467
Jewish Legion 470
Jewish National Home 463, 469, 470, 498
Jewish society 477
Jewish state 16, 20, 273, 361, 468, 471, 472, 475, 488, 499, 511, 569, 570, 573
Jewish Virtual Library (JVL) 371, 470
jihad, jihadism 9, 83, 111, 112, 117, 119, 121-123, 126, 140, 149, 151, 156, 167, 168, 174, 176-179, 181-185, 249, 257, 258, 275, 277, 279, 283, 286, 288, 289, 295, 296, 298, 304-306, 308, 311, 313-320, 328, 329, 332, 338, 342, 347, 375, 385, 388, 391, 435, 447, 451, 459-461, 478, 514, 519, 522, 535, 541-543, 545, 546, 548, 549, 551, 555, 559, 562, 563
jizyah 286
Johnson, Chalmers 483, 551, 556
Johnson, Douglas V. 99
Johnson, Lyndon 43, 45, 48, 58, 481, 500, 512, 513, 567
Joint Chiefs of Staff (JCS) 501

Joint Comprehensive Plan of Action (JCPOA) 366, 368, 369
Joint Military Command (Egypt, Syria, Jordan) 35
Joint Special Operations Command (JSOC) 484, 546
Jordan: protectorate 464, 514
Jordanian Air Force 44, 55, 464
Jordanian Embassy (in Iraq) 202, 234, 277
Jordanian enlistments 98, 465
Jordanian ground forces 464
Journal of Palestine Studies (JPS) 21, 25, 30, 49, 78, 90, 149, 250, 252, 253, 255, 345, 400, 559
Judgment Day (End Time) 192, 286, 300
Jumayyil, Amin 80, 85, 492
Jumayyil, Bashir 73, 77, 80, 86, 89, 396, 398, 492, 516
Jumayyil, Pierre 396
Junblat, Walid 258, 401
jurisprudent cleric (*velayat-e faqih*) 93
Justice and Development Party (AKP) 343, 345, 346, 349, 351, 352, 413
JVL (*see* Jewish Virtual Library)

Kahan Commission 79, 398
Kahan Report 80, 90
Kahan, Yitzhak 79
Kanat, Kilic 346, 350
Kandil, Hazem 337, 411
Kaplan, Fred 368, 477
KAR (*see* Kurdish Autonomous Region)
Karachi Airport 163
Karamah 54

594

596

286, 295, 296, 316-320, 322, 326-329, 526, 551, 558
Lahhud, Amil 87, 89, 249, 396, 397
Lakkis, Hasan 257
Lamb, Franklin 82
Land of the Two Rivers 462
Landis, Joshua 335, 389
Lang, Hans Peter 251
Langley Airbase 324
Lashkar-e Taiba 162, 164
Lawrence, T. E. 11, 462
Lawson, Fred H. 267, 402, 450
Lawton, Timothy 440
Le Billon, Philippe 372, 425, 505
Le Monde Diplomatique 112
League of the Followers of Truth 313
League of Nations 12, 14, 15, 471
League of the Righteous 372, 373, 378
Lears, Jackson 543, 545
Lebanese army 30, 83, 86, 252, 332, 396, 400, 401, 482, 487, 535
Lebanese cabinet 401
Lebanese Civil War of 1975-90 72, 74, 87, 492
Lebanese Compromise 396
Lebanese Constitution 89, 397
Lebanese forces 82, 247, 251, 259, 402
Lebanese Ministry of Defense 82
Lebanese Parliament 88, 89, 247, 248, 257, 397, 400
Lebanese Presidency 259, 402, 403
Lebanese-Israeli Accord of 5/17/83 85
Legrenzi, Matteo 267, 402, 450

LEHI (Stern Gang) 18-23, 28, 29
Leiken, Robert 328
Lenczowski, George 21, 22, 26, 38, 40, 430
lesser pilgrimage 438
Leverett, Flynt 383
Levitsky, Steven 476
Lewis, Anthony 78
Lewis, Jessica 306
Lia, Brynjar 546, 563
Libi, Abu Yahya al 328
Libya Dawn 162, 292, 299, 300, 311
Libya Government of National Accord 314
Lieberman, Avigdor 347
Lifeline to India 404
Likud 197, 474, 475, 476
Lilienthal, Alfred 44
Lindsey, Ursula 340, 461
L'Institut d'Études Politiques de Paris 231
Lippman, Thomas W. 488
liquid natural gas (LNG) 450
Lisbon massacre 467
Lister, Charles 169, 170, 171, 179, 284, 337, 383, 384, 389, 426, 493, 494, 541, 542, 545
Livni, Tzipi 478
Lloyd George, David 14, 470
Lloyd, Selwyn 37
Lloyds of London 105
Long Commission 84, 517
loya jirga 163
LRB (*see The London Review of Books*)
Luce, Edward 166, 313
Lukoil 230
Lund, Arun 335
Lustick, Ian 49
Luttwak, Edward 19, 297, 481

597

Lynch, Marc 274, 486, 560

Ma'ariv 79
Mabhuh, Mahmud 130, 131, 152
MacDill Air Force Base (Tampa) 546
Mackey, Sandra 92, 93, 96, 98-101, 103, 105-108, 110, 139, 144, 359
Madrid train attacks 327
Mahdi (Shiite) 360
Mahdi Army (*Jaysh al Mahdi*) (JAM) 205, 207, 215, 217, 219, 221, 233, 237, 238, 242, 263, 364, 380
Mahdi, Muhammad al 360
Majid, 'Ali Hasan al 106
Makinen, James 251
Makover, Meshulam 29
Malik, Tashfin 310
Maliki, Nuri al 180, 213, 214, 216-231, 238, 242, 243, 244, 249, 281, 364, 371-374, 376-378, 380, 424, 487, 497, 543
Mallon, Thomas 555
Mamelukes 366
Mamluk, 'Ali 536
Mandean 374
Manning, Michael 485
Mansour, Camille 73, 75
Mansur, 'Adli 458
Mansur, Akhtar 163. 165, 166, 334
Manuel I (Portugal) 467
Maqdisi, Abu Muhammad al 279, 286
Maras Massacre 344
March 14 Coalition 257, 401, 484
March 8 Coalition 257, 401
Marean, Curtis 1

Margalit, Avishai 18, 20, 38, 43, 471
Margolis, Eric 100, 163, 165
Marj al Sultan air base 389
Marj Dabiq, Battle of 366
marji' al taqlid (source of emulation) 399
Marolda, Edward 105
Maronite (Catholic) 72, 78, 83, 86, 87, 89, 248, 258, 259, 394, 396, 398, 402, 403, 516, 552, 565
Marr, Phoebe 212, 520
Marsh Arabs 147
Marshall Plan 480, 485
Marshall, George 480
Martinez, Jose Ciro 384
Marwan, Ashraf 71
Mashhadani tribe 215
massacre 21, 23, 26, 30, 32, 55, 77-79, 86, 90, 148, 158, 164, 262, 319, 331, 336, 338, 340, 341, 344, 349, 369, 382, 391, 398, 403, 405, 407, 467, 525
Masum, Fu'ad 231
Mateos, Susana Bastos 468
Mathews, Jessica 168, 486, 547
Mattson, Roger 512, 567
Mawsil Dam 171, 240, 287, 289, 316, 424
May, Renee 323
Maysalun, Battle of 463
Mazzetti, Mark 440
MB (*see* Muslim Brotherhood)
McArthur, Shirl 504
McCaffrey, Barry 217
McCants, William 310, 329
McChrystal, Stanley 188
McClatchy 129, 171, 173, 182, 191, 229, 250, 266, 287, 293, 330, 341, 387, 424, 427, 493

McDowall, David 108
McFarlane, Robert 81, 83, 104, 111, 246
McGoldrick, Jamie 454
McGovern, George 216
McMahon, Sir Henry 8
McNulty, Tim 82
Mearsheimer, John J. 192, 483, 502
Mecca 8, 11, 95, 106, 285, 308, 438, 439, 440, 443, 449
Mecca Agreement 150
Medes 408
Meese, Edwin 112
Mehsud, Baitullah 161, 162
Mehsud, Hakimullah 162, 163
Meir, Golda 21, 59, 60, 464, 473, 474, 500, 501, 567
MEJ (*see Middle East Journal*)
MEK (*see* Mujahedeen e-Khalq)
Melhem, Hisham 310
Mendel, Yonatan 114, 155
MEP (*see Middle East Policy*)
MER (*see Middle East Report*)
Merkel, Angela 353
Merrick, Roger 61
MHP (Turkish Nationalist) 352
Middle East Airlines 115
Middle East Journal (MEJ) 42, 77, 105, 106, 202
Middle East Policy (*MEP*) 19, 26, 28, 46, 47, 49, 52, 55, 97, 99, 100, 106-108, 118, 121, 128, 132, 133, 139, 148, 149, 153, 154, 159, 162, 171, 173, 184, 203, 210, 214, 231, 257, 267, 268, 274, 276, 279, 280-283, 285, 294, 296, 301, 305, 328, 329, 331, 332, 338-341, 345, 346, 348-350, 363, 364, 367, 368, 372, 378, 389, 401, 402, 410, 412-414, 419, 425-429, 431, 436, 443, 446, 447, 449, 450, 452, 475, 488, 494, 504, 505, 507, 525, 530, 533, 546, 547, 551, 552, 555, 563, 566
Middle East Policy Council 174
Middle East power struggle 174, 274, 444, 455, 466, 514, 526, 536, 538, 561
Middle East Quarterly 117
Middle East Quartet 124
Middle East Report (*MER*) 47, 80, 100, 108, 112, 132-134, 139, 142, 184, 211, 217, 230, 246, 247, 254, 326, 330, 331, 342, 354, 384, 386, 389, 411, 417, 447, 465, 506, 517, 529
Midhat, Ahmad (Pasha) 138
Milani, Mohsen 364
military coup (Egypt) 33
military coup (Iraq) 33
military coup (Syria) 33
Military-Industrial Complex 431, 485, 486, 558
Miqati, Najib 257
Mish'al, Khalid 119, 122, 133, 135, 153, 345, 447, 449
Mizrahim 476
MIT 255
MNF (*see* UN Multinational Force)
Modesto Bee 232
Mogelson, Luke 310, 312, 372, 380, 425, 429, 543
Mollet, Guy 37
Monaco, Lisa 186
Mongol Empire/Mongols 271, 369, 466, 536, 536
Monitor Online 221, 281

599

Monophysite (Eastern Orthodox) Christianity 403
Monroe Doctrine 478, 548
Montgomery, Field Marshall Bernard 24
Moore, George C. (Curt) 111
Moore, Pete 230
Morgan, J.P. 88
Moroccan forces 65
Morris, Benny 21, 25, 30
Moshe Dayan Center 12
Mosque of the Prophet 453
Mossad 117-119, 129, 152, 249, 259, 326, 371
Mossadeq, Mohammad 96, 360, 495, 557, 558
Moussa, Amr 130
Mu'awiyah bin Abi Sufyan 359, 445
Mu'awwad, Rene 246
Mubarak, Husni 130, 308, 318, 339, 442, 449, 453, 456-459, 462, 494
Mubarak, Jamal 457
Mueller, Kayla 283
Mughniyah, 'Imad 253, 256, 258, 402
Mughniyah, Jihad 258
Muhajir, Abu Hamzah al (Abu Ayyub al Masri) 215, 218, 231, 280, 282
Muhammad 'Ali 7, 272, 408, 564
Muhammad bin Salman 440, 448, 450, 452, 453
Muhammadun 238
Muhy al Din, Zakariyya 49
Mujahedeen-e Khalq (MEK) 97, 103, 104, 146, 226, 365
Mujahidin Army 228, 332, 553
Mukalla Airport 265
Multinational Force (Iraq) 220

Multinational Force (MNF) (Lebanon) 76, 78, 398, 516
Mumbai 162, 510
Munich Olympics 115, 126
Mursi, Muhammad 132, 153, 293, 339, 340, 343, 347, 443, 457-460, 494, 495, 527
Murtaji, 'Abd al Muhsin 43
Musawi, 'Abbas 247
Musharraf, Pervez 159, 161
Muslim Brotherhood (MB) 26, 53, 117, 132, 148, 153, 265, 274, 286, 293, 296, 304, 317, 328, 329, 337-343, 346, 348, 351, 382, 384, 385, 443, 446-449, 457-459, 461, 465, 473, 507, 527, 536
Muslim, Saleh 427, 429
Mustansiriyyah University 92, 241
Mutawakkil 405
Mutlaq, Salih al 211, 230
Myers, Richard 198
Myerson, Morris 59

Nabatiyyah 82
Nagl, John A. 209
Najaf Airport 222
Najaf seminary (Iraq) 394
Naji, Abu Bakr 169, 303
Najibullah, Muhammed 157
Najjar, Muhammad al 447
nakbah 472
Nakhlah, Emile 257
Napoleon 510
Nashashibis 15
Nasr, Vali 89, 93, 108, 198, 212, 257, 376, 394, 395, 436
Nasrallah, Hasan 247, 249, 252, 253, 256, 257, 267, 393, 402
National Enquirer 246

369, 409, 442, 448, 449, 468, 473, 474, 486, 489, 490, 492, 500-505, 514, 518, 550, 551, 554, 567-569

Nujayfi, Athil al 358

Nuqrashi, Mahmud 337

Nur Party 340, 461

Nusrah 169, 172, 173, 176, 177, 179-182, 185, 187, 258, 274, 279, 283-285, 287, 301, 308, 312, 316, 330-336, 341, 342, 348, 349, 352, 386, 387, 391, 392, 423, 432, 433, 448, 476, 487, 494, 507. 519, 526, 527, 533, 541, 543, 557, 561, 562

Nusaybah, Ghanim 135

Nusayr, Al Sayyid 317

Nuwas, Dhu 403

NY (*see The New Yorker*)

NYR (*see The New York Review of Books*)

NYTM (see *The New York Times Magazine*)

O'Ballance, Edgar 66

O'Driscoll, Dylan 378

O'Neill, Paul 195

Obama, Barack 130, 135, 136, 162, 165, 166, 169-177, 179, 180, 182-187, 230, 231, 268, 298, 309, 365, 366, 431, 442, 468, 475, 478, 486, 489, 490-498, 502-504, 508, 542, 545, 546, 551, 556, 557, 561-563, 568

Ocalan, Abdullah 346, 348, 349, 410-414, 426, 427, 429, 506

Occupied Territories (OT) 22, 46, 119, 127, 466, 476

Odierno, Raymond 221

Office for Reconstruction and Humanitarian Assistance (ORHA) 192, 197, 199, 200

offshore balancing 175

oil depot at Jiyyah 254

oil pipelines 214, 218, 240

Oil-for-Food Program 197, 198, 201

Olmert, Ehud 253, 475

Omar, Mullah Muhammad 158, 159, 163, 165, 166, 319, 320

Omer, Mohammed 154

Ong, Betty 323

OPEC (*see* Organization of Petroleum Exporting Countries)

Open Society of Justice Initiative (OSJI) 175

Operation Dignity (Libya) 311

Oren, Amir 465

Organization of Monotheism and Holy War 279

Organization of Petroleum Exporting Countries (OPEC) 66, 67, 416, 453

ORHA (*see* Office for Reconstruction and Humanitarian Assistance)

Osirak nuclear reactor 96, 98, 474

Oslo Accord 118, 119, 132, 148, 318, 529

OT (*see* Occupied Terrirories)

Otis Airbase 323

Ottaway, David 150

Ottaway, Marina 458

Ottoman Empire 3, 7-9, 11, 91, 272, 273, 337, 343, 345, 357, 359, 404, 408, 462, 470, 510, 524

Oxfam 241

604

Revolutionary People's
Liberation Party/Front 348
Reza'i, Farhad 328
Rice, Condoleezza 196, 203,
211, 420, 484
Ricks, Thomas 203, 220, 520
Riedel, Bruce 291
Rikhye, Indar 42
Rivlin, Reuven 475, 477
Robertson, Pat 192
Robinson, Eugene 498
Robinson, Glenn 127, 149
Rodenbeck, Max 152, 254, 372
Rogan, Tom 533
Rogers, Mike 177
Rogers, William P. 58-60
Rojava 424, 428, 429
Romano, David 349
Romney, Willard "Mitt" 551
Roosevelt, Franklin 191, 479,
488, 499, 550
Rose, Charlie 135
Rosen, Nir 216, 219
Rosiny, Stefan 276, 283, 285,
288, 290, 296, 305, 329, 331,
332, 428, 446
Roth, Kenneth 561, 562
Rothschild, Walter 470
Rouhani, Hassan 362, 364-368,
446, 496
Rove, Karl 193
Roy, Sara 118, 119, 124, 154,
559
Royal Dutch Shell 222, 224, 226
RPP (see Republican People's
Party)
Rubaysh, Ibrahim al 176
Rubin, Michael 413
Rumley, Grant 150

Rumsfeld, Donald 101, 102, 141,
192, 196, 198, 200, 203, 216,
232, 324, 325, 551
Rushayd, Zaki Bani 341
Russian airliner, crash of 308,
433, 461
Russian air force 182, 259, 319,
336, 352, 353, 390, 392, 433-
437, 533, 574
Russian Ambassador to Turkey
assassinated 544
Russian arms supply 513
Russian ground troups 434, 534
Russian intervention in Syria
367, 388, 389, 431
Russian jet fighter shot down
530, 531
Russian Jews 60
Russian Navy 436
Russiapedia 60
Ruthven, Malise 169, 179, 278,
279, 281, 296, 303, 339, 439,
443, 453, 560
Ryan, Randolph 554

Sa'd, Ja'far Muhammad 266
Sa'dat, Ahmad 120
Saddam Husayn 92-95, 98-103,
106, 108-110, 112, 139, 141-
147, 189-197, 200-202, 204,
206, 208, 213, 216, 219, 220,
222, 224, 226, 229, 233-242,
276, 278-282, 289, 296, 304,
313, 370, 373, 377, 378, 416,
417, 419, 422, 493, 497, 505,
517-519, 522, 525, 553-555,
559, 566
Sadr, Muhammad al 235
Sa'id, Nuri al 12, 370
Sa'iqah, Al 55
Sa'ud, Muhammad Ibn 438

606

Sa'adon, Ilan 117

Sabah, Fahd al Ahmad al 140

Sabra-Shatila massacre 78, 79, 86, 90, 398

Sachs, Jeffrey D. 555

Sachs, Natan 504

Sadat, Anwar al 57-62, 64, 65, 68-70, 116, 317, 318, 338, 455, 462, 501, 514, 515, 564

Sadr, Muhammad Baqir al 91, 92

Sadr, Muqtada al 202, 205, 207, 208, 212, 213, 218, 219, 229, 233, 235-238, 242, 249, 279, 378, 380, 497

Sadr, Musa 383, 394, 395

Sadrists 210, 212, 217, 221, 223, 229, 231, 235

Saeed, Hafiz Muhammed 164

Safavid Dynasty 2, 3, 91, 272, 273, 359, 361, 443, 524, 564

Safire, William 416

Sahwah (*see* The Awakening)

Sa'id, Nuri al 370

Salafi 152, 155, 157, 213, 277, 279, 286, 289, 295, 298, 300, 302, 303, 305, 316, 319, 340, 374, 406, 419, 439, 447, 448, 457, 459, 524

Salah al Din (Saladin) 404, 408

Sale, Richard 141

Salih-Hadi faction 175

Salih, 'Ali 'Abdallah (Zaydi) 260-269, 406, 407, 446, 450

Salim, 'Izz al Din 206

Sallal, 'Abdallah al 405

Sallouch, Bassel 524

Salomon, Erika 497

Samarra'i, Ibrahim al 282

Samarra'i, Iyad al 227

Samii, Abbas William 252

Sammu' 54

Samuel, Sir Herbert 14

San Remo Conference 9

Sanchez, Ricardo 205, 208

sanctions 88, 89, 102, 124, 147, 158, 184, 193, 194, 200, 228, 229, 235, 239-241, 246, 263, 291, 391, 320, 327, 363, 364, 366, 368, 371, 392, 397, 409, 419, 420, 447, 490, 495, 496, 500, 504, 518, 520, 553, 554, 560

Sanctions Committee 194

Sanger, David 546

Sarkhi, Mahmud al 214

Sarkis, Ilyas 396

Sarkozy, Nicolas 226, 229

Sassanian Dynasty 3, 361, 403

Saspartas, Avi 117

SATF (*see* Special Anti-Terrorism Forces)

Satloff, Steven S. 290

Saudi air force 102, 260, 264, 268, 269, 449- 451, 490, 491

Saudi Arabian Monetary Agency 450

Saudi Aramco 368, 451

Saudi forces 267, 450, 518, 534

Saudi Arabia News Agency 187, 494

Saudi Economic Council 453

Saudi National Guard 144, 319, 443, 534

Saudi subsidy to Egypt 461

Saudi-Wahhabi alliance 438, 442

Savak 360

Savichi Kurds 197

Sawers, John 315

SCAF (*see* Supreme Command of the Armed Forces) (Egypt)

Scahill, Jeremy 329, 484, 555

Schanzer, Jonathan 117, 148, 149

608

Twin Towers 167
Twitter 294, 309

U Thant 42
UAE (seven tribal entities) 445
UAE Air Force 447, 459
UAE forces 267, 449, 450
UAE Navy 268
UAR (*see* United Arab Republic)
'Ubayd, 'Abd al Karim 246
'Ubaydi, Harith al 227
Ullman, Harlan 566
Ulrichsen, Kristian 222, 262, 407
ultimatums to Israel 30, 38, 40,
    69, 76, 515
ummah 364
UN Assistance Mission for Iraq
    207
UN Charter 505
UN Disengagement and
    Observer Forces (UNDOF)
    69, 333
UN Educational, Scientific, and
    Cultural Organization
    (UNESCO) 131, 475, 485,
    566
UN Expeditionary Force (UNEF)
    39, 40, 42
UN General Assembly (UNGA)
    20, 29, 39, 42, 49, 115, 129,
    131, 471, 475, 499, 503, 504,
    516, 479, 499, 521
UN headquarters in Iraq 207,
    234, 277
UN High Commissioner for
    Refugees (UNHCR) 128, 243,
    465
UN High Commissioner on
    Human Rights 130, 451, 537
UN Human Rights Council 129,
    131, 499

UN Interim Force in Lebanon
    (UNIFIL) 246, 251, 252, 255,
    400
UN Monitoring, Verification,
    and Inspection Commission
    (UNMOVIC) 197
UN Multinational Force (MNF)
    76, 78, 398, 516
UN Refugee Commission 388
UN Relief and Works Agency
    for the Palestinian Refugees
    in the Near East (UNRWA)
    33, 126, 128, 134, 388, 472
UN Sanctions Committee on Iraq
    194
UN Secretary General (UNSYG)
    42, 129, 135, 198, 232, 301,
    420, 436, 477
UN Security Council (UNSC)
    34, 38, 39, 42, 49, 68, 78, 102,
    125, 128, 130, 143, 145, 147,
    158, 183, 197, 198, 207, 212,
    220, 355, 386, 399, 401, 406,
    473, 491, 501, 502, 515
UN Special Tribunal for
    Lebanon 402
UNEF (*see* UN Expeditionary
    Force)
UNESCO (*see* UN Educational,
    Scientific, and Cultural
    Organization)
UNGA (*see* UN General
    Assembly)
UNGA Resolution 181 (1947)
    16, 21, 31, 117, 469, 471, 499,
    521
UNGA Resolution 194 (1948)
    29, 48
UNGA Resolution 302 (IV)
    (1949) 128, 472

614

UNSC Resolution 2334 (2016)
568
UNSCOP 17, 20, 21
'Urabi, Ahmad 6
Urduni, Abu Turab al 322
Urquhart, Brian 65
US Air Force (USAF) 84, 159,
160, 165, 170, 171-174, 179,
181-184, 186-188, 194, 198,
199, 202, 267, 285, 287, 294-
296, 298, 302, 307, 309, 310,
312, 313, 315, 318, 327, 348,
349, 351, 352, 357, 370, 376-
379, 407, 411, 419, 424, 425,
428, 430, 483, 487, 488, 496,
506, 407, 542, 544, 552, 560,
574
US bases worldwide 485
US commitment to the security
of Israel 547
US Cyber Command 186
US Consulate in Jiddah 314
US Dissent Channel 187
US Drone War 168, 170, 175-
177, 185, 188, 263, 555, 557,
566
US arms embargo 81, 101, 366,
369
US Embassy (Baghdad) 208, 556
US Embassy (Beirut) 80, 82, 482
US Embassy (Cairo) 340
US Embassy (Islamabad) 317
US Embassy (Kabul) 166
US Embassy (Kenya) 320
US Embassy (Riyadh) 440
US Embassy (San'a') 261, 407
US Embassy (Tanzania) 320
US Embassy (Tehran) 94, 97,
112
US hawks 556

US House of Representatives
171, 197, 255
US Joint Special Operation
Command (JSOC) 484, 546
US Legation (Beirut) 565
US Marine barracks bombing 83,
84, 245, 400, 482, 516
US Massive Ordnance Penetrator
367
US Navy 73, 82, 84, 86, 105-
107, 167, 172, 193, 267, 269,
482, 483, 488, 492, 512, 516,
517, 546, 547, 552, 566
US policy 90, 96, 184, 378, 454,
455, 483, 484, 488, 491-493,
500, 546
US Presidency 565
US Provincial Reconstruction
Teams 216
US recognition of Syria-Lebanon
treaties 396, 493
US resistance to admitting World
War II refugees 467
US Senate 136, 146, 197, 504
US Special Operations
Command (USSOCOM) 177,
329, 484, 546
US subsidy 111, 153, 180, 263,
494, 535, 568
US Supreme Court 480, 496, 498
Usher, Graham 149
USS Abraham Lincoln 496
USS Carl Vinson 547
USS Caron 84
USS Cole 168, 261, 320, 406
USS Liberty 500, 512, 567
USS New Jersey 82, 84, 516
USS Quincy 488
USS Stark, 104
USS Vincennes 108

618

Left to right: Lebanese Prime Minister Saeb Salam, Lebanese Parliament President Kamel El-Asaad, Lebanese President Suleiman Frangieh, US Secretary of State William P. Rogers, Lebanese Foreign Minister Khalil Abouhamad, American Ambassador to Lebanon William Buffum.

Visit by US Secretary of State William P. Rogers to Lebanon, May 3-4, 1971. Left to right: President Frangieh, Secretary Rogers, the Author (interpreter), Lebanese official (anon).